EXPLORING CULTURES
A Prentice Hall Series in Anthropology

The Legacy of Mesoamerica

History and Culture of a Native American Civilization

ROBERT M. CARMACK
University at Albany – State University of New York

JANINE GASCO
Institute for Mesoamerican Studies

GARY H. GOSSEN
University at Albany – State University of New York

with contributions from
George A. Broadwell, Louise M. Burkhart, Liliana R. Goldin, John S. Justeson, Brenda Rosenbaum, Michael E. Smith

PRENTICE HALL, Upper Saddle River, New Jersey 07458

Library of Congress Cataloging-in-Publication Data

The legacy of Mesoamerica: history and culture of a Native American civilization/[edited by] Robert M. Carmack, Janine Gasco, Gary H. Gossen.
p. cm.—(Exploring cultures)
Includes bibliographical references (p. 481) and index.
ISBN 0-13-337445-9
1. Indians of Mexico—History. 2. Indians of Central America—History. 3. Indians of Mexico. 4. Indians of Central America. 5. Mexico—Civilization. 6. Central America—Civilization. I. Carmack, Robert M. II. Gasco, Janine. III. Gossen, Gary H. IV. Series.
F1219.L44 1995
972'.00497—dc20 94-31722
CIP

Acquisitions Editor: Nancy Roberts
Copyeditor: Eleanor Walter
Buyer: Mary Ann Gloriande
Editorial Assistant: Pat Naturale
Editorial/Production Supervision
and Interior Design: Mary Kathryn Bsales/Rob DeGeorge

Simon & Schuster/A Viacom Company
Upper Saddle River, New Jersey 07458

Printed in the United States of America

10 9 8 7 6 5 4 3 2 1

ISBN 0-13-337445-9

Prentice-Hall International (UK) Limited, *London*
Prentice-Hall of Australia Pty. Limited, *Sydney*
Prentice-Hall Canada Inc., *Toronto*
Prentice-Hall Hispanoamericana, S.A., *Mexico*
Prentice-Hall of India Private Limited, *New Delhi*
Prentice-Hall of Japan, Inc., *Tokyo*
Simon & Schuster Asia Pte. Ltd., *Singapore*
Editora Prentice-Hall do Brasil, Ltda., *Rio de Janeiro*

Contents

Preface

We invite our readers to share the urgency and passion that we feel toward the content of this volume. We offer here a broad appreciation of why the native peoples of Mexico and Central America have attracted the attention of scholars, chroniclers, and travelers for centuries, and why in our time this interest shows no signs of abating.

MESOAMERICA IN WESTERN INTELLECTUAL HISTORY

The encounter of the old and new worlds, which commenced in a sustained fashion in 1492, can be said to have fundamentally changed the course of human history. This encounter not only provided the opportunity for the ascendancy of Spain and Portugal to the role of being the first truly global powers, but also, in a real sense, initiated the globalization of humanity under European hegemony—a pattern that, for better or worse, remains with us to this day. Although the Caribbean Basin was the stage for the early and cataclysmic period of initial contact—which resulted in nothing less than the virtual annihilation of hundreds of thousands of Caribbean Indians, essentially the entire population, by 1550—the institutionalization of Spain's New World enterprise took root only with the conquest of Mesoamerica and the creation of New Spain, and subsequently the parallel enterprise in Peru. By 1600, fundamental Western ideas and practices concerning modernity, social progress, "tutelage" of the vanquished, bureaucratic rationalism, and economic and political dependency under the global system we know as colonialism were firmly in place—complete with all of that system's atrocities and social asymmetries. Indeed, Mesoamerica's radically truncated and transformed Indian communities, forced to live under Spain's "missionary state," became what might be called prototypes of colonized peoples, a social condition that would eventually characterize much of Asia, Africa, North and South America, and the Pacific in the ensuing centuries.

Aside from the particulars of this period, which will be discussed elsewhere in this text, it should be remembered that the sixteenth-century theological and philosophical debates regarding the "moral status" of the Amerindians were in large part focused on data that came from New Spain (Mexico). These discussions, which came to influence not only Crown and Church policy in America but also the very foundations of Western ideas about human nature, carried in their wake nothing less than the dawn of modern social science—that is, the attempt to understand human variation in what was the beginning of a truly global comparative perspective (Klor de Alva, 1988).

Sixteenth-century Mesoamerican data provided the first major, modern ethnographic reports, perhaps best exemplified by Bernardino de Sahagún's enormous corpus, in which we have a comprehensive and objective description of the customs, social organization, economy, and arts of the Nahuatl world, all of it set down in the native language with Spanish translation. This is not distant from the goals of modern ethonography. It was thus set down for all to see (but few saw the work since it was suppressed) that Spain had in fact encountered and destroyed a high civilization, comparable in some ways to Europe itself. Not only did Sahagún and others achieve a certain detachment of their descriptions from their missionary and political agenda; some also came to appraise the moral status of the colonial enterprise itself. Father Bartolomé de las Casas, who had witnessed first-hand Spain's atrocities of the early Contact period in the Caribbean and later in what is now southern Mexico and Guatemala, wrote one of the most influential political treatises of sixteenth-century Europe (*A Brief Description of the Destruction of the Indies)* as a critique of his own country's systematic destruction and cruel exploitation of Amerindians in the Caribbean and in Mesoamerica. In this work, as in many other theological and political works of the period, we are able to discern a clear pattern of cultural critique and relativism, a distancing of the observer from his own culture. Needless to say, these were exceptional individuals and their ideas were unpopular at the time; however, it is important to note that these contemporary-sounding reports and reflections about human nature, the human condition, and human variation came from sixteenth-century Spaniards who were writing of Mesoamerica. Thus, in addition to the vast material wealth and enormously important food, fiber, and medicinal plant cultigens that flowed from the New World to the Old World, there also came from America the challenge to reflect upon the origins, interrelations, givenness, mutability, internal coherence, and moral value of myriad human social forms that were unfamiliar to the Old World.

To this brief sketch of what we believe to be important contributions of Mesoamerica to the formative period of modern Western intellectual history must be added the major contributions by colonial Spanish scholars to the lexicography, transcription, translation, and grammatical analysis of Mesoamerican and other Native American languages. This is noteworthy because it was a Spaniard, Father Nebrija, who in 1492 wrote the first grammar of Castilian; this was also the first grammar of any vulgate Latin language. Hence, Spain's influential Renaissance scholarship in philology and descriptive linguistics continued with major works on the languages of the New World, establishing—largely with Mesoamerican data—a remarkable corpus of written testimonies in native languages with sophisticated translations. If one also considers that the ancient Mesoamericans themselves possessed several forms of pictographic, ideographic, and phonetic writing systems that date to at least the beginning of the Christian era, it becomes clear that, in terms of both native written testimony and early Contact period textual and linguistic materials, Mesoamerica has what are by far the oldest and most comprehensive written records of any region of the New World. It is therefore not surprising that scholars with an interest in problems of evolution and continuity of Native American civilization and of America's place in the whole flow of human history have found in Mesoamerica an extremely fruitful focus for such research. The singular power of the region to elicit our scholarly and general human interest stems not only from the great diversity and temporal depth of its cultural forms, but also from the fact that Mesoamericans themselves have spoken eloquently and often of their own world. This testimony begins with the glyphic texts and calendrical notations that date from the Late Formative period (400 B.C. to A.D. 200) and continues vigorously into the present. This constitutes a written record, rendered in several different media and writing systems, that spans over 2,000 years.

If one also considers the massive contribution of modern archaeologists, epigraphers, ethnologists, linguists, and ethnohistorians to the construction of the cultural history of the region, it becomes clear that Mesoamerica ranks as the best-known and best-documented cultural tradition of the New World. This uniquely rich documentation confers upon the region the quality of a "benchmark" that makes it possible, using data from Mesoamerica, to mount credible comparisons on innumerable topics both within the Americas and with the Old World.

MESOAMERICA IN THE HISTORY OF CULTURAL STUDIES

Because of Mesoamerica's centrality in Western scholarly reflection and romantic imagination, it will come as no surprise to the reader to find that the region has played an important role in the history of cultural studies themselves. We use the phrase "cultural studies" in its broad sense, which includes both humanistic and scientific studies of human variation in time and space.

We have already observed that systematic ethnographic reporting can, without forcing the issue, be traced back to Sahagún's pioneering work in the mid-sixteenth century. The comprehensiveness of his Mexican corpus and his commentaries on its meaning, together with his consistent attention to the importance of testimonies and texts written in Nahuatl, give his work a precocious modernity.

The ancient civilizations of Mexico and Central America figured prominently as themes in the work of European and U.S. antiquarians, natural historians, philologists, and folklorists, beginning as early as the late eighteenth century. Such scholars as the German naturalist Alexander von Humboldt and Spanish archaeologists Diego García de Palacio and Antonio del Río traveled extensively in the region and were among the first modern observers to take the region's "antiquities" seriously as subjects of scientific interest. Indeed, one can attribute to these scholars a central role in the beginning of systematic scientific collection and classification as these activities are understood in the modern era.

The middle and late nineteenth century saw the study of native Mexican and Central American culture blossom with the work of such scholars as the Frenchman Brasseur de Bourborg (rediscoverer and translator of the famous Quiché Maya *Popol Vuh*), Americans John Stephens *(Incidents of Travel in Yucatan)* and Daniel Brinton (*Aboriginal American Authors and Their Productions; Especially Those in Native Languages: A Chapter in the History of Literature)*, the British scholar Lord Kingsborough *(Antiquities of Mexico, Comprising Facsimiles of Ancient Mexican Paintings and Hieroglyphs)*, and the great German ethnologist Eduard Seler *(Collected Works in Mesoamerican Linguistics and Archaeology)*. With the advent of the Mexican Revolution in the early twentieth century, Mexico began to turn its own scholarly energies to the rediscovery of its past, most notably represented, perhaps, by the work of Manuel Gamio *(La población del valle de Teotihuacan, Mexico)*, who is recognized as the founder of modern Mexican anthropology. This brief recital of major precursors to modern Mesoamerican studies is meant to provide a perspective from which to appreciate the continuity and vitality of scholarly interest in the region's culture history—an enterprise that has, of course, exploded in the twentieth century (for more on this topic, see Chapter 1). This century of research in the area has produced some major discoveries and insights that are recognized as core themes not only in Mesoamerican studies but also within cultural studies as a whole.

What are these major ideas and approaches that owe their formulation and systematization to the peculiarly rich cultural traditions of Mesoamerica?

The first theme that bears a distinctive Mesoamerican pedigree concerns the *methodology of culture history.* Beginning with Sahagún's efforts to elicit testimony from contemporary Nahuatl speakers for the purpose of reconstructing the recent and ancient past, Mesoamerican studies have a long tradition of using written and oral testimony from living culture bearers, together with ethnographic analogies drawn from contemporary observation and other complementary strategies, for the purpose of synthesizing an account of historical lifestyles that are no longer extant. The modern manifestation of this multifaceted culture historical approach—the combined use of archaeology, ethnohistoric documents, oral history, art history, ethnography, historical linguistics, and biological anthropology—is attributed to the German-born American ethnologist, Franz Boas, who with his students (among them Mexico's own Manuel Gamio) made this an emblematic "Americanist" approach. Although Boas forged this methodology in the early twentieth century as a pragmatic strategy for reconstructing culture histories for all of the societies of the aboriginal New World that did not have written historical accounts of their own past, it has without doubt been used with singular success in Mesoamerica. This has been the case in large part because all of the desirable primary data sources abound in the region: omnipresent archaeological remains of millennia of human occupation; written testimonies from some groups, dating back as early as the time of Christ; abundant ethnohistoric sources dating from the earliest years of European contact; and millions of contemporary native people who, even today, speak more than 80 different languages belonging to several macrofamilies and live in thousands of distinctive communities. In short, the region has all of the elements necessary for providing scholars with the opportunity to learn a great deal about an enormously diverse and ancient center of high civilization whose innovations (particularly plant cultigens) influenced much of the aboriginal New World and, subsequently, the Old World as well. Readers may be their own judge as to the degree of success that has been achieved toward this scholarly goal, but surely no other region of the Americas has such potential for bringing together diverse strategies of historical inquiry for the pursuit of a common enterprise.

A second achievement of Mesoamerican studies with respect to the whole of cultural studies has been a major contribution to the *theory of the evolution of state-level societies and empires*—their rise, decline, and transformation—in long historical perspective. Although the issue of cultural evolution has been of interest to social theorists and philosophers for several centuries, it can be said without exaggeration that Mesoamerica and the Andes, together with the Middle East—all of which possess comparably deep and rich archaeological sequences that span social forms from pre-agricultural communities to multiethnic empires—have provided the best empirical foundation for a general theoretical understanding of major evolutionary trends in human history. Much of this important body of research has focused on Mesoamerican data. Many of the major contributors have been archaeologists, who have for the most part worked within the cultural evolutionist framework.

A third equally important contribution to Mesoamerican studies and to cultural studies as a whole is the *theory of peasantry.* Just who are those tens of millions who have lived (and continue to live today) at the social, economic, political, and ideological peripheries of states? How are their communities, economies, customs, and identities linked to the macropolities under whose shadow they live? Are they autonomous and benignly marginalized or are they benighted pawns of elite centers? Perhaps the most influential debates on this issue within twentieth-century anthropology have focused on Mesoamerican data and have involved such major figures as Robert Redfield, Oscar Lewis, Eric Wolf, and Rodolfo Stavenhagen.

The evolution, dynamics, and heterogeneous composition of states are closely linked to a fourth contribution of Mesoamerican studies to anthropological and historical literature: *the study of colonialism, ethnicity, syncretism, and social change.* How did native peoples cope with their new status as colonized subjects of a European nation? What changed and to what extent when Spain destroyed the symbolic capital and the political and economic power of the native states of Mesoamerica? Did this affect the elite groups differently than the peasants? men differently than women? urban centers differently than small villages? What new social and biological forms emerged in the course of the encounter? How was resistance to the new masters orchestrated? What happened to the supernatural world of the vanquished? What, in fact, distinguishes "Indian identity" from "national identity"? How are these identities related to each other?

These questions mattered a great deal to colonial authorities and missionaries, just as they are of concern to government officials in the region today. Since Mesoamerica was an early and prototypical case of a modern state system that attempted to absorb hundreds of ethnically diverse communities, studies of that system have contributed much to our knowledge of the dynamics of culture change.

A fifth contribution to general cultural and social research that has a particularly strong tie to Mesoamerica concerns the *uses of social science in the formation and implementation of public policy of European-modeled states toward their ethnic minorities.* Specifically, the body of policy legislation and applied practice that is known as *indigenismo* has since the early twentieth century evolved in Mexico and, to a lesser extent, in Peru and Guatemala as a guiding agenda for Indian policy. As a corollary of *indigenista* ideology, social research becomes the servant of the national interest and an instrument for social change, nation-building, and community development. Perhaps nowhere in the world has this policy role of social research been more thoroughly articulated and successfully practiced than in Mexico. Many nations of the developing world of the late twentieth century look to Mexico as a source of ideas for deploying the scarce resources that are available for research in such a way that practical benefits for the nation and its people will be forthcoming.

A sixth major contribution of Mesoamerican studies to cultural studies as a whole lies in the fields of *linguistics, epigraphy, and art history.* The extraordinary recent discoveries of the linguists and epigraphers who study texts written in the hand of ancient Mesoamericans have extended the testimony of these peoples back to the beginning of the Christian era. Through such texts, now credibly rendered in translation, the Mesoamericans themselves tell us in their own writing systems what their world signified to them.

MESOAMERICA AND THE STRUGGLE FOR PHYSICAL AND SOCIAL SURVIVAL

It is evident from what we have considered above that Mesoamerica has contributed a great deal to the wealth and political ascendancy of the West and to the development of Western thought in general and the social sciences in particular. But when we acknowledge the region's gifts to us in the form of wealth, labor, plant cultigens, and ideas, we must also recognize what they have cost: Native Mesoamericans have endured more than four centuries of various forms of oppression and exploitation in the course of their encounter with the outside world. In this asymmetrical contact situation, they have seldom acted as passive victims.

From their first contact with European peoples in the sixteenth century to the Zapatista Movement that Maya Indians launched in January 1994, large numbers of the cultural and biological descendants of the prehispanic Mesoamerican peoples have struggled to preserve their cultural identity. In stating this we do not mean to imply the romantic notion of some mystical persistence of the Mesoamerican peoples and their cultural traditions. In the chapters to follow, we will document their struggles to survive and maintain a dignified identity in the face of hundreds of years of oppression. The Mesoamerican cultural tradition is a living, vibrant social phenomenon and has survived in a diversity of expressions only as a result of the unrelenting resistance—in many instances, violent resistance—to outside imperialists by the Mesoamericans themselves.

The physical and social survival of the Mesoamerican Indians is sufficiently noteworthy to serve as both inspiration and model for other native peoples around the world who have suffered the ravages of colonization and "modernization." We are not arguing that the Mesoamerican tradition has survived intact, or that the Mesoamericans have always played a key role in every social development in Mexico and Central America. Nevertheless, the Mesoamericans' ability to adapt their cultural traditions to the dramatically changing social milieu in which they live and, when necessary, to attempt actively to transform that milieu, has rightfully captured the attention of the world community.

With respect to the physical survival of the Mesoamerican Indians within Mexico and Central America, we should note first that the absolute numbers of Indians has substantially increased through time since the catastrophic losses following first Spanish contact. The accompanying table summarizes the changes in absolute numbers of Indians in the region for the close of the prehispanic era (A.D. 1520), the time of independence from Spain (1800), the eve of the Mexican Revolution (1900), the beginning of the modern development phase (1950), and the present (1990).

As the table indicates, in Mexico almost 10 million people now identify themselves as Indians, and they make up 11 percent of that country's total population. In Central America, almost 6 million people identify themselves as Indians, amounting to approximately 24 percent of its population (most of them in Guatemala). Remarkably, despite the massive population losses associated with the conquest and colonization of the region, the survivors of the Mesoamerican world now represent more than one-half the total aboriginal population from the time of Spanish contact. This demographic recovery constitutes a survival record perhaps unsurpassed by any other group of peoples suffering cataclysmic population losses in the annals of modern history.

The Mesoamericans' record for social survival is as impressive as their record of

Changing Native Population in the Mesoamerican Region
(in millions of Indians)

Year	*1520*	*1800*	*1900*	*1950*	*1990*
Mexico	21.4	3.7	2.1	2.9	9.5
Central America	5.7	0.6	1.3	3.8	5.9
Totals	27.1	4.3	3.4	6.7	15.4

Note: None of these population figures is highly reliable and should be considered only approximations. This is especially true for the prehispanic period (1520), for which some scholars would lower Mexico's 21 million figure to 10 million or less. But even the more recent figures are best seen as estimates since they reflect the varying definitions of what constitutes Indian identity through time and from country to country.

physical survival. Many of the forms of social resistance that the Mesoamericans have practiced during the past 500 years are comparable to those of other native peoples around the world: closing off communities to outside influence, passive obedience or active disobedience to the mandates of outside powers, subtle syncretization of alien cultural forms with native cultures, rebellious nativistic movements, and many others. Large numbers of aboriginal peoples have actively participated in twentieth-century revolutionary movements in places like Russia, China, and Vietnam, but none more effectively or in greater numbers than the Mesoamericans. The first revolution of the twentieth century took place not in Russia but in Mexico, and as we will see, the native Mesoamericans played a crucial role in that social upheaval. Similarly, the most recent twentieth-century revolutions have been occurring in the Central American countries of Nicaragua, El Salvador, and Guatemala, where native Mesoamericans once again have been major players.

Undeniably, the revolutions that have shaken the world during the twentieth century constitute some of the most important events in modern world history. Given this historical fact, we think it is time that the Mesoamericans are given recognition for their significant revolutionary activities in Mexico and Central America. In this regard, it is worth noting that the Maya Zapatista Movement currently in progress in southern Mexico promises to force the democratization of Mexico's entire political process (for the Zapatista Movement, see the Epilogue).

MESOAMERICA AND MODERN NORTH AMERICA

We conclude this preface by commenting briefly on why we, as scholars and citizens of the New World, should care about the cultural and social history of Mesoamerica as a segment of general knowledge that may be relevant to our everyday lives, now and in the future. We wish to move beyond academic and intellectual concerns to observe that the region has already profoundly influenced the world we live in. Indeed, some of the most familiar tastes and sights that make up our everyday lives derive from Native Mesoamerican and Mexican origins. For example, some of the staple ingredients in a McDonald's fast food lunch—french fries, ketchup, and chocolate shakes—come from plants that were domesticated by Native Americans—potatoes, tomatoes, and cacao. Chocolate (cacao) and tomatoes were native Mesoamerican cultigens, and potatoes were originally domesticated in Andean South America. Furthermore, the cattle that provide the beef to make the hamburgers are fed on maize (corn), the dietary staple of the ancient and modern peoples of Mesoamerica.

The social and economic history of maize, a Mesoamerican plant domesticate, is extraordinary in itself. It has become the principal food crop of many nations of Africa and Asia. In our own culture it appears in many forms, from tacos and tortilla chips (taken from Mexican cuisine) and cornbread (adapted from North American Indians) to the corn syrup that is ubiquitous in our processed foods. Maize and products derived from it make a multimillion-dollar contribution to the annual U.S. export economy.

Our homes, too, have been influenced by Mesoamerican traditions. The "ranch-style" houses so common in our modern suburbs developed from the modest one-story ranch houses of northern Mexico, which in turn were derived from Spanish house styles, modified during the Colonial period by the use of Mesoamerican building materials. Both Spanish and ancient Mesoamerican architectural styles included public and private outdoor living spaces. We have borrowed the names and concepts of "plaza" and "patio" and made them our own in the form of shopping plazas and backyard patios.

And around the world, what image is more associated with the United States than the western cowboy? Time and again our athletes choose to march into the Olympic

Games wearing the familiar cowboy hat. Yet the mythical "cowboy culture" that we celebrate as our own in literature, movies, and the arts bears the indelible imprint of its origins in northern Mexican cattle culture. The traditional cowboy outfit—broad-brimmed hat, kerchief, chaps, spurs, "cowboy" boots, and "western" saddle—is of Mexican origin. And so are dozens of words, borrowed from Spanish, that are associated with cowboy life and culture: ranch *(rancho)*; corral *(corral)*; buckaroo (from *vaquero*, meaning "cowboy"); bronco (from *bronco*, meaning "hoarse," "resistant," "untamed"); and rodeo *(rodeo)*. To this list we must add "chili," the quintessential dish of Southwestern U.S. cuisine and mainstay of cattle drivers. This dish is nothing less than a slightly altered adaptation of a generic bean, chili, tomato, and meat stew that existed in Mesoamerica long before Spain invaded Mexico.

We could go on to enumerate the influences of our southern neighbors on U.S. music, art, and other areas of our daily lives; however, suffice it to say that many regions of our country have a long history of interaction with the peoples of Mesoamerica. This began with the ancient trade networks between Mesoamerican and North American native groups and continued with the shared experience of exploration and efforts at colonization by Spain (large areas of our South and West were first explored by Spain between 1540 and 1570, decades before the founding of Jamestown). The pattern of close association continues with the current influx into our cities of millions of Mexican and Central American immigrants and refugees.

The United States shares a highly permeable 2,000-mile border with Mexico, and the flow of people, goods, and ideas across it has had a powerful impact on our society. This is reflected in a simple but startling demographic fact: East Los Angeles ranks second only to Mexico City itself among Mexican urban populations. Mexican Americans make up the majority of what is the largest non-English-speaking population of the United States. Indeed, the United States is the sixth-ranking Spanish-speaking nation in the world. Furthermore, the Mexican Spanish-speaking segment of U.S. society is growing faster than any other minority or immigrant group in this country. All of this leads to the obvious conclusion that ancient and modern Mesoamericans have long been a significant presence in U.S. culture and society, a pattern that shows no signs of abating in the near or distant future. Mesoamericans are thus, literally and figuratively, our fellow Americans. We have every reason to become well acquainted with them.

Canada, Mexico, and the United States have recently formalized the North American Free Trade Agreement. Modern Mesoamericans will now join us as members of one of the three major economic and trading blocs in the world: North America, Europe, and Asia. This suggests that the twenty-first century will inevitably bring Mexico, our "distant neighbor," into our very midst with a shared set of economic interests and opportunities. As English-speaking North Americans, we will obviously have much to gain in appreciating and understanding the ancient and modern legacy of Mesoamerican civilization.

ACKNOWLEDGMENTS

The authors wish to extend their gratitude to all the members of the Institute for Mesoamerican Studies (IMS) who contributed their time and talents to the creation of this book. We also wish to give very special acknowledgment to Cynthia Heath-Smith, former Research Director of IMS, who labored tirelessly and efficiently to coordinate the assembling of the text itself, the obtainment of permissions for many of the illustrations, and the initial editing of the manuscript on the campus of the University at Albany–SUNY.

The contributors below provided illustrations from their personal collections, as indicated by figure numbers listed:

Louise Burkhart: Figures 2.6, 2.13, 5.3, 5.4, 5.6, 5.12.

Robert Carmack: Figures 1.5, 1.6, 1.7, 1.13, 6.8, 7.4, 8.5.

Alfredo Rosenbaum: Figures 9.6, 9.7.

Brenda Rosenbaum: Figure 9.9.

Michael Smith: Figures 1.1, 1.4, 2.2, 2.11, 2.14, 2.18, 2.19, 7.11, 8.4.

Ellen Cesarski prepared artwork specifically for the following figures of the book: Figures 1.2, 1.3, 1.8, 1.11, 1.12, 2.3 (map), 2.5 (map), 2.7, 2.9 (map), 2.17 (map), 4.1 (map), 5.1 (map), 6.1 (map), 7.1 (map), 7.7 (map), 8.1, 8.6, 11.1, 11.3, 12.7.

The individuals and institutions below went out of their way to assist and provide us with illustrative materials, in many cases waiving or drastically reducing their regular fees:

Frances F. Berdan

E. Bradford Burns

Susan Danford, The John Carter Brown Library, Brown University

Enrique Florescano

Jeffrey Jay Foxx

David A. Freidel

Ian Graham

Merle Green Robertson

Gillett G. Griffin

Debra Nagao

Alex Ross

Linda Schele

Finally, we would like to thank the following reviewers for their helpful suggestions and useful insights: Robert R. Alvarez, Arizona State University; Robert V. Kemper, Southern Methodist University; Karl H. Schwerin, University of New Mexico; Albert Wahrhaftig, Sonoma State University; and Alaka Wali, University of Maryland.

Chapter 1 Introduction

The Spanish explorers and conquistadors who first made contact with the Mesoamerican world were surprised by its complexity and grandeur, for they had become accustomed to the simpler ways of the previously subjugated natives of the Caribbean islands. Their testimony constitutes an informative beginning place for our study of the Mesoamerican world, whose origins, condition at European contact, and transformations resulting from colonization and (more recently) modernization are the subject of this text.

SPANISH FIRST IMPRESSIONS OF MESOAMERICA

The Spaniards were extremely impressed with the level of cultural development achieved by the Mesoamerican peoples, and in reviewing their first impressions the reader should take particular note of the complexity and diversity of Mesoamerica. Let us begin with Columbus and his fourth voyage to the New World.

Columbus Meets the Maya during His Fourth Voyage

The first Europeans to make contact with Mesoamerican peoples were Christopher Columbus and his men during their fourth voyage to the New World. Columbus began the voyage in 1502. Departing from Spain, he touched down on the island of Hispaniola (present-day Haiti and Dominican Republic), and then sailed directly to the Bay Islands located off the coast of Honduras. While he was at one of the islands, a large canoe of "Indians" arrived, bearing merchandise brought from areas to the west. Many years later, Columbus's son Fernando described the canoe and its people as follows:

> [The canoe was as] long as a galley and eight feet wide, made of a single tree trunk. . . . Amidship it had a palm-leaf awning like that which the Venetian gondolas carry; this gave complete protection against the rain and waves. Under this awning were the children and women and all the baggage and merchandise. There were twenty-five paddlers. . . . [The Admiral] took aboard the costliest and handsomest things in that cargo: cotton mantles and sleeveless shirts embroidered and painted in different designs and colors; breechclouts of the same design and cloth as the shawls worn by the women in the canoe, being like the shawls worn by the Moorish women of Granada; long wooden swords with a groove on each side where the edge should be, in which were fastened with cord and pitch, flint knives that cut like steel; hatchets resembling the stone hatchets used by the other Indians, but made of good copper; and hawk's bells of copper, and crucibles to melt it. For provisions they had such roots and grains as the Indians of Española eat, also a wine made of maize that tasted like English beer. They had as well many of the almonds [cacao beans] which the Indians of New Spain use as currency. . . . (Keen 1959:231–232)

Columbus was impressed by the cultural refinement of the natives in the canoe, for he had not seen a people like them before in the New World. He seized the leader of the boat, an old man named Yumbe, who became translator for Columbus with the peoples they later met along the coast of Honduras. Yumbe is a Maya name, which suggests that Columbus had stumbled onto a group of Maya long-distance traders from the Mesoamerican world.

Columbus apparently did not fully understand the significance of the Maya traders or the complex world from which they came, and he sailed east toward lower Central America in search of the hoped-for passageway to the Orient. As a result, he encountered indigenous peoples culturally similar to the natives already known to him in Hispaniola and the other Caribbean islands. His decision to explore lower Central America established a pattern followed by subsequent explorers, who during the next two decades initiated the first permanent Spanish settlements in the area known today as Panama.

The Spaniards Make Contact with the Powerful Kingdoms of Mesoamerica

Exploration of Mesoamerica by the Spaniards began between 1517 and 1519 (for details, see Chapter 4), as first Hernández de Córdova, then Juan de Grijalva, and finally Hernán Cortés sailed around the Yucatán Peninsula and northward along the Gulf Coast of Mexico. In 1519, while Cortés and his men were camped with the Totonac Indians of Veracruz, they witnessed the arrival of a group of Aztec tax collectors. The Spaniards were astonished by the extreme deference with which the Totonacs served the Aztecs, and began to understand—perhaps for the first time—just how politically complex and culturally diverse the newly discovered world of native peoples really was. The point was driven home even more forcefully to the Spaniards as they began their history-making journey from the Veracruz coast to the Central Basin of Mexico. At each step along the way they encountered economically richer, culturally more sophisticated, and politically more powerful peoples. Beyond Totonac country, they felt they were entering "a different sort of country," one in which the gleaming plastered stone buildings of the towns and fortresses reminded them of Spain itself.

In places like Tlaxcala, Cholula, and Huejotzinco, the Spaniards were surprised to find cosmopolitan and highly politicized peoples. Their robust kingdoms were populated by over 100,000 subjects each, and they vied with one another for power by employing elaborate forms of diplomacy, intrigue, and warfare. Territories were defended with high walls and fortifications. Armies in the tens of thousands were organized into diverse ranks and squadrons, each with its own insignia and dress code. Cities as large as in Spain bustled with people engaged in daily trade, administrative affairs, and religious ritual. The native societies were profoundly stratified, not only between noble and commoner, but also between rich and poor, freeman and slave. Cortés captured the cosmopolitan nature of these societies with the following description of Tlaxcala:

> The city is indeed so great and marvellous that though I abstain from describing many things about it, yet the little that I shall recount is, I think, almost incredible. It is much larger than Granada, and much better fortified. Its houses are as fine and its inhabitants far more numerous than those of Granada when that city was captured. Its provisions and food are likewise very superior—including such things as bread, fowl, game, fish and other excellent vegetables and produce which they eat. There is a market in this city in which more than thirty thousand people daily are occupied in buying and selling, and this in addition to other similar shops which there are in all parts of the city. Nothing is lacking in this market of what they are wont to use, whether utensils, garments, footwear or the like. There is gold, silver and precious stones, and jewellers' shops selling other ornaments made of feathers, as well arranged as in any market in the world. There is earthenware of many kinds and excellent quality, as fine as any in Spain. Wood, charcoal, medicinal and sweet smelling herbs are sold in large quantities. There are booths for washing your hair and barbers to shave you: there are also public baths. Finally, good order and an efficient police system are maintained among them, and they behave as people of sense and reason: the foremost city of Africa cannot rival them. (Cortés 1962:50–51)

The Tlaxcalans, Cholutecans, and other peoples of the area were able to describe for Cortés what the Aztec heartland was like. Nevertheless, the Spaniards were unprepared for what they saw when in November 1519 they finally reached the Basin of Mexico and entered the Aztec capital of Tenochtitlán. Cortés later wrote of the Aztec capital (Figure 1.1):

Figure 1.1 The island city of Tenochtitlán at the time of Spanish contact. From the painting by Miguel Covarrubias in the Museo Nacional de Antropología, Mexico City.

> The great city of Tenochtitlan is built in the midst of this salt lake, and it is two leagues from the heart of the city to any point on the mainland. Four causeways lead to it, all made by hand and some twelve feet wide. The city itself is as large as Seville or Córdova. The principal streets are very broad and straight, the majority of them being of beaten earth, but a few and at least half the smaller thoroughfares are waterways along which they pass in their canoes. (Cortés 1962:86)

Cortés, an astute observer, attempted to place the Aztec capital in the wider context of Mesoamerica as a whole and even of the Old World. He described in great detail the pomp and ceremony surrounding Motecuhzoma, the ruler of the Aztec empire, who, he said, rivaled "the sultans themselves or other eastern potentates." Cortés recounted how Motecuhzoma was attended by literally thousands of retainers, who were not permitted to wear sandals in his presence or see his face. The Aztec ruler changed attire four times a day, never wearing the same clothing more than once. Wherever he went he was carried on jewel-studded litters by men of the highest noble rank. Hundreds of young men and women served his meals, which included up to three hundred different dishes. Motecuhzoma conducted imperial business in the royal palace, amusing himself during breaks by strolling through the surrounding gardens and parks stocked with every variety of plant and animal known to the native world.

Motecuhzoma's wealth in gold and other metal pieces; precious stone jewelry; exquisite feather, stone, wood, and bone crafted items; beautiful cloths; and innumerable other objects was so great that Cortés was "doubtful whether any of all the known princes of the world possesses such treasures in such quantity." Cortés estimated the city's main market to be twice as large as the one in Salamanca. The quality of Aztec maize, in both grain size and taste, was said to be superior to that of "all the other islands or the mainland." The multicolored cotton cloth was as good as any in Spain, and on a par with the silks of Granada. Cortés also marvelled at the number of commercial goods being exchanged in Tenochtitlán, brought there by thousands of canoes bound for the city from every direction along the network of canals. All goods that entered the city were taxed. In the marketplaces themselves every conceivable item and service were available, from barbering to prostitution, and large numbers of skilled and unskilled laborers gathered there "waiting to be hired by the day."

In an attempt to put Aztec society into broader perspective, Cortés summarized his observations as follows:

> Finally, to avoid prolixity in telling all the wonders of this city, I will simply say that the manner of living among the people is very similar to that in Spain, and considering that this is a barbarous nation shut off from a knowledge of the true God or communication with enlightened nations, one may well marvel at the orderliness and good government which is everywhere maintained. (Cortés 1962:93–94)

The Spaniards quickly determined that the Aztec empire was vast, extending for hundreds of miles in all directions, and that, as Cortés attested, "Motecuhzoma was feared by all both present and distant more than any other monarch in the world." Still, the Spaniards were well aware that they had seen only a small part of the Mesoamerican world, and that many other kingdoms, large and small, were yet to be explored and subdued.

With the fall of Tenochtitlán to the Spaniards in 1521 (see Chapter 4), Cortés began to send his captains on military expeditions from the Basin of Mexico to contact and, if necessary, conquer the diverse peoples and kingdoms of Mesoamerica. For example, expeditions were sent to the great province called Michoacán in the west and further north from there to the province of Cihuatán, "which it is affirmed had an island inhabited solely by women"; and to the rebellious province of Huaxteca in the northeast. Other expeditions were dispatched to the southern provinces of Mesoamerica, such as Oaxaca, Chiapas, and "the very rich lands" of Higueras (Honduras). One of the most important expeditions was entrusted to Cortés' courageous but ruthless captain, Pedro de Alvarado, who was sent to the "rich and splendid lands inhabited by new and different races" in the provinces of Utatlán and Guatemala.

DEFINING "MESOAMERICA" AND OTHER IMPORTANT TERMS

We have referred to the world encountered by Cortés and his band as "Mesoamerica." What do we mean by this term? To what will it refer in the chapters to follow? We should begin by noting that the term *Mesoamerica* has varied widely in meaning; in fact, no term is more debated in Mesoamerican studies than Mesoamerica itself. We do not propose to settle the debate, but rather to define our terms and try to employ them in clear and consistent fashion. We are aware that the Mesoamericans themselves are sensitive about how such terms are used, and in the chapters to follow we have tried to keep their interests in mind as well.

Literally, the term Mesoamerica means "Middle America," and was at one time widely used to refer exclusively to the aboriginal cultures of the region, whether in their pristine prehispanic or acculturated modern forms. That is to say, Mesoamerica had a geographic reference: the region where the ancient Mesoamerican cultures flourished prior to the coming of the Spaniards. This usage was problematic for mestizo, European, and even indigenous peoples who had little or nothing to do with the so-called Mesoamerican cultures but have resided in the region for centuries. In this text, for the most part, we avoid using the term strictly as a geographic region or culture area.

A more flexible and useful definition of Mesoamerica, we think, is as a particular historical tradition of aboriginal cultures (sometimes referred to as a "civilization"). It is understood that the tradition was constantly undergoing transformation prior to the coming of the Spaniards, and has continued to undergo change and adaptation since Spanish contact. The creators of this rich historical tradition—both the original, prehispanic version and the posthispanic, modified variants—may properly be termed "Mesoamericans." From our perspective, Mesoamerica, whether past or present, cannot be adequately defined by a list of essential traits or ideas; rather, we must examine the relationship through time between these ideas and the social and material processes involved in their creation. Both the cultural tradition and the processes by which Mesoamerica has changed are worth tracing because they have profoundly influenced the participating peoples of Mexico and Central America, whether they be aboriginals, mestizos, Africans, or Europeans.

It must be emphasized that Mesoamerica, as we employ the term, does not refer to a fixed or static cultural system. From at least 1000 B.C. onward, the Mesoamerican cultural tradition has been a complex mix of regional and local cultures, and in a state of continual flux. This was even more the case after the Spanish cultural traditions—and later European and North American traditions—were imposed on the Mesoamerican peoples and further fragmented their cultures. Nevertheless, the legacy of the Mesoamerican cultural tradition has been sufficiently cohesive, unique, and influential in the history of the region to warrant its identification with a special term.

Despite the unity of the Mesoamerican cultural tradition, the Mesoamericans have perhaps never seen themselves as a single people sharing a common culture. During prehispanic times the widest identifying units for most Mesoamericans were the political systems to which they were subject, whether empires, kingdoms, city-states, or chiefdoms. Furthermore, most Mesoamericans have been strongly localistic, and collective identities based on ethnic group, community, and lineage were probably even stronger than those based on political affiliation.

For millions of Mesoamericans in the region, this continues to be true today, as their collective identity comes more from the village, hamlet, region, or language group to which they belong than from the nation-state in whose territory they reside. In most contexts and time periods, then, Mesoamericans have tended to see themselves mainly as first, members of a lineage; second, participants in a community; third, speakers of a common language; and finally, if at all, as Mexicans, Central Americans, or Mesoamericans.

Like the term Mesoamerica, *Indian* is another controversial term debated within Mesoamerican studies. As is well known, this term was incorrectly applied to the native peoples of Mesoamerica and elsewhere by Columbus and later Spanish explorers. The Spaniards continued to refer to the Mesoamericans during the colonial period as Indians (in the Spanish form, "indios"), and its usage persisted in the nation-states of Mexico and Central America after independence. Therein lies the controversy, for many Mesoamericans today resent being called Indians. The term, they say, is not only a misnomer but worse, a device employed by the ruling classes to keep the native peoples in a subordinate ("neo-colonial") social position.

Various alternate labels have been suggested by scholars and Mesoamericans alike to replace Indian, such as "aborigine," "indigene," "natural," "native," and "Native American." Some Mesoamericans prefer to be identified by either generic ethnic designations—such as "Maya," "Nahua," "Otomí," "Pipil"—or local community eponyms—for example, "San Juaneros" or "Ixtahuacanos" (people from the community of San Juan, or the community of Ixtahuacán). Given the controversy, the term Indian should be used with care and an effort made to determine how it has been used to further the political and economic interests of both the Mesoamericans and their external oppressors.

Another controversial term, especially for the Mesoamericans themselves, is *conquest.* The Mesoamericans accept that they were invaded by Spaniards and defeated in wars against them, but insist that they were never conquered by the Spaniards or anyone else. They argue that they did not willingly submit to domination by outsiders, and have continued to struggle against the aggressors down to the present time. Considerable evidence will be presented in this book to support this claim, although, as the reader will discover, we nevertheless employ the term conquest to refer to the bloody clashes that took place during the sixteenth century between the Spaniards and Mesoamericans.

Although we are sympathetic to arguments made by Mesoamericans about the importance of terminology, terms like "Indian" and "conquest" are universally employed in North American scholarly discourse, and it seems to us that it would be overly pedantic to excise them from our account. Ironically, some native Mesoamericans insist on being called Indians in order to dramatize the oppression to which they have been subjected since initial contact with the Europeans. The word conquest is universally applied in the social sciences to refer to political clashes like the ones that took place in Mesoamerica during the sixteenth century. We hasten to add, however, that "Indian," as we use the term, carries no connotation of racial or cultural inferiority, and that "conquest" does not mean that the native Mesoamericans have ceased to resist all means to subjugate them. We trust it will be obvious to the reader of the pages to follow that our respect and admiration for the Mesoamerican Indians and their cultures are genuine and grounded in a clear understanding of their history.

Finally, we wish to mention a few other, less controversial terminological problems. The most important of these, perhaps, has to do with orthography: how to spell or represent native terms and expressions. Linguists, of course, have a universal phonetic alphabet by which they record and analyze the diverse languages of the world, including those spoken by Mesoamericans. Other scholars, such as ethnologists, archaeologists, geographers, and historians, have developed orthographies that do not always correspond perfectly with the linguists' phonetic system. In part this is a practical matter of being able to write native terms in the everyday alphabets of the scholars' home countries (English, Spanish, German, etc.). The countries of the Mesoamerican region, especially Mexico and Guatemala, have stressed the importance of developing alphabets for the native languages that are easily adapted to Spanish. Recently, the Mesoamerican Indians themselves have taken a renewed interest in developing their own ways of writing the native languages which are, after all, part of their own cultural heritage. Fortunately, a growing number of native scholars are being trained in the science of linguistics, and consequently now express more of an interest in finding a universal graphic system to transcribe the Mesoamerican languages than in developing a unique "native" alphabet for each language.

For the most part in this text, we follow standard scholarly usage in representing native terms and expressions. Except for Chapter 11 on the Mesoamerican languages, we write the names of native persons, places, and things in their Anglo-American rather than truly phonetic forms. Similarly, we render Spanish terms and expressions—which have been incorporated into the Mesoamerican tradition in large numbers—with English glosses where possible. We use accent marks for Spanish names in those cases where correct pronunciation by the reader might otherwise be difficult.

THE PHYSICAL SETTING OF ABORIGINAL MESOAMERICA

Having seen how the Spaniards viewed the Mesoamericans, and having defined "Mesoamerica" and other terms, let us now turn to the physical setting in which the Mesoamericans developed their elaborate cultural tradition. In this section, we begin with a brief examination of the broad geographic conditions within which the Mesoamericans developed their distinctive civilization, after which a series of special "natural areas" will be delineated. We will also briefly attempt to characterize the Mesoamericans in biological terms, arguing in the process that these biological characteristics represent adaptations by the aboriginal peoples to the environmental conditions of the region.

The Highland and Lowland Division

Few places in the world of equivalent size vary as much as the Mesoamerican region in its landforms, climate, flora and fauna, soils, and vegetation. Indeed, this geographic diversity is thought to be closely linked to the origin of agriculture and evolution of the state within the region. The "natural areas" into which the region is subdivided provide widely divergent adaptive challenges to the inhabitants, whether aboriginal Mesoamericans or the modern mixed populations of whites, mestizos, and Indians in Mexico and Central America. We are particularly interested in the responses to these environmental challenges through time by the native Mesoamericans, and how these responses help explain the social history and cultural patterns that will be reviewed in the chapters to follow. It is likely, too, that adaptations to the more general features of Mesoamerican geography have provided the ecological basis for the many shared cultural features that gave the peoples of the Middle American region a common identity and set them apart from other native peoples in North and South America.

One useful scheme divides the region into three distinct geographic zones, as shown in Box 1.1.

Generally speaking, the Mesoamerican peoples have adapted to the highland/lowland divide by means of two major adaptive or ecological systems, defined in terms of their respective agricultural, demographic, and settlement pattern regimes.

Box 1.1 *Three Geographic Zones of Middle America*

Broad contrasts in elevation divide the region into the following three distinct geographic zones (Sanders and Price 1968:101–105) (Figure 1.2):

Tierra Fría zone ("cold lands"), 2,000 to 2,800 meters elevation.

Tierra Templada zone ("temperate lands"), 1,000 to 2,000 meters elevation.

Tierra Caliente zone ("hot lands"), 0 to 1,000 meters elevation.

These three zones can be further subdivided into geographically diverse subzones on the basis of variations in land elevation and the relative amount of rainfall received. The resulting zones and subzones define conditions that have greatly affected the production of the main cultivated plants in Mesoamerica, and thus played an important role in the history of the region. For example, the way maize (corn) is grown will vary considerably depending upon the subzones; in arid subzones, it usually will not grow at all unless irrigated. Similarly, cacao does not do well in Tierra Templada zones, and requires irrigation in subhumid subzones or arid Tierra Caliente subzones. Cotton grows well only in arid and subhumid Tierra Caliente subzones.

It is customary to simplify the geography of the region by referring to both the Tierra Fría and Tierra Templada zones as "highlands," and the Tierra Caliente zone as "lowlands." This broad highland versus lowland division is thought to have been historically the region's most fundamental geographic division.

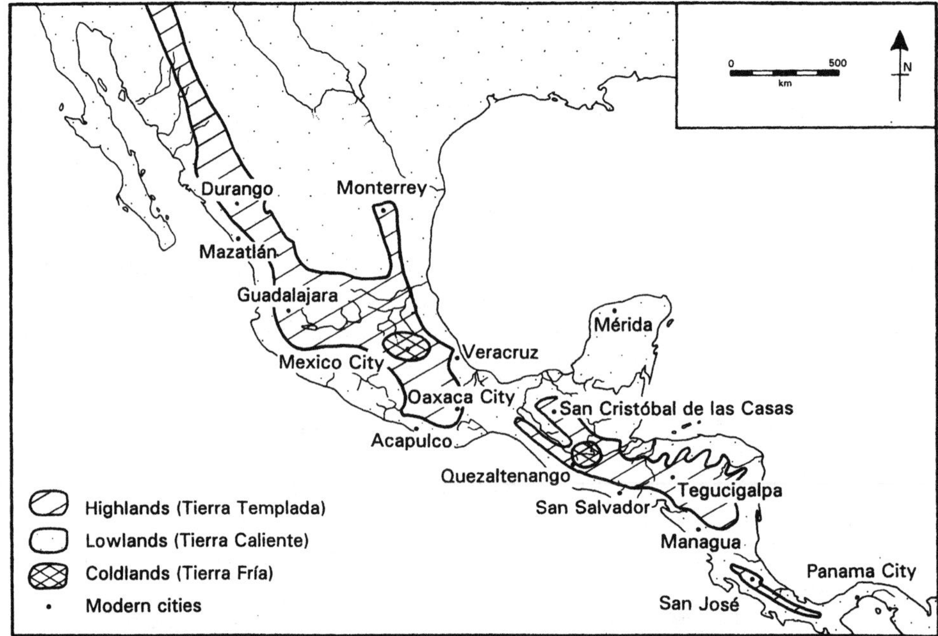

Figure 1.2 The three major geographic zones of Mesoamerica. After Robert C. West, "The Natural Regions of Middle America," *The Handbook of Middle American Indians, Volume I: Natural Environment and Early Cultures,* volume editor Robert C. West, general editor Robert Wauchope. Austin, TX: University of Texas Press, 1964, p. 365.

Highlands. The Mesoamericans associated with the highland ecological system have been concentrated mainly in the Central Plateau of Mexico, the mountainous areas of Oaxaca, and the intermontaine basins of Chiapas and Guatemala. The most fertile soils of the region are found in the highlands, especially within the larger basins, valleys, and plateaus. The soil fertility of the highlands is primarily the result of sedimentation in extinct lakes and volcanic action. Periodic volcanic eruptions have carried ash and cinder into the numerous large valleys and basins of the highlands.

Maize, beans, squash, amaranth, maguey, and other crops were produced in the highlands, employing an intensive agricultural technology. In aboriginal times technological intensification took the form of terracing, irrigation, and short-term fallowing (dry farming).

Highland populations in the region have always been concentrated in the valleys and basins, in aboriginal times at densities of 100 persons per square kilometer or more. They also have tended to be nucleated in urban centers, both "towns," with thousands of persons, and "cities," with tens of thousands of inhabitants. Population densities in the highland urban centers during aboriginal times were invariably greater than 2,000 persons per square kilometer. Overall, the total population of the highland peoples of contact-period Mesoamerica may have numbered over 20 million persons, the vast majority of them residing in the highlands of Mexico.

Most of the minerals of importance to the aboriginal peoples of Mesoamerica occurred naturally in the highlands. Among these were metals (gold, silver, copper), obsidian, jadeite and other serpentine stones, amber, and volcanic stone for grinding tools. Salt, a necessary element in the diet of all peoples, came mostly from the lowlands, although there were a few briny sinks in the highlands from which salt could be extracted.

Lowlands. The Mesoamerican peoples associated with the lowland ecological system have been concentrated mainly along the eastern (Gulf of Mexico and Caribbean) and western (Pacific) coasts of the region. Soil fertility varies widely in the coastal lowland zones. Along the eastern coast, particularly in the Yucatán Peninsula, the limestone soils are generally thin and relatively infertile. The soils in the western lowlands tend to be more fertile as a result of volcanic deposition, especially in the piedmont areas. In general, the most fertile lowland soils consist of alluvial deposits formed by rivers flowing from the volcanic highlands down through the lowlands on their way to the two oceans.

The aboriginal inhabitants of lowland settings have usually adopted the slash-and-burn (swidden) system of horticulture. This system is based on an extensive technology in which the natural vegetation is cut and burned, after which maize, beans, and squash seeds are planted in holes punched by a simple digging stick. The Mesoamerican "trilogy" (maize, beans, and squash) is complemented in the lowlands with chiles, root crops (yucca, camote, sweet potatoes), and fruit trees (zapote, papaya, breadnut, cacao).

Lowland populations have tended to be more evenly scattered across the landscape than in the highlands, overall densities in prehispanic times typically ranging from five to thirty persons per square kilometer. The characteristic settlement pattern in the lowlands, even today, consists of a ceremonial-type center surrounded by dependent rural hamlets. Some urbanization has always existed in the lowlands, but generally in the form of towns rather than cities. At Spanish contact, the population of the lowlands together numbered around 6 million persons, roughly 20 percent of the total Mesoamerican population at that time.

The lowlands provided many exotic items of importance to the Mesoamericans. For example, bright feathers from tropical birds and pelts of the ocelot and other cats were obtained in large numbers. Hardwoods were available for construction and canoe-making. From other trees rubber, copal incense, and dyes were extracted, while paper was made from the bark of a large fig tree and an aromatic medicine from the balsam tree. There were many other dye plants in this area, including indigo, annatto, and genipap. Tobacco was cultivated and made into "rolled cigars," while coca was grown in the far southern part of the lowland area.

It must be emphasized that the ecological systems of Mesoamerica, both past and present, were far more diverse than the general highland-lowland types just described. For example, recent research has shown that considerable intensification of agriculture—including terracing and "raised field" gardening—existed in some tropical lowland areas long before Spanish contact. Furthermore, within the highlands important ecological differences have always existed between temperate (Tierra Templada) and cold (Tierra Fría) zones. For example, in the cold highlands located at elevations above 2,000 meters, the maize growing season is shortened and the pulque-producing maguey plant grows well. It is undoubtedly significant that the most powerful political systems in the region, both past and present, have been located in the cold highlands.

Other important ecological differences result from the contrast between arid and humid lowland subzones. In the arid lowlands aboriginal Mesoamericans had to irrigate in order to obtain dependable maize production, while cacao could not be effectively grown even with irrigation. In contrast, cotton flourished in arid lowland zones. These and other ecological considerations help explain why some of the most powerful lowland political systems of Mesoamerica were located in dry lowland subzones.

Figure 1.3 The natural areas of Mesoamerica. After Robert C. West, "The Natural Regions of Middle America," *The Handbook of Middle American Indians, Volume I: Natural Environment and Early Cultures,* volume editor Robert C. West, general editor Robert Wauchope. Austin, TX: University of Texas Press, 1964, p. 368.

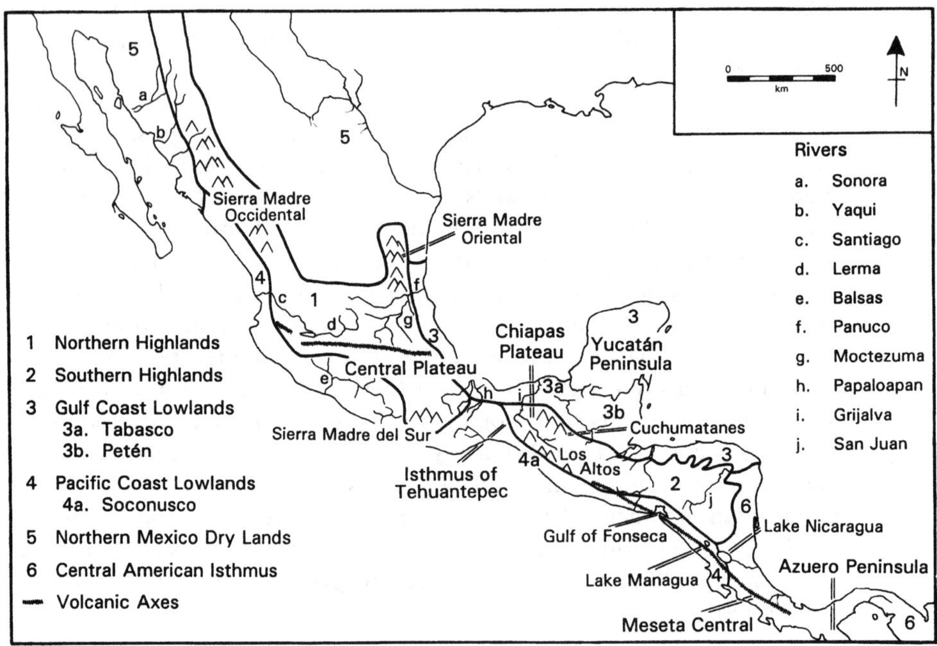

Natural Areas

With the basic highland-lowland division in mind, we now briefly describe Mesoamerica's "natural areas"; that is to say, subregional geographic divisions that define the critically important natural conditions for the inhabitants of the region. For the purposes of our study, five main natural areas stand out (West 1964): (1) Northern Highlands, (2) Southern Highlands, (3) Gulf Coast Lowlands, (4) Pacific Coast Lowlands, and (5) Northern Mexico Dry Lands (Figure 1.3). The geographic conditions of these five areas differ markedly from one another, and the peoples of the Mesoamerican region have had to adapt to them in fundamentally different ways.

Northern Highlands. The Northern Highland area is composed of the Mesa Central, or Central Plateau, and the highlands of Oaxaca and Guerrero. The Central Plateau has been a major focus of human activity within the Mesoamerican region for several thousand years. This remains true today—Mexico City is not only the largest and most important city of Mexico, but it is now (or shortly will be) the largest city in the world (Figure 1.4).

The Central Plateau is marked by volcanic features and unique hydrological patterns. A line of high volcanos, some of them still active, forms the southern rim; on the eastern flank is the Sierra Madre Oriental, while the Sierra Madre Occidental forms the western escarpment. The plateau itself consists of large, flat basins, many of which once contained lakes, and eroded volcanic peaks. Among the largest basins are Mexico, Puebla, Toluca, Guadalajara, and a series of linked basins that form the Bajío of Guanajuato. Many of the lakes no longer

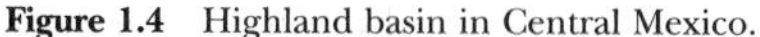

Figure 1.4 Highland basin in Central Mexico.

exist, some because of sedimentation and desiccation, and others, such as the five lakes in the Valley of Mexico, because they have been artificially drained. A few lakes, such as Lake Pátzcuaro in Michoacán, are still viable.

Much of the plateau itself lies in Tierra Templada, although the higher basins and surrounding mountains are Tierra Fría zones. Several of the volcanic peaks—such as Orizaba, Popocatepetl, Iztacchihuatl—are snow-covered year round, and ice has been obtained from these peaks for centuries.

The Central Plateau is drained by three major river systems. With its headwaters in the Toluca Basin just west of Mexico City, the Lerma River flows west to the Pacific, forming the longest river system in the region. Tributaries of the Balsas River also drain into the Pacific, and flow from basins in the southeastern portion of the plateau. The Panuco River and its tributary, the Moctezuma River, form one of the largest drainage systems of Mexico's Atlantic watershed. Both have their headwaters in the northeastern part of the Central Plateau.

In the volcanic range that forms the southern boundary of the Central Plateau, overlooking the Balsas Depression—formed by the Balsas River—and south of the Balsas River, lies the second highland zone of this area, the Sierra Madre del Sur in Guerrero and the Mesa del Sur in Oaxaca. In contrast to the Central Plateau, there are few large, flat basins in this zone, which is instead covered by rugged mountain peaks and small, deep valleys. The Valley of Oaxaca, the largest basin, supported dense populations in the past and continues to do so today.

Much of the Central Plateau has been denuded of vegetation as a result of human activities. Once the area was covered with evergreen and deciduous oak forests. At higher elevation the mixed pine-oak forests gave way to stands of pines, firs, and junipers. At lower elevations grasses, scrub oak, cactus, acacia, and pirul (introduced from Peru in the sixteenth century) now dominate. The southern part of the Northern Highlands, like the Central Plateau, once had large expanses of oak-pine forests. Humid mountain peaks, however, supported cloud-forest vegetation, and in lower-lying arid valleys xerophytes (acacia and cacti) predominate.

Neotropical (South American) fauna have invaded the Northern Highlands, including small numbers of such mammals as the peccary, tapir, spider monkey, jaguar, anteater, and armadillo. The Nearctic (North American) mammals native to the highlands include white-tailed deer, rabbits, squirrels, cougar, and puma. The deer and peccary may have been the main mammals hunted and eaten in fairly large numbers by Mesoamericans of the Northern Highlands in aboriginal times. Migratory birds (ducks, geese, teals), amphibians (frogs, salamanders), and small fish inhabited the many lakes of the Northern Highlands in times past, and were an important food source for aboriginal Mesoamericans.

Southern Highlands. South of the Isthmus of Tehuantepec (Figure 1.5) is a complex highland area framed by two mountain chains, a geologically older northern one and a younger southern one. The northern chain begins with the Chiapas plateau and continues southeast as the Cuchumatanes and folded Alta

Figure 1.5 Isthmus of Tehuantepec depression.

Verapaz mountains of Guatemala. The intermontaine basins and plateaus formed by the northern chain—for instance, San Cristobal (Chiapas), Sacapulas (Guatemala)—are few in number and small (Figure 1.6). The southern chain, volcanic in origin, begins with the Sierra Madre of Chiapas, continues as the Los Altos of Guatemala and the mountains of eastern Guatemala, Honduras, and

Figure 1.6 Highland mountains and valleys in Guatemala.

northern Nicaragua. This southern chain provides the structural framework for numerous basins, valleys, and plateaus—for instance, Quezaltenango, Quiché, Guatemala, Comayagua (the first three in Guatemala, the last in Honduras). In El Salvador and Nicaragua the southern volcanic chain is located in a transisthmian depression, and the basins and valleys are either low (for instance, Zapotitlán and San Salvador in El Salvador) or occupied by freshwater lakes (lakes Managua and Nicaragua in Nicaragua).

Most of the Southern Highlands fall into the Tierra Templada zone, although there is a small zone of Tierra Fría in Chiapas and western Guatemala. The highlands have mostly subhumid subzones, with fringes of humid pockets and a few arid river valleys (Grijalva in Chiapas, Motagua in Guatemala, and Catacamas in Honduras). In the western parts of the Southern Highlands, there is a distinct dry period (December through April), while in eastern parts rainfall tends to occur year round.

Natural vegetation in the Southern Highlands mainly consists of mountain forest, typically of oaks and pines. Nearctic animals are less common in this area than in the Northern Highlands, while Neotropical animals (tapirs, monkeys, etc.) are more common. Some bright-feathered trogan birds are found exclusively in the Southern Highlands, notably the quetzal.

Gulf Coast Lowlands. This lowland area is part of a coastal plain that runs along the Gulf Coast of Mexico all the way to South America. The broad central zone is made up of the Tabasco Plains, the Petén Lowlands, and the Yucatán Peninsula. Narrower coasts are found to the north in Tamaulipas and Veracruz (Mexico) and south in Guatemala and northern Honduras. In the past the area was covered with dense evergreen rain forest, broken in places by savanna grasslands (eastern Tabasco, northern Yucatán, southern Petén). In many places the coastal plains are cut by rivers flowing from the adjacent highlands, forming deltas and levees as the rivers slow down on their course to the Gulf of Mexico and the Caribbean Sea (especially in Tamaulipas, Tabasco, Belize, and the Gulf coasts of Guatemala and Honduras). Long stretches of the northern shoreline have "barrier beaches" that enclose lagoons and tidal swamps, while offshore sand bars and reefs are common, especially off the west coast of Yucatán and the coast of Belize.

The Gulf Coast Lowlands are Tierra Caliente (hot lands). Temperatures are high year round, and rainfall is heavy. Most of the area is humid, and rain falls during all months of the year. While humid, some zones, such as the Petén, are drier during the first two or three months of the year. Northern Yucatán is a subhumid subzone to the east and arid subzone to the west.

The natural vegetation of most of the Gulf Coast Lowlands is tropical forest. A canopy is formed by giant mahogany, ceiba, and wild fig trees, while below are smaller but useful trees such as the palm, ramón (breadnut), rubber, mamey, sapodilla, and logwood. The patches of savanna are covered with grass and pines, except in northwestern Yucatán, where the vegetation is xerophytic scrub.

The fauna of the Gulf Coast area consists largely of Neotropical animals.

Most of the mammals are arboreal—monkey, sloth, opossum, coati—but there are also ground dwellers such as the tapir, peccary, brocket deer, and paca. The main predators are the jaguar, ocelot, and jaguarundi. Bright-feathered birds are numerous (some 500 species), including macaws, parrots, toucans, and trogons. Game birds, such as the tinamou and cassarow, and numerous migratory waterfowl are common. Several varieties of poisonous snakes infest the area, while other reptiles like the iguana and marine turtle (five species) are good sources of food. The waters off the coast of the northern lowlands (especially the coast of Tabasco, the west coast of Yucatán, and the coast of Belize) are rich in fish (for instance, mullets, grey snappers), crabs, shrimp, oysters, and the manatee sea mammal.

Pacific Coast Lowlands. The Pacific coastal side, starting in the north at Sinaloa and extending southward to the Nicoya Peninsula, forms a second Mesoamerican lowland area. This natural area consists of plains, hills, and volcanic slopes, which in some zones, such as Soconusco and Guatemala, is divided into distinct piedmont and plains areas. The Pacific Coast Lowland area is generally traversed by relatively short, fast-flowing rivers that lay down smaller levee and delta depositions than in the Caribbean lowlands. The largest of these rivers are the Lerma-Santiago and Balsas of central Mexico. The coastline has many tidal swamp zones, the most extensive being in El Salvador (Gulf of Fonseca, Jilquilisco Lagoon), Guatemala, and Soconusco. Some of these tidal areas form natural canals that were probably used as aquatic transportation routes in aboriginal times. High winds offshore make ocean travel very dangerous on the Pacific side, but the winds also stir up the coastal waters and enhance the availability of marine life.

The Pacific Coast Lowlands are Tierra Caliente, but they receive less annual rainfall than the Caribbean lowlands and have a distinct dry season. Most of the area is subhumid, although the piedmont is largely humid and the coastal plain may vary from subhumid to arid. The rainfall pattern results in a natural deciduous forest cover of palm, broad-leaf, fig, and dyewood trees. Savannas along the Pacific Coast are small and scattered, and may be artificial creations by humans. In the piedmont and river floodplains, the natural vegetation has the appearance of rain forest, with giant guanacaste, ceiba, mahogany, and cedar trees. The natural vegetation of the coastal plains is deciduous forest, or thorny scrub in arid areas. The tidal swamp zones have mangrove forests. The fauna of the Pacific Coast Lowlands is predominantly Neotropical, and similar to the animals of the Gulf Coast Lowlands already described.

Northern Mexico Dry Lands. This was the largest arid zone of the entire region, and stretched across the northern part of present-day Mexico on the eastern and western sides of the Sierra Madre Occidental. This area always served as a corridor between the Mesoamericans and the village farmers of the southwestern United States (for instance, the Pueblo peoples), although travel has never been easy in this desert country (Figure 1.7).

Figure 1.7 High plateau country of Northern Mexico.

The part of the Northern Dry Lands on the eastern side of the Sierra Madre Occidental is an extension of the Central Plateau, and topographically consists of a long series of high desert basins. Some of the basins were once covered with lakes, but by the time of Spanish contact most were dry and many caked with salt at their lowest points. Daytime temperatures tend to be very high in this zone, but nighttime temperatures often drop below freezing during winter. These temperature extremes, combined with very low precipitation, produce an extremely harsh environment. In the section immediately adjacent to the Sierra Madre Occidental, the natural setting is more favorable, as daytime temperatures are lower, rainfall is higher, and numerous streams flowing from the foothills leave fertile alluvial deposits along the margins of the basins.

On the western side of the Sierra Madre Occidental, in the present-day Mexican states of Sonora and Sinaloa, is found a much lower extension of the Northern Mexico Dry Lands. Temperatures in this zone are higher than anywhere else in the entire region, even though winter frosts sometimes occur; rainfall is even scarcer than in the higher zone on the eastern side of the mountains. The harsh environment is ameliorated somewhat by large rivers that flow westward across this desert zone from the Sierra Madre Occidental. Such rivers as the Sinaloa, Fuerte, Yaqui, and Sonora create narrow valleys in which rich alluvial soils are deposited two times each year.

Vegetation in the eastern part of the Northern Dry Lands area is xerophytic, made up largely of low, widely dispersed plants such as yucca, agaves, and cacti (including the edible prickly-pear cactus). Clumps of mesquite (its pods are edible) and yucca trees can be found in places with alluvial deposits. Peyote occurs naturally in the zone. Adjacent to the mountains, the streams are lined with cypress, cottonwood, mesquite, and willow trees. In the low desert zone west of the Sierra Madre Occidental, the vegetation is more lush and arboreal. Furthermore, the rich river valleys here have been cultivated for maize, beans, and other crops since before Spanish contact. Nearctic animals such as deer and rabbits were once abundant in the more lush parts of the area, and provided an important component of the inhabitants' diet in aboriginal times. A few Neotropical animals were also present, such as the jaguar, peccary, and armadillo.

A sixth natural area, which largely falls outside the region occupied by the Mesoamericans but nevertheless has been important to them, is the Central American Isthmus. It is described in Box 1.2.

Box 1.2 *Central American Isthmus*

The narrow territory of present-day Nicaragua, Costa Rica, and Panama forms a "bridge" that connects Middle America with South America, and this natural area has played an important role in the history of the Mesoamerican peoples. The Central American Isthmus is constituted by a central highland zone, formed by a continuation of the Southern Highland volcanic axis, flanked by Caribbean and Pacific lowlands that are structurally part of the Pacific Coast and Gulf Coast Lowlands already described. The most distinguishing natural feature of the area is its narrowness; it is less than 100 kilometers wide in many places. The highland strip occupies a relatively reduced part of the Isthmus area, and except for the Meseta Central of Costa Rica, the highland basins are relatively small and low in elevation. Furthermore, the isthmus highlands are broken in several places, making coast-to-coast travel relatively easy in the area. The coastal lowlands on both sides of the isthmus are more mountainous than in their northern extensions, and in many places the mountain cliffs drop off into the sea. These coastlines are also very irregular, with numerous peninsulas, gulfs, lagoons, cays, and reefs.

The isthmus is predominantly a Tierra Caliente humid subzone, in both the highlands (except for the Tierra Templada zone of the Meseta Central in Costa Rica) and the two coastal lowlands. Some areas of the Caribbean and Pacific lowlands are the wettest in the entire region. Rain falls throughout the year in most of the isthmus, although in southern Nicaragua, Guanacaste, the Meseta Central of Costa Rica, and the Pacific Coast east of Azuero in Panama there is a distinct dry period resulting in subhumid conditions.

Not surprisingly, the natural vegetation of most of the isthmus is tropical rain forest, the strip of highland mountain forest again being the major exception. Two important savanna zones are Guanacaste in northwestern Costa Rica and Panama's "interior," stretching west of the Canal zone and north of the Azuero peninsula. As might be expected, the isthmus fauna is predominantly Neotropical.

The Central American Isthmus area is endowed with important exotic natural resources that have long been of interest to the Mesoamerican peoples. Perhaps the most important of these in aboriginal times was gold, substantial veins of which exist in the Guanacaste, Osa, and Chiriquí mountains. Other isthmian resources were typical of lowland areas: hardwoods, animal pelts, bright plumage, sea shells (including the murex shell from which purple dye was extracted), salt, cacao, cotton, and special medicinal and narcotic plants (including coca).

Biological Characteristics of the Mesoamericans

It should be stated from the outset that biological differences did not provide an important basis for social distinctions in the Mesoamerican world prior to the coming of the Spaniards. In general, the Mesoamericans themselves gave little social importance to skin color or biological features. Nor did the Spanish conquistadors observe major physical differences between the various Mesoamerican peoples, certainly none comparable to the rather dramatic contrasts found in the Old World between Europeans, Africans, and Asians. Instead, the Spaniards described the Mesoamerican peoples as being racially similar, made up of relatively homogeneous, small, brown-skinned peoples. For example, in one report by the first explorers of Yucatán, the Maya were described as of "middle height and well proportioned," while the Emperor Motecuhzoma was portrayed by one of Cortés's soldiers as "of good height and well proportioned, slender and spare of flesh, not very swarthy, but of the natural colour and shade of an Indian." Both Spanish and native sources agree, however, that artificial alteration of physical appearance was of the utmost social importance in the Mesoamerican world. Social status was marked by facial painting; body scarification; hair styling; and pierced noses, ears, and lips, in which adornments were placed.

Modern biological studies reveal that the Mesoamericans share many genetic features with Asian peoples. Nevertheless, the aboriginal Mesoamericans also had external physical features that differentiated them genetically from the Asians—as, for example, high frequencies of the convex nose, eyes devoid of the mongoloid fold, and wavy hair. Studies of genetically linked blood types reveal that the aboriginal Mesoamericans lacked the blood Type B found among Asians, and were perhaps universally blood Type O. This suggests that the Mesoamericans had long been separated from their relatives in Asia, and that they were biologically quite homogeneous.

In aboriginal times, there must have been considerable genetic contact between populations within the Mesoamerican region but limited contact outside of it. One modest biological variation that existed within the Mesoamerican region was that the populations in the northern part tended to be larger and stockier than those in the southern part. This difference may have been primarily due to the fact that on average, northern peoples inhabited highland settings, while their southern counterparts were widely distributed across lowland zones.

The arrival of the Spaniards to the region in the sixteenth century initiated a complex process of biological and demographic change for the native Mesoamerican populations. The indigenous populations were subjected to the Old World diseases, against which they lacked strong natural immunities. At the same time, miscegenation (interbreeding) began to take place, creating new types of people with mixed biological ancestry.

For the native populations of the Americas, including the Mesoamericans, contact with the Europeans and the African slaves resulted in demographic disaster. In many areas of the Mesoamerican region, 90 percent or more of the indigenous population died during the first decades of Spanish rule, leaving survivors with profoundly disrupted social systems. While in some areas the native populations began to recover by late in the sixteenth century, in other areas the recovery did not begin until the eighteenth century, and in still other places the Indian populations eventually disappeared altogether.

The presence of Spaniards and Africans—most of whom were men—led to unions with the native Mesoamericans throughout the region. This resulted in postcontact populations made up not only of Spaniards and Indians, but also of a host of biologically mixed peoples who did not fit neatly into either Spanish or Indian racial types (mestizos) (Figure 1.7). In time this process of miscegenation became even more complex, as new immigrants came to the region from other parts of Europe, Asia, and the Middle East.

The population of the Mesoamerican region today is a reflection of its demographic history. In many areas the population has remained predominantly Indian, and the twentieth-century natives have expanded to their prehispanic demographic levels. In such cases, it took over 400 years for the native populations to recover from the demographic disaster begun in the sixteenth century. In other areas the immigrant population as well as the mixed populations have grown at a more rapid pace. This is true in many of the region's urban centers, where a glance at a crowded street reveals the complex biological makeup of much of the region's modern populations.

PAST STUDIES OF MESOAMERICA

The summary of Mesoamerican history and culture to follow in this text builds on the labor of numerous scholars who have gone before us. Because the legacy of past studies is not of information alone but also of particular interpretations of that information, we have chosen to organize the following historical sketch according to the diverse approaches to Mesoamerica that have been taken through time. We warn the reader that space does not permit us to do justice to the full history of Mesoamerican studies, and that the account here is meant to be illustrative rather than exhaustive.

Let us begin our review with the "Romanticists," writers who approached the study of Mesoamerica with preconceived notions, usually based on religious or philosophical ideas. Next we discuss the "Scientific Precursors," students of Mesoamerica who employed a more systematic and objective approach. They became particularly influential toward the end of the nineteenth century, and began to replace religious ideas with scientific theories. A modern scientific approach emerged gradually during the twentieth century, carried forward at first by the "Culture Historians," and after 1950 by the "Cultural Evolutionists." The historical and evolutionary approaches continue to be influential in Mesoamerican studies today, and we will argue in the final section to this introduction that our own approach in general terms might be seen as a synthesis of these two approaches.

Romanticists

From the time of Columbus to the present day, an unending stream of Western writers have concocted fanciful explanations for the origin and cultural achievements of the Mesoamerican Indians. We refer to them as Romanticists because their ideas have been highly speculative, and for the most part based on preconceived religious notions about how the world ought to be. Almost all these explanations are ethnocentric, rooted in the belief that cultural sophistication could only be achieved by Europeans, and therefore Mesoamerica's cultural developments must have resulted from ideas originating outside the region. The romantic explanations of Mesoamerica have not stood the test of time, but they continue to be proposed and to have ardent followers even today.

Sundry priests, scholars, and dilettantes at one time or another have proposed nearly every conceivable place in the Old World as the original homeland of the Mesoamericans: Phoenicia, Egypt, Israel, India, China, Africa, Ireland, Germany, and even Rome. Not surprisingly, most of the first Spanish priests who administered in the Mesoamerican region were of the opinion that the Indians were derived from biblical peoples. The most common view was that the Indians had descended from wandering Hebrews, and in particular the Lost Ten Tribes of Israel. This view was not universally accepted, however, as illustrated by the case of the erudite Franciscan priest, Juan de Torquemada (A.D. 1564–1624). Torquemada (1943:I:25), who labored for many years in Mexico, rejected the claim that the Indians were descended from the Hebrews, noting that "if these Indians were Jews, why only in the Indies have they forgotten their language, their law, their ceremonies, their Messiah and finally their Judaism?" Nevertheless, Torquemada's own explanation of the Mesoamericans was both biblical and racist: As a dark-skinned people, they must have descended from Noah's son, Ham.

In more recent times, the Church of Jesus Christ of Latter Day Saints (the Mormons) teach as part of their official doctrine that certain descendants of Noah, Judah, and Joseph emigrated from the Middle East to the New World many centuries before Christ, laying the foundation for the Mesoamerican cultures of Mexico and Central America. The doctrine retains racist features, in claiming that the less righteous immigrants failed to prosper and became dark-skinned (the Lamanites), while the righteous prospered and remained light-skinned (the Nephites).

Quetzalcoatl, the Mesoamerican priestly ruler and feathered serpent deity, has been a particularly appealing figure for the Romanticists working within the biblical tradition. Some of the early Spanish and native documents describe Quetzalcoatl as a light-skinned, bearded, holy man. Catholic scholars have often identified him with St. Thomas or St. Bartholomew, who, according to tradition, travelled to India and beyond into the Americas to do missionary work. Mormon scholars find in Quetzalcoatl evidence for their belief that Jesus Christ visited the

Americas in ancient times, citing as evidence the Mesoamerican tradition that Quetzalcoatl was a holy man whose symbol was the serpent (the Bible associates Jesus Christ with the serpent lifted up by Moses).

Almost as popular as the biblical tradition among Romanticists has been the idea that the Mesoamerican Indians came from continents that long ago sank to the bottom of the sea. It is noteworthy that the Lost Continent advocates share with the biblical Romanticists the belief that the Mesoamericans could not have developed their elaborate civilization independently. The most common version of the Lost Continent tradition is that a large continent known as Atlantis once existed in the ocean west of Europe, inhabited by an energetic people who created advanced civilization (Figure 1.8). Massive earthquakes and floods caused Atlantis to sink to the bottom of the ocean, but not before its inhabitants escaped to America and other continents and gave rise to the major civilizations of the ancient world. The story of Atlantis was an old one going back to Plato, who wrote that it had been told to Solon by Egyptian priests many years before. With the "discovery" of America by Columbus, interest in Atlantis was revived, some Spaniards claiming that America was the remains of the sunken continent mentioned by Plato. Box 1.3 discusses some of the more interesting theories about the Lost Continent origin of the Mesoamerican peoples.

Figure 1.8 Hypothetical map of ancient lost continents. After Robert Wauchope, *Lost Tribes and Sunken Continents: Myth and Method in the Study of American Indians.* Chicago, IL: University of Chicago Press, 1962, p. 37.

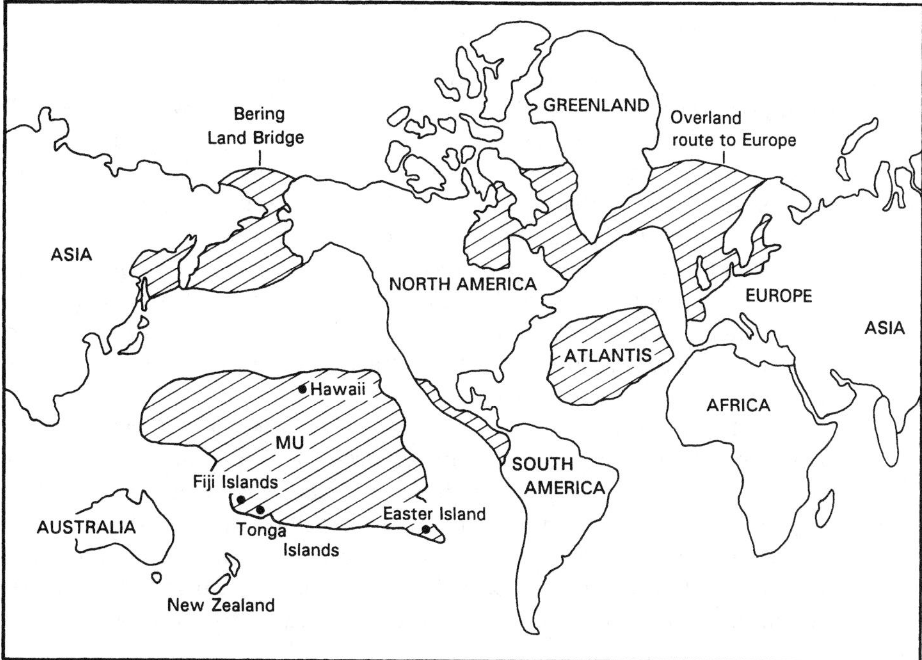

Box 1.3 *Lost-Continent Romanticists*

The idea that the Mesoamerican and other advanced civilizations originated in Atlantis was popularized by a series of remarkably romantic figures. One of these was Ignatius T.T. Donnelly, a U.S. Congressman who in his 1880 book, *Atlantis: The Antediluvian World,* argued that Plato's Atlantis was not only real, but the original Garden of Eden and the place from which Mexico and all the continents were populated. By 1949 Donnelly's book had already undergone fifty printings! An even more remarkable proponent of the Atlantis tale was the French physician and adventurer, Augustus Le Plongeon. During visits to Yucatán, Mexico, Le Plongeon became interested in the Maya culture. An erroneous reading of one of the Maya codices (scroll books) led Le Plongeon to believe that he had found a lost history of Atlantis. The history allegedly described how Atlantis was split by civil war, the losing faction fleeing the continent and going on to found the Egyptian and Maya civilizations. In contrast with other Romanticists, Le Plongeon argued that the Mesoamericans colonized Egypt rather than the reverse!

A few of the Atlantis advocates, such as the Scottish mythologist Lewis Spence (1925), attempted to square the tale with scientific findings. But most of the believers in Atlantis were hopelessly speculative. This was the case with Helena Blavatsky, the founder of the Theosophy religion, who claimed that one of the seven "Root Races" of humanity came from Atlantis. Upon fleeing the sinking continent, she said, the Atlantis race gave rise to various groups of people, among them Cro-Magnons, Semites, and the "handsome 8-feet tall" Toltecs of ancient Mexico!

The most outrageous of the Lost Continent Romanticists, however, was James Churchward, who created a continent in the Pacific Ocean out of whole cloth. "Colonel" Churchward's so-called "Continent of Mu" was said to measure 5,000 miles long and 3,000 miles wide. About 80,000 years ago its inhabitants began to emigrate in waves, headed for the utmost bounds of the world. One of these migratory groups, the so-called "Quetzals," was made up of "stalwart, young adventurers with milk-white skins, blue eyes, and light flaxen hair." They settled in Yucatán and gave rise to the great Maya civilization.

The romantic tradition lives on today, most strikingly in the preposterous writings of Erich von Daniken. Von Daniken has achieved a large following by proposing that ancient astronauts from faraway galaxies visited the ancient Mesoamericans and introduced them to many technological and ideological innovations. A principal piece of evidence for von Daniken's theory is an image portrayed on the lid of a tomb at the Maya site of Palenque, Mexico (Figure 1.9). Von Daniken argues that this image can be none other than an ancient astronaut sitting at the controls, ready for take-off! Like so many Romanticists before him, von Daniken seems to assume that the Maya and other Mesoamerican peoples were incapable of creating complex cultures on their own, and so needed enlightenment from faraway places.

The old romantic notion that ancient Mesoamerica was deeply influenced by peoples from Africa has recently resurfaced in a somewhat repackaged form. This may be seen as part of an effort to better understand the rich cultural heritage of Africa and to recognize the many contributions that Africans have made to Western civilization. For some zealous proponents of African culture, the effort has developed into a form of Afrocentrism. They have speculated that the Mesoamerican cultures were influenced by Africans who came to the Americas before Span-

Figure 1.9 Sarcophagus lid from the Classic-period Maya site of Palenque, Mexico. According to von Daniken, this carving portrays an ancient astronaut. Courtesy of Merle Greene Robertson, Copyright © 1973.

ish contact, and introduced important elements of the African cultures to the Mesoamerican civilization. According to one claim, the main African influence occurred during the time of the Olmecs (ca. 900–400 B.C.), as suggested by the reputed African-like facial features of the large stone heads carved by Olmec artists.

Like many other romantic notions, the idea of an African origin for the Mesoamerican civilization stems more from ideological agenda than from scientific evidence. To date there is no archaeological evidence to support the claim that Africans somehow influenced the Olmecs or any other prehispanic Mesoamerican peoples.

Scientific Precursors

Not all the early writers on the Mesoamerican Indians were Romanticists. For example, the famous sixteenth-century Dominican missionary, Bartolomé de Las Casas (1958:105:69–72), rejected the romantic notion that the Indians were descended from the Lost Tribes of Israel on the grounds that the languages and cultures of Mesoamerica were unlike those of the ancient Hebrews. He argued instead that the New World was only an extension of the posterior part of Oriental India, and that the Indians were thus "natural" to the American continent (Figure 1.10). Another Spanish priest, the Jesuit José de Acosta (A.D. 1540–1600), also denied any connection between the American Indians and biblical peoples. Like Las Casas, Acosta (1880:I:4) concluded on rational grounds that the New World must have been connected with the Old World, and that its first inhabitants immigrated there "by land, which might be done without consideration in changing little by little their lands and habitations."

Objective thinkers like Las Casas and Acosta, of course, were the exceptions until the nineteenth century, when more "positivistic" scholars gradually began to push aside the highly fanciful and religious interpretations of Mesoamerica being put forward by the Romanticists. In growing numbers, the Scientific Precursors began to argue that the Mesoamerican peoples had developed their civilization independently from the peoples of the Old World or Lost Continents. Nevertheless, a truly scientific orientation came slowly, at first consisting mainly of applying somewhat more secular and systematic techniques to the study of Mesoamerica.

The forerunners to the scholars who would later produce modern accounts of Mesoamerica were men (and with few exceptions they were all males) like Alexander von Humboldt, John Lloyd Stephens, and Charles Etienne Brasseur de Bourbourg, to name a few. These men kept the study of Mesoamerican history and culture alive and provided new perspectives on the topic, although it is doubtful that they much advanced our knowledge beyond where the Spaniards had left it in previous centuries.

Humboldt, the son of a Prussian major, was perhaps the most renowned scientist of his time. He travelled throughout the Americas during the first years of the nineteenth century, making observations on geological and other physical

Figure 1.10 Painting of the Defender of the Indians, Fray Bartolomé de Las Casas. James A. Magner, *Men of Mexico,* 2nd ed. Salem, N.H.: Books for Libraries, Ayer Company Publishers, 1968.

features of the two continents. In Mexico he studied firsthand numerous archaeological remains and native codices, which he correctly interpreted as "fragments of history." In Humboldt's (1814) account of his studies in Mexico, he concluded that the evidence failed to support the claim that the Mesoamericans had descended from biblical peoples. Rather, in physical appearance and culture they were closest to the Asiatics. He particularly called attention to the similarity between the ancient Mexican calendar cycle of fifty-two years and the Asiatic calendrical cycle of sixty years. In addition, six of the Mexican day signs corresponded with the Zodiac signs of Asia; namely, tiger, rabbit, serpent, monkey, dog, and bird. Humboldt's scientific credentials and objective methods of studying ancient Mesoamerica inspired all the subsequent Scientific Precursors.

Another influential precursor was the North American lawyer, John Lloyd Stephens. Travelling throughout southern Mexico and Central America between 1839 and 1841, Stephens and his artist colleague, Frederick Catherwood, made systematic observations, drawings, and maps of many of the most important archaeological sites in the southern Mesoamerican region (Stephens 1841). The drawings and descriptions provided new information on ancient Maya architecture, settlement patterns, religious symbols, calendrics, and hieroglyphic writing. Although Stephens erroneously thought that most of the remains dated from the period of Spanish contact, he correctly concluded that the original sites were built by the ancestors of the natives who still inhabited the area during the nineteenth century. This conclusion motivated Stephens to record the customs of these native peoples—for example, their making ritual offerings inside caves—which in turn inspired subsequent students of Mesoamerica to search for persisting native customs in order to reconstruct the aboriginal past.

Box 1.4 tells about one of the key transitional figures between the Romanticists and the Precursors, the French scholar and priest, Brasseur de Bourbourg.

The final decades of the nineteenth century and beginning decades of the twentieth century laid the groundwork for the development of a truly modern approach to Mesoamerican studies. The number of scholars engaged in this study greatly expanded, and the methods of research became increasingly specialized. In particular, formal excavations of archaeological sites helped create a Mesoamerican "archaeology," while expertise in documentary texts and written native languages helped give rise to a Mesoamerican "ethnohistory." Most studies of aboriginal Mesoamerica have been carried forward in recent years by

Box 1.4 *Brasseur de Bourbourg*

Brasseur de Bourbourg served as parish priest in Guatemala for many years in the mid-nineteenth century, during which time he also travelled extensively in Mexico. He obtained copies of numerous native documents important for studying the aboriginal Mesoamerican cultures. Brasseur was erudite, and probably had access to more documentary and archaeological information on Mesoamerica than anyone of his time. Unfortunately, many of his interpretations of history lacked objectivity, and in some cases were downright speculative. For example, in Brasseur's (1857–1859) writings petty Mesoamerican kingdoms were transformed into powerful empires, small towns into huge cities, minor priests into mighty prophets, and princely revolts into bourgeois revolutions. Nevertheless, Brasseur's general summary of events taking place in Mexico and Central America before the conquest was profoundly secular in orientation, and possibly constituted the most exhaustive historical treatise on the subject ever attempted up to that time. Unfortunately, during the last years of his life Brasseur yielded to the lure of the Lost Continent of Atlantis tale in order to explain the origins of the Mesoamerican civilization. He died a broken man, his new "theories" rejected by the emerging scientific community in Europe and the United States.

archaeologists and ethnohistorians, although other specialists such as linguists, epigraphers, geographers, historians, and ethnographers have also made significant contributions. As already noted, many of these diverse scholars at first applied a culture history theoretical model to their studies of ancient Mesoamerica.

Culture Historians

The approach to Mesoamerica taken by the Culture Historians represented an important advance over that of the Romanticists and Precursors, who tended to explain the aboriginal cultures as transplants (diffusions) from somewhere else—usually Asia, Europe, or a Lost Continent. Most Culture Historians, in contrast, accepted the indigenous source of the Mesoamerican cultures, and concentrated on determining the origins and changes of the cultures within the Mesoamerican region. Mesoamerica was viewed as a unified geographic area in which the diverse peoples shared distinctive customs or cultural traits. These traits set them apart from the peoples of other "culture areas." Culture areas were thought to have common historical traditions, the study of which would constitute a way to explain the particular combination of traits that characterized each area.

The Mexican scholar Paul Kirchhoff (1943) provided the definitive application of the culture historical approach to the pre-Spanish natives of Mesoamerica. Kirchhoff placed most of the peoples of Mexico and Central America within the "Mesoamerican" culture area, and defined the area by the languages spoken and the presence of a long list of cultural traits. Essential or diagnostic traits of the Mesoamerican culture area for Kirchhoff included lake gardens (*chinampas*), cacao, bark paper, obsidian-edged swords, stepped pyramids, writing, solar calendars, ritualized human sacrifice, and long-distance trade. The native peoples in the northern part of Mexico, on the one hand, and the southeastern part of Central America, on the other, were said to have spoken different languages and to have exhibited distinct cultural traits. Thus, they constituted separate culture areas from Mesoamerica: the "Southwest" culture area to the north, and the "Chibcha" culture area to the south (Figure 1.11).

Much of the research on Mesoamerica by the Culture Historians centered on the so-called Olmec culture, initially reconstructed through excavations at the archaeological site of La Venta in Tabasco, Mexico. The Olmec culture provided the Culture Historians with a key to the origin of the Mesoamerican civilization. Olmec culture was known to be very old (it was thought to have appeared around 900 B.C.), yet it already exhibited most of the essential traits of the Mesoamerican culture area—for instance, pyramids, carved monuments, sacred calendars, exquisite jade, and pottery craft items. Quite understandably, the Culture Historians concluded that the Olmec culture was the "mother culture" from which all other Mesoamerican cultures descended.

For several decades a focal point of Mesoamerican studies consisted of tracing out the historical connections between the Olmec culture and other cul-

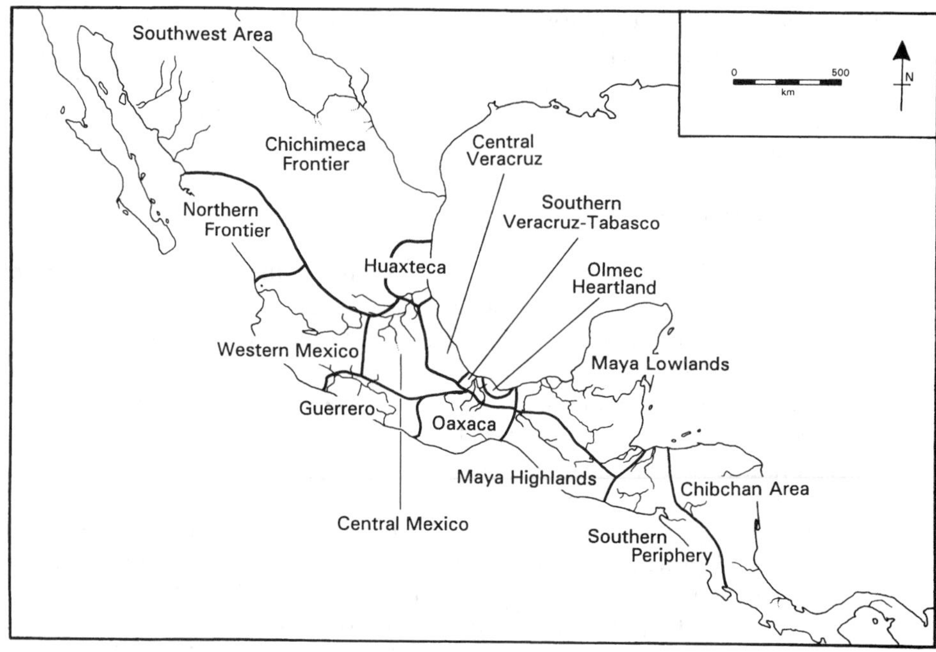

Figure 1.11 Mesoamerican Culture Area and its main sub-areas. After Gordon R. Willey, et al., "The Patterns of Farming Life and Civilization," in *The Handbook of Middle American Indians, Volume I: Natural Environment and Early Cultures,* volume editor Robert C. West, general editor Robert Wauchope. Austin, TX: University of Texas Press, 1964, p. 461.

tures appearing through time within the region. For example, the Mexican archaeologist-artist, Miguel Covarrubias (1957), was able to demonstrate that the various Mesoamerican rain deities were derived from an original Olmec were-jaguar deity (Figure 1.12). Other scholars found historical links between the Olmec calendrical system and those of the Maya and Zapotecs. Special attention was given to Olmec religious, artistic, and intellectual expressions rather than to the material conditions that might have influenced the development of those expressions. As one Culture Historian put it, "The most uniquely distinctive Mesoamerican features are not so much material as they are ideological, and it was this ideological realm—a kind of Mesoamerican world view" that was developed early on by the Olmecs and gave Mesoamerica its traditional unity (Willey 1966:108).

Another focus of the Culture Historians was the traditional Indian community of contemporary Mexico and Central America. Numerous "ethnographic" studies of individual Indian communities revealed that many of the Mesoamerican cultural traits had persisted into modern times. In an important summary of the community studies, Sol Tax (1952) argued that the Mesoamerican culture area had remained largely intact despite modifications resulting from contacts with modern forces from the outside. In the 1960s and 1970s a more general summary of over half a century of culture historical studies on Mesoamerica appeared

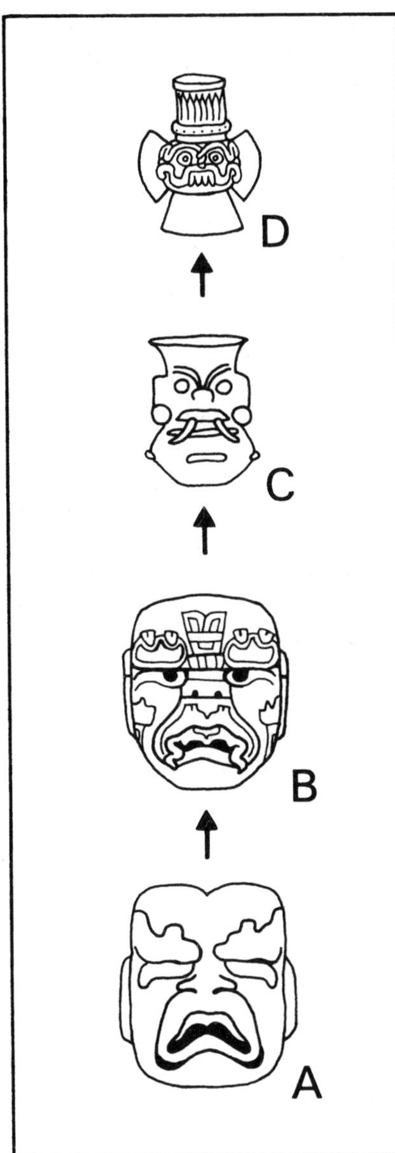

Figure 1.12 Sequence (steps A–D) by which the Olmec were-jaguar motif was transformed into later religious motifs of Mesoamerica. Adapted from Miguel Covarrubias, *Indian Art of Mexico and Central America.* New York, NY: Alfred A. Knopf, 1957, p. 62.

in the twelve-volume *Handbook of Middle American Indians.* The *Handbook* essays dealt with both aboriginal and contemporary culture areas of Mesoamerica.

In retrospect, it is clear that the Culture Historians tended to see culture as consisting of values and ideas, and thus were concerned with the *essential* features rather than the *material* determinants of the Mesoamerican cultures. For this reason the culture historical approach has been widely criticized as "idealist." Another tendency was to study contemporary Indian communities as isolated, self-contained units in which traditional cultural traits only gradually changed through contact with outside peoples, a process known as "acculturation." Eventually, it was recognized that the focus on isolated communities resulted in a theory that was too static and insufficiently historical.

Cultural Evolutionists

By the mid-twentieth century, a general turning away from culture history was taking place in Mesoamerican studies, partly because that approach focused on ideas rather than behavior and partly because it described cultural differences between peoples and areas without providing an explanation of these differences. There emerged in the social sciences a larger theoretical movement that focused attention more on behavior than on ideas; specifically, the behaviors by which human groups exploit their material environment. Cultures, according to this perspective, are seen as adaptive mechanisms by which human populations conform to ever-changing environmental conditions. The adaptive changes engaged in by groups of people constitute cultural evolution, and result in either divergence or convergence between cultures. Studies of particular cultural divergences are referred to as "specific evolution," while examples of cultural convergence—demonstrated by comparing different cases of adaptation around the world—are termed "general evolution."

An important early application of the cultural evolutionary approach to aboriginal Mesoamerica was made by the American anthropologist Julian Steward (1949). Steward presented an evolutionary sequence for Mesoamerica consisting of the following developmental stages:

> *Hunting and Gathering.* Simple food-gathering technology gives rise to bands of hunters and gatherers.
>
> *Incipient Agriculture.* Domestication of plants lays the foundation for settled village life.
>
> *Formative.* Increasingly intense farming provides the basis for the growth of villages into towns.
>
> *Regional Florescence.* Complex irrigation works promote population growth, cities, and highly stratified society.
>
> *Cyclical Conquests.* Use of metals and increase in trade create conditions for endemic warfare between societies.

Steward compared the specific Maya and Central Mexican evolutionary sequences in Mesoamerica with similar sequences in other regions of the world where ancient civilizations had developed, and argued for their convergent evolution. He found the explanation of evolutionary convergence in the application of similar irrigation and other advanced subsistence technologies to similar ecological conditions in the regions where these diverse peoples lived; in particular, the semi-arid river valleys of Mesopotamia, Egypt, China, Peru, and Mexico. The Mesoamerican civilization, then, was defined not in terms of shared cultural traits but rather as a series of evolving stages resulting from adaptive responses to particular environmental settings.

Following Steward's lead, the evolutionary approach has been widely used in the study of Mesoamerican cultures. For example, while the Culture Historians had defined the aboriginal lowland Maya as virtually unique in their cultural patterns and historical development, cultural evolutionists like William Sanders and Barbara Price (1968) argued that far from being unique, the Maya advances were actually based on ecological adaptations common to Mesoamerica as a whole. Specifically, populations in Central Mexico had adapted to the semi-arid conditions of the Teotihuacán Valley by constructing an elaborate irrigation system, and upon this material foundation built the powerful, urban Teotihuacán civilization. Evolutionarily advanced Teotihuacán became the material basis for the development of advanced cultural features by the lowland Maya located far to the south (Figure 1.13). The subsequent collapse of the Teotihuacán civilization around A.D. 700, followed by transition to a new evolutionary stage in Central Mexico, were again used to explain the dramatic Maya cultural collapse 200 years later in the southern lowlands. Sanders and Price concluded that without the evolutionary developments of Teotihuacán, Maya cultural evolution would have remained at a chiefdom stage, which is precisely what happened to many of the peoples falling outside the Mesoamerican regional sphere.

Figure 1.13 Partially excavated Teotihuacán-type building at the Classic-period Maya site of Tikal.

The Cultural Evolutionists brought the Mesoamericans down to earth, so to speak, and forced scholars to see the region's cultures rooted in material factors and generically similar to cultures throughout the world. Rather than cultural configurations or world views determining behavior, behavior oriented to the production of food determines or at least conditions culture. The Cultural Evolutionists also shifted the scope of Mesoamerican studies away from the isolated Indian communities to macrosocial units, such as ecologically diverse regions and nation-states. One manifestation of this shift was the adoption of "dependency" theory to explain the evolution of contemporary Indian cultures. Indian communities in certain regions of Mexico and Guatemala, for example, were now seen as being dependent on national economic and political powers, which in turn were dependent upon world powers like the United States and Europe. From this perspective, Mesoamerican culture is seen as an adaptive response to external political and economic forces rather than a historical legacy of ideas, rules, and values for living.

THE APPROACH TAKEN IN THIS TEXT

A few comments about our own approach to Mesoamerica need to be made. As should be obvious from the preceding review of past studies, we eschew romantic notions of Lost Tribes or Lost Continents to explain developments in Mesoamerica. Nor do we generally adhere to strictly culture historical or cultural evolutionary arguments, although like most modern students of Mesoamerica we have been influenced by those arguments. Rather, we are guided by more recent theoretical ideas that have influenced the social sciences in general and Mesoamerican studies in particular. Let us briefly explain.

The anthropologist Norman Schwartz (1983), in an insightful summary of recent Mesoamerican studies, notes the split mentioned above between studies that focus on the essential ideas of culture and those with a focus on the material determinants of culture. For the idealist students of Mesoamerica, the culture history model has evolved into the use of more sophisticated models of culture such as structuralism, semiotics, phenomenology, and even more recently, discourse analysis. These scholars stress that Mesoamerican cultures, in both their prehispanic and contemporary forms, are conceptual systems that cannot be explained as mere responses to underlying material or political conditions. As systems, the Mesoamerican cultures have "inner logics" that fundamentally affect how they change.

While the cultural evolutionary approach continues to be influential in Mesoamerican studies, it also has undergone considerable modification in more recent times. For example, neo-Marxists stress the importance of material production and the "superstructural" nature of Mesoamerican ideas. Similarly, ecologists, who derive their ideas from biology, treat Mesoamerican cultures as special behavioral responses to energy exchanges and demographic challenges. Dependency theory has largely given way to world system theory, according to which prehispanic Mesoamerica is seen as a world system in its own right, and post-conquest Mesoamericans as part of a worldwide class of exploited proletariats created by global capitalism. Even more so than the Cultural Evolutionists who preceded them, these recent materialists have tended to portray the Mesoamerican cultures as secondary derivations from behaviors oriented toward physical and political survival.

Schwartz goes on to argue that we can no longer study the Mesoamerican cultures as isolated communities or ignore the impact of external powers on local Indian groups. Social classes based on the unequal distribution of economic means have always played an important role in determining the characteristics of the Mesoamerican cultures, both ancient and contemporary. As Schwartz puts it:

> Identity, tradition, and culture become tactics in a game of power rather than primary irreducible determinants of change and continuity. [The Mesoamerican] Tradition is no longer a manifestation of a particular world view but rather an expression of sectarian interests, a labile adaptation to an environment, and a dependent variable. (Schwartz 1983:355)

And yet, cultures are not merely responses to material and political forces; they have their own logic and historical existence. What we need, Schwartz concludes, are theories that take into account both material and ideological factors, as well as microsocial and macrosocial settings. For Mesoamerica, as elsewhere, the "patterns of behavior and choices between alternatives are . . . the result of a complex interplay between ideas, rules, psychological and material resources, and situation circumstances" (Schwartz 1983:353; see also Gossen 1986).

The kind of synthesis between materialist and idealist theories called for by Schwartz and others is emerging not only in Mesoamerican studies but in all the social sciences. In anthropology, for example, Sherry Ortner (1984) describes recent theoretical trends that take account of both the idealists' concern for agency and ideas and the Marxists' concern for economic domination and inequality. Cultural ideas and material forces are brought together through "practices," the special kind of behavior based on the human capacity to respond to both cultural ideals *and* changing material conditions. This kind of "interactive" theory, then, shifts our attention away from culture or material conditions per se toward the processes by which humans create and reproduce cultures in response to material conditions. Cultures, Mesoamerican or otherwise, are seen not only as objective structures or systems but also as human products in the making. Because this approach requires us to see cultures as dynamic, always being transformed as circumstances change, it necessarily leads to a perspective that is historical rather than static. It also requires that local developments be seen in terms of their regional and even global contexts.

Consistent with recent trends in theory, we attempt to present the Mesoamerican cultures in terms of both the symbols and meanings by which they are constituted, and the material and behavioral contexts within which these ideas are created and transformed. We are interested as much in *how* the Mesoamerican cultures have been created as in *what* they are like. We accept the role of agency on the part of the Mesoamericans, and where possible specify which individuals and groups created the cultural patterns and the reasons they did so. Our approach is therefore patently historical: We study the Mesoamerican cultures from their beginnings to their most recent manifestations. We also consciously relate local developments of Mesoamerican culture to regional, national, and global forces. We think these characteristics are all in the best tradition of broadly defined recent theory, and therefore of Mesoamerican studies as now practiced.

ORGANIZATION OF THE TEXT

As already mentioned, the focus of this text is on the Mesoamerican Indians, and we define Mesoamerica as a cultural tradition or civilization rather than a geographic region of peoples. The reader will find in the chapters to follow information about non-Indian inhabitants of the Mexican and Central American region; nevertheless, our emphasis is on the native Mesoamericans—their social institutions and cultural patterns, and the changing relations with each other and with the peoples of radically different cultural traditions surrounding them. This emphasis is by design, and should not be interpreted as disinterest in the millions of mestizos, blacks, whites, and other ethnic peoples who now make up the majority of the Mexican and Central American populations. We trust that the text will make clear that some of these non-Indian peoples have exercised controlling power over the native American peoples for almost 500 years. This historical fact, of course, is not new, and has been stressed again and again in the publications on Mexico and Central America. Our book carries an additional message: that there existed a dynamic, highly developed Mesoamerican civilization before the coming of the Europeans; that the Mesoamericans resisted conquest from the beginning, and have continued to resist assimilation of their civilization ever since; and that the peoples of the region, both Indian and non-Indian, continue to be profoundly influenced by the legacy of that civilization.

The preface is designed to alert the reader to the significance of Mesoamerica for the rest of the world and for the studies of native peoples in general. We claim that Mesoamerica's contribution to world history is much greater than heretofore recognized, and in the preface we make the case for this claim.

The first unit of the book is made up of six chapters that together constitute a historical overview of Mesoamerican culture from prehispanic to modern times. For each period we describe the cultural characteristics of Mesoamerica, as well as the historical processes by which these characteristics were created and transformed through time.

The six chapters of the second unit also take historical developments into consideration, but the primary focus is on a series of topics of current interest and special importance to Mesoamerican studies. We pay more direct attention to cultural features of the Mesoamerican tradition in this unit than in the first unit, particularly in the chapters on language, religion, and literature. Nevertheless, in the chapters on gender and political economy special emphasis is given to the social and material forces that condition these cultural features.

In the epilogue we discuss the rebellion by Maya speakers that broke out in Chiapas, Mexico, on January 1, 1994. Not only does the rebellion constitute an update to the history of Mesoamerica presented in this text, but it is also a concrete example of why knowledge about Mesoamerica is essential to an understanding of a world that is increasingly interconnected.

One of our main goals in writing this text is to make sure that the Mesoamericans' own perspectives are represented throughout. Another is to summarize as much as possible the best scholarship available on Mesoamerica from the international scholarly community. We are also determined to integrate our findings on Mesoamerica into a single, cohesive narrative—a text.

The complexity of scholarship about Mesoamerica and of the Mesoamerican cultural tradition itself was a compelling factor in our deciding to write this text as a collective effort. The authors of record (Carmack, Gasco, and Gossen) were responsible for ensuring the overall integration of the text, and for preparing the preface, introduction, epilogue, and part or all of eight of the chapters. The other contributing authors—Broadwell, Burkhart, Goldin, Justeson, Rosenbaum, and Smith—prepared part or all of seven of the chapters. Together, we attempt to capture both the glory and the tragedy of the Mesoamerican peoples in their tri-millennial quest to make sense out of their changing world.

SUGGESTED READINGS

DÍAZ DEL CASTILLO, BERNAL 1956 *The Discovery and Conquest of Mexico, 1517–1521.* New York: Grove Press.

GRAHAM, JOHN A. (ed.) 1966 *Ancient Mesoamerica: Selected Readings.* Palo Alto, Calif.: Peek Publications.

HELMS, MARY W. 1982 *Middle America: A Culture History of Heartland and Frontiers.* New York: University Press of America.

KENDALL, CARL, JOHN HAWKINS, AND LAUREL BOSSEN (eds.) 1983 *Heritage of Conquest Thirty Years Later.* Albuquerque: University of New Mexico Press.

SANDERS, WILLIAM T., AND BARBARA J. PRICE 1968 *Mesoamerica: The Evolution of a Civilization.* New York: Random House.

WAUCHOPE, ROBERT (ed.) 1962 *Lost Tribes & Sunken Continents: Myth and Method in the Study of American Indians.* Chicago: University of Chicago Press. 1964–1978 *Handbook of Middle American Indians,* vols. 1–15. Austin: University of Texas Press.

WEST, ROBERT C., AND JOHN P. AUGELLI 1989 *Middle America: Its Lands and Peoples.* Englewood Cliffs, N.J.: Prentice Hall.

WOLF, ERIC 1959 *Sons of the Shaking Earth: The People of Mexico and Guatemala, Their Land, History, and Culture.* Chicago: University of Chicago Press.

Unit I
An Historical Overview of the Mesoamerican Peoples

The six chapters in this unit are designed to provide an overview of the origin, development, and transformation of the Mesoamerican cultural tradition. The summaries for each historical period are general and focus on the processes by which Mesoamerica as social system and cultural tradition was constituted and reconstituted through time. We attempt to give roughly equal coverage to the six time periods into which the unit is divided (prehistoric, contact, conquest, colonial, liberal, and modern periods); however, it must be recognized that the periods are somewhat arbitrary and the coverage for each is far from comprehensive. The long history of Mesoamerica prior to the contact period, the so-called prehistoric period, in particular receives less attention than it deserves, partly because several archaeological summaries of that period already exist (see the recommended readings at the end of chapter 2). Nevertheless, we trust that our account strikes an appropriate balance between historical periods and cultural developments.

Chapter 2
Origins and Development of Mesoamerican Civilization

> At daylight the clouds still hung over the forest; as the sun rose they cleared away. . . . The branches of the trees were dripping wet, and the ground very muddy. Trudging once more over the district which contained the principal monuments, we were startled by the immensity of the work before us. . . . The woods were so dense that it was almost hopeless to think of penetrating them. . . . It is impossible to describe the interest with which I explored these ruins. The ground was entirely new; there were no guide-books or guides; the whole was a virgin soil. . . . We stopped to cut away branches and vines which concealed the face of a monument. The beauty of the sculpture, the solemn stillness of monkeys and the chattering of parrots, the desolation of the city, and the mystery that hung over it, all created an interest higher, if possible, than I had ever felt among the ruins of the Old World. (Stephens 1841, v. 1:117–120)

With these words the nineteenth-century explorer John L. Stephens described his initial reaction to the ruined Maya city of Copán. Stephens and his fellow traveller, artist Frederick Catherwood, were the first explorers to describe the lost cities of the Maya to American and European audiences. These spectacular ruins, which had lain abandoned in the jungle for almost a millennium, excited the public's imagination (Figure 2.1), and a number of farfetched theories arose attributing the construction of the cities to the ancient Greeks, Egyptians, the Lost Tribes of Israel, and even refugees from the mythical continent of Atlantis. Some of these were discussed in Chapter 1. Against these popular notions, Stephens had the correct explanation from the start:

> We are not warranted in going back to any ancient nation of the Old World for the builders of these cities. . . . There are strong reasons to believe them the creation of the same races who inhabited the country at the time of the Spanish conquest, or of some not very distant progenitors. (Stephens 1843, v. 1:50)

These ancestral Maya peoples and their contemporaries throughout Mesoamerica not only built the ancient cities discovered by Stephens and Catherwood, they also forged a distinctive civilization whose legacy survives throughout Mesoamerica today. The antecedents of Mesoamerican culture can be traced back to the Pleistocene Ice Age over 10,000 years ago, when the first hunters and gatherers arrived in Central America. Some time between 8000 and 5000 B.C., during the Archaic period, the descendants of the earliest inhabitants brought about what was probably the single most important innovation in Mesoamerican history—the domestication of maize or corn. The initial impact of maize cultivation was minimal, but after several thousand years the crop had improved to the point where people could assume a new lifestyle based upon year-round settled villages and maize agriculture. This point signals the start of the Formative period in Mesoamerica (2000 B.C.–A.D. 200).

The Formative period saw the origin of Mesoamerica as a distinctive cultural entity. Widely scattered peoples speaking a variety of languages were united as Mesoamericans by two key traits—their reliance upon maize agriculture, and

Figure 2.1 Ruins of the Classic-period Maya city of Copan, Honduras, as captured in an 1843 engraving by artist Frederick Catherwood. Reprinted with permission from John L. Stephens, *Incidents of Travel in Central America, Chiapas and Yucatan, Vol. I*. New York, NY, Dover Publications, 1969, p. 154.

FALLEN IDOL.

their common participation in a new religious tradition focused on the earth and fertility. All later Mesoamerican cultures were built on these twin foundations of maize and religion. The following Classic period (A.D. 200–900) was characterized by the growth and expansion of cities and states. Mesoamerican societies grew in complexity as they developed writing, calendars, urban planning, social stratification, powerful kings, state-sponsored cults, and other hallmarks of civilization. The final episode of the Precolumbian past—the Postclassic period (A.D. 900–1519)—saw a continuation of these patterns of social complexity, but the large and powerful theocratic states of the Classic period gave way to smaller and more secular and commercially oriented city-states.

Mesoamerica in 1519 was a distinctive cultural tradition whose many diverse peoples shared this heritage. In this chapter we review the history of Precolumbian Mesoamerica, starting with the arrival of Pleistocene hunters and ending with the arrival of Europeans in 1519. Our goal is to identify and discuss the major changes and innovations that together created the Mesoamerican world of 1519.

EARLY INHABITANTS OF MESOAMERICA

Paleoindian Hunter-Gatherers

The earliest people to inhabit Mesoamerica arrived at the end of the Pleistocene epoch (also known as the Ice Age), sometime between 40,000 and 10,000 B.C. (Figure 2.2). They were part of several migrations of peoples who crossed from Asia to the New World over a land bridge that linked Siberia and Alaska. This land bridge, called Beringea, was formed by the lowering of sea levels owing to the formation of enormous glaciers. The end of the Pleistocene Ice Age was marked by increasing temperature, which had major environmental impacts on the New World. The glaciers that had covered much of North America melted, leading to a rise in sea levels and the flooding of Beringea, putting an end to the Asian migrations. Vegetation, landforms, and surface water all changed dramatically in response to the climatic shifts, leading to the extinction of many Pleistocene animal species (including mammoths and mastodons) and modifications of the habits and ranges of many others. These changes had important effects on the new settlers from Asia.

Scholars are currently divided on the timing of the arrival of the first Asian immigrants. The most likely scenario has the migrations beginning in the time range of 40,000 to 30,000 B.C., and continuing up to the flooding of the Bering land bridge around 9000 B.C. These early settlers had a primitive stone tool technology, but they managed to adapt to the varied late Pleistocene environments of the New World as some populations travelled the length of the American continents as far as southern Chile. Archaeological sites from this time period are the remains of temporary campsites of mobile hunter-gatherers. Among the sites with radiocarbon dates older than 10,000 B.C. are Meadowcroft Rockshelter in Penn-

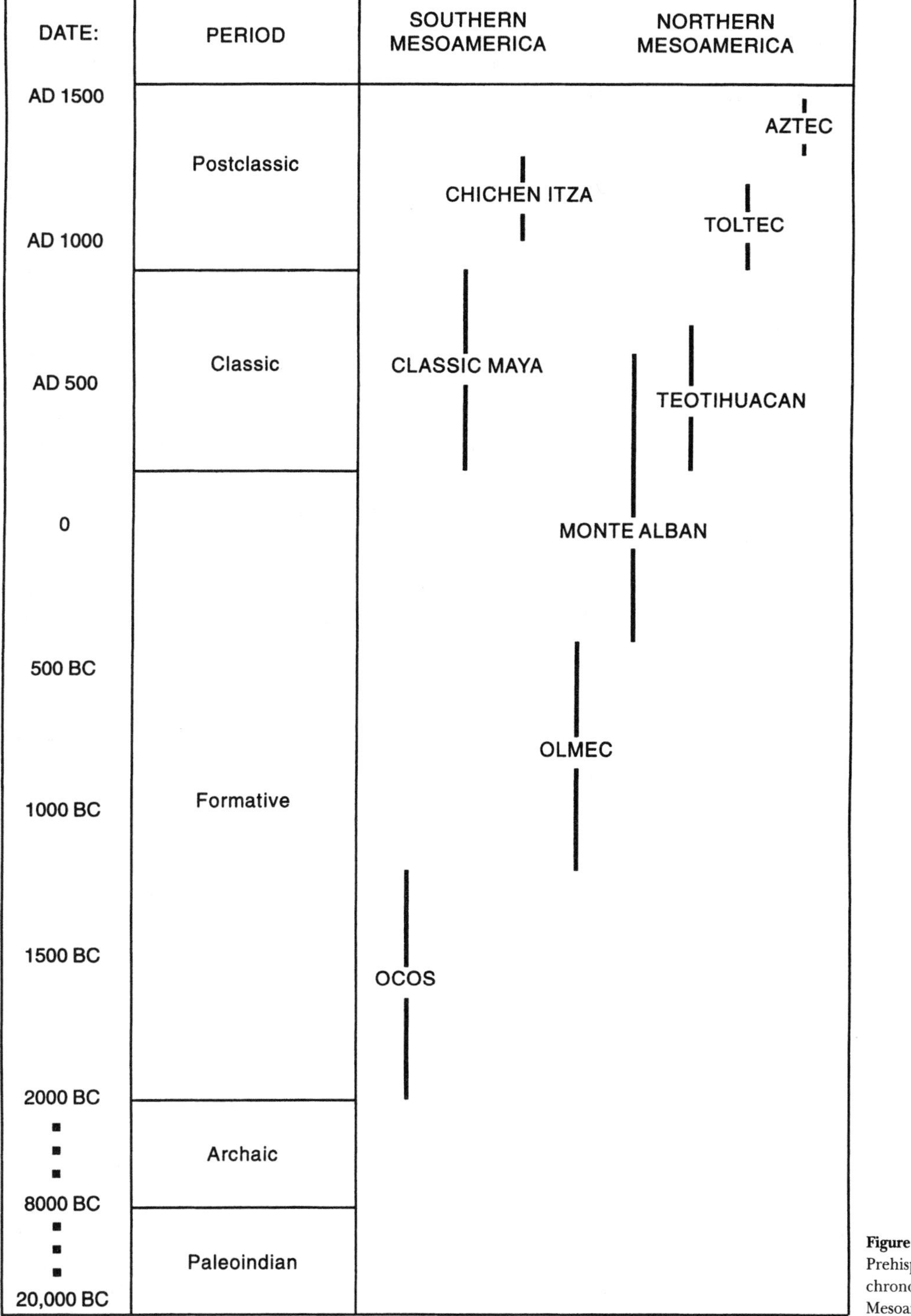

Figure 2.2 Prehispanic chronology of Mesoamerica.

sylvania, Pedra Furada in Brazil, Monte Verde in Chile, and several sites in Mexico. The most extensively studied Mexican sites were excavated by José Luis Lorenzo and Lorena Mirambell. El Cedral (in the Mexican state of San Luis Potosí) was a campsite at a freshwater spring in which stone and bone tools were found around a hearth dating to between 20,000 and 30,000 B.C. Tlapacoya, in the Valley of Mexico, was a settlement at the edge of a lake with remains of stone tools, animal bones, and hearths dating to around 19,000 B.C. (Figure 2.3).

The very end of the Pleistocene epoch saw the spread of the mammoth-hunting Clovis culture throughout North America and northern Middle America. Like Clovis sites in the United States, those in Middle America illustrate the proficiency of these ancient hunters, who used well-made stone tools to kill and butcher huge mammoths. The site of Santa Isabel Iztapan in the Valley of Mexico consists of the remains of two butchered mammoths together with the stone tools used to process them; the site is dated to 9000 B.C. At nearby Tepexpan, a complete female skeleton dating to around 8000 B.C. was preserved (although the excavation report called her "Tepexpan man"!). The post-Pleistocene environmental changes after 9000 B.C.—rising sea levels, changing vegetation, and extinction of mammoths and other species—forced the Paleoindian peoples to modify their diets and activities, leading to an increased reliance upon plant foods. An important result of these modifications was the domestication of food plants, which led eventually to the start of farming in Middle America.

Figure 2.3 Locations of major Paleoindian- and Archaic-period sites.

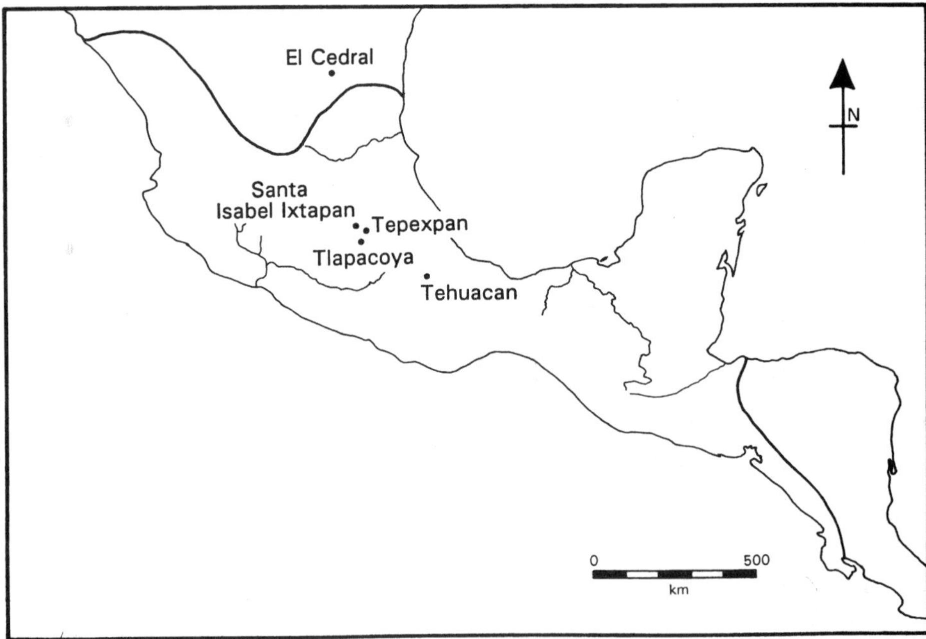

Plant Domestication

Domestication is the process by which wild plants evolve into domesticated crops as humans select for traits that will make the plants more useful. Domesticated crops have a different genetic makeup than their wild ancestors, and generally cannot survive in the wild. Independent episodes of domestication took place in several parts of the world in the aftermath of the Pleistocene, including Middle America, the Near East, sub-Saharan Africa, southeast Asia, north China, the Andes, and the Amazon basin. Plant domestication in Middle America was particularly significant not only because it established a pattern for the development of Mesoamerican cultures in the subsequent Formative period, but also because some of the resulting crops are among the most important food crops in the world today.

Domestication of Mesoamerican plants took place during the Archaic period, between 8000 and 2000 B.C. Unfortunately, archaeologists have little direct evidence for the early stage of the process, although its results are clear. By around 5000 B.C., the suite of Mesoamerican domesticates—maize, beans, squash, tomatoes, chiles, avocado, and other plants (see Table 2.1)—had already been transformed from their wild ancestors into useful food sources. Excavations by archaeologist Richard MacNeish at dry cave sites in Tamaulipas and the Tehuacán Valley in Puebla uncovered the earliest domesticates in Middle America. Between 7000 and 5000 B.C., beans and bottle gourds (used as containers) first appeared in Tamaulipas, while work in the Tehuacán Valley uncovered chiles, avocado, squash, and amaranth at this time.

The earliest remains of maize are from Tehuacán around 5000 B.C., by

Table 2.1 Mesoamerican Domesticated Plants

COMMON NAME	*SCIENTIFIC NAME*	*COMMON NAME*	*SCIENTIFIC NAME*
Seed Plants		tuna cactus	*Opuntia*
maize	*Zea mays*	mamey	*Calocarpum mammosum*
beans	*Phaseolus* (four species)	chicosapote	*Achras sapote*
amaranth	*Amaranthus cruentus*	Mexican cherry	*Prunus capuli*
sunflower	*Helianthus annuus*	hog plum	*Spondias mombin*
chía	*Salvia hispanica*	guava	*Psidium guajava*
Tuber Plants		vanilla	*Vanilla planifolia*
jícama	*Pachyrrhizus erosus*	Fiber Plants	
Vegetables		agaves	*Agaves* (at least five species)
squash	*Cucurbita* (four species)	cotton)	*Gossypium hirsutum*
tomato	*Lycopersicon esculetum*	Condiments	
husk tomato	*Physalis xiocarpa*	chile pepper	*Capsicum* (various species)
chayote	*Sechium edule*	Dye Plants	
Fruits		indigo	*Indigofera suffruticosa*
avocado	*Persia americana*	Ceremonial Plants	
cacao (chocolate)	*Theobroma cacao*	copal	*Protium copal*
papaya	*Carica papaya*		

Note: Adapted from West and Augelli (1989:220).

which time the crop (*Zea mays*) had evolved fully from its wild ancestor teosinte (*Zea mexicanus*) through processes of cultural selection and genetic mutation (Figure 2.4). The nutritional quality of maize was so great that it became the most important staple of the regional diet, from early times until the present (see Box 2.1). In contrast to its variety of domesticated plants, Middle America was the home to very few species of domesticated animals. Only dogs, turkeys, and possibly bees, all used for food, were domesticated in the area.

Although maize and the other food crops were available and used from at least 5000 B.C., a fully agricultural economy did not develop in the region until after 2000 B.C. The hunter-gatherers of the Archaic period continued their nomadic lifestyle for several thousand years after the appearance of domesticates, merely adding these crops to their repertoire of wild resources. This contrasts with the process of agricultural evolution in other parts of the world, where plant domestication was almost always soon followed by the start of a fully settled, or sedentary, agricultural lifestyle. The reason for this delay in Middle America is simple: While the earliest maize was very nutritious, the tiny corncobs did not produce enough food to permit storage, sedentism, and a fully agricultural lifestyle. During the 3,000 years after 5000 B.C., the hunter-gatherers continued their deliberate selection for larger, more productive plants, and eventually maize became productive enough to serve as the principal agricultural staple for permanent village dwellers.

The Beginnings of Village Life

During the last 3,000 years of the Archaic period, peoples throughout Middle America gradually adopted a more sedentary lifestyle. The expansion of sedentism was one of the most far-reaching changes in ancient human history (in Middle America and elsewhere), as it set the scene for an agricultural way of life and

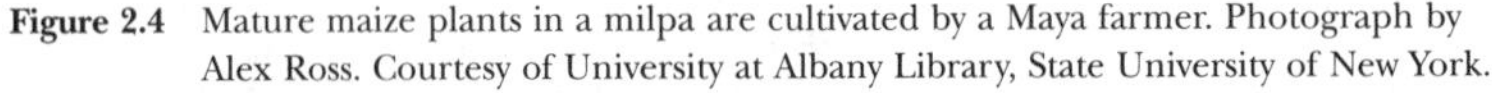

Figure 2.4 Mature maize plants in a milpa are cultivated by a Maya farmer. Photograph by Alex Ross. Courtesy of University at Albany Library, State University of New York.

Box 2.1 *Maize*

Why was maize so important to the ancient Mesoamericans, and why does it continue to be the primary food in modern Mesoamerica? The answer lies in a combination of the plant's nutritional qualities and the lack of domesticated animals in ancient Mesoamerica. In most areas of the world, traditional diets provide most of their calories through high-carbohydrate, low-protein, staple grains, but most rely on domesticated animals like cattle or pigs for their protein. This dietary strategy would not work well in Mesoamerica because of the paucity of domesticated animals (only turkeys and dogs were available). In order to meet their protein needs, Mesoamericans domesticated maize and then developed methods of preparing and serving the food to turn it into an adequate and complete source of protein.

Maize has high concentrations of most of the essential amino acids that the human body needs to synthesize proteins, but two are lacking and one is chemically bound and not readily available. In order to supply the missing amino acids, Mesoamericans eat beans with their tortillas (or other forms of maize); beans have high concentrations of the missing nutrients. To free the chemically bound acid, Mesoamericans soak their maize in an alkali solution (normally made by simply adding powdered lime—calcium carbonate—to water) before grinding the kernels. These two practices are deeply ingrained cultural traits that not only produce delicious meals but also ensure that maize provides adequate protein for human needs. The Mesoamerican diet, from Formative times until the present, is one of the few traditional world cuisines that can provide adequate protein without heavy supplements of meat or other animal protein sources.

Given the nutritional and cultural importance of maize, it is not surprising that Mesoamerican peoples long ago devised many different ways of serving the food. Tortillas, flat maize cakes roasted on a clay griddle, have been the most prevalent form of maize from the Classic period to the present day. In addition to being flavorful and easy to eat, tortillas have the advantage of portability—they can be cooked ahead of time and then carried to eat later, in the field or on the road. Tamales are balls of coarse maize dough steamed in large pots, often with chile or meat filling. This was probably the major way maize was eaten before the invention of the tortilla. Atole, a thin gruel of finely ground maize, often flavored with fruit or sugar, is a popular breakfast food; pozole, a soup made with large maize kernels (hominy), is a common evening food. Maize is also eaten fresh on the cob, but this method does not involve alkali soaking and therefore does not provide the nutritional benefits of the other maize foods.

The methods of tortilla preparation, well-documented in ethnographic accounts of modern traditional behavior, have probably changed little in 2,000 years. The ears of maize are typically left to dry on the plants. In the fall, the dried maize is harvested and then shelled; it is stored sometimes on the cob and sometimes as dried kernels. To prepare tortillas, the dried kernels are soaked in the alkali solution in a clay pot, and then ground by hand on a stone mill or metate. The moist ground flour or dough is then patted into shape by hand and the tortillas are cooked on a clay griddle and stored in a basket or wrapped in cloth. Maize grinding stones are common artifacts at Mesoamerican archaeological sites, and clay griddles are typically either absent (at early sites) or ubiquitous (at later sites). This traditional method of food preparation is quite arduous; grinding the maize to make several dozen tortillas for the daily meals of a family of six requires four to five hours of physical labor. The domestic activities and schedules of women in traditional Mesoamerican societies are thus heavily conditioned by the requirements of maize grinding.

the later evolution of cities and states. Over the same period, other important changes were taking place—populations were growing, people were becoming more and more dependent on domesticated plants, and people began storing food. Archaeologists believe that these changes were all linked.

The earliest evidence in the region for possible sedentism comes from lowland zones—the Pacific Coast, the Gulf Coast, and the Caribbean coast of

Belize. Clay housefloors dating to between 3000 and 2500 B.C. have been found in shell middens at the site of Puerto Marquez in Guerrero and at Tlacuachero in Chiapas. In coastal Veracruz, a preceramic village may have existed as early as 3000 B.C. at the site of Palo Hueco, and the remains of late Archaic camps have been found in northern Belize.

Other possible early village sites are found in certain regions of the highlands where environmental conditions existed that enabled people to become sedentary prior to dependence on agriculture. One such area is the Basin of Mexico, where villages may have existed along the shores of lakes and lagoons between 5000 and 3000 B.C. Elsewhere in the highlands, in the Tehuacán Valley and in Oaxaca, evidence for sedentism also dates to the late Archaic period, but in these regions settled village life was linked to the development of agriculture.

We know very little about these earliest villages. There does not appear to have been much variation among houses within villages, and within the various subregions there is no evidence of a hierarchy of communities. The general consensus among archaeologists is that the earliest Middle American villages were egalitarian and autonomous. Even though some of the earliest settlements were based on exploitation of wild resources in lowland zones, by the end of the Archaic period populations in lowland as well as highland areas were increasingly dependent upon cultivated plants, particularly maize. By around 2000 B.C., the village farming tradition was firmly in place in many parts of the region.

MESOAMERICA DEFINES ITSELF: THE FORMATIVE PERIOD

The 2,000 years of the Formative period (also called the Preclassic period) (2000 B.C.–A.D. 200) were a time of rapid and far-reaching cultural change throughout Middle America. Archaeologists usually divide this time span into three subperiods. The Early Formative period (2000–1200 B.C.) saw the initial settlement of most areas of the region by farming peoples. In a few areas, early villages grew in size and complexity to reach the level of social organization known as the chiefdom. The succeeding Middle Formative period (1200–400 B.C.) is notable for three main historical developments. Complex chiefdoms emerged in many more parts of Middle America; one chiefdom in particular—the Olmec—developed into a major polity whose cultural influence was felt over large areas; and a common religious iconography spread throughout the region. In the Late Formative period (400 B.C.–A.D. 200), the Olmec and other Middle Formative polities collapsed, to be replaced by larger and more complex societies—the first Mesoamerican states. Formative period sites are shown in Figure 2.5.

The Early Formative Period

The transition from the Archaic to the Formative periods was marked by the introduction of fired ceramics and the growth of sedentary agricultural villages. Both domestication and sedentism had existed in the Archaic period, but it was

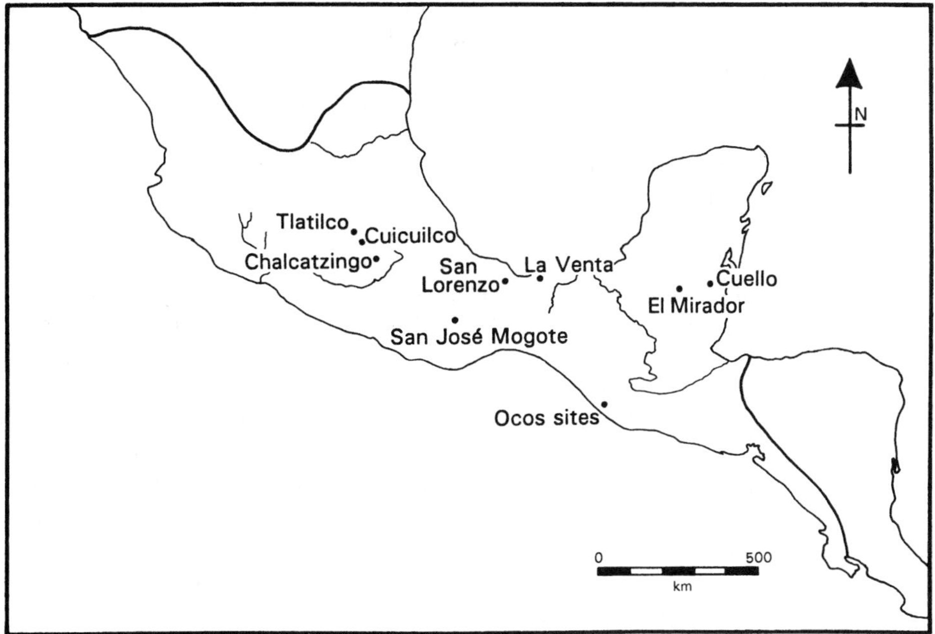

Figure 2.5 Locations of major Formative-period sites.

not until around 2000 B.C. that maize and other domesticated crops became sufficiently productive to support whole villages as the major portion of the diet. The foundation of the first agricultural villages coincided closely with the introduction of pottery throughout the region. These two trends have a logical link: It is simply not practical for nomadic peoples to carry around ceramic pots, whereas sedentary peoples require a large number of sturdy vessels for food storage, and fired clay pots serve this purpose well. Fired clay was also used to produce figurines—small images of persons, gods, and animals. The forms and designs of these figurines suggest that they were used in rituals of fertility and curing. The theme of agricultural fertility was one of the earliest and most fundamental components of Mesoamerican religion, and its appearance at Early Formative villages marks the emergence of the Mesoamerican religious tradition (see Chapter 8).

The earliest well-documented and securely dated pottery in the region forms a tradition called Ocos. Ocos pottery proper is found along the Pacific Coast of Chiapas and Guatemala, but Ocos-related pottery occurs across a wide area of Middle America, from the Gulf Coast of Veracruz to El Salvador and Honduras. This distribution suggests that for the first time there was widespread contact and communication among regional villages, and pottery provides material evidence for the emergence of Mesoamerica as a distinctive culture in the Early Formative period.

Whereas most Early Formative villages were small settlements with little evidence for social ranking, craft specialization, or other elements of social complexity, recent research at Ocos sites in coastal Chiapas by John Clark and Michael Blake suggests that simple chiefdoms developed in this area early on. The presence of an elaborate central residence larger than others (probably of the chief), evidence for limited specialization in the manufacture of pottery and possibly other items, and the existence of a two-level hierarchy of settlements all point to a society that had developed beyond the level of other Early Formative groups in Middle America.

In Central Mexico many Early Formative sites have been located in regional archaeological surveys, but few of these sites have been excavated. Excavations of burials at the site of Tlatilco in Mexico City (by both archaeologists and looters) reveal the existence of a tradition of sophisticated pottery vessels used as burial offerings. In the absence of excavations of houses and settlements, however, it is difficult to reconstruct the nature of Early Formative society in the area.

In the Valley of Oaxaca a long-term interdisciplinary archaeological project directed by Kent Flannery and Joyce Marcus has provided the most complete and extensive information on Early Formative villages anywhere in Middle America. A number of these sites have been excavated, revealing the rapid expansion of farming villages throughout the Valley. Toward the end of the Early Formative period, evidence for social complexity began to appear in Oaxaca, including large residences, public ceremonial buildings, and the beginnings of craft specialization.

The Olmecs

In the last centuries of the Early Formative period and throughout the Middle Formative, the Olmec culture flourished along the Gulf Coast. At the site of San Lorenzo, a small farming village existed as early as 1500 B.C. In its early years the village at San Lorenzo was similar to villages elsewhere in the region, and its inhabitants used Ocos-like pottery. Beginning around 1350 B.C., however, there is evidence for increasing cultural complexity at San Lorenzo. Most striking is the massive public works project begun at this time, which involved the reshaping of the natural hill upon which San Lorenzo sits. Large quantities of fill were used to turn the hill into a level plateau, and construction was begun on a symmetrical system of ridges that jut out from the main plateau.

By 1150 B.C. most of the features that characterized the fully developed "Olmec civilization" were present at San Lorenzo. These include colossal stone heads—thought to be portraits of rulers—for which the Olmec are most famous (Figure 2.6), as well as other stone sculptures, hollow ceramic figurines with baby faces, ceramic vessels decorated with iconographic motifs, public architecture, and a series of stone drains that were linked to artificially constructed ponds. San Lorenzo also had the first Mesoamerican ball court.

These characteristics indicate that by as early as 1350 B.C., a level of sociopolitical complexity was reached at San Lorenzo far beyond what had existed previously. An elite group had emerged with the power to mobilize the labor force necessary for major public works projects and for the transport of stone for

Figure 2.6 Giant Olmec head from the site of La Venta, Mexico.

monumental sculpture. Although we do not know a great deal about these earliest Olmec leaders, the iconography on Olmec sculpture indicates that they were considered to be of divine descent and imbued with supernatural powers. Moreover, access to positions of leadership may have been hereditary.

San Lorenzo dominated the Olmec heartland for several hundred years, but by 900 B.C. its importance began to fade, and the site of La Venta became a major Olmec center. Other Olmec centers contemporary with La Venta were Laguna de los Cerros and Tres Zapotes, but little work has been done at these sites. At La Venta large quantities of stone sculpture as well as smaller portable artifacts such as jade figurines and celts have been found. Monumental architecture, rich tombs and offerings, and buried large mosaic masks all indicate that La Venta was an elite residential area as well as a ceremonial center. Current research by Rebecca González Lauck promises to provide us with a more complete view of society at La Venta. By the end of the Middle Formative period, La Venta was in decline, and the era of widespread Olmec influence on the emerging Mesoamerican cultural tradition came to an end.

Linguists Lyle Campbell and Terrance Kaufman have postulated that the Olmecs spoke a Mixe-Zoquean language. Whereas these languages are limited to highland Oaxaca and the Isthmus of Tehuantepec today, in Olmec times Mixe-Zoque speakers were most likely distributed across a wide area of southern Middle America extending from the Gulf Coast, across the Isthmus of Tehuantepec, and down the Pacific Coast of Chiapas and Guatemala. In the Late Formative period, descendants of the Olmecs played a significant role in the development of the earliest Mesoamerican writing and directly influenced the evolution of the Maya writing system. An important key to this is the recently discovered La Mojarra Stela 1 (see Chapter 11).

Other Middle Formative Chiefdoms

The Olmecs were not the only complex society in Middle Formative Mesoamerica. Chiefdoms emerged in various areas, and a network of trade and interaction linked the Olmecs with their contemporaries in Oaxaca and Central Mexico. Olmec-style iconography appears at sites from El Salvador to the Valley of Mexico, and this distribution has generated a number of interpretations. Formerly, many scholars thought that the widespread distribution of these symbols indicated that the Olmecs had conquered or somehow controlled contemporaneous cultures in other parts of Mesoamerica. Recent fieldwork at sites that were supposedly Olmec "colonies" or "subjects" has produced a different view of Middle Formative cultures and interactions. A number of supposed Olmec symbols turn out to be more common at non-Olmec sites than they are in the Olmec heartland.

During the Middle Formative period the elites of several powerful chiefdoms were in contact with one another through trade networks and personal visits, and the participants in this network used a common system of emblems and religious symbols to proclaim their positions and power. The Gulf Coast Olmecs were merely one of these chiefdoms, although they were clearly the most complex and powerful polity at the time. Since much of this widely shared iconography has no greater association with the Olmecs than with chiefdoms in Oaxaca or Central Mexico, David Grove and others prefer to call it the "X-Complex" rather than the Olmec style per se (Figure 2.7).

Two well-studied Middle Formative chiefdoms outside of the Gulf Coast were centered at San José Mogote in the Valley of Oaxaca, and at Chalcatzingo in Morelos. In these and a few other areas, important changes began to occur in the

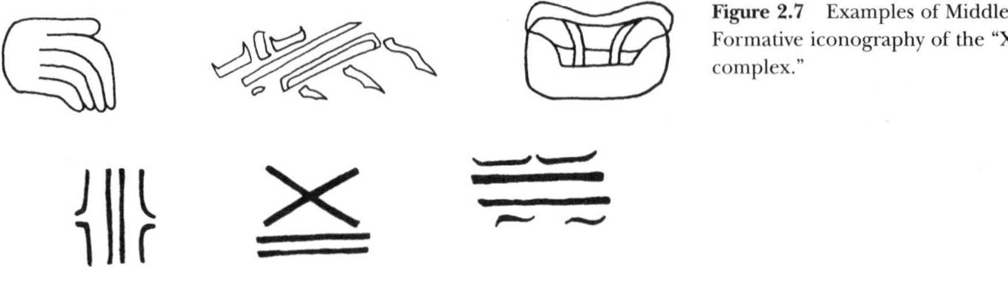

Figure 2.7 Examples of Middle Formative iconography of the "X-complex."

Box 2.2 *Mesoamerican Calendars*

Beginning sometime in the Formative period, Mesoamerican peoples began making use of three distinctive calendars. The ritual or sacred almanac consisted of a combination of two cycles, one of thirteen numbers and a second of twenty named days, corresponding to deities, which together created a 260-day cycle (13 × 20). The specific names for the days varied from region to region, depending on the language spoken, but the meanings for the day names were similar across Mesoamerica. The 260-day sacred almanac was used (and still is used in some Maya communities) for religious and divinitory purposes. An individual's destiny was closely tied to his or her birthday as expressed in the ritual almanac.

The second Mesoamerican calendar corresponded to the solar year. The solar calendar was made up of eighteen months of twenty days plus an additional five-day period, which produces a solar year of 365 days. The months in the solar calendar had patron deities who influenced people and events.

For the ancient Mesoamericans, each day was named with reference to both the sacred almanac and the solar cycle. This is not really so different from our own system, in which we have one cycle of seven day names (Monday through Sunday) and a second cycle of twelve months that have between 28 and 31 days. In our system, the most complete way to express a particular day is to say "Friday, September 23." Similarly, for the Yucatec Maya, for example, a particular day might be called "3 Imix" (for the ritual almanac) "15 Zac" (for the solar year). The combination of the ritual and solar cycles created a third calendrical cycle called the calendar round, which was fifty-two years long. This means that a given combination of day designations from the ritual and solar cycles–for example, "3 Imix, 15 Zac" occurs only once every fifty-two years.

last centuries of the Early Formative period. These include the construction of public structures, the relatively rapid growth of villages, the development of craft specialization, increases in long-distance exchange, the development of a calendrical system and writing (see Box 2.2), and the emergence of social stratification.

By the Middle Formative period, a hierarchy of settlements existed in the Valley of Oaxaca: a primary center, San José Mogote; a series of secondary centers, all of which had public architecture; and tertiary centers, which were small villages with no public architecture. Elites had access to valuable trade goods, they lived in larger houses than did the common people, and they were buried in more elaborate tombs. A sacrificed prisoner is depicted on a carved stone monument at San José Mogote, suggesting that political relations among chiefdoms included an element of violence. Archaeologists have also identified what might be a small defensive wall, again suggesting inter-community rivalries.

Chalcatzingo, a center in what is today the state of Morelos, is notable for its large civic-ceremonial precinct and its Olmec-style monumental stone art. Archaeologist David Grove argues that by the Middle Formative period, Chalcatzingo was ruled by a chief with close connections to the Gulf Coast Olmecs and other contemporary chiefdoms in the highlands. These connections included the exchange of goods, stylistic emulation, and perhaps marriage alliances. Variations in burial treatment at Chalcatzingo suggest significant levels of social stratification and ascribed status.

In the Maya lowlands, it is not until the Middle Formative period that the first good evidence for agricultural villages appears. Excavations by Norman Hammond at the site of Cuello in Belize have shown that this early Maya village was inhabited by maize farmers who lived in pole-and-thatch houses. Toward the end of the Middle Formative period, population growth in the Maya lowlands was rapid, and at sites in the Petén, the Yucatán Peninsula, and Belize, ceramics are quite similar, belonging to what is called the Mamon tradition. This uniformity in the pottery suggests that there was widespread contact across the region.

The first evidence for public architecture in the Maya lowlands occurs in the Middle Formative period. A large ceremonial structure, consisting of three temples sitting atop a terraced platform, was constructed at the site of Nakbé in the northern Petén. Overall there is little evidence for social ranking at these early Maya sites. In the Maya lowlands, very few Olmec-style artifacts have been recovered, and most Maya villages did not participate in the network of interacting Middle Formative chiefdoms that included the Gulf Coast, Oaxaca, and Central Mexico.

Late Formative Developments

After the collapse of Chalcatzingo and other Middle Formative Central Mexican chiefdoms, Cuicuilco and Teotihuacán became the preeminent polities. During the final two centuries B.C., each began construction of huge temple platforms, the first truly monumental buildings in Central Mexico. Cuicuilco, with its large circular-step pyramid, grew into a city of perhaps 20,000 inhabitants by the time of Christ. Then in the first century A.D., a nearby volcano, Mount Xitle, erupted and buried the settlement under 20 feet of lava, leaving only the top of the pyramid visible. Archaeologists had to use dynamite to excavate parts of Cuicuilco, most of which remains covered with volcanic rock in the southern part of Mexico City. The destruction of Cuicuilco in the Late Formative period enabled Teotihuacán to become the dominant power in Central Mexico by the beginning of the Classic period.

During the Late Formative period in the Valley of Oaxaca, the organization of settlements underwent a major change as the hilltop settlement of Monte Albán was established. This urban center would serve as a regional capital until late in the Classic period, around A.D. 700. According to Richard Blanton, Monte Albán may have been established by a confederation of Valley chiefdoms. The site's founders, who probably came from many of the Valley's communities, established an administrative center in a neutral location. The hilltop location in the central part of the Valley was far from the most productive farming lands, but it was centrally located and offered a commanding observation point for the entire valley. At this time other changes also took place in Oaxacan society. Population grew at a rapid pace, a market system developed, agricultural intensification took place, and Monte Albán became an urban center and capital of the Zapotec state. Political domination by Monte Albán was achieved, in part, through violence: One building at the site is adorned with

***Box 2.3** Mesoamerican Technology*

The Mesoamericans are sometimes described as having employed a "Stone Age" technology because of the prevalence of stone tools and the very limited and late development of metallurgy. Although this description is technically correct, it does not follow that Mesoamerican technology was crude or simple. A brief look at two areas of technology—tools and agriculture—illustrates some of the ingenuity and diversity of ancient Mesoamerican technological development.

With the exception of a small number of Postclassic cultures that used metal tools (see below), Mesoamerican peoples relied upon chipped stone for such cutting tools as knives, drills, scrapers, axes, arrow points, swords, etc. The preferred stone was obsidian, a form of volcanic glass. The primary tool, known as a prismatic blade, was difficult to manufacture, and it took archaeologists many years of experimentation to figure out how the Mesoamericans produced them. The great benefit of prismatic blades was their sharpness; microscopic tests have shown that these blades are often sharper than a modern surgeon's scalpel (archaeologists who analyze obsidian blades can be recognized from the bandages on their fingers!). Because of the great skill required to make blades, obsidian knapping was probably a specialized occupation in ancient Mesoamerica. The study of obsidian is helpful to archaeologists not only for its insights into tool technology but also for the analysis of trade routes. Obsidian occurs only in a limited number of highland locations, and each geological source has a distinct chemical profile or fingerprint that allows artifacts to be traced to their point of origin.

Metallurgy was first developed in the New World in the Andes mountains of South America, where a tradition several thousand years old has been identified by archaeologists. The technology was introduced into Mesoamerica by contact with South American cultures. Gold and silver working were brought into southern Mesoamerica during the Classic period from craftspersons in Central America, and copper and bronze technology were introduced into western Mexico in the Early Postclassic period through sea contact with South America. Once Mesoamerican cultures had adopted metalworking, they developed new techniques to suit their interests. Most metallurgy was devoted to ornamental and ritual objects like plaques, bells, and jewelry. In western Mexico, however, a tradition of bronze tools (including axes, chisels, awls, and sewing needles) developed in the Postclassic period, and this tradition was spreading to Central Mexico at the time of Spanish conquest.

Some of the most impressive technological advances of ancient Mesoamerica were in the realm of agriculture. As populations grew and centralized states expanded in the Classic and Postclassic periods, Mesoamerican farmers responded by devising new, more productive farming methods. The primary methods—irrigation, terracing, and raised fields—produced more food per unit of land compared to simple rainfall agriculture, but at the cost of increased labor inputs per unit of food output. The process of devising and adopting such methods is known as agricultural intensification, and this process was associated with population growth, political centralization, and urbanization. Simple irrigation canals and dams were first used in the Middle Formative period, but widespread use of irrigation did not occur until Classic times. By the time of Spanish conquest, the Aztecs had achieved the ability to elevate canals on aqueducts to carry water over low areas, a difficult engineering task.

Raised fields, a method of reclaiming swamps for crop cultivation, were one of the most fascinating elements of Mesoamerican technology. Raised fields were first devised in the Maya lowlands in the Formative period, and then saw heavy use supporting the high population densities of the Classic period Maya. The Aztecs later adopted this technology in the swampy lakes around their capital Tenochtitlán (Aztec raised fields are known as chinampas). Raised fields are constructed by piling up sediment and organic material from the swamp on long rectangular platforms, leaving canals filled with water between the fields. Crops planted on the field produce well, since they receive abundant water from the canals and the soils are fertilized by periodic applications of muck or organic matter from the swamp. This is a very highly productive agricultural method that was almost completely abandoned in the lowlands after the Maya collapse.

By the time archaeologists first recognized the remains of ancient raised fields in the Maya lowlands in the 1970s, there was only one place where this farming system was still practiced—in Xochimilco, just south of Mexico City. The Aztec system of raised fields had been used continuously since the Spanish conquest, and archaeologists looked to Xochimilco for clues as to how the method worked. They soon realized that raised fields in tropical lowland areas were somewhat different from the Central Mexican highland system, and archaeologists and agronomists began rebuilding Maya raised fields to study their construction and use. A similar program of experimental raised field construction was being undertaken in the southern Andes of Peru and Bolivia, where the ancient Inca and Tihuanaco civilizations had also used raised fields. In both Mesoamerica and the Andes, the modern experiments not only provided clues to the ancient technology, but also led to programs to reintroduce raised field cultivation as a sustainable agricultural method for modern peoples. This is a fascinating case of ancient technology providing a direct impetus for modern economic development.

carved stones depicting over 300 prisoners who had been killed; many of them had also been dismembered. Monte Albán was partially protected by defensive walls.

The Late Formative period (and the subsequent Protoclassic-Terminal Formative period) was a time of rapid population growth and cultural development in the Maya lowlands. During this period many of the traits that would characterize Classic Maya civilization developed. Communities that had been small-scale, egalitarian villages grew into centers with large populations and massive civic-ceremonial architecture. The archaeological evidence from the Late Formative period is much more complete than for earlier periods, and it provides us with clues for understanding the important changes that were taking place in Maya society. During the Late Formative period the Maya began to experiment with more intensive forms of agriculture, digging irrigation canals and reclaiming wetlands by constructing raised fields. Increased agricultural production allowed for even greater population growth. These agricultural projects also point to more centralized control over labor. At some centers massive construction projects were undertaken. At El Mirador the largest structure known in the Maya area was built in the Late Formative period (see Box 2.3).

Other evidence for the consolidation of religious and political power in the hands of the Maya elite includes the large stucco masks that adorned the faces of many Late Formative temple-pyramids (Figure 2.8). Linda Schele and David Friedel interpret the masks as attempts by Maya rulers to be identified with deities and supernatural powers. Many of these structures also served as the funerary monuments for Maya leaders. These developments signal the growing link between political power and religion as Mesoamerican rulers took control over religious ritual and belief systems. The culmination of this trend came with the powerful states of the succeeding Classic period.

Figure 2.8 Temple-pyramid with stucco god masks at the Late Formative-period Maya town of Cerros, Belize. Courtesy of David A. Freidel.

THE CLASSIC CIVILIZATIONS

Beginning around A.D. 200, an era traditionally called the Classic period began (see Figure 2.2). This was a time of Mesoamerican cultural florescence (Figure 2.9). It should be pointed out that the use of the term "Classic" is not an altogether satisfactory term, given what we now know about cultural complexity in both the Formative and Postclassic periods. Despite some attempts to introduce more neutral terminology that might better reflect the historical stages in Mesoamerican prehistory, the current period names—Formative (or Preclassic), Classic, and Postclassic—are so embedded in the literature that archaeologists continue to use them extensively. These terms now refer to time periods rather than to developmental stages.

Teotihuacán

The destruction of Teotihuacán's main rival, Cuicuilco, in the first century A.D. led to a period of explosive urban growth at Teotihuacán. The huge pyramids of the moon and sun were constructed, and the city's rulers laid out an entire city of 20 square kilometers following a regular grid pattern around the north-south axis of the "Street of the Dead" (the names of structures, streets, and the city itself were given to the ruined structures a millennium later by the Aztecs; the original names remain unknown). By A.D. 500, the city had grown to over 150,000 people and was the largest city in the world outside of China.

The precise location of Teotihuacán may have been chosen because the central portion of the site lies above a network of natural caves. The entrance to

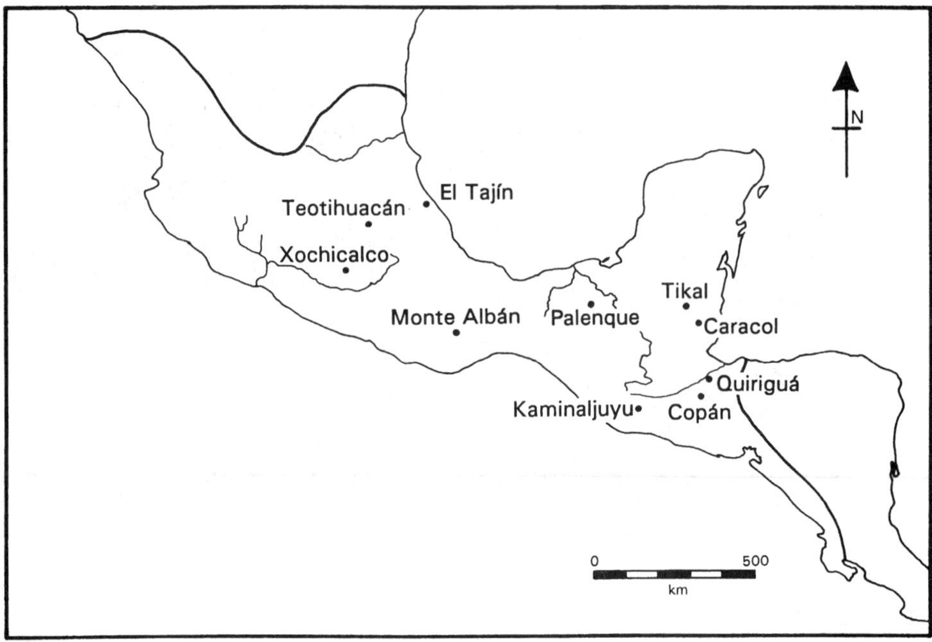

Figure 2.9 Locations of major Classic- and Epiclassic-period sites.

the largest cave is near the base of the central staircase of the Pyramid of the Sun, and this cave leads to a chamber directly under the top of the pyramid. Its passage was modified in ancient times and the cave was used for rituals. For Mesoamericans, caves had sacred qualities; they were viewed as entrances to the underworld, and the sun, moon, and even humans emerged from caves in the mythological past. Even after its demise, Teotihuacán continued to be viewed as a sacred place. Teotihuacán, whose name means "city of the gods" in the Nahuatl language, was the place where the sun was born, according to Aztec myths.

Settlement at Teotihuacán was laid out in a roughly concentric pattern. Major temples, elite residences, and civic buildings including a market were located along the Street of the Dead. These were surrounded by a zone of densely packed apartment compounds that housed the bulk of the city's populace, and this area was in turn surrounded by a zone of scattered huts that housed farmers (Figure 2.10).

Archaeologists have used housing patterns at Teotihuacán to reconstruct aspects of ancient urban social organization. The vast majority of the city's population lived in apartment compounds. These were large, rectangular stone buildings with a single entrance leading to a central courtyard. Passages led off the courtyard to smaller residential units or apartments housing several families each. Some of the courtyards had small pyramid-temple models that served as shrines for religious offerings. Much of the craft production that took place in Teotihuacán was carried out within the apartment compounds. Archaeologists have found evidence for the specialized production of obsidian tools, ceramic vessels and figurines, and jewelry in many of the apartment compounds.

Some of the Teotihuacán apartment compounds are larger and more sumptuous than most, and these have been interpreted as elite residences. Most of these are located in the central part of the city, close to the Street of the Dead. At the opposite end of the social scale, archaeologists have found evidence of small, insubstantial structures around the outer edges of the city, which were probably houses for the poorest inhabitants of Teotihuacán.

With a population of some 150,000 persons, inhabiting over 2,000 separate residential structures, Teotihuacán needed a regular and abundant food supply. Many of the urban residents were farmers who had to walk out to their fields each day. The city was located in an area of natural springs, and water from these was channeled and used to irrigate highly productive agricultural plots at the edges of town.

Several lines of evidence point to a powerful government that regulated many aspects of life and society at ancient Teotihuacán. The city's regular grid plan signals a high degree of urban planning, which could only have been accom-

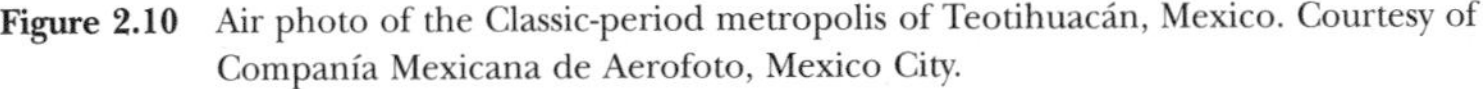
Figure 2.10 Air photo of the Classic-period metropolis of Teotihuacán, Mexico. Courtesy of Compania Mexicana de Aerofoto, Mexico City.

plished by a strong central authority. As the city grew in size early in the Classic period, many rural farmers were forced to abandon their homes and move into the expanding urban settlement. While we are not sure of the reasons for this policy, it is likely that only a strong centralized government could carry out such a practice. As Teotihuacán grew in size and complexity, its economic and political influence spread throughout much of Mesoamerica. The foreign influence of Teotihuacán was of three types: a political empire in highland Central Mexico, a trading network throughout much of Mesoamerica, and a sphere of ideological or religious influence even more widespread than the trade system.

Teotihuacán's armies conquered an empire that covered most of the central Mexican highlands. Within this area, formerly dispersed settlements were congregated into a small number of towns to aid administration and control of the conquered population. Many of these new towns were built in imitation of Teotihuacán itself, with a similar cardinal orientation (16 degrees east of north), grid plan, and use of a major central avenue.

Beyond the borders of its empire, Teotihuacán merchants engaged in an active trade with many areas of Mesoamerica. Green-tinted obsidian artifacts from the Teotihuacán-controlled Pachuca source are found at Classic sites as far south as Honduras, and Teotihuacán-style pottery is abundant in many areas. At distant sites such as Kaminaljuyú in highland Guatemala, structures were built in the distinctive Teotihuacán style, perhaps as residences for merchants from the central Mexican city. At least one neighborhood of foreign merchants has been excavated at Teotihuacán itself, providing strong evidence for the importance of the city's international trade networks. The ideological significance of Teotihuacán as a major religious and political center spread beyond its far-flung trade network. Teotihuacán-style incense burners were used in local rituals in many parts of southern Mesoamerica, and iconographic signs of Teotihuacán's religions and political power became incorporated into Classic Maya iconography as symbols of military prowess.

The end of Teotihuacán came rather suddenly in the seventh century A.D., when the city was burned and destroyed by its inhabitants. The evidence of destruction by fire is revealed in many of the excavations that have been done in various parts of the city. The burning was quite selective, with religious and administrative structures receiving the most damage and residences the least. This suggests internal revolt rather than external invasion as the means of destruction, although the reasons or causes for the revolt are not known. Even after destruction of the major buildings along the Street of the Dead, a sizable population remained within the city, and people continued to inhabit the area through the Aztec period and up to the present.

The Classic Maya

We have seen that the antecedents of Classic Maya civilization appeared in the Late Formative period, but in the southern lowlands the Classic period was a time of cultural florescence. During the Classic period the population reached its peak, building construction was extensive, and there was widespread elaboration of a set of traits that were uniquely Maya and associated with Maya elites. These traits include sophisticated calendrical, mathematical, and astronomical systems; writing; and masonry architecture using the corbeled arch, an architectural innovation that formed a vault (Figure 2.11).

The Classic period in the Maya area typically is subdivided into Early (ca. A.D. 200–600) and Late (A.D. 600–900) subperiods. This division reflects what is often called the Classic "hiatus," a period of several decades in the late sixth century in which there was a significant slowdown in the construction of buildings and the erection of stone monuments. This slowdown may have been a local response to changing conditions elsewhere in Mesoamerica—particularly the decline of the powerful Teotihuacán empire in Central Mexico. The beginning of the Late Classic period marks the end of the hiatus and a period of renewed vigor in Maya society.

A number of ideas once held about the Classic Maya have been revised in recent years as new evidence has come to light. Once the Maya were perceived to be a peaceful people; the common people were thought to have lived in dispersed settlements, practicing simple slash-and-burn horticulture while a priestly class resided in empty ceremonial centers, conducting rituals based on an obsession with time. Archaeological fieldwork in the 1960s and 1970s and then glyphic decipherment in the 1970s and 1980s have modified this picture considerably. We now know that the Maya, like other Mesoamerican groups, engaged in warfare, took

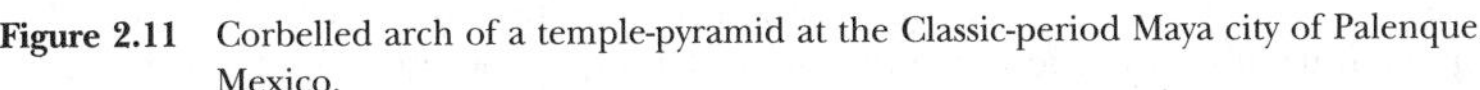

Figure 2.11 Corbelled arch of a temple-pyramid at the Classic-period Maya city of Palenque, Mexico.

Box 2.4 *The Long Count Calendar*

Sometime in the Late Formative period a system of dating was developed that we call the long count. The long count system allowed for much more precise dating than did other dating methods (such as the calendar round) because it was a linear count of days rather than a repeating cycle. The Classic Maya made greater use of the long count system than did any other group, although the system was developed initially by non-Maya peoples (probably Mixe-Zoqueans) before the beginning of the Classic period.

The long count system was based on a hierarchy of progressively larger units of time that were tied primarily to the vigesimal—or base 20—system of mathematics. To depict numbers from 1 to 20 a system of bars and dots were used, with a dot equalling 1 and a bar equalling 5. With a combination of bars and dots, numbers up to 20 could be recorded. Each Maya long count date has five notations that represent the following units of time:

kin = 1 day

uinal = 20 days (or 20 kin)

tun = 360 days (or 18 uinals)

katun = 7,200 days (or 20 tuns) (approximately 20 years)

baktun = 144,000 days (or 20 katuns) (approximately 400 years)

Each long count date, then, tells us how many kin, uinals, tuns, katuns, and baktuns have passed since the beginning of the current "great cycle" (a period of approximately 5,128 solar years), which began on a mythical starting date of zero in 3114 B.C. in our own calendrical system. A long count date of 9.15.5.0.0 simply means that 9 baktuns, 15 katuns, 5 tuns, 0 uinals, and 0 kin have passed since the Maya zero date, or 3114 B.C. in our calendar.

The earliest long count dates currently known come from the site of Chiapa de Corzo (36 B.C.) and Tres Zapotes (31 B.C.). But as we mentioned earlier, the Classic Maya made the most extensive use of the long count system. Hundreds of long count dates appear on stelae during the eighth and ninth baktun cycles. The decline of the Classic Maya of the southern lowlands took place during the ninth baktun cycle, and the last long count date of 10.4.0.0.0 (A.D. 909) was recorded at the site of Toniná.

prisoners, and in many cases sacrificed them. The population in the lowlands was large and many areas were densely populated. A number of agricultural systems in addition to slash-and-burn were practiced by the lowland Maya, including the construction of raised fields in wetland areas, terracing, arboriculture, and kitchen gardens. Maya sites once thought to be vacant ceremonial precincts are now known to have been true urban centers with a variety of functions (see Box 2.5).

Our understanding of the events of the Classic period in the Maya lowlands has increased markedly in recent years as more and more of the Maya writing system has been deciphered (see Chapter 11). Inscriptions appear primarily on stelae, but they also are found on stucco facades, on wooden or stone lintels above doorways, on stairways, and on pottery. These inscriptions provide information on dynastic histories of Maya rulers, the political alliances forged between and among centers, warfare, and ritual life.

Although cities across a wide area of the Maya lowlands shared a common culture, the area was never unified politically. Instead, several regional states existed within the Maya lowlands, with each region composed of a capital city and numerous smaller subject cities, towns, and villages. The composition of each region was fluid as centers were alternatively warring with each other and joining in alliances. The Classic Maya regional states were in a continuous process of expansion and contraction owing to changing fortunes in warfare, statecraft, and exchange.

For reasons that are still not completely understood, Classic Maya civilization in the southern lowlands collapsed between A.D. 800 and 900. While the popular image of the mysterious vanished Maya civilization is not entirely accurate—Maya peoples continued to live in certain areas within the southern lowlands after the collapse—the religious and state institutions that held society together during the Late Formative and Classic periods stopped functioning around A.D. 800. The first evidence for the impending collapse was the cessation of construction activity at sites in the western portion of the southern lowlands. No long count dates (see Box 2.4) were recorded at sites along the Usumacinta River after A.D. 840. All but a few centers were virtually abandoned by A.D. 900 or shortly thereafter.

The causes of the collapse of Classic Maya civilization have eluded archaeologists for many years. It is now generally agreed that no single factor can account for the collapse; instead, several related factors contributed to the failure of elite institutions. Demographic and ecological stress clearly played a role. The rapid increase in population in the lowlands meant that much more food needed to be grown to feed the population. In the fragile tropical ecosystem, the implementation of more intensive forms of agriculture may have upset an already delicate ecological balance and led to depletion of nutrients in soils. Skeletal evidence indicates that Late Classic populations suffered from malnutrition and other chronic diseases. The environment simply could not sustain indefinitely the large populations of the Late Classic period.

Several aspects of Maya social organization also contributed to the collapse. The gap between elites and commoners increased during the Late Classic period. As the elite population grew, its demands on the remainder of the population increased. The boom in the construction of new buildings, monuments, and other public works may have produced greater frictions within Maya society and growing resentment on the part of the commoners. If elites played a management role in the intensive agricultural systems, any failure in food production also would have been blamed on the elites. Warfare was another significant cause of the Classic Maya collapse. Evidence now suggests that warfare between Maya polities increased during the Late Classic period. Moreover, the nature of warfare may have changed, with territorial expansion replacing the capturing of prisoners as a goal in battle.

In addition to these growing problems in Classic Maya society, external pressures added to the disruptions of the ninth century. The intrusion of outsiders into the lowland Maya area was once thought to have been a major factor in the Maya collapse. Evidence for foreign intrusion at some sites is clear—particularly in the western lowlands (along the Usumacinta River)—but it is now believed that the intruders found an already unstable Maya society and merely took advantage of an existing situation rather than being the main cause of the decline. It is likely that the intruders were Putun or Chontal Maya from the Tabasco region. Some combination of these factors was responsible for the collapse of Classic Maya society in the southern lowlands, although it is likely that the precise combination of factors varied from region to region.

The collapse of Classic Maya civilization in the southern lowlands did not mean that the area was left entirely uninhabited. The population decline was dramatic owing to both increased mortality rates and emigration, as elites and others apparently fled to northern Yucatán. Yet some of the population remained, choosing to live not in the abandoned cities but in the rural areas. By the Postclassic period a thriving, if smaller and radically reorganized, Maya society survived with settlements located primarily in the lake area of the central Petén. Further north, in the Yucatán Peninsula, Maya centers such as Uxmal, Edzná, Sayil, and Labná thrived for one or more centuries.

A brief look at three of the largest and most intensively studied Classic Maya cities will provide a fuller view of Classic Maya culture and illustrate both similarities and differences among Maya cities.

Tikal. Tikal is the largest known Maya center—the main residential area covers 23 square kilometers, and over 3,000 structures have been mapped—and it has been studied intensively by scores of archaeologists for many years (Figure 2.12). Located in the Petén jungle of Guatemala, Tikal had a population of 50,000 at its peak in the Late Classic period. From the numerous stelae and inscriptions found on buildings, epigraphers have been able to reconstruct the political and dynastic history of Tikal in some detail. A single dynasty ruled at Tikal from the Early Classic period to the ultimate demise of the center, and we know the names of many of the rulers and some details about their lives.

By the Late Formative period, Tikal was already developing into an important regional center. During the Early Classic period, Tikal emerged as the dominant center of the central lowlands after defeating its major rival, neighboring Uaxactún. Tikal prospered and grew; it controlled trade routes and had great influence over its neighbors. There were important links between Tikal and Teotihuacán; Maya rulers adopted Teotihuacán imagery—perhaps to enhance their own prestige—and Teotihuacán-style pottery and other artifacts became popular at the site.

The Classic hiatus hit Tikal hard, and for over 100 years, between the mid-sixth and late seventh centuries, monumental construction virtually ceased. Tikal's problems may have been exacerbated by attacks from a belligerent neighbor; according to inscriptions at the nearby city of Caracol, this polity defeated Tikal during hostilities in the mid-sixth century. Caracol was unable to assume a dominant role in the region for very long, and by the late 600s Tikal once again emerged as a powerful center. With the accession of a new ruler, Ah Cacaw, in A.D. 692, an ambitious building program was initiated at Tikal. Indeed, most of the buildings we see today at Tikal were built by Ah Cacaw and his two successors, currently known as Rulers B and C.

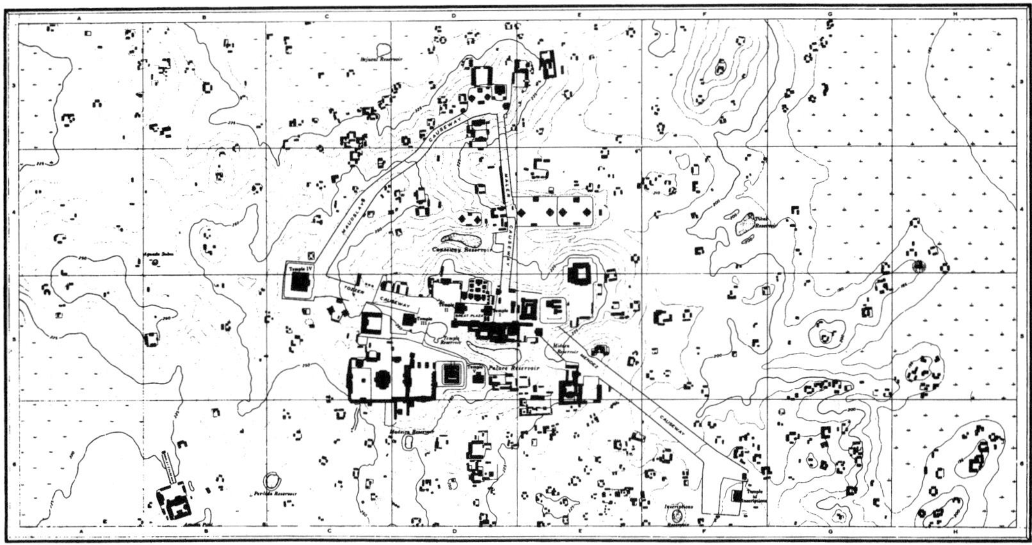

Figure 2.12 The central portion of the Classic-period Maya city of Tikal, Guatemala. Courtesy of The University Museum, University of Pennsylvania.

During the Late Classic period Tikal once again became an expansionistic power, using the strategy of combining alliance-making with the use of force. Male members of Tikal's ruling dynasty were installed as leaders of some subject towns while females married into dynastic families of others, thereby cementing alliances. At the same time, war was waged against cities like Calakmul, which had once been antagonistic toward Tikal.

The last flurry of building at Tikal was commissioned by Ruler C, who came to power in A.D. 768 and who is also the last Tikal ruler to be identified. Subsequently, Tikal fell into another period of decline; this time it would not recover. The last dated monument at the site was erected in A.D. 869.

Palenque. Palenque occupies a dramatic natural setting, nestled in the hills of Chiapas overlooking the Gulf Coast plain. Much of what we see today at the site of Palenque was constructed during the reigns of its two most notable rulers: Pacal, or Shield, and his oldest son, Chan-Bahlum, or Snake-Jaguar. Pacal and Chan-Bahlum ruled for most of the seventh century, although inscriptions at the site date the beginnings of Palenque's dynastic history at A.D. 431.

Palenque stands apart from other Classic Maya sites for its unique architectural style and its beautiful bas-relief sculpture, in both stone and stucco, which includes some of the longest Classic Maya texts. The rulers of Palenque were particularly concerned with legitimizing their positions as rulers, and many of the texts focus on family trees. This has made it possible to reconstruct the complete dynastic history of the site. As a result we know for certain that two women—Pacal's mother, Lady Zac Kuk, and his great-grandmother, Lady Kanal-Ikal—ruled at Palenque.

Innovations by architects at Palenque enabled them to construct rooms with thinner walls and greater interior space, creating rooms that were lighter and better ventilated than the small, dark rooms found at other sites. This allowed artists to incorporate carved stone panels into the walls on the interiors of the temples. At Palenque, unlike most other Classic Maya centers, sculptors did not erect freestanding stone monuments or stelae, as their work could be displayed on building interiors.

Palenque was not a large settlement like Tikal, yet it clearly was a prominent political and religious center in the Late Classic period. The site is dominated by the Temple of the Inscriptions—the funerary monument to Pacal—and a network of buildings called the Palace (Figure 2.13). Deep within the Temple of the Inscriptions is Pacal's tomb. His coffin, made of stone, is so massive that it had to be put in place before the pyramid was constructed. The coffin lid depicts Pacal's journey to the underworld. The tomb can be reached by climbing down a narrow, vaulted stairway that begins at the top of the temple.

The descendants of Pacal and Chan-Bahlum ruled at Palenque until the late 700s, but by late in the century one or more of its subject towns had broken away, suggesting that Palenque was losing power over centers it once dominated. The forces that led to the Maya collapse hit Palenque early—its last dated monument was erected in A.D. 799.

Copán. The Copán Valley, located in Honduras at the southeastern edge of the Maya area, was first settled in the Early and Middle Formative periods. In the Early Classic period the site of Copán grew into an important Maya city, and

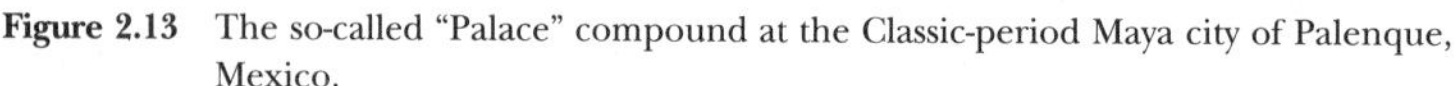

Figure 2.13 The so-called "Palace" compound at the Classic-period Maya city of Palenque, Mexico.

most of what is visible at the site today was built during the Late Classic period. Situated in a highland valley at around 2,000 feet above sea level, Copán is one of the few Classic Maya centers in an upland region.

According to inscriptions at Copán, the ruling dynasty was founded in A.D. 426, and all subsequent rulers, sixteen in all, based their legitimacy on their descent from the first ruler, Yax-Kuk-Mo', or Blue Quetzal Macaw. Copán has been the focus of extensive research in recent years; the ceremonial precinct as well as several outlying residential districts have been excavated, and epigraphers have made important advances in the decipherment of the numerous hieroglyphic texts at the site.

At Copán, like Palenque and Tikal, we now know the identities of the rulers who were responsible for leading the city to greatness during the Late Classic period. For most of the seventh century Copán was ruled by its twelfth ruler, Smoke-Imix-God K, a contemporary of Pacal at Palenque and Ah Cacaw at Tikal. Under this ruler, Copán expanded its territory to its greatest extent, bringing neighboring Quirigua and other centers into its orbit. Smoke-Imix-God K's successor and son, 18 Rabbit, was responsible for transforming much of Copán's ceremonial center into the form that we see it in today. All of the stelae in the Great Plaza were commissioned and erected under 18 Rabbit. Indeed, Copán is most noted for the artistic quality of stelae, unusual in Maya art because they were sculpted in the round (Figure 2.14).

18 Rabbit met an untimely end when he was captured and sacrificed by the ruler of Copán's former subject city, Quirigua, in A.D. 738. This act naturally ended the creative works of 18 Rabbit, and apparently temporarily diminished the power of Copán's ruling dynasty—no structures or stelae were erected during the reign of 18 Rabbit's successor. The death of Copán's ruler did not, however, result in any great changes in the everyday life of most of Copán's citizens; archaeologists cannot detect any changes in social and economic activities associated with 18 Rabbit's demise. By the reign of the son of 18 Rabbit's successor, Copán's ruling dynasty had reestablished its position of strength, although this was not to last.

The sixteenth and penultimate ruler of Copán, Yax-Pac or First Dawn, came to power in A.D. 763. Yax-Pac began an ambitious building program at Copán, but he ruled in a time of crisis. By Yax-Pac's reign, overpopulation had put a strain on the valley's resources, and noble families were increasingly competing with the ruling family for power. When Yax-Pac died, probably in early A.D. 820, dynastic rule at Copán was close to collapse; this was the date on the last monument erected at the site. Although the city center and outlying neighborhoods continued to be occupied for another hundred years or so, centralized political control and all of the activities it had engendered had come to an end.

Other Classic Civilizations

Although Teotihuacán and the lowland Maya were the largest civilizations of the Classic period, several other areas of Mesoamerica also supported large state-level societies at this time. In the Valley of Oaxaca, the Zapotec hilltop city of Monte

Figure 2.14 Stela A at the Classic-period Maya city of Copán, Honduras.

Albán became capital of a powerful state. Evidence from stone monuments indicates that the use of force was sometimes needed to subjugate neighboring as well as distant polities. Monte Albán apparently had a good relationship with Teotihuacán. Depictions of what appear to be diplomatic meetings between Teotihuacán "ambassadors" and Zapotec lords were recorded on stone monuments at Monte Albán, and Zapotec merchants lived in their own barrio at Teotihuacán. After A.D. 600, however, Monte Albán suffered a period of decline, and its territory began to shrink as subject towns gained strength and broke away from its control. By A.D. 700 Monte Albán had lost its dominant position in the Valley, and by A.D. 800 portions of the site—including the Great Plaza—were no longer in use. Nevertheless, part of the site and the surrounding area continued to be used into the Postclassic period.

The interval between the destruction of Teotihuacán and the rise of the Aztec empire over five centuries later saw the rise and fall of a succession of militaristic cities and states in northern Mesoamerica. The two centuries after the fall of Teotihuacán (between A.D. 750 and 950) are known as the Epiclassic period in Central Mexico. During this period a number of large cities sprang up to fill the political and economic vacuum left by the fall of the Teotihuacán empire. In addition to the remnant city at Teotihuacán itself (still a major city of 30,000 inhabitants), impressive urban centers were found at Xochicalco in Morelos, Teotenango in the Toluca Valley, and Cacaxtla in the Puebla-Tlaxcala Valley. These were mountaintop cities whose fortifications and iconography attest to the prevalence of warfare at this time (Figures 2.15, 2.16).

On the Gulf Coast, the center of El Tajín is an important site that gained prominence during the Classic period. Closely linked to Teotihuacán in the early part of the Classic period, El Tajín reached its peak of development after the fall of Teotihuacán. The site is noted for being a center of the ball game cult, and many of the artifacts recovered during excavations at the site are paraphernalia used in the ball game.

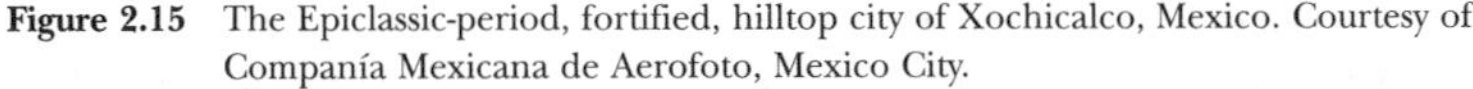

Figure 2.15 The Epiclassic-period, fortified, hilltop city of Xochicalco, Mexico. Courtesy of Companía Mexicana de Aerofoto, Mexico City.

Figure 2.16 Ritualized battle as depicted in a mural at the Epiclassic-period city of Cacaxtla, Mexico. Courtesy of Debra Nagao.

Box 2.5 *Changing Views of Mesoamerican Cities*

Forty years ago most Mesoamericanists believed that the Classic Maya did not have true cities. Sites with large architecture were thought to be "empty ceremonial centers" inhabited only by priests, and the Maya were mentioned along with Old Kingdom Egypt as the only ancient civilizations that lacked urban centers. Today nearly all Mesoamericanists would describe the Maya as an urban society with true cities and towns. This reversal of opinion came about partly as a result of archaeological fieldwork at Maya cities and partly as a result of changes in our definition of the term *urban.*

The fieldwork most responsible for showing that Maya sites were indeed true cities was the University of Pennsylvania Tikal Project in the late 1950s and early 1960s. Most earlier archaeological work at Maya sites had concentrated solely on the monumental architecture found in the centers of sites. The great innovation of the Tikal Project was to extend coverage outward from the site's center with a systematic program of mapping and excavations (directed by William Haviland and Dennis Puleston). Archaeologists learned that the jungle surrounding the pyramids and palaces was filled with low mounds that were the remains of commoner houses. Tikal was not an "empty" center at all but a city with a population of 50,000 or more. The fieldwork at Tikal was part of a larger reorientation of archaeological research in Mesoamerica and elsewhere in the 1960s away from an exclusive concern with "temples and tombs" and toward a focus on ancient society and culture, including commoner households and rural areas.

Even after the residential neighborhoods of Maya sites were identified, mapped, and excavated, some scholars still suggested that these settlements were not "true cities" like Teotihuacán or Tenochtitlán. This interpretation was based upon a definition of cities as large settlements with very dense populations and complex social institutions. In comparison with Teotihuacán (Figure 2.10), Tikal (Figure 2.12) certainly had a smaller population, a far lower population density, and more limited expressions of social and economic complexity. But does this mean that Tikal was not really an urban settlement?

During the 1970s a new functional definition of urbanism was embraced by anthropologists and other social scientists. Rather than viewing cities as settlements with lots of people, the functional perspective defines cities as settlements that fulfill various functions or roles for a hinterland. These functions can be economic (the city as a center for manufacturing or trade), administrative (the city as a center for government), religious (the city as a setting for important temples), or cultural (the city as a center for the arts or education). This definition of urbanism leads to the notion that there are different types of cities, some of which have large, dense populations and others of which do not.

When the functional view of urbanism was applied to ancient Mesoamerica (initially by Richard Blanton and Joyce Marcus), it became obvious that there was more than one "type" of ancient Mesoamerican city. Tikal, Palenque, Copán, and other large Maya centers were cities whose major functions were in the realm of administration (as shown by palaces) and religion (large temple-pyramids), whereas Teotihuacán was an urban center where economic functions predominated, although administrative and religious functions were also important.

Among Mesoamerican cities there is enormous variation in such features as city size, population density, degree of formal planning, amount of ceremonial space, presence of fortifications, topographic setting, arrangement of housing, etc. (compare Figures 2.11, 2.12, 2.14, 2.15, 2.17). But does this great variety of urban form mask an underlying similarity in urban function? Today many archaeologists believe that apart from a few exceptions, Mesoamerican urban centers functioned primarily in the realms of administration and religion. Nearly all Mesoamerican cities were built around a city center consisting of large buildings carefully arranged around one or more open public plazas. The most common types of central buildings were palace compounds and temple-pyramids. The central focus of the plaza and the size of temples and palaces relative to other structures point to the dominance of religion and administration. In cases where written records provide clues to urban function (such as ethnohistoric descriptions of Aztec cities, or the content of glyphic inscriptions at Classic Maya cities), administration and religion also stand out, providing additional support for this model. Outside of the city center, spatial patterns show considerable variation, but in most cases population density is not extremely high. The exceptions to this pattern are Teotihuacán and Tenochtitlán, Central Mexican imperial capitals with strong economic orientations and very large, dense populations. Nevertheless, these two cities were also important administrative and religious centers for their hinterlands, and the functional approach to urbanism provides insights into all of the urban centers of ancient Mesoamerica.

POSTCLASSIC CITY-STATES

The Postclassic period, from the fall of the Classic civilizations through the Spanish conquest (see Figure 2.2), is often characterized as a time of secularization in Mesoamerica. This does not mean that religion ceased to be important to the Mesoamerican peoples, but that the civil and particularly commercial elements of society became more important than they had been previously. Political power was less intertwined with supernatural power, and economic and commercial affairs became more independent of state control. One of the major forces bringing about these changes was the expansion of market systems and long-distance exchange among Postclassic polities. The Aztec and Tarascan empires emerged as dominant powers in northern Mesoamerica in the Late Postclassic period, but many small Postclassic states throughout Mesoamerica were unable to expand their territories in the same manner as the large Classic states like Teotihuacán or Monte Albán. Instead, political control by individual states was limited to smaller areas. At the same time, the boundaries between small polities became increasingly permeable to both commercial and cultural exchange and interaction. Art styles, for example, exhibit greater unity across all of Mesoamerica than ever before. Technological innovations, such as the use of the bow and arrow and of cotton quilted armor, were adopted throughout the region.

Much of what we know about life in the Postclassic period comes from written documents, and the analysis and interpretation of these documents is known as ethnohistory. These ethnohistoric sources are discussed at greater length in chapters 3 and 12. In the remainder of this chapter we emphasize Postclassic historical changes as revealed by archaeological fieldwork.

Northern Mesoamerica

In the tenth century, Tula emerged as the largest urban center since the fall of Teotihuacán (Figure 2.17). Tula was the home of the Toltecs, a shadowy group about which archaeology and ethnohistory are in disagreement. According to Aztec native historical accounts, the Toltecs were wise and great. They were devout, and invented all of the useful arts and crafts. Their capital, Tula, was a magnificent metropolis, the center of a large empire covering much of highland Central Mexico. The Toltec dynasty was revered by the Aztecs, and the rulers of the later Aztec city-states traced their descent and legitimacy back to the Toltec kings.

Archaeology paints another picture. While Tula had some impressive public architecture, including pyramids with monumental sculptures, ballcourts, and a series of colonnaded halls, it was a far cry from the size and grandeur of

Figure 2.17 Locations of major Postclassic-period sites.

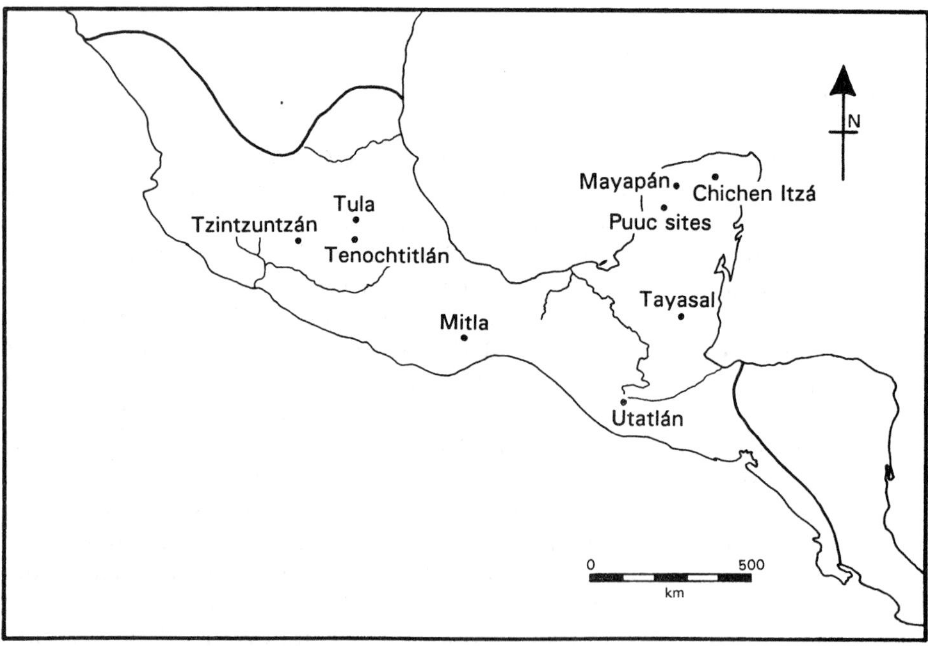

earlier cities like Teotihuacán or Xochicalco. There is no material evidence for a Toltec empire, and the lack of some key Postclassic trade goods (such as Fine Orange pottery) at Tula suggests that the city was off the beaten track of the busy international trade networks of the time. Until further research is carried out, it is difficult to know what to make of the different views that archaeology and the written documents provide of Tula and the Toltecs. At some point around A.D. 1150, Tula was abandoned and the scene was set for the rise of the Aztecs.

In West Mexico, the Tarascan or Purépecha state ruled over a vast territory that rivaled the Aztec empire in territory. The Tarascans ruled from their capital at Tzintzuntzán on the shores of Lake Pátzcuaro in Michoacán. By the Late Postclassic period, Tzintzuntzán was an important city with as many as 35,000 people. Within the city were the burial-temple platforms of kings; other religious shrines; civil-administrative buildings; storehouses; artisan workshops; and the residences of elites, commoners, and foreigners.

Aztec attempts to conquer Tarascan territories were met with stiff resistance. The Tarascans had a well-trained military, and they maintained forts along their borders. West Mexico is well known for the metal goods that were produced there, including copper, bronze, and gold objects.

Oaxaca

Prior to the Postclassic period, the Oaxaca region had been dominated to a great extent by events taking place in the Valley of Oaxaca, an area populated by the Zapotecs. But in the Postclassic period, the Mixtecs, who inhabited much of Oaxaca outside of the central Valley of Oaxaca, began to have a much greater influence on the other Mesoamericans.

After the decline of Monte Albán, the Valley of Oaxaca was divided into a large number of independent city-states, none of which exercised absolute control over the valley in the way that Monte Albán had done in the Classic period. Although the Postclassic occupation of Monte Albán was relatively small, it had impressive architecture, and the site wielded considerable political power because it was home to an important Zapotec royal family. Mitla, also in the eastern part of the valley, is the best-known Postclassic site in the Oaxaca Valley. Mitla was occupied continuously from the Early Formative period, but the center's florescence took place in the Postclassic period. It was during the Late Postclassic period that the most important—and beautiful—building complexes were constructed. Described in the sixteeth century as having two of the most impressive and famous buildings in New Spain, Mitla is noted for the intricate mosaic veneer on the facades of buildings and for its murals (Figure 2.18). It is thought that Mitla was a Zapotec religious center.

Many sites in the Valley of Oaxaca show evidence of Mixtec influence in the Postclassic period, although the precise nature of this influence is the subject of ongoing debate. By the early part of the Postclassic period, the Mixtecs were becoming an increasingly important and influential force among Mesoamericans.

Figure 2.18 Stone mosaic facade of a palace building at the Postclassic-period city of Mitla, Mexico.

This is particularly true of artistic styles. According to both Mixtec and Zapotec historical traditions, intermarriage between Mixtec and Zapotec noble families strengthened ties between the two groups, and this—rather than intrusive Mixtec populations—may best explain Mixtec presence and influence in the valley.

The Yucatán Peninsula

During the Late Classic through Early Postclassic periods of the Maya collapse, cities in the northern Yucatán Peninsula carried on much of the southern Classic Maya tradition. These centers, which did not suffer the effects of the collapse, are best known for their unique architectural styles, with intricate mosaic designs on building facades and frequent depictions of Chac (rain god) masks over doorways and at the corners of buildings. The Puuc area sites of Uxmal, Sayil, and Labná are the most elaborate examples. These centers fell into decline within a hundred years of the collapse in the southern lowlands, perhaps for many of the same reasons.

Chichén Itzá emerged as the dominant Maya center in the Yucatán Peninsula early in the Postclassic period. Although Chichén Itzá was a small site during the Classic period, after A.D. 1000 the site emerged as an important regional center. Many archaeologists believe that the rise of Chichén Itzá at that time was linked to events taking place at Tula, the Toltec capital. The period between 1000 and 1250 at Chichén Itzá is sometimes referred to as the Toltec period because of a number of architectural and artistic similarities between Chichén Itzá and

Tula, including several close architectural parallels, similar sculptural styles, the use of columns that depict warriors, and the presence of distinctive carved figures known as chacmools. While the physical similarities between Tula and the northern portion of Chichén Itzá are striking, the precise nature of the relationship between the two centers is poorly understood and hotly debated. One view derives from central Mexican and Yucatec native histories, which claim that in A.D. 987 Topiltzín Quetzalcoatl, a high priest in the Quetzalcoatl cult at Tula, was expelled from Tula after a power struggle with Tezcatlipoca. In the same year Kukulkán (the term for Quetzalcoatl in the Yucatec Maya language) is said to have arrived at the site of Chichén Itzá along with a group of intruders called the Itzá. In this view, the architectural and artistic similarities between Tula and Chichén Itzá result from either the direct presence of Toltecs or else the influence of a foreign Maya group who had close contact with the Toltecs.

An alternative view is that the construction of the so-called Toltec-style buildings at Chichén Itzá actually preceded construction at Tula. Unfortunately, the lack of a solid archaeological chronology for Chichén Itzá and the resulting difficulty of dating the architecture prevent resolution of the conflicting interpretations of the "Toltec" presence at the site. Current research on dating and architecture should help solve the problem.

Whatever the correct explanation for the relationship between Tula and Chichén Itzá, there is little debate about the ultimate demise of Chichén Itzá late in the twelfth century. At that time the city was sacked by a rival Maya group from the city of Mayapán. Mayapán succeeded Chichén Itzá as the primary center of the Yucatán, a position it held until the mid-1400s. Mayapán, which dominated the Yucatán Peninsula for over two centuries, was a poor imitation of Chichén Itzá. Construction methods were shoddy and as a result, many of the buildings are poorly preserved. The city was walled—mute testimony to the increased levels of militarism that characterized Postclassic Yucatán.

Like Chichén Itzá before it, Mayapán's downfall was brought about through a violent attack. In this case, the attack was led by members of the Xiu lineage, and again, there is evidence that the city was sacked and burned. According to various chronicles, Mayapán fell in 1441. Mayapán was the last Yucatecan center that was able to dominate the peninsula. Subsequently, the region was divided into numerous small, independent, petty polities.

Coastal towns on the Yucatán Peninsula, particularly those along the eastern coast, flourished in the Late Postclassic period, in large part because of the importance of sea-based commerce. The Island of Cozumel not only served as a center for trade, but also was the site of an important shrine to Ix Chel, goddess of medicine and patron deity of women. On the mainland, Tulum and other towns were busy seaports whose buildings were adorned with colorful murals depicting ceremonial scenes.

In contrast to the well-documented polities and events of northern Yucatán, little is known about the Maya who remained in the southern lowlands following the Classic collapse. Most of the known settlement in the Postclassic period was concentrated in the central Petén, on the shores of a chain of lakes—

Lakes Petén Itzá, Yaxhá, and Macanché. According to the Yucatecan chronicles, the Itzá survivors of the sacking of Chichén Itzá fled to the Petén and established a new capital on an island in Lake Petén Itzá. From their capital of Noh Petén—or Tayasal, as it was called by the Spaniards, the Itzá came to dominate the southern Maya lowlands. In terms of both political organization and artistic and architectural styles, there were strong similarities between the Late Postclassic centers in the Petén and in northern Yucatán. Noh Petén was one of the last Maya centers to fall to the Spaniards—its leaders successfully resisted Spanish efforts at conquest until 1697. But that story will be told in Chapter 4.

The Highland Maya

The Postclassic period in the highlands of Guatemala and Chiapas was a volatile time of warfare, migration, and social upheaval. Most cities were located in defensible positions on ridge-tops or plateaus and were surrounded with walls. The Late Postclassic polities were influenced by Central Mexican cultures, in some cases borrowing Nahua terms for kin groups, adopting Central Mexican art styles, or adding Central Mexican deities to their pantheon. The ruling dynasties of these Postclassic Maya states all claimed descent from the Toltecs.

During the fourteeth and fifteenth centuries, the Quiché capital of Utatlán (or K'umarcaaj) was a large, nucleated city situated on an inaccessible plateau reachable only by a causeway and bridge from the east and a steep stairway from the west. The site consists of several plaza groups made up of an open courtyard bounded by a temple, a council or administrative building, and a palace or residential building. The various plaza groups were most likely occupied by the major Quiché lineages as identified in ethnohistoric sources. Several adjacent plateaus—in equally defensible positions—were settled by related lineage groups.

Several decades before the arrival of the Spaniards, the Quiché empire began to crumble. By the late fifteenth century, Quiché hegemony was seriously threatened by the Cakchiquels, who had broken away and founded their own capital at the site of Iximché in the late 1400s. Like Utatlán, Iximché was situated in a defensible location, surrounded on three sides by steep ravines.

The Rise of the Aztecs

We use the term *Aztec* to refer to the Nahuatl-speaking peoples of highland Central Mexico at the time of the Spanish conquest. There were several distinct Aztec ethnic groups, of which the Mexica are the best known. These groups originated in northern Mexico, migrating south into the central Mexican highlands in the twelfth and thirteenth centuries. Scholars are divided as to whether their reported home, Aztlán, was a real or mythical place. When the Nahuatl-speakers arrived in Central Mexico after the fall of Tula, they founded towns and set up dynasties, leading to the development of a series of city-states that continued as the dominant political form through the time of the Spanish conquest. These new city-states were successful economically and politically, and this period witnessed a great surge of population growth caused by both immigration and natural increase.

Like other Mesoamerican city-state systems, such as the Mixtec or perhaps the Classic Maya, the Aztec polities interacted with each other through a combination of peaceful and aggressive practices. By the early fifteenth century, several Aztec polities had succeeded in establishing small-scale empires consisting of networks of conquered city-states. These include Texcoco, capital of the Acolhua group in the eastern Valley of Mexico; Azcapotzalco, capital of the Tepanecs in the western Valley; and Cuauhnahuac, head city of the Tlahuica in Morelos.

The Mexica, who were to become the dominant polity by the end of the century, were originally vassals of the Tepanec king. Their tribute to the Tepanecs was service as mercenaries in their wars of conquest. In 1428, the Mexica banded together with the Acolhua and several other groups to overthrow the Tepanec empire and establish an alliance of three polities: Tenochtitlán (Mexica), Texcoco (Acolhua), and Tlacopán (a dissident Tepanec polity). This "Triple Alliance," known today as the Aztec empire, began a systematic campaign of militaristic expansion soon after 1428. The combined armies began by conquering areas in

Box 2.6 *Archaeology and Mesoamerican Peasants*

It is only natural that archaeologists studying the complex societies of Mesoamerica and elsewhere have focused most of their attention on cities and urban centers. These are the largest archaeological sites, they contain the most impressive architectural remains, and they exhibit the most complete evidence for ancient social complexity. Nevertheless, in the past two decades an increasing number of archaeologists have turned their attention to rural areas that were the hinterlands of ancient cities. Archaeological fieldwork on rural areas has taken two forms. First, regional settlement pattern surveys that became common in the 1960s and 1970s following initial projects directed by Gordon Willey and William Sanders provided information on the number, size, and location of rural sites across the landscape. More recently, archaeologists such as David Webster and Michael Smith have furnished more detailed data on rural life by excavating peasant houses in Maya and Aztec hinterland areas.

This growing archaeological attention to peasants and rural areas is important for rounding out our view of ancient Mesoamerican societies. Peasants are rural farming peoples who are part of larger state-level societies. They typically provide labor, food, and other products for urban elites and state institutions. Research around the world shows that in some ancient states peasants were heavily exploited, had little freedom, and lived a hard, dull life, while in other cases peasants were well-off economically and had considerable control over their own lives and destiny. One of the goals of archaeological research on Mesoamerican peasants is to document the conditions of peasant households and communities in order to provide more complete interpretations of ancient Mesoamerican societies.

A comparison of Teotihuacán and the Aztecs illustrates some of the variation among Mesoamerican peasants. As urban settlements, Teotihuacán and Tenochtitlán shared many characteristics, but their overall societies were quite different politically and economically, and these differences influenced the nature of rural settlement during the Classic and Late Postclassic periods. Teotihuacán was a powerful polity whose rulers dominated their subjects in both city and countryside. Many rural villagers had been forcibly moved into the city early in the Classic period, leaving a small number of scattered peasant villages in the hinterland. Excavations at one of these villages suggest a meager standard of living, with villagers imitating urban styles in both artifacts and architecture. There is little evidence of economic activities apart from food production. These were poor peasants with few independent economic resources or opportunities.

Rural conditions in the Aztec period were quite different. Archaeological surveys located many more rural sites, with a nearly continuous distribution of hamlets and villages in some areas. Compared to Teotihuacán, Aztec city-states had less power to dominate or exploit their commoners, and the growth of market systems gave rural Aztecs ready access to goods and exchange opportunities. Excavations at two rural sites in Morelos reveal thriving rural economies where peasant households obtained large numbers of exotic goods including obsidian, foreign pottery, and bronze tools. In addition to growing maize and other food crops using agricultural terracing, farmers cultivated cotton, which was spun and woven into cloth for both tribute payments (to nobles and city-states) and exchange in the marketplace (textiles served as a form of money for the Aztecs). Although these peasants lived in small adobe houses with stone floors (Figure 2.19), they were well-off economically in the commercialized city-state economy of Aztec Central Mexico.

Knowledge of Aztec peasants is important not only to provide a complete picture of Aztec society, but also to understand the nature of change after the Spanish conquest. Aztec cities were destroyed by the Spaniards, states and empires were dismantled, and the Aztec nobility were co-opted into the Spanish colonial system (see Chapter 4), leaving rural peasants as the repositories of the Mesoamerican cultural tradition. These people were accustomed to paying tribute to nobles and to conforming to the laws of states. Age-old peasant strategies of surviving within the context of states and empires served them well under Spanish rule, when tribute and law continued as institutions controlling peasant life. In fact, for many rural Aztecs the Spanish conquest had only a minimal effect on their lives—one set of overlords was simply replaced by another. The peasant lifeway had a long history in ancient Mesoamerica, and archaeological research is now bringing to view these previously ignored rural Mesoamericans.

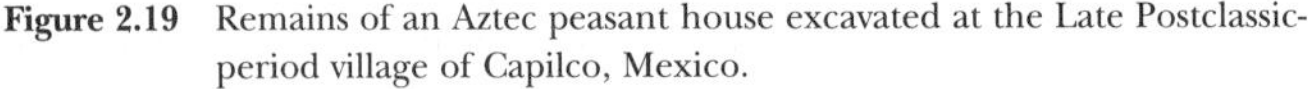

Figure 2.19 Remains of an Aztec peasant house excavated at the Late Postclassic-period village of Capilco, Mexico.

the Valley of Mexico, and then moved beyond to incorporate ever-greater areas of Mesoamerica. When Cortés and the conquering Spaniards arrived in Mexico in 1519, the Aztec empire covered much of Mesoamerica, and areas not conquered by the empire were influenced by the Aztecs through trade and other institutions. The organization of Mesoamerica in 1519 is the theme of Chapter 3.

ANCIENT MESOAMERICA

Mesoamerican civilization was forged by processes of change among many different peoples over a time span of millennia. The following changes stand out as the most important developments that shaped the course of cultural evolution of ancient Mesoamerica. First, the domestication of maize provided a secure nutritional and agricultural foundation for the emergence of Mesoamerican civilization. Second, the rise of settled village life and the spread of early religious concepts brought about the coalescence of Mesoamerican culture in the Formative period. Third, the evolution of state-level societies characterized by writing, cities, social stratification, and powerful kings signalled the development of truly complex civilizations in the Classic period. Finally, the Postclassic period witnessed the continuing political and economic development of these societies, particularly the emergence of smaller polities (city-states) in which markets and commercial forces came to the fore as dominant institutions. By the arrival of Cortés and the Spanish conquerors in 1519, Mesoamerica was a distinctive cultural tradition whose heritage shaped the continuing historical development of the area in the colonial, national, and modern epochs (see Box 2.6).

SUGGESTED READINGS

BLANTON, RICHARD E., S. A. KOWALEWSKI, GARY FEINMAN, AND LAURA FINSTEN 1992 *Ancient Mesoamerica: A Comparison of Change in Three Regions*, 2nd ed. New York: Cambridge University Press.

DIEHL, RICHARD A., AND JANET CATHERINE BERLO (eds.) 1989 *Mesoamerica After the Decline of Teotihuacan: A.D. 700–900.* Washington, D.C.: Dumbarton Oaks.

FLANNERY, KENT V. (ed.) 1976 *The Early Mesoamerican Village.* New York: Academic Press.

FLANNERY, KENT V., AND JOYCE MARCUS (eds.) 1983 *The Cloud People.* New York: Academic Press.

MILLON, RENÉ 1973 *Urbanization at Teotihuacan, Mexico*, vol. 1, The Teotihuacan Map. Austin: University of Texas Press.

MORLEY, SYLVANUS G., GEORGE W. BRAINERD, AND ROBERT J. SHARER 1983 *The Maya*, 4th ed. Stanford, Calif.: Stanford University Press.

SANDERS, WILLIAM T., JEFFREY R. PARSONS, AND ROBERT S. SANTLEY 1979 *The Basin of Mexico: Ecological Processes in the Evolution of a Civilization.* New York: Academic Press.

SCHELE, LINDA, AND MARY E. MILLER 1986 *The Blood of Kings: Dynasty and Ritual in Maya Art.* Fort Worth, Texas: Kimball Art Museum.

SHARER, ROBERT J., AND DAVID C. GROVE (eds.) 1989 *Regional Perspectives on the Olmec.* New York: Cambridge University Press.

WEAVER, MURIEL PORTER 1993 *The Aztecs, Maya, and Their Predecessors*, 3rd ed. Orlando, Fla.: Academic Press.

Chapter 3 Mesoamerica at Spanish Contact

The Mesoamerican world that confronted the Spanish conquistadors at the beginning of the sixteenth century was extremely complex, the result of a long development as outlined in the preceding chapter. We will begin our discussion of Mesoamerica at Spanish contact with a brief description of its social and cultural complexity, although rather quickly our focus will shift to Mesoamerica as a whole. We want to see Mesoamerica as an interconnected world in which events taking place in one social unit affected those in another, however distant they might have been from one another. Such an approach will help simplify for us the complexity of Mesoamerica, while also putting into relief the underlying cohesiveness and unity that has allowed the peoples of the region to resist cultural destruction during the centuries following Spanish contact.

Our reconstruction of contact period Mesoamerica is based primarily on ethnohistory research (documentary studies). The two most important documentary sources are (1) Spanish accounts, provided by the first explorers, conquerors, and colonizers of the region, and (2) written accounts left to us by the Mesoamericans themselves (see Chapter 12 for a discussion of these latter documents). Useful supplementary information comes from (3) the archaeological remains of the Mesoamerican settlements from the time of Spanish contact, and (4) linguistic and cultural patterns that the descendants of those original Mesoamericans successfully preserved through five difficult centuries of "colonization." Based on these various sources of information, we want to answer the question of what the Mesoamerican world was like on the eve of contact with the Spaniards.

COMPLEXITY OF THE MESOAMERICAN WORLD

Let us begin our account with a brief review of the social and cultural diversity that characterized the contact period Mesoamerican world. At this point, our goal is to perceive the complexity of Mesoamerica in extremely broad terms. More detail and analysis of this complexity will be given in the sections to follow.

City-States and Empires

Most scholars argue that the fundamental building blocks of the Mesoamerican world at contact were large towns and their dependent rural communities. The rural communities were made up of kinship groups, often patrilineal in descent, which together formed a commoner class of peasants. The elite ruling class and its attendants resided in the politically dominant towns where they exercised authority over the rural commoners. Scholars have long debated whether these units in Mesoamerica constituted chiefdoms or states. It now seems clear, however, that chiefdoms and states are only models by which we try to understand a continuum of ancient Mesoamerican political groups, and that no specific feature can demarcate one unit as chiefdom or another as state. Any given political unit in Mesoamerica, then, might fall toward either the chiefdom or the state end of the continuum, depending upon the degree to which the ruling group's authority was accepted as superior to all other forms of authority.

Many social units in Mesoamerica at the time of contact fell on the chiefdom end of the continuum, but the majority of them—numbering perhaps several hundred—fell on the state end. The latter are usually referred to by scholars as "city-states." Each city-state had a ruler or joint rulers, appointed by the "royal" lineage to act as the supreme authority over the political center and dependent rural communities. For example, at least fifty city-states existed in the Valley of Mexico alone, each supreme ruler being called by the term *tlatoani* ("he who speaks"; plural, *tlatoque*). In contrast, about thirty city-states were found in highland Guatemala, where each maximum ruler was given the title *ajpop* ("he of the mat").

Mesoamerica, however, did not simply consist of a large number of equal and autonomous city-states. Throughout the region powerful imperial states (empires) used conquest or other means to subjugate formerly independent chiefdoms, city-states, and even empires. The Mexica or Aztec empire is the best-known imperial state, but there were perhaps another twenty notable examples in Mesoamerica from the contact period. Many of these empires were modelled after the legendary Toltec empire of Central Mexico, which had collapsed 300 years before the coming of the Spaniards (for details, see Chapter 2). Several successor states became "epigonal" Toltec empires, employing conquest and tribute collection as part of a mission to civilize Mesoamerica in the name of great Toltec rulers of the past such as Topiltzín Quetzalcoatl. At least some of the imperial rulers claiming Toltec connections were actually usurpers from small city-states or even chiefdoms located on the margins of Mesoamerica. Driven at first to expand in order to survive, these upstart rulers later created elaborate militaristic political visions, synthesizing ideas from their own marginal political units and from the more "civilized" Mesoamerican political tradition.

Imperial states like the Aztec empire were influential throughout Mesoamerica, and were able to significantly affect political units falling outside their direct control. A kind of core and periphery dependency relationship was created by such entities, which became a defining characteristic of Mesoamerica at the time of Spanish contact.

Ethnic Groups

Mesoamerica is often described as a single "culture area," and long lists of cultural "traits" were supposedly shared by the peoples of the area. Indeed, many cultural patterns were common to the peoples of Mesoamerica, but it must also be emphasized that there was much cultural diversity within the region as well (and linguistic diversity, as discussed in Chapter 11).

Much of the cultural diversity of Mesoamerica was an expression of an incredibly complex ethnic mosaic found throughout the region. Mesoamerican ethnic groups—often referred to in the account to follow as "peoples"—were usually defined on linguistic grounds. Nevertheless, other important criteria were used to define ethnicity in Mesoamerica, such as occupation (for instance, merchants, artisans), style of life (rustic vs. civilized), relations of descent (lineage affiliation), religious cult (shared patron deity), and historical origins (such as emigration from a common sacred homeland). Ethnic "peoples" existed by the thousands throughout Mesoamerica, and they influenced all aspects of social life there.

Many of the Mesoamerican city-states had their origins in ethnic groups, and each group's particular language, deity, and general vision of the world continued to be influential long after political relations had become dominant over ethnic bonds. For example, in Central Mexico most of the city-states were organized by "chichimec" groups, the term *chichimec* being an ethnic designation that meant something like "nomadic peoples from the north." The Aztecs and several other chichimec groups spoke Nahuatl, but some ethnic chichimecs spoke unrelated languages such as Otomí and Tarascan. In contrast, the ethnic groups that formed the Maya city-states of highland Guatemala were usually referred to as "amak's," their defining criterion being emigration from a common homeland in the "East." The Maya amak' groups spoke diverse languages, but shared a common identity through affiliation in lineage systems that united them into kin groups of varying size.

Most city-states and all imperial states of Mesoamerica were multiethnic, which raises the question of the extent to which state religion and ideology superseded internal ethnic cultural differences. Scholars have pointed out that Mesoamerican states such as the Aztec empire did not actively seek to impose their own gods and particular cultural practices on other peoples. Recent research indicates, however, that the ruling ethnic groups tended to reformulate their particular patron deity cults as religious ideologies promoting broad imperial interests. Ideologies stressing war and human sacrifice were widely promoted by states throughout Mesoamerica, although the particular features of each ideology varied greatly. We also know that ethnic groups within the core areas of the larger states were often assimilated to the dominant imperial culture, while in the marginal or peripheral areas ethnic groups often remained segregated as culturally distinct peoples.

Regional Cultures

Beyond the cultural variation in Mesoamerica, which was based on ethnic and political organization, were broader cultural differences of regional importance. Archaeologists in particular have called attention to this regional diversity, and have shown that it existed in Mesoamerica long before Spanish contact. Each regional culture was characterized by distinctive language and cultural patterns promoted by highly influential groups inhabiting the region. A prototypical case would be the Zapotec peoples who built the Monte Albán city and later nearby towns in the Valley of Oaxaca, and in the process promoted a regional culture inherited by the peoples of Oaxaca at the time of Spanish contact. The most important regional cultures of Mesoamerica, according to one prominent scheme, were as follows: Maya highlands, Maya lowlands, southern periphery, southern Veracruz-Tabasco, Oaxaca, Central Mexico, central Veracruz, Huaxteca, Guerrero, western Mexico, and the northern frontier (see the section on ecology in Chapter 1 for the geographic characteristics of these regions).

In summary, Mesoamerica at the time of Spanish contact comprised highly diverse component parts: numerous city-states, empires, ethnic groups, and regional cultures.

MESOAMERICA AS A WORLD SYSTEM

One way scholars have tried to simplify and make sense out of the diversity and complexity of Mesoamerica is to apply world system theory to it. This theory, developed by Immanuel Wallerstein (1976) to explain historical developments in Europe, posits that for several thousand years the societies of the Old World were embedded in large intersocietal networks known as world systems. Europe in the fifteenth and sixteenth centuries was in the process of being formed into a world system, the consequences of which were to be felt in all regions of the globe. The coming of the Europeans to Mesoamerica truly initiated a clash of "worlds," because, as we shall now see, Mesoamerica was also a world system at the time of its "discovery" by the Europeans.

A first step in seeing Mesoamerica as a world system at the time of contact with Europe is to recognize that some of its component societies were dominant over others, and that as a result its diverse units formed an integrated, stratified world. A second step is to understand that the Mesoamerican region was not under the political control of a single empire, but rather was an arena of competing independent political units. The most powerful Mesoamerican state at the time of Spanish contact was the Aztec empire, yet it controlled less than half of the territory in the Mesoamerican region. Furthermore, other powerful, independent empires co-existed with the Aztecs. Mesoamerica at contact was tied together primarily through economic bonds, and thus constituted a "world economy" rather than a "world empire," despite occasional claims by the Aztecs that they ruled over the entire "civilized" world known to them.

Students of Mesoamerica recognize that Central Mexico was its most influential area, or in world system terms, its dominant core. As we will see, however, the Mesoamerican world had other *core zones* in West Mexico, Oaxaca, and Yucatán-Guatemala. Adjacent to the core zones were found the socially dominated *peripheral zones* of Mesoamerica, in such places as northwestern Mexico, northeastern Mexico, and southeastern Central America. The main *semi-peripheral zones* of the Mesoamerican world system can be identified primarily with zones specialized in trade and other commercial activities. The semi-peripheral zones functioned to bind the Mesoamerican world into a common economic system, largely by mediating between the unequal core and peripheral units. The most important semi-peripheral unit in Mesoamerica at contact was probably Xicalanco on the Gulf Coast of southern Mexico, but other key semi-peripheral units existed in northwest Mexico and along the Caribbean and Pacific coasts of Central America (Figure 3.1).

Relationships between core, periphery, and semi-periphery in the Mesoamerican world system were determined to an important extent by the flow of luxury goods, such as cotton garments, jade pieces, cacao beans, animal skins, tropical bird feathers, and gold ornaments. These "preciosities" were the life-blood of the core states, for they were used to legitimize the authority of the rulers and reward the loyal cadres of warriors and state officials who dominated the intersocietal networks. The peripheral peoples were pressed by the core societies to yield their precious resources. The mechanisms used in this unequal exchange process included ceremonial gift giving and mediated trade within semi-peripheral zones, as well as military threat, outright conquest, and tributary demands.

The exchange of goods between core and periphery societies, which underwrote the stratified structure of the Mesoamerican world system, has been summarized as follows:

> . . . a consequence of the growth of powerful core states in ancient Mesoamerica was a widespread stimulation of trade, a reorientating of priorities in many places toward production and exchange in the world system arena . . . [A]s powerful core states develop they must stimulate increased production of the luxury goods used to reward cadre. These heightened demands ripple outward, beyond territories conquered by the emergent cores, influencing production strategies over a broad area and thus incorporating more and more local groups into [the periphery of] a Mesoamerican world economy. (Blanton and Feinman 1984:678)

The core states of Mesoamerica expropriated not only the preciosities of the peripheral peoples, but also their labor. In the core zones, most subject commoners were required to specialize in the production of bulk goods, especially

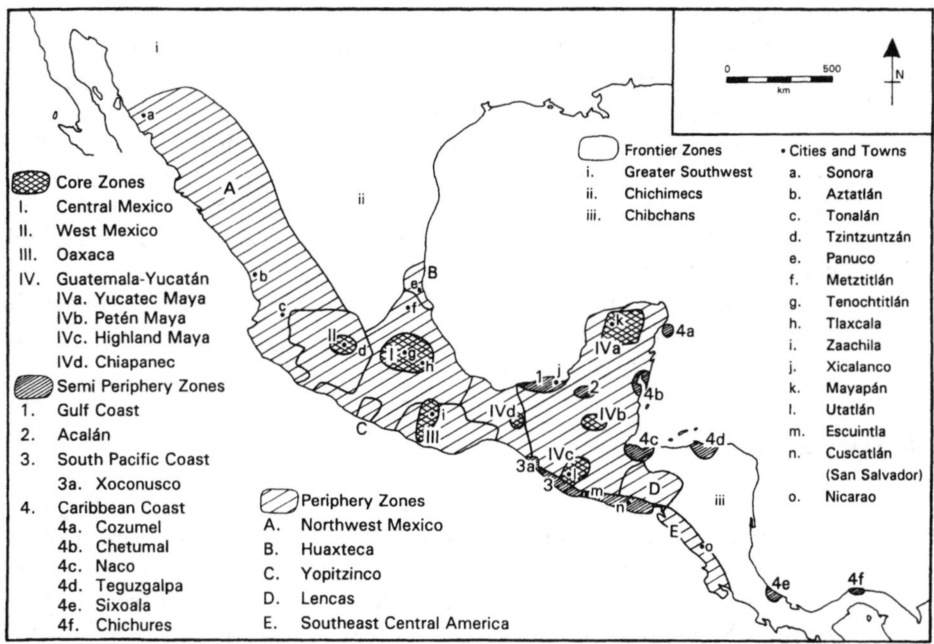

Figure 3.1 Core, Semi-Periphery and Periphery zones of the Mesoamerican World System.

"grains" such as maize, beans, and amaranth. In the peripheral zones, the demand for preciosities forced the peoples there to expand production of these items, or of other items that could then be traded farther afield for the desired goods. In particular, the prodigious demand for cotton garments by the core societies—it is estimated that over 3 million articles of cotton cloth flowed into Central Mexico alone each year—meant that much of the labor-intensive cultivation of cotton, spinning of it into thread, and weaving of the thread into cloth was shifted away from the core to the periphery.

It is likely that at the time of Spanish contact all societies located within the territorial boundaries created by the Mesoamerican world system, however small or undeveloped, had been incorporated into the exchange network either as core, periphery, or semi-periphery. Outside the boundaries of Mesoamerica were found *frontier* peoples, divided into hundreds, perhaps thousands, of smaller, less complex social networks. Although few if any of the frontier societies were so small or isolated as to qualify as simple bands ("mini-systems," in world system terms), many of them were organized on a tribal level of development and were politically weak. In general, the frontier peoples were of limited economic or political interest to the Mesoamericans—in part, no doubt, because they controlled few luxury items and in part because their fragmented social networks would have made it difficult to subdue and incorporate them into the Mesoamerican world system.

The frontier peoples to the north and south of Mesoamerica were influenced by, and in turn exercised influence on, the Mesoamerican world, although their relationships with Mesoamerican peoples were neither systematic nor highly significant. To the north of Mesoamerica the frontier consisted largely of peoples speaking languages of the Uto-Aztecan family (Cora, Huichol, Piman, Mayo), and were widely known to the Mesoamericans as chichimecs. To the south, the frontier peoples mainly spoke Chibchan languages (Paya, Sumu, Huétar, Talamanca, Boruca, Guaymí). It is not known whether the Mesoamericans had a special term by which they referred to these chibchan peoples, but they were undoubtedly considered culturally foreign and socially backward.

Let us now review some of the diagnostic characteristics of the three main structural units—core, semi-periphery, periphery—within the Mesoamerican world system, starting with the core states.

MESOAMERICAN CORE

Although the Aztec empire was clearly the most powerful and influential political unit within the Mesoamerican world system at the time of Spanish contact, there were many other core states that competed with the Aztecs for military, economic, and cultural dominance. Like the Aztecs, these societies were organized into states with imperial tendencies, and thus were able to fend off other strong states while exploiting (peripheralizing) the hundreds of less-powerful city-states and chiefdoms that dotted the landscape throughout the Mesoamerican region.

Competition among core states was most intense and resulted in the most complex intersocietal networks in four special geographic subregions of Mesoamerica, which we shall refer to as "core zones." The strongest of the four, Central Mexico, was built upon the foundation of the ecologically rich Basin of Mexico, the Mesoamerican zone most agriculturally fertile and free of physical barriers to communication. The Nahuatl (Aztec) language was spoken by the majority of inhabitants in the zone, and this facilitated intercommunication between the many states making up this interacting network.

The other three core zones were less ecologically propitious than Central Mexico, but were also areas with favorable ecological conditions. The West Mexico core zone had a strong ecological base in the "symbiotic" relationships established between the highland Lake Pátzcuaro basin and the lowland Balsas river system. The Tarascan language (also known as Purépecha) was spoken throughout most of the subregion, and this facilitated the thorough domination of the zone by the Tarascan empire. The Oaxaca core zone was also ecologically diversified, and was based on the economic integration of a highland area (Mixteca Alta), a large highland river valley (Valley of Oaxaca), and two important lowland plains (Oaxaca Pacific Coast and Isthmus of Tehuantepec). The Mixtec and Zapotec languages were widely spoken in Oaxaca, and their historical connection, while somewhat distant, provided at least a minimal basis for intercommunication throughout the zone at the time of contact. The Maya core zone stretched from Guatemala to Yucatán, and was an ecologically diversified subregion made up of southern highland river basins, a central area of lakes and tropical lowlands, and northern lowland plains. Virtually all the peoples of this zone spoke languages belonging to the Maya family, and these languages, despite differences, shared enough common features to permit limited but crucial intercommunication between the numerous states of the subregion.

Let us now examine more closely each of the four main core zones of Mesoamerica (see the map in Figure 3.1).

Central Mexico Core Zone

The Central Mexico core zone was dominated by a confederated empire composed of the allied Mexican, Texcocan, and Tlacopan states (see Chapter 2) (Figure 3.2). The Mexican state achieved dominance over the other two, and its city of Tenochtitlán, inhabited by approximately 200,000 persons, became the capital of the empire.

Figure 3.2 Central element of the Aztec calendar stone, denoting the Sun deity, the cyclic creations of the world, and the ascension to power of the Aztec in A.D. 1427. After Richard F. Townsend, *State and Cosmos in the Art of Tenochtitlan.* Washington, D.C.: Dumbarton Oaks, 1979, p. 64.

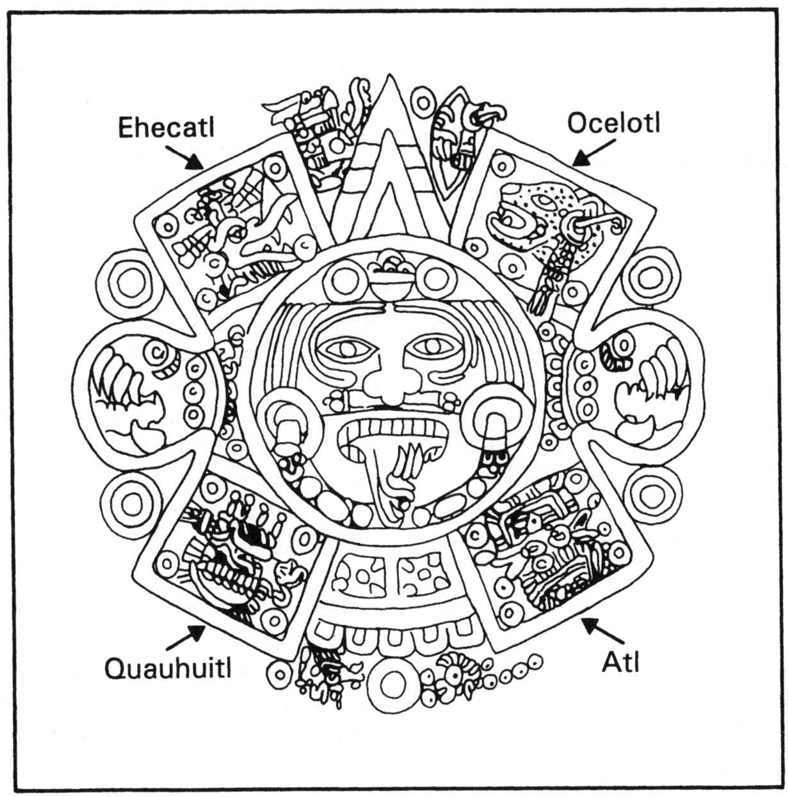

The Aztec empire ruled over approximately fifty city-states (*altepetl*) within the Basin itself. The subordinate city-states (for example, Culhuacán, Huexotla, Azcapotzalco) shared many of the institutions, benefits, and liabilities of the empire, and even though they had tribute obligations they are properly seen as core units within the Central Mexico zone. At the time of contact with the Spaniards, most of the peoples in the Basin spoke Nahuatl, the language of the empire.

The Aztec empire ruled over about 250 more city-states located outside the Basin, which were administered as thirty-eight tribute-paying provinces. Most of the provinces were close to the Basin of Mexico, but some of them, such as Yoaltepec (Guerrero coast), Coixtlahuacán (Oaxaca highlands), and Xoconusco (Chiapas coast), were far removed from the imperial heartland. The lingua franca of the provinces was Nahuatl, but most of the peoples there spoke other Mesoamerican languages such as Otomí, Mazatec, Matlazinca, Totonac, Mixtec, and Zapotec. Roughly 100 additional city-states located outside the Central Basin were subject to Aztec political and military controls as "client states," and were probably in the process of being organized into provinces. The client states paid tributes to the empire, but their main imperial role was to serve as buffers against the empire's chief military competitors. The peoples of the client states were as linguistically diverse as those in the provinces. Both the formal provinces and the client states can be seen as peripheral units in terms of their relations with the Aztec empire and the Central Mexico core zone as a whole.

There was considerable competition among the states that made up the Aztec empire, and this was manifested in the form of wars from time to time. But the sharpest conflicts within the Central Mexico core zone took place between the Aztec empire and a series of politically independent states located adjacent to the Basin. The most important competitors to the Aztec empire were Tlaxcala, Huejotzinco, and Metztitlán. These states shared basic imperial and cultural features with the Aztecs (for example, they had similar origin myths, deities, and calendar systems), but nevertheless were engaged in protracted military struggles with the Aztec empire and with each other. They also participated in ritual warfare ("flower wars") with one another, staging battles designed to provide captives for sacrifice to their respective patron deities. The rulers of the hostile states in the Central Mexico core zone attended each other's important ceremonies, at which times they exchanged elite gifts and other prestations. They also intermarried, although most elite marriages probably took place within imperial domains.

Huejotzinco, Tlaxcala, and Metztitlán were located in mountainous zones quite close to the center of the Aztec empire. Although relatively poor in natural resources, they stood in the way of the empire's access to the resources of the rich coastal lowlands to the east. Tlaxcala had traditionally been active in trade with the Gulf Coast peoples, and the Aztecs were apparently interested in taking control of their trading routes. The Aztec armies attacked the three states on many occasions, sometimes in alliance with one or the other of the three, but were never able to militarily dominate them (Huejotzinco apparently fell to the Aztecs shortly before Spanish contact).

In part this was as a result of the defensive nature of their mountain strongholds, but it was also a result of the fact that internally these states were profoundly militarized, unified, and determined to maintain political independence. All three states had within their ranks fierce mercenary soldiers, especially from Otomí and Chalca ethnic groups, who had previously been driven from their homelands by the Aztec armies. The peoples of Huejotzinco and Tlaxcala spoke Nahuatl, the Aztec language, while Otomí appears to have been the primary language of the people of Metztitlán.

There is some indication that the Aztecs may have considered all-out war against these hostile states to have been more costly than the limited tributes they would get in return. The Aztecs' strategy appears to have been increasingly that of isolating the three states by conquering their weaker neighbors, while engaging the states themselves in a kind of low-intensity, highly ritualized warfare. Nevertheless, relations between these states and the Aztec empire were profoundly competitive, and they set the tone for the entire Mesoamerican world system.

West Mexico Core Zone

Like Central Mexico, West Mexico was dominated by a single empire, which we will refer to as the Tarascan empire (Figure 3.3). The West Mexico core zone, however, was unique in that its empire had no serious competitor states within

Figure 3.3 Temple mound at the Tarascan capital of Tzintzuntzán in West Mexico. After Ignacio Marquina, *Arquitectura prehispánica,* Mexico City, Mexico: Instituto Nacional de Antropología e Historia, 1951, p. 256.

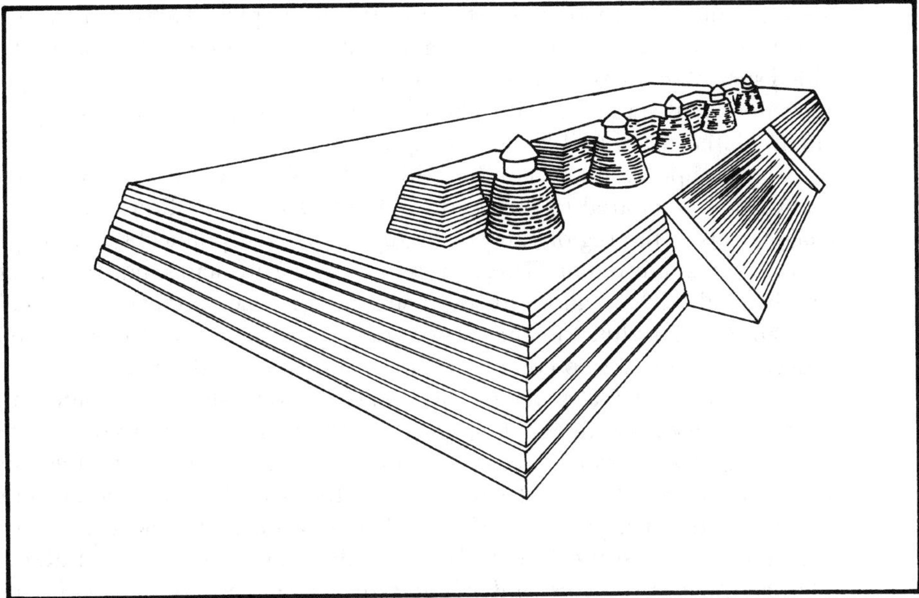

the zone. The boundaries of the Tarascan empire corresponded roughly with the modern state of Michoacán, a vast territory of mountains, plateaus, river basins, and coastal plains enclosed by the Balsas and Lerma-Santiago river systems. The capital of the empire was Tzintzuntzán, a city of about 35,000 inhabitants located in the highland Lake Pátzcuaro basin.

The Tarascan empire was originally formed through the political and military unification of some eight city-states located within the Pátzcuaro basin. Later, it expanded by conquering an additional seven city-states adjacent to the basin, and eventually took control of many other political groups located in more distant areas. The Tarascan empire was more centralized and unified than the Aztec empire, and its subjugated city-states retained little autonomy. Administration of the empire was divided into four regions whose authorities ruled directly over the local units rather than through a provincial organization. Nevertheless, a few client states located along the frontiers of the empire, especially the eastern borders, were allowed to retain their own authorities. They were considered by the empire to be allies rather than subjects, and their tributary obligations took the form of military service and provision of captive slaves and sacrificial victims. Together, the tribute-paying units of the four regions, along with the client states, made up an important part of the periphery of the West Mexico core zone.

The Tarascan language and culture were totally dominant in the Pátzcuaro and surrounding basins, and were being assimilated by most of the peoples of the empire. The strong ethnic character of the empire is thought to have been a response by the imperial heartland to the relatively limited ecological base of the Pátzcuaro basin and, therefore, the need to ensure access to resources over a much wider area through cultural assimilation. Nevertheless, some ethnic "segregation" existed within the empire. There were a few foreign enclaves (for example, Cuitlatecs and Nahuatls) within the core zone that provided special services such as artisanry, trade, and spying. Along the imperial frontiers the client states tended to be multiethnic, made up mainly of Otomí, Mazahuan, Matlazincan, and Nahua groups.

Competition and conflict within the West Mexico zone was muted, especially when compared to the Central Mexico zone. The Tarascan empire had no major rivals in the region, and its highly centralized political system kept internal conflict at a minimum. There were no powerful states north or east of the empire, although smaller city-states such as the Nahua-speaking Coca, Tecuexe, Cazcán, and Zacaluta (in the present-day Mexican states of Jalisco, Colima, and Guerrero) were able to contain Tarascan advances in these areas.

The principal rivals of the Tarascans were the Aztecs, and this intense *external* rivalry undoubtedly helps explain the relative *internal* cohesiveness of the West Mexico core zone: A unified empire was necessary if the Tarascans were to compete successfully with the Aztecs. The Tarascans became one of the most militarized states of all Mesoamerica, and they more than held their own in many wars fought against the Aztecs. To the south and west, where the Tarascan empire abutted Aztec provinces and client states, fortifications were constructed and client states organized to defend against Aztec incursions. Even though Tarascan rulers at times attended Aztec ceremonies in Tenochtitlán, and presumably vice versa, nonmilitary contacts between the two great powers were minimal. As far as we know, there was no intermarriage between the respective royal families, and direct trade was virtually nonexistent (nevertheless, considerable trade through intermediaries flourished). Long-distance merchants from the two empires could not cross each other's imperial boundaries, and even ambassadors under royal escort entered each other's territory at great risk to their personal safety.

The West Mexico core zone, then, was a special case within the Mesoamerican world system. Its only imperial state was militarily powerful, but turned inward. Beyond the Aztecs and other close neighbors, the Tarascans appear to have shown little interest in the rest of Mesoamerica. They were not renowned as traders, although they produced superb metal objects that may have been traded over great distances within Mesoamerica—in part, perhaps, by sea along the Pacific Coast. Tarascan culture shared many of the characteristics of the Mesoamerican "world" culture, but it was also parochial compared to other imperial states. Many of the Tarascan religious beliefs and art forms were unfamiliar to the rest of Mesoamerica and, surprisingly, the Tarascans had no writing system.

Oaxaca Core Zone

The core zone in what is today the state of Oaxaca, Mexico, contrasted dramatically with the Central and West Mexican core zones in not having a dominant imperial state. Instead, the zone was divided into about fifty small kingdoms or city-states, whose territorial boundaries and political alliances were constantly shifting. These states were concentrated in roughly equal numbers in the Mixtec highlands and the Valley of Oaxaca. The highland city-states were made up primarily of Mixtec speakers, while the peoples of the Valley of Oaxaca mostly spoke Zapotec (an important minority of the Valley inhabitants spoke Mixtec). The Mixtecs also controlled a few additional city-states in the eastern and coastal lowlands, as did the Zapotecs in the Isthmus of Tehuantepec lowlands. Other peoples in the area spoke languages that were neither Mixtec nor Zapotec: Chocho, Chinantec, Mixe, Zoque, Chatino, Amuzgo. For the most part, these peoples were outside the direct control of core states and formed the main periphery of the Oaxaca core zone.

Within the Mixtec highlands, the ruling line of the Tilontongo city-state was particularly prestigious, and the rulers of many of the other states in the area traced genealogy from that line. The Mixtec codices make special reference to a ruler, 8 Deer "Tiger Claw," of that line, who is said to have conquered many towns and peoples and established the important kingdom of Tututepec on the coast. He was finally killed while attempting to conquer certain city-states in the Valley of Oaxaca. The sharing of a common royal lineage provided the Mixtec states with considerable cultural unity, a unity reinforced by extensive intermarriage between the different ruling families. Despite such bonds, warfare between the Mixtec states was widespread.

In the Oaxaca Valley many of the Zapotec states recognized Zaachila as the most revered and powerful state. The Zaachila rulers collected tribute from several city-states in the valley, and in a few places established provinces by appointing their regional authorities to govern over the local peoples. As in the case of Tilontongo, however, Zaachila's preeminence appears to have been based more on cultural sharing than on military domination. The Zaachila state was probably heir to the historic Monte Albán Zapotec political system, and as such was characterized by an especially close blending of politics and religion. Despite Zaachila's prestige and numerous interdynastic marriages, the states of the Valley remained largely independent of one another, and warfare between them was endemic.

Archaeological evidence indicates that the highland Mixtec states were able to dominate and perhaps peripheralize many of the Valley Zapotec peoples (see Chapter 2). Members of the royal family from the Mixtec kingdom of Yanhuitlán gained a measure of control over the Zaachila state through marriage into its dynastic line, while other Zapotec city-states were conquered and ruled over by Mixtecs from the mountainous highlands. Mixtec ceramics, metalwork, carvings, and painted figures have been found at many sites in the Valley of Oaxaca, most notably at Monte Albán (Tomb 7) and Zaachila. It is unlikely that Mixtec control over the Zapotecs in the Valley of Oaxaca was very long lasting, but it resulted in considerable creative synthesis of the Mixtec and Zapotec cultures.

The Oaxaca zone developed a series of relationships with states in the other core zones of the Mesoamerican world system. The Mixtec kings claimed descent from the Toltec ruling line, and maintained political ties with rulers of city-states in Central Mexico who made similar claims. The Aztec armies conquered many Mixtec and Zapotec states, organizing them into the tribute-paying provinces of Coixtlahuaca and Coyolapán. The Aztecs set up a garrison at Guaxacac (from which comes the name Oaxaca) in the Valley, intermarried with the ruling families of important Mixtec and Zapotec kingdoms, and made Nahuatl the lingua franca for the zone's ruling classes. Nevertheless, control over the zone by the Aztec empire was weak, and rebellion against Aztec rule by the Mixtec and Zapotec city-states, often in alliance with one another, was widespread at the time of Spanish contact.

The Oaxaca core zone was famous for its artisans: working within the so-called "Mixtec-Puebla" art tradition, they produced some of the most exquisite and widely distributed preciosities of the Mesoamerican world (Figure 3.4). Various cities of the Central Mexico core zone had wards of resident Mixtec artisans, who not only manufactured crafts but also taught their skills to Aztec artisans. In addition, Oaxaca polychrome ceramics, gold pieces, bone carvings, and other objects circulated widely within the larger Mesoamerican world.

Maya Core Zone

This southernmost core zone comprised diverse city-states and empires occupying the areas of present-day Guatemala and Yucatán Peninsula. The Maya zone was structurally more like Central Mexico than West Mexico or Oaxaca, and like the Central Mexico zone, it exercised powerful influence over a large area of Mesoamerica (the Central American part). One of the zone's main characteristics

Figure 3.4 Mixtec artist-scribe as portrayed in the Codex Vindobonensis. After Jill Leslie Furst, *Codex Vindobonensis Mexicanus I: A Commentary,* Publication No. 4. Albany, NY: Institute for Mesoamerican Studies, State University of New York, 1978, p. 125.

was that its constituent peoples, in both the core and the periphery, were overwhelmingly Maya in language and culture. Another defining characteristic was the relative weakness of ties between its highland and lowland core states, although important political and economic exchanges certainly did take place between them (Figure 3.5).

Broadly speaking, the Maya core states were distributed in three geographic areas: the southern highlands (present-day Chiapas and Guatemala), the central lake and tropical lowlands (Petén, Belize), and the northern lowlands (Campeche, Yucatán, and Quintana Roo). More than thirty distinct Maya languages were spoken in these three areas, the majority of them in the southern highlands (for example, Tzotzil, Jacaltec, Mam, Ixil, Quiché, Cakchiquel, and Pokomam). The languages of the central lake area and northern lowlands were fewer in number and more similar to one another (Lacandón, Chol, Mopán, Itzá, and Yucatec). Most of the core states incorporated speakers of diverse Maya languages, and in some cases non-Maya speakers as well.

In the southern highlands, the Quiché Maya created an imperial state, centered on its capital of K'umarcaaj (also known as Utatlán) of around 10,000 to 15,000 inhabitants. Through conquest the Quiché subjugated most surrounding Maya and non-Maya city-states, organizing them into approximately thirty tribute-paying provinces. The Quiché empire also competed in military and economic terms with other Maya core states of the southern highlands, such as the Cakchiquel and Tzutujil states. These highland empires were able to peripheralize numerous less powerful city-states and chiefdoms through warfare, trade, and

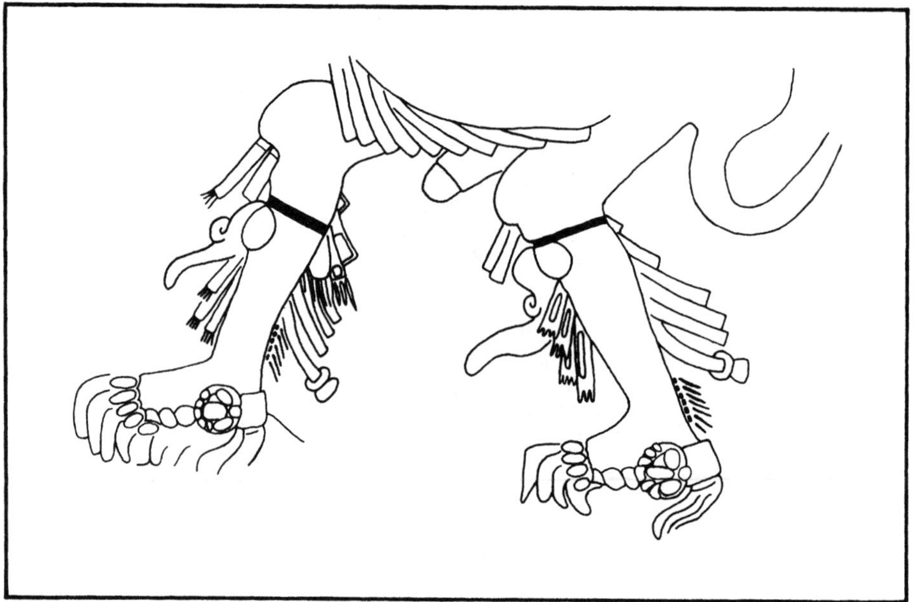

Figure 3.5 Monkey figure from a painted mural at the Quiché-Maya capital of Utatlán, Guatemala. Redrawn from *The Quiché Mayas of Utatlán: The Evolution of a Highland Guatemala Kingdom,* by Robert Carmack. Copyright © 1981 by the University of Oklahoma Press.

aggressive diplomacy. Most of these peripheral peoples were also Maya speakers—Tzotzils, Tzeltals, and Mams to the west; Ixils and Pokomams to the north and east. To the south the peripheral peoples mainly consisted of non-Maya-speaking Pipils (Nahua) and Xinca. The Mangue-speaking Chiapanecs formed perhaps the only non-Maya imperial state within this core zone. The Chiapanecs, from their capital city near Chiapa de Corzo, dominated Zoque-speaking peoples on their western flank and applied military pressures against the Tzotzil Maya to the east.

Core states were not as numerous in the central lake and northern lowland areas as in the southern highlands, and many of the Maya peoples there occupied peripheral and semi-peripheral positions within the larger zone. Perhaps the only core state within the central area was that of the Itzá-Maya, whose capital of Tah Itzá was built on an island within Lake Petén. The Itzá rulers collected tribute from dispersed farming groups residing on the mainland surrounding the lake. The Itzá language was very similar to Yucatecan-Maya, and these two language groups engaged in extensive trade (using the Mopán Maya of Belize as intermediaries). Less powerful Maya peoples who spoke Chol and Lacandón languages were located in the territory surrounding the Itzá state. They were apparently peripheralized by the Itzá through threats of war and actual military conflict.

In the northern lowlands of Yucatán, most of the peoples at one time had been subject to the powerful Mayapán "empire," centered on a small city of 11,000 inhabitants in the northwestern part of the peninsula. By the time of the Spanish conquest, however, that empire had fragmented into smaller political units. Some sixteen of the independent units (for example, Maní, Sotuta, Champotón, etc.) had built up small core states that competed with one another for power and tribute goods. They partially peripheralized the other, more simply organized political groups (such as Chakán, Chikinchel, and Uaymil).

Most interaction between the southern highland and northern lowland Maya core states took the form of trade, especially long-distance trade carried out by specialized merchants who moved merchandise both by land and by sea. Jade, obsidian, grinding stones, metals, and quetzal feathers from the highlands were exchanged for textiles, pottery, slaves, honey, and cacao from the lowlands. Relations between the highland and lowland areas were difficult to maintain, in part because travel through the dense tropical jungle of the Petén and surrounding environs was so arduous. The Itzá were perhaps reluctant mediators between the southern highland and northern lowland sections of the core zone. Nevertheless, some direct contacts existed, for rulers of the highland core states claimed genealogical ties with "Maya-Toltec" rulers in the Tabasco and Yucatán areas, and they periodically sent ambassadors to those places as a means of bolstering their own authority.

Both the southern highland and northern lowland Maya states traded extensively with the Oaxaca and Central Mexico core zones, mostly through the mediation of outside long-distance merchants. Maya and Aztec merchants travelled to special markets on the coasts of Guatemala and Tabasco, where they exchanged goods under highly formal conditions. The Aztecs and Quiché probably engaged in military skirmishes, as when they struggled for control over the Xoconusco area. As a result, considerable military tension existed between the Aztec and Quiché empires, and marriages between their royal families were arranged, presumably to help ease the tensions. Trade between the Maya core states and the peripheral peoples southeast of the Guatemala-Yucatán zone involved direct exchanges carried out under the auspices of Maya merchants. Apparently, the Maya states were also able to apply considerable military and political pressure on the peoples of the southeastern periphery.

THE MESOAMERICAN SEMI-PERIPHERY

Societies that help mediate unequal relations between core and periphery form the semi-periphery. Semi-peripheral units tend to be innovative in the development of social institutions, in part because they assimilate cultural patterns from both core and peripheral units. Within the Mesoamerican world system, the societies that specialized in arranging and promoting trade between foreign peoples can be seen as the key semi-peripheral units. Zones where open trade takes place are often referred to as "ports of trade," a term that may be appropriate for Mesoamerica as long as it is remembered that Mesoamerican trading centers were not necessarily seaports or politically neutral. In the Mesoamerican trading centers, exotic religious cults often flourished and served to attract pilgrims from near and far. Trade and religion went together especially well in the Mesoamerican semi-periphery.

Most of the Mesoamerican semi-peripheral zones were located away from the core centers, in some cases on the borders between different core zones and always adjacent to large peripheral areas. Thus, for example, the famous port of trade zone in the southern Gulf Coast of Mexico was situated near the boundaries of the Aztec empire to the west and the Maya core states to the east. In contrast, the Casas Grandes trading center (destroyed around A.D. 1350) was located far to the northwest of the Mesoamerican core zones, but near important peripheral peoples of that area. The monumental architecture of Casas Grandes included workshops, warehouses, a large marketplace, apartment buildings, and a ball court. Local products such as painted ceramics, copper ornaments, and exotic feathers attracted traders from afar, who in turn brought to Casas Grandes luxury items such as turquoise and other rare stones desired in the Mesoamerican core zones. A cult dedicated to the Quetzalcoatl deity apparently existed at Casas Grandes, perhaps making it a "holy city."

A few semi-peripheral units may have existed within the core zones themselves, although surrounded by powerful core states it was very difficult for them to maintain political independence. Most of them, in fact, were incorporated into empires and thus lost or radically altered their ability to mediate relations between core and periphery. For example, Tlatelolco, a merchant city-state that maintained considerable independence even within the Aztec empire, eventually was subjected to the full weight of Aztec rule in A.D. 1473.

Let us now turn to the main semi-peripheral zones of Mesoamerica and their individual ports of trade (see the map in Figure 3.1).

Gulf Coast

The area of the present-day Mexican state of Tabasco was the setting for the largest and most important semi-peripheral zone in Mesoamerica. This zone was situated on a major transportation route where the Grijalva, Usumacinta, and Candelaria river systems and numerous lagoons made travel by canoe highly efficient. A series of small city-states in the area functioned as ports of trade, beginning with Coatzacoalco to the west and extending eastward to Xicalanco and beyond that to Champotón (Campeche). Foreign merchants visited these ports of trade from all directions: Aztecs from Central Mexico, Tzotzil and Quiché Maya from highland Chiapas and Guatemala, Chontal Maya from Acalán, and Yucatecan Maya from the Peninsula. Gulf Coast merchants were known as "Putuns," a name possibly taken from the people of Putunchán, one of the important ports of trade located in the central part of the zone near Xicalanco.

Much of the trade within the Gulf Coast consisted of formal exchanges between merchants representing the interests of hostile core states, mediated by the ruling officials of the ports of trade. Trade of this kind usually involved exchanging manufactured goods (cloth, pottery, gold ornaments, precious-stone jewelry) for valuable raw materials (feathers, jade, skins, salt, slaves). There were regular marketplaces in the zone as well, where considerable trade of a more "open" nature took place. The local peoples produced large quantities of cacao beans, which allowed them to profit handsomely from the trade zone. They also travelled long distances by canoe to exchange merchandise in ports of trade elsewhere, especially in Yucatán and along the Caribbean coast.

The port of trade societies were politically independent, and oriented toward trade rather than war and conquest. The governing class was made up of merchants organized into political councils. Women could reach high positions of authority, although male relatives are said to have assumed their administrative duties. Foreign merchants formed residential wards in the port of trade towns, and no doubt exercised influence in political matters. This was especially true of the Aztec merchants residing in Xicalanco, who apparently served in the governing councils and had the backing of warriors stationed in the area. Nevertheless, political neutrality was an important characteristic of the ports of trade of the area, for without it the trade between merchants from powerful competing states would not have been possible.

The Chontal Maya language was spoken by most peoples in the Gulf Coast, and it also served as one of the trade languages employed by the merchants and officials doing business in the zone. Nevertheless, Nahuatl was also spoken by virtually all members of the merchant class, and native Nahuatl speakers resided in every port of trade town. In eight of these towns (the largest was Cimatán), native Nahuatl speakers made up the majority of the residents.

The peoples of the Gulf Coast zone were considered by their neighbors to be particularly wealthy, cosmopolitan, and friendly toward outsiders. The merchant class surrounded itself with fine works of art—painted codices, pottery, jewelry, murals, statues—executed in the current Mesoamerican "international" art style. We know little about their religion, except that it had many similarities with the religion of the Yucatecan Mayas.

Box 3.1 describes the semi-peripheral trading zone of Acalán, similar in many ways to Xicalanco.

South Pacific Coast

The Pacific Coast from Xoconusco southward formed a long strip in which a string of trading centers were located. Unfortunately, we know little about this zone at the time of contact, and some scholars question the presence there of true ports of trade. Xoconusco itself (Soconusco, the coastal part of Chiapas, Mexico) had been a neutral port of trade zone where merchants from the mutually hostile Aztec and Quiché Maya empires could engage in administered trade. About fifty years before the coming of the Spaniards, the Quiché and Aztecs began to vie for political control over the Xoconusco area. The Quiché conquered some of the eastern towns (Ayutla, Tapachula, Mazatán), but shortly thereafter the Aztecs gained control over the entire Xoconusco area. Aztec historical sources indicate that these conquests were carried out by long-distance merchants from the Tlatelolco city-state who had been attacked by the native peoples of Xoconusco.

Box 3.1 *The Trading Center of Acalán*

Acalán ("the place of canoes") was an independent city-state that specialized in trade and was located along the tributaries of the River Candelaria in what is today Campeche, Mexico. The capital of Acalán was Itzamkanac, a merchant town of perhaps 10,000 inhabitants. This town was too far inland to have been a true seaport, but its merchants were Putuns, middlemen who travelled far and wide to link up with vital trading routes. The Acalán merchants regularly moved by canoe to the Gulf Coast area to trade, and perhaps from there around the Yucatán Peninsula to still more distant ports of trade. They also trekked overland to trade with Yucatecan-Maya peoples to the north, and to the south at least as far as the small Nito port of trade on the Caribbean coast. At Nito the Acaláns had their own permanent commercial agents and residential ward.

The Acalán city-state was governed by an independent merchant class. The paramount ruler was also the leading merchant, and he was subject to the will of merchant councils representing the interests of the four wards into which the capital was divided. The merchant class oversaw the production of portable trade goods, such as cacao, cotton cloth, dyes, body paint, and pine resin.

The native tongue of the Acalán people was Chontal Maya, but many members of the ruling class had Nahuatl names and could speak the Nahuatl language. The Spaniards claimed that the Acaláns were better proportioned and more refined than their neighbors. The patron deity of the ruler of Itzamkanac was Kukulchán (the Chontal equivalent of Quetzalcoatl). Patron deities of the town's four quarters were also prominent in the Acalán pantheon: Ikchaua, patron of cacao and merchants; Ix Chel, patroness of weaving, childbirth, and women; Tabay, patron of hunters; and Cabtanilcab, of unknown identity. The goddess Ix Chel was of special importance, and the Acaláns sacrificed maidens especially raised for that purpose in her honor.

Even though Xoconusco became a tributary province of the Aztec empire, apparently it continued to function as a trading zone. Aztec merchants traded there and, despite Aztec political control, so did merchants from Oaxaca, Chiapas, and Guatemala. The Aztec merchants also used the zone as a base for launching trading expeditions further south along the Pacific Coast.

The Xoconuscan peoples themselves produced large quantities of cacao and were actively engaged in trade. Archaeological remains in the area suggest that Xoconuscan society was less stratified or politically centralized than the societies of the core zones. They may have been organized as chiefdoms rather than states. Most of the inhabitants of the zone spoke Mixe-Zoquean languages, although Mangue- and Pipil-speaking minorities were also present. At Spanish contact, Nahuatl was the lingua franca of the Xoconusco zone.

Suchitepequez on the western coast of Guatemala, like Xoconusco, was an area of cacao production and trade. Aztec merchants travelled there not only to trade their wares but also to spy for the empire. Special trading centers must have existed in Suchitepequez because the Aztec merchants were not welcome in the capitals of the Maya core states to the north. The situation may have been the reverse of that in Xoconusco: In Suchitepequez, the coastal trading centers were subject to Quiché political authority but Aztec and other foreign merchants were permitted to visit for purposes of trade. The Quiché established colonies of

Nahua speakers in the area, no doubt to better exploit the trade networks that had long operated there.

We know that both Aztec and Maya long-distance traders passed through Escuintla in the central part of the Guatemalan coast on their way to points further south. Additional trade centers or ports of trade, then, must have existed along the Pacific Coast of eastern Guatemala, El Salvador, and Nicaragua. Unfortunately, our historical sources do not indicate where such centers might have been located or how they were politically organized.

Caribbean Coast

A series of trading centers were located along the Caribbean coast of the Yucatán Peninsula and the Central American Isthmus, and together they made up still another important Mesoamerican semi-peripheral zone. The Caribbean trading centers were established in strategic locations so as to exploit local resources and link up the core zones of Mesoamerica with the large southeastern periphery and, beyond that, the lower Central American frontier. Gold was one of the main precious items that moved through this network, circulating all the way from Panama to Yucatán and from there to the rest of Mesoamerica.

The island of Cozumel just off the Caribbean coastline of the Yucatán Peninsula was organized as a small port of trade at the time of Spanish contact. Special platforms were built at various points on the island so as to be out of reach of the floodwaters, and thus provide safe storage for trade goods. In addition, causeways extended from the water's edge to the central town, where it is thought that the formal trading took place. This central town was probably the site of the famous Ix Chel goddess' shrine, to which religious pilgrimages were directed.

Archaeologists excavating at the island sites argue that the inhabitants of Cozumel were a pragmatic people. They invested in warehouses, stone streets, and modest residences rather than massive temples, shrines, or palaces. Even the Ix Chel cult had a practical side, for its speaking idol could issue flexible instructions to meet the changing needs of the trade-oriented Cozumel inhabitants. As might be expected of a port of trade, the people of Cozumel for the most part received the first Spanish visitors in a friendly manner, and tried to trade with them. They even requested "letters of recommendation," which they hoped would bring commercial benefits from subsequent Spanish visits!

Located further south along the Caribbean coastline were two other well-known ports of trade, Chetumal and Nito. Both were strategically placed for receiving goods from the interior by way of major river systems and providing easy access to the Caribbean Sea. They were also cacao-producing areas. Murals found at the Chetumal site were painted in a modified version of the Mesoamerican international art style, and Ikchaua, the merchant god, was among the deities prominently portrayed in the mural scenes (Figure 3.6). As noted in Box 3.1 above, the Nito trading center had resident merchants and agents from Acalán and elsewhere.

Figure 3.6 Drawing of painted murals at Santa Rita, Chetumal, in the Semi-Periphery of the Caribbean Coast; the head of the merchant deity appears on the right side facing the drummer. Adapted from J. Eric Thompson, "Merchant Gods of Middle America," *Summa Antropología en Homenaje a Roberto J. Weitlaner.* Mexico City, Mexico: Instituto Nacional de Antropología e Historia, 1966.

The largest and most important of the port of trade zones along the Central American coast was found in the Ulua river valley of present-day Honduras. Ulua was similar in many ways to the Gulf Coast zone, in that travel was mostly by canoe and abundant cacao was produced in the environs. One of the most important ports of trade in the zone was located at Naco in the Chamelecón Valley just south of the Ulua delta. Naco apparently served as a crossroads for merchants from Yucatán to the north, highland Guatemala to the west, and traders from Central American ports of trade further to the south. As an inland port, Naco saw goods such as obsidian, gold, jade, cacao beans, and feathers move through by both overland and sea routes. The commoner population of Naco most likely spoke Chol or Chortí Maya, both of which are close relatives of the Chontal-Maya language spoken in the Gulf Coast and Acalán. Archaeologists working at Naco suggest that an enclave of Nahuatl speakers or Nahuatl-influenced Maya governed this trading town (see Figure 3.7).

Other trading centers were located south of the Ulua zone along the Caribbean coast of Central America, although we know little about them. One possible center, Papayeca, was established in the Taguzgalpa area of eastern Honduras, near the Agalta Valley gold deposits. The rulers of Papayeca spoke a lan-

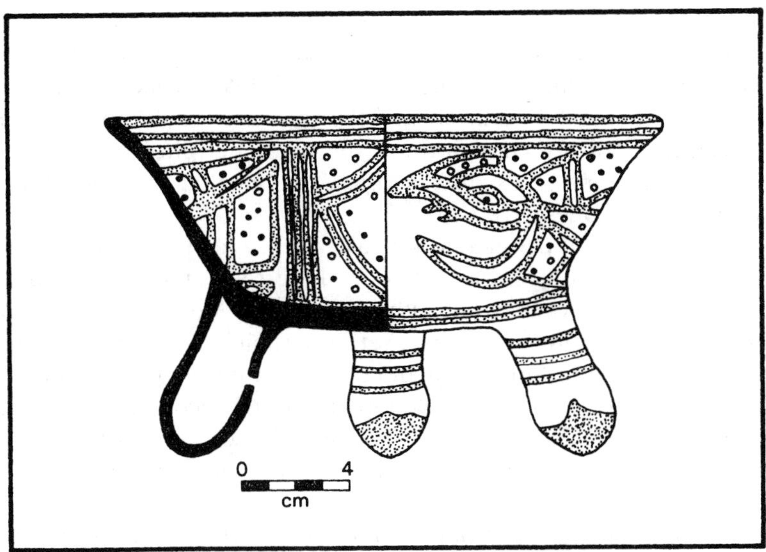

Figure 3.7 Painted ceramic vessel from Naco, Honduras, in the northern part of the Central American periphery. After Anthony Wonderley, "Imagery in Household Pottery from 'La Gran Provincia de Naco,'" in *Interaction on the Southeast Mesoamerican Frontier*, ed. E. Robinson, BAR International Series, 327. Oxford, England: BAR, 1987, p. 310.

guage similar to the Aztec language, and they apparently exchanged "gold and other valuables" directly with Aztec merchants. Still farther south along the Caribbean coast in the Sixoala Valley of present-day Costa Rica was another trade center of Nahuatl speakers, known to the Chibchan-speaking peoples of the area as Siguas ("foreigners"). The ruler of the Siguas bore the Aztec name of Iztolín, and was said to be a "Mexica-Chichimeca." The Siguas traded gold taken from the Sixoala riverbeds to the Aztecs, either directly through Aztec merchants or indirectly through Chontal seaborne merchants.

Finally, we have tantalizing evidence of a group of people living near Nombre de Diós (the place where the Panama Canal now flows into the Caribbean Sea) who, according to the Spanish conquistadors, in pre-contact times had travelled in canoes from Honduras to colonize the site. They spoke a different language from the other natives of Panama, and were called "Chuchures." The Chuchures were probably traders, most likely Chontal or Nahuatl speakers. If so, they would have formed the southernmost outpost of semi-peripheral peoples within the Mesoamerican world system.

THE MESOAMERICAN PERIPHERY

Mesoamerican peripheral societies actively participated in the economic, political, and cultural life of the Mesoamerican world, but from a weak and subordinate position. Whether through military conquest or threat of conquest, forced political alliance, or unequal ceremonial and market exchanges, the peripheral societies were structurally linked to the core states of Mesoamerica. The powerful empires and kingdoms that so impressed the Spaniards could not have come into being or continued to function without the many peripheral peoples who provided the labor, raw materials, and sacrificial victims that sustained the complex Mesoamerican core zones.

Many peripheral peoples, as we have already seen, were incorporated into the imperial states as subject provinces. In these cases, they were exploited and peripheralized in a direct manner. Other peoples of Mesoamerica retained varying degrees of political independence, yet were subject to indirect and more subtle forms of domination. Most of them confronted unrelenting military pressure from the core states, as well as exploitation through economic exchanges. The "meddling" of the core states kept the peripheral peoples, whether administered provinces or dependent societies, politically weak, economically exploited, and culturally backward.

The Mesoamerican periphery should be distinguished from the so-called frontier areas, which were made up of peoples outside the Mesoamerican world system located primarily in northern Mexico and southern Central America. The frontier peoples were politically and economically influenced but not structurally transformed by the Mesoamerican world. Frontier peoples, however, could affect developments in Mesoamerica, not only by making war on its peripheral peoples but also by exposing them to new ideas and practices. The Aztecs originally were a frontier people who were later integrated into the Northwest Mexico periphery; subsequently migrated to Central Mexico, where they became a core state; and finally developed the dominant imperial state of the Mesoamerican core (see Chapter 2).

Let us briefly examine some of the most important peripheral zones of the Mesoamerican world system, beginning with Northwest Mexico (see the map in Figure 3.1).

Northwest Mexico Periphery

Northwest Mexico was an area rich in resources of interest to the Mesoamerican world, especially copper, gold and silver; turquoise and other precious stones; cotton; sea shells; aquatic birds; salt; peyote; and other desert flora and fauna. These valuable raw materials were extracted and processed by peripheral peoples in the Northwest, and exchanged for manufactured goods coming from the core zones of Mesoamerica. The raw materials were concentrated in two main areas of the Northwest: one along the Pacific Coast, the other on the eastern flanks of the Sierra Madre.

At the time of Spanish contact, the peoples who extracted and processed the raw materials were concentrated in greater numbers along the coast than the eastern side of the mountains. They were generally organized as city-states, and shared many Mesoamerican cultural patterns. Their closest ties to a core zone were probably with West Mexico and the Tarascan empire. Trade with the Aztec empire and other Central Mexico core states may have been impeded along the coast by the Tarascans, but it continued to operate along the Sierra Madre route.

The most powerful city-states of the Northwest area were in the southern part, in what are today the Mexican states of Jalisco, Colima, and Nayarit. Most of these peoples spoke languages similar to Nahuatl. City-states like Tonalán (Guadalajara) and Cazcán were relatively large and highly militaristic. They could field armies of several thousand warriors, and may have built cities occupied by up to 10,000 inhabitants. They shared several "advanced" Mesoamerican features—for example, copper hoes, obsidian-blade swords, markets, and public buildings and houses constructed of stone. Their religious pantheons featured familiar Mesoamerican deities, and human sacrifice and cannibalism were part of the ritual system.

The city-states under discussion received strong military and economic pressure from the Tarascan empire just to the south, and many of the above-mentioned Mesoamerican features may have been responses to Tarascan meddling. The Tarascans no doubt found ways to drain off the scarce goods produced in the area, especially cotton, metals (gold, silver, copper), salt, honey, and cacao. The southern part of the Northwest periphery, then, was rather directly dominated by the Tarascan core state.

City-states further to the north, such as at Chametla, Aztatlán, and Culiacán, were made up of peoples speaking Cora and Cahita languages, both close relatives of the Nahuatl language. These peoples probably had little direct contact with the Tarascans, and therefore were perhaps influenced by more indirect means from other Mesoamerican core zones. Apparently, they traded with the core societies of Central Mexico, as suggested by the polychrome ceramics and copper and gold ornaments fashioned within the Central Mexico art style found at archaeological sites in the area. Although these city-states were smaller than the ones southward, some of the military units may have numbered a few thousand persons. Political rulers in the area were carried about in litters, and enjoyed high (noble) status.

In general, the peripheral peoples in the northern part of the zone supplied the Mesoamerican world with similar products to those yielded by their neighbors in the southern part. In return they received manufactured goods, and in the process assimilated Mesoamerican cultural features. Craft goods rendered in the late Mesoamerican "international" art style and complex religious ideas about deities and human sacrifice were typically Mesoamerican (Figure 3.8). It is noteworthy, however, that these northern peoples failed to produce stone architecture or sculpted monuments.

Scholars once thought that the line between Northwest Mesoamerica and the non-Mesoamerican frontier was located at the Río Fuerte in Sinaloa. Recent historical and archaeological evidence indicates, however, that the Mesoamerican periphery extended into the main river valleys of Sonora. The Opata-speaking inhabitants of Sonora were organized as city-states similar to the peripheral units just described. They must have provided an important connecting link between the Northwest Mesoamerican periphery and the aboriginal peoples of what is

Figure 3.8 Figure painted on a pottery vessel from Sinaloa, Mexico, in typical Mesoamerican style. After Charles J. Kelley, "The Mobile Merchants of Molino," in *Ripples in the Chichimec Sea*, eds. Frances Joan Mathien and Randall McGuire. (Carbondale, IL: Southern Illinois University Press, 1986, p. 87.

today the southwestern United States. In fact, some archaeologists argue that the Northwest periphery at one time extended all the way to the southwestern United States, from which socially complex peoples such as the Hohokam and Anasazi exported turquoise and cotton cloth to Mesoamerica. In the process these southwestern peoples took on certain Mesoamerican features, and according to some scholars became peripheral units of that world system. Trade between the Northwest periphery that we have been describing and the Greater Southwest area remained intact at the time of Spanish contact, but it had been reduced to sporadic exchanges best characterized as frontier relations.

The Huaxteca

The people of the Huaxteca formed a special periphery in the northeastern part of Mesoamerica. Although Nahua speakers inhabited the northern and southern parts of the Huaxteca, most inhabitants of the area spoke Huaxtec, a distant lin-

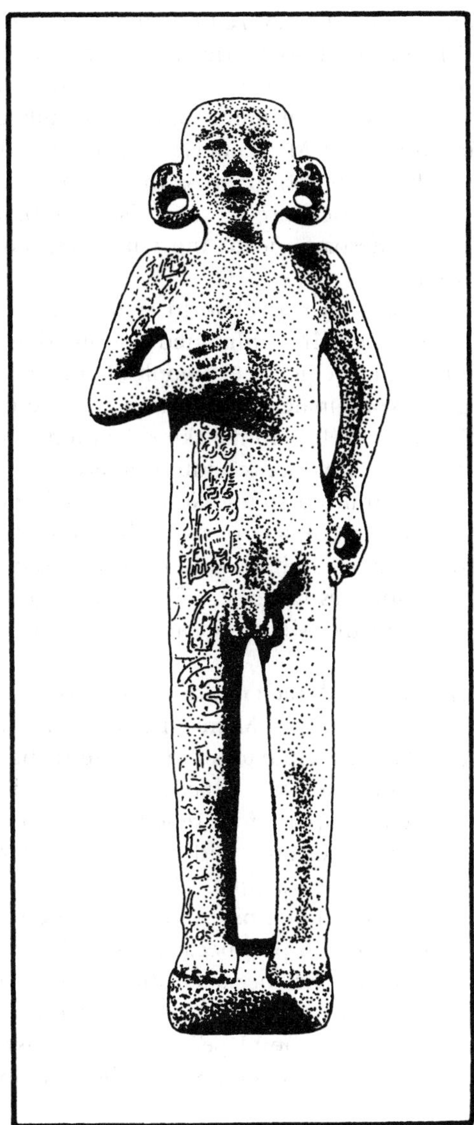

Figure 3.9 Huaxtec carved statue of an unclothed man with tatoos on one side of his body. Drawing by Ellen Cesarski.

guistic relative of the Maya family. It is surprising to find Maya speakers so far removed from their sister languages to the south, but some scholars think that the Huaxtecs at one time inhabited the entire east coast of Mexico and had been geographically contiguous with the Maya zone.

The Huaxtecs seem to exhibit "archaic" cultural features, suggesting that their entry into the Mesoamerican world system may have come relatively late. Core peoples like the Aztecs considered the Huaxtecs to be exotic. The Huaxtecs painted their hair different colors, filed their teeth, wore a kind of conical head cover, revealed genital parts in public, and were revered for shamanistic and other magical practices (Figure 3.9). Well-known Mesoamerican gods were conceptualized by the Huaxtecs in anachronistic ways. For example, Tlazolteotl, the Aztec goddess of sensuality, was for the Huaxtecs a primeval mother fertility goddess. The Huaxtecs were mentioned in an ancient Mesoamerican myth that describes the settling of Mexico by peoples who came from across the sea and landed at the Huaxtec port of Panuco. Whether or not there was any historical basis to the myth, it suggests that in the minds of Mesoamericans the Huaxtecs were a remnant of their civilization's ancient past.

From the perspective of Mesoamerica as a world system, the Huaxtecs were rather typical of peripheral peoples. They inhabited a somewhat isolated area, and were in close contact with frontier chichimec peoples falling outside the civilized world. The area was rich in exotic materials of interest to the core societies, especially rubber, bark cloth, turtle shells, animal skins, feathers, and shells. The Huaxtecs were politically weak, being fragmented into numerous small chiefdoms rather than consolidated into centralized states. Nevertheless, larger political units existed on the borders with Metztitlán, a core state with which the Huaxtecs were at times allied. Huaxtec public architecture mirrored the political situation: It was relatively small and unimpressive except for a few larger, well-fortified sites along the southern border in the Metztitlán area. As far as we know, the Huaxtecs had no writing system.

Even prior to the emergence of the Aztec empire, there was considerable direct exploitation of the Huaxtecs by the Central Mexican city-states. The Aztecs themselves are said to have first attacked the Huaxtecs during the reign of Motecuhzoma I (A.D. 1440–1468), in retaliation for the Huaxtecs' having killed merchants trading in the area. The Huaxtecs apparently relied heavily on magical rites to win this battle; they were defeated, however, and many men, women, and children were killed by the victorious Aztec warriors. Only when the Huaxtec chiefs agreed to pay handsome tributes to the empire did the killing stop. Wars between the Huaxtecs and Aztecs continued, in part because many Huaxtec political groups remained independent and in part because others rebelled against imperial rule. The wars were opportunities for the Aztecs to carry off booty, slaves, and sacrificial victims. Like other peripheral peoples, the Huaxtecs were subjected to degrading stereotypes: The Aztecs referred to them as disgusting drunkards and sodomists.

The Yope and Lenca, described in boxes 3.2 and 3.3, were peripheral peoples similar to the Huaxtecs.

Southeastern Central America Periphery

The southeastern periphery of Mesoamerica comprised a string of city-states occupying the Pacific Coast zone from the eastern part of Guatemala down to the Nicoya Peninsula of Costa Rica. The northern section of this zone, in what are today Guatemala and El Salvador, was occupied mainly by groups speaking Pipil,

Box 3.2 *Yopitzinco*

Yopitzinco, an isolated mountainous zone located in what is today the state of Guerrero, was similar in some ways to the Huaxteca zone just described. Guerrero was probably the region of greatest linguistic diversity in all Mesoamerica, and included peoples speaking Nahua, Tarascan, Tlapanec, Cuitlatec, and other languages now extinct. The Yope, inhabitants of Yopitzinco, spoke the Tlapanec language. Most of Yopitzinco's neighbors, including other Tlapanec speakers, were conquered by either the Aztecs or the Tarascans. Some of these conquered peoples paid regular imperial tributes, while others were required to man military garrisons established on the borders between the two hostile empires. The Aztecs also colonized one of Guerrero's northern provinces with 9,000 families from Central Mexico.

In Mesoamerican terms the inhabitants of Yopitzinco were a rather unsophisticated people. They were a mountain folk famous for their hunting prowess and use of the bow and arrow. Until marriage neither men nor women wore clothing. They were known to be fierce warriors who beheaded and flayed the skins of captives. Politically, the Yope were organized into loose chiefdoms or "tribes" rather than centralized states, and they totally lacked urban centers. The Yope were identified as the people of Xipe Totec, the red god of the Eastern sun and vegetative renewal. In Xipe's honor gladiatorial rituals were performed, during which sacrificial animals and humans were flayed and their skins donned by red-painted ritual specialists. Xipe Totec was an important deity throughout Mesoamerica at the time of Spanish contact, and was especially revered by the Aztec emperors. The Yope were given special religious status because of their close association with the Xipe deity.

The Yopitzinco area was poor in the kinds of raw materials that interested the Mesoamerican core peoples, although jaguar, lion, and wolf pelts extracted from the area circulated in the wider exchange system. The Yope were only weakly incorporated into the periphery of the Mesoamerican world system—in part, no doubt, because of the dearth of resources in the area. Culturally, they lacked many of the features common to other peoples of Mesoamerica. Nevertheless, as noted, they were the source of important religious ideas and practices that apparently were taken over and used for imperial purposes by the core states. Yopitzinco was also a source of slaves and sacrificial victims for the more powerful societies of Central and West Mexico.

Strategically located on the border between the Aztecs and the Tarascans, the Yope were subject to political manipulation by these two imperial powers. The Aztecs, in particular, regularly invited the Yope chiefs to witness their bloodiest and most impressive sacrificial celebrations in Tenochtitlán, at which times they would shower their rustic guests with expensive gifts. The underlying message must have been clear to the visitors: It would be useless to oppose the Aztecs, and therefore they should hold the line against the Tarascans. As with other peripheral peoples, the Aztecs employed ethnic stereotyping to keep the Yope in place, referring to them as untrained barbarians: "just like the Otomí only worse"!

Box 3.3 *The Lenca*

Scholars have long debated the position relative to Mesoamerica of the Lenca peoples of southwestern Honduras and eastern El Salvador. Some scholars think that they were part of the Mesoamerican world, others a buffer or frontier to Mesoamerica, and still others part of an entirely different cultural world. The Lenca language shares several features with the major language families of Mesoamerica, but appears not to have demonstrable genetic ties with any of them. Nevertheless, the Lenca had a long history of interaction with Maya societies from the Guatemala-Yucatán core zone of Mesoamerica, and at Spanish contact shared important cultural patterns with the Mesoamerican world (for example, the 365-day solar calendar divided into eighteen "months," and high temple mounds). From a world system perspective the Lenca are best seen as forming a relatively independent periphery of Mesoamerica, similar in important ways to the Huaxtecs and Yope.

Politically, the Lenca were organized as simple city-states or chiefdoms, each political unit exercising authority over a single river valley. The political ruler, high priest, chief justice, and other officials formed a Lenca ruling class that was internally united by bonds of kinship and marriage. Nevertheless, the various political units engaged one another in warfare, in a never-ending struggle to increase territorial holdings, tribute goods, and slaves. Still, in some areas certain periods were set aside during which warfare was banned. In many cases the Lenca political divisions were correlated with language dialects, the different dialects providing each unit with a degree of ethnic homogeneity. At the time of Spanish contact, for example, the Care dialect was spoken around Gracias a Diós, Colo in the Agaltec Valley, and Potón in eastern El Salvador and northern Nicaragua. These and other "languages" mentioned in the documentary sources were apparently dialectical variants of the same Lenca language.

The Lenca had features typically associated with peripheral peoples. They were politically fragmented, limited in power, and politically transitional between chiefdom and state levels. Archaeologists have shown that the Lenca constructed little monumental public architecture, except for military fortifications, and most construction was of adobe rather than stone. Many Lenca groups inhabited isolated mountain zones adjacent to non-Mesoamerican tribal peoples such as the Jicaque, Paya, and Sumu. Lenca territory was relatively poor in resources of interest to the Mesoamerican world, although it yielded some honey and cacao. Because the Lenca were numerous—they may have numbered over 500,000 persons—they may have been an important source of slaves for neighboring core states. In the northeastern part of Honduras, the Lenca occupied strategic territories with important gold and other mineral deposits.

Unfortunately, we have little information about the process by which the Lenca were integrated as periphery into the Mesoamerican world system. They apparently fought wars on unequal terms against the neighboring Maya and Pipil city-states. No doubt the Lenca also engaged in trade with semi-peripheral peoples in the ports of trade at places like Naco and the Pacific Coast. In order to have something to trade for the salt and manufactured goods they desired, the Lenca must have intensified the labor that went into the production of larger quantities of honey, animal skins, and woven cloth. A more direct form of exploitation of the Lenca occurred in the Olancho and Agalta mining areas, where under the authority of Nahua-speaking overlords they labored to extract gold and other precious metals.

a language closely related to Nahuatl. The southern section, along the coasts of Nicaragua and Nicoya, was inhabited by groups speaking the Chorotega and Subtiaba languages and additional groups of Pipil speakers (the Nicarao). The closest linguistic relatives of these three languages—Chorotega, Subtiaba, and Pipil—were found to the north, adjacent to the Mesoamerican core zones.

There has been much confusion about the relationship between the southeastern peoples and Mesoamerica. They have been variously referred to as "buffer," "frontier," or "intermediate" peoples relative to Mesoamerica. The evidence suggests, however, that they were integrated into the Mesoamerican world system. They were subject to political and economic pressures from the Mesoamerican core states, and they shared many typical peripheral characteristics. In particular, they were under pressure to provide the Mesoamerican world with raw materials and unprocessed goods such as cotton, cacao, feathers, animal skins, and dyes.

Politically, most peoples of the southeastern periphery were organized as city-states, which engaged in continual struggles with one another over power and position relative to the more powerful core states. The largest city-states were found among the Pipils in such places as Escuintla, Mita, Izalco, and Cuzcatlán. The Pipil city-states interacted more directly with the neighboring Maya core states than did the other peoples of the Southeast, and correspondingly assimilated more core-like features. South of the Pipils the city-states were smaller, as exemplified by the Subtiaba of Maribio, the Chorotega of Diriangen and Nicoya, and the Nicarao of Quauhcapolca.

In most cases, the southeastern city-states were governed by a ruler of noble status, who was subject to advice and consent from political councils made up of older men elected for set periods of time. Together, the rulers and councils selected war chiefs to lead the people in time of war. This somewhat decentralized form of government differed from the more centrally organized core states of Mesoamerica. The southeastern town centers were also smaller and less nucleated than their counterparts in the core zones. Architectural differences existed too, as exemplified by the fact that most of the public buildings in the Southeast were constructed of earth rather than stone.

Some scholars have argued that the Nicarao and Chorotega engaged in external relations primarily with non-Mesoamerican peoples to the south rather than the Mesoamerican peoples to the north. This has been particularly suggested for the Chorotega, who were politically weaker than the Nicarao and were considered by the Spaniards to be "crude . . . and subject to (the rule of) their women" (Chapman 1960:86). Nevertheless, the cultural ideas and practices of the Chorotega were clearly Mesoamerican, and they actively engaged other Mesoamerican units in trade, political alliance, and warfare. In short, they formed part of the southeastern periphery of Mesoamerica.

The Nicarao were even more clearly tied into the Mesoamerican world system. Many of their cultural patterns—such as the 260-day calendar system, elaborate pantheon of deities, and ritual human sacrifices—were fully Mesoamerican. Cultural similarities of this kind with the rest of Mesoamerica would not have been possible without constant interaction between the Nicarao and the core units of that world. This conclusion is confirmed by maps shown to the Spanish conquistadors, which portrayed routes used by Aztec and Putun merchants travelling to "Nicaragua" in order to trade. Indeed, the Nicarao had well-developed markets, where the most important Mesoamerican preciosities circulated, including cacao money. The Nicarao traded with merchants from the Mesoamerican core states, most likely in special ports of trade located along the Pacific Coast.

As noted above, the Nicarao and Chorotega societies were politically weaker than the Pipil city-states farther to the north. Nevertheless, it is likely that they were organized on a state rather than chiefdom level, as both the Nicarao and Chorotega had well-established tributary systems and standing armies. Furthermore, as in the core states, noble status was required for holding highest public office.

On the Caribbean side of the present-day Central American countries of Honduras, Nicaragua, Costa Rica, and Panama—to the east of the Pipil, Chorotega and Nicarao city-states—were located peoples who clearly fell outside the Mesoamerican world system. From the perspective of Mesoamerica, they constituted its southeastern frontier. Most of these peoples spoke Chibchan languages, and were linked together into small world systems of their own. Generally, their political groups took the form of chiefdoms, whose elite leaders travelled throughout the area exchanging gold and other valuable objects with one another. As frontier peoples to Mesoamerica, they exercised some influence on that world. For example, the Nicarao custom of chewing coca, no doubt, was borrowed from the Chibchan frontier peoples. Nevertheless, cultural influence moved mostly from Mesoamerica to the small tribes and chiefdoms making up the Chibchan worlds of the Central American Isthmus, rather than vice versa.

CASE STUDY: THE AZTECS OF CENTRAL MEXICO

We have seen that the Aztec empire was not only the dominant state of the Central Mexico core zone but also profoundly influential in the other core zones as well. It was, in fact, one of the most militarily powerful states in Mesoamerican history (see Chapter 2). Nevertheless, the Aztec empire shared many features with the other units of the Mesoamerican world system, and a brief summary of its political economy and religion will serve to illustrate the nature of the Mesoamerican world system in general and the core states in particular.

Political Economy

Although the Aztecs utilized a technology that was largely "Stone Age," their material productive capacity was truly astounding. They provided food for over 200,000 inhabitants in the city of Tenochtitlán and more than 1 million people residing in the central Basin. They erected monumental structures in the numerous cities of the Basin. Their stone and mortar constructions included thousands of public buildings (see Box 3.4); a huge hydraulic system of dikes, causeways,

Box 3.4 *Tenochtitlán*

The Aztec imperial capital Tenochtitlán was founded on a swampy island in Lake Texcoco in 1325. According to Aztec history, the wandering Mexica chose the city's site when they saw an omen from their god Huitzilopochtli: an eagle seated on a cactus eating a snake (this image is now the national symbol of Mexico). Tenochtitlán's island location in the densely settled Valley of Mexico provided excellent opportunities for commerce, and the city prospered and grew. It became the imperial capital upon formation of the Aztec empire in 1428; by 1519, the city covered 13 square kilometers with a population of around 200,000. Much of Tenochtitlán was destroyed when the Spaniards invaded; Mexico City was built over the ruins.

Tenochtitlán was criss-crossed by many canals filled with busy canoe traffic. Dikes kept the salty waters of Lake Texcoco separate from the fresh water surrounding the city, permitting cultivation of *chinampas* or raised fields on the outskirts (see Box 2.3, pp. 55–56). Urban residents included nobles and commoners engaged in a variety of occupations such as artisans, merchants, bureaucrats, farmers, and priests. The great marketplace at Tlatelolco, Tenochtitlán's smaller twin city, was attended by over 60,000 persons daily. Political and religious activities were centered in the Sacred Precinct, a large walled compound filled with temples, palaces, and other civic buildings including the "Templo Mayor," an impressive temple-pyramid that was the symbolic center of the Aztec empire and cosmos. This formed the nucleus for the rest of the city, whose streets, canals, and buildings were all built with a common grid orientation matching that of the Sacred Precinct.

The rulers of Tenochtitlán drew on older Mesoamerican traditions of urban planning as they designed the city, but they also innovated. The great size, dense population, and strict grid layout were features that mirrored the earlier imperial capitals of Teotihuacán and Tula. The Aztecs also called upon an older Mesoamerican urban tradition not evident at Teotihuacán in founding a sacred city constructed around a central ceremonial precinct dominated by large pyramids and shrines. In this respect Tenochtitlán resembled Tikal, Monte Albán, or Xochicalco more than Teotihuacán (see Box 2.5, pp.70–71).

Tenochtitlán exceeded Teotihuacán and other earlier Mesoamerican cities, however, in size, scale, and the importance of marketplaces and market trade. Tenochtitlán's *pochteca* or merchants travelled farther and traded a wider variety of goods with a greater number of foreign towns than any earlier merchants had, and the number and size of marketplaces in Tenochtitlán and Tlatelolco far surpassed other Mesoamerican cities. The Templo Mayor, although not as massive as the Pyramid of the Sun at Teotihuacán, was far more elaborately decorated and contained many times the number of rich offerings of earlier temple-pyramids. The richness of the construction and offerings at the Templo Mayor reflects the opulence and prosperity of Tenochtitlán, prosperity that was created and sustained by both commercial activity and tribute payments from conquered provinces.

Today Tenochtitlán lies buried under Mexico City. In the past few decades, archaeologists have made numerous discoveries in connection with the expansion of the Mexico City underground metro system. By far the most spectacular archaeological finds have come from the excavations of the Templo Mayor, in the heart of Mexico City, between 1978 and 1988. The Templo Mayor and its elegant museum, open to visitors year-round, are impressive testimonies to the greatness that was Tenochtitlán in 1519.

canals, and aqueducts; and an extensive system of irrigation channels in the hilly country surrounding the central lake area (Figure 3.10).

The Aztecs were heirs to centuries of Mesoamerican developments with respect to food production. The many cultigens available to them included maize, beans, squash, chile, chía, amaranth, and maguey. Domesticated dogs and turkeys and wild game provided a ready supply of meat, although diet for commoners was predominantly vegetarian, especially maize and beans. Swidden agriculture (*tlacolol*) was practiced along the foothills, while the flat areas and river beds were worked into complex irrigation systems of agriculture. Especially productive were the lake gardens (*chinampa*), which began to fill in much of the southern shoreline of the great lakes. The chinampas could produce seven crops per year, and it has been estimated that they may have provided over half of the basic food needs of Tenochtitlán, the other half coming from foods brought in as tribute from the

Figure 3.10 Central Basin of Mexico, showing the system of dikes and causeways associated with the Aztec capital of Tenochtitlán. From Geoffrey W. Conrad and Arthur A. Demarest, *Religion and Empire: the dynamics of Aztec and Inca expansionism*, p. 12. Copyright © Cambridge University Press 1984. Reprinted with the permission of Cambridge University Press.

imperial provinces. Agriculture was supplemented by hunting game in the hinterlands and migratory water birds on the lakes, as well as by fishing in the lakes. The Aztecs also gathered locusts, grubs, fish eggs, lizards, honey, "a green like scum formed by water fly eggs," and the spirulina algae. The flesh of human sacrificial victims was consumed, too, especially by members of the ruling class.

The Aztecs' surplus agricultural system underwrote a highly advanced industry of craft manufacturing. The most complex of the manufactures—featherworking, metallurgy, painting, and lapidaries—were worked by artisans of guild-like organizations whose members lived together in special residential wards. These master craftspeople manufactured exquisite adornments and objects used by the noble class, as well as the ornate and architecturally fine buildings that gave the cities of the central Basin their impressive, metropolitan aura.

In Aztec society, the ruling class exercised considerable control over the production of these goods and the means to produce them. The ruling class took the agricultural surpluses from producers in the Basin and beyond, expropriated the labor of commoners in order to build monumental public works, and accumulated masses of raw materials and artisan goods from the peoples in the imperial provinces. Control over the main means of production—lands, raw materials, laborers—by the Aztec ruling class was especially evident in the central Basin, while in the provinces to a much greater degree the means of production remained under control of local rulers and the producers themselves.

The tributary system dominated the Aztec economy, even though commodity production and trade in markets were important. Most commodity producers, including farmers working the lake gardens near the cities, obtained essential goods from the central markets. Tribute payers residing in more distant places also acquired food, raw materials, and other necessary goods in local and regional markets. The full-time Aztec merchants exchanged a wide variety of goods in both regional markets and distant ports of trade, apparently providing for their own subsistence needs in local markets. Land, slaves, carriers, and luxury items all circulated to some extent in the markets, although always within limits laid down by the ruling class.

The main tribute takers formed a nobility (*pipiltin*) whose status could be inherited from either parent (or both). Nevertheless, some tribute rights were specifically attached to administrative office, and others may have been purchased (that is, were personal property). Many of the lands, tributary goods and labor services were grants from the king and other high officials to noblemen and, in a few cases, to commoners of high achievement in war or other state activities.

The tribute payers were hereditary commoners (*macehualtin*) who formed the bulk of the lower-class residents of the town and country wards (*calpulli*). They were "free" artisans and peasants, subject to the demands of public officials, including the priests, noble houses, and perhaps, in some cases, private landlords. The tenancy of other commoners was so closely tied to certain parcels of land that the tenants themselves were included in any transferral of these lands. Aztec scholars have determined that a sharp division did not exist in Aztec society between free and tenant commoners, at least for the last decades of the pre-contact period. Virtually all lands, including those within the calpulli, came under control of the noble class, and the internal organization of commoner wards and hamlets fell under the direct authority of these nobles.

Free commoners could sell themselves as slaves (*tlacotin*), but they were also subject to being made slaves for criminal acts or capture in warfare. Slavery was not rare, and a thriving slave trade existed in Central Mexico. Slaves did not pay tributes, but their labor and subsistence were subject to direct control by the overlords. Commoners as well as nobility could own slaves. Slaves could even have other slaves subject to them, and could marry and thereby procreate children free of slave status. The carriers (*tlameme*), so critical to a world without draft animals, were in some cases hired laborers, but many of them must have been slaves or tenant commoners who were assigned this specific service obligation.

The full-time merchants (*pochteca*) and artisans (*tolteca*) were also subject to tribute and payments, but of commodities and services rather than subsistence goods or manual labor. They could achieve a rank just below noble status, which allowed them to own private property, accumulate wealth, wear fine clothing, and carry out rituals involving human sacrifice. Nevertheless, the professional merchants were carefully supervised by the ruling class, and were required to demonstrate public humility and obeisance in the company of true nobility.

The supreme ruler of the Aztec empire and the rulers of the empire's constituent city-states bore the title of *tlatoani* (plural, *tlatoque*). The tlatoani was primarily a secular figure who ruled over the affairs of state from a palace outside the religious precinct. He had many ritual obligations too, but religious theology and daily ritual were left largely in the hands of a full-time priesthood. The tlatoani was above all a military leader, and his first act upon taking office was to launch a military campaign in which he would demonstrate his military capabilities by capturing prisoners. Furthermore, he was in charge of a government largely dominated by military men. Most of the highest positions in the state hierarchy were military, especially a council of four commanders to which the tlatoani had belonged before his "election" as supreme ruler. Functionaries in charge of other matters of state participated in much larger but less prestigious councils, each subject to the dictates of the tlatoani and his military commanders.

At the time of Spanish contact, the selection of the tlatoani was in the hands of a small coterie of royal lineage officials. During an earlier period in Aztec history, this selection had required the approval of the tlatoque from Texcoco, Tlacopan, and other city-states subject to the Alliance, but in A.D. 1503 Motecuhzoma II was selected supreme tlatoani without participation by the other rulers. He thus became monarch of an empire that extended throughout much of Mesoamerica; assisted by a handful of close advisers, he ruled over a government whose officials numbered in the thousands.

Ideology and Religion

Some scholars claim that what really made the Aztec political economy work was an ideology that tied the ancient religious traditions of Mesoamerica to the expansionist strategies of the emerging empire (Conrad and Demarest 1984; Sanders and Price 1968). This ideology was created by the first leaders of the empire, such as Itzcoatl and Tlacaelel, who in A.D. 1428 burned the ancient books in order to erase the memory of the past and began to reorganize Central Mexican myth, ritual, and history. They "rationalized" the entire religious system, making it more supportive of the new political order. While the modifications were designed primarily to legitimize the authority and tributary rights of the first leaders, Aztec religion took on a life of its own and influenced developments within the empire and the Mesoamerican world as a whole.

The central figure in the Aztec religion was Huitzilopochtli, the hero-deity of the Mexica. Huitzilopochtli ("humming bird on the left") was melded with the ancient Mesoamerican war and hunting gods, such as Tezcatlipoca ("smoking mirror") and Tonatiuh ("he who goes forth shining," the sun), and was thus moved to the center of the cosmos as patron of war and human sacrifice. Huitzilopochtli thus symbolized the Aztecs' responsibility for maintaining the life of the sun by feeding it sacrificial blood. The implication of this was that the Aztecs were required to relentlessly take captives through warfare, and sacrifice them before the gods in order to preserve the universe from the threat of cosmic destruction. Between A.D. 1428 and Spanish contact in 1519, these powerful ideas were expressed in newly inscribed books, carved and painted in art works, and taught at the elite schools (*calmecac*).

The myth of the solar struggle gave the Aztecs a religious orientation that may have significantly differed from many of the other Mesoamerican states, at least at first, and was used to justify the Aztecs' aggressive military expansion. Political economic goals, such as outdoing other states in the competition for tribute, marched in step with ideological goals, imbuing the Aztec warriors with the cosmic mission of winning sacrificial victims to feed the gods. The extraordinarily strong ideological bent of Aztec religion appears to have resulted in major contradictions that may have weakened the empire in the long run. For example, Aztec military expansion led to the destruction of thousands of people at the sacrificial block, thus creating deep resentment on the part of the conquered peoples as well as the loss of invaluable producers and laborers.

Virtually all aspects of Aztec religion helped serve the interests of the ruling class because imperial policy and sacred cosmology were thoroughly integrated. Major events, such as important conquests or succession to the highest political offices, were draped in the sacred trappings of the cosmos: rulers dressed in the attire of deities, dancers moving in the cosmic counter-clockwise direction, dates of political importance identified with universal cycles of time, etc. Aztec religion, of course, expressed concerns besides the political ones, but interests of the state were inevitably present in every aspect of myth and ritual.

According to Aztec mythology, creation was a cyclic process, consisting of a series of periods or "Suns," each ending in destruction, the most recent Sun to end in earthquakes. Ometeuctli ("lord two") and Omecihuatl ("lady two"), the dualistic (male-female) creator couple, were said to have initiated creation by bringing forth four active deities associated with the cardinal directions: Tezcatlipoca (north), Xipe Totec (east), Quetzalcoatl (west), and Huitzilopochtli (south). These deities then created human beings and the other elements of the world. Human sacrifice began when a lowly god with pustules (Nanahuatzín) cast himself into the fire at Teotihuacán, followed by an arrogant rich god (Tecciste-catl), both then rising to the sky as sun and moon. They were given orbital movement by the auto-sacrifice of the other gods and a strong wind from Ehecatl, the wind god.

The Mexican historian Miguel León-Portilla has argued that myths of this kind were synthesized out of preexisting myths by certain Aztec priestly wisemen (*tlamatinime*), who claimed to be adding to the original ideas of the Toltec priest-ruler, Topiltzín Quetzalcoatl. The Aztec wisemen were able to determine the origin of the world, its stabilization through dualistic balancing, and its cyclic transformations with the passage of time. They further conceptualized the world as being composed of four basic elements (earth, wind, fire, and water), spatially divided into four quarters (each associated with one of the cardinal points). As they conceived the world, it was not a tranquil place but an arena in which diverse and powerful sacred forces were in perpetual struggle for supremacy.

As already indicated, these "metaphysical" ideas in Aztec religion were not solely the philosophical speculations of sages, but also were elements of a practical ideology being promoted by hardened military rulers. Thus, for example, the universalism associated with abstract creative powers might be seen as an expression on a highly symbolic level of the imperial quest for universal domination of the known Mesoamerican world. The violent destruction and reconstruction of the Suns or cosmic periods, especially that of the emerging fifth Sun—when the homely god jumps into the fire and initiates the obligation to feed the sun with blood—recapitulates in symbolic form the history of the Mexica, at first an obscure people who went on to military greatness. We should note, too, that a cosmology in which a myriad of deities and other forces competed for supremacy was consistent with the real Mesoamerican world of struggling ethnic groups, city-states, and empires.

The cosmological division of the world into four sections, each associated with a cardinal direction, was a very ancient pattern in Mesoamerica, and therefore could not have been a simple expression of the territorial divisions of the Aztec empire. Nevertheless, as Aztec specialist Richard Townsend has pointed out, the Aztecs used the idea of the four cosmic quarters as a general model of the Mesoamerican world and the empire's relationship to that world. In particular, the cosmological Eastern quarter, which was warm and fruitful, was associated with the empire's most successful provincial units in the east. The Northern and Western quarters, cosmically linked with cold, death, and the underworld, were associated with the enemies of the Aztec empire, specifically the hated Tarascans to the west and the recalcitrant chichimecs to the north. The earth itself (Tlaltecuhtli) was cosmically viewed as the back of an alligator floating on a great sea, whose life-giving heart was the very center of the world. Not surprisingly, the Aztecs associated their glorious capital of Tenochtitlán with the "heart" and center of this reptilian earth. Finally, the Aztecs' cosmic view of the world as being divided into thirteen celestial and nine underworld levels might well have been symbolic expression of the highly stratified nature of Aztec imperial society and the Mesoamerican world as a whole.

Aztec society had other dimensions besides the imperial one, of course, and the complex pantheon of Aztec religion must have provided symbolic expression of the diverse groups and categories of which that pluralistic society was constituted. For example, the Huitzilopochtli deity was the patron of warriors, and as such came to represent the highly militarized ruling class as well as the military units themselves. As noted above, this deity provided the main rationale for conducting military actions, collecting tribute, and ritually sacrificing human beings, three of the most important preoccupations of the Aztecs. Other Aztec war deities with ancient genealogies in Mesoamerica were Tonatiuh (the Sun, an aspect of Huitzilopochtli also), Mixcoatl (the Milky Way), and the all-powerful, all-seeing warrior and sorcerer of the night, Tezcatlipoca.

Tlaloc, the Aztec rain deity, was patron of the agriculturalists, who were largely free and tenant commoners. Tlaloc's consort was Chalchiuhtlicue, the woman with the jade skirt; and his helper-children were known as the Tlaloque, the little sprinklers. Tlaloc's domain was said to be located in the Eastern paradise, hovering over the mountain tops. Tlaloc was depicted with goggle eyes and a snarling upper jaw, symbols that linked him to rain gods present in the most ancient of Mesoamerican traditions. Tlaloc shared a spot alongside Huitzilopochtli in the main temple of Tenochtitlán, presumably to provide legitimization of the critical but unequal relationship between the ruling and commoner classes. Together these deities symbolically expressed the Aztecs' propagandistic claim that they had achieved cosmic balance between noble and commoner, warfare and agriculture, life and death, civilization and barbarism.

Little children were sacrificed to the rain deities because their teardrops imitated rain and they were small, like the Tlaloque helpers. In general, both human and vegetative fertility were closely associated with commoners and women in Aztec religion. The ancestral "mothers" and "grandmothers" of the Aztecs were patron goddesses of earth, birth, and curing (Teteo Innan, Toci, Coatlicue, Xochiquetzal). The red deity Xipe Totec represented the renewal of the vegetation layer at springtime, but was more masculine and militant than the fertility goddesses. Victims sacrificed in Xipe's honor were flayed, and the skins ceremonially donned (for the origin of this deity in Yopitzinco, see Box 3.2 above).

Quetzalcoatl, the "feathered serpent" deity, was patron of the supreme ruler and of priests (Figure 3.11). To the Aztecs, this deity represented Topiltzín Quetzalcoatl, the legendary priest-ruler of the ancient Toltecs. According to Aztec history, Topiltzín left Central Mexico in the ninth century for the East coast, where he is alleged either to have died and been apotheosized as the Morning Star or to have set sail on the ocean with a promise to return. The legitimacy of the Aztec rulers was based on their claimed genealogical right to stand in for Topiltzín. As patron of the priests, Quetzalcoatl symbolized the abounding wisdom, knowledge, and art of the Toltecs, handed down to the priesthood. "He embodied all that the Mexica characterized as 'civilization'" (Berdan 1982:130). The

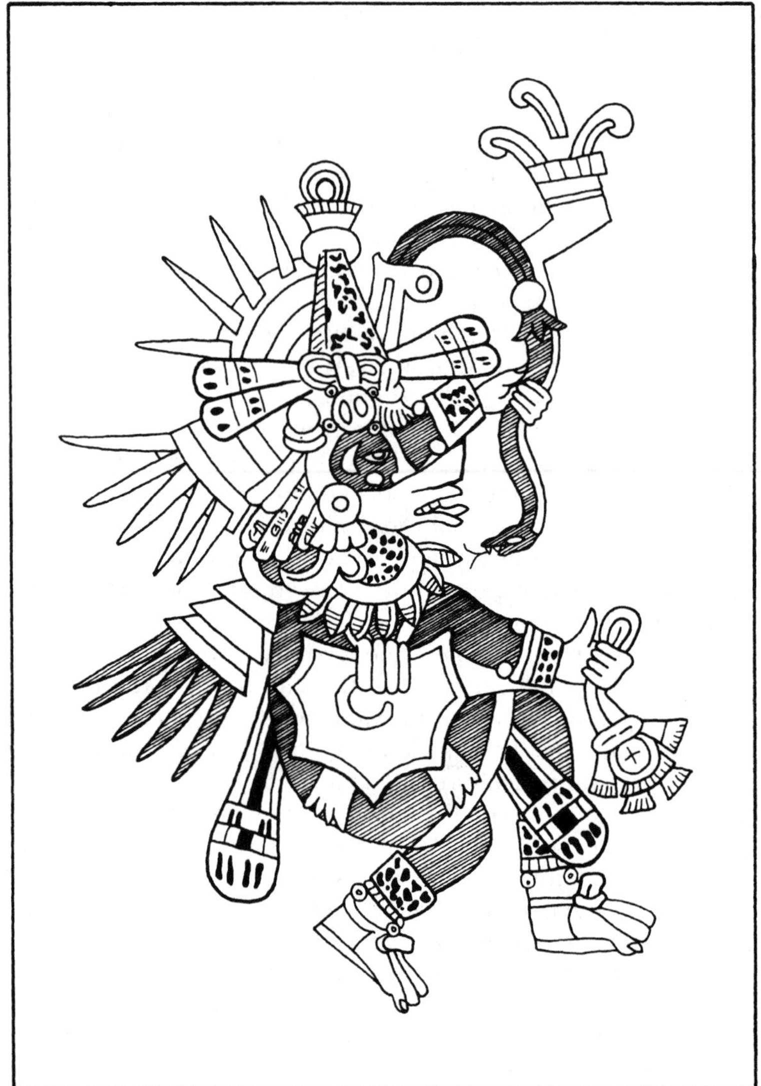

Figure 3.11 The Aztec deity, Quetzalcoatl, the "Feathered Serpent." After the *Codex Borbonicus.* Graz, Austria: Akademische Druck- und Verlansanstalt, 1974, folio 22.

Aztecs usually portrayed Quetzalcoatl wearing a mask with a bird's beak, conical headdress, and garment bearing a sea shell. Ehecatl, the Aztec wind and rain deity, was another aspect of Quetzalcoatl, and Ehecatl's temple at Tenochtitlán was cylindrical in shape.

The professional artisans and merchants also had patron deities that bore the special symbols traditionally associated with these two "middle-level" occupations. Yacatecuhtli, the most important patron deity of the merchants, was portrayed as a traveller, usually carrying a staff and backpack. Yacatecuhtli was represented as having a long nose, the nose symbolizing the merchants moving forward during their long trading journeys.

Some of the Aztec wisemen apparently went beyond the otiose creator deities to conceptualize an even more abstract universal creative power. It was a dualistic power, having both male and female aspects, sometimes associated with the creator couple and sometimes with Tezcatlipoca, the source of all natural forces and human strength. As H. B. Nicholson (1971:411) has said, "In the conception of the leading religious thinkers, all the deities may have been considered merely aspects of this fundamental divine power." With this omnipresent, abstract creative power we are brought once again to the issue of religion and ideology. While some scholars think this abstraction to be a projection of Christian ideas back onto Aztec religion, it may well have been a pre-Spanish religious expression of the Aztec dream to create a "universal" empire out of the intangible but socially very real Mesoamerican world.

REFLECTIONS ON MESOAMERICA AS A WORLD SYSTEM

It seems reasonable to conclude from our study that Mesoamerica provides a good fit with the idea that it was an integrated world at the time of Spanish contact. We were able to define a Mesoamerican core; in fact, several core zones, in which powerful states exploited weaker societies and interacted with one another in highly competitive ways; a periphery, made up of peoples subject to exploitation, whether directly under imperial rule or formally outside it; and a semiperiphery of trading zones where hostile core states as well as core and peripheral units could actively engage one another in economic exchanges. We found that despite the broad hegemonic power of the Aztec empire, there were many independent states in Mesoamerica, including other powerful empires.

The Mesoamerican world then, was a "world economy" rather than a "world empire," and its relationships of widest scope were the economic ones of trade, gift exchange, forced production, and market control. Of course, political relations also extended outward to engulf the Mesoamerican region, as the city-states and empires exercised influence on one another through never-ending struggles for power and relative economic advantage. Cultural patterns corresponding to the individual city-states (as well as to the core, periphery, and semiperipheral divisions) existed, although these distinctions are harder to draw than the economic and political ones.

Having argued that the world system model fits the Mesoamerican case well, certain caveats are in order. It is particularly important to keep in mind that we are using extremely broad conceptual categories. Concepts such as "core," for example, allow us to discuss together highly disparate political groups, from the huge Aztec empire to the rather small Mixtec states of highland Oaxaca. There is much to be gained from viewing these societies together as parts of great regional structures that defined much of social life in ancient Mesoamerica. It cannot be denied, however, that the differences between the individual societies were also important for understanding social life in ancient Mesoamerica. The "periphery" is an even broader concept, for we have applied the term to social groups of vastly different political organization (from tribes and chiefdoms to city-states), and with diverse connections to Mesoamerica as a whole (from imperial provinces to largely independent peoples such as the Lenca).

Some scholars will argue that our account of Mesoamerica tends to stress economic and political relations over cultural analysis. That is a valid point, and we recognize that the preceding reconstruction of Mesoamerica at Spanish contact devotes more systematic attention to economic and political matters than to cultural issues. Nevertheless, the world system approach clearly does not leave out culture, and, in fact, its focus on political and economic structures provides an essential context for the analysis of Mesoamerica's diverse cultures. Even at the broadest level of the Mesoamerican world system we would expect to find cultural expressions that could be understood only in their "world" context. The Aztec case is particularly relevant to this issue, since it suggests the possibility that the Aztec intellectuals (and probably their counterparts in other Mesoamerican core societies) had developed the idea of highly abstract, invisible powers transcending the complex pantheons of deities that characterized Mesoamerica's diverse religions. By taking this first step in the creation of universal deity, the Mesoamericans were perhaps engaging in a kind of cultural "rationalization" that might well have been inspired by the quite rational economic and political relationships binding Mesoamerica into a single world system.

The issue of cultural rationalization leads to questions about where the Mesoamerican world was headed at the time it so violently collided with the emerging world system of Europe. In the history of the Old World, ancient world economies similar in type to Mesoamerica were often transformed into world empires, as one powerful state would manage to dominate all others and gain political control over the entire economic network. The rulers of the Aztec empire certainly were aware of the possibility of taking control of the larger Mesoamerican world, and boasted at times of already having accomplished just that. But as we have seen, they failed in their attempt to create a universal empire, and there is good evidence that they were far from ever doing so. After all, even close neighboring states were able to maintain independence from the Aztec empire, and more distant imperial powers such as the Quiché Maya of Guatemala were probably more than equal to the task of preventing Aztec domination of the highland Maya core zone. Even political groups already incorporated into the provincial structure of the Aztec empire—as, for example, city-states in the Oaxaca area—were a constant threat to regain political independence through military means. There is some evidence, too, that the Aztecs had come to realize that subjugation of the semi-peripheral trading zones might have been profoundly crippling to the larger economy. Perhaps their military takeover of the Xoconusco port of trade zone taught them that valuable lesson.

It seems likely, then, that Mesoamerica was destined to remain a world economy for many years more. Of course, changes would take place in the relative position of the individual units within the Mesoamerican world. New core states would emerge, old ones would drop into the periphery or semi-periphery, and former frontier peoples would be brought into the periphery. Unfortunately, we shall never know the transformations that might have taken place, and instead are left to ponder the legacy of an incredibly vibrant world system that has reverberated down through the corridors of time in Mexico and the countries of Central America.

SUGGESTED READINGS

BERDAN, FRANCES F., RICHARD E. BLANTON, ELIZABETH H. BOONE, MARY G. HODGE, AND MICHAEL E. SMITH 1993 *Aztec Imperial Strategies.* Washington, D.C.: Dumbarton Oaks.

CARMACK, ROBERT M. 1981 *The Quiché Mayas of Utatlan: The Evolution of a Highland Guatemala Kingdom.* Norman: University of Oklahoma Press.

FOWLER, WILLIAM R. JR. 1989 *The Cultural Evolution of Ancient Nahua Civilizations: The Pipil-Nicarao of Central America.* Norman: University of Oklahoma Press.

HODGE, MARY G., AND MICHAEL E. SMITH (eds.) 1994 *Economies and Polities in the Aztec Realm.* Albany: State University of New York, Institute for Mesoamerican Studies.

POLLARD, HELEN P. 1993 *Tariacuri's Legacy: The Prehispanic Tarascan State.* Norman: University of Oklahoma Press.

SCHOLES, FRANCE V., AND RALPH L. ROYS 1968 *The Maya Chontal Indians of Acalan-Tixchel: A Contribution to the History and Ethnography of the Yucatan Peninsula.* Norman: University of Oklahoma Press.

SPORES, RONALD 1967 *The Mixtec Kings and Their People.* Norman: University of Oklahoma Press.

TOWNSEND, RICHARD F. 1993 *The Aztecs.* London: Thames and Hudson.

VOORHIES, BARBARA (ed.) 1989 *Ancient Trade and Tribute: Economies of the Soconusco Region of Mesoamerica.* Salt Lake City: University of Utah Press.

WALLERSTEIN, IMMANUEL 1976 *The Modern World-System: Capitalist Agriculture and the Origins of the European World-Economy in the Sixteenth Century.* New York: Academic Press.

WHITECOTTON, JOSEPH W. 1977 *The Zapotecs: Princes, Priests, and Peasants.* Norman: University of Oklahoma Press.

Chapter 4 Mesoamerica and Spain: The Conquest

For three centuries, the Mesoamericans were part of a vast colonial empire ruled by Spain. Spanish domination profoundly altered the culture and history of Mesoamerica's indigenous peoples: Old World infectious diseases, combined with violence and exploitation, killed millions of people; new technologies and new plants and animals had a deep impact on local economic and ecological adaptations; new social and religious customs were imposed. Spanish rule also introduced new categories of people into the social scene: Spaniards and other Europeans; the Africans they brought as slaves; and people whose heritage mixed Indian, European, and African ancestry in every possible combination. The native people who survived these upheavals found themselves at the bottom end of a new social hierarchy, with power concentrated in the hands of the foreigners and their descendants.

In this chapter we present a historical overview of the Spanish invasion, in order to explain how this small European nation came to rule over the densely populated, socially complex, and highly militarized Mesoamerican world described in the preceding chapter (Figure 4.1). Particular attention is given to the beliefs and motivations of the actors on both sides of the conflict. We begin by examining events in Spain's history that led up to the country's colonial enterprise and affected its course in many ways.

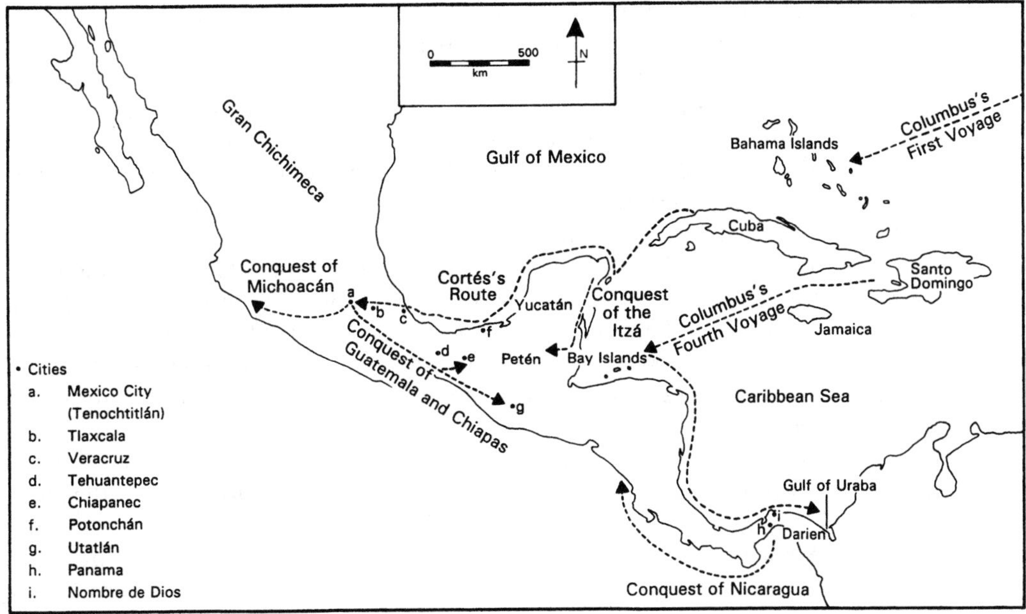

Figure 4.1 The main routes by which the Spaniards conquered the Mesoamerican world.

THE ORIGINS OF SPANISH IMPERIALISM

Spanish imperialism grew out of the Christian "reconquest," or *reconquista*, of Spain from the Moors. The Moors were Muslims of North African descent, whose Arab and Berber ancestors had conquered most of the Iberian Peninsula between A.D. 711 and 718. The Moorish rulers in Spain presided over a cosmopolitan, multiethnic society in which Jews and Christians were tolerated and permitted to practice their religions. Many Spanish Christians, however, found rule by these foreign "infidels" unacceptable, and bands of independent Christians challenged Moorish rule from their bases in mountainous northern Spain.

During the ninth century, the originally united Muslim state fractured into many small and competing kingdoms. Thereafter, Christian armies from the north were able to confront their Muslim enemy one faction at a time. Between A.D. 850 and 1250 the balance of power gradually shifted until the only remaining Moorish kingdom was Granada, a wealthy mountain stronghold in the south of Spain. The rest of the peninsula was dominated by the Christian kingdoms of Portugal in the west, Castile in the north and center, and Aragon in the northeast.

For the Christians, the conflict with the Moors was a holy war: The Islamic religion was seen as evil and the Muslim way of life as sinful. Spanish soldiers believed that Saint James, the patron saint of Spain, not only sanctioned their quest but often appeared before them on a white horse, leading them into battle. Religious faith and military zeal went hand in hand; these in turn were barely distinguishable from political and economic ambitions. That Christ's soldiers should enjoy the material spoils of victory, appropriating the wealth and property of vanquished Moors, was seen as no more than their due reward.

Over the centuries of the *reconquista,* Spanish Christian society came to glorify military achievement. Lacking ancestral ties to particular pieces of territory, the aristocracy was highly mobile, counting its wealth in herds of domestic animals rather than agricultural land. The knights who conquered a territory would move in as its new overlords, being rewarded for their military service with rights to tribute and labor from the subject population. Soldiers recruited from the peasant class would be given parcels of land in the new territory, which they owned outright (in contrast to the serfdom prevailing elsewhere in Europe). The Christian kings found their power always circumscribed by the need to placate the nobles, on whose military prowess they depended for the conquest of additional lands; as a result, there was a constant tension between the central authority of the monarch and the local concerns of the feudal lords.

After a long hiatus marked by the Black Death and by factional disputes within the Christian kingdoms, the reconquest resumed in 1455 under King Henry VI of Castile. In 1469 Henry's eighteen-year-old half-sister and heir, Isabella, married seventeen-year-old Ferdinand, heir to the throne of the much weaker kingdom of Aragon. After much political intrigue, including a civil war in Castile, the couple emerged as the powerful rulers of a united Spain. They succeeded in limiting the influence of both their own nobles and the pope. Themselves very pious, they used religion as an effective means of promoting national unity. They established the Spanish Inquisition as a tool for enforcing religious conformity among Spanish Christians—including increasing numbers of *conversos,* or converts from Judaism, and *moriscos,* or Christianized Moors, thousands of whom would be executed as heretics. The couple's close ally Francisco Jiménez de Cisneros, a Franciscan priest and Isabella's confessor, raised the standards of orthodoxy and austerity among the religious orders, especially the Franciscans, and sought to revitalize the religious faith of the entire populace. Appointed Archbishop of Toledo in 1495 and Inquisitor General in 1507, Cisneros was the most powerful individual in Spain apart from the king and queen themselves. He twice served briefly as regent of Castile, following Isabella's death in 1504 and Ferdinand's in 1516.

Isabella and Ferdinand sponsored scholarship in the humanities, earning an international reputation as patrons of learning. Among their circle of learned associates was Antonio de Nebrija, a *converso* scholar who in 1492 published the first grammar of a modern, spoken language, as opposed to Latin and Greek. Nebrija's *Grammar of the Castilian Language* elevated Castile's dialect of Spanish to a privileged position previously restricted to those ancient languages. It thus helped to legitimize Castile's supremacy over the rest of Spain, and beyond: When first presented with the book, Isabella reportedly asked its purpose; the Bishop of Ávila, speaking on Nebrija's behalf, explained, "language is the perfect instrument of empire."

His words were apt, for the year 1492 launched Spain on its way toward becoming the world's most powerful state. Early that year, Isabella and Ferdinand had seen the *reconquista* come to an end: The forces of Christian Spain marched victorious into Granada on January 2.

With the Moorish frontier closed at last, Spain's heavily militaristic and aristocratic society might have settled down to focus on internal economic development. The towns were already dominated by a middle class of tradespeople and entrepreneurs; production of certain goods, especially wool and leather, was in the process of industrialization. However, other events of 1492 steered the nation onto a different track.

On March 30, 1492, Isabella and Ferdinand signed a decree demanding that all Jews be expelled from Spain within four months. A campaign to force Muslims to convert began in 1499, with an edict of expulsion following in 1502. Prior to the fall of Granada, Jews actually had fared better in Spain than elsewhere in Europe. Spanish Christians knew that any Jews or Muslims expelled from Christian-held territory would have been welcomed in Moorish lands, where their skills and assets would only strengthen the power of the Moorish rulers. But after the conquest of Granada there was no longer any such refuge, and in the climate of religious fervor that accompanied the culmination of the *reconquista*, Spain's rulers opted to impose their faith on all their subjects.

Between 120,000 and 150,000 Spanish Jews left the country; today's Sephardic Jews are descended from these exiles. Thousands more, like the majority of the Moors, chose to convert to Christianity, at least in name, rather than leave their homes and property. As *conversos*, the descendants of Jewish families often continued to practice at least some Jewish customs in secret, and were always at risk of being tried by the Inquisition for real or alleged Judaic practices. Some were attracted to Christian religious orders, such as that of the Franciscans, that were somewhat compatible with their own traditions of scholarship, prophecy, and mysticism. Scholars from *converso* families contributed significantly to the sixteenth-century flowering of Spain's universities.

The departure of the majority of Spain's Jews took a tremendous toll on Spain's economy. Jewish merchants and financiers had dominated the middle class; without their skills and trading networks, Spain's commerce was devastated. Jewish traders were replaced not by upwardly mobile Spanish Christians but by foreigners who took their profits out of the country. What had been a thriving and industrializing commercial system sank into centuries-long stagnation.

On August 3, 1492, a Genoese mariner named Christopher Columbus set sail from Spain on a voyage sponsored by Isabella and Ferdinand. The goal of the enterprise was to discover a westward route to Asia and to claim Spanish sovereignty over any previously unknown lands found along the way. For the Spanish rulers, such a route—and their control over it—would facilitate trade for such items as silk and spices as well as giving them access to whatever riches might lie in undiscovered lands.

Their interests were more than economic, however, for Columbus and his Spanish patrons envisioned a worldwide religious crusade. They hoped that with a Spanish-controlled route to Asia, the struggle against Islam could be continued beyond Spain's borders. The abandoned medieval crusade to establish Christian control over the Holy Lands, which were then part of the Ottoman Empire of the Turks, could be restarted under Spanish leadership, financed by new wealth from the western trade. In effect, a westward passage would allow Christian armies to sneak up on the Turks (and other Islamic peoples) from behind, rather than having to battle their way eastward through the Turks' formidable defenses. Furthermore, the non-Islamic peoples of Asia might be converted to Christianity. Such conversions would not only be pleasing to God. The new converts, potentially numbering in the millions, would also swell the ranks of the Christian armies as they passed westward toward what might be the ultimate battle between the followers of Christ and the followers of Mohammed.

But on October 12, Columbus and his men stumbled upon an island in the Caribbean. That island proved to be one of many, that lay adjacent to two large continents. Instead of establishing new links to Asia, Isabella and Ferdinand found themselves presiding over a massive project of exploration, invasion, and conquest, as the lands Columbus mistook for the "Indies" were forcibly transformed into colonies of Spain.

SPAIN'S COLONIAL ENTERPRISE BEGINS

The leaders of Spain believed that they had a God-given right to dominate non-Christian peoples and bring to them the word of Christ; the fact that the "new" lands were revealed to Columbus while he sailed under the Spanish flag was proof enough of divine intent. Spanish claims were further legitimized by Pope Alexander VI, himself a Spaniard, who issued a papal bull in 1493 giving Spain the right to explore westward and southward and claim any territory not already under Christian rulership.

This ran afoul of Portugal, which was engaged in expeditions in the eastern Atlantic and along the coasts of Africa. In 1493 Spain and Portugal agreed to divide between themselves the right to explore and conquer unknown parts of the world. This Treaty of Tordesillas declared a line of demarcation, which passed through the Atlantic Ocean 370 leagues west of the Cape Verde Islands (which Portugal already claimed). Spain had rights to everything to the west of this line; Portugal over all lands to the east. Spain, though intending to claim all of America, had inadvertently yielded to Portugal the eastward-projecting mass of Brazil.

Once Spain's rights to American territory had thus been formally recognized, the process of invading and conquering these lands could be treated juridically as a process of pacification. Native peoples who declined to recognize Spanish dominion were by definition rebelling against their lawful rulers and thus inviting violent retaliation and suppression. Native groups that submitted peacefully to Spanish rule were merely performing their duty as Spanish subjects. This "myth of pacification" served to justify the Spanish invasion and mask its accompanying brutality behind a façade of legitimate statecraft.

The *reconquista* had won back previously Christian territories from the descendants of Muslim invaders. The conquest of America was an aggressive campaign against peoples who had never heard of, let alone threatened, Spain. However, for many Spaniards the invasion of America was a logical continuation of their struggle against the Moors—led, like that campaign, by their warrior patron Saint James. The new frontier provided new employment for soldiers and new opportunities for sons of the aristocracy to rule over territory and subjects that they had helped to conquer. Spain had been purged of Jews and Muslims, and the new lands also would be uniformly Christian. Indeed, the prospect of converting the native peoples of America was compatible with the plan to convert Asia: The Church would be that much more fortified against the Muslim threat.

Also, the economic decline of Spain could be temporarily stalled by an influx of wealth from America. Although the cities of gold that filled Spanish dreams never materialized, Spanish colonists extracted enough silver, gold, and other precious substances to enrich their homeland. However, the result of flooding Europe's markets with American silver was similar to what would happen if a modern nation sought to offset economic problems by printing additional currency: It set off a cycle of inflation that only furthered Spain's long-term decline.

Thus, even though millions of pounds of silver poured into Spain, its New World colonies were never profitable. Under the Habsburgs, Spain concentrated its energies and wealth on expensive military campaigns throughout Europe instead of developing successful commercial and industrial enterprises as the northern European powers were doing. The Dutch, British, and French, unhappy with the pope's having essentially given the New World to Spain and Portugal, sought to gain America's wealth through control of commerce and banking—and through outright piracy. In the end, Spain's royal coffers were nothing more than a funnel through which New World silver flowed on its way to the pockets of northern European merchants and bankers.

Spanish attention, following the example of Columbus's voyages, focused at first upon the Caribbean islands, especially the island of Hispaniola—today shared by the nations of Haiti and the Dominican Republic—where the settlement of Santo Domingo was established in 1496. The native inhabitants of the islands, divided among many small polities with no standing armies or other organized defensive forces, were ill prepared to ward off the Spanish invasion.

Spain's rulers rewarded successful conquerors with rights to tribute in goods and labor from the native people. This reward system, which had precedents in the *reconquista,* was called *encomienda*; an individual who held an *encomienda* grant was an *encomendero. Encomenderos* comprised a colonial aristocracy that from the beginning found its interests often in conflict with those of both the Spanish Crown and the Church. *Encomenderos* were officially charged with seeing to the religious instruction of the native people entrusted to them; their frequent indifference to this demand was one source of friction between them and their rulers.

The consuming purpose of the early colonists was the search for gold, which overrode any concern for the long-term integrity of a colonial society. The islands contained some placer deposits of gold, and the native people were compelled to work the gold fields for the enrichment of their new overlords. Already facing massive population loss owing to disease, these people saw their survival further threatened by this forced labor and other abuses: beatings, rapes, murders. They also suffered from a nutritional crisis resulting from the disruption of their agriculture, hunting, and fishing.

Such problems only made the people more susceptible to the Old World infectious diseases that European invaders and their African slaves inadvertently introduced to the Americas. Never having been exposed to these bacterial and viral agents, the native people had no natural immunity to the diseases they caused. Mortality rates when a new disease first struck were as high as one-third of the population, with the sickness affecting healthy adults as severely as children and the elderly. Owing to a combination of brutality, exploitation, and disease, within three decades of Columbus's first landfall very few native people of the islands were left alive. A more extensive account of the demographic consequences for the Mesoamericans of the European contact period can be found in Box 4.1.

The status of native people under Spanish colonial rule was inherently

Box 4.1 *The Demographic Consequences Of European Contact*

A pre-contact indigenous population that some estimate as high as 27.1 million in Mexico alone was reduced to around 1.2 million in the first century of Spanish rule, after which it began a gradual rebound (see the Preface for estimated figures). During the conquest years, warfare was directly responsible for the deaths of many Indians, and in the years immediately after the conquest slavery and the harsh treatment of Indians in the mines and in other Spanish enterprises accounted for many more deaths. Random acts of torture and murder, whether for the purpose of "sport" or to maintain a state of terror, were responsible for additional deaths. In terms of sheer numbers, however, most of the deaths were the result of infectious diseases previously unknown in the Americas. The biggest killers were smallpox, measles, typhus, bubonic plague, yellow fever, and malaria. In many areas, native populations were already weakened by early epidemics before they had to fight the Spanish invaders.

The process of *mestizaje* also affected native demographics. Mestizos were neither Spanish nor Indian—they were the children of unions between Spaniards and Indians (usually a Spanish father and an Indian mother). Indians and Africans also formed unions, giving birth to children who were classified as mixed-race rather than natives. Thus, Indian populations declined in areas where *mestizaje* was high, even if Indian mortality rates were relatively low.

Within colonial Mesoamerica there was significant variability in demographic patterns in different regions. Generally, populations in the lowland regions suffered greater declines than did the highland populations, although the causes for this are still not well understood. Throughout much of colonial Mesoamerica this pattern has had a long-term impact, and today Indian populations are typically much greater in highland areas than in the lowlands. Thus, in the highlands of Oaxaca, Chiapas, and Guatemala, Indians constitute the majority of the population even today.

The impact of high mortality rates in the years just preceding and following the Spanish conquest was profound. In many areas as much as 90 to 95 percent of the native population died within the first fifty to seventy-five years following contact, disrupting all aspects of native life. Communities were left with no legitimate leaders, children without parents or even close relatives to care for them, and entire families died out.

Spaniards often explained the epidemics as punishment wrought by God. Native practices before the conquest—the worship of false gods, human sacrifice, polygyny, and so forth—were now being avenged. Certain sympathetic priests, however, asserted that it was the Spaniards who were being punished for their ill treatment of the native people. The Indians, now baptized as Christians, would go to heaven, but the rapacious colonists would be deprived of a native population to labor for them.

It is difficult to determine how the Mesoamericans themselves explained these diseases. At least some insight is provided by the answers to a questionnaire that Spain's King Philip II sent to all the communities in the colony in the late 1570s—just after a particularly severe epidemic. Asked about the health of their people, elders in a number of Indian towns blamed the high mortality rate on the changes in lifestyle that had followed the Spanish conquest. People no longer followed the strict behavioral regimen of their ancestors. They ate too much meat, dressed too warmly, married too young. Behaviors such as these caused people to become weak and easily susceptible to illness. Indirectly, these elders were blaming the Spaniards, who had introduced domestic animals like sheep and pigs, wool (for warmer clothing and blankets), and previously unknown garments such as shirts and coats. Similarly, Catholic priests, trying to prevent premarital sex, encouraged the Mesoamericans to marry in their mid-teens. The ancestors' way of life had been more rigorous and virtuous. In contrast to the Spanish idea that the Indians were being punished for the "sins of the ancestors," these Indians blamed their decline on the adoption of Spanish ways.

Some native documents provide particularly vivid descriptions of epidemics and their effects on the population. The *Book of Chilam Balam of Chumayel*, from the Yucatán Peninsula, speaks as follows:

> There was then no sickness then;
> They had no aching bones then;
> They had no high fever then;
> They had no pustule fever [smallpox] then;
> They had no burning chests then;
> They had no abdominal pains then;
> They had no consumption then;
> They had no headaches then;
> The course of humanity was orderly then;
> The foreigners made it otherwise
> When they arrived here.
> They brought shameful things
> When they came. (Roys 1933:22)

In the *Annals of the Cakchiquels* an epidemic that struck in 1519 is described in equally vivid terms:

> It happened that during the twenty-fifth year [1519] the plague began, oh, my sons! First they became ill of a cough, they suffered from nosebleeds and illness of the bladder. It was truly terrible, the number of dead there were in that period. . . . Little by little heavy shadows and black night enveloped our fathers and grandfathers and us also, oh, my sons! when the plague raged. . . . Great was the stench of the dead. After our fathers and grandfathers succumbed, half of the people fled to the fields. The dogs and the vultures devoured the bodies. The mortality was terrible. Your grandfathers died, and with them died the son of the king and his brothers and kinsmen. So it was that we became orphans, oh, my sons! So we became when we were young. All of us were thus. We were born to die! (Recinos 1980:119-120).

problematic. At first treated unambiguously as potential slaves—Columbus being the first to enslave Indians—under Isabella's orders they were soon declared citizens of the Spanish Crown with corresponding legal rights. However, since the Crown had the right to tax its subjects, and also had somehow to reward conquerors for their service, it was considered acceptable to require tribute from these new subjects. But heavy tribute requirements could amount to virtual slavery. Furthermore, an illegal slave trade flourished, and slavery long remained a legal option when dealing with peoples who resisted Spanish domination or who were believed to practice cannibalism. False accusations of cannibalism were used to justify slave-raiding campaigns. The nature and extent of service that Spaniards could legitimately extract from Indians remained a major issue of contention.

Christian evangelization was a second major issue. Religious fervor played such a key role in promoting Spanish unity and legitimizing Spanish imperialism that the conversion of the Indians was a top priority for the Crown, especially for pious Isabella. How could the Indians be brought to the faith? Were they capable of becoming fully Christian? How could the material needs and desires of Crown and colonists be reconciled with the spiritual needs of the native people? So rapidly were the island natives decimated that these questions were barely considered before it was too late.

In Spain, Isabella's death in 1504 ushered in another era of factionalism and instability. As a result of a series of deaths in the royal lineage, Isabella and Ferdinand's daughter, Juana, ended up inheriting the throne of Castile. Juana was married to Archduke Philip of Burgundy, a member of Europe's powerful Habsburg dynasty. Philip's father, Maximilian, was ruler of the Holy Roman Empire, a confederation of feudal states in Central Europe whose princes traditionally elected their so-called "emperor."

Many Spanish nobles allied themselves with Philip in order to curtail Ferdinand's claims to his dead wife's dominions and to boost trading links with Habsburg possessions in the Netherlands. The ensuing disputes are too complex to be treated in detail here, but the upshot was that, what with Philip's death in 1506 and Juana's alleged insanity, after Ferdinand died in 1516 the Spanish crown passed to the eldest son of Philip and Juana, young Charles of Ghent.

Charles, born in 1500, had grown up in the Netherlands. He did not speak Spanish and had never set foot in his mother's homeland until he arrived as king in 1517, bringing with him a bevy of Flemish advisers. Two years later, Charles's grandfather Maximilian died and Charles was elected to succeed him as Holy Roman Emperor. This further linked Spain to the fortunes of other European lands—lands that would soon be torn apart by the religious wars of the Protestant Reformation. A man of the Renaissance, Charles opened Spain's closed and conservative society to humanistic influences from elsewhere in Europe. Not all Spaniards wished to see this virtual foreigner upon their throne, however, and he did not secure his control over the Crown until 1522.

By 1520 the limited quantities of gold that the Caribbean islands had held were nearly gone. Lacking both gold and the native laborers to extract it, the Spanish colonists had to turn to new enterprises. As the native population dwindled, trade in African slaves had become widespread. With Africa as the new source of forced labor, an economy based on livestock ranching and agriculture began to develop. The Spanish settlers, descendants of the original *encomenderos*, came to constitute a landed gentry, a small, elite group living off of the work of a large subject population of African slaves and free African and mulatto wage laborers.

Some Spaniards, however, unwilling to settle for the increasingly limited options offered by the island colonies, looked toward the vast, unconquered mainland as a potential source of new opportunities. On his fourth voyage in 1502, Columbus had encountered an elite Maya merchant and his entourage sailing near the coast of Honduras, their large ocean-going canoe laden with rich goods (see Chapter 1). Since then, Spaniards had known that the mainland was home to peoples whose societies were more complex and whose material goods more sophisticated than those of the island natives.

The Spanish conquest and occupation of the mainland was staged from strongholds in Central Mexico and Panama. Most of Mesoamerica was brought under Spanish control by Spanish forces originating in Central Mexico. But even before their struggle with the Aztecs in Central Mexico had begun, the Spaniards already had established towns in Darién and the Panamanian Isthmus.

The Spanish occupation of the mainland began in 1510 with the foundation of Santa María de Antigua del Darién (in modern Colombia). In 1519, six years after Santa María's founder, Vasco Núnez de Balboa, first saw the Pacific Ocean, the new settlement of Panama was established on the Pacific side of the isthmus, a short distance from the Caribbean port of Nombre de Dios; Spanish treatment of the native population was harsh. Under the brutal leadership of governor Pedro Arias de Avila, Spaniards raided native settlements for gold and slaves, and soon the indigenous population had virtually disappeared.

Spanish expansion into Nicaragua, Costa Rica, and Honduras was carried out primarily by forces based in Panama. The native peoples of these regions also suffered from heavy-handed treatment by their conquerors. Indians throughout lower Central America were captured and sold as slaves during the first decades of colonial rule, but nowhere was the slave trade as lucrative as in Nicaragua. Tens of thousands of Nicaraguan Indians were taken as slaves; most were transported to Peru, but large numbers died en route. In 1542 Indian slavery was officially outlawed, although Indians continued to be enslaved in subsequent years. When the Indian slave trade died out around 1550, it was not because the Spaniards were concerned about the legal ramifications of their actions but because there were so few Indians left.

Once the slave trade had died out and the isthmus and the rest of lower Central America were firmly under Spanish control, the Caribbean and Pacific port cities in Panama served primarily as a locus of movement of people and goods from Spain, New Spain, and the Caribbean to Peru and the rest of Pacific South America.

THE DEBATE OVER INDIAN RIGHTS

The disastrous effects of Spanish rule in the Caribbean caused a small number of contemporary observers to question Spain's right to govern these lands. How could Christians, charged with bringing the Word of God to these fellow humans, justify their presence in the face of such widespread suffering and abuse? In 1511, a Dominican priest named Antonio de Montesinos preached a famous sermon to the Spanish colonists of Hispaniola. He asked them, "Are these Indians not humans? Do they not have rational souls? Are you not obliged to love them as you love yourselves?" The *encomenderos* were outraged that a priest would dare to criticize their behavior. And thus was born a campaign for the human rights of the Indians.

An alliance between priests and the powerless that foreshadowed today's liberation theology, the movement was phrased in terms of Christian religion and tended to take a paternalistic view of the Indians as helpless victims. Nevertheless, the arguments of Montesinos and his followers speak across the centuries to anyone concerned about human rights and the survival of indigenous peoples.

The most influential convert to Montesinos's views was the Spanish adventurer-turned-Dominican-priest Bartolomé de Las Casas. Las Casas would come to view the entire Spanish enterprise in America as unjust and illegal. Although he would also play an important role among the native people of Mesoamerica as a missionary and the first bishop of Chiapas (see Chapter 5), he is most famous for his activities in Spain, where he publicized the brutal effects of Spanish colonialism. In Spain he found an ally in Francisco de Vitoria, a Dominican priest who was one of the country's foremost theologians.

Although Vitoria never visited America, he lent his immense knowledge of Classical philosophy and medieval theology, plus his skill in logic and rhetoric, to the cause of Indian rights. He concluded that the Indians were civilized people with full rights to their own territories. They were not irrational or otherwise mentally deficient. Customs that offended Spanish sensibilities were not unknown among Old World civilizations and, however shocking, did not provide grounds for invasion and conquest.

Las Casas's own writings went beyond Vitoria's careful reasonings, and into polemical, sensationalized accounts of Spanish brutality. His treatise entitled "A Brief Relation of the Destruction of the Indies" was printed in several European languages and helped give rise to the so-called "black legend" regarding the injustices associated with Spanish domination (Figure 4.2). To these European readers, the tract was less relevant as a description of the distant colonies than as a warning about their own possible fate, given Charles V's control over Habsburg and Holy Roman Empire lands outside of Spain and his intentions to enlarge these holdings. Las Casas's work thus helped to stir up anti-Spanish (and in Protestant territories, anti-Catholic) sentiment throughout Europe.

Las Casas never went so far as to doubt that the Indians would benefit from the Christian religion, but he argued that the only proper way to introduce

Figure 4.2 Title page of Las Casas's "Brief Relation on the Destruction of the Indies," Spanish edition, Seville, 1552. *Source:* Courtesy of the John Carter Brown Library at Brown University.

them to that faith was through peaceful contact—there was no justification for violent conquest. In his book entitled "Of the Only Way to Attract All Peoples to the True Religion," he proposed that missionaries should enter Indian territory unarmed and unaccompanied by soldiers. If they were welcomed and permitted to preach, the Indians—being as intelligent and rational as any other people—would soon be persuaded that Christianity was indeed superior to their traditional forms of worship. And if not, then so be it; the priests should depart in peace and hope that future ventures might prove more successful.

Charles V, troubled by the assertions of Las Casas and Vitoria, summoned a group of theologians to present arguments on both sides of these issues. This famous debate occurred at Valladolid, Spain, in 1550 and 1551. Las Casas was the spokesman for the anti-colonial side. His opponent was Juan Ginés de Sepúlveda, a distinguished theologian and historian. Sepúlveda based his arguments on the ancient Greek philosopher Aristotle's theory of natural slavery. He claimed that the Indians were by nature brutish and irrational and therefore inferior to Europeans. Not only did Europeans have the right to conquer and enslave them, but the Indians would actually benefit from their own subjection by being provided with superior behavioral models. Las Casas countered that the Indians were fully rational, of equal or superior capacity to all other peoples. Since the judges of the debate did not leave a record of their decision, we do not know who was considered the winner.

The pro-Indian movement, despite the stir it caused in Europe, did little to improve the lot of native people in the colonies. Las Casas and his allies had some impact on official Spanish policies, but these efforts to mollify the damage wrought by colonial rule were often ignored by the colonists who were supposed to enforce them. The whole controversy over whether the conquest was justified was little more than a game of words, since almost all of Mesoamerica was already under Spanish control by the time of the Valladolid debates, and there was no way that the conquerers were going to pack their bags and return home. Franciscan priests criticized Las Casas for focusing his energy on these philosophical debates instead of living among the native people and helping to defend them against their more immediate Spanish neighbors.

Some scholars have claimed that the pro-Indian movement of Las Casas and his allies indirectly promoted African slavery. Since their efforts contributed to the outlawing of Indian slavery (in law if not always in practice), Spanish colonists who wanted to own slaves had to look elsewhere. The African people sold as slaves by Portuguese traders were, for these colonists, a convenient source of forced labor.

It is true that Las Casas and Vitoria saw nothing inherently wrong with the enslavement of Africans; Vitoria even admitted that he would be willing to own such a slave. The pro-Indian movement's most effective argument against Indian slavery was not based on a belief in human equality. Rather, it was based on legalistic principles regarding the nature and authority of Spanish rule in the Americas. Spain could not claim jurisdiction over the Indies and simultaneously enslave their inhabitants, any more than the Spanish king could arbitrarily enslave citizens of his own nation. In Africa, however, where Spain had no territories and claimed no jurisdiction, Portuguese treatment of the native people, whether benign or brutal, was of no concern to Spain. African people had no rights that were legally recognized by Spain. Thus, if an African person had the misfortune to end up transported to the Indies, she or he had no legal grounds on which to claim mistreatment.

Although the movement for Indian rights was of limited benefit for the natives of the Spanish colonies—and did nothing to promote fair treatment of Africans—it did have a long-range impact on European intellectual currents. The efforts by Las Casas and his allies to describe and analyze native cultural patterns—in order more effectively to defend them—were among the first attempts to create systematic accounts of other cultures. Their insistence that these cultural patterns were valid in respect to the societies that practiced them was an early expression of cultural relativism—the idea that any particular cultural trait must be understood in relation to the rest of the culture, within which it makes sense.

In a broad sense, as Europeans learned about the Americas they were led to question many of their traditional assumptions about human nature. The very existence of a "New World" forced radical adjustments to a mindset that had always assumed that the world was composed of a trinity of continents: Europe, Africa, and Asia. A theology that explained everything in terms of the Bible and the accrued contemplations of medieval scholars was hard pressed to reduce all of the new knowledge to its traditional categories of thought.

Accounts of the native cultures were often highly distorted, alternately exalting and vilifying indigenous customs, but nevertheless they challenged Europeans to think in new ways about their own cultures and their own social structures. It became possible to imagine that one's own cultural patterns were arbitrary and might be changed. The accomplishments of native American civilizations were admired; at the same time, the native people were envied for their (presumed) freedom from some of the restrictions that circumscribed life in Europe. Critiques of European customs were phrased in terms of comparisons with native America. For example, Michel de Montaigne's essay "On Cannibalism," though based on an inaccurate conception of native Brazilian peoples, nevertheless constituted a brilliant satire of the author's sixteenth-century French society. As much as any other factor, the existence of America and its peoples drove European thought out of the Middle Ages and into the modern age.

It was the Aztec civilization, with its sophisticated art and oratory, its centralized state and extravagant court life, and its bloody rituals of human sacrifice and cannibalism, that provided European commentators with their most frequently cited examples of both native accomplishments and native depravity. Both Las Casas and Sepúlveda drew principally on Aztec ethnographic data in constructing their arguments for and against the legitimacy of native cultures. The need to justify the Aztec practices of human sacrifice and cannibalism was perhaps the greatest challenge that Las Casas faced in the debate. He insisted that the number of victims (Sepúlveda claimed 20,000 a year) had been grossly exaggerated—otherwise the land could not have been so populous as it was when the Spanish first arrived. Las Casas asserted that the number must have been less than 100 or even less than fifty. And even a century's total of victims amounted to fewer native lives than the Spaniards had sacrificed to their precious "goddess of greed" every year since their conquests began.

We now turn to the Spanish campaign against the Aztecs. Spain's victory over the Mexica capital of Tenochtitlán brought with it military control over a massive part of Mesoamerica, already organized into a tribute-producing empire. The story of this campaign is one of the great dramatic narratives of European colonial expansion; as such, it has accumulated elements of legend, with the conquering Cortés potrayed in heroic terms and the native people depicted as too paralyzed by their fatalistic religious beliefs to mount an effective resistance. Because of the many contradictions among the various versions of this story, both

Spanish and native, it is not possible to construct one single "true" account of what really happened. The following synopsis is based on a critical examination of native and Spanish sources.

THE CAMPAIGN AGAINST THE AZTECS

In February 1519 Hernán Cortés left the colony of Cuba on an expedition to explore the nearby mainland. Cortés had come to the Caribbean in 1504, from Extremadura in western Spain. He had participated in the campaign to take control of Cuba, and served as secretary to Diego Velásquez, Cuba's first colonial governor. The 1519 expedition, funded largely with Cortés's own money, consisted of eleven ships and over 500 men, sixteen horses, and a few cannons.

The first landfall was the island of Cozumel off the east coast of the Yucatán Peninsula. Here Cortés discovered Gerónimo de Aguilar, a Spaniard who had survived a shipwreck eight years earlier. Held captive by the local Maya on the mainland in the intervening years, Aguilar had learned to speak the Yucatec Maya language. After he joined Cortés he became an interpreter for the expedition. Another Spaniard who had survived the shipwreck was Gonzalo de Guerrero. Guerrero, however, had married a Maya woman and was living as a Maya. Unlike Aguilar, Guerrero had no interest in rejoining his compatriots; instead he chose to fight the Spanish invaders, and he reportedly died fighting on the Maya side.

After sailing westward around the Yucatán Peninsula, Cortés's expedition stopped at Potonchán, near the mouth of the Grijalva River in what is today the Mexican state of Tabasco. After initial hostilities, the local native leaders offered Cortés gifts, including several young women. One of these women was Malintzín, a native speaker of Nahuatl whose mother and stepfather had sold her into slavery among the Tabascan Indians, from whom she had learned the local Maya tongue. Malintzín (also called Marina, her Spanish name, and Malinche) and Aguilar were able to translate for Cortés's group from Maya to Nahuatl to Spanish (and vice versa). Marginalized by her own people, Malintzín threw her lot in with the Spaniards and proved an invaluable assistant to Cortés, especially as she quickly mastered Spanish. She eventually became Cortés's lover and bore him a son, Martín.

On Good Friday, April 19, 1519, Cortés landed near what is today the city of Veracruz. Here he had his first encounter with representatives of Motecuhzoma, the Aztec ruler. According to a native account written down in the 1550s, Motecuhzoma's emissaries brought special gifts to Cortés, which included complete costumes of three of the Aztecs' most important deities: Quetzalcoatl, Tezcatlipoca, and Tlaloc (see the discussion of these deities in Chapter 3). These costumes were made up of headdresses of precious gold and feathers, masks of turquoise; and ornaments of jade, gold, and seashells (Figure 4.3). Motecuhzoma

Figure 4.3 Motecuhzoma's emissaries present gifts to Cortés. To Cortés's left stands his Nahua interpreter, Malintzín. *Florentine Codex*, Book 12, folio 8v. Reprinted with permission from Fray Bernardino de Sahagún, *Historia General de las cosas de Nueva España,* Códice florentino. Facsimile of the Codex Florentinus of the Biblioteca Medicea Laurenciana, supervised by the Archivo General de la Nación (AGN) de México, Florence, Italy, 1979.

may have been seeking to establish a social relationship with the strangers through the exchange of gifts, while impressing them with his wealth. He may also have thought that these unexpected, peculiar-looking strangers were deities of some sort, or had been sent by some god. Their leader's reaction to the divine array would reveal what sort of god he represented. Reportedly, the messengers dressed Cortés up in the costume of Quetzalcoatl. It is highly unlikely that the Spaniard actually permitted this. In any case, his subsequent behavior diverged sharply from the model of the wise and priestly Quetzalcoatl: Rather than reciprocating with rich gifts of his own, Cortés had the messengers shackled and then demonstrated the power of the Spanish guns.

When the emissaries returned to Motecuhzoma with their report, the ruler was terrified and astounded:

> ... when he heard how the gun, at [the Spaniards'] command, discharged [the shot]; how it resounded as if it thundered when it went off. It indeed bereft one of strength; it shut off one's ears. And when it discharged, something like a round pebble came forth from within. Fire went showering forth; sparks went blazing forth. And its smoke smelled very foul; it had a fetid odor which verily wounded the head. And when [the shot] struck a mountain, it was as if it were destroyed, dissolved. And a tree was pulverized; it was as if it vanished; it was as if someone blew it away.

The emissaries also told of the Spaniards' armor, horses, and personal appearance:

> All iron was their war array. In iron they clothed themselves. With iron they covered their heads. Iron were their swords. Iron were their crossbows. Iron were their shields. Iron were their lances.
>
> And those which bore them on their backs, their deer, were as tall as roof terraces.
>
> And their bodies were everywhere covered; only their faces appeared. They were very white; they had chalky faces; they had yellow hair, though the hair of some was black. Long were their beards; they also were yellow. They were yellow-bearded. (Sahagún 1975:19)

Motecuhzoma sent more emissaries, wizards who offered the Spaniards food soaked in the blood of sacrificed captives. If the Spaniards had indeed been gods, they would have relished such dishes. But they were nauseated at the very smell, and instead chose to eat ordinary foods—tortillas, eggs, turkeys, and a variety of local fruits. But despite this evidence of the Spaniards' humanity, the wizards found that their magical spells had no effect upon the strangers.

While the native people wondered who and what the Spaniards were, the Spaniards themselves were beset with internal dissensions. Many in Cortés's party were eager to continue to the Aztec capital, but others were dissatisfied with Cortés, believing he had exceeded his orders, and still others had fallen ill. Cortés managed to have himself declared leader of the newly founded Spanish town of La Villa Rica de la Vera Cruz ("the rich town of the true cross," today's Veracruz), and as such, he claimed that he was no longer subject to Cuba's governor, Velásquez, but instead responsible directly to the King of Spain. The newly established *cabildo* (town council) of Vera Cruz sent emissaries to Spain to lobby for Crown support for Cortés at the same time that Velásquez was asserting new powers for himself on the mainland and continuing his efforts to contain Cortés. With several of Cortés's men threatening to desert and return to Cuba, Cortés took bold steps: He had two of the men executed and he sunk his ships, thus preventing any further attempts by his men to desert.

Before moving inland, Cortés made his first alliance with a native group, the Totonac Indians who lived in the town of Cempoala and who were weary of Aztec domination. In August 1519 the expedition began its journey toward Tenochtitlán, accompanied by a large party of Totonacs.

Within two weeks Cortés's party was in Tlaxcala, a powerful independent state that had never fallen to the Aztecs (See the account in Chapter 1). The Tlaxcalans decided to ally themselves with Cortés, and they provided him with several thousand warriors (Figure 4.4). The party moved next into Cholula, where they were initially received favorably, but it soon became clear that the Cholulans were preparing an ambush. The Spaniards, however, captured Cholulan leaders and then reportedly massacred thousands of Cholula warriors. Subsequently the Cholulans declared their loyalty to the Spanish king.

Shared enmity toward the Aztecs was the most important reason why these and other indigenous polities allied themselves with Cortés. Having themselves been taken by surprise by Spanish weapons and Spanish tactics, they recognized that these could be a potent force against their own enemies. In allying himself with these groups, Cortés began the process that would lead to his ultimate victory. His small army of Spaniards could have had no hope of conquering Mexico. But what he did was organize and oversee a joint uprising of the Aztecs' traditional enemies and subject states tired of paying tribute to Aztec overlords.

In early November 1519 Cortés's party, now made up of around 350 Spaniards and several thousand Tlaxcalan warriors, made the last leg of the journey to Tenochtitlán. As they approached the city, Motecuhzoma sent noblemen to present Cortés with more rich gifts. But instead of feeling humiliated that they had nothing of like value with which to reciprocate, the Spaniards only longed for more. Their reaction to the golden treasures is described in a native account:

Figure 4.4 Two of Tlaxcala's four principal lords declare their alliance with Cortés. The scrolls in front of the faces represent speech. *Florentine Codex*, Book 12, folio 21v. Reprinted with permission from Fray Bernardino de Sahagún, *Historia General de las cosas de Nueva España,* Códice florentino. Facsimile of the Codex Florentinus of the Biblioteca Medicea Laurenciana, supervised by the Archivo General de la Nación (AGN) de México, Florence, Italy, 1979.

> They gave them golden banners, precious feather streamers, and golden necklaces.
>
> And when they had given them these, they appeared to smile; they were greatly contented, gladdened. As if they were monkeys they seized upon the gold. It was as if their hearts were satisfied, brightened, calmed. For in truth they thirsted mightily for gold; they stuffed themselves with it; they starved for it; they lusted for it like pigs.
>
> And they went about lifting on high the golden banners; they went moving them back and forth; they went taking them to themselves. It was as if they babbled. What they said was gibberish (Sahagún 1975:31).

Bernal Díaz del Castillo, one of the Spanish soldiers accompanying Cortés, later penned a lengthy account of his experiences. When he and his fellows caught their first glimpse of the Basin of Mexico, they thought it looked like something out of Spain's popular romances of chivalry:

> . . . when we saw so many cities and villages built in the water and other great towns on dry land, and that straight and level Causeway going towards Mexico, we were amazed and said that it was like the enchantments they tell of in the legend of Amadis, on account of the great towers and cues [temples] and buildings rising from the water, and all built of masonry. And some of our soldiers even asked whether the things that we saw were not a dream. (Díaz del Castillo 1956:190–191)

On November 8, 1519, Cortés and his party entered the great city of Tenochtitlán, and Cortés and Motecuhzoma met face to face (Figure 4.5). At first, Motecuhzoma welcomed the Spaniards, treating them as honored guests and allowing them to reside in the imperial palace of his father, Axayacatl. Although some later accounts depict Motecuhzoma as extremely fearful, it is unlikely that at this point he felt very insecure: At a word from him, his armies could have conquered the Spaniards and Tlaxcalans or driven them out of the city.

But Cortés soon executed a daring ploy that Motecuhzoma could not have foreseen. Word of an attack on a small group of Spaniards on the Gulf Coast served as a pretext for Cortés to take Motecuhzoma prisoner and keep him in the Spaniards' quarters. Both Cortés and Motecuhzoma tried to maintain the charade that Motecuhzoma had willingly moved in to reside with the Spaniards: Motecuhzoma knew that his authority over his subjects was now very tenuous; Cortés knew that if he openly challenged Motecuhzoma the Spaniards would be killed or driven out.

Cortés and the Spaniards effectively governed Motecuhzoma's kingdom for five months, issuing orders, collecting tribute, and attempting to suppress the elaborate sacrificial rituals. In April 1520 the situation changed when it was learned that a fleet of eighteen ships sent by Governor Velásquez had landed on the Gulf Coast. The leader, Pánfilo de Narváez, had orders to arrest Cortés and bring him to Cuba to stand trial. Cortés's response was to try to win Narváez and his men over to his side through a combination of bribery and armed attack. The latter was accomplished when a force, led by Cortés, attacked Narváez's troops as

Figure 4.5 The first meeting between Motecuhzoma and Cortés. The native artist highlights the crucial role of Malintzín, Cortés's Nahua interpreter. *Florentine Codex*, Book 12, 26r. Reprinted with permission from Fray Bernardino de Sahagún, *Historia General de las cosas de Nueva España,* Códice florentino. Facsimile of the Codex Florentinus of the Biblioteca Medicea Laurenciana, supervised by the Archivo General de la Nación (AGN) de México, Florence, Italy, 1979.

they slept. Narváez was captured and his men surrendered to Cortés, thus increasing the size of Cortés's force.

Meanwhile, in Tenochtitlán, Pedro de Alvarado, whom Cortés had left in charge, was losing control of the situation. Alvarado flew into a rage upon hearing of the celebration of a traditional Aztec festival in honor of Huitzilopochtli that was to include human sacrifice, even though he had initially given permission for the ceremony to take place. Alvarado ordered his men to attack the defenseless participants, and hundreds of Mexica were massacred. This prompted retaliation against the Spaniards: There were attempts to burn the palace where they were housed, and several Spaniards were killed. At this moment, Cortés and his entourage, which included several thousand Tlaxcalan warriors, returned to Tenochtitlán. The Mexica allowed them to join Alvarado and Motecuhzoma, but attacks on the Spanish compound continued.

In the midst of growing tension, members of the Mexica ruling elite, who had long opposed Motecuhzoma's cooperation with the Spaniards, decided to depose Motecuhzoma and elect his brother, Cuitlahuac, to succeed him. Cortés, who had not imagined that the native "king" could be so easily removed from office, found himself with a useless hostage. In late June, Motecuhzoma was killed. Spanish accounts claim that he was stoned by his former subjects; native accounts claim he was murdered by the Spaniards. The situation for the Spaniards was grim, and Cortés decided to retreat (Figure 4.6).

Figure 4.6 The *noche triste*. The Spaniards, with their Tlaxcalan allies, begin their flight from the city. A man standing atop a temple and a woman drawing water from a canal raise the alarm. *Florentine Codex*, Book 12, 42v. Reprinted with permission from Fray Bernardino de Sahagún, *Historia General de las cosas de Nueva España,* Códice florentino. Facsimile of the Codex Florentinus of the Biblioteca Medicea Laurenciana, supervised by the Archivo General de la Nación (AGN) de México, Florence, Italy, 1979.

The night of the Spaniards' retreat, usually identified as June 30, 1520, has come to be called the *noche triste* (the night of sorrows) because of the high casualty figures on both sides of the conflict. As the Spaniards and their Tlaxcalan allies attempted to flee the island of Tenochtitlán on the causeways, they were attacked by Aztec warriors. Many were killed, and many others drowned in the lake, some of them weighed down by the gold they had looted from Motecuhzoma's treasury. What was left of Cortés's troops made their way back to the safety of Tlaxcala.

In the following months Cortés strengthened his position east of the Basin of Mexico by carrying out raids and making new allies. Several hundred Spanish reinforcements arrived from Jamaica and Cuba, and the foundation of a garrison along the road to Veracruz established control over routes to the south. By late December Cortés and his troops were making the final preparations for an assault on Tenochtitlán. By now Cortés had a force of over 700 Spaniards and an estimated 75,000 Tlaxcalan allies as well as eighty-six horses and fifteen cannons.

In the meantime, the people of Tenochtitlán may have experienced their first encounter with an Old World infectious disease: smallpox (Figure 4.7). It is

Figure 4.7 The smallpox epidemic. A woman, possibly a doctor, attempts to comfort a sick man; other sufferers lie helpless on their sleeping-mats. *Florentine Codex*, Book 12, 53v. Reprinted with permission from Fray Bernardino de Sahagún, *Historia General de las cosas de Nueva España,* Códice Florentino. Facsimile of the Codex Florentinus of the Biblioteca Medicea Laurenciana, supervised by the Archivo General de la Nación (AGN) de México, Florence, Italy, 1979.

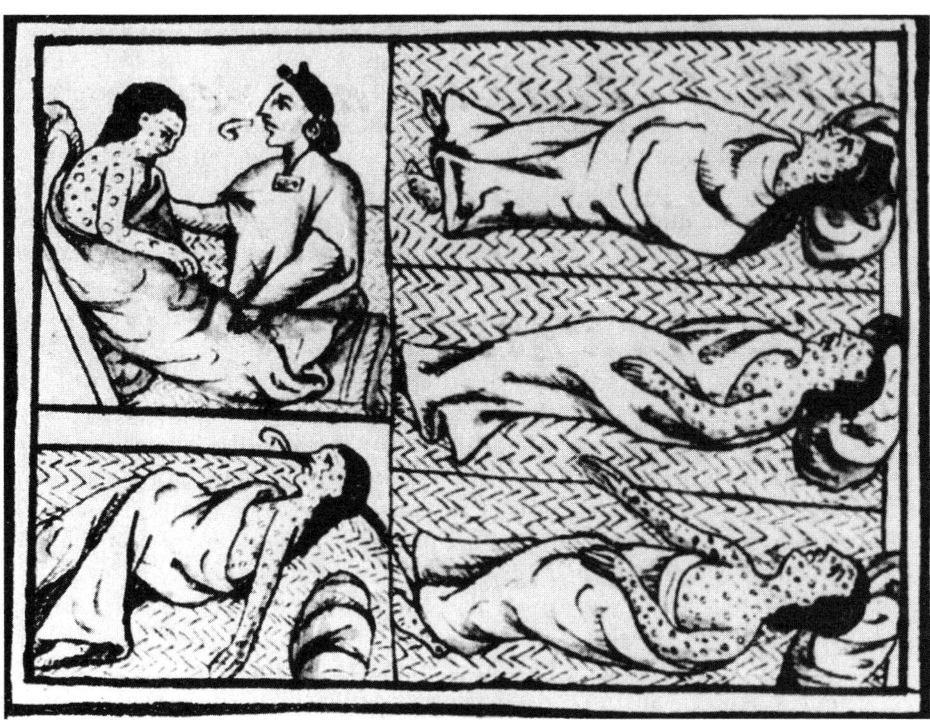

not entirely certain that this epidemic struck in 1520. The accounts of Cortés and other conquistadors do not mention it; it is possible that the epidemic did not occur until after Spanish control was established the following year. However, the principal native history of the conquest, as well as other native documents and an important chronicle written by a Spanish priest in 1541, place the smallpox outbreak in 1520 after the *noche triste* retreat and before Cortés's final campaign. In addition to causing population losses, the epidemic could have had a severely demoralizing effect on the survivors, who had never before experienced widespread suffering from infectious disease. The native chronicle gives this account of the disease's progress:

> No longer could they walk; they only lay in their abodes, in their beds. No longer could they move; no longer could they bestir themselves; no longer could they raise themselves, no longer could they stretch themselves out on their sides, no longer could they stretch themselves out face down, no longer could they stretch themselves out on their backs. And when they bestirred themselves, much did they cry out. There was much perishing. Like a covering, covering-like, were the pustules. Indeed many people died of them, and many just died of hunger; there was no one to take care of another; there was no one to attend to another.
>
> And on some, each pustule was placed on them only far apart; they did not cause much suffering, neither did many die of them. And many people were harmed by them on their faces; their faces were roughened. Of some, the eyes were injured; they were blinded. (Sahagún 1975:83)

This account is an accurate description of how smallpox afflicts its victims. The most severely ill, those with a great many pustules, are unable to move about. If a whole family or neighborhood is stricken, such that no one is able to tend to the ill, people are as likely to die of thirst or starvation as of the virus itself. People with relatively few pustules are likely to survive, but may be left scarred by pockmarks or even blind.

The new Mexica ruler, Cuitlahuac, also died between the *noche triste* and the Spanish assault. It has often been assumed that he died of smallpox, but no source states this explicitly. Cuitlahuac was succeeded by Cuauhtemoc, a nephew of Motecuhzoma selected for his prowess in war. Cuauhtemoc led a valiant resistance against Cortés and his allies.

Cortés's strategy for the final assault on Tenochtitlán involved first subduing settlements along the lakeshore, which effectively isolated Tenochtitlán. A blockade kept fresh water and food from reaching the island city. People had to drink the briny water of the lake, and when their food stores ran out they were reduced to eating such things as marsh grass and worms. The final blow was struck through a combined effort by lake and land. Spanish and Tlaxcalan foot soldiers, who approached Tenochtitlán by the three major causeways, were aided by thirteen sailing vessels that had been constructed under Spanish supervision, disassembled, and then reconstructed on the shore of Lake Texcoco (Figure 4.8).

The final battle for Tenochtitlán lasted for almost three months. Differences between Spanish and native military tactics, as well as the element of sur-

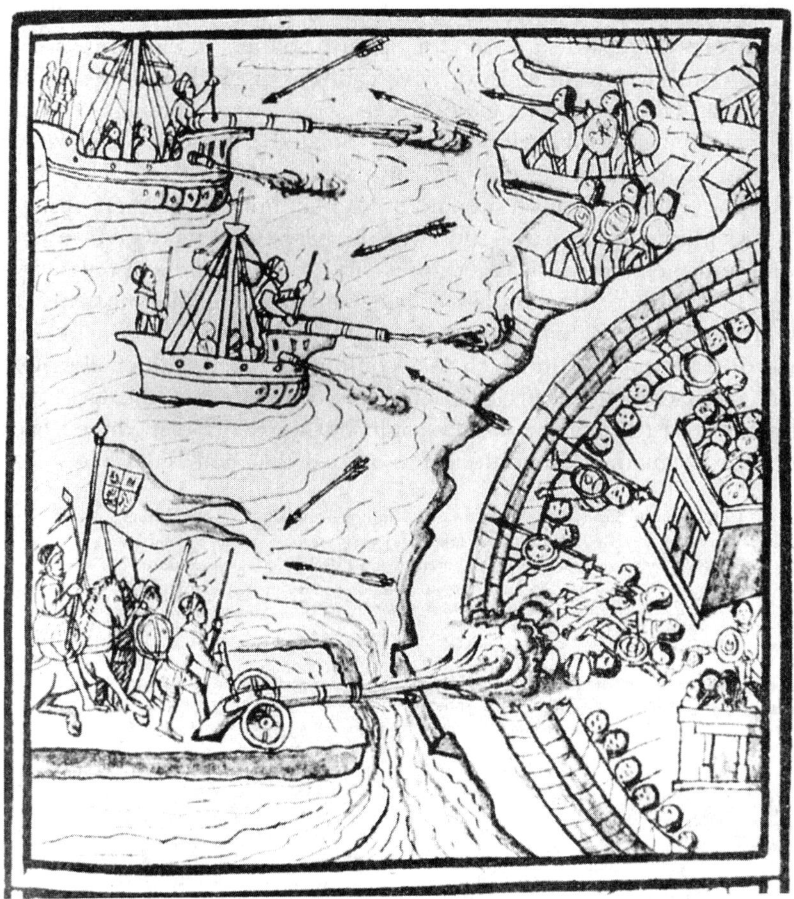

Figure 4.8 The siege of Tenochtitlán. The Spaniards attack from their ships, while Mexica soldiers fight back from canoes and from the city's walls and rooftops. *Florentine Codex*, Book 12, 56r. Reprinted with permission from Fray Bernardino de Sahagún, *Historia General de las cosas de Nueva España,* Códice florentino. Facsimile of the Codex Florentinus of the Biblioteca Medicea Laurenciana, supervised by the Archivo General de la Nación (AGN) de México, Florence, Italy, 1979.

prise fostered by Spanish horses, huge dogs, cannons, and guns (which were so clumsy and inaccurate that they caused relatively few actual casualties), had favored the Spaniards in their earlier battles against native groups. The goal of native warfare was not to kill or maim the enemy upon the battlefield but to seize uninjured prisoners to take home as captives. Soldiers fought one-on-one, seeking to display their individual prowess rather than to maximize the other side's casualties. In contrast, the Spaniards fought as a closed and—to native warriors—impenetrable rank, while indiscriminately killing and wounding warriors and even unarmed civilians. On an open battlefield, a small group of Spaniards was able to vanquish a much larger native army.

The conquest of the island city, however, posed a greater challenge. In the narrow streets there was no space for Spanish soldiers to close ranks. Horses had limited footing. It was difficult to move cannons around, and equally difficult to find clear targets amid the tangle of streets, canals, and buildings. Mexica warriors could carry out guerrilla-style attacks on isolated parties of Spaniards and their allies, then disappear along the familiar alleyways (Figure 4.9). They also learned quickly how to dodge cannon fire and how to kill horses with their obsidian-bladed swords. Captured Spaniards—and even horses—were sacrificed atop the great pyramid and their heads displayed on a rack, to the distress of fellow Spaniards.

To conquer Tenochtitlán, Cortés and his allies had virtually to level it. They proceeded bit by bit, tearing down buildings and filling in canals in order to provide a flat surface on which they could move freely and challenge their enemies to open combat. The city's defenders, weakened by the lack of food and fresh water, resisted as long as they could but were gradually driven back.

Historian Inga Clendinnen has argued that both sides allowed the battle

Figure 4.9 Fighting in the city streets: Mexica warriors unhorse and kill a Spanish soldier. *Florentine Codex*, Book 12, 58r. Reprinted with permission from Fray Bernardino de Sahagún, *Historia General de las cosas de Nueva España*, Códice florentino. Facsimile of the Codex Florentinus of the Biblioteca Medicea Laurenciana, supervised by the Archivo General de la Nación (AGN) de México, Florence, Italy, 1979.

to drag on longer than they wanted. Cultural differences made each side unable to understand the other's behavior, including behaviors that symbolized victory or defeat. They did not know how to terminate a kind of warfare that was previously unknown to both sides, or how to negotiate terms with an enemy whose actions seemed so alien and unpredictable. Cortés ended up destroying much of the beautiful city he coveted; the Mexica, not knowing how to negotiate their own surrender, were driven to a level of desperation they had never known was possible.

Finally, on August 13, 1521, Cuauhtemoc was taken prisoner by the Spaniards as he attempted to leave the city by canoe. The battle was over, though not the killing: The Tlaxcalans went on to perpetrate a massacre of their long-time enemies so brutal that even Cortés claimed to be shocked by it—although they had learned of such behavior only when Cortés directed the earlier massacre at Cholula. One hundred thousand or more Mexica may have died during the siege and subsequent massacre. A Mexica account describes the conquered city:

> Broken spears lie in the roads;
> we have torn our hair in our grief.
> The houses are roofless now, and their walls
> are red with blood.
>
> Worms are swarming in the streets and plazas,
> and the walls are splattered with gore.
> The water has turned red, as if it were dyed,
> and when we drink it,
> it has the taste of brine.
>
> We have pounded our hands in despair
> against the adobe walls,
> for our inheritance, our city, is lost and dead.
> The shields of our warriors were its defense,
> but they could not save it. (León-Portilla 1962:137–138)

With the defeat of the Aztec state, virtually all of the territories subsumed under what had once been the Aztec empire also were now under de facto Spanish rule. The native allies who joined with Cortés in order to free themselves from Mexica rule would now find themselves subject to overlords whose demands were even more burdensome.

THE CONQUEST OF MICHOACÁN

Once the Aztec empire was firmly under Spanish control, the Spaniards began their expansion to other areas of Mesoamerica. To the west and north of the Basin of Mexico, in what is today the state of Michoacán, was the powerful Tarascan or Purépecha state. From their capital at Tzintzuntzán on Lake Pátzcuaro, the Tarascans maintained an independent polity that had successfully resisted every attempt by the Aztecs to impinge upon its territory (see Chapter 3).

Before any official contacts between Tarascans and Spaniards took place, a smallpox epidemic hit Michoacán, and one of its first victims was the Tarascan ruler or Cazonci, Zuangua. He was succeeded by one of his sons, Tzintzicha Tangachoan, and as the new Cazonci, this young man was faced with difficult decisions about how he would respond to the Spaniards.

The first face-to-face contacts between Spaniards and the Tarascans took place in February 1521, before Tenochtitlán had fallen. A year later Cristóbal de Olid was sent by Cortés to explore in the region. Initial contacts between the Tarascans and the Spaniards were friendly, although Olid ultimately failed to subdue the region. In 1525 the Cazonci converted to Christianity, formally accepted Spanish domination, and requested that friars be sent to Michoacán. The Cazonci apparently hoped that peaceful acceptance of Spanish rule would result in his maintaining some degree of autonomy. But this was not to be.

In 1528 Nuño de Guzmán, who would earn a reputation as one of the most ruthless conquistadors and treasure-seekers in New Spain, took the office of President of the Audiencia of Mexico, the colony's first ruling body. Early on, he began pressing the Cazonci to turn over more gold and silver, and he had the Cazonci imprisoned in Mexico City on more than one occasion, holding him for ransom. But what must have at one time seemed an inexhaustible source of gold and silver was now in short supply. In 1529–30 Guzmán organized a large expedition, made up of both Spaniards and Indian allies, to bring Michoacán more firmly under Spanish control.

Guzmán's expedition quickly made its way from Mexico City to Tzintzuntzán, leaving looted and burned towns and tortured victims in its wake. Shortly after arriving in the Tarascan capital, Guzmán took the Cazonci prisoner, and he was put on trial for a number of offenses—the most serious being interference with the *encomienda* system and ordering the killing of several Spaniards. After being tortured by Guzmán, the Cazonci confessed guilt. His sentence was harsh—he was to be dragged through town behind a horse and burned at the stake. With the death of the Cazonci, the great Tarascan kingdom ended.

THE MAYA AREA

A situation quite different from that of Central Mexico confronted the Spaniards in the Maya region, where no single group dominated large territories (see Chapter 3). Within the Maya area were numerous small polities that were often at war against each other. Here, the Spaniards faced a more protracted battle. It was simply not possible to gain control of the Maya area except through a series of campaigns that could subjugate each region one by one. This process took over 175 years.

In Chiapas initial contact may have occurred as early as 1522, but it was not until 1524 that a small group of Spaniards, led by Luis Marín, made a concerted effort to bring the Tzotzil Maya and the neighboring Chiapanecs, a non-Maya group, under Spanish control. While the Spaniards apparently achieved some military success, their failure to establish a Spanish community in the region rendered any military victories meaningless.

The definitive conquest of the area occurred during the 1527–28 campaigns of Diego Mazariegos, in which the Zoques, the Chiapanecs, and the Tzotzil and Tzeltal Maya were pacified. By 1535 a Spanish town, Ciudad Real (today San Cristóbal de Las Casas), was established in Chiapas and within a few years the outlying areas also were under Spanish control.

The Yucatán Peninsula was not brought under Spanish control until 1547, although initial contacts between Spaniards and Maya there had taken place several years before Cortés's arrival in Central Mexico. Early expeditions were received with hostility and did not succeed in establishing any permanent Spanish presence. There is good evidence that the peninsula was hit by a series of epidemics before the first party of conquistadors, under Francisco de Montejo, arrived in 1527. Initially, Montejo and his men were received in peace, but within months they met with considerable opposition. After two years Montejo left to renew supplies and enlist more men.

Montejo's second campaign took place between 1531 and 1534. This time, he concentrated more on the west coast of the peninsula. After some initial successes this campaign, too, met with defeat. Toward the end of the campaign word reached the expedition of the riches to be found in Peru. By this time it was clear that there was no gold in Yucatán, and most of Montejo's men abandoned him to go to Peru. Now left vulnerable to attacks by the Maya, Montejo was forced to withdraw.

The final campaign to pacify Yucatán was carried out by Montejo's son, Francisco de Montejo the Younger, from 1540 to 1547. Although much of the Yucatán Peninsula was under Spanish control by 1545, uprisings occurred for the next two years. Even then, Spanish control was not complete, for many Indians fled south to the Petén. The Maya in the Petén would successfully resist Spanish domination for another 150 years.

The Spanish invasion of Guatemala was preceded by a smallpox epidemic in 1520. Three years later, in December 1523, Pedro de Alvarado was commissioned by Cortés to lead a group of over 400 Spanish soldiers and hundreds of Tlaxcalan warriors south to Guatemala. En route Alvarado and his troops successfully subdued Mixtecs in Oaxaca, Zapotecs in Tehuantepec, and Mixe-Zoque groups in Soconusco.

As in Central Mexico, in Guatemala the Spaniards were aided by a polarized situation that had been created by the existence of a powerful and expansionist state, the Quiché. The Quiché Maya had made many enemies during the course of expansion; by 1523 their power was waning, but many groups that had once been subjugated by them were willing to join with the Spaniards to ensure their defeat.

Alvarado's first encounters with the Quiché warriors came in early 1524 in battles on the Pacific piedmont and in the highlands of western Guatemala. During hostilities near Xelajú (today Quetzaltenango), the Quiché leader, Tecum, was killed (Figure 4.10). A passage from a Quiché document, the *Títulos de la Casa Ixquin-Nehaib*, describes the personal battle between Tecum and Alvarado in vivid detail. Told from a Quiché point of view, this version casts the encounter in mythological terms. In attacking Alvarado, Tecum is transformed into a valiant eagle; in death he becomes a resplendent quetzal bird whose beauty astonishes the Spanish leader. Even in defeat the native hero is glorified (see Box 4.2 for the full text on the death of Tecum from the Quiché perspective).

After this defeat, the Quiché invited the Spaniards to return with them to their capital, Gumarcaaj or Utatlán. Once there, Alvarado realized that the Spaniards had been led into a trap, and he and his men slipped away, taking several Quiché lords prisoner. Alvarado then fought to bring the area surrounding Utatlán under control, and Utatlán itself was burned. Here the Spaniards were aided by the Cakchiquel Maya, enemies of the Quiché.

With the conquest of the Quiché complete, Alvarado founded the first Spanish capital in Guatemala at the Cakchiquel city of Iximché on July 25, 1524. At first the Cakchiquels welcomed the Spaniards, but Alvarado's increasing demands soon led the Cakchiquel to revolt. In fact, a general revolt against the Spaniards took place in 1526.

One by one, the other Maya groups of the Guatemalan highlands fell to

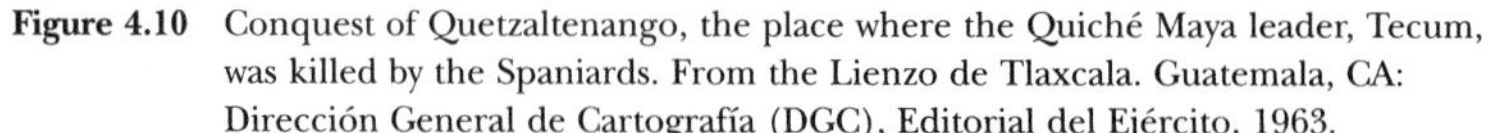

Figure 4.10 Conquest of Quetzaltenango, the place where the Quiché Maya leader, Tecum, was killed by the Spaniards. From the Lienzo de Tlaxcala. Guatemala, CA: Dirección General de Cartografía (DGC), Editorial del Ejército, 1963.

Box 4.2 *The Death of Tecum*

> . . . this captain [Tecum] brought many people from many towns, ten thousand Indians in all, all came armed with their bows and arrows, slings, lances and other arms. And Captain Tecum, before leaving his town and in front of the chiefs, demonstrated his courage and his spirit and he put on wings with which he flew and his two arms and legs were covered with feathers and he wore a crown, and on his chest he wore a very large emerald which looked like a mirror, and he wore another on his forehead. And another on his back. He looked very gallant. This captain flew like an eagle, he was a great nobleman and a great sorcerer. . . . [after a battle of many hours] the Spaniards killed many Indians, there was no count of those whom they killed, not a single Spaniard died, only the Indians who had been brought by Captain Tecum and much blood ran from all the Indians. . . . And then Captain Tecum flew up, he came like an eagle full of feathers that grew from his body, they were not artificial; he wore wings which also sprang from his body and he wore three crowns, one was of gold, another of pearls and another of diamonds and emeralds. This Captain Tecum came with the intention of killing Tunadiu [Alvarado] who came on horseback and he hit the horse instead of the Adelantado and he cut off the head of the horse with one lance. It was not a lance of iron but of shiny stone and this captain had placed a spell on it. And when he saw that it was not the Adelantado but the horse who had died he returned to fly overhead. . . . Then the Adelantado awaited him with his lance and he impaled this Captain Tecum with it. . . . [Captain Tecum] appeared covered with quetzal feathers and very beautiful plumes, for which reason this town of Quetzaltenango ["Quetzal fortress"] was given its name, because here is where the death of this Captain Tecum came to pass. And immediately the Adelantado called to all his soldiers to come and see the beauty of the quetzal Indian. Then the Adelantado told his soldiers that he had never seen another Indian as gallant and as noble and covered with such beautiful quetzal feathers, in Mexico, nor in Tlaxcala, nor in any of the towns that he had conquered. . . . And as the rest of the Indians saw that the Spaniards had killed their captain, they fled, and immediately the Adelantado Don Pedro de Alvarado, seeing that the soldiers of this Captain Tecum were fleeing, said that they also should die, and the Spanish soldiers pursued the Indians and caught up with them and killed all of them. There were so many Indians that they killed that they made a river of blood . . . all the water became blood and the day became red because of the great bloodshed that day. (Recinos 1984:89–94)

the Spanish invaders. The Tzutujil, the Mam, the Pokomam, the Chortí, and others were all under Spanish control within a few years.

For almost 200 years after the first contact between Spaniards and the Maya of the Yucatán Peninsula, the dense forests of the Petén served as a zone of refuge for Maya fleeing Spanish rule in the northern part of the peninsula. In fact, the movement of peoples between northern Yucatán and the Petén had begun well before the arrival of the Spaniards (see Chapter 2). The Itzá were one of the groups who, according to native tradition, fled to the Petén lakes region after the demise of Chichén Itzá and/or Mayapán. There they established a capital, Noh Petén, on the island where the modern town of Flores lies today. In the sixteenth century, the Itzá polity was composed of a confederacy of four territorial groups, with the Canek lineage in control of the most powerful group.

The Spaniards showed little interest in the Petén during the sixteenth century, but several attempts were made in the seventeenth century to bring the Itzá under Spanish rule. The Spaniards were not successful until 1697, and the fascinating story of the final conquest of the Itzá is worth recounting.

For many years the influence of Maya prophecies in the conquest of the Itzá has received attention. It has been argued that the Maya view of cyclical history meant that certain events were destined to be repeated at specific dates within calendrical cycles. The year 1697 has long been thought to be one such date, a date that was destined to bring political collapse. According to this view, the conquest of 1697 was inevitable; the Itzá simply surrendered knowing that any attempt to resist the Spaniards would be futile. Recent research by ethnohistorian Grant Jones has led him to call into question this interpretation, suggesting that the situation was, in fact, more complex.

Jones does not deny that the Itzá were influenced by prophecies and a cyclical view of history but argues that, in the case of the events of 1697, it was the Spaniards, in particular a certain Franciscan priest, who took advantage of their knowledge of Maya beliefs to try to negotiate a peaceful surrender. Subsequent events make it clear that, contrary to some reports, these efforts did not succeed.

The Itzá put up a valiant fight, and it was only after the Spaniards slaughtered huge numbers of Indians that they succeeded in taking the city. One report states that the Spaniards killed "such an innumerable quantity that the dead bodies of the Indians appeared as an island in the lake."

If the Itzá did not surrender to the Spaniards peacefully, then what was the role of prophecy in these events? Jones suggests that internal struggles within the confederacy had disrupted the existing balance of power in which Canek (leader of the ruling lineage) enjoyed a dominant position. The year 1697 was, in fact, seen by the Itzá as a year of political collapse foretold by the prophecies, but it was interpreted as the time when the local ruling dynasty would change, not the time to submit to Spanish rule. Canek's lineage had ruled over the Itzá for 256 years, which constituted an entire calendrical cycle, and rival lineages sought a change of command. Canek himself, it seems, had agreed to surrender in the hope that the Spaniards would let him remain in power as governor. But his strongest rivals had effectively seized power, and they were the ones who put up the resistance to the Spanish army. Thus, despite the decades of cautious negotiations aimed at a peaceful surrender, the last independent Mesoamerican kingdom came to a violent end. Canek, his hopes of alliance shattered, ended up a prisoner in Guatemala City.

SUGGESTED READINGS

CLENDINNEN, INGA 1991 "Fierce and Unnatural Cruelty": Cortés and the conquest of Mexico. *Representations* 33:65–100.

COLUMBUS, CHRISTOPHER 1989 *The Diario of Christopher Columbus's First Voyage to America, 1492–1493.* Edited and translated by Oliver Dunn and James E. Kelley, Jr. Norman: University of Oklahoma Press.

CORTÉS, HERNÁN 1986 *Letters from Mexico.* Edited and translated by Anthony Pagden. New Haven: Yale University Press.

DÍAZ DEL CASTILLO, BERNAL 1956 *The Discovery and*

Conquest of Mexico. Edited and translated by A. P. Maudslay. New York: Farrar, Straus and Giroux.

ELLIOT, J. H. 1963 *Imperial Spain 1469–1716.* New York: New American Library.

GIBSON, CHARLES 1966 *Spain in America.* New York: Harper and Row.

GREENBLATT, STEPHEN 1991 *Marvelous Possessions: The Wonder of the New World.* Chicago: University of Chicago Press.

HANKE, LEWIS 1949 *The Spanish Struggle for Justice in the Conquest of America.* Philadelphia: University of Pennsylvania Press.

LAS CASAS, BARTOLOMÉ DE 1992 *The Devastation of the Indies: A Brief Account.* Edited by Bill Donovan. Translated by Herma Briffault. Baltimore: Johns Hopkins University Press.

LEÓN-PORTILLA, MIGUEL 1992 *The Broken Spears: The Aztec Account of the Conquest of Mexico.* Boston: Beacon Press.

WARREN, J. BENEDICT 1985 *The Conquest of Michoacán: The Spanish Domination of the Tarascan Kingdom in Western Mexico, 1521–1530.* Norman: University of Oklahoma Press.

Chapter 5 The Colonial Period in Mesoamerica

Despite the trauma of the conquest and the demographic collapse that occurred over the course of the sixteenth century, the native peoples of Mesoamerica survived. Their populations eventually rebounded, and at the end of the Colonial period they still accounted for the majority of the region's inhabitants.

Ruled by Spain for three centuries, the peoples of Mesoamerica underwent the usual fate of a colonized people: They were systematically impoverished, their resources and productive capacity redirected toward the enrichment of the invaders and their descendants. However, in some ways Spain pursued a policy of indirect rule, allowing the native people to run many of their own affairs within limits set by the colonizers.

This chapter begins by describing how Spain ruled and administered its Mesoamerican territories and then discusses the colonial institutions that had direct impact on the native people, with particular attention to the role of the Catholic Church. We then examine colonial society, first giving an overview of the social makeup of the colony as a whole and then focusing on the way of life that developed in the surviving native communities.

THE COLONIAL REGIME

The Spanish king was, in all respects—economic, political, and religious—the supreme ruler over Spain and its territories. A portion of all the wealth generated in the Indies was destined for the royal treasury. The king and his advisers also had ultimate political power, overseeing the appointment of all high-ranking colonial officials. In addition, the Crown had been granted extraordinary privileges by the pope, which meant that the Spanish king controlled all the ecclesiastical affairs in his domain. But despite all this power and the vast wealth of the empire, the "golden age" of Spain was fleeting.

Crown strategies for controlling and profiting from its empire were based on maintaining strict monopolistic powers over the movement of goods and people between Spain and its colonies. Ideally, the colonies would provide raw materials as well as ready markets for goods manufactured in Spain. The House of Trade (*Casa de Contratación*) was created in 1503 to grant licenses to all ships and merchants bound for the Indies, to monitor imports and exports, and to provide permits to all passengers travelling to the New World.

The first years of Spanish colonial rule in the Mesoamerican region were marked by power struggles over the spoils of victory. The Crown, always fearful that the development of an aristocracy in the colonies would threaten its own power, actively sought to create a highly centralized colonial government directly under its control. But from the beginning of Spanish occupation, intense rivalries developed among the many Spanish factions over control of the vast resources that the New World offered—whether they be precious metals or Indian labor. Strong animosities existed between the Crown and the conquistadors, between Crown-appointed officials and colonists, and between members of the clergy and colonists. Arguments raged over the status of the native population: Were Indians to be treated as humans? Could they be enslaved? The implementation of various laws intended to protect the Indians provoked outraged responses from colonists.

The most notorious example of this was the attempted implementation of the New Laws of 1542–43, a set of laws that had been heavily promoted by the Dominican activist Bartolomé de Las Casas (see Chapter 4). These laws were intended to end certain abuses against the native people. At the heart of the New Laws was a new attempt by the Crown to regulate and ultimately to eliminate the *encomienda* system.

We have already seen that the *encomienda* system had originated in medieval Spain and had been introduced in the Caribbean, where it was at least partially responsible for the demise of much of the native population there. On the Mesoamerican mainland, as elsewhere, the *encomienda* system consisted of rewarding Spaniards (initially the conquistadors) for service to the king by "commending" or entrusting to them the tribute and labor of a given group of Indians—usually the Indians of a specific town. The Spanish *encomenderos* were charged with the Christianization of the Indians in return for their goods and labor.

The merits of the *encomienda* system on the mainland—after its disastrous effects in the Caribbean—were hotly debated, with the Crown opposed to it on principle but grudgingly allowing conquistadors to be given *encomiendas* as rewards for their part in the conquest.

A few *encomiendas* were granted to very high-ranking Indians, in recognition of their status and in an attempt to pacify individuals who might otherwise pose a challenge to Spanish rule. For example, doña Isabel de Motecuhzoma was granted the important town of Tlacopan (or Tacuba) in *encomienda.* She was the eldest surviving child of the Aztec emperor Motecuhzoma with his principal wife. According to some accounts, she was also the widow of Cuauhtemoc. The last of her three Spanish husbands made a prolonged but ultimately unsuccessful effort to secure the perpetual continuation of her *encomienda* rights for the couple's descendants, on the grounds that his wife was the legitimate heir of her father's throne.

The New Laws prohibited slavery of Indians, regulated the tribute that could be paid by Indians to their *encomenderos,* and, most important, forbade the granting of any new *encomiendas* and prohibited the inheritance of those already in existence. Throughout the colonies, the New Laws were met with outrage on the part of the Spanish colonists. In Peru their implementation resulted in the death of the viceroy followed by several years of civil war. In New Spain the portion of the New Laws that prohibited new *encomiendas* and the inheritance of *encomiendas* was simply not enforced.

After several years of instability, a governing apparatus was put into place that was based on the organization of government in Spain. Sixteenth-century Spain did not recognize a separation of church and state. Spanish—as well as Spanish colonial—government was divided into five branches: civil, judicial, military, treasury, and ecclesiastical. The jurisdictional units for the five branches of government were not necessarily the same, and the powers of officials—the king as well as some lower-ranking officials—were broad, often cross-cutting the various branches. We will briefly outline the civil and ecclesiastical administrations.

The Spanish Crown ruled its American colonies with the help of the Council of the Indies, which was charged with overseeing Spain's New World possessions. In the colonies royal power was delegated to viceroys. By the 1540s there were two viceroyalties in the Americas, New Spain, and Peru. Within the viceroyalties were smaller jurisdictions called Audiencias ruled by a group of Crown-appointed judges or *oidores.* Different regions of Mesoamerica fell under the jurisdictions of the Audiencias of Mexico, created in 1527; Guatemala, created in 1543; and Guadalajara, created in 1548 (Figure 5.1).

Smaller political units were kingdoms *(reinos)* and provinces *(provincias),* which were ruled by governors; even smaller units, called *corregimientos* and *alcaldías mayores,* were governed by lesser-ranking officials, *corregidores* and *alcaldes mayores,* who were subordinate to the governors. A special category of *corregidor,* the *corregidor de indios,* was responsible for the administration of Indian towns. Finally, municipalities—both Spanish and Indian—were governed by a group of officials collectively called the *cabildo,* or town council. In addition to this hierarchy of officials, the Crown regularly appointed royal inspectors *(visitadores)* who conducted inspections *(visitas)* and filed reports directly to the king. The king also was kept informed about the performance of colonial officials through a program of investigations *(residendias)* whereby testimony was given by any interested party about the behavior of officials during their term of office.

Figure 5.1 The main Spanish colonial jurisdictions established in Mesoamerica during the 16th century. After Howard F. Cline, "Introductory Notes on Territorial Divisions of Middle America," *The Handbook of Middle American Indians, Volume 12: Guide to Ethnohistorical Sources, Pt. 1,* volume editor Howard F. Cline, general editor Robert Wauchope. Austin, TX: University of Texas Press, 1972, p. 25.

In the eighteenth century, after the French Bourbon dynasty replaced the Habsburg dynasty on the Spanish throne, the administrative organization of Spain and its colonies was overhauled. In the colonies one of the changes made by Bourbon King Charles III was the introduction, in 1786, of the intendancy system developed in France to strengthen royal control. This resulted in the creation of new jurisdictions that replaced, and in many cases crosscut, previous divisions. Similarly, the new office of intendant replaced the offices of governor, *alcalde mayor*, and *corregidor*. The establishment of the intendancy system was intended to bring governance in the colonies under more direct control by Spain: Intendants were to be Spanish-born and they reported directly to officials in Spain.

The ecclesiastical administration of Spain's colonies was carried out by two groups within the Roman Catholic Church: the secular clergy (so named because they live in the world at large), made up of clerics in the ecclesiastical hierarchy that extends from the pope to parish priests; and the regular clergy (so called because they live according to a rule or *regla*), which comprises the mendicant orders (those who live from donations and alms, such as the Franciscans, Dominicans, Augustinians, Mercedarians, etc.) and the Society of Jesus, or Jesuits.

For most of the Colonial period, the entire region of the prehispanic

Mesoamerican world fell within the Archdiocese of Mexico, headed by the Archbishop of Mexico, although after 1745 portions of southern Mesoamerica became part of the newly created Archdiocese of Guatemala with its own archbishop. Diocesan divisions within Mesoamerica included, at various times, Guadalajara, Michoacán, Mexico, Tlaxcala, Antequera (Oaxaca), Chiapa, Yucatán, Verapaz, Trujillo, and León, each administered by a bishop. Within the dioceses were smaller divisions, the parishes, administered by parish priests.

The regular clergy came to the Spanish colonies with the specific mission of bringing Christianity to the Indian communities. In the New World members of the religious orders lived primarily among the Indians, learning the native languages and ministering to the native population through missions, schools, and hospitals. Originally the regulars were expected to return to Spain once the conversion of the Indians was completed, but, with the exception of the Society of Jesus, whose members were expelled from Spain's colonies (and Spain itself) in 1767, the religious orders remained in the colonies throughout the Colonial period and into the Republican and modern periods.

In 1571 the Holy Office of the Inquisition was established in Mexico City to investigate and punish religious crimes. Native people were exempt from prosecution by the Inquisition. Inquisition-like proceedings carried out by bishops in Mexico and Yucatán during the 1530s and 1540s had, it was thought, gone too far, with Indians being tortured and even executed. By 1571 the opinion prevailed that the Indians had been brought into the Catholic faith too recently to be held to the same standards as Spanish Christians. This policy would remain in effect until the Inquisition was dissolved at the end of the Colonial period.

However, Spaniards of Jewish ancestry who may have hoped that their move to the colony might grant them some religious freedom found themselves once again under perpetual scrutiny and suspicion. People from European countries where Protestantism was common, such as the French printers who ran some of Mexico's first publishing houses, were also viewed with suspicion. And people of African and mixed descent were subject to investigation, even though they might have much less familiarity with Christian teachings than the Indians around them. The Inquisition's *autos de fe,* or rituals of penitence and reconciliation, became a feature of New Spain's public life, and those convicted of religious crimes were occasionally burned at the stake.

CIVIL-RELIGIOUS INSTITUTIONS AFFECTING THE NATIVE POPULATION

For the Spaniards the wealth of the Indies was not confined exclusively to precious metals and other goods; the large Indian populations themselves were viewed as a valuable resource. As a result, many of the institutions imposed by the Spaniards were designed to allow Spanish colonists to use native labor. Ultimately, any wealth generated by Indian labor (or by any other means) would benefit the king of Spain, as he was guaranteed to receive one-fifth of anything coming out of the Indies.

In establishing official policies regarding the treatment of the Indians, the Crown was torn between what was genuinely felt to be an obligation to promote the well-being of the Indians on the one hand and its ultimate desire to generate revenues from the colonies on the other. Unfortunately for the Indians, even when Crown policies were clearly intended for their benefit, local officials often failed to implement them out of indifference if not open hostility. The unwillingness of Crown officials to enforce the laws is well-illustrated in the phrase *obedezco pero no cumplo* ("I obey but do not execute")—the speaker acknowledges the king's authority but refuses to carry out his commands. Cortés reportedly uttered this phrase when he received orders from King Charles V that, among other things, explicitly forbade him from distributing *encomiendas* in Central Mexico. He may have been the first to express this sentiment in colonial Mesoamerica, but he was certainly not the last.

One of the earliest Spanish institutions to have a direct economic impact on the Indians was the *encomienda* system. Initially, *encomiendas* were a great source of wealth for Spaniards, with native communities furnishing large amounts of goods to their *encomendero.* An *encomendero* of the highland Guatemala town of Huehuetenango received the following items in tribute in 1530–31 (Kramer, Lovell, and Lutz 1991:274):

800 lengths of cotton cloth
400 loincloths
400 jackets
400 blouses
400 skirts
400 sandals
400 reed mats
400 woven mats
unspecified amounts of corn, beans, chile, and salt
108–126 large jugs of honey
2,268 turkeys

The Crown repeatedly tried to eliminate the *encomienda* system, but with little success. In some areas the Crown was successful in revoking *encomiendas*; in these cases an Indian town or province became, in effect, an *encomienda* of the Crown. In other areas, however, *encomiendas* held by generation after generation of Spaniards persisted until well into the eighteenth century.

In the 1550s Indian slavery was abolished, and that, together with a new policy that prevented *encomenderos* from demanding labor from the Indians they held (they could still receive goods), presented the Crown with a serious dilemma: Who was going to provide the labor required for the various colonial enterprises? The *repartimiento* system was implemented to solve this problem.

Repartimiento was essentially a system of forced labor that provided the Spaniards with a new means for exploiting native people. Under *repartimiento,* Indian communities were required to provide labor for public projects such as building and road construction and maintenance, for agricultural work, for work in the mines, and as porters. The law required that *repartimiento* laborers be paid. The system was easily abused, however, with Spanish officials and their friends using the labor drafts for private endeavors and finding ways to cheat the Indians out of the wages they had earned.

A variation of the *repartimiento* of labor was the *repartimiento* of goods, in which the Indians were forced to purchase goods from unscrupulous Spanish officials at exorbitant prices. Often these were items the Indians neither needed nor wanted, such as Spanish shoes, although sometimes the goods were actually the raw materials that the natives needed to produce items for tribute payments. For example, a native community that was charged tribute in textiles might be forced to purchase—at high prices—the cotton or wool needed to produce the textiles. Another variation of this form of *repartimiento* consisted of Spaniards providing raw materials (such as raw cotton) to Indian weavers in return for the right to purchase the finished product—and often the purchase price was well below market value.

Among the most disruptive of the Spanish institutions was the program of *congregación* or *reducción.* These forced resettlement programs were instituted throughout New Spain in the sixteenth century. They were intended to aid the clergy in "civilizing" previously dispersed native populations by congregating them into new, densely populated villages where the activities of the natives could be more easily monitored.

In addition to providing their *encomenderos* with goods and labor and providing labor for *repartimiento,* native communities also were taxed through the colonial tribute system. Indians, as vassals to the king, were required to pay annual tribute either directly to the Crown or to their *encomenderos.* In the latter case, a portion of the tribute collected by the *encomendero* was paid to the king. Initially tribute payments were made in goods, but gradually payments in money replaced payments in goods. By the mid-eighteenth century payment in goods was made illegal.

We saw in chapters 2 and 3 that at the time of Spanish contact expansionist powers like the Aztecs collected tribute from conquered regions. In fact, some of the earliest colonial tribute assessments may well have been based on existing Aztec tribute collection documents. But eventually the tribute demands of the Spaniards were much more debilitating than prehispanic tribute payments. The demographic decline meant that there were fewer and fewer Indians, but reductions in tribute payments usually lagged far behind population decline. In colonial documents we find many examples of native communities requesting that they be excused from tribute payments because they simply did not have the resources to pay.

In addition to the many abusive policies forced upon the Indians, many

Spanish economic enterprises in colonial Mesoamerica affected the native populations, as well. Among the enterprises that would have the greatest impact on native societies were mining, the hacienda system, and the textile factories or *obrajes*.

From the beginning, the Spaniards were obsessed with a desire to obtain gold and silver, and by the mid-sixteenth century large deposits of silver were being mined in several areas of Mesoamerica, primarily in the north in the areas around Zacatecas, Guanajuato, San Luis Potosí, and Pachuca. Mining was one arena where the Crown and the colonists were of one mind—no holds were barred to ensure that the mines were as productive as possible. Beyond the wealth generated by the silver itself—even after the king had received his fifth—fortunes also could be made by the entrepreneurs who provided the food and other goods for the mining camps. Labor for the mines was provided largely by the Indian population—at first through *repartimiento* labor and later through wage labor. Wages were good, but the risks were high, and many natives lost their lives as they toiled in the unhealthy atmosphere of the mines.

With the gradual demise of the *encomienda* in many parts of Mesoamerica, Spanish access to large tracts of land shifted to outright ownership of landed estates called haciendas. In less-populated areas—primarily in the north—haciendas were large and focused primarily on livestock. In other areas they were often smaller and more diverse with livestock and agricultural components. In many regions, the growth of the haciendas was achieved at the expense of the native communities as Spaniards took control of what were formerly Indian lands. In theory official policies prevented Spaniards from taking Indian lands, but in practice Spaniards were able to acquire these lands through a variety of means. Indian leaders sometimes willingly sold community properties to Spaniards. Another common practice involved the Crown policy of selling what were deemed to be vacant lands to make money for the royal treasury. The demographic collapse of the native population left many areas with low population densities. Lands that were underpopulated—even though they might be used for hunting and other activities by native communities—could be declared vacant and then legally sold to Spaniards.

The labor for haciendas was often supplied by native workers who had left their communities. A situation of debt-servitude frequently developed when these people were given wages in advance and were then required to remain on the hacienda until the debt was paid off. In other cases, however, a share-cropping arrangement existed whereby laborers were provided with access to a portion of the hacienda lands to cultivate in exchange for handing over part of their crop and perhaps providing the owner with other services. In still other cases, natives temporarily left their communities to work on haciendas to earn the cash they needed to meet their tribute demands.

Obrajes were textile factories that produced coarse cloth for consumption within New Spain. Finer cloth was imported. The *obrajes* tended to be located in the cities in Central Mexico, and they had little impact outside this area. The bulk of the work force in the *obrajes* was made up of Indians who had left their com-

Figure 5.2 Indian textile workers in an *obraje*. This illustration by a native artist is from the *Codex Osuna*, a set of documents prepared in 1565 as a report on the Spanish and native governments of Mexico City. *Códice Osuna*. Mexico City, Mexico: Instituto Indigenista Interamericano, 1947, p. 258.

munities. Working conditions were unhealthy, and treatment of native workers was harsh (Figure 5.2).

EVANGELIZATION: ISSUES AND IMPLICATIONS

The colonial institution that had the most profound effects upon indigenous life in colonial Mesoamerica was the Catholic Church. Most Spanish colonists were content to enrich themselves by the Indians' labor, satisfied if the Indians stayed peaceful and displayed some minimal evidence of Christianity. But men of the Church sought to extend colonial authority into the most intimate aspects of native life—from the selection of marriage partners to the expression of sexual desire.

Many books have been written about the Christian evangelization of Mesoamerica. Recently, scholars have questioned a number of traditional assumptions, especially the notion that Mesoamerica was "spiritually conquered" by Christian missionaries, and have begun to see the native people as playing an active role in formulating their own understandings of Christianity. Rather than include here a detailed discussion of missionary methodologies—the subject of numerous previous studies—we have chosen to discuss some of the broader political and social issues involved in the evangelization of colonial Mesoamerica.

The missionary friars of the mendicant orders had tremendous influence and prestige during the early decades of Spanish rule in Mexico. The recent reforms initiated in Spain by Jiménez de Cisneros had filled the religious orders with well-educated men who took their vows and duties seriously. They enjoyed the favor of a king who was determined to prevent a repetition of the disastrous colonization of the Caribbean. And, for the most part, they found themselves welcome among the native people. A few friars, who had dreamed of becoming martyrs at the hands of savage Indians, were actually disappointed by the graciousness and generosity with which they were received (Figure 5.3).

Figure 5.3 Indo-Christian art: A native artist painted this portrait of fray Martín de Valencia, the leader of New Spain's first official mission of Franciscan friars, in the Franciscan friary at Tlalmanalco (southeast of Mexico City); it probably dates to the late 1580s.

Were these missionaries mere tools of Spanish imperialism, helping to transform Mesoamericans into compliant colonial subjects, or did they sincerely believe that the native people would benefit from their preaching of the Christian gospel? Just as we cannot fully separate the Spanish soldier's lust for gold from his desire to glorify his God, we must understand that, while these distinctions may be meaningful to us, people of the sixteenth century did not think in these terms. The majority of the missionaries believed that the Spanish conquest, despite its attendant evils, was justified precisely because, and to the extent that, the native people were brought into the Christian fold. And it was only by bringing them under colonial rule and reorganizing their lifestyle along European lines that the salvation of their souls could be achieved.

The position of many of the friars, especially the Franciscans, could be described as pro-imperialist but anti-colonialist. That is, they supported Spanish rule in principle and condoned the military conquest, but they objected to the actual colonization of these territories by large numbers of Spaniards. They hoped to insulate the native people from what they saw as the corrupting influence of Spanish colonists, whom the friars did not consider model Christians. They hoped that New Spain might remain a predominantly Indian society, but Christianized by the friars and ruled by a viceroy appointed by the Spanish king. These concerns led the friars often to side with New Spain's viceroys against the settler aristocracy and against the secular ecclesiastical hierarchy, which sought to administer New Spain according to the same system of tithes and parishes that operated in Spain. Many native people adhered to the position of these friars, declaring loyalty to the king—to them a distant but potentially benevolent figure—while objecting to specific policies and to particular abuses perpetrated by local Spaniards.

Contrasting with this majority opinion was the more radical position taken by Bartolomé de Las Casas and some of his fellow Dominicans. As we discussed in Chapter 4, Las Casas believed that the end—Christian evangelization—did not justify the means—violent conquest. Missionaries should do their work without the assistance of invading armies. Las Casas convinced Charles V to allow him to try out his program in Tuzulutlán, an as yet unconquered area of Guatemala. During the 1540s he and other Dominicans succeeded in bringing the area under Spanish control without military intervention, while introducing Christianity among the indigenous people. In recognition of the Dominicans' achievement, Charles changed the region's name from Tuzulutlán, which means "the land of war," to Verapaz, or "true peace." He granted the Dominicans full administrative authority over this district, which for the next three centuries remained a theocratic mini-state operating within the larger colony.

The situation in Verapaz was an extreme example of a pattern that emerged throughout colonial Mesoamerica: an alliance between the religious orders and the native communities. This is one dimension of a colonial political scene that was far more complex than a simple struggle of Spaniards against Indians. The ties that bound friars and Indians to one another were often phrased in terms of kinship, with the friars represented as stern but compassionate fathers to their innocent but oft-misguided Indian children. This terminology helped to obscure what was in reality a relationship of mutual dependence. The Indians fed and clothed the friars, built their convents and churches, and provided a power base to back up the friars' various political intrigues—many of which, such as a campaign to prevent the ecclesiastical hierarchy from forcing the Indians to pay tithes, benefitted both friars and Indians.

The friars taught the native nobles to read and write and to master the forms of rhetoric with which they could petition Crown or Council on their own behalf. Since they sometimes petitioned for more friars, or to prevent friars from being removed from their communities, such skills worked also to the friars' advantage. The friars trained commoners to exploit the new tools and technologies introduced from Europe—to the frustration of Spanish artisans who had hoped to monopolize these industries. They acted as advocates and interpreters before the colonial government. Although they sometimes resorted to corporal punishment to impose their will, with rare exceptions they refrained from the forms of economic and sexual exploitation Indians all too often experienced at Spanish hands—including those of secular clergy. It is no wonder that the native people, shrewdly appraising the friars as the best friends they were likely to find among the emigrants from Europe, welcomed their presence.

But what about conversion? Did the Indians become Christians? Perhaps the best answer to that question is both "yes" and "no." Yes, they were baptized—almost all of them within a few decades after their particular territory had been brought under Spanish rule. Yes, they participated in Christian worship and eventually came to think of themselves as Christian people who no longer worshipped the gods of their ancestors. Yes, Christian churches replaced the old temples as the centers of community religious life (Figure 5.4). Yes, they were sincerely devoted to the sacred beings of Catholic Christianity: Christ, the Virgin Mary, the various saints.

But they did not undergo a conversion experience, in the sense of responding to a personal spiritual crisis by consciously and intentionally replacing one entire belief system with another. The fact that in Mesoamerica the social structure of the native communities generally remained intact, with local leaders retaining control over community affairs, probably helped to keep people from experiencing the transition to Spanish rule as a traumatic crisis in their own lives. Traditional religion was more a matter of collective, community rites and celebrations than of an individualized, personal faith. Christianity too would be above all a collective, public enterprise associated with the identity of the community—now centered on a patron saint rather than a tutelary divinity.

The native people interpreted Christianity in terms that were more or less compatible with their own cultures. This process was facilitated by the fact that the friars preached to them in their own languages. Friars, in collaboration with native assistants, produced many books and manuscripts in the native languages (Figure 5.5). The process of translation subtly altered Christian concepts and

Figure 5.4 Colonial church in the town of San Pedro y San Pablo Teposcolula, Oaxaca. The resident Dominican friars ministered to the town's native population from the large, arcaded open chapel, now partially ruined.

brought them more in line with indigenous understandings. For example, in the Nahuatl language the word *tlahtlacolli* was used to convey the Christian concept of "sin." The Nahuatl word meant "error" or "crime" or "destruction" in a much broader sense and alluded to a general process of disintegration and decay that affected all social and natural orders. The translation thus had the effect of watering down the Christian notion of personal moral responsibility and relating individual behavior to broader processes that were not seen as necessarily evil (See Chapters 8 and 12).

Also, native people had no concept of a "religion" or a "faith" as such, as a clearly defined entity separable from the rest of culture, and thus did not comprehend what it was they were supposed to be giving up and taking on. Priests were too few and too awkward in the native languages to explain to everyone the theological and philosophical underpinnings of Christianity in terms they would understand; most religious instruction occurred on a rudimentary level.

To the native people, Christianity appeared to be primarily a set of practices, many of which resembled their traditional practices of prayer, offerings, processions, dramas, fasting, and the use of sacred images. It was on these expressive and often collective behaviors that the native people focused, sometimes with notable enthusiasm. Christianization proceeded as a process of addition and sub-

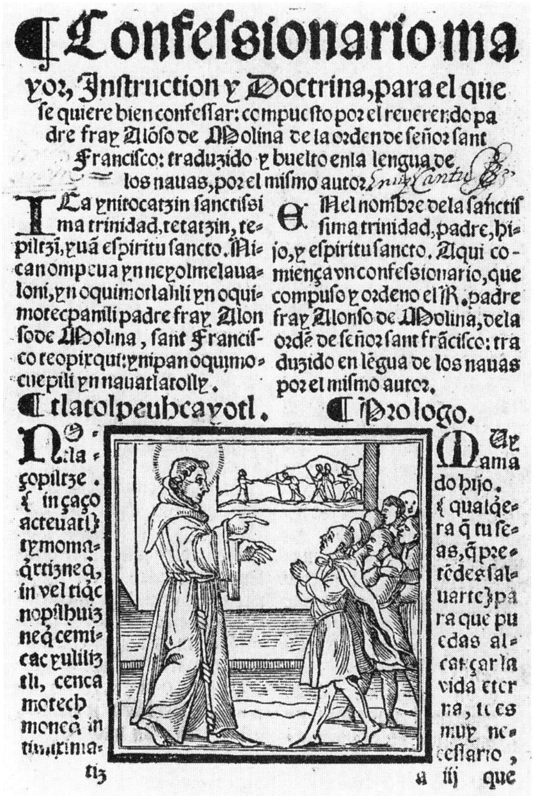

Figure 5.5 The first page of a 1565 confession manual printed in both Spanish and Nahuatl. The woodcut depicts a Franciscan friar accompanied by Indian children. From Alonso de Molina, *Confessionario mayor, en lengua Mexicana y Castellana*. Courtesy of the John Carter Brown Library at Brown University.

stitution within the existing repertoire of devotional practices. Priests who lamented that instead of a thousand gods the Indians now had a thousand and one, the Christian god having simply been added to the native deities, had indeed perceived an aspect of this process. Over time, new prayers, new images, new songs, new penances, and new festivals were adopted while many of the old practices were abandoned. But there was never a sudden and total substitution of a new *faith* for an old.

Given that Christianity was not perceived as a spiritually compelling new faith, what motivated people to make even these changes in their traditional devotions? With the exception of the native priesthood, most people had little to lose and much to gain by joining the Church. We have already seen that the presence and support of the friars benefitted the native communities. Other factors may also be noted. The Spaniards attributed their military success to their god, just as native people did when they were victorious in warfare. The conquest itself thus was a compelling endorsement of the efficacy of Christian worship. The new god was obviously more powerful than the old ones, and many people came to accept the Christian view that their old deities were demons unworthy of service (Figure 5.6).

Another important factor was the Spanish policy regarding indigenous

Figure 5.6 This relief by a native sculptor decorates a sixteenth-century chapel in San Andrés Calpan, now in the state of Puebla, Mexico. It shows the archangel Saint Michael's victory over the Devil. This story was told to native people as an explanation for the origin of their gods, whom the friars claimed were really devils.

rulers. The native nobles were allowed to retain their rank and position and to hold government offices at the city and town level. However, Spanish officials were more willing to support and cooperate with local rulers who showed themselves to be devotees of Christian worship. Those who failed to accept Christianity soon found themselves passed over in favor of young men from the friars' schools, who knew how to read and write and could speak some Spanish. Some of these upstarts were not even born into noble rank! Within a generation, the indigenous nobility had been brought into the Church, and the common people tended to follow the example of their leaders.

Some scholars have suggested that Mesoamericans were relieved to give up the more bloody aspects of their religion, such as human sacrifice, and to turn from their cruel gods to the compassionate figures of Christ and the saints. There may be some truth in this view, but it is difficult to assess how much of a factor this was. For one thing, human sacrifice had been most closely associated with the cult of war, which became obsolete as Spanish rule turned traditional enemies into peaceful neighbors. Many of the old gods had been relatively benevolent providers of water, food, health, and children. The relationship between the native communities and their new Christian patron-deities retained—and still retains today—a contractual character, according to which the community provides service in exchange for the saint's protection and support: No reward is bestowed without adequate payment.

But we can say one thing with more certainty. As the native people became more and more impoverished and oppressed, the Christian teachings that made a virtue of poverty and promised an easier existence after death became meaningful to people whose ancestors had never thought in those terms. Indian Christianity developed into a religion of the poor, and the words with which Jesus of Nazareth had challenged the status quo of an earlier colonial regime became readily available tools of protest.

The missionary friars, though at first thrilled at the Indians' enthusiastic reception of Christian worship, soon were disillusioned by what they perceived as a superficial conversion. To them, all Indian worship was either Christian or pagan; either the Indians had truly converted or they remained in thrall to the Devil. They did not understand that the Indians could be perfectly sincere in their devotion to Christ and yet continue to mingle with their Christian practices elements that the friars considered to be idolatrous. Nor did they understand the extent to which Christian devotions took on indigenous characteristics when translated across cultures, just as native practices labeled as pagan took on new meanings when redirected toward Christian figures. They did not understand that native spirituality was closely linked to collective experiences generated by elaborate ritual, rather than to private prayer and contemplation.

The friars attributed the shortcomings they saw in native religion to shortcomings of the Indians themselves. They characterized the Indians as weak and sensual, childish, more attracted by outward appearances than by inward meanings. Blind to the spiritual aspects of native religion, they concluded that the Indian personality lacked a spiritual dimension. Recall that the friars holding these views were the Indians' staunchest defenders, far less prejudiced against them than were most other Europeans in the colony—many of whom equated the Indians with brute animals.

This view of the Indians echoed the attitude that many urban and educated Europeans took toward people of the lower classes, especially rural peasants. By labelling the Indians in this way, the friars placed them into a familiar category. They could then talk about, preach to, and interact with Indians according to the same tactics they would use with uneducated peasants in their European homelands. They could thus, in a sense, deny the immense cultural differences separating them from the native peoples.

The friars' attitude had other important implications. Most significant, the belief that the Indians were spiritually inferior justified a policy of keeping them out of the priesthood. With very rare exceptions—most of these among the Jesuits and in frontier regions—Indian men in colonial Mesoamerica were not allowed to become priests. Indian women were only very rarely allowed to become nuns, even though some chose to live like nuns and even entered convents as servants and companions to the more privileged daughters of Spaniards. This policy reinforced the colonial status quo, helping to keep the Indians in a dependent, inferior position relative to Europeans and their descendants (the same exclusionary policy applied to persons of mestizo and mulatto background).

Priests perpetually feared that the Indians would rebel against Christianity and revert to their pagan ways. It is interesting to note that when religious uprisings did occur, their participants usually did not try to revive the cults of the ancestors but instead sought to form their own Christian cults, under native leadership. They did not reject Christianity as such, although they developed highly unconventional versions of it. Rather, they rejected the established Church's right to govern their religious life, rebelling against the priests who remained always foreigners to the native communities. These movements sometimes began as reactions against particularly abusive or negligent priests. Typically, individual Indians would take on the identity of Christ, the Virgin Mary, or other saints, while a cadre of native priests arose to serve them and administer the sacraments. This recurrent desire to give an Indian face to Christian religion has its roots in the failure of the early mission Church to integrate Indians into the priesthood. For an example of a native religious movement, see Box 5.1.

Box 5.1 *The Tzeltal Revolt, Chiapas, 1712*

One day in May 1712 María López, a thirteen-year-old Tzeltal Maya girl from the town of Cancuc, was walking along the outskirts of her town when she experienced an apparition of the Virgin Mary. As Agustín López, María's father, later described the encounter, the Virgin said to the girl, "María, you are my daughter." María responded, "Yes, Lady, you are my mother." The Virgin then told her, "Daughter, make a cross on this place and mark the earth. It is my will that a shrine be made here for me to live in with you." When María told her husband and parents what had happened, her mother encouraged her to tell the townspeople of the miracle and her father erected a cross on the site that the Virgin had designated. With the support of the town's native leaders, the whole populace turned out to help build a small chapel on the site. The Virgin continued to visit María, appearing to her in a hidden room within the chapel.

María's apparition experience followed a standard European pattern: The Virgin Mary or another saint appears to a worshipper, often a shepherd boy or a young woman, on the edge of town and asks that a chapel be built on the spot. However, in eighteenth-century Chiapas there was little chance that an Indian girl's personal religious experience would be considered authentic by the local Spanish ecclesiastical authorities. In June, Fray Simón de Lara, the Dominican priest in charge of Cancuc, heard of these events and came to investigate. He denounced the new cult as the work of the Devil and flogged María and her father with forty lashes each. However, he did not dare to anger the townspeople by tearing down the chapel.

Later that month, sixteen citizens from Cancuc went to see the bishop of Chiapas. They told him of the miracle and requested permission to maintain the chapel and have a priest say Mass there. The bishop had them imprisoned in Ciudad Real, the capital of Chiapas, and declared that he would send soldiers to burn the shrine if the townspeople did not tear it down. The religious authorities' next step was to imprison some of Cancuc's town officials and install more obedient replacements.

Meanwhile, people from other native towns were flocking to Cancuc to make offerings at the chapel and listen to María convey messages from the Virgin. María's father organized an inner circle of cult leaders. These included men from other villages, some of whom had held religious offices and had had negative experiences with Spanish priests. One, a Tzotzil man named Sebastián Gómez from the town of San Pedro Chenalhó, carried with him a small statue of Saint Peter. Gómez claimed that he had gone to heaven and had spoken with the Holy Trinity, the Virgin Mary, Jesus Christ, and Saint Peter. Saint Peter had given him the authority to ordain literate Indians as priests and had told him that the Indians were now free from Spanish rule and no longer had to pay tribute. What had apparently begun as a local attempt at community religious revitalization within the framework of the Catholic Church was—because of the authorities' repressive responses—escalating into a rebellion against the Church and the Spanish colonial state. Warned that his life was in danger, Fray Simón de Lara fled the town.

The imprisoned Cancuc officials escaped and returned home, ousting the men who had been appointed in their places. The townspeople removed the religious images from their main church and took them to the new chapel. Using ceremonies that imitated the Mass and the rite of baptism, Sebastián Gómez took on the role of Indian bishop and began ordaining rebel priests. The new priests, and María herself, dressed in priestly vestments taken from the old church. María became known as María de la Candelaria, after the Virgen de la Candelaria (Candelaria is a Spanish name for the festival of the purification of Mary.) Cancuc was renamed Ciudad Real Cancuc, symbolizing that the town was to replace the Spanish city of Ciudad Real as the political center of the region.

In early August the cult leaders sent a letter, written in Tzeltal Maya, around to the leaders of other communities in the region. The letter read, in part:

> I, the Virgin of Our Lady of the Rosary, command you to come to the town of Cancuc. Bring all the silver from your church, and the ornaments and bells, with all the coffers and drums, and all the books and money of the confraternities, because now there is neither God nor King.

The letter was signed, "The Most Holy Virgin Mary of the Cross."

That the cult leaders framed their call to war as orders from the Virgin Mary demonstrates how the political rebellion continued to be conceived in religious terms. Throughout the revolt, the participants held to the ceremonial forms and institutional structures of the Catholic Church. The rebel priests conducted masses, baptisms, and marriages; the communities celebrated Catholic festivals with processions and other customary practices. The rebels were attempting to legitimize their movement by associating it with the objects, behaviors, and words that they had learned to consider sacred, while also usurping control over these symbols of authority as a way of declaring independence from Spanish rule. The attempted power reversal is well illustrated by María López's role as the cult's spiritual leader—an Indian girl represented the antithesis of the adult male Spaniards who controlled the colonial Church and government. The cult simultaneously drew on older Maya beliefs about the supernatural; for example, one source indicates that some of the men chosen as military leaders were shamans believed to have powerful *naguales*, or spirit guardians.

In all, people from twenty native towns joined Cancuc in the revolt. Thirteen of these shared Cancuc's Tzeltal Maya language; five were Tzotzil and two were Chol. Two of the Tzotzil towns, Santa Marta and San Pedro Chenalhó, had seen local miracle-based cults discounted and forcibly suppressed by the Church only the preceding year. Because of the prevalence of Tzeltal speakers, the movement is often called the Tzeltal Revolt, even though some Tzeltal communities remained loyal to the Spanish king. The rebels began raiding non-Indian communities, killing priests and militiamen. Some of the women were taken back to Cancuc, where they were forcibly married to Maya men: The Virgin had declared, through María, that in the future there would be no difference between Spaniards and natives. The rebels also attacked Indian towns that refused to join the uprising. At one point, Spanish defenders claimed to have faced an army of 6,000 Maya, but this estimate was probably exaggerated.

An army of Spanish, mixed-race, and native militiamen eventually suppressed the revolt. Toribio de Cosío, president of the Audiencia of Guatemala, came to Ciudad Real in September 1712 to oversee the campaign. After he issued an offer of amnesty in November, a number of the rebel villages put down their arms; others were forcibly occupied by the Spanish-led army. In February 1713, the last of the rebel soldiers abandoned the cause. Cosío then supervised the execution of dozens of captured rebel leaders and the floggings of many more. Others were exiled or barred from future public office. New officials were appointed in all of the towns. Cancuc was destroyed and its residents forcibly resettled on a new site.

Cosío attempted to prevent further violence by issuing a series of edicts. Native leaders were forbidden to publicize any new miracles or to purchase gunpowder. The economic situation of the Chiapas highlands was also addressed: Several of the edicts were intended to limit and better regulate the economic exploitation of the Indians by, for example, reducing the *repartimiento* labor drafts imposed on some of the towns and demanding that cattle ranchers sell beef to the Indians at fair prices. These and later reform efforts had little effect, however. Ethnic relations remained polarized and the native population remained impoverished.

Toward the end of the revolt, María López had fled Cancuc. She and other members of her family had gone into hiding near the rebel town of Yajalón. They spent the next three years in hiding, growing food for themselves, their presence known only to a few people from Yajalón who remained loyal to the cult. María continued to commune daily with the Virgin in a small chapel built by her father. Early in 1716, she died from complications brought on by her first pregnancy. Two weeks after her death, the hiding place was discovered. María's father and two other family members were arrested and executed, the last of the rebels to be put to death. Sebastián Gómez, the rebel bishop who claimed to have visited heaven, was never found.

(Based on Gosner 1992:122–159; see also Bricker 1981:59–69.)

COLONIAL SOCIETY

The social structure of colonial Mesoamerica was based on the hierarchical ranking of categories of people that were defined in ethnic and racial terms. We have seen that in the wake of the *reconquista* in Spain, the Spaniards became increasingly intolerant of anyone who was not Catholic, and from this intolerance the doctrine of *limpieza de sangre* (purity of blood) was born. In Spain, anyone who could not demonstrate that he or she was descended from pure Christian stock, untainted by Jewish or Moorish blood, was unable to hold noble status and prohibited from taking part in many other activities.

In the New World this intolerance translated into legal discrimination against people of mixed ethnic ancestry, and a complex nomenclature was developed to deal with the wide array of possible backgrounds any individual might have. During the course of the Colonial period the number of categories soared, perhaps numbering in the hundreds. These different categories were called *castas,* or castes (Figure 5.7). Skin color was of prime importance in the ultimate determination of one's status, and the possibilities for upward mobility were certainly higher for individuals with lighter skin.

We should point out, though, that these discriminations were based not on a biologically or genetically based concept of "race" but on legalistic cate-

Figure 5.7 These paintings are from a series illustrating different *castas*, or social and ethnic categories, in eighteenth-century New Spain. A) A Spanish man with an Indian woman produce a mestizo child; B) the child of a Spanish man with an African woman is a mulatto; C) a man of African descent and his Indian partner produce a *sambaigo*, a category also called *zambo* or *sambo*. Pedro Alonso O'Crouley, *A Description of the Kingdom of New Spain*, ed. and trans. by Seán Galvin. San Francisco, CA: John Howell Books, 1972.

gories. As the colonial overlords of the land, Spaniards enjoyed the highest level of legal privilege. Indians, as the original inhabitants of the land, had claim to legal rights, including some special privileges. African slaves had no recognized legal rights, but free persons of African or partially African descent were citizens of the colony with some legal status. Determining the status of persons of mixed ancestry was a thorny legal problem. Since the darkness or lightness of a person's skin happened to correspond, to some extent, to these status levels, it became a convenient index to a person's place in the social and legal hierarchy.

Historian Magnus Morner has reduced the number of *castas* to six broad categories: Peninsular Spaniards, Creoles, Mestizos, Mulattoes-*Zambos*-Free Blacks, Slaves, and Indians. At the top of the *casta* hierarchy were pure-blooded Spaniards who had been born in Spain. Referred to as "peninsulars"—because they had been born on the Iberian Peninsula—members of this group almost always held the best positions, in both civil and religious life, and they were the most prestigious members of the community.

Creoles had the same ancestry as the peninsular Spaniards, but they were born in the New World and this relegated them to a lower status than peninsulars. This reflected the belief among Europeans that the American climate and general environment was detrimental, rendering anyone born there inherently inferior—even if their parents were from Europe. This belief functioned, we may note, to help maintain the Spanish king's power, since he could continue to appoint administrators whom he personally knew and trusted. As a result, few creoles ever attained the highest church and government positions. Despite this secondary status, they enjoyed a privileged position in colonial society and belonged to the ranks of the colonial aristocracy, particularly in the more provincial areas.

Ranking well below the creoles in social status were the mestizos—the offspring of Spanish and Indian parents. In most cases, mestizos had a Spanish father and an Indian mother. During the years of Spanish exploration and invasion, it was quite common for Spanish men to take Indian women as lovers and occasionally as wives (particularly when the woman came from a noble Indian family). But from the beginning, mestizos were discriminated against: They were prohibited from holding *encomiendas* and they were not allowed to hold certain public offices. Generally, they were not allowed to enter the priesthood. While some mestizos—primarily those descended from prominent conquistadors—held comfortable positions in colonial society, the large majority were poor and uneducated.

Mulattoes, the offspring of Spanish and African parents, occupied a lower position in colonial society than did mestizos. For many legal purposes, mulattoes occupied the same position as did free Africans and so-called *zambos*, who were the offspring of Africans and Indians.

Occupying the bottom rungs in society were the African slaves. The holding of enslaved Africans remained legal in New Spain until independence from Spain was won in 1820, although the slave trade diminished after the mid-seventeenth century. Most Spanish and creole families throughout the colony had

African slaves in their households; large numbers were exploited as laborers in coastal plantation regions and in mining areas.

Where Indians fit into this hierarchy is somewhat problematic. In some places and times they were treated even worse than slaves. For example, Indians were sometimes worked to death in the mines, their lives being considered of no value; owners of slaves would, at the very least, seek to protect their investment by keeping their workers alive. For the most part, however, the status of black slaves was, indeed, lower. In fact, members of the native nobility sometimes had African slaves in their households.

Although Indians had low social status and were looked down upon by anyone who could claim at least some Spanish descent, they did have some legal rights and protections not available to other residents of the colony. For example, they were able to govern their own communities, they maintained community ownership of land, and they were exempt from prosecution for religious crimes. They also were obliged to pay tribute to the Crown, which other persons—though subject to Church tithes and other taxes—did not have to do. Indians had a unique status in the colonies: They were, in effect, wards of the Church and Crown, and as such were to be protected from unscrupulous colonists to the extent that this was possible.

Although all Indians were included in this single legal category, there were complex internal divisions within native society. The Spaniards, coming from a hierarchical society themselves, were quick to recognize the existence of a native nobility. Particularly in the early part of the Colonial period, the Spaniards relied heavily on native elites to implement colonial policies. In return for their cooperation, members of the native nobility were given special privileges that set them apart from the common people. They were granted coats of arms and were allowed to wear Spanish dress, to carry firearms, and to ride horses.

LIFE IN THE CORPORATE COMMUNITY

Under colonial rule, the region that had been the site of the prehispanic Mesoamerican world remained culturally diverse, its native people speaking many languages and pursuing a wide variety of local customs. Native communities were all subjected to similar influences from the Church and the colonial administration, but the ways that they responded—accepting some of these influences, reshaping others, and rejecting still others—varied considerably across colonial Mesoamerica.

Our knowledge of indigenous life in colonial Mesoamerica has been greatly expanded over the last couple of decades, thanks to pioneering studies of original documents written by Indians in their own languages. These sources include historical annals, city council records, wills, bills of sale, and court testimony. To date, most of this research has focused on documents written in Nahuatl, which make up by far the largest body of colonial text material in any Mesoamerican language. However, a few scholars have recently begun to locate and analyze similar materials written in other languages, such as Yucatec Maya, Zapotec, Mixtec, Cakchiquel, and Quiché. (See Chapter 12 for a more extensive discussion of literacy and native-language texts).

Historian Nancy Farriss has described Indian life under colonial rule as "the collective enterprise of survival" (Farriss 1984). This phrase is useful because it focuses our attention on two points. First, for those Indians who remained in the native towns, life remained very much oriented toward the community as a corporate entity. Most land was held in common by the community as a whole or by its constituent wards. Government officials were selected by the community and were expected to use their office for the community's benefit, not for personal prestige or financial gain. The most important religious events were community affairs.

Perhaps most significant, people drew their primary sense of identity from their membership in a particular community. The concept of community was very strong; that is, the "idea" of community was highly developed and associated with powerful emotional ties. This social and territorial unit, which the Nahuas called the *altepetl*, the Yucatec Maya called the *cah*, and the Mixtecs called the *sina yya*, had deep roots in preconquest times. Though often referred to in English as a "city-state," the traditional corporate community was often not very large or very urbanized. What was more important was the idea of a group of people who shared ancestral rights to a particular piece of land, which they occupied as a settled and permanent community. They shared an identity based on their association with this particular place. Most people married within their own community. People thought of themselves not as Indians, or Nahua, or Zapotecs, but as Teposcolulans, or Tlapanecans, or Pantitecans—depending on whatever their home community happened to be called.

The second point is that these corporate communities were engaged in a struggle to survive. Spanish colonization had devastating effects not only on population levels but on all aspects of native life. The political system was reorganized so that native people had no power beyond their own communities. The economy was reorganized in order to siphon wealth away from the native people and into Spanish hands. A European world view and Roman Catholic religion made significant inroads, even though they never completely supplanted native belief systems. In order to survive, native people had to make tremendous changes and adaptations in their lifestyle and develop complex strategies of self-defense and mutual support. This is not to say that life in native communities was always harmonious, with everyone working together for the good of the community. Conflicts within communities—between individuals, kinship groups, or political factions—over access to power and resources were common.

But the native communities did survive, through the Colonial period and in many cases up to the present day. We can attribute at least part of that success to their collectivist orientation. By working together for their mutual support and often presenting a united front against outside forces, the townsfolk helped to ensure the survival of the community as a whole. At the same time, however, this strong community affiliation tended to prevent people from reaching across their borders and forming broader alliances to address common problems.

Community Government

The colonial authorities grouped the native communities into townships called *municipios.* The largest settlement in each *municipio* was designated as the *cabecera,* or head community. The other communities then became subjects, or sujetos, of this head community. For administrative purposes, jurisdiction trickled down to the subject towns through the governing officials of the *cabecera.* In turn, tribute payments, legal disputes, and other matters passed first from the subject towns to the *cabecera* and from there to higher, Spanish-controlled, levels of administration. Interestingly, although Spanish administrators viewed this organization in terms of a hierarchy of greater and lesser towns, native people took a different view. For them, each town was essentially an equal and independent unit of the same type. The *cabecera* had certain rights and duties for the sake of convenient administration, but generally it was not seen as inherently dominant over the other towns around it.

The colonial administration, by incorporating the native community into its structure, helped ensure the survival of that institution. One could argue that the Spanish rulers caused it to survive, that they kept the native communities intact precisely because their existence facilitated the colonial program of indirect rule. It was easier for the Spanish authorities to allow the native communities to govern their own local affairs than it would have been to introduce an entirely new sociopolitical organization at all levels of native society. For Indians to identify with their local communities, rather than uniting more broadly along class or ethnic lines, also served the Spanish strategy of "divide and conquer."

But we can also look at this in another way. The native people probably would not have tolerated the complete dissolution of their communities. The Spaniards would have had to contend with constant rebellions and uprisings; perhaps they would have been driven out of Mesoamerica completely. The system that developed was a compromise. Native people gave up the intercommunity, regional patterns of integration that had existed at the time of the conquest, which were inherently weaker than local affiliations and were quickly undermined by colonial policies. But the Spaniards acknowledged the status of the individual community as a self-governing entity with rights to its communal property. If they had not, there might have been no colony.

In the early colonial years, political power within native communities was wielded by members of the traditional ruling families—descendants of the prehispanic *tlatoque* in Nahua regions, the *halach uinic* in Yucatán, and the *yaa tnuhu* in the Mixtec area, as well as members of other high-ranking noble families. These leaders came to be called *caciques* by Spaniards who had learned this word for "chief" from the Arawaks of the West Indies and applied it to the leaders of native communities throughout the Spanish colonies. Within a few decades of the conquest, however, the Spaniards imposed a system of community government that was based on the model of town government in Spain.

By the mid-sixteenth century, native communities were governed by a municipal council called a *cabildo* (Figure 5.8). The *cabildo* consisted of a hierarchy of offices. Men from the community were elected to these offices, typically for terms of one year. In theory, all tribute-paying men of the community—that is, all married men and widowers—had the right to both hold office and vote in *cabildo* elections. In many cases, however, the traditional ruling families managed to hold a monopoly on the highest community offices. Similarly, elites often were able to manipulate elections, sometimes by limiting voting rights to those who already held office, or by only allowing members of the nobility to vote.

The most prestigious office was that of *gobernador*, or governor. After him came the *alcalde*, or judge, of which there were one or two, followed by between two and four *regidores*, or councilmen. Below these there were several variously named lesser offices, whose incumbents served as notaries, constables, policemen, wardens of the town jail, church stewards, tribute collectors, and messengers. A municipal building, constructed on the town's central plaza opposite or adjacent to the church, housed the *cabildo* offices and the jail.

At first, the traditional office of hereditary ruler was combined with the new office of governor, with no abrupt change in leadership. However, the political structure did change as the *cabildo* system took shape. The governor had to share his power with the other officials. And since *cabildo* officials were subject to yearly elections and the local priest and the local Spanish *corregidor* or *encomendero* could veto *cabildo* appointments, men who hoped to remain in office had to cooperate with the colonial administration. Unlike preconquest rulers, colonial governors often served only for short terms. But some managed to hold office continually for many years. For example, Antonio Valeriano, a noted Nahua scholar who spoke Latin and collaborated on some of the great works of sixteenth-century Nahuatl literature (see Chapter 12), served for eight years as governor of his hometown of Azcapotzalco and then became the Indian governor of Mexico City for twenty-three years, retiring only when his health failed. A commoner by birth, Valeriano was able to pursue this political career thanks to his marriage to a daughter of Mexico City's traditional royal dynasty.

According to law, *cabildo* officials were supposed to be Indians from the community. But mestizos, typically the sons of local Mesoamerican noblewomen who had married Spaniards, were occasionally elected, their ability to function in both Spanish and Indian worlds being seen as an asset by their Indian supporters. And sometimes outsiders would move into a community and gain office through aggressive politicking, as we know from court cases in which disgruntled locals challenged the authority of these usurpers.

The *cabildo* members had jurisdiction over all affairs that were internal to the community. They could imprison offenders, impose taxes and fines, assign community lands to needy families, rent out community lands to raise money, and grant permits allowing individual merchants or craftsmen to pursue their trade in the community. They could allocate community funds to such projects as build-

Figure 5.8 The members of Mexico City's native *cabildo* receive staffs of office, plus advice on good leadership, from Luis de Velasco, viceroy of New Spain from 1551–1564. *Códice Osuna.* Mexico City, Mexico: Instituto Indigenista Interamericano, 1947, p. 198.

ing roads, maintaining the town hall and the church, and financing religious festivals. Non-Indians who wished to take up residence in the town had to petition the *cabildo* for permission—which was often denied. *Cabildo* officers also had the unpleasant tasks of collecting tribute payments and assigning local men to the labor drafts required under the *repartimiento* system. For an example of a *cabildo* in action, see Box 5.2.

Box 5.2 *Ana Gets a New House Site: San Miguel Tocuillan, 1583.*

An unusually detailed Nahuatl record of a land transfer provides insight into how colonial town government operated. This document comes from the town of San Miguel Tocuillan, a lakeshore community located near the larger town of Texcoco, to the east of Mexico City. Written by the town notary, this record was intended for local use; it is not directed to Spanish officials and assumes that the persons mentioned are known to the reader.

The text tells of a woman named Ana who, along with her husband, Juan, and their small son, also named Juan, has been staying for a month in the home of her older brother, Juan Miguel, who is a member of the town's council or *cabildo.* It is possible that they lost their former residence because of flooding: The brother's house is described as being on high ground. Ana decides to petition the council for a plot of land on which she and her husband can build themselves a new home. Her brother goes off to gather four other members of the town council, telling his sister:

> "Don't worry, younger sister. Let me go and get them right away, and you be making a tortilla or two. There's nothing for you to worry about; there's *pulque* for them to drink when they come."

Juan Miguel returns with the councilmen, and Ana invites them in and serves a snack. After they have eaten, she asks them for a piece of the town's communal land, which she describes as belonging to the town's patron saint. Following the customary rules for polite speech, she expresses herself very humbly:

> "I have summoned you for a negligible matter. Here is what we beg, that we might apply for a bit of the land of our precious father the saint San Miguel, for we want to put up a little hut there. I don't have many children; the only one I have is little Juan alone. May we?"

The councilmen agree to grant her request, and the entire group immediately heads out to find a suitable piece of land. Ana chooses the spot, and a square lot is measured out. The rest of the proceedings are recorded as follows:

> Then Ana said, "Thank you very much; we appreciate your generosity."
>
> Then the rulers said, "Let it begin right away; don't let the stone concern you, but let it quickly be prepared to begin the foundation."
>
> Then Ana said, "Let's go back and you must enjoy a bit more *pulque*."
>
> Then the rulers said, "What more do we wish? We've already had enough."
>
> And Ana wept, and her husband wept, when they were given the land.
>
> Then Ana said, "Candles will be burnt, and I will continue to provide incense for my precious father the saint San Miguel, because it is on his land that I am building my house."
>
> Then Juan Miguel said, "We thank you on behalf of your precious father. Let it always remain this way."
>
> When all five lords had spoken, everyone embraced.

The notary and all five councilmen signed the document. All six men have simple Spanish saints' names as their surnames—such as Juan Miguel—but all claim for themselves the noble title "don."

An indigenous perspective pervades this account. Rather than just summarizing the results, the notary has meticulously recorded the words spoken (or allegedly spoken) by the parties involved throughout the process. This reflects the continuing importance of oral expression in native life: Written documents exist to record what people say, not to replace the spoken word with impersonal prose.

The conduct of public life is highly ceremonialized: People do not simply carry on a conversation, but give formal little speeches. The parties share food and drink before getting down to business. They treat one another with much respect. The successful petitioners weep in a ritualized display of humility and gratitude. All parties embrace at the close of business.

Religious beliefs are closely tied up with this economic transaction: The land "belongs" to Saint Michael; Ana promises to make offerings to the saint as if in fulfillment of a religious vow; her brother invokes San Miguel as the symbolic father of the *cabildo* members.

Finally, we also see a native woman acting independently and negotiating the local political scene to her own and her family's advantage. True, as sister of a councilman Ana had an "in" with the officeholders, but rather than letting her older brother speak for her she presents her own case. Her husband stands by and lets her do the talking. She knows the right things to do and say, and is duly rewarded: Having asked for land on which to build a "little hut," she is allowed to choose the site herself and is promised a sturdy house with a stone foundation.

(Adapted from Lockhart 1991:66–74)

If a legal dispute crossed community lines—perhaps a Spanish rancher was running cattle on community land, or people in one town were diverting water from irrigation canals claimed by another town—the case would move up to the Indian courts run by the Spanish colonial administration. Indians did not hesitate to pursue their claims in these higher courts. Indian plaintiffs often were successful in their lawsuits, even when they were up against Spanish defendants. The Indians quickly gained a reputation as being excessively litigious, ready to run before the court after the slightest injury.

Social Structure and the Family

Throughout the Colonial period, the basic division of native society into nobles and commoners remained intact. It was reinforced by the colonial government's recognition of the nobles' right to govern and to receive tribute from their vassals. Although the degree of wealth differentiation between nobles and commoners shrank over time, status differences within native society continued to be important throughout the Colonial period. The nobility saw their wealth diminish as they lost control over resources to Spaniards and as community lands were appropriated by non-Indians. Also, some of the wealthier nobles were siphoned off into mainstream society as high-ranking women wed Spaniards and raised children who identified with the dominant culture. But in many parts of colonial Mesoamerica, marked status differences between nobles and commoners were retained (Figure 5.9).

Another long-term effect of colonial rule was the breakdown of traditional family systems in favor of a nuclear family model promoted by both Church and state. This process proceeded at different rates in different areas, with some aspects of extended family and lineage organization surviving to the present in rural regions.

Colonial authorities believed that the Indians would be easier to supervise and control if divided into small nuclear households. The authority of the elders would be reduced if their adult children were separated from their influence. Also, since tribute levels and labor drafts were assessed on the basis of how many male heads of household resided in the community, it worked to the Spaniards' advantage if young Indian men married and set up their own homes.

Priests, seeking to keep young people from engaging in premarital sexual relations, also encouraged them to marry young. Whereas in preconquest times people generally married around age nineteen or twenty, during the Colonial period marriage often occurred during the mid-teens, or even younger for girls. With the Church controlling the wedding ceremony and imposing new restrictions on the choice of marriage partners, family elders found their authority over their kin even further undermined (Figure 5.10).

Colonialism also had an impact on gender relations. The trend toward male-headed nuclear families reduced some of the autonomy native women had traditionally enjoyed as members of extended kin groups. The age difference between wives and husbands widened. A young girl of fourteen or fifteen, living

Figure 5.9 These paintings from 1774 show the differences in dress between A) Indian *caciques*, or members of the native elite, and B) commoners. Pedro Alonso O'Crouley, *A Description of the Kingdom of New Spain*, ed. and trans. by Seán Galvin. San Francisco, CA: John Howell Books, 1972.

Figure 5.10 This woodcut from 1565 depicts a Franciscan priest presiding over a native wedding ceremony. The bridegroom wears the traditional native-style cape knotted over his colonial-style tunic; the bride wears the long, loose blouse and skirt characteristic of Nahua women before and after the Spanish conquest. From Alonso de Molina, *Confessionario mayor, en lengua Mexicana y Castellana*, folio 57r. Courtesy of the John Carter Brown Library at Brown University.

alone with a husband a few years older, obviously did not have the same power base as a woman of twenty wed to a man her own age and surrounded by a network of supportive relatives. Over a period of generations, the balance of power shifted somewhat in favor of male dominance. However, gender relations in native communities tended to remain more egalitarian than those that prevailed in Spanish and mestizo contexts.

This shift can be seen, for example, in Nahuatl documents from Central Mexico analyzed by anthropologist Susan Kellogg. Records from the sixteenth century show Nahua women being very active in the colonial courts, acting as plaintiffs in lawsuits and presenting their own testimony. In their wills, they pass property to a wide variety of relatives including siblings and cousins—that is, members of their own family who were not related by blood to these women's husbands. In the seventeenth century, women rarely pursued lawsuits in their own right but instead were represented in court by their husbands or fathers. And in their wills, they left nearly all of their possessions to their husbands and children, following Spanish patterns that favored nuclear family ties over broader networks of kin relations.

At baptism, every Indian child received a Spanish first name. These were always the names of Catholic saints, some of which were so popular that a small town might have many Anas, Isabels, Juans, and Pedros. Other names used by native people reflect differences in rank and in the degree of Spanish influence operative in any given area. Native names came into use as individual surnames; some then became established as family surnames. These native names were passed down from one's ancestors or from preconquest naming traditions. For example, before the conquest the Nahua often referred to their daughters according to their order of birth: Tiacapán for the eldest, Tlaco for the middle one, Xoco for the youngest, Mocel for an only daughter. In the colonial records appear women with such names as María Tiacapán, Barbara Tlaco, Ana Xoco, and Angelina Mocel. Other names derived from the day-signs of the traditional calendar: hence, Martín Ocelotl, (Martin Jaguar). Some native nobles chose to use traditional lordly titles as their second names. In general, the farther people were from the centers of Spanish power, the greater the extent to which these indigenous names were maintained.

The historian James Lockhart has found that when native people did take on Spanish surnames, their usage tended to correlate with social status. High-ranking noble families sometimes adopted a name associated with the Spanish nobility, such as Mendoza, Velasco, or Pimentel. Nobles also made frequent use of the Spanish title "don" (or "doña" for women), prefixing this to their name: For example, don Diego de Mendoza was the native ruler of Tlatelolco from 1549 to 1562. Somewhat less prestigious were Spanish surnames derived from Catholic religion, such as de la Cruz ("of the Cross") or San Miguel. And people of humbler status, or even nobles in smaller towns (such as the *cabildo* members discussed in Box 5.2), might have as their second name a typical saint's name (without the San), such that in effect they had two first names: Ana Juana, Pedro Martín. Last names of this sort were less likely to be passed along as family surnames.

One European institution that proved enormously popular with native Mesoamericans was the Catholic custom of godparenthood. In standard Church practice, a child is sponsored at baptism by a couple who then share the parents' responsibility for the child's religious education and, if necessary, material needs. As this institution was adapted by Mesoamericans, these ritual kinship ties came to focus less on the relationship between child and godparents and more on the relationship between the two adult couples. The practice is therefore called *compadrazgo*, or "co-parenthood." Adults linked in this manner call each other *compadres*, "co-parents" or "co-fathers," and *comadres*, "co-mothers."

We can easily understand why this institution proved useful to the native people. The recurrent epidemics left many people widowed or orphaned. Men were often away from home for long periods because of *repartimiento* obligations or wage labor; some died or became disabled while working at dangerous tasks such as mining. *Compadrazgo* gave families a mechanism for helping to ensure their mutual survival. Parents knew that if one or both of them died, they could rely on their co-parents to look after the children. It also gave people more economic security: If the whole family should fall into need, their co-parents could be relied on to share whatever resources they might have. Co-parents also helped to pay the costs of the children's courtship and wedding.

It was to a family's advantage to have many co-parents and to have close ties with them. A pattern developed by which, instead of a child's having only the godparents who sponsored her or him at baptism, additional sponsors would be chosen at other important rituals in the child's life, especially confirmation and marriage. Parents could manipulate the system in various ways, choosing to intensify ties with a small circle of ritual kin (for example, by having the same couple sponsor a number of their children), or to develop more extensive ties by involving as many other couples as possible. They could also choose whether to seek alliances with people of their own socioeconomic status, thus promoting solidarity among equals, or to invite people of higher rank, such as local nobles or wealthy non-Indians, into their circle. This had economic advantages, for one could then approach this wealthier couple if in need of a loan, and they might help their sponsored child to find a job. For the higher-ranking couple, to be sought out in this way was a source of prestige.

In a sense, the native people used these forms of ritual kinship, which were approved by the Church, to compensate for the loss of their more traditional patterns of extended kinship ties. *Compadrazgo* relationships were marked by a great deal of formality and respect, and thus provided a context in which customs of polite behavior and formal speech-making, developed to the status of a fine art in preconquest times, could continue to flourish.

Economy

The economic activities that members of native communities engaged in varied tremendously across colonial Mesoamerica, reflecting both the traditional differences that had existed at the time of the Spanish invasion and the variable influence of Spanish interference in local affairs. At one end of the spectrum are the more isolated—usually highland—communities where subsistence agriculture, little changed from the precolumbian past, has remained the dominant activity of most residents up to the present day. At the other extreme are communities whose economies were transformed because they were located near Spanish population centers or in areas where Spanish enterprises came to dominate the local economy. In these cases, the introduction of new crops and new technologies together with a foreign work ethic—reliance on wage labor—thoroughly disrupted traditional economic relations. The experience of most native communities, of course, lies somewhere between these two extremes.

The traditional agricultural system, and its reliance on the cultivation of maize and other indigenous crops, prevailed in many communities throughout the Colonial period, but it was quickly supplemented with the introduction—and ready acceptance by the natives—of European fruits and vegetables. Similarly, European animals, particularly chickens, pigs, and goats, were quickly adopted by Indian families. In some areas simple European agricultural technology, such as the ox-driven plow, became an essential part of native agricultural technology.

The *repartimiento* system of forced labor was clearly a disruptive influence within the Indian communities, but the concept of what was essentially a labor tax was not a foreign one for Mesoamerican Indians. As with tribute, communities had been compelled to provide labor to dominant powers, whether they be regional capitals or the powerful Aztec or Quiché empires, in precolumbian times. It does seem likely, however, that the levels of forced labor under the Spaniards increased and were much more burdensome, particularly in light of the disastrous population decline that reduced the size of the potential labor force so precipitously. The decline of the *repartimiento* system cleared the way for what was a truly new form of economic relationship: wage labor.

The idea of selling one's labor for money must have seemed strange to the Mesoamerican natives when it was first introduced. We do not know what proportion of the Indians participated in this system by the close of the Colonial period, but surely a large number were compelled to work for others at one time or another. Many who had managed to survive and support families by growing enough food for their own sustenance found the situation increasingly difficult in the eighteenth century. By the mid-eighteenth century communities that had paid tribute for over 200 years in the goods they produced were now forced to pay tribute in money. At the same time, pressures on land were also increasing owing to larger Indian (and non-Indian) populations and increased Spanish takeovers of Indian lands. In the face of such pressures, many Indians were forced to turn to Spanish enterprises—the local hacienda, sugar plantation, or textile factory—to make ends meet.

Religion

Indian parishes were called *doctrinas*, or "doctrines," rather than the usual Spanish term *parroquia*. This difference in terminology highlights the continuing sense, on the part of the Spaniards, that the native people were still in the process of being indoctrinated and were not fully comparable to Spanish Christians. In general, only the larger native communities had resident priests. Smaller communities would receive occasional visits from priests who lived in other towns. On these visits the priest would celebrate Mass, baptize new babies, conduct marriage ceremonies, and hear confessions. Native people often complained about priests who neglected their duties and rarely showed up in the smaller towns, or who acted abusively—charging exorbitant fees for administering the sacraments, beating people, molesting women—when they did come. Priests fluent in the languages of their native parishioners were always in short supply.

The native people were able to exercise considerable control over their own religious life. Persons from the community handled many day-to-day affairs and also organized the community festivals. The most important religious official was called the *fiscal*. He acted as an assistant or deputy to the priest. The *fiscal* oversaw local matters such as teaching the catechism to children; making sure that everyone attended Mass; and keeping records of baptisms, marriages, and burials. Today these parish record books are valuable sources of information on demography, family structure, and naming patterns.

Other religious officials included the sacristan, who supervised the maintenance of the church building and its ornaments. A choirmaster, or *maestro de coro,* was in charge of musical performances (Figure 5.11). Music was such an integral part of native worship that this position brought considerable status. He and the members of the choir, both singers and musicians, sometimes enjoyed special privileges such as exemptions from paying tribute or the payment of a salary. However, these salaries were only a small fraction of what choir members in the Spaniards' churches received. Other minor officials, often designated even in non-Nahua areas by the Nahuatl term *teopan tlaca,* or "church people," were responsible for such tasks as preparing bodies for burial and digging the graves, cleaning the church grounds, and providing fresh flowers and other decorations. The carrying out of these various religious duties was often hampered when people had to leave their communities to find wage labor.

Figure 5.11 Two Nahua *cantores,* or choir members, rehearse their music in this native painting from the *Florentine Codex.* Native choirs sang Latin chants during Church services and also prepared music for religious festivals, when native-language songs were sung to the accompaniment of drums and other traditional instruments. *Florentine Codex,* Book 10, folio 19r. Reprinted, with permission, from Fray Bernardino de Sahagún, *Historia General de las cosas de Nueva España,* Códice florentino. Facsimile of the Codex Florentinus of the Biblioteca Medicea Laurenciana, supervised by the Archivo General de la Nación (AGN) de México, Florence, Italy, 1979.

The most important institution in native religious life was the *cofradía*, the religious brotherhood or confraternity. Like *compadrazgo*, this was a European institution that native people took over and adapted to their own purposes. The *cofradía* was a voluntary organization—that is, members joined by their own choice. Each confraternity was devoted to some aspect of Catholic belief. For example, a town might have one or more confraternities devoted to the Virgin Mary in her various forms (such as the Assumption, the Rosary, or the Immaculate Conception), one devoted to the Souls in Purgatory, another devoted to the Passion of Christ, another devoted to the Eucharist, and another devoted to Saint Francis or some other saint. A small village might have just two or three of these organizations, but a larger town might have a dozen and a city would have several attached to each of its neighborhood churches.

Members of a confraternity contributed yearly dues to a communal coffer. The funds were used to pay for the funerals of any members who passed away (not a trivial matter in times of epidemic disease); to finance Masses for the souls of the dead; and to purchase the candles, flowers, costumes, and other paraphernalia needed for religious festivals that the group sponsored. The members also took care of the holy images housed in the local church. They manufactured ornate vestments and processional platforms to be used when the images were brought out of the church during festivals. They acted in a general sense as mutual aid societies, caring for impoverished or orphaned members.

Each confraternity was responsible for the public celebration associated with its designated devotion. For example, a confraternity dedicated to the Passion of Christ would conduct elaborate processions on Good Friday and act out a dramatization of the Crucifixion. A confraternity devoted to the Virgin of the Assumption would hold a large procession on August 15, parading around the town with images of the Virgin Mary. They might stage a show in which an actor playing Mary would be lifted into the air on a platform raised by pulleys, thus representing her ascent into heaven. Confraternities devoted to the Souls in Purgatory would have their special day on November 2, the Feast of All Souls, when they would make offerings of food and flowers in the community's cemetery and hire a priest to say Masses for the dead.

Cofradías were formally instituted and overseen by the Catholic Church: The native people were not free to invent their own. However, as they operated at the local level these organizations did allow people to organize their religious celebrations much as they chose. The collective orientation undoubtedly appealed to the native people, allowing them to come together in groups dedicated to a common purpose. The confraternities counterbalanced the authority of the priest—an isolated foreigner—with that of local groups who controlled their own funds and whose ceremonial rights and duties were inscribed in official statutes. Women, whom the priests barred from offices such as *fiscal* and choirmaster, were able to take on informal leadership roles within the confraternities, thereby gaining prestige in the community while participating actively in religious celebrations.

The Catholic saints were regarded as community sponsors and protectors. Under a colonial policy, the name of each town's patron saint was combined with the town's traditional name to yield a composite designation—for example, San Miguel Tocuillan or San Andrés Calpan. The town's identity became closely linked to that of the saint in the minds of its residents as well, as seen in the land document in Box 5.2 where the saint is treated as the owner of the town's communal property. The centering of religious devotion around community patron saints makes sense in a political and social context where the community was the most important unit (Figure 5.12).

Because they did not see any necessary contradiction between Christian worship and their own traditions, native people supplemented their Christian devotions with many other practices that were more indigenous in character or that freely combined Christian and native elements. This was particularly true in regard to concerns that were not adequately addressed within the rudimentary form of Christianity that the native people were taught. Issues of personal, family, and group survival were the most prevalent concerns. These were dealt with through rituals surrounding the birth of a child; through a wide range of curing techniques; and through rites intended to ensure success in agriculture, hunting, or other subsistence pursuits. Curers, midwives, and conjurers of the weather—people who were credited with control over winds, rain, and hailstorms—enjoyed considerable prestige and operated as informal religious authorities.

From the viewpoint of the Catholic priests, such practitioners were in league with the Devil. The practitioners themselves, however, often claimed that their powers were given to them by God or a saint, whom they encountered in a vision. They used formulas from Christian prayers in their incantations, and sometimes explained misfortune in reference to Catholic supernaturals, claiming, for example, that the sick person had angered a particular saint. At the same time, they invoked preconquest deities, often using complex metaphors that masked these deities' identity behind a kind of secret language. They sometimes used psychogenic substances, such as peyote or hallucinogenic mushrooms, in their quest for supernatural knowledge. They made offerings at ancient shrines, and in some areas continued to observe the ancient 260-day ritual calendar.

At the household level, religious devotions centered around a family altar, which in Nahuatl was called the *santocalli*, or "saints' house." Here again, Christian worship combined with non-Christian customs. A housewife would often begin her day by ritually sweeping her patio and offering fire or incense to the four directions, but the same woman might later be seen kneeling before her altar and reciting the Hail Mary and other Catholic prayers in her own language. Images of saints, crucifixes, rosaries, and other religious objects were purchased, treated with reverence, and bequeathed to one's heirs. Native wills sometimes specify who will receive such objects and demand that the inheritor show proper reverence by making offerings or sweeping around the altar. But the saints' images might share the altar with an ancient figurine that had been passed down from the family's ancestors or that someone had discovered somewhere. Even an oddly shaped stone someone happened to dig up in his field might be placed on the altar as a manifestation of divine essence. Offerings of food and fresh flowers would be made to all of these revered objects.

Figure 5.12 In the Nahua town of Tepoztlan, south of Mexico City, a native sculptor decorated the sixteenth-century church with this large relief carving of the Virgin Mary, Tepoztlan's patron saint.

Today, the principal saint worshipped throughout Mexico, by native people and mestizos alike, is Our Lady of Guadalupe, an advocation of the Blessed Virgin Mary. The origin of this colonial cult is outlined in Box 5.3.

One final aspect of native religious life that needs to be addressed is the ritual use of alcohol. This is a sensitive subject, because the stereotype of the "drunken Indian" is a powerful one throughout the Americas and carries with it

Box 5.3 *The Virgin of Guadalupe*

The popular legend associated with this cult asserts that it began in 1531 when the Virgin appeared several times to a Nahua commoner named Juan Diego. Intercepting him as he walked past the hill of Tepeyacac, on the lakeshore north of Mexico City, she spoke to him in Nahuatl and told him to go to the bishop, who at the time was the Franciscan friar Juan de Zumárraga, and ask that a shrine be built for her on that site. To provide proof of her presence, she had Juan Diego gather into his mantle the flowers that were blooming on the hillside. When he shook out his mantle in front of the bishop, the Virgin's image appeared miraculously impressed upon the cloth. Zumárraga kneeled before it, and soon a new shrine was built to house the image. According to tradition, this cloth image is the same one revered today at the basilica at Tepeyacac, which now lies in the northern part of Mexico City's huge urban sprawl.

Controversy has long surrounded the origins of this cult, for authentic sixteenth-century documents supporting the traditional legend have never been found. The date of the shrine's origin is unclear, though it was surely founded by Spanish devotees of the original Virgin of Guadalupe, Spain's principal shrine to the Virgin Mary. The cult image at the Spanish shrine is a statue of the Madonna and Child. The first cult image in Mexico may have been a copy of this statue, later superseded by the cloth image known today. In contrast to Spain's Guadalupe, this image depicts the Virgin of the Immaculate Conception: She stands alone, hands joined as if in prayer, upon a crescent moon and surrounded by beams of light.

The documents that do exist indicate that the Mexican shrine first became popular in the mid-1550s, when significant numbers of Spaniards from the city started going there to worship. Furthermore, according to this documentation the cult image these Spaniards were revering had recently been painted by a native artist. Stylistically, the cult image does closely resemble the work of native artists from the mid- to late sixteenth century, much of which was based on woodcuts imported from Spain. It is known that these artists sometimes painted religious images on cloth.

Another popular claim, that the shrine stood on the site where an Aztec mother goddess had previously been worshipped, such that the identity of this goddess merged with that of the Virgin, is also impossible to substantiate. It is probable, though, that some form of preconquest shrine did stand on this site. It was by no means unusual for colonial chapels and churches to be built on or near the ruins of preconquest temples.

The earliest versions of the legend appear to date from the early seventeenth century, and it was not widely known until it was popularized by creole priests in the middle of that century (Figure 5.13). However, it is interesting that the earliest known versions are in the Nahuatl language. Parts of the story are told in a native style, with elements that fit very well with indigenous conceptions of encounters with the supernatural. This suggests that native people, even if only a few literate nobles who worked with Spanish priests, had something to do with the development of the legend—that it was not simply invented by creoles. But the basic outline of the story bears a strong resemblance to European legends about miraculous images. Apparently, this basic legend form was adapted to fit the Mexican context and an image that already existed—and to which people were attributing miracles.

Despite the popular belief that the shrine immediately became a focus of native religious devotion, it appears from historical records that Indian participation in the cult was limited until priests began, in the later seventeenth century, to propagate the cult in native communities. Until this time, as James Lockhart has noted, Indians would have had little interest in a saint's cult whose focus lay outside of their own communities and whose shrine was not under native jurisdiction. Native people participated in the worship of the Virgin, but they preferred their own local images housed in their own churches and tended by their own confraternities.

However, by the late seventeenth and eighteenth centuries the old community boundaries were weakening; many Indians spoke Spanish as well as their native language; and many were spending long periods outside of their own communities, working as wage laborers. Away from home, they interacted as individuals with Spaniards and with Indians from other communities. When their priests encouraged them to take up the Guadalupan devotion, they could now identify with a cult that represented the larger colonial society centering on the capital city, and that spoke to them as individuals and as Indians rather than as members of local ethnic groups.

Today, the Virgin of Guadalupe is herself viewed as a mestizo or Indian woman—the "dark" *(morena)* virgin. The story of her apparition to a humble Indian is an important national myth, symbolizing the merging of Spanish and Indian cultures, under divine sanction, into the Catholic and mestizo nation. But it was not until Mexico gained its independence from Spain that the cult began to function as an expression of national identity. (See Chapter 8 for more on the cult.)

HVEI
TLAMAHVIÇOLTICA
OMONEXITI IN ILHVICAC TLATÓCA
ÇIHVAPILLI
SANTA MARIA
TOTLAÇONANTZIN
GVADALVPE IN NICAN HVEI ALTEPE-
NAHVAC MEXICO ITOCAYOCAN TEPEYACAC.

Impreſſo con licencia en MEXICO: en la Imprenta de Iuan Ruyz.
Año de 1649.

Figure 5.13 Title page from the first published Nahuatl account of the Our Lady of Guadalupe apparition legend. The title reads: "By means of a great wonder appeared the royal noblewoman of heaven, Saint Mary, our precious mother, here on the outskirts of the great city of Mexico, in the place called Tepeyacac." From Luis Lasso de la Vega, *Hvei Tlamahviçoltica . . .*, 1649. Courtesy of the John Carter Brown Library at Brown University.

connotations of laziness and violence that contribute to prejudices against native people. But we should not gloss over a significant issue just because it has been so often misused and misunderstood.

During the Colonial period, Spanish observers frequently expressed dismay at the disorderly public drunkenness they saw in the native communities. Priests strove to curb such behavior by preaching against it and punishing participants. But such efforts had little impact on a behavior pattern that was becoming an integral part of native religious festivals. The communal experience of religious ceremony was expressed and enhanced by collective drinking: Sharing drinks with one's fellows reinforced community ties, while the drunken state itself transported one beyond the mundane level of nonritual life, providing a sense of being temporarily taken over by a sacred force beyond one's control. Catholic figures—in particular, certain images of the Virgin Mary—became associated with the maguey plant, whose fermented juice, *pulque*, was the most important native brew.

Spaniards consumed substantial quantities of alcohol themselves, but they admired the man who could "hold his liquor," who might partake on a daily basis but never showed signs of losing his self-control. Indians did not share the European ideal of the independent, rational, self-determining, and self-controlled individual. They exploited alcohol's capacity to alter and dissolve people's sense of individual identity, and chose to get riotously and publicly drunk on special occasions rather than drinking "moderately" and in private. This difference in the use of alcohol may have had more to do with the image of the "drunken Indian" than actual levels of consumption.

That alcohol provided some solace to the oppressed and some escape from daily hardships may also be assumed. We may further note that, given Spanish attitudes toward the Indians' drinking, this behavior was a form of resistance against colonialism, a refusal to obey the Spaniards' rules and act the way they wanted Indians to act. People who were too drunk or too hung over to labor effectively for their Spanish masters were, after all, refusing to cooperate with their own exploitation.

Unfortunately, this was a behavior pattern that also took a toll on the lives and health of native people. Traditional alcoholic beverages such as *pulque* were low in alcohol content and rich in vitamins. The Spaniards introduced wine and hard liquor, which had much higher levels of alcohol and provided little or no nutritive benefit. They also introduced the technique of distillation, which would turn maguey juice into the much stronger mescal and tequila. In the presence of these stronger drinks and in the absence of preconquest social controls over drinking, it was all too easy for native people, also faced with the hardships imposed by colonial rule, to become addicted to alcohol. Alcohol sometimes brought out aggressive behavior that would be directed against one's fellow Indians, often women. The corporate community was not always a peaceable place.

Native people who remained in the corporate communities faced an often diminishing resource base and onerous demands for tribute and labor. Their own officials sometimes ruled them unfairly. But they had the advantage of various support structures that helped to ensure that, although they might share their neighbors' poverty, they would be able at least to survive. Emotional ties within the community, reinforced by marriage patterns, ritual kinship, and collective religious life, provided a potent psychological armature that helped people to defend themselves against pressures for assimilation to the dominant culture. Legal protections granted to the native communities under colonial law—most significant, the rights to their communal lands—gave them some economic security, even though they often had to go to court to defend those rights.

People who left their communities merged into the burgeoning mass of Spanish speakers of mixed Indian, African, and Spanish descent; their children ceased to identify with Indian cultures or to speak the native languages. After the end of the Colonial period, many native towns also would gradually lose their indigenous character and merge into the dominant mestizo or Ladino society, a process that continues to the present day. But where indigenous people do survive today, their colonial ancestors lived in these corporate communities and engaged in the collective enterprise of survival that we have described.

NATIVE REBELLIONS

Native response to the imposition of Spanish colonial rule was never passive, and in much of this chapter we have seen how Indians coped with Spanish domination in creative ways, holding on to elements of their prehispanic heritage and adapting Spanish institutions to meet their own needs. But throughout the Colonial period, and right up to the present day, native groups in many parts of Mesoamerica have openly rebelled against authorities when their situations became intolerable. The following are just a few examples of native revolts that took place during the Colonial period.

We saw in Chapter 4 that the Itzá Maya of the Petén effectively resisted Spanish rule until the closing years of the seventeenth century. East and northeast of Itzá territory, in the area that today makes up central and northern Belize, the Spaniards also encountered strong Maya resistance. This region initially came under Spanish control in the early 1540s, but local Maya joined in a widespread revolt throughout the Yucatán Peninsula in 1546 and 1547. The Spaniards were determined to maintain control of the region, however, resettling rebellious Maya into *reducción* settlements. Again, in the 1630s, rebellions broke out, culminating in a major revolt in 1638 that was orchestrated by the Indians of Tipú. Over the next forty years Maya communities were deserted, and the entire region was virtually free of Spanish control. Spaniards regained control of the area in the late 1670s, but for a variety of reasons, most of the Maya population was moved to Lake Petén Itzá following the Spanish conquest of the Itzá. The entire region eventually came under British control.

In the town of Tehuantepec (Oaxaca), an abusive Spanish *alcalde mayor* was stoned to death in 1660 by angry Zapotecs. The rebels burned municipal buildings and captured Spanish weapons. With an Indian government installed in Tehuantepec, the uprising spread to other towns, nearby Nejapa and the highland towns of Ixtepeji and Villa Alta. Indian supporters of the revolt may have numbered as many as 10,000 in over twenty towns. In a letter to the viceroy, leaders of the rebellion explained that they remained loyal to the king of Spain but were unwilling to submit to harsh treatment, excessive tribute, and the demands of *repartimiento*. Within a year, the revolt had been violently suppressed; the leaders were condemned to death, their bodies quartered and displayed in prominent places within the communities.

Perhaps the most well-known native rebellion of the Colonial period is the so-called Tzeltal rebellion of highland Chiapas in 1712 (see Box 5.1 above). This rebellion was the culmination of events that began several years earlier with roots in the almost two centuries of economic abuse by Spaniards and the development of a native Christianity that horrified some members of the Spanish clergy. Beginning in 1706, the Virgin Mary appeared to Tzotzil and Tzeltal Indians in several highland communities. In each case the Virgin offered to help the Indians, and a cult was created around her image. These apparitions happened at a time when Spanish friars and priests were increasingly intolerant of any deviation from Spanish Catholicism. Church response to the Virgin cults was swift and decisive; church officials destroyed chapels dedicated to the Virgin, images of the Virgin were removed, and Indian devotees were punished. The most serious threat to Spanish authority took place in 1712, when a Virgin cult in the Tzeltal town of Cancuc developed into a large-scale uprising.

There were numerous other native rebellions in colonial Mesoamerica. None of them was successful for very long, and many never received widespread support. Spaniards always maintained an advantage since they controlled the weapons, and punishment for rebels was always severe.

SUGGESTED READINGS

CHANCE, JOHN K. 1989 *Conquest of the Sierra: Spaniards and Indians in Colonial Oaxaca.* Norman: University of Oklahoma Press.

CLINE, S. L. 1986 *Colonial Culhuacan, 1580–1600: A Social History of an Aztec Town.* Albuquerque: University of New Mexico Press.

FARRISS, NANCY M. 1984 *Maya Society Under Colonial Rule: The Collective Enterprise of Survival.* Princeton, N.J.: Princeton University Press.

GOSNER, KEVIN 1992 *Soldiers of the Virgin: The Moral Economy of a Colonial Maya Rebellion.* Tucson: University of Arizona Press.

GRUZINSKI, SERGE 1989 *Man-Gods in the Mexican Highlands: Indian Power and Colonial Society, 1520–1800.* Translated by Eileen Corrigan. Stanford, Calif.: Stanford University Press.

JONES, GRANT D. 1989 *Maya Resistance to Spanish Rule: Time and History on a Colonial Frontier.* Albuquerque: University of New Mexico Press.

LOCKHART, JAMES 1992 *The Nahuas After the Conquest: A Social and Cultural History of the Indians of Central Mexico, Sixteenth through Eighteenth Centuries.* Stanford, Calif.: Stanford University Press.

LOVELL, W. GEORGE 1985 *Conquest and Survival in Colonial Guatemala: A Historical Geography of the Cuchumatán Highlands, 1500-1821.* Kingston and Montreal: McGill-Queen's University Press.

SPORES, RONALD 1984 *The Mixtecs in Ancient and Colonial Times.* Norman: University of Oklahoma Press.

TAYLOR, WILLIAM B. 1979 *Drinking, Homicide, and Rebellion in Colonial Mexican Villages.* Stanford, Calif.: Stanford University Press.

Chapter 6
Mesoamericans in the Era of Liberal Reforms

Any effort to synthesize the social history of the Mesoamericans from independence to the beginning of the modern era must necessarily be carefully framed and qualified. Although the beginning of this period is clearly marked by political and state-level events that established the region's independent nations whose political boundaries we recognize today, it could be argued that the end of the period—the radical break with the creole past, as symbolized by the emblematic Mexican Revolution (1910)—did not occur in all of the region at the same time or in the same ways or on the same scale.

In Guatemala, for example, typically nineteenth-century liberal political and social forms appeared to find closure with the revolutionary events of the mid-twentieth century; in Honduras, to take another example, the radical break with institutions of the past is still in the process of taking place. Thus, in this chapter we are considering nineteenth-century and early twentieth-century social and political adjustments to the post-colonial order that evolved in similar ways throughout the region, but with decidedly different chronologies and national characteristics. We intend to examine the general trends and patterns of the region as a whole rather than on the basis of individual countries.

In keeping with the overall theme of the volume, our focus will be on the biological and cultural descendants of ancient Mesoamerica, a world whose coherent social system, as we have seen, was broken into a hundred pieces by the Spanish colonial regime. The Mesoamerican "Indians" were segregated into isolated rural communities during the Colonial period, where they were deprived of native leadership at regional and national levels and sorely exploited by the colonial ruling class. The new creole and mestizo leaders of the post-independence period and the liberal reforms that they advocated resulted in exploitation of the Mesoamerican Indians as severe as that by the Spanish colonialists, and these so-called liberals were perhaps even less sympathetic to the native cultures than had been the Spaniards.

Our story of the Mesoamericans in the period of liberal dominance, then, cannot be a saga of glory or triumph. Nevertheless, it will be shown that the Mesoamerican cultural tradition continued to provide an important reservoir from which the native peoples of the region could draw in their struggle to survive as ethnically distinct groups within the independent states of Mexico and Central America. We will learn, too, that the Mesoamericans contributed in concrete ways to the important social movements of the region far more than is generally recognized.

NINETEENTH-CENTURY SOCIAL HISTORY: FROM INDEPENDENCE TO DICTATORSHIP

The Break from Spain

The emergence of the modern states of Mexico and Central America between 1810 and 1825 came through a domino-like set of events, many of which began violently in Europe and reached America almost as a distant echo. The close of the eighteenth century brought the last gasp of the millennium-old vision of the Holy Roman Empire. Underwritten by the waning idea of the divine right of kings to hold both political and religious authority on behalf of universal Roman Catholic Christendom, France and Spain in the late eighteenth century were besieged by the rising economic and political power of the Protestant nations of northern Europe, particularly Britain, and by the perceived threat of the Russian and Ottoman empires in the east. The U.S. independence movement beginning in 1776 was also being watched with the greatest of interest by Spanish-American creole leaders and intellectuals. These external political and economic forces, together with the growing favor being enjoyed by Enlightenment ideals of individual and collective rights and freedoms under secular state authority, led to a violent end to the eighteenth-century political order of Europe. The French Revolution of 1789 and the subsequent continental firestorm of the Napoleonic Wars brought with them the fall, in 1807, of the faltering Bourbon monarchy of Spain. Carlos IV's abdication, the Napoleonic occupation and defeat, followed by the restoration in 1817 of a greatly weakened monarch, Fernando VII, created a full decade of political vacuum that enabled most of Spain's vast empire in America to mobilize for a clean break from Europe.

The ideologies of the American and French revolutions were conscious models for Latin America's independence movements (1810–1825), yet it is important to note that the "nationalist period" of Latin American history was dotted with early pan-national experiments, notably Iturbide's Mexican–Central American empire (1822–1823) and Simón Bolívar's confederation of Gran Colombia (1819–1830). These experiments failed, but the ideology of unity persisted even when unity could not be achieved—notably in the case of the Central American Federation, which lasted from 1823 to 1839 (Figure 6.1).

Nationalism in Mexico and Central America was intimately linked with the effort of creoles to forge a home for themselves in a region divested of the authority of the Spanish Crown. The creoles, who were left in power when Spain departed, naturally sought to stay in power. They accomplished their goal by creating states in which it made sense—at least to themselves and to Europe and to the United States—that they should be the heirs apparent of the Spanish colonial order. The creole ascendancy effectively produced the map of the modern Mesoamerican region. The seat of the old viceroyalty of Mexico became the dominant new nation. The old Captaincy General of Guatemala, however grudgingly, was broken into the lesser nations of Guatemala, Honduras, El Salvador, Nicaragua, and Costa Rica.

If the first quarter of the nineteenth century witnessed the forging of the political identity of the modern nations of the region, their essential ethnic composition long antedated their existence as nations and continues even today. Mex-

Figure 6.1 Political divisions of Mexico and Central America shortly after Independence. After Jorge L. Tamayo, *Geografía Moderna de México,* 2nd ed. Mexico City, Mexico: Editorial Trillas, 1981, p. 365.

ico emerged from the Colonial period as the quintessential mestizo core of New Spain, with significant enclaves of unmixed Spanish settlements in the north, and large parts of the central, southern, and western sections of the region effectively segregated into Indian and mestizo communities. In particular, the Mexican states of Yucatán, Chiapas, and Oaxaca contained many thousands of ethnically Indian hamlets and villages. This demographic pattern continued into Guatemala, where the northwestern and central highlands were overwhelming Indian, with large towns and cities being mestizo and creole (Figure 6.2). Pacific and Caribbean Guatemala was of mixed Indian and mestizo composition. By 1800, the southern provinces of New Spain, under the jurisdiction of the Captaincy General of Guatemala—El Salvador, Honduras, Nicaragua, and Costa Rica—had acquired their essential mestizo character that persists today, with the exception of a major presence of mixed Afro-Americans along the eastern coasts of Honduras, Nicaragua, and Costa Rica.

The Caribbean rimland, from Costa Rica north to Belize—a region that had not been of particular economic interest to Spain—remained sparsely populated with remnant Indian populations and a growing influx of West Indian Afro-Americans who emigrated there as free laborers in search of jobs when slavery was abolished in the Caribbean. These Afro-Caribbean populations, including the mixed Indian and African group known as the Black Caribs or Garífunas (who arrived as deportees in 1797), occupied a thin band of the coastal areas of Cen-

Figure 6.2 Spreading coffee beans for drying on a Guatemalan plantation in the 19th century. Courtesy of E. Bradford Burns. Reprinted from E. Bradford Burns, *Eadward Muybridge in Guatemala, 1875: The Photographer as Social Recorder.* Berkeley, CA: University of California Press, 1986, p. 118.

tral America and were significantly augmented throughout the nineteenth century as commercial agriculture and railroad and port facilities were developed there and related employment became available. The Pacific Coast of Central America (particularly in Nicaragua) and Mexico also had a significant Afro-American demographic presence, some dating from early in the Colonial period in relation to sugar and cotton plantation agriculture. Other black immigrants, along with significant numbers of Chinese, arrived in the nineteenth century to work in the construction of railroads, telegraph systems, and port facilities.

Centralism, Federalism, *Caudillos*, and *Caciques*

The administrative centers of the Mesoamerican region's new nations, once formed, typically did not enjoy effective territorial and political sovereignty. One of the reasons was demographic. Most of the new nations of the region had a series of noncontiguous heartland settlement areas, separated by vast hinterlands. This noncontiguous, nucleated settlement pattern led to various political expressions of regionalism, for authority systems were in effect local, not national. To some extent, then, the new nations were fictions, and central governments had neither the communication and transportation systems nor the political control to exert effective national authority. Regionalism was thus related to the important current of federalism as a model for governing. The powerful creole elites, however, lived in the old capital cities and provincial capitals. This old aristocracy of land, army, and Church interests was linked by ties of kinship and common interests in such a way that their power bases, the national and provincial capitals, expressed a political preference for central authority, which was usually conservative, pro-clerical, and favorably disposed to large landholding interests. The political expression of centralist elements was also conservative in the sense that suggests that power and tradition beget wisdom and, for this reason, ought to rule. Alliance with the army, therefore, became an important part of the centralist political strategy, for military coercion was an effective way of enforcing the right of conservatives to rule.

Federalists were skeptical of the centralist vision and generally followed U.S. models of regionally based consensus, with the central government being more a bureaucratic and ceremonial than a policy-making entity. Federalism tended to be politically "liberal" in the sense of valuing individual and regional expressions of self-interest. This meant that social and economic sectors beneath the landholding aristocracy were entitled to political expression, the acquisition of property, education, and general participation in "social progress." Federalism and liberalism, most typically associated with the presidencies of Benito Juárez of Mexico (1854–1862; 1867–1872) (Figure 6.3) and Justo Rufino Barrios of Guatemala (1873–1885) (Figure 6.4) also tended to favor the secular state and diminished legal and economic power for the Catholic Church. So great was the antipathy of the Mexican conservative elite for the liberal reforms that they looked in desperation for help from abroad, which led France, for reasons of its

Figure 6.3 Painting of Benito Juárez, the great Liberal reformer of Mexico. James A. Magner, *Men of Mexico,* 2nd ed. Salem, N.H.: Books for Libraries, Ayer Company Publishers, 1968.

own, to help install a short-lived and ill-fated monarchy in Mexico (1867–1872) under the Archduke Maximilian of Austria.

The oscillation between federalist and centralist models was the great leitmotif of nineteenth-century political life in all of the region from Costa Rica to Mexico. The pattern of oscillation yielded periods of liberal "reform," such as the eras of Juárez and Barrios, in which liberal, federalist models encouraged diffusion of economic and political authority from central to regional governments.

The oscillating pattern of centralism and federalism also tended, in centralist periods, to emphasize development of urban centers and their access to port cities. This lack of interest in the hinterland, beyond its economic utility, had an obvious result: The hinterland was never fully incorporated into national cultural and political life. The social and economic relations between city and

Figure 6.4 Justo Rufino Barrios, the Liberal strongman of Guatemala.

countryside became progressively more unidirectional, with wealth flowing out of the countryside into the cities and abroad, thus concentrating status and privilege and development priorities in the urban centers. This phenomenon had a great deal to do with Mexico's loss, under the long rule of centralist President Antonio López de Santa Anna, of half of its national territory to the United States in 1848. It is useful in understanding the origins of the U.S. Hispanic Southwest to realize that Santa Anna and his followers regarded the far north and its inhabitants as irrelevant to the national interest, for both economic and demographic reasons. Their priorities lay with the urban heartland and the agricultural, ranching, and mining resources of Mexico's Central Basin.

The poles of centralism and federalism were also related to other themes in national life in the region. Under the centralist mode, the emphasis was on economic development and creation of a commercial infrastructure (communication and transportation) in the already dominant urban areas and in those areas suitable for large-scale, capital-intensive, and labor-intensive agricultural production. Under the federalist program, the emphasis was on the extension of political and social participation to broader sectors of society. Yet both centralism and federalism coincided in their commitment to the positivist agenda of progress via economic growth and applied science. If anything, both models created new opportunities for the creole establishment to dominate national life, both in the capitals and in the provinces. The rural and urban poor, largely of mestizo and Indian background, found themselves economically and socially more marginalized under both modern systems than they had been in the closing years of the Colonial period.

Although the constitutions of the new nations generally followed French and U.S. models, the political traditions of the region's states were not generally democratic. Rather, they were personalistic and authoritarian, with a strong military infrastructure that often became one with the political system. The long-lived regimes of dictators Rafael Carrera (1844–1865) of Guatemala and Porfirio Díaz (1872–1910) of Mexico exemplified this tradition. It is easy to find the roots of this system in the structure of the older colonial society, whose strong infrastructure was actually appropriated by the new creole *caudillos* ("strong men"). In the older system as well as its derivate forms after independence, both liberal and conservative, the military was always at the disposal of the political authorities to safeguard and underwrite their right to rule.

The tradition of authoritarian, personalistic rule allied with military force was based on the charismatic leadership qualities of one individual, the *caudillo*. The support from the army was usually obtained through reciprocal favors. The compliance of the army in supporting the *caudillos* was encouraged by the opportunities for social and economic mobility for mestizos that were available through military careers. This was a singularly successful way—often the only way—for ambitious mestizos to penetrate the relatively impermeable social networks of the creole aristocracy and new professional classes. The creoles needed the army to guarantee their own positions of political and economic power. The cost to the creoles consisted of granting privileges—substantial salaries as well as access to their own family networks through intermarriage. In this manner, upwardly mobile mestizo army officers became economically, politically, and socially allied with the creole elite. Often it was the case that mestizo officers in effect tended the creoles' interests in the provinces while the creoles themselves, who preferred urban life, lived well in the cities and occasionally visited their country estates. Sometimes the mestizo army officers became national leaders themselves and, with their military affiliations, were able to take power and remain in power. This pattern crossed the federalist-centralist dichotomy in a way that allowed mestizos to reach positions of national authority under both centralist and federalist rubrics.

The local expression of *caudillo* was the *cacique*, a small-scale version of the nondemocratic, authoritarian ruler at the community level (not to be confused with the native elite class of the Colonial period, also known as *caciques*).

This system of personalistic local authority characterized both mestizo and Indian communities, and often, in the latter case, involved the descendants of the old Indian elite families who had enjoyed, during the Colonial period, privileges and exemptions from the tribute system in exchange for serving as intermediaries, labor provisioners, and tribute collectors for the Crown. As these small-scale strong-man fiefdoms evolved in the region, it was often the case (as it was at the regional and national levels with the system of *caudillos*) that reciprocity greased the system through such favors—from the *cacique*—as loans, legal assistance, marriage arrangements, jobs, and scriptorial services. *Caudillos* and *caciques* were also involved in ritual kinship links with their subalterns through the system of *compadrazgo*, whereby the *caudillo* or *cacique* would become godparent, patron, and protector of the client's child in the ritual of baptism. The client, in turn, owed absolute loyalty to his patron in all matters pertaining to defending his privileges and right to absolute political authority in local affairs. This mode of local political authority, while often informal, nevertheless proved to be an effective way of guaranteeing local stability in the ebb and flow of national politics.

Forces Leading to Stable Dictatorship

The intellectual universe of the independence movement and the subsequent formulation of national agendas and priorities were strongly influenced by French positivism. It was a world view and policy template that emphasized the ideal of inevitable progress and modernization through science and reason. Following closely the ideals of general social evolution, the models to be emulated were European. Latin America was "behind" in the world hierarchy of power, progress, and prosperity and felt obliged to "catch up." These ideals, as interpreted by creoles in Mexico and Central America, could best be achieved through economic development of their backward regions. Thus, capitalist development, with relatively few regulatory constraints, became the policy focus of most nineteenth-century governments of the region, both liberal and conservative. Whatever brought economic growth, urban development, increased production for export markets, and "civilization" was good. This meant that education and expanded social inclusion for skilled technicians were desirable, but not so much so as to keep "progress" from favoring the privileges of the old creole elite.

The ideology of positivism created the new professional ideal of engineering (applied science). Applied scientists and technicians, known generally as *científicos* (scientists), were essential for the creation of the commercial infrastructure that would make economic progress possible. Architects, agronomists, electrical engineers, railroad technicians, and road engineers became respectable and their professions prestigious and well remunerated. The creole aristocrats' preference for gentleman farming and ranching, army careers, and the priesthood was amplified to include the newly desirable category of *científico*. To this day, few titles before one's name are more honorable or likely to impress than *Ingeniero* (literally "engineer", but also referring to college degrees in all applied sciences).

While significant numbers of the new elite sector of *científicos* came from creole and mestizo stock within the region, tens of thousands of trained technicians and applied scientists were imported from Western Europe and the United States. Many of these professional newcomers became citizens of their adopted nations. They, too, along with the high-ranking army officers of mestizo background, were admitted to elite creole economic, political, and social networks.

Along with the *científicos* who immigrated to Mexico and Central America in the nineteenth century to build the railroads, telegraph lines, port facilities, and roads and to plant vast new expanses of land with commercial cash crops such as cotton, henequen, coffee, and bananas, there also came significant waves of nonprofessional new immigrants from Europe in search of jobs and opportunity in the climate of the region's burgeoning new export industries. Significant numbers of Asians and West Indian Afro-Caribbeans also came in search of jobs. The Chinese were particularly important as labor for the feverish pace of railroad construction. The West Indian immigrants were actually preferred as laborers for the banana plantations because these were mostly owned by North Americans who found it easier to deal with Afro-Caribbean English speakers than with local Spanish speakers. Although the old creole elite did not lose out on the direct and indirect benefits of the fever for economic development and modernization, the mestizo and Indian poor turned out the big losers. Increasingly, the power structure totally excluded these elements of the population, even though they comprised an overwhelming majority of the population. In contrast, the newly arrived *científicos* did extremely well. In some cases, their success eclipsed the privileges of the old creole elite. It was not uncommon at the end of the nineteenth century to have railroad and telegraph facilities wholly in the hands of North American and English companies. Guatemala's enormous expansion of coffee production included vast tracts that were owned by newly arrived German immigrants. North American corporations and individuals controlled much of Mexico's rail infrastructure and a majority of the henequen plantations in Yucatán. Even Costa Rica permitted Minor Keith, the North American engineer who built the railroad that linked the highlands to the Atlantic port city of Limón, to acquire almost full economic control of it. Whose party was it? Certainly not the sharecroppers' and plantation workers' down the road.

The ideologies of liberalism and positivism, operating in the name of social progress and economic growth, displaced millions of the region's rural poor, both mestizo and Indian. Their traditional land base eroded, facilitated by government policies that encouraged privatization of communal property and easy alienation of it for cash. The frenzy for development of production for export also led to government policies that facilitated encroachment on and outright appropriation of small landholdings of Indian and mestizo peasants. Land that had hitherto been deemed marginal suddenly became prime land for coffee, henequen, banana, and beef production for the export market to the United States. Once the rural poor saw themselves without a source of subsistence, millions of them became attached to large cattle ranches and commercial agriculture operations in what was essentially debt slavery. Their wages were never sufficient to pay their debts for housing, food, and emergency cash needs. The company store became the agent of bondage.

It hardly comes as a surprise, therefore, that the truncated and impoverished Indian communities that managed to survive these predations retrenched and retreated from other than obligatory contact with national cultures. In particular, in both Guatemala and Mexico renewed emphasis was placed upon the highly local, ethnically segregated civil and religious community organizations that developed during the Colonial period in accordance with Crown dictates. It is worth noting the irony that the very institutional formulas that were intended to *integrate* Indian communities into colonial society became defense mechanisms that facilitated their exclusion from participation in national life in the post-independence period. Nevertheless, scholars have pointed out that the so-called "closed corporate" Indian community was a form of social organization that was never fully closed during the Colonial period, and was becoming even less closed during the turbulent years of the nineteenth century. If it ever existed, the option for the Indians of isolation within closed communities, shielded from the dramatic political and economic changes being promoted by liberal dictators like Porfirio Díaz in Mexico, was rapidly disappearing.

For those displaced rural people who were already outside the confines of Indian communities, the main option was migration to the cities, either directly from their eroded communities or indirectly via the haciendas and plantations. Great numbers fled to the anonymity of the cities, especially the major cities and provincial capitals, which indeed had been the main beneficiaries of the economic "progress" that was created by the priorities of both centralist and federalist governments. In and around the cities were to be found real (and sometimes fictional) sources of employment in the manual labor and service sectors of the economy. Thus, the fruit of positivism and liberalism was none other than the creation of a new rural and urban proletariat. Migrants poured into the major cities, for there was little economic opportunity elsewhere, short of returning to the plantations and haciendas from which they had fled.

Without recourse to the channels of grievance that, however convoluted, were available to them in the Colonial period, the rural poor in nineteenth- and early twentieth-century Mexico and Central America reached what was surely their most tragic moment since the sixteenth century. The class system had admitted a few carefully edited newcomers to the elite sectors, while the growth of the middle class progressed slowly, even in the urban centers. The rural and urban poor constituted the overwhelming majority of the population in all of the region except perhaps Costa Rica.

It was thus in this period that the Mexican and Central American cities took on their current mosaic of elite cores and suburbs, with interlaced working-class and slum barrios. It was also during this period that because of the new transportation networks, deliberately built by the United States to link Mexico to

U.S. markets, the United States became a popular destination for the displaced rural and urban poor, particularly from Mexico. They found employment largely in the growing commercial agriculture economies of the southern, western, and southwestern parts of the United States. The greatly expanding U.S. rail network also provided employment opportunities for Mexican laborers, creating sizable Mexican-American communities in places like Denver, Chicago, Philadelphia, and Kansas City. It is clear, therefore, that the events we are discussing in this chapter came to influence quite directly the demography of many U.S. cities as well as the vast region that would become known in our time as the Sun Belt.

On the wave of positivism and with the economic development that accompanied the expansion of agricultural export production came a huge flow of foreign capital to Mexico and Central America. Frequently the production units themselves (cattle ranches, henequen, banana, cotton, and coffee plantations), as well as the processing and shipping facilities, were completely controlled by foreigners or by newly arrived, wealthy immigrants. Governments, whether centralist or federalist, conservative or liberal, tended to look benignly on this phenomenon. Why? Because foreign control seemed a small price to pay for the economic transformation and commercial infrastructure—railroads, power plants, and telegraph systems—that would bring progress. The irony, of course, is the very one that haunts the region to this day: It was development that mobilized a continent to provide raw materials, fiber, food, meat, and minerals to supply industrial Europe and the United States without creating the capacity for self-sufficiency in the production of industrial goods and technical skills on which they had become dependent.

MESOAMERICANS AND THE INDEPENDENCE MOVEMENTS

The independence movements in Mexico and Central America were led primarily by creoles in order to retain political privileges over the Indian peasants and mestizo masses who, it was feared, might otherwise rebel against colonial rule and usher in genuinely revolutionary changes. This was a justified fear, since by the time of independence there were over 2 million mestizos and almost 5 million Indians in the former Mesoamerican region, compared to only about 120,000 creoles. Indeed, as we shall now see, in Mexico shortly before independence Indians and mestizos by the thousands participated in major uprisings that threatened to become class wars between the haves and have-nots, and similar uprisings on a smaller scale broke out in Central America around the same time.

Hidalgo and the Mexican Independence Movement

The great hero of the independence movement in Mexico was Father Miguel Hidalgo, whose name is recalled each September 15 when from the balcony of the National Palace the president of the republic repeats Hidalgo's legendary cry: "Mexicanos, viva México" ("Mexicans, long live Mexico"). In September 1810,

Hidalgo, priest of the Dolores parish in the Bajío (just north of the Central Basin), incited his followers to rebel against the French usurpers of the Spanish Crown and to strike for independence. Father Hidalgo was a creole (his father was a Spaniard), and his call to independence was part of a creole plan to replace the ruling *peninsulares* (Spaniards, also known as *gachupines*) with the creoles themselves. However, the band of men who made up Hidalgo's followers on that day in 1810, as well as the tens of thousands who joined his cause in the ensuing months, were made up largely of Indians and mestizos, and their goal was much more radical: to end tributes, forced labor, discrimination, landlessness, and political subjugation (Figure 6.5; for places mentioned in the account to follow, see the map in Figure 6.1).

Hidalgo seized the image of the Virgin of Guadalupe as his banner and led several hundred men in the takeover of Dolores; then San Miguel, the hometown of Hidalgo's creole military chief, Ignacio Allende; and shortly thereafter the town of Celaya. At this time Hidalgo assumed the title of "Captain-General of America," and with a force that had swelled to over 25,000 men marched on the rich mining center of Guanajuato. The Spaniards of Guanajuato retreated to the protection of the town's granary *(alhóndiga)*, which was stormed and overrun by the furious Hidalgo "horde." The rebels had lost at least 2,000 men in the assault, which they soon avenged by hacking to death 400 to 600 men, women, and children found inside the granary. The town was sacked, everything of value being carried off by Hidalgo's rude warriors. Shortly thereafter, Hidalgo's band took Valladolid (later renamed Morelia), as their numbers swelled to around 80,000 men.

At this point Hidalgo turned his army toward Mexico City, the capital and main stronghold of the Spanish establishment. The rebels met a small but well-trained Spanish contingent in the mountains between Toluca and Mexico City. The Spanish forces inflicted very heavy casualties on the rebels (2,000 to 4,000 rebel warriors were killed), and as a result Hidalgo decided not to march on the capital. He directed his army instead to Guadalajara, which was taken without a fight. In Guadalajara, the rebels quietly executed hundreds of gachupines (Spaniards), while recruiting thousands of new rebel fighters from the surrounding Indian communities and haciendas.

After the capture of Guadalajara, events began to turn against Hidalgo. Most creoles had come to see the movement as a "caste war," a life-and-death struggle between Indians and mestizos on one side and whites on the other. The creoles rallied to the side of the Spaniards, and among them were many creoles who had originally joined Hidalgo's movement. The Spanish forces under the ruthless General Félix Calleja retook Guanajuato, where they proceeded to slaughter anyone suspected of being even sympathetic to the rebel cause. Next the Spaniards marched on Guadalajara, which Hidalgo decided to defend with the full force of his vast hordes. During fighting on the grassy plains outside the city, a Spanish cannonball struck one of Hidalgo's ammunition wagons, which blew up, killing many of the rebel soldiers and setting fire to the plains. Hidalgo was forced to retreat, losing over 1,000 men as well as control of Guadalajara.

The rebel forces fled to the north, where Allende stripped Hidalgo of his

Figure 6.5 Mural painting of Miguel Hidalgo and his band of followers. Mural by Juan O'Gorman. Courtesy of the Organization of American States, Columbus Memorial Library.

military command, and began to seek support from friends on the U.S. side of the border. At this point, both Hidalgo and Allende were betrayed by a former rebel lieutenant, who led them into a trap laid by the Spanish forces. They were captured at a small desert village named Our Lady of Guadalupe Baján. Hidalgo was taken to Chihuahua, where he was tried, denied his priesthood, and executed in July 1811. Hidalgo was then beheaded, along with other rebel leaders, and his head placed in an iron cage on one of the four corners of the granary roof in Guanajuato. The main threat of the caste war had ended for the time being, even though the idea of independence remained very much alive.

Hidalgo's rebellion was viewed primarily as an Indian uprising at the time, which is one of the reasons why the creoles abandoned the movement so quickly. The term used to refer to the Indians at the time, "indios," was highly ambiguous (indeed, it still is in Mexico), and under the rubric were included poor, underclass, rural mestizos. Indeed, Hidalgo's ragged army was made up of mestizos, mulattoes, and poor creoles, as well as Indians. Nevertheless, it is a fact that tens of thousands of Indians from the Bajío and western Mexico did take up arms under Hidalgo. We know little about their ethnic identities, but most of them appear to have been Nahua and Otomí speakers. Enemies of the movement referred to Hidalgo's Indians as "Chichimecs," arguing that they were wild savages very different from the civilized Indians of the central and southern zones of Mexico. More likely, however, they were descendants of aboriginal groups who had once been part of the prehispanic Mesoamerican world, albeit the northwestern periphery of that world (see Chapter 3 for information on that periphery).

The native peoples to the south of the Bajío in central and southern Mexico largely rejected Hidalgo's call to arms. The historian John Tutino (1986) claims that this rejection helps explain the failure of the Hidalgo forces to take Mexico City: The rebels were not supported with either warriors or supplies by the Indians in areas like Toluca and Morelos on the road to the capital. The Indians in these areas had retained their community organizations intact, and had worked out a stable symbiosis with neighboring haciendas. While these Indians provided much of the labor needed by the haciendas, the haciendas in turn protected the Indians' local autonomy and, within limits, community lands. Thus, the Indians nearer to the capital were able to maintain strong peasant communities and traditional Mesoamerican cultures. In contrast, the Indians of the Bajío and Guadalajara area who joined with Hidalgo were subject to irresistible commercial forces that disrupted the communities, proletarianized the able-bodied men, and shattered the traditional Mesoamerican cultures. They were much more attracted to Hidalgo's movement and had much less to lose from it than the communities of Indians located adjacent to the Basin of Mexico.

The thousands of Indians from the north and west who followed Hidalgo were attracted to him as a charismatic religious leader whose message was sympathetic to their repressed social condition. Hidalgo played to the Indians' religious inclinations by adopting the Virgin of Guadalupe as the movement's key symbol, a symbol deeply meaningful to the Indians. On a more practical level, as priest of Dolores, Hidalgo was widely respected for having promoted a series of "development" projects to help the Indians. Among the projects—which were managed by the Indians themselves—could be found commercial pottery making, cultivation of silkworms, and the growing of grapes for wine and olives for oil. Hidalgo struck a responsive chord with the struggling Indians of the Bajío when he spoke of his movement as a "reconquest," of undoing some of the wrongs done to the Indians by the Spanish conquistadors. He pronounced in favor of eliminating the hated tribute payments and of finding lands for the Indians (Hidalgo's Indians were allowed to keep properties taken from Spaniards during the war). Hidalgo was not a revolutionary, and we must not exaggerate the extent to which his movement was carried out on behalf of the Indians. Yet, the Indians believed he was on their side, and they became his faithful, even fanatical, followers.

The anthropologist Victor Turner (1974) has pointed out that the Hidalgo rebellion had all the characteristics of nativistic movements found so widely around the world in conjunction with modern European expansion. The Hidalgo movement emerged after the long Colonial period with its rigidly ordered, relatively unchanging social structure; it was followed by another prolonged period of struggle and change that would initiate a newly structured world along "revolutionary" lines. The rebellion, then, may be seen as a period of breaking down past structures and experimenting with new ideas and ways of behaving. Hidalgo addressed a host of material and spiritual needs deeply felt by his lowly Indian and mestizo followers, needs that had been hidden and repressed for centuries. "Liminal" figures like Hidalgo deal in sacred symbols, and Hidalgo was the principal prophet by and for whom the great symbols of the Mexican independence movement were created. For this reason, and regardless of what the true facts about Hidalgo the man might be, he became and has remained the accepted father of the Mexican nation and the object of unending praise and artistic expression.

Hidalgo himself seems to have been inspired by the dynamic events of the movement to fulfill his role as prophet. As the movement progressed he modified his original creole goal of replacing Spanish with creole rulers, and adopted more radical ideas about the importance of the indigenous past for the Mexican nation and the need to restore Indian rights. The basic creole plan for the new nation advocated a return to the conquistadors, the supposed ancestors of the creoles, and thus this creation of a nation would include the Indians and mestizos only as servants. Hidalgo and other leaders of the movement, in contrast, went back further in search of the roots of the new nation, all the way to the prehispanic period. According to this more nativistic vision, the independence movement would be a reconquest, reversing the initial Spanish conquest and restoring the pristine Mesoamerican way of life. The primary beneficiaries of the new nation would be the Indians.

Hidalgo, of course, could not go that far, even though as nativistic prophet he opened a whole new discourse about the need to incorporate the Indians and mestizos into the emerging nation. Hidalgo understood that Mesoamerican symbols and practices could not meet all the needs of the socially and culturally differentiated Indians of his day, and even less the needs of the creoles and mestizos who would also form part of the nation. Whether consciously or not, he turned to popular Christian religion, and particularly to the symbol of Our Lady of Guadalupe. The Virgin's alleged association with the ancient Aztec earth goddess, as well as her female gender as counter to Spanish patriarchal domination, made her a compelling symbol to the Indians. But Guadalupe also appealed to the creoles and mestizos, for whom she symbolized important universal principles such as fraternity and equality as found within popular Christianity. Hidalgo's selection of the Virgin of Guadalupe as the key symbol of his movement, then, was prophetic in that it offered on a religious level the means of uniting both creole and Indian. Unfortunately, as Turner explains, the liminal ideas of prophets usually do not win battles, as was so tragically the case with Hidalgo's remarkable ideas.

Hidalgo's independence movement in Mexico was carried on after his death by others, particularly by another parish priest from the Michoacán area, José María Morelos. Morelos's followers were primarily mestizos and mulattoes rather than Indians, recruited largely from among the peons working on haciendas in the lowland zones of Michoacán and Guerrero. Morelos, in fact, forbade his followers to use the term "indio," which he felt helped perpetuate the colonial caste system. Nevertheless, he envisioned a Mexican nation that would revere its Mesoamerican ancestry and give the native peoples their rightful place within it. At a rebel constitutional assembly in Chilpancingo (Guerrero) in 1813, Morelos stated:

> Spirits of Motecuhzoma, Cacamatzín, Cuauhtemoc, Xicotencatl, and Calzontzín! Take pride in this august assembly, and celebrate this happy moment in which your sons have congregated to avenge your insults! After August 12, 1521, comes September 8, 1813! The first date tightened the chains of our slavery in Mexico-Tenochtitlán; the second broke them forever in the town of Chilpancingo. . . . We are therefore going to restore the Mexican Empire! (Cumberland 1968:125)

Morelos's army was much smaller than Hidalgo's, and it never posed a serious threat to the Spaniards and their creole allies. Like Hidalgo, Morelos attempted to strike against Mexico City, but again failed to find support among the Indian peasantry in the areas surrounding the Central Basin. Even in the area of the present-day state of Morelos (named after this independence hero), which 100 years later would become the center of the Mexican Revolution, the Nahuatl-speaking Indians remained ensconced within their communities and did not support the Morelos rebellion. Morelos was captured and executed by the Spaniards in 1815.

Following the death of Morelos, Mexico's independence movement fell into the hands of more conservative creole leaders, who feared not only "revolutionary" rebels like Hidalgo and Morelos but also the liberal reformers in Spain. These creoles convinced the remaining rebel leaders that their own more moderate plan for independence would include social justice for Indians and mestizos. Under the leadership of a creole military official, Agustín de Iturbide, the creoles took possession of Mexico City in September 1821 against only token opposition from the Spaniards. Mexico was now in the hands of creoles who would try to revive the very colonial system that leaders like Hidalgo and Morelos and their Indian and mestizo followers had struggled so hard to disrupt.

The Independence Movements in Central America

The independence movements in Central America were much more responses to external factors than in Mexico, and produced no large-scale civil war. Conservative creoles led these movements, in part out of opposition to the liberal policies emanating from Spain and in part because they were inspired by Iturbide's actions in Mexico. They declared independence in Guatemala on September 15, 1821, and five months later under pressure from Iturbide accepted annexation by the Mexican "empire." Opposition to these decisions came largely from liberal creoles and mestizos concentrated in the southern provinces of Central America, where resentment of political dominance by Guatemala was strong. Rebellious Salvadorans eventually had to be brought into line by Mexican troops. At this point, events in Mexico once again determined the fate of Central America, as the Mexican empire crumbled and Central America declared independence for a second time in July 1823 (Chiapas decided to remain with Mexico). Subsequently, the Federation of Central American States was founded under the leadership of creole and mestizo liberals.

Central America experienced no large Hidalgo-type nativistic movement, but many Indian rebellions broke out prior to independence and indirectly contributed to its eventual success. These uprisings not only demonstrated the weakness of the Spanish regime, but also convinced the creoles that if they did not take matters into their own hands a popular "revolution" might ensue. As one scholar has observed (Jonas 1974:119): "It is frequently said that Central American independence was an achievement of the *criollos* alone. Insofar as *ladinos* and Indians participated in various phases of the movement, and insofar as their participation forced the *criollos* to take up the cry for independence, this was not the case."

Indian uprisings in the decade prior to independence were focused on the issue of tribute payments, which had been abolished by Spain in 1811, reimposed in 1814, and removed once again in 1820. Many Indian communities refused to pay tributes after 1811, and their inhabitants violently resisted attempts by Spanish and Crown officials to force them to comply. Nativistic rebellions on a local scale were endemic throughout the highlands of Guatemala during these years, and widespread in El Salvador and Nicaragua. The rebellions by Indians in Nicaragua were particularly threatening to Spanish rule. Between 1811 and 1812, bands of rebels numbering over 12,000 men (mostly Subtiaba and Pipil Indians from León, Masaya, and Rivas) were able to temporarily seize the reins of local government from the ruling Spaniards and creoles. The rebel bands formed weak alliances under native leaders, among whom were several priests. The rebels armed themselves and demanded an end to such hated colonial practices as tribute payment, forced labor, and slavery. The movement was all but destroyed in 1811, however, when local creole collaborators jumped sides and aided contingents of Spanish soldiers sent from Olancho (Honduras), San Miguel (El Salvador), and Cartago (Costa Rica) to put down the rebellion. Nevertheless, led by a Subtiaba priest, Tomás Ruiz, the Nicaraguan rebels participated in the Belén "conspiracy" in Guatemala (1813), designed to free their incarcerated comrades, initiate a colony-wide military uprising, and declare independence.

For an account of the Central American rebellion from the independence period that has received the most attention, see Box 6.1 on the Atanasio Tzul rebellion in Guatemala and see the map in Figure 6.1 for places mentioned below.

Box 6.1 *The Atanasio Tzul Rebellion*

As with so many other native uprisings of the time, the immediate cause of the Tzul uprising was the refusal of the Quiché Maya Indians of San Miguel Totonicapán to pay tributes. Already in 1816 the community's Indian alcalde, Atanasio Tzul, had refused to collect the tributes for the Crown, and in subsequent years as governor he had personally travelled to the colonial capital (Santiago de Guatemala) in order to obtain official papers exonerating the Indians from further payments. Atanasio was considered to be a cacique in Totonicapán, a status that gave him particularly strong legitimacy among the Indians there. Furthermore, he was the head of a large and powerful clan located just to the northwest of the town center, and was a direct descendant of royal officials who had been sent from the capital of the Quiché empire to rule over the Totonicapán province in aboriginal times.

By 1820 the Indians of the larger Totonicapán area had rebelled against further payment of tributes. Atanasio Tzul became the focal point of the movement, assisted by Lucas Aguilar, an Indian of commoner status in Totonicapán. Leaders from surrounding Indian communities such as San Francisco El Alto, Chiquimula, and Momostenango coordinated efforts with Tzul to do away with the tribute payments, and if necessary cast aside the regional Spanish officials. On July 5, Tzul and his followers drove out the regional Spanish authority *(alcalde mayor)*, threatened and then deposed the local native authorities, and took charge of regional government. In an elaborate ceremony celebrated with processions, dancing, and music, Atanasio Tzul was crowned "King of the Quiché" under a feathered canopy, and Aguilar was made "President." Tzul's crown was taken from Saint Joseph's statue, and he donned Spanish hat, pants, shoes, and sword. His wife Felipa was named queen, and given the crown of Saint Cecilia. Messages sent to Tzul from Indians in the surrounding towns clearly indicate that Atanasio's crowning was taken seriously by thousands of Quiché Maya Indians, who began to address him with honorary titles such as "Our Lord" and "Your Grace."

Atanasio Tzul's reign as king of the Quiché was short-lived. The Spaniards organized an army of over 1,000 men made up of soldiers from Spanish towns in the highlands, and marched on Totonicapán almost exactly one month after Tzul's crowning. The town was taken without opposition, although rebels from surrounding communities attacked the Spanish soldiers with slings, stones, and machetes from positions on the mountains above the road leading into Totonicapán. The Spanish soldiers looted many homes in Totonicapán, and dozens of Indians were whipped and threatened. Tzul, Aguilar, and other native leaders were carried off as prisoners to Quezaltenango, where they were tried for sedition. Although found guilty, Tzul and the other Quiché leaders were pardoned seven months later.

The Tzul rebellion has been largely discounted in scholarly discussions of Central America's independence movement. Some have argued that it had nothing to do with independence from Spain, but was merely another "colonial riot" against abuses by the Spaniards and their creole collaborators. Even its nativistic features have been denied, with the argument that Atanasio Tzul was only assuming the role of the deposed regional Spanish authority and dramatizing his loyalty to the Spanish king by taking the crown of a Catholic saint. It has been noted too that the rebellion was restricted to the Totonicapán area, and hence should be seen as the product of a colonial system that forced the Indians into relatively closed, isolated communities. These are all important points, and it must be conceded that Tzul and his followers were heavily influenced by Spanish institutions, remained respectful of the Spanish Crown, and indeed were unable to marshal broad enough support to keep the movement going for very long.

The Guatemalan historian Daniel Contreras, however, argues persuasively that the Tzul rebellion must be seen as part of the larger independence movement of 1821. After all, he says, in their own way the Indians were struggling to liberate themselves from the repression of the Spanish system and thus added their "grain" to the success of the larger movement. He points out that the creole officials on the scene considered the rebellion to be much more than a local riot; it was a true premeditated conspiracy that could easily become a general insurrection. Those officials understood, too, what many modern-day scholars tend to overlook: that the Indians had never lost the desire to be free of colonial rule, and thus had persisted as a partially digested Indian "nation," not strictly autonomous but nevertheless culturally distinct from the Spanish, creole, and mestizo peoples who dominated them. Too often, Contreras observes, Indian rebellions are seen as "caste wars," racial vendettas, rather than the liberation movements that they are. Contreras concludes:

> . . . it is not possible to deny the similarity in goals between the creole and Indian groups: a change in the political, economic, and social regime. Therefore, if one wants to obtain the complete picture of the total historical development of our political emancipation (Central American Independence), one cannot forget the Indian rebellions. (Contreras 1951:69)

The Tzul rebellion, like others from this time period in Central America, was strongly nativistic despite denials by some scholars and even by Atanasio Tzul himself in testimony to Spanish magistrates (under the circumstances, it is understandable that he would deny trying to organize a countergovernment to the royal colonial regime!). The idea of restoring the old Quiché kingdom was very much alive among the Indians of the western highlands at that time, as proven by the widespread acceptance of Atanasio as king by Indians from other communities. Furthermore, subsequent to independence these same Indians continued to struggle to establish their own native "king." Even though Atanasio Tzul did not seem to express in his person all the characteristics typical of a nativistic prophet, his royal ancestry was still revered and must have been a source of enormous charisma. And, despite the many Spanish elements that found their way into Tzul's coronation ceremony, we can be certain that most of the deeper meanings associated with the processions, crowning, and ritual language were profoundly Mesoamerican.

MESOAMERICAN INDIANS UNDER LIBERAL RULE

The profound changes described above for Mexico and Central America during the century following the independence movements and collapse of Spanish rule resulted in major transformations in the social life and cultural patterns of the remnant Mesoamerican peoples. The question arises as to just how, in fact, the Mesoamerican Indians were affected by the turbulent conditions of the post-independence period. As we shall now see, the situation of the Indians under creole rule remained highly oppressive, and became progressively worse as liberal policies were implemented.

The Plight of Mestizos and Mesoamericans

The post-independence struggles between individual power-seeking creole *caudillos,* each supported by Indian and mestizo dependents, became political "schools" for the mestizos and, to a lesser extent, the Indians. The mestizos especially took advantage of the unusually chaotic conditions after independence to become acquainted with regional power, and to achieve their first positions of political leadership. Eventually, *caudillos* from the mestizo sector would achieve power at the national level, notably in the cases of Benito Juárez and Porfirio Díaz in Mexico, and Rafael Carrera in Guatemala.

In his book, *Sons of the Shaking Earth* (1959), Eric Wolf points out that the relative gains in power by the mestizos after independence as compared with the Indians were correlated with the contrasting ethical systems that guided the two groups in their struggle for survival. The mestizo ethic placed stress on entrepreneurial skills, and the drive for power and self-improvement. The Mesoamerican Indians' ethical system was based more on traditional Mesoamerican principles, and in some ways was in a dialectical relationship with the mestizo system. Compared to the mestizos, for example, the Indians were less open to change, less willing to take risks, less socially ambitious, more oriented to collective goals, and far less articulate in the Spanish language. These differences gave the mestizos a comparative advantage over the Indians as the two groups struggled against creole repression during the long liberal period.

The differences between mestizos and Mesoamericans were partly based on social class. The mestizos shared a common social alienation and exclusion, and thus formed a marginal lower-class division within liberal society. They functioned in a wide variety of low-prestige occupations, such as petty officials, small ranchers, low-level priests, humble artisans, petty traders, half-employed paupers, cattle rustlers, and town thieves. The Mesoamerican Indians also shared a common alienation from the dominant creole world, but their lower-class status was more clearly defined for them in ethnic terms—at times legally—as members of the inferior native caste. The Indians were less economically diversified than the mestizos, most of them working in agriculture as either peasant cultivators or hacienda peons. Compared to the mestizos, the Indians' community differences in language and custom made it more difficult to unite into larger political groups on the basis of common class or ethnicity. Only on a few occasions were the Mesoamerican Indians able to challenge the creole establishment (as described below under nativistic movements).

The identification of the mestizos and Indians as culturally distinct sectors in liberal society theoretically made both of them eligible candidates to serve as symbols of the emerging nations of Mexico and Central America. In Mexico during the early years following independence, a few enlightened creoles proposed that the new nation adopt the Indians as an ethnic symbol. One creole leader even suggested that a descendant of Motecuhzoma be crowned emperor of a new Mexican empire, after which the monarch would take a wife from among the "whites," thus binding the races together. These suggestions did not prevail, and, as might be expected, the Spanish and creole whites emerged as the identifying ethnic symbol. Hernán Cortés was glorified and hailed as the true founder of the Mexican nation.

Later, when upwardly mobile mestizos began to challenge creole leadership in Mexico, the creole rulers hit upon the idea of massive immigration of Europeans (particularly the French) and North Americans as a means of preserving the country's ethnically white identity—and not coincidentally, preserving the creole's political control. Of this policy, a modern Mexican scholar has remarked, "it seems inconceivable that our creole liberators were willing to hand us over to the North Americans or English rather than accept an Indian (identity) for Mexico" (Aguirre 1983:328). In the end, of course, the mestizos could not be denied, and during the Díaz period they began to replace the whites as the symbol of national ethnic identity. Consistent with Díaz's liberal positivism, however, ethnicity was now seen more in cultural than in racial terms. The Mexican mestizo was said to combine the progressive ideas of the whites and the fighting spirit of the Indians.

In Central America a national identity based on the image of the white creole remained strong throughout the entire liberal period, and even mestizos (ladinos) found it hard to gain ethnic recognition within the budding national cultures. Indian ethnicity was totally discounted, creating a pathetic situation in which the native peoples of Central America had become foreigners in their own land.

Consequences of the Liberal Reforms for Mesoamerican Indians

Even before independence was achieved from Spain, beginning with the Bourbon reforms at the end of the Colonial period and continuing through the entire nineteenth century and into the early twentieth century, the Mesoamerican Indians were under pressure from the liberal faction of the creoles to assimilate into the wider colonial and later national society. Liberal attempts to "reform" the Indians were specifically aimed at forcing them to adopt the Spanish language, become orthodox Catholics, work for wages, and generally replace native practices and beliefs with Western ways.

In contrast, the conservative faction of the creoles benefitted from keeping the Indians as an inferior "caste," and therefore tended to oppose reforms that would modify the natives' social condition. This explains why most Mesoamerican Indians preferred conservative "centralism" to liberal "federalism."

The conservative creoles were interested in freezing the Indians in their inferior caste-like colonial status. As long as the Indians paid tributes in the form of goods and services, the conservative creoles were content to let them organize the kind of rural communities they pleased. Octavio Paz points out that in post-independence Mexico the conservative creole *caudillos* were heirs to the old Spanish order, and actually employed Spanish colonial law in dealing with the Indians. Among other things this meant that the Indians would be legally differentiated from both the creoles and the mestizos, and as a result would occupy a secure even if inferior position in society.

Liberal reform programs were stronger in post-independence Mexico than in Central America, especially during the first fifty years. The pivotal liberal figure was Benito Juárez, a mestizo from Oaxaca with Zapotec Indian ancestry. Juárez attempted to establish a more just society in Mexico, including justice for Indians. He courageously resisted the American invasion of the national territory, and led the struggle to eliminate the conservative-backed Maximilian monarchy. But even Juárez's fair-minded liberal policies worked to benefit the mestizos at the expense of the Indians. Similarly, Porfirio Díaz (Figure 6.6), another mestizo liberal with Indian (Mixtec) blood, carried out policies that were detrimental to the Indians of Mexico despite the father image many Indians had of him. As Octavio Paz explains, the political philosophy behind the liberal reforms negated Mexico's Indian past, and therefore was necessarily sterile and empty. In Mexico, Paz said (1961:133), "The past returned, decked out in the trappings of progress, science, and republican laws . . . (an) imposition of juridical and cultural forms which not only did not express our true nature but actually smothered and immobilized it."

It is not surprising, then, that the Indians of Mexico reacted so negatively to the liberal reforms. Indian rebellion was endemic, sometimes under the leadership of mestizo *caudillos* who claimed Mesoamerican ancestry. These rebellions should be seen as violent rejections of the ruling powers, and thus true liberation movements. The rebellious Indians were inspired by noble goals such as community autonomy, preservation of land rights, and cultural preservation. The creoles understood just how radical the rebellions were to their own long-range goals, and this fact helped push the conservative and liberal factions into common cause and in the end tipped the balance toward the liberal policy of Indian suppression.

The liberal reforms had similar consequences in Central America, although many of the native rebellions there were smaller in scope and came later in time. The most important uprising took place in Guatemala, where the mestizo *caudillo* Rafael Carrera led a massive movement against the liberals. He was supported not only by poor mestizos from the eastern part of the country but also by tens of thousands of Maya Indians from the western highlands (Figure 6.7). The Carrera rebellion resulted in thirty years of conservative rule in Guatemala, which in turn brought relative peace with the Indians. Finally, in the latter part of the nineteenth century the *caudillo* Justo Rufino Barrios was able to reestablish liberal rule in Guatemala, and this again touched off widespread

Figure 6.6 Porfirio Díaz, mestizo caudillo and Liberal dictator of Mexico. James A. Magner, *Men of Mexico,* 2nd ed. Salem, N.H.: Books for Libraries, Ayer Company Publishers, 1968.

native rebellions in that country as well as similar conflicts in El Salvador and Nicaragua.

The dramatic liberal program introduced by Barrios and other dictators in Central America has been hailed by many as laying the foundation for nationhood in that region. From the perspective of the Mesoamerican Indians, however, the program was a repressive, sterile imposition. As in Mexico, the Central American liberal regimes applied excessive force against the Indians and lower-class

Figure 6.7 Rafael Carrera, conservative dictator of Guatemala.

mestizos in order to ensure the availability of cheap labor for the burgeoning capitalist enterprises (coffee and banana plantations) being established in the region.

Let us now attempt to understand the impact of the liberal reform programs on the local Indian communities by examining events taking place during the nineteenth century in the Maya community of Momostenango, Guatemala.

Momostenango, Guatemala

Momostenango was a rather marginal province of the Quiché Maya empire during prehispanic times in Guatemala. Its inhabitants paid tributes of gold, mined from the mountains in the area, as well as lime and agricultural products to the rulers at the imperial capital of Utatlán. After the conquest Momostenango became one of about 700 Indian communities under Spanish rule in the Captaincy General of Guatemala. While Momostenango's tributary obligations to the Spaniards were not particularly onerous, they were considered to be an undesirable burden by the local inhabitants who rose up in open rebellion against them toward the end of the Colonial period.

Following independence, the Momostenango Indians rallied behind the mestizo *caudillo* Rafael Carrera, and during the 1840s helped him seize the presidency of the Republic and maintain a dictatorial hold over it. The Momostecans considered Carrera to be their personal lord and patron, and served him faithfully as client soldiers and tributaries. Carrera, in turn, allowed the Momostecans to retain considerable political and cultural autonomy. Social conditions in Momostenango under Carrera's conservative rule are clearly revealed by a series of court cases dating from that period of time, the records of which are now preserved in the municipal archives (Carmack 1973:210–214).

The court records show, for example, that as late as the 1860s the ancient Quiché Maya pattern of rural clans and cantons had remained intact. Customary native law was still operating in Momostenango, and it enjoyed the respect of the entire Indian sector of the community. The Momostenango Indians were able to retain these cultural traditions despite the fact that all the municipal and regional authorities were either creoles or mestizos (the latter were referred to as "ladinos" in the court records). Special Indian judges were introduced in important legal cases, as had been done during the Colonial period, and Spanish colonial laws relative to the Indians were in use. Consistent with the thinking of the conservatives, the Indian judges dealt with the Indians paternalistically. One judge, for example, stated that the Indians had the right to receive special treatment because they were "ignorant, not ever having been taught the Gospel."

The liberal reforms carried out in Guatemala in the 1870s under the direction of Justo Rufino Barrios resulted in the loss of nearly half of Momostenango's best agricultural lands, and led to the forced labor of hundreds of Momostecans on the new coffee plantations of the Pacific Coast. Creole and mestizo authorities were put in charge of virtually all activities in Momostenango, in a drastic reduction of the community's autonomy from the Carrera years. Momostenango's Indians rose up against liberal authority in 1876, and fought a bitter guerrilla war to preserve their traditional way of life. The liberal armies, however, ruthlessly quashed the native rebellion, after which they executed the rebel leaders and burned the homes of collaborators. Momostenango's Indians were then subjected to years of suffocating control under a series of liberal dictators.

The social conditions of the Momostenango Indians under the repressive liberal regime are dramatically revealed by a murder that took place in the community in the early morning hours one day in February 1899 (Figure 6.8). While the Indian Timoteo was attending the wake of his sister at the house of his in-laws, an Indian militia lieutenant named Fermín led a patrol of soldiers into the house, embraced Timoteo, and then plunged a knife into his heart. Lt. Fermín was taken into custody a few hours later by the mestizo *alcalde.* Acting as justice of the peace, the alcalde had the body examined by an "expert," took testimony from the many witnesses to the stabbing, and remitted the case and the prisoner to the Court of First Instance in the regional capital of Totonicapán. The father of Timoteo employed the services of a highly skilled and educated mestizo lawyer to prosecute the murderer, while Lt. Fermín's defense was made by an educated

Figure 6.8 Parade of local police and militia in the town center of Momostenango in 1968.

local Indian. The court proceedings lasted for eight months, and resulted in a guilty verdict for Fermín. He was sentenced to ten years in prison for murdering Timoteo, and an appeal to a higher court was rejected. Finally, in 1901 President Manuel Estrada Cabrera pardoned Fermín, and he was freed from prison in 1904.

The case demonstrates that most of the Indians involved in the dramatic events were active participants in the local militia organization. Besides Lt. Fermín and his Indian patrol members, it appears that Timoteo, his male in-laws, and the local Indian "lawyer" were also militiamen. All the principal Indian actors appear to have been significantly acculturated to mestizo ways: They spoke Spanish, were active in the commercial sphere, had familiarity with the legal system, and depended on ties of friendship more than kinship relations. Even the manner in which the crime was committed—in a public setting and with a knife—was mestizo rather than Indian, for murder in rural Momostenango usually was interpreted as an act of witchcraft. The motives behind the crime were not traditional native motives either, but the more typical mestizo ones of jealousy over women or insults against personal dignity.

The court record also makes clear that the law being applied by the authorities in this case no longer made legal distinctions between Indians and mestizos. In fact, the Indian defender of the accused presented an elegant argument to the effect that "moral" considerations were not relevant, only legal ones, as befitted "modern legislation." It is evident, too, that some Indians were active participants in the liberal establishment itself, as with Lt. Fermín, the militia head, and the educated Indian who acted as legal defense.

Liberal reforms in Guatemala, then, introduced major changes into the community of Momostenango. The Indians were being transformed in thought, language, custom, and social position. The great majority of them were subordinated to the political control of mestizo rulers and were being severely exploited economically on the coffee plantations where they were forced to work. The impact of liberalism on the Indian communities of Mexico was similar to that of Momostenango, as shown by the case of Tepoztlán, Mexico in Box 6.2. (See the map in Figure 6.1 for the location of Tepoztlán.)

Box 6.2 *Tepoztlán, Mexico, and the Liberal Reforms*

Oscar Lewis's classic account of Tepoztlán, Mexico, *Life in a Mexican Village* (1963), provides a brief social history of that community during the liberal period. In prehispanic times Tepoztlán had been a city-state within one of the Aztec provinces, paying tributes largely in paper, lime, cotton cloth, and turkeys. During the Colonial period, Tepoztlán became subject to the Spanish governor residing in Cuernavaca. Tributes were paid in maize and money, as well as in the form of onerous labor in the mines of Taxco and nearby sugar haciendas. A large group of local officials, including local *caciques* who were descended from the prehispanic ruling class, was also supported by tribute payments.

Conditions for the common people worsened following independence. The *caciques*, Church, and haciendas all increased their monopoly hold on the land properties of the area, and the "tithes" now demanded by the Church surpassed in amount what the Tepoztecans had paid as tributes during the Colonial period. The local *cacique* Indians collaborated with the ruling creoles, enhancing the former's wealth and power over the local population. Most Tepoztecans became poor peasants, forced to labor part time on plantations as peons for pitifully low wages.

The liberal reforms of Benito Juárez divided the community; most of the inhabitants sided with the conservative Church, which had lost its property. A few, however, sided with the liberal government, and formed a military unit that fought bravely in the war to drive the French out of Mexico. Nevertheless, under continued liberal rule the *caciques* grew even more powerful while the Tepoztecan peasants became poorer. Rebellious action by the peasants was common, but most rebels would be quickly rounded up, imprisoned, and either banished from the community or forced to serve in the army.

By the Porfirio Díaz period, the vast majority of the Tepoztlán Indians had become landless. They were not permitted to use the communal lands, and thus had no alternative but to labor on the nearby sugar plantations, mainly as indebted peons. These native peons were positioned at the bottom of a highly stratified society, exploited not only by the upper-class mestizos and creoles of the region but also by the local cacique rulers. The old custom of collecting religious taxes was reinstituted, as was obligatory participation in an elaborate calendar of religious ceremonies and fiestas. As a result, many of the poorer Tepoztecans became increasingly critical of the Church, a clear prelude to the strong anti-Church ideas that erupted later in the Mexican Revolution.

The account to follow was related to Lewis by a small landholder who still remembered the Díaz years, and provides a graphic view of what life was like in Tepoztlán during the liberal period:

> The thing that was truly scarce was work. And so during the difficult times from January to May and from August to September the stronger among us went to work on the sugar plantations . . . in the state of Morelos. The owners of the plantations were *gachupines* (Spaniards), and they mistreated the Indians, kicking and insulting them. These plantations also robbed the nearby villages of their lands. This is what happened to Tepoztlán. We lost some of our best lands. The rich here had their lands and produced good crops, but the poor had no lands. The poor ate chile and salt and some beans. Meat was had once a month at best. . . . The local government was in the hands of *caciques.* (Cacique) Vicente Ortega held power for many years, with the support of the state authorities among whom he had ties of *compadrazgo.* There were no political parties or opposition groups allowed. . . . Anyone who opposed his rule might be sent to prison in Quintana Roo. (Lewis 1963:95)

As this account makes clear, the Indians of Tepoztlán were profoundly exploited by the liberal regimes. In the process they were becoming secularized, and losing many of their native cultural ideas and practices.

NATIVISTIC MOVEMENTS IN THE MESOAMERICAN REGION

While the economies of Europe and the United States appropriated Mexico and Central America as producers of food and fiber and other raw materials, there remained the visage of the region's very considerable Mesoamerican Indian population. Among those millions of Indians who remained, a response was inevitable. Without access to the written word, these poor and marginalized peoples were nevertheless quite aware of what was happening to them and around them. In particular, they took advantage of "openings" in national and regional events (such as the U.S.-Mexico war between 1846 and 1848) to mount massive and vigorous expressions of Indian identity and protest before the altar of liberal reform.

Mexico and the Central American countries experienced hundreds of these articulate movements of social criticism; political activism, and violent protest from the Indian communities, beginning with the period of independence and continuing on through the extended liberal period. These social movements typically addressed longstanding economic and political grievances against the local representatives of the national powers, and they nearly always advocated their causes by demanding religious and political autonomy as well as recognition of their native ethnic identity. A few of the movements created national panic, as when Hidalgo led his bands of Indians and mestizos against weakened Spanish rule in 1810, or when masses of Maya Indians in Yucatán rebelled against national rule just at the time that Mexico was losing large parts of its northern territory to the United States (see Box 6.3 below). Indians from one community would rise up in arms against the creole and mestizo oppressors, usually joined by those from other communities in the region—especially where the Indians comprised the majority populations in their respective regions. The Indians frequently justified this militancy by mobilizing Mesoamerican symbols in the name of native separatism, and for this reason the rebellions are often referred to as "nativistic" movements.

Such nativistic movements were violently suppressed by state military mobilization, as we already learned in the case of the independence movements, but some of them proved to be rather long-lasting. They expressed in poignant terms the reality of certain regions with hidden "majorities"—the Indians, especially those within their communities, but also many now living outside the communities—who had been allowed participation in national economic and political life only as servants to the ruling class. Not enough attention has been given to the nativistic features of these movements, especially features that helped the Mesoamerican Indians to defend themselves against creole and mestizo reformers intent on destroying their historically derived social and cultural integrity.

The nativistic movements of nineteenth- and early twentieth-century Mexico and Central America were not just cathartic expressions, for they also provided a basis by which the Indians could adapt their own social and cultural traditions to the social changes being forced on them by the liberal reformers. This helps explain why, through time, these movements tended to expand in territorial scope and assimilate more of the dominant creole-mestizo culture. We have the paradox, then, of movements that helped the Mesoamerican Indians preserve their cultural heritage at the same time that they united them in larger political organizations and incorporated more creole and mestizo culture than ever before.

Nativistic movements similar to those carried out by the Indians of the Mesoamerican region have been reported throughout the world, as native peoples opposed attempts by agents of the modern world to impose liberal policies and capitalist economic systems. Comparative studies of these nativistic movements demonstrate that they share some base features:

1. The movements are led by "prophets," charismatic representatives of traditional native elites who lost dominant power under European colonization and now seek to regain it through violent means.
2. The prophet leaders employ magical means to counter the overwhelming technological and military advantages of the European and national exploiters.
3. The prophets and their followers are guided by beliefs about a return to the original native society (hence the term "nativistic"); specifically, a utopian society in which there would be no whites but only natives.
4. The movement draws upon those elements from the traditional native cultures that can be "syncretized" with European elements, creating new, more adaptive cultural codes.
5. When the prophets fail and the uprisings are put down (as was usually the case), the disappointed native peoples subsequently become more willing to engage in secular, even revolutionary forms of opposition to the dominant classes.

Nativistic movements as we are using the term are not revolutionary movements. Their proponents marshal local kinship and village groups behind charismatic leaders, in contrast with revolutionary movements in which great classes of peasants or proletariats are united under radical modernizers. We agree with social scientists like Franz Fanon, however, that nativistic movements may prepare the way for later revolutions by creating hope, solidarity, and politicization among exploited native peoples. As we shall see in the next chapter, this is precisely what happened in the region during the twentieth century.

With these general characteristics of nativistic movements in mind, and recalling the Hidalgo and Tzul cases from the independence period, let us turn to examples of prototypical nativistic movements by the Mesoamericans during the liberal period. The first example is a movement carried out by the Pipil Indians of Nonualco in El Salvador shortly after independence (see the map in Figure 6.1 for places mentioned in the following account).

The Nonualco Insurrection

Nonualco was an important province within the southeastern periphery of Mesoamerica in prehispanic times. Located in a valley of the central piedmont zone southeast of present-day San Salvador, Nonualco probably exercised political control over the Jiquilisco Bay on the Pacific Coast. Its population was made up of over 5,000 Pipil-speaking (Nahua) people and perhaps some Lenca speakers as well. Nonualcans produced maize, beans, and chiles; extracted fish, salt, and cotton as tribute goods from their coastal subjects; and traded for other items such as cacao, honey, and obsidian. At the time of the Spanish conquest, Nonualco had apparently been subjugated by the Pipil state of Cuzcatlán, whose capital was near present-day San Salvador. Nonualcans probably paid tributes to the Cuzcatlán rulers in the form of foods, including fish, and cotton cloth.

Following the conquest, the Nonualcans were concentrated into several communities, among them Santiago, San Pedro, and San Juan Nonualco, and forced to pay tributes to Spanish *encomenderos* (overlords). Still in the sixteenth century, cacao production was introduced into the area, and cacao beans became one of the main tribute items paid by Nonualcans to the Spaniards. The indigo plant, which produced a blue dye, soon replaced cacao as the main commercial crop in the area, and the Nonualco Indians were forced to provide labor on the Spanish and creole indigo plantations. These indigo estates disrupted community life in Nonualco by encroaching into communal lands and draining off labor.

Toward the end of the Colonial period, the population of the three Nonualcan communities numbered over 4,000 persons, about 700 of them mestizos. These communities were surrounded by at least nine indigo and sugar-producing plantations. Relations between the Indians and the plantations were tense, and in 1789 the Nonualcans rose up in opposition to the low wages being paid by the indigo plantation owners. The rebellion was quickly put down, however, by the Spanish authorities. Between 1812 and 1814 the Nonualcans again rebelled, this time to protest the reinstatement of tributes by the Spanish Crown and the forced recruitment of Nonualco men into the creole armies organized to help El Salvador sever its ties with Guatemala.

Despite the many disruptions, the Nonualco communities survived the Colonial period surprisingly well, and confronted the post-independence liberal reforms with their traditional institutions reasonably intact. Pipil was widely spoken, although Spanish had become the language of public discourse. The system of ancient clans *(calpulli)* continued to operate in the communities, some clans having over 200 members. Native leadership was still in place, based in part on a continuation of the ancient noble and commoner status distinction. Lands had been lost to the indigo estates, but a significant portion of the communal lands were preserved. Trade was flourishing, and the Nonualcans were considered to be "rich" Indians.

By the 1830s the liberals had been in power for several years in El Salvador, and their policy of favoring the indigo plantations was seen by the Indians as highly oppressive. The Salvadoran province was on the verge of civil war between the liberal and conservative creoles, with Indians being forced to fight for interests in which they had no stake. In 1833 the Nonualcans rose up against the local creole authorities and plantation owners. They were led by Atanasio Aquino, a commoner Pipil Indian from Santiago Nonualco who had worked as a peon on the indigo estates. From the beginning, the uprising had strong nativistic features, as Aquino assumed traditional Pipil titles and dress. He called for an end to creole domination over the Indians, and mobilized the Indians and many mestizos from surrounding communities. The rebels quickly overpowered the main creole towns and estates of the area, as well as in the adjacent area of San Vicente.

Aquino's army soon swelled to 3,000 warriors, and easily beat back several military contingents sent by the government to put down the rebellion. Aquino took the title of "General Commander of the Liberation Forces," proclaiming a free and autonomous Nonualco territory. He replaced the creole authorities with Indians, and laid down a severe legal code to govern the affairs of the nearly independent territory (for example, thieves were to have their hands cut off). It is generally conceded by scholars that Aquino's rebel army could have taken the Salvadoran capital had they wished to. Aquino, however, made no attempt to extend his control beyond the Nonualco area, not even to other Indian communities in the west that were sympathetic to his movement. A commission of Indians as far away as highland Guatemala came to negotiate with Aquino over the possibility of a pan-Indian union. But Aquino's political vision was local rather than regional.

The creoles and most of the mestizos were profoundly frightened by Aquino and his Indian "terrorists." They regrouped, and reinforced by soldiers from Guatemala, managed to raise an army of 5,000 men that marched on Nonualco. The rebels were quickly routed and Aquino captured. The rebellion had lasted less than four months. Aquino was imprisoned, and after the formality of a trial, was executed. His head was cut off, put in a stone cage, and placed on a prominent hilltop for public viewing.

Atanasio Aquino was a remarkably charismatic leader. He was deeply religious, and medallions of the saints dangled from his neck. His Christian beliefs were tightly interwoven with native "superstitions." He was an extremely brave warrior and excellent horseman. His fighting prowess was enhanced, he claimed, by a secret narcotic (probably coca) that he chewed in battle. Like Atanasio Tzul twelve years earlier, Aquino had himself crowned "king," using Saint Joseph's crown for this purpose. There is some evidence that Aquino believed in the ancient Mesoamerican idea of companion animals (naguals), and that his companion was the tiger (ocelot) (see p. 313). He used a tiger skin as a saddle, and while in prison referred to himself as "a tiger without claws or fangs." During his rise to power, Aquino was able to integrate in his person both native and Spanish elements, and consequently to become an archetypically nativistic prophet.

Events calmed down in Nonualco after the death of Aquino. By mid-century, coffee replaced indigo as El Salvador's main export crop, and has remained so ever since. In 1879 the liberals passed laws that made it possible for coffee owners to acquire additional lands from the Indian communities. Even though the Nonualco area largely fell outside the coffee zone, its native inhabitants were adversely affected by the new laws, and joined in widespread Indian rebellions in 1885. The center of native rebellion, however, had begun to shift to the western Izalco area, where Indian unrest would again turn into a major conflagration in 1932 (as described in the next chapter).

The classic example of nineteenth-century nativistic movements in the region is the "Caste War of Yucatán," described in Box 6.3.

Box 6.3 *The Caste War of Yucatán*

In his classic study, *The Caste War of Yucatan* (1964), Nelson Reed describes conditions in Yucatán during the first half of the ninteenth century that were typical of that period for Mexico and Central America as a whole. After independence, the creole *caudillos* of Yucatán competed with one another for regional power, rationalizing personal conflicts as contests over liberal versus conservative ideals. The contests particularly pitted *caudillos* from the city of Campeche against their counterparts in the capital city of Mérida. Large numbers of Maya Indians were recruited as soldiers in the *caudillo* armies, and fighting alongside the mestizos they received on-the-job training in warfare and other creole practices.

The liberal *caudillos* of Yucatán began to push hard to expand plantation agriculture, especially the henequen industry, in the western part of the Peninsula and sugar in the eastern part. Under the auspices of liberal reform, the land and labor of the huge Maya peasantry inhabiting the Peninsula were exploited. Thousands of Maya were trapped on the plantations as peons; thousands of others fled to the Quintana Roo frontier zone, where they established independent peasant communities and became known as the Huits ("the loincloth people"). The Catholic Church was suppressed by the liberals too, and this diminished the ruling creoles' control over the Maya and hence gave greater freedom for the latter to persevere in their traditional Maya religious practices.

Around mid-century (1850), over 100,000 of the Huits in the eastern frontier finally rose up against liberal rule, and a "caste war" ensued with the Indians on one side and the now-united creoles and mestizos on the other. For the Maya, the goal was to win freedom from what had become an intolerably repressive system of rule. The Maya rebels succeeded in liberating a large area of Yucatán from Mexican control, but eventually retreated to Quintana Roo where they established a separate "nation" known as the "Empire of the Cross." The independent Maya empire survived for over fifty years. The rallying symbol in both war and political organization for the Maya was a series of sacred crosses dressed in huipils, which they claimed had suddenly appeared near a sacred well (cenote) in Chan Santa Cruz. The crosses spoke to the charismatic leaders of the movement, and instructed them on how to make war against the creoles.

The movement's message was strongly nativistic, and a rejection of the liberal attempt to destroy the identity and cultural patterns that the Maya had struggled to preserve throughout the centuries of domination, first by the Spaniards, and later by the peninsular creoles. The society created by the rebellious "people of the cross" was a fascinating syncretic organization, constituted by a surprisingly large number of cultural patterns similar to those of the prehispanic Maya. Political leadership was vested in a prophet ruler (Tatich) who received messages from the talking idols (the crosses); society was stratified into the ancient division between lords, commoners, and slaves (the slaves were white captives); and the old Maya dispersed settlement pattern was instituted, consisting of a politico-ceremonial center surrounded by numerous small agricultural villages (Figure 6.9). Nevertheless, important cultural patterns from the creole world were also woven into the rebel institutions. For example, creole-type military companies became important units of the social system; public administration was performed by secretaries and ecclesiastical officials similar to those found in creole society; and a Spanish-type cathedral was constructed on the spot where the crosses first appeared, and within it masses and rituals dedicated to the saints were regularly carried out.

In the creole and mestizo areas of Yucatán beyond the Empire of the Cross, the henequen industry was expanded and the nonrebellious Maya were drawn further into the liberal system as indebted laborers. After Porfirio Díaz came to power in Mexico, the central government was able to gain control over the caudillo struggles in Yucatán by appointing loyal military leaders as governors of the state. General Bravo, one of these governors, defeated the hapless army of the Maya empire around the turn of the century, and once again incorporated Quintana Roo into Mexican territory. Despite defeat, the rebel Maya had succeeded in making an important political point through their fifty-year struggle: They were determined to survive as Mayas in spite of all attempts by the Mexican overlords to destroy their way of life.

Figure 6.9 Drawing of the town layout at Chan Santa Cruz, the capital of the rebellious Maya of Yucatán. Reprinted from *The Caste War of Yucatan* by Nelson Reed with the permission of the publishers, Stanford University Press. © 1964 by the Board of Trustees of the Leland Stanford Junior University.

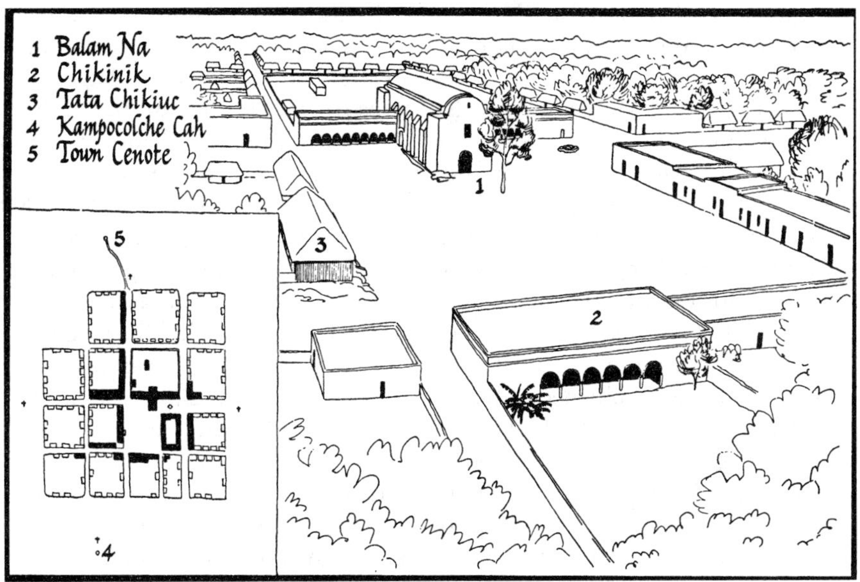

The Yaqui Wars

Let us turn now to the example of the Yaqui Indians of Sonora, Mexico, who have a long history of rebellious activity against outside rule (see the map in Figure 6.1 for the location of the Yaqui during the period under discussion). Occupying the banks of the Yaqui River, they formed part of the northwest periphery of Mesoamerica in prehispanic times. The Yaqui fiercely resisted conquest by the Spaniards, and remained outside colonial control until voluntarily submitting to the authority of the Jesuit missionaries in the early part of the seventeenth century. For 120 years the Yaqui lived peacefully in model villages organized by the Jesuits, governed by their own native authorities. With the increasing encroachment of miners and ranchers into their territory in the eighteenth century, however, the Yaqui joined with the Mayo in a violent and bloody uprising against the Spaniards in 1740. Later, after the Jesuits were expelled from Mexico (1767), the Yaqui dispersed themselves widely throughout the northwest area and thus evaded effective Spanish control. Consequently, they did not take sides or participate directly in Mexico's independence movements.

Liberal policy toward the Yaqui throughout the nineteenth century and into the early twentieth century called for their integration into Mexican society, access by outsiders to their fertile river lands, and expropriation of their labor for use on adjacent mines and cattle haciendas. The Yaqui never acceded to this policy, and repeatedly resisted every attempt to dominate them. Preservation of Yaqui identity, language, religion, and political system provided the underlying nativistic theme of their unrelenting struggle for autonomy.

The first major Yaqui rebellion following independence took place in 1828 in response to an attempt by Mexican liberals to subject the Yaqui to local, regional, and national authorities, and divide their lands into individual plots. The rebellion was led by a highly charismatic leader, "Captain General" Juan Banderas, who rallied the native forces in the names of Father Hidalgo, the Virgin of Guadalupe, and Motecuhzoma. Banderas sought to unite all the native groups of the northwest in order to drive the Mexican whites out of the area. Understandably, the rebellion was interpreted by the Mexican creoles and mestizos as a "race war." Banderas and his forces were effective in preventing the liberals from carrying out reforms in Yaqui country, and they managed to roam throughout Sonora, terrorizing the resident white settlers. Organized Yaqui military actions ended, however, when Banderas was captured and executed in 1833.

The following decades saw renewed efforts by the liberal governments to put the Yaqui under political control, but continued opposition by the militarily organized Yaqui blocked all such attempts. Nevertheless, the area eventually became surrounded by Mexican mines, haciendas, and ranches, and the Yaqui increasingly were drawn away from their communities into wage labor (but not peonage). In 1873, a new charismatic leader named Cajeme emerged from among the Yaqui, and led them once again into open rebellion.

Cajeme, who had previously served in the state militia, was a good organizer, and helped the Yaqui rebuild their communities and become more self-reliant. Under Cajeme the Yaqui regained political and territorial control over the river valley that had always defined their homeland. They adopted an openly nativistic strategy to revitalize the ancient communal land tenure system, calendar of rituals, and council form of government. Many of these practices actually dated from the Colonial period, but since the Jesuit missionaries had originally allowed the Yaqui to blend Spanish with aboriginal ways, the revitalized patterns also had roots in the prehispanic cultures.

Yaqui claims to autonomy were totally rejected by the Porfirio Díaz regime, which had important commercial plans for developing the area. Contingents from the Mexican army launched military campaigns against the Yaqui beginning in 1879, and finally captured and executed Cajeme in 1887. The Yaqui continued the struggle through guerrilla warfare after that, until in 1903 Díaz turned to the ultimate solution of the Yaqui problem: the mass deportation of thousands of Yaqui men, women, and children to Yucatán and other select areas of southern Mexico. Many Yaqui fled to the cities of the northwest and exile communities near Tucson, Arizona. In the meantime, the Yaqui homeland was resettled by mestizo colonists and prepared for large-scale, irrigated commercial agriculture. The liberals had finally gained control of the Yaqui river valley, but the remarkable Yaqui people never did yield to liberal authority.

GROWING U.S. INFLUENCE IN THE REGION

U.S. interference in the affairs of Mexico and Central America has a long history, extending back to the last decades of the Colonial period and continuing on into the twentieth century. As early as 1786, Thomas Jefferson expressed the official U.S. attitude toward the region: "Our confederacy must be viewed as the nest, from which all America, North and South, is to be peopled" (Cockcroft 1983:49). Still in the eighteenth century, U.S. merchants and contrabanders broke through the Spanish trade monopoly to sell their wares at huge profits in Mexico and Central America. U.S. commercial representatives began to appear in the major ports of trade of the region; and U.S. political agents engaged in military intrigue, pressuring the colonies to cast aside Spanish control. And no sooner had Mexico and Central America achieved independence than U.S. (along with British and other European) merchants were aggressively maneuvering to dominate trade with these countries at the expense of British and other merchants. The political meddling began immediately as well—the first U.S. ambassador to Mexico referred to the Mexicans as "ignorant and debauched," and correspondingly tried to tell them how to run their government. In Central America the new federation was based on the U.S. model, and on one or two occasions states like El Salvador, Honduras, and Nicaragua went so far as to request admission to the U.S. Union.

Despite President Monroe's warning to the European powers in 1823 to stay out of the region, Mexico and Central America were repeatedly invaded during the nineteenth century by the European powers, especially England. The worst offender, however, was the United States. Texas was annexed in 1845, and in 1846 the United States invaded Mexico with the excuse of collecting debts owed its citizens from the time of the independence wars. U.S. soldiers succeeded in occupying Mexico City, at the cost of some 50,000 Mexican lives, and forced the Mexican government to cede almost half of its territory (in the "Treaty" of Guadalupe). William Walker, the filibusterer from California, invaded Nicaragua in 1855, and ruled it as a slave state for two years with U.S. official recognition. In 1861, at a time when the United States was preoccupied with its Civil War, Spain invaded Mexico, only to be replaced in 1862 as invaders by the French; they occupied the country until 1867, when they were driven out by Benito Juárez's nationalist forces. Veterans of the U.S. Civil War aided the Juárez forces, and Juárez offered important concessions to the United States in exchange for its recognition of the new Mexican government.

The most important concessions to the United States, however, were made by liberal dictators in Mexico and Central America after the 1870s. Porfirio Díaz not only made it legal for U.S. citizens to own property in Mexico, but personally saw to it that U.S. companies were given contracts to build the major rail lines throughout the country. With Díaz's open-door economic policy, U.S. investors soon dominated mining, oil production, and export agriculture in Mexico. Even the textbooks used in Mexican schools were written by U.S. authors and published by the Appleton Publishing Company (Cockcroft 1983:88).

In Central America, the United States intervened almost at will in the region's governmental affairs. For example, the United States in 1906 forced a Guatemalan dictator to end his war with the other Central American countries; in 1909 made a Nicaraguan dictator resign from office when he dared challenge U.S. power; in 1912 appointed an acting president of Honduras in order to protect U.S. banana interests; and in 1917 ousted a Costa Rican president who refused to make special concessions to U.S. banana and oil companies. As a direct result of such interventions, the Central American countries became known as "Banana Republics" (La Feber 1983).

The liberals, then, opened the door to foreign investment during the nineteenth century; in the early part of the twentieth century, their successors allowed the United States and other foreigners to take virtual control of the political and economic affairs of the states in the region.

U.S. investments in the region were primarily concentrated in mining, oil, and agriculture. As might be expected, the investments were oriented toward production for exports, especially to the United States. But the investments were also accompanied by the heavy infusion of advanced technologies—especially machine-driven tools and infrastructural improvements—mainly in railroads, shipping, irrigation systems, and building construction. In northern Mexico mining was stepped up, largely under the auspices of U.S. companies such as Anaconda, and by 1911 the country had become the second leading producer of silver in the world (Figure 6.10). The exploitation of Mexican oil was dominated by U.S.

Figure 6.10 Mining complex built up in Pachuca, Mexico, during the 19th century.
George Pickow/Superstock.

and British companies (Figure 6.11). As of 1921, production of crude oil in Mexico accounted for about one-fourth of the world's supply, and 70 percent of it was in American hands. Most of the eighty largest industries of Mexico in 1911 were U.S.-owned, many of them specialized in commercial agriculture. U.S. companies, for example, owned and operated the majority of the sugar plantations of Morelos, the most productive sugar cane area in the world, and the lucrative henequen (fiber) plantations of Yucatán. Largely because of foreign mining and agricultural operations, foreigners succeeded in gaining rights to almost 20 percent of Mexico's total land surface. Also early in the century, Mexico became linked to the U.S. market through a vast network of railroad lines, built and controlled by U.S. investors.

In Central America, coffee was the leading export item, accounting for over 50 percent of the area's export values in 1917, and foreign investors increasingly monopolized its production, processing, and shipping (Figure 6.12). As in Mexico, mining was foreign-owned and -operated in Central America—although with the exception of the Nicaraguan gold mines near Puerto Cabezas, the yields were not substantial. U.S. control of the area's economy was most visibly manifested in the growing power of the United Fruit Company (UFCO). Formed around the turn of the century as a U.S. exporter of bananas, UFCO eventually came to monopolize not only banana production in Central America but also the area's railroad, shipping, and communication systems. The UFCO received huge land concessions from all the Central American countries and exercised enormous influence over economic and political matters there, even though the company was exclusively U.S.-owned, and its substantial profits were largely remitted to the parent company in Boston.

Figure 6.11 Oil fields of Veracruz, Mexico, around the turn of the 20th century.

Politically, the countries of the region were ruled by dictators manipulated behind the scenes by foreign powers. Populist slogans helped create an image for the dictators of the strong father figure, and this image was used to keep the poorer sectors in line. Nevertheless, dictators throughout the region created large armies and highly coercive rural police forces that they could call upon if necessary to maintain the status quo. One observer has referred to the Díaz regime in Mexico around 1910 as "not so much a nation as a company store." The regime made Mexico safe so that U.S. investors and other foreigners could reap huge profits. The role of Porfirio Díaz as keeper of the store in Mexico applies equally well to such Central American dictators as Manuel Estrada Cabrera (1898–1920) and Jorge Ubico (1931–1944) in Guatemala, Maximiliano Hernández (1931–1944) in El Salvador, Tiburcio Carías Andino (1932–1948) in Honduras, Anastasio Somoza García (1936–1956) in Nicaragua, and even the somewhat more democratic Cleto Gonzáles and Ricardo Jiménez (1906–1936) in Costa Rica.

This does not mean that peace and harmony reigned at the top of the

Figure 6.12 Carts for transporting coffee from the Pacific coastal plantations to the seaports in 19th century Guatemala. Courtesy of E. Bradford Burns. Reprinted from E. Bradford Burns, *Eadward Muybridge in Guatemala, 1875: The Photographer as Social Recorder.* Berkeley, CA: University of California Press, 1986, p. 126.

political "store," and, in fact, the United States intervened on many occasions in order to orchestrate developments in the region. Some of the political problems originated from local capitalists who opposed domination by foreign investors, others from conflicts between manufacturing and agricultural interests, and still others from middle-class intellectuals and professionals blocked from power by the dictatorial regimes. The dictators themselves often outlived their usefulness to the foreign powers, and the latter did not hesitate to negotiate their downfall. In Mexico, for example, the United States facilitated Porfirio Díaz's departure from power in 1911, later maneuvering behind the scenes to have him replaced by the wealthy creole, Francisco Madero. Failing at this, the United States landed the marines in Veracruz in 1914 in an effort to bring down Victoriano de la Huerta, who was being supported by its British competitors.

Political intervention by the United States in the first three decades of the twentieth century was even more blatant in the case of the Central American countries. The pattern was set early on in Panama, where in 1903, with the backing of President Theodore Roosevelt, U.S. troops negotiated Panama's political separation from Colombia and concessions for U.S. ownership and construction of a canal connecting the two oceans (the canal was completed in 1914). An even more egregious U.S. intervention took place in Nicaragua, which was occupied by the U.S. marines between 1912 and 1933 (except for a short period between 1925 and 1927 when the marines were withdrawn).

The U.S.-dominated capitalism of early twentieth-century Mexico and Central America brought dramatic economic growth to the region, but it failed to promote the well-being of common people. Peasants by the hundreds of thousands were drawn into wage labor, much of it required as debt cancellation and all of it miserably low paying. Most of these rural workers were people of color: Mesoamerican Indians, mestizos, and blacks. They profoundly resented the economic exploitation to which they were subjected and the racist discrimination heaped upon them by the foreign and national capitalists. The United States, for its part, seemed to show no interest in the plight of the Indians or other exploited peoples from whom its entrepreneurs extracted exorbitant profits. Neither did it recognize that increasingly this rural sector—part peasant and part proletariat—was becoming a tinderbox waiting to burst into flames.

Even the industrial workers, most of whom had emigrated from the rural zones to occupy the manufacturing jobs in the burgeoning cities of the region, were subject to severe economic exploitation and racial discrimination. In Mexico many of them labored in mining and textile manufacturing, and by 1910 they already made up around 15 percent of the economically active population. Influenced by intellectuals in the city, the workers began to be radicalized, and toward the end of the Díaz period engaged in dozens of (illegal) strikes. In Central America the urban workers constituted a smaller percentage of economic society, perhaps 10 percent of the labor force in the 1920s. But they were sorely repressed by the Central American regimes, and by the 1920s began to form radical unions and engage in wildcat strikes. They were soon joined by rural laborers from the United Fruit Company's banana plantations, who in the 1930s became the premier radical sector of Central American society.

In retrospect, it seems clear that already in the early part of the twentieth century the societies of the region under powerful U.S. influence were developing conditions that could lead to revolutionary actions more radical than the nativistic movements of the nineteenth century. "Revolution" as we use the term contrasts with "reform," and refers to those violent actions by which socially dominated classes seek to break the bonds that hold them down and in the process cast aside the ruling classes. If in reform change comes from above (led by the upper classes), in revolution it comes from below (the lower classes take the lead). The modern era was initiated in the region by the twentieth century's first "socialist" revolution, which like a volcano erupted in Mexico's countryside in 1910. But that is a topic for the chapter to follow.

SUGGESTED READINGS

CARMACK, ROBERT M. 1983 Spanish-Indian Relations in Highland Guatemala, 1800–1944. In *Spaniards and Indians in Southeastern Mesoamerica: Essays on the History of Ethnic Relations*, edited by M. J. MacLeod and R. Wasserstrom, pp. 215–252. Lincoln: University of Nebraska Press.

KATZ, FRIEDRICH (ed.) 1988 *Riot, Rebellion, and Revolution: Rural Social Conflict in Mexico.* Princeton, N.J.: Princeton University Press.

KINCAID, A. DOUGLAS 1987 Peasants into Rebels: Community and Class in Rural El Salvador. *Comparative Study of Society and History* 29:466–494.

LA FEBER, WALTER 1983 *Inevitable Revolutions: The United States in Central America.* New York: W.W. Norton.

LEWIS, OSCAR 1963 *Life in a Mexican Village: Tepoztlán Restudied.* Urbana: University of Illinois Press.

MCCREERY, DAVID J. 1989 Atanasio Tzul, Lucas Aguilar, and the Indian Kingdom of Totonicapán. In *The Human Tradition in Latin America: The Nineteenth Century,* edited by J. Ewell and W. H. Beezley, pp. 39–58. Wilmington, Del.: SR Books.

PAZ, OCTAVIO 1961 *The Labyrinth of Solitude.* New York: Grove Press.

REED, NELSON 1964 *The Caste War of Yucatan.* Stanford, Calif.: Stanford University Press.

SMITH, CAROL A. (ed.) 1990 *Guatemalan Indians and the State: 1540–1988.* Austin: University of Texas Press.

SPICER, EDWARD H. 1962 *Cycles of Conquest: The Impact of Spain, Mexico, and the United States on the Indians of the Southwest, 1533–1960.* Tucson: University of Arizona Press.

Chapter 7 Mesoamericans in the Modern Era

Globally, the twentieth century has been a time of reaping the harvest of seeds sown by nineteenth- and early twentieth-century capitalism and the liberal reforms used to justify it. This has been as true for the Mesoamericans of Mexico and Central America as for native peoples elsewhere. Liberal programs evolved into more sophisticated and carefully planned "developmental" strategies, while widespread opposition to the injustices accompanying residual old-fashioned liberalism and the new developmental reforms led to "socialist revolutions" throughout the region.

The revolutionaries and development agents of twentieth-century Mexico and Central America have barely taken the Mesoamericans into account in their haste to create modern nation-states, although they have at least paid lip service to the preservation of their fading cultural traditions. Even the "indigenist" programs sponsored by agents of the modern world were largely designed to assimilate them as underclass minorities. Not surprisingly, the Mesoamericans have resisted the loss of their cultural heritage.

We begin our discussion with a summary of social changes taking place in the region during the twentieth century. We will then examine revolutions and developmental reforms from the perspective of how the Mesoamerican Indians have both affected and been affected by these broad social processes.

SUMMARY OF TWENTIETH-CENTURY SOCIAL HISTORY

Comparative studies of revolutions in the twentieth century—especially the Russian, Chinese, and Vietnamese cases—have given us a much better understanding of the social forces that lead to revolutions and the key participants in them. Three central findings about revolutions seem particularly relevant to twentieth-century social developments in the region that continues to be the homeland of the Mesoamerican Indians (Wolf 1969):

1. Revolutions tend to take place in societies in which large peasant sectors have been strongly affected by capitalist forces. These forces break down the old landlord-peasant ties, and free up middle peasants and proletarianized peasants to participate in revolutionary actions.
2. Peasant uprisings take on larger dimensions when leadership is provided by ambitious middle-class radicals—such as teachers, military officers, merchants, and bureaucrats—who have become frustrated by barriers to their attempted rise in power. These leaders and their urban followers meet up with the rebellious peasants in the countryside, from where they march to battle, usually under "socialist" banners.
3. Corrupt regimes highly dependent on outside powers tend to have weak legitimacy, easily crumble in the face of determined internal opposition, and create political vacuums that revolutionaries try to fill.

We shall attempt to show in this chapter that these three conditions have consistently emerged in the Mesoamerican region during the twentieth century (Figure 7.1).

The Mexican Revolution

Revolution first broke out in Mexico in 1910 with the electoral challenge to Porfirio Díaz by the conservative reformer, Francisco Madero. The conflict was initially between members of the ruling class, and it led to the departure of Díaz and the replacement of Madero by another conservative, Victoriano de la Huerta. It eventually unleashed genuine revolutionary forces under the leadership of Pancho Villa in the north (Figure 7.2) and Emiliano Zapata in the south (Figure 7.3). Venustiano Carranza and Alvaro Obregón led two other somewhat more middle-of-the road forces. These various factions captured the government in 1914, but then began fighting among themselves. The more moderate Carranza and Obregón factions formed an alliance, and integrating their armies in 1920 finally achieved victory over the Villa and Zapata factions after years of bitter warfare.

From the outbreak of violence in 1910, the struggle was highly destructive of human life and material goods. Perhaps as many as 2 million Mexicans died, many of them after being taken prisoner and others from disease and wounds. Civilians were robbed, cattle slaughtered and eaten by soldiers, and in the chaos of war manufacturing declined and agricultural production almost

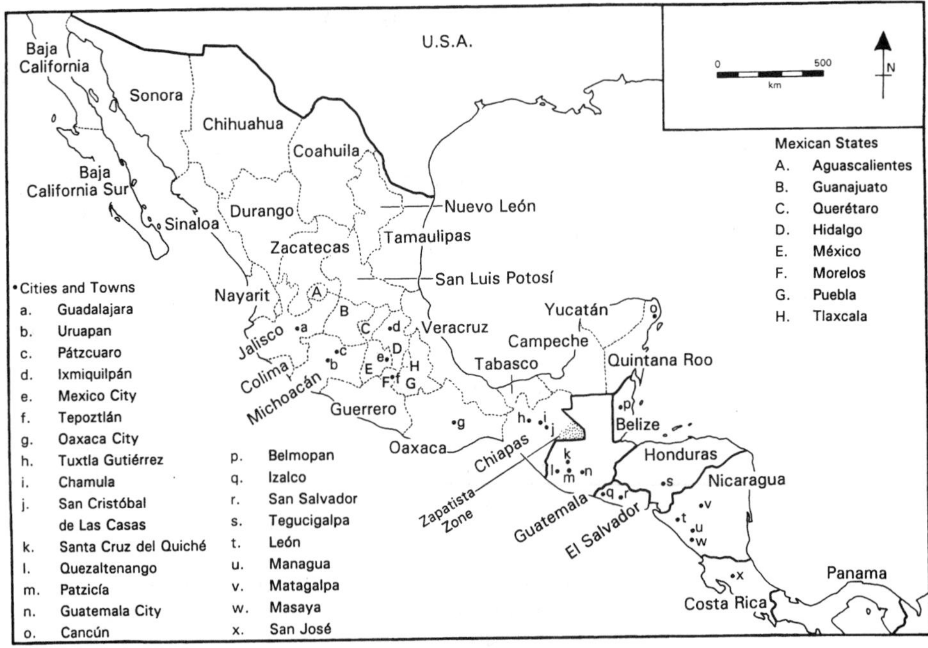

Figure 7.1 Political states of modern Mexico and Central America; also shown are places mentioned in the text.

came to a standstill. The country fell even more deeply in debt to U.S. and other foreign investors.

The most important political developments during the period were the creation of a Constitution in 1917 and the welding together of the peasants, workers, and military groups into a single political organization. The Constitution laid down truly revolutionary laws in the areas of labor relations, elections, education, and civil freedoms. While the progressive laws of the Constitution came from Obregón's side of the alliance, it was the more conservative Carranza who became president, and he failed to carry out most of the Constitution's provisions. Carranza tried, illegally, to extend his own presidency; he was driven out of office and killed, while Obregón became president of Mexico. The peaceful succession from Obregón to Elías Calles in 1924 symbolized the solidification of the revolutionary government and the end of the most violent phase of the Mexican revolution.

The radical social changes called for in the 1917 Constitution were only gradually implemented in the years following 1924, most of them during the presidency of Lázaro Cárdenas (1934–1940). Opposition to the changes was fierce. For example, curtailment of the Catholic Church's economic and political powers led to deep hostility on the part of the priesthood and its loyal followers. In the Guadalajara area, loyalists to the Church launched the so-called "Cristero" movement, which included guerrilla warfare against the revolutionary government. At one point all the bishops and archbishops were expelled from Mexico, and in 1926 Church buildings were closed throughout the country. The expro-

Figure 7.2 Pancho Villa, leader of the revolutionary forces in northern Mexico. Courtesy of Culver Pictures.

priation of the foreign-controlled oil fields by Cárdenas in 1938 was another policy decision that evoked intense opposition to the revolutionary government. U.S. and British oil companies, backed by their respective home governments, threat-

Figure 7.3 Emiliano Zapata, leader of the peasant revolutionary forces in southern Mexico. Courtesy of the Organization of American States, Columbus Memorial Library.

ened the use of force and attempted various forms of blackmail in an attempt to roll back the government's action. These countries tried to block the shipping of oil from Mexico, but such obstructive actions failed and petroleum production began to flourish under Mexican control.

Perhaps the most radical change instituted by the revolutionary government was the redistribution of land to the peasants and rural proletariats. Lands were turned over to the villages as "ejidos," communal properties to which use rights were given to the landless. The bulk of the redistribution was carried out by Cárdenas, and at the end of his term in 1940 approximately 2 million people in 15,000 villages had received lands and now controlled production on about 50 percent of Mexico's croplands. The peasants seemingly had gained the lands for which they had fought so long and hard.

The conditions mentioned above as being associated with twentieth-century revolutions around the world were all present in the case of the Mexican Revolution. The driving force of the revolution, particularly in its early stages, was the peasants, the majority of whom lined up behind Zapata. These peasants generally had been forced off their lands and made to work for capitalist enterprises—especially sugar plantations, in the case of Zapata's followers. The Villa forces tended to be more proletarianized, and many of them were not peasants at all but cowhands, miners, and migrant farmworkers. Most of the revolutionary leaders themselves were from the middle class, as in the case of Zapata and many captains of the Villa, Carranza, and Obregón forces. Villa himself came from the lower class, but Carranza and Obregón, whose movements were more reformist than revolutionary, had ties to the landlord class.

It is clear that the Mexican Revolution was precipitated by the weakness of the dependent Díaz regime, and further fomented by the clumsy attempts on the part of the United States and England to name his successor (first Madero, then Huerta, and finally Carranza). Not only did the collapse of authority at the center create a vacuum into which the revolutionaries rushed, but outside meddling gave the movement a strong anti-foreign and pro-nationalist tint. The idea of Mexico as an independent, "revolutionary" country would provide political legitimacy for the new government in the years ahead.

Central American Revolutions

Full-scale revolution erupted in Central America half a century later than in Mexico (see below), although several aborted revolutionary movements broke out shortly after events finally began to calm down in Mexico. In 1920, for example, when the Guatemalan dictator Manuel Estrada Cabrera was pushed out of office with U.S. help after twenty-two years of rule, peasant forces were unleashed in the western part of the country, which had definite revolutionary overtones. Even though the movement was quickly quashed, the rebels harbored strong anti-foreign ideas as a result of the many concessions that for years had been given to the German coffee growers and the United Fruit Company in Guatemala.

More serious revolutionary movements, even though also aborted, took place in Nicaragua and El Salvador. The Nicaraguan movement was brought on by the ouster in 1909 of José Santos Zelaya, a liberal caudillo with strong nationalist leanings, and the subsequent occupation of the country by U.S. troops from 1912 on. Under the leadership of military officers sympathetic to Zelaya and his liberal cause, bands of peasants in the northern part of the country rose up against the U.S. forces and their Nicaraguan puppet leaders. The movement became more radical in 1927, when Augusto Sandino, a middle-class mestizo who had earlier become politicized while residing in Mexico, assumed its leadership after his superior commanders began to collaborate with the U.S.-backed regime. Employing the techniques of guerrilla warfare and anti-imperialist ideals, Sandino's "revolutionaries" were able to hold the U.S. Marines at bay until elections were held and the U.S. forces departed in 1933. Sandino maintained ties with the communist parties of Central America and with President Calles in Mexico, but his ideology was primarily nationalist and not particularly radical. He was assassinated in 1934, apparently by members of the National Guard unit left behind when the U.S. military pulled out of the country.

The Salvadoran movement was precipitated by a military coup against a moderate president in 1931, and the cancellation of municipal elections the following year. Urban workers in the capital city of San Salvador, under the leadership of Farabundo Martí and the Communist Party, went out on strike, at the same time that bands of peasants in the coffee-rich Izalco area rebelled against the local landlords and government authorities. General Maximiliano Martínez took charge of putting down the "communist revolution," with full backing from the U.S. and Canadian governments (warships were quickly dispatched to the area). Leaders of the urban strike, including Martí, were rounded up and executed, while 10,000 to 30,000 of the western peasants were hunted down and killed in the days following the uprising. This ended both the revolutionary movement and the political vacuum in El Salvador, as General Martínez stridently launched thirteen years of dictatorial rule.

At this time in Central America, revolutionary conditions apparently were not as fully developed as in Mexico. In particular, capitalist penetration into the peasant communities was more localized and not as extensive. The middle-class leaders seem to have commanded much smaller followings among the urban working classes than in Mexico. Certainly, corrupt and dependent political regimes abounded in Central America at the time, and successions from one dictator to another brought on periods of considerable confusion and instability. In general, however, military caudillos, usually with U.S. help, tended to fill these periods of political void in Central America, and restored "order" more effectively than in the case of Mexico.

By the 1960s conditions for revolution in Central America had greatly accelerated, and full-blown revolutionary movements broke out in the area. In Central America, as had been the case in Mexico, proletarianized peasants played a major role in these revolutionary events, mediated by Marxist radicals and their working-class supporters from the urban zones. Corrupt military regimes lacking broad legitimacy were precipitating factors, along with blatant political meddling by the United States. Cuba provided a new element that figured into the revolutionary equation, serving as both model for socialist revolutions "Latin–American style" and source of military and economic aid to the Central American revolutionaries.

Let us now briefly trace the more recent revolutionary developments in Guatemala, El Salvador, and Nicaragua.

Guatemala. In many ways the Guatemalan Revolution can be understood as the legacy of the U.S.-orchestrated overthrow of the country's legitimate government in 1954, and subsequent U.S. backing of a long succession of anti-communist military regimes. The Guatemalan army virtually took over the state, serving the interests of foreign and local capitalists and its own generals, who increasingly used office to acquire personal wealth. As the state became more repressive, opposition from the lower and middle classes intensified. In the 1960s a group of young army officers broke with their commanders, and formed bands of revolutionary guerrillas in the eastern area of the country. They were joined by proletarianized mestizo peasants there, and together they achieved widespread popularity throughout the country. The movement was ruthlessly smashed, however, under the direction of Colonel Carlos Arana, assisted by U.S. Green Berets and unrelenting local death squads. An estimated 10,000 people were killed—many of them innocent victims—particularly students, union leaders, and peasants from the eastern zone.

The military government went on to create a permanent state of terror in Guatemala, losing any legitimacy it might have enjoyed and creating dissent from all social sectors, even from members of the capitalist class. Toward the end of the 1970s, guerrilla fighting erupted again, this time in the western highlands where the majority of Maya Indians reside. Most of the guerrilla leaders were urban Marxists affiliated with the earlier movement in the east, but now they were joined by several thousand Indian soldiers and aided by hundreds of thousands of sympathizers from the Indian communities. The war between the revolutionaries and the Guatemalan army was nearly won by the insurgents toward the close of the 1970s, at which time in desperation the army adopted a program of scorched earth and genocidal tactics against the Indian communities. Over 400 villages were wiped out, and more than 50,000 people killed, most of them Indians and many of them women and children. Eventually, over 1 million people were forced to flee their homes as refugees, either within Guatemala or in other countries (especially Mexico, but also the United States, Nicaragua, and Costa Rica).

By 1985 the Guatemalan army's ruthless counterinsurgency tactics had broken the back of the revolution, and the entire western highlands became a militarized zone of bases, strategic hamlets, and "civil" patrols. The revolutionaries continued to fight, but any threat that they might be able to topple the government had been eliminated. Civilian presidents were elected in 1985 and 1991, even though the military continued to control much of what went on in the country. In keeping with the Central American Peace Accords, in 1993 the guerrilla units and the government finally agreed to begin negotiations on an end to what had become a thirty-year war.

El Salvador. El Salvador's revolution was not precipitated by one singularly important political event, but rather slowly gathered steam during the 1970s and finally burst open around 1980. Key developments along the way that led to the conflagration were the fraudulent elections in 1972, when José Napoleón Duarte of the Christian Democratic Party was denied the presidency; the collapse of a reform junta in 1979; and the assassination of Archbishop Oscar Arnulfo Romero and later of four U.S. nuns in 1980. The critical factor bringing on the revolution, however, was the total domination of Salvadoran society by the army. The army not only made sure that its generals would be "elected" each term, but also secured the interests of foreign and national capitalists by ruthlessly repressing all opposition to the regime from the lower classes. In 1979 alone over 600 people were murdered by the army and its allied death squads.

The guerrilla forces began to organize as early as 1972, expanding in numbers until in 1980 they totalled around 7,000 men and women and could count on support from another 200,000 sympathizers. The revolutionaries were grouped together under the Farabundo Martí National Liberation Front (FMLN), an umbrella organization whose leadership was provided by Marxist-oriented intellectuals and radical urban workers. Most of the recruits were landless peasants, many of whom had been politically awakened by the new "liberation theology" taught in Christian base communities. The revolutionaries became an effective military force that fought the well-trained and financed Salvadoran army to a standstill. On several occasions they launched major offensives throughout the country in hopes of igniting a general insurrection.

As is well known, the U.S. government financed, trained, and provided military leadership for the Salvadoran army in its war against "communism." It also maneuvered behind the scenes to ensure the election of Duarte in the 1984 general election, in the belief that the moderate Christian Democrats would be able to mediate between the reactionary generals and the radical FMLN commanders. Duarte did win the election, but the war dragged on. The FMLN leaders finally agreed to participate in the national elections of 1989, which were won by the conservative candidate, Alfredo Cristiani (the leftist candidate received only 3 percent of the popular vote). Surprisingly, Cristiani was open to negotiation with the revolutionaries, and through the auspices of the United Nations peace was finally agreed to in 1992. The war ended in El Salvador some twenty years and 50,000 deaths after the first revolutionary organizations made their appearance.

Nicaragua. The essential factor leading to revolution in Nicaragua was the highly corrupt, U.S.-dependent regime of Anastasio Somoza Debayle. Somoza used the government for personal gain, as he and his relatives and cronies amassed huge fortunes in property and business holdings. The Somoza regime lacked legitimacy among the important social sectors of Nicaragua—even the capitalists resented his personal meddling in the country's commercial affairs. Political control was maintained by means of a highly corrupt National Guard and the unfailing support of the United States. The National Guard was a 7,000-strong army and police force directly under Somoza's control (his sons usually held its highest command posts), that used terror and extortion to keep the population in line. Precipitating events leading to the revolutionary explosion against the Somoza regime were the devastating earthquake in 1972 (Somoza was accused of personally benefitting from the incoming foreign assistance); Somoza's fraudulent re-election in 1974; and the assassination in 1978 of his leading political opponent, newspaper editor Pedro Joaquín Chamorro (it was widely believed that Somoza was responsible for Chamorro's death).

Revolutionary opposition to the Somoza regime started as early as 1961, with the founding of the Sandinista National Liberation Front (FSLN) by a group of middle-class radicals from the Matagalpa Highlands. Following the Cuban model, the small band of revolutionaries engaged in guerrilla-like attacks against the National Guard and gradually won to their side large numbers of Nicaragua's highly proletarianized peasants. By the 1970s the FSLN was able to recruit several thousand middle-class youth and urban workers to its cause, and began to launch bold military offensives against the regime. For example, in 1978 the rebels seized the National Palace and forced Somoza to accede to several exorbitant demands. Finally, the FSLN forces initiated attacks on all the major cities of Nicaragua, preceded in almost every case by local insurrections—beginning with a four-day uprising in the Monimbó ward of Masaya in February 1978 (Figure 7.4). The United States withdrew its support of Somoza late in 1978, and attempted to negotiate a compromise designed to prevent a FSLN takeover of the government. The compromise failed, FSLN forces launched a final offensive from Costa Rica, and in July 1979 Somoza fled to Miami as the Sandinistas occupied the capital of Managua.

The victorious Sandinistas attempted to create a socialist state in which both private enterprise and civil liberties would be respected. They were opposed at every step by the United States, which cut off all aid and organized a counterrevolutionary group of dissident National Guardsmen and Nicaraguan peasants known as the Contras. By 1983 the Contras were infiltrating Nicaragua from Honduras, and in response the Sandinistas began to further militarize and harden

Figure 7.4 Masks worn by Sandinistas during the 1978 insurrection at Monimbó, Masaya, Nicaragua.

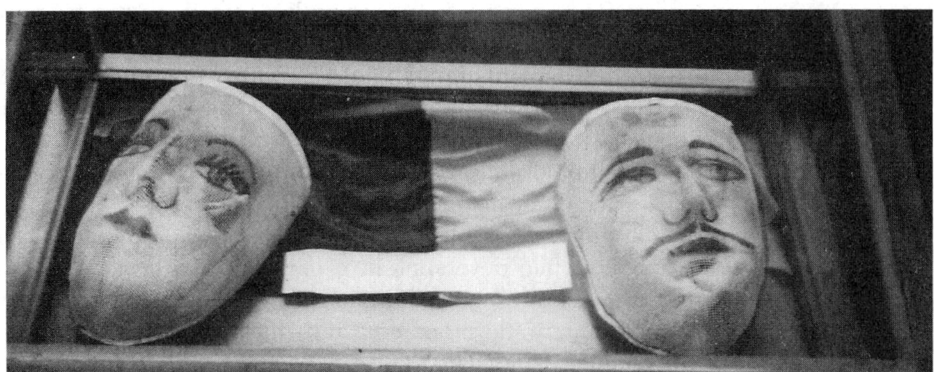

their control over society. Nevertheless, elections were held in 1984, in which Daniel Ortega, the FSLN candidate, won 67 percent of the vote. Through the mediation of Mexico, Costa Rica, and other countries, the Sandinistas and Contras finally agreed to a cease-fire in 1988. New elections were held in 1990, and the Nicaraguan Opposition Party (UNO) candidate, Violeta Chamorro (the wife of the newspaper editor who had been assassinated in 1978), was victorious over Daniel Ortega of the FSLN party with almost 60 percent of the vote. President Chamorro agreed to allow the Sandinistas to retain control over the army, and a degree of reconciliation began to take place in Nicaragua after thirty years of civil war.

Modernization through Development

Revolution is one common path to modernization in the twentieth century; another is development. "Development," as we shall use the term, consists of planned change, especially change resulting from economic measures taken by governments and collaborating entrepreneurs. The developmental approach to change is more gradual than the revolutionary approach, and tends to be more conservative. It may avoid much of the violence associated with revolution, but it has costs, particularly the costs of deep social inequalities and widespread poverty. As we shall now see, the developmental approach to modernization has been widely applied in the region of Mexico and Central America, and as elsewhere in the world, its costs have been high.

Mexico. Octavio Paz (1985) has commented that there are two kinds of revolution, one resulting because of development, as in England and France, and one from the *lack of* development, as in Russia and China. The Mexican Revolution, he explains, was of the second kind. Indeed, even after the immensely important changes brought by the Mexican Revolution, as of 1940 an estimated 60 percent of the peasants in Mexico still did not have enough lands to sustain themselves and 50 percent of all cultivable lands remained under the control of the large landowners (*latifundistas*). Industry continued to be dominated by foreigners, despite the fact that by law majority ownership had to be in the hands of Mexican capitalists. The state for its part mainly controlled infrastructural works such as highways and electrical and irrigation systems. Urban workers were brought into the massive Confederation of Mexican Workers Union (CTM) but were subject to the strict control of the state, and real wages were declining. The revolutionaries successfully fought a civil war, established a strong state, and created the image of a united nation, but development in the modern sense of the term was yet to be achieved.

Under the guidance of the Institutionalized Revolutionary Party (PRI), after 1940 Mexico launched development programs of such magnitude and success that they became known as the "Mexican miracle." Goals were shifted from public welfare to economic development, and during the 1950s and 1960s economic growth exceeded 6 percent per year. Industrial production was stressed, especially of consumer goods such as food, clothing, televisions, and cars. Government agencies proliferated, and the population grew at the prodigious annual rate of more than 3 percent. Urbanization proceeded apace as peasants streamed into the cities to work in the factories, especially in Mexico City. By 1960 the urban workers and middle classes made up 40 percent of the total population of the country. Mexico was becoming modern, and new ideas about progress as measured by the consumption of material goods were replacing the earlier revolutionary ones of liberation through class conflict.

In retrospect, we can see that Mexico's modernization was achieved at very high costs. The country became heavily dependent on the United States and other industrialized countries. Economic growth was largely financed by foreign companies, which drained off a large portion of the huge profits from Mexican industry. Furthermore, imports far exceeded exports, and Mexico developed a serious trade imbalance and one of the largest foreign debts in the world. At the same time, the gap between rich and poor widened. Mexican capitalists affiliated with foreign companies grew in wealth and importance, while the vast majority of the massive peasantry possessed either lands too small for their own subsistence or none at all. The land problem affected those peasants working collective *ejido* lands as well, and almost the entire rural population was forced to find work on large commercial farms and plantations in Mexico or as "braceros" (migrant farmers) in the United States. Economic conditions were not as prosperous for the middle class or urban labor class as they appeared either, since below the elite sectors of both classes were to be found most of the class members struggling against inflation and low wages.

The ruling party and its administrative organ, the Mexican state, took on authoritarian, corrupt, and repressive characteristics. As Octavio Paz says, the system became a veritable "pyramid" of power. The presidents of Mexico were chosen and essentially appointed by PRI, and they thoroughly dominated the legislative and judicial branches. The party and the army closed ranks, and even after the army became more professional and less politically active, powerful military, police, and paramilitary units were organized to control, by terror if necessary, opposition to the state and its "institutionalized revolutionary" policies. Indeed, in 1958 a large strike in Mexico City was ruthlessly put down by the army, and again in 1968 a crowd of 400,000 anti-government demonstrators in the Tlatelolco square was brutally fired upon by security forces; 300 or more persons were killed (Figure 7.5). Guerrilla fighting broke out in the rural zones during the 1970s, although the rebel bands were never able to coordinate their efforts in the face of relentless search and destroy forays by the state security forces.

Since 1970 Mexico has made an attempt to open up its political and economic systems and return to the revolutionary goals. PRI allowed minority parties to compete in elections on a fairer basis, and even recognized the existence of the Communist Party. The country established relations with Fidel Castro in Cuba and Salvador Allende in Chile, and generally closed ranks with the Third World bloc as it tried to chart a more independent foreign policy course with respect to

Figure 7.5 Demonstrators confront the Mexican army near the Plaza of Three Cultures, Tlatelolco, Mexico in 1968. Courtesy of Bettman Archives.

the United States The discovery of rich new oil reserves revived hope in the economy, and the decision was made to use funds from petroleum sales to pay off the foreign debt and diversify the economy. In particular, production was moved away from lighter consumer to heavier capital goods (such as machinery) and to intensify agriculture—the goal being self-sufficiency in food. These reforms led to some developmental "progress" in Mexico, but hard economic times throughout the world in the 1970s and 1980s—in Mexico inflation rates rose into the 20 to 30 percentiles and the foreign debt mushroomed to the tens of billions of dollars—meant that in many ways the country's problems would remain much as the development programs of the 1960s had left them.

Central America. The Central American countries paralleled Mexico in their attempt to modernize through development after the 1940s, but they differed in not yet having experienced major revolutionary change. To some extent, then, they more closely followed Paz's model of revolution that takes place because of development rather than the lack of it. Growth and economic development became important goals in all the Central American countries beginning in the 1950s, spurred on by the Alliance for Progress and the Central American Common Market (CACM). By the 1970s, developmental reforms had already produced social conditions that precipitated the radical revolutions described above for the region. As with Mexico, developmental reform in Central America resulted in economic and political dependency on the United States and other highly developed countries, very large peasantries strongly repressed by the military establishments, and fairly large middle classes spiraling downward in social status and economic well-being.

In parallel with Mexico, developmental programs at first brought overall growth and prosperity to the Central American countries. Gross national product (GNP) increased in the region for the three decades from 1950 to 1980 by an average of 6 percent per year. Growth was especially high in export goods produced by commercial agriculture, the five leading products being coffee, cotton, bananas, sugar, and beef. Growth in manufactured products was almost as great, but most of these products were funneled into the CACM. The withdrawal of Honduras from the CACM and its subsequent disintegration toward the end of the 1970s, however, was a sign of the negative growth and profound economic problems the Central American countries began to experience in the 1980s.

In only two instances were serious efforts made to institute lasting developmental reforms in Central America, the first in Guatemala (1944–1954) and the second in Costa Rica (1948 onward). In the other countries of the region—El Salvador, Honduras, and Nicaragua—major reform was never seriously undertaken. In El Salvador, for example, a political cycle was reenacted in which young military officers would lead coups against corrupt superiors, institute minor social and economic reforms, only to succumb to the temptations of power and become vulnerable to a repetition of the cycle. The situation was similar in Honduras, where early in the 1960s and again in the 1970s military leaders won power and undertook just enough land reform to counter the threat of unrest among the peasantry. In Nicaragua, the conditions calling for reform—such as a large underclass exploited by a prosperous capitalist class and sizable middle class—were present, but the Somoza dynasty was more interested in personal wealth than meaningful developmental reform, despite lip service to the Alliance for Progress.

Guatemala's major effort to modernize began in 1944, when students, professionals, merchants, and young military officers from the emerging urban middle class seized the reins of power from the dictator Jorge Ubico and formed their own "revolutionary" government. During the next ten years the reformers attempted to change Guatemala from a dependent, racist state typical of the nineteenth century to a modern, independent, capitalist state. Under presidents Juan José Arévalo and Jacobo Arbenz, the government challenged U.S. hegemony over Guatemala as well as the large landowners' control of land and the Church's hold on the population's conscience.

Guatemala became more democratic than at any time in its history, with free elections, a viable congress, competing political parties (even the Communist Party became legal), organized unions and peasant leagues, and an independent course in foreign affairs. Much effort went into modernizing the economy, as forced labor was eliminated, a fair labor code enacted, and in 1952 an agrarian reform law instituted. The land reform led to the expropriation of about 1 million acres of land from the largest plantation owners, and these lands were turned over to 100,000 landless peasant families. The peasant communities were strongly affected by the reforms, as the newly formed political parties pitted up-and-coming progressive leaders against the traditional elders. Concurrently, the peasant leagues and agrarian councils provided opposition to the traditional authorities responsible for order within and between the rural communities. Modernization was beginning to make headway in the countryside of Guatemala.

The government and its modernizing reforms were sharply contested by groups that had benefitted from the past dictatorial system: large landowners, led by the United Fruit Company, which lost about one-half million acres of idle lands; the older generation of army officers, who opposed the erosion of their influence in the countryside; the Church, which saw in the government a communist threat; and the U.S. State Department, which feared that its domination of the Guatemalan state was being weakened and so denounced Guatemala's leaders as communists. The U.S. Central Intelligence Agency (CIA) organized, trained, and led a clandestine band of dissident Guatemalan soldiers and mercenaries in a coup that overthrew the Arbenz government in 1954. One historian described the reasons for the coup as follows: "The Guatemalan 'revolution' threatened the favoured monopoly position of U.S. capital, presenting a challenge perceived in Washington not solely as a threat to the UFCo but also as a potential menace to U.S. hegemony throughout Latin America" (Handy 1984:147).

Development and reform did not entirely end in Guatemala with the 1954 coup, but subsequent years were characterized by repressive military rule, the massive accumulation of wealth for the few, and dire poverty for the many.

Costa Rica's attempt to modernize through developmental reforms (beginning in 1948) was not as bold as Guatemala's, but as we shall see in Box 7.1, it turned out to be more practical and longer lasting.

Box 7.1 *The Figueres Reforms in Costa Rica*

In Costa Rica, in the years preceding 1948, a powerful populist president, Rafael Angel Calderón, managed to form alliances with both radical plantation workers and conservative coffee barons. This unusual coalition made it possible for Calderón to push through important social reforms, such as a labor code, social security program, and universal education. As Calderón began to move toward greater control of the state, however, opposition coalesced against him among members of the urban middle class. When Calderón and his followers attempted to annul the 1948 election results, an uprising took place under the leadership of José Figueres, a coffee farmer with connections to the U.S. State Department (Figure 7.6).

The Figueres-led rebels initiated a two-month long civil war, or "revolution" as they called it, with backing from the United States (the U.S. government saw the revolt as an anti-communist movement). The victors went on to create a new constitution that modified the labor and electoral codes, outlawed the Communist Party, nationalized the banks, and, most dramatic of all, abolished the army. The leaders of this reform movement soon organized the National Liberation Party (PLN), and in 1952 Figueres was elected president under the new party's banner. In the years following 1952 opposition parties managed to win presidential elections from time to time, but the PLN reformers clearly dominated the political field through a series of economic, political, and social welfare programs. As a result, Costa Rica experienced almost thirty years of relative peace, growth, and prosperity. In most indices of health, education, and economic well-being, by the 1970s Costa Rica surpassed not only the other Central American countries but Mexico as well.

Figure 7.6 Followers of Pepe Figueres in the 1948 Costa Rican uprising. Reprinted, with permission, from Victor Hugo Acuña, *Conflicto y Reforma en Costa Rica: 1940–1949,* Nuestra Historia (17) San José, Costa Rica: Universidad Estatal a Distancia, 1991.

PARTICIPATION IN THE TWENTIETH-CENTURY REVOLUTIONS BY MESOAMERICAN INDIANS

We turn now to the role played by the heirs to the Mesoamerican civilization—the Indians of Mexico and Central America—in the revolutionary movements described above (see the map in Figure 7.7 for places mentioned below in connection with revolutionary actions in the region).

The Mexican Revolution

Octavio Paz (1985) claims that the Mexican Revolution was an authentic popular movement to bring change, but that it had no clear ideology. It was, instead, a countercultural movement, a search for national culture. Heroes of the revolution such as Pancho Villa and Emiliano Zapata would become symbols of a new, more national culture. They were the inspiration for novels about the revolution and majestic public murals painted by artists like Diego Rivera and José Clemente Orozco.

The denigrated Mesoamericans were also elevated to a position of moral inspiration, and historical figures like Cuauhtemoc and Benito Juárez (who had Zapotec ancestry) were collectively glorified. The Spaniards, in contrast, were vilified, and the figure of Hernán Cortés was transformed into a bow-legged, chinless cretin. The agrarian reform and other changes made by the revolutionary

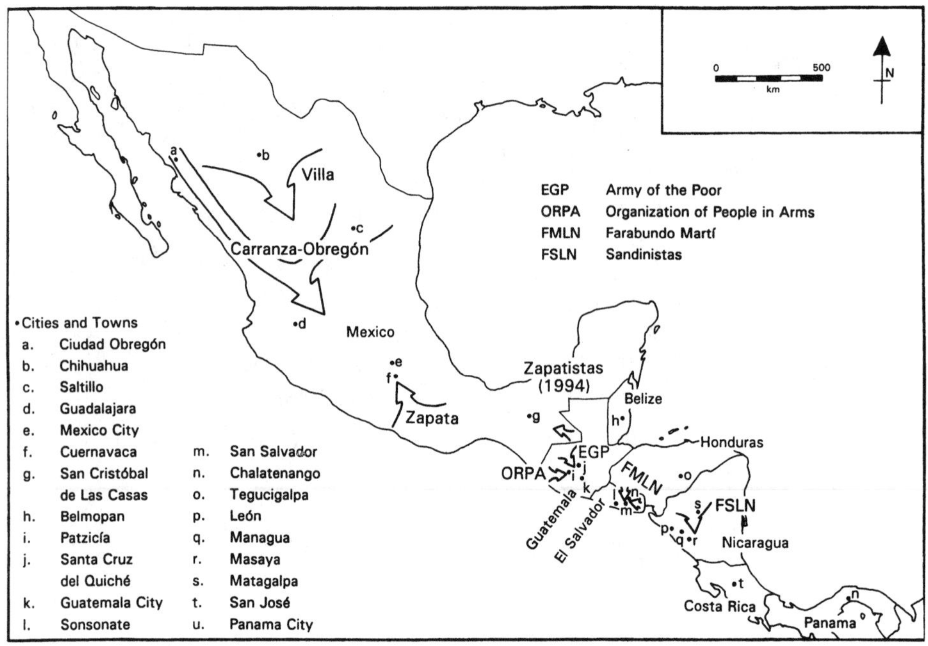

Figure 7.7 Places and regions of action in the Mexican and Central American revolutions.

government were rationalized to some extent as ways to restore the Indians to their rightful place in history. There was even some thought of elevating the Mesoamericans to the position of ethnic symbol of Mexican identity, and indeed Mesoamerican culture and art styles became the object of study and admiration. On a more practical level, certain native institutions, such as the Indians' communal land tenure system (ejidos), became sources of legitimization for the revolutionary programs. In the end, however, this modern-day version of nativism was overshadowed by ideas about mestizo ethnic identity, non-Indian revolutionary heroes, socialism, and anti-Americanism. Later, programmatic concern for the Indians would grow in importance as the revolution turned to development and reform after the 1940s.

The Mesoamerican Indians actively participated in the Mexican Revolution, but not equally in every region; overall their impact, while important, was not decisive to the outcome. The expansion of haciendas and plantations in the rural areas during the Díaz period had greatly affected the native peoples of Mexico by the eve of the revolution. In the northern states, the Mesoamericans lost most of their best lands, and this forced them to labor as peons on the large estates. Communities were destroyed and native identities lost. In the central and southern states, the Mesoamericans survived with more of their communities and native cultures intact. In some communities the elders continued to govern by consensus, religious fiestas were conducted according to traditional ceremonial calendars, lands were held communally, and native language and identity remained strong.

Even in these cases, however, the surrounding commercial plantations tended to exert strong pressure on the native communities to yield their lands and laborers.

Only the Zapatista wing of the revolutionary movement in Mexico received much backing from the Mesoamerican peasant communities. In contrast, the Villista wing was supported primarily by rural proletariats, most of whom no doubt had native ancestry but now identified "racially" and culturally with the mestizos. The more moderate constitutionalist wing of Carranza and Obregón received much of its support from hacienda peons, rural middle-class farmers, and eventually urban workers. It is not coincidental, then, that the Zapatistas were the most radical of the revolutionary bands, or that they placed the greatest stress on the Indian heritage. They became the only revolutionary group to represent the interests of the Mesoamericans, despite the fact that Zapata himself was a mestizo and many Mesoamericans failed to join his movement.

Followers of Zapata were scattered throughout Mexico, but the core area of the movement was the state of Morelos.

The Zapatistas of Morelos. Morelos society on the eve of the revolution was still deeply divided between the "civilized people" and the "macehuales"; that is to say, the mestizos and the Indians. Most of the Indians by then spoke Spanish, but Nahuatl was the language of the elders and in some communities it continued to be the everyday language (in 1910 about 9 percent of the population in the state spoke a native tongue). Dress was an important social marker, the Indian men wearing breeches and coarse cotton shirts, the Indian women wraparound skirts and huipils (blouses). The Indian villages had their own traditional ways, symbolized by elaborate ceremonies in honor of the saints, with food, drink, and music. Large families—in reality, lineages—provided the essential internal relations for the Indians, as did innumerable *compadrazgo* relationships actuated during ceremonial occasions.

New economic barriers between the mestizos and Indians were being created that were less rigid than the traditional ones, but effective just the same. The estate owners, government administrators, merchants, and professionals were all considered to be civilized people, while the *milpa* farmers and part-time peons on the plantations were thought to be uncivilized Indians. Permanent peons residing on the plantations were distinguished from the Indians, being dubbed "little creoles." Most of the middle-level farmers and money-lenders were mestizos, but a few Indians also engaged in these economic pursuits. Through social climbing, Indians could in theory become "civilized." In fact, it was not uncommon for well-to-do Indians to wear trousers rather than breeches and to move from the rural villages to the town centers, although they were subject to ridicule by the poorer Indians.

The Zapatista movement in Morelos was led by mestizos from the middle level who had close connections with the Indian communities. The Zapata family were merchants and horse breakers, while other revolutionary chiefs worked as ranchers, artisans, storekeepers, and one as a Protestant preacher. Their followers, who swelled to well over 40,000 soldiers at one point, were Indian peasants who tilled communal lands and worked part-time as peons on the large sugar plantations (Figure 7.8). In most cases, entire communities of young Indian men (and some women) would join one of the revolutionary bands as a group, although later individual switching from one band to another took place. The upper-class mestizos of Morelos, of course, opposed the Zapatistas from start to finish, even though at first they tried to reach some kind of an understanding with them. Later on, members of the mestizo elite were forced to abandon Morelos, taking with them as much wealth as they could. Many of the middle-level mestizos served as intermediaries between the wealthy elite and the rebellious communities during the military period, but most of them personally opposed the revolution. The permanent peons on the plantations were too compromised to turn against their bosses, and for the most part did not support the revolutionary cause.

The Zapatistas were not strongly motivated by abstract ideology. The early uprisings were highly practical affairs, directed against greedy plantation owners and government officials who had made it impossible for the peasants to live off the land or maintain community autonomy. The initial fighting helped bring on the downfall of Porfirio Díaz as well as other far-reaching political developments, but despite important victories the Zapatistas were content to retreat to Morelos and institute the kind of local land and political reforms for which they had rebelled in the first place. These actions revealed the peasant base of the movement, and the practical but limited nature of the Zapatista goals. Later, pro-Díaz and then pro-Carranza constitutionalist armies brutally retaliated against the Zap-

Figure 7.8 Zapatista revolutionaries fight the federal troops at Milpa Alta, Federal District of Mexico. From *Life and Death in Milpa Alta: A Nahuatl Chronicle of Díaz and Zapata,* translated and edited by Fernando Horcasitas. Copyright © 1972 by the University of Oklahoma Press.

atistas in Morelos for their rebellious actions. Men, women, and children were killed by the thousands, and other thousands were carried off in exile to cities and faraway areas. The Indian communities were ransacked, looted, and burned; cattle were slaughtered, and fields destroyed. The Zapatistas were moved to battle again, and once more for explicitly practical reasons: to defend their very lives and homes in the face of possible extermination at the hands of the government forces.

The Zapatista movement became widely known in Mexico for its nativistic character. One overt symbol employed was the image of the Virgin of Guadalupe, carried on battle flags and sewn into wide-brimmed hats. Guadalupe stood for the preservation of Indian identity and the inviolate linkage between native peoples and the land, symbolic relationships with deep roots in Mexican history. Opponents of the movement used the nativistic character of the movement to raise the specter of a new "caste war" and of invasion of the capital by "savages" from the south.

Zapatista nativism, however, was quite general in character, as might be expected of a movement led by mestizos and supported by native Mesoamericans who had been strongly influenced by modern forces. Much of the nativism that can be detected was implicit rather than explicit. For example, we recognize native cultural patterns in the Zapatistas' sense of moral outrage at being deprived of ancestral lands and self-sufficiency; the unswerving efforts to restore communal property and political autonomy; the legitimization of military authority on the basis of community service and personal ties to *cacique* leaders; the integration of religious ritual and political action (Zapata set aside village lands to be worked in support of rituals to the saints); the guerrilla form of warfare, in which the fighting was always closely articulated with the milpa cycle and community life; and the use of discussion and consensus in making decisions.

The assassination of Zapata in April 1919 ended the movement as an effective revolutionary force. Perhaps the excessive reliance on Zapata as father figure by the Morelos peasants should be seen as still another nativistic feature of the movement. At any rate, the Zapatistas were defeated, and there seemed little to show for their long and bloody struggle. Most of the plantation owners were able to recoup lands and privileges with the help of the constitutional authorities in Mexico City. The villagers were left landless, their communities ravaged, and the population depleted by one-half as a result of deaths in the war and forced migration. The Indians had demonstrated their willingness to fight for their native identity and way of life, but powerful acculturation forces were unleashed in the process of their fighting under mestizo leaders against mestizo enemies. By the time President Cárdenas restored lands to the impoverished peasants of Morelos in the 1930s, it was too late to prevent the loss of additional Mesoamerican cultural elements.

Reaction to the Zapatista movement was very different in other states with large Indian populations as we shall see in Box 7.2.

Box 7.2 *Revolution in Oaxaca*

The Zapatistas of Morelos proved to be the most consistently radical Mesoamerican group of the Mexican Revolution. There were many native Mesoamerican recruits to the Zapatista movement from surrounding states such as Puebla, Tlaxcala, and Guerrero, but in these states the Mesoamericans' militancy tended to be sporadic and kept under control by local conservative caudillos. In other states, such as Michoacán, revolutionary activity on the part of the native Mesoamericans was largely confined to postwar conflicts over lands being redistributed as part of the agrarian reforms. Revolutionary actions were notably weak or absent in the southern states of Mexico, where native Mesoamericans made up higher percentages of the population. In fact, most of the native peoples in the south took a conservative stance relative to the radical wing of the revolution. The Oaxaca case might serve as an illustration of the conservatism of Mesoamericans in such southern states as Chiapas, Tabasco, and Yucatán.

Oaxaca on the eve of the Mexican Revolution had a huge peasant population (about 87 percent of the total state population), made up mostly of Mesoamericans who spoke the Zapotec, Mixtec, Cuicatec, and other native languages. Except for scattered local uprisings in 1911, however, the Oaxacan Indians failed to respond positively to the revolutionary call. Many of them joined a conservative movement that opposed radical change while calling for state sovereignty. The Indian recruits to the sovereignty army were organized along Zapatista lines by village units, each with its own chief, but the causes and consequences were totally different. In fact, Carranza's constitutionalist army, against which the Oaxacans were supposedly fighting, was able to recruit soldiers from among these very same peasant Indians.

Ronald Waterbury (1975) has observed that the contrast in responses to the revolution by native peasants in Morelos on the one hand and the Oaxaca natives on the other can be traced to the profoundly different economic and cultural conditions in the two areas. The haciendas and plantations of Oaxaca were much weaker and less capitalistic than in Morelos, and as a result the Oaxaca Indians had retained far more of their lands, languages, and customs. Organized native communities existed in both areas, but were more internally cohesive in Oaxaca than in Morelos. Economic conditions in Morelos left the Indians with little choice but to rebel, and their years of experience working on the plantations had resulted in extra-village relations and ideas that made a regional movement feasible. The Indians of Oaxaca, in contrast, generally retained the lands and resources necessary to survive on their own, and they closed themselves off to the outside by re-creating small cultural worlds with roots extending back into the past. They had more to lose than to gain from joining the revolution, and in the end rejected the Zapatista call for radical change.

The Central American Revolutions

As noted above, the Indians participated in the aborted revolutions of Central America during the early part of the twentieth century, but paid a high price for that participation. In El Salvador, for example, thousands of Pipil Indians from the Izalco area took part in the uprising of 1931, but the counterattack by the government was so brutal that it became dangerous to speak a native language or be seen in traditional native dress. Not surprisingly, the Indians of El Salvador began to mask their traditional cultural practices and identity in the years following the rebellion. They also became more conservative about radical causes, which, as they had learned the hard way, were particularly risky for poor peasants like themselves.

In Guatemala, the Indians were active participants in uprisings with revolutionary overtones at the fall of the dictators Manuel Estrada Cabrera in 1920 and Jorge Ubico in 1944. In the 1920 uprising, rebellious Quiché Maya peasants from the Totonicapán area were quickly rounded up and executed without trial. In the 1944 rebellion, Cakchiquel Maya peasants from Patzicía, who had killed a few mestizo families in the area, were hunted down like animals and "uncountable numbers" of them were summarily executed. These were terrifying political lessons for the Indians of Guatemala, who became extremely suspicious of radical movements in the years that followed.

The Sandino rebellion in Nicaragua involved only limited participation by Indians. Most of the guerrilla fighting took place in the Segovia province, away from the Pacific coastal zone where the Mesoamerican Indians were historically concentrated. It is likely that Sandino's followers were more mestizo than Indian and more proletariat than peasant. That is to say, the Sandino revolutionary force was similar to the Villa rather than the Zapata faction of the Mexican Revolution. Nevertheless, Sandino himself was from the village of Niquinohomo on the Pacific Coast, and his mother was Indian. Furthermore, he identified with the Mesoamerican heritage, and saw the movement as a way to promote not only the cause of Nicaragua but also its native peoples (Figure 7.9).

The more recent revolutionary movements in Central America have differed greatly from one another in terms of the degree to which the Mesoamericans participated. In the case of Guatemala, however, Indian involvement in the phase of the revolution that began in the second half of the 1970s has been pervasive and profoundly important. The revolutions in El Salvador and Nicaragua, in contrast, had relatively little to do with the Indians, either as direct participants or as inspiration for the struggles.

This raises the question as to whether or not the presence or absence of the Mesoamerican Indians made a significant difference in the outcome of the Central American revolutions. For example, did the Guatemalan Revolution, where the participation of Mesoamericans was pervasive, differ from the revolutions in El Salvador and Nicaragua, where Indian participation was limited? The answer to this questions is yes, as is suggested by the solemn fact that the Guatemalan Revolution has been going on longer than the other two and that a peaceful solution to it has yet to be achieved. Clearly, the Indian factor has prolonged the struggle in Guatemala. The Guatemalan Revolution has also been the bloodiest in terms of the loss of human life, perhaps double the losses in El Salvador and Nicaragua. This can be attributed partly to the racist, "ethnic cleansing" policy of the government forces in the Guatemalan struggle. We should note, too, that the ideology employed by the Guatemalan revolutionaries has been more syncretic and less rigidly Marxist than in El Salvador and Nicaragua. The Guatemalan insurgents have had to accommodate ideology to the important Indian component, and this has resulted in attempts to incorporate nativistic ideas into the revolutionary program.

Guatemala. What makes Guatemala's revolution unique is the overwhelming presence of the Maya Indians in that country. These Indians make up

Figure 7.9 Augusto Sandino, the Nicaraguan revolutionary. Courtesy of Bettman Archives.

over half of the population, most of them peasants concentrated in the central and western highlands. Indian participation in the prolonged revolutionary movement was slow in coming, but by the 1970s the Maya Indians began to join the insurgents in impressive numbers.

The two most important guerrilla organizations in Guatemala—the Guerrilla Army of the Poor (EGP) and the Organization of the People in Arms (ORPA)—were established squarely in Indian zones, and the bulk of the guerrilla soldiers and most civilian support of a logistical nature came from the Indian sector. At the high point of guerrilla activity around 1980, a few thousand Indian soldiers joined the insurgent forces, and up to a quarter of a million civilian Indians provided support of various kinds. Furthermore, most of the civilians killed in the counterinsurgency war were Indians (estimated at about 75,000 persons for the years between 1978 and 1985), as were almost all of the refugees, both inside Guatemala (estimated at 1 million persons) and outside the country (about 150,000 persons, mostly in Mexico and the United States).

The guerrilla leaders themselves, most of them mestizos from the urban middle class, have recognized that the Indian presence has been a major factor in Guatemala's revolution. One of the guerrilla spokespersons wrote that the Guatemalan Revolution is "unique" because the Indians are heirs to highly developed prehispanic native cultures, and in the face of weakly developed Spanish capitalism were able to reconstitute through time many of their native organizational and cultural patterns. Therefore, this guerrilla leader went on to explain, orthodox Marxist revolutionary ideology about class warfare is an inappropriate model for the revolution because "'ethnic-nationalism' constitutes one of the essential factors for any possible revolutionary change" (EGP 1982).

The counterinsurgency forces organized by the Guatemalan military establishment have not only recognized but exaggerated the importance of the Indian factor in the revolution. According to interviews with army officers fighting against the guerrillas, the army's most critical task was to eradicate the Indians' world view and replace it with a modern, "cosmopolitan" view. Beginning in the mid-1980s, the army began to lay down a structure of civil patrols, model villages, and development poles in the Indian area in order to transform the thinking and behavior of Guatemala's Indians. This highly repressive military apparatus constitutes concrete evidence of the importance Guatemala's political establishment attaches to the Indians and their involvement in the civil war.

Scholars have pointed out that the peasants most strongly identified as Indians have been at the very center of revolutionary action in Guatemala, and their joining one side or the other would probably be decisive to the eventual outcome of the war. The majority of the over 5 million Guatemalan Indians are Maya. They speak Maya languages and are cultural heirs to the Mesoamerican traditions of the past. But they are highly diversified in social terms, and Maya from these social divisions have responded differently to the revolutionary struggle. While the individuals making up these diverse sectors are all identified as Indians in Guatemala, in varying degrees they retain elements of the Maya cultural tradition and tend to manifest divergent "affinities" for revolutionary action.

The largest social sector of Maya are the peasants who inhabit tightly integrated communities. They tend to hold to traditional native cultures, which clash on most points with revolutionary ideology. For these Maya, power is expressed more as a supernatural than a secular phenomenon. Their enemies are defined in local rather than national terms, and often are identified as neighboring lineages, hamlets, or villages; social change is conceptualized in terms of cyclic rather than linear time. Obviously, the "traditional" Indians of this sector are not oriented toward revolutionary activities, and, in fact, with few exceptions have not joined the guerrilla movements.

Indians from other sectors hold to versions of Maya culture that seem better suited to revolutionary action. For example, it is well known that Indian leadership within the guerrilla organizations has been largely provided by the much smaller sector of urbanized, educated Maya Indians. One example would be Pablo Ceto, an Ixil-speaking Maya Indian who attended high school in the town of Santa Cruz del Quiché during the 1970s, and who later became a leader in an EGP guerrilla unit. While in Santa Cruz and before joining with the guerrillas, Ceto organized a study group of town Indians intent on discovering their Maya roots. Anthropologists were invited to help the group identify nativistic elements consistent with the needs of the embattled Indians. Ceto went on to take a leadership role in the Committee for Peasant Unity (CUC), a political organization made up mostly of Indian and poor mestizo peasants and workers. At first, CUC's work was devoted to organizing and educating rural workers and peasants in an attempt to improve their general social conditions, but under relentless attack from the army the organization went underground and merged with the guerrilla movement.

Indian leaders like Ceto came to understand that remnants of the ancient Maya culture could serve as powerful symbols for the revolution. An important source of Maya symbolism was the *Popol Vuh,* the so-called "bible" of the Quiché Maya (see chapters 12 and 13). The Popol Vuh, for example, tells the story of a greedy and pompous giant Macaw bird claiming to be the sun. The bird is brought down from its high perch by humble orphan twins who mortally wound it with pellets from a blowgun. Cast in the emerging nativistic ideology of the revolution, the self-aggrandizing macaw bird metaphorically could stand for the wealth-seeking military rulers of Guatemala, while the orphans who humble that arrogant bird could represent the poor Indians fighting against the military regime. Metaphors of this kind have enormous motivational power among both the educated and peasant Maya of Guatemala.

Perhaps even more important than the educated town Indians for the Guatemalan revolution have been the Maya of the proletarianized rural sector. Jeffrey Paige (1983) has noted that, as with the revolution in Vietnam, the insurgents in Guatemala enjoyed their greatest success in gaining recruits precisely in rural areas where the Maya Indians had previously been transformed "from hacienda to migratory labor estate and from Indian to proletarian." We still do not know much about the revolutionary ideas by which these proletarianized Indians are motivated, but the scanty evidence now available suggests that they too can be inspired by the great Mesoamerican tradition. Consider the soliloquy delivered by a Quiché Maya guerrilla leader as shown in a recent documentary film entitled "When the Mountains Tremble":

> Guatemala is at war. The road that led to that war is over 400 years old. It led us up into the mountains when the Spaniards invaded and tried to wipe out our Indian culture. Our ancestors preserved our customs. We grew corn and our numbers increased. We say that every road has a coming and a going, a leaving and a returning. Now we're coming down out of the mountains. We're going back down to the towns and cities. We are reclaiming our rights. But we don't travel this road alone. There can be no returning unless everyone, Indians and non-Indians go together. All of us together will make a new Guatemala. All of us together will reclaim our rights. The road is returning. Together we will win.

The leader and the people to whom he addressed the speech were representative of the hundreds of thousands of Maya peasants who in recent years have been proletarianized on the coffee, sugar, and cotton plantations of Guatemala. In these few phrases we find echoes of both their recent travails and the ancient Mesoamerican traditions. In particular, the metaphor of the modern Indian's history as a "road" takes us back to the Popol Vuh and a prayer therein that refers to the journey of life as a dangerous "Green road, the Green Path" trod by the ancient Maya despite its many pitfalls and snares.

Nicaragua. The peoples identified as Indians in Nicaragua today are the Miskito, Sumu, and Rama of the Caribbean coast, descendants of tribal peoples who lived outside the prehispanic Mesoamerican world. Making up about 4 percent of the national population, these coastal Indians form a small minority of relatively isolated natives similar to indigenous groups such as the Talamanca and Kuna found in the countries of Costa Rica and Panama. In Nicaragua, these native groups took no part in the revolutionary war against the Somoza regime, and later vigorously resisted attempts by the Sandinista government to integrate them into the emerging socialist society. MISURASATA (Miskito-Sumu-Rama-Sandinista), the organization set up by the Sandinistas to bring the Indians into the revolutionary fold, was taken over by Indian leaders like Steadman Fagoth, whose goals were Indian self-determination rather than national integration. When MISURASATA began to cozy up to the Contras, the Sandinistas declared it a counterrevolutionary force and began resettling the Indians inland, away from their coastal villages. This further alienated the Indians, and despite later gestures of good will the Sandinistas were never able to gain their confidence.

Nicaragua's native Mesoamerican population had become largely invisible by the time of the Sandinista revolution. Perhaps 20 percent of the population retained Indian biological features and traces of Mesoamerican heritage, but they were generally identified as mestizos rather than Indians. Nicaragua's revolutionaries concluded that the Indians had already lost their communal lands and native identity by the time Augusto Sandino launched his rebellion in the 1920s, and that in the process of becoming mestizo peasants had developed greater revolutionary "consciousness" than their Indian ancestors. According to Sandinista ideology, Indian identity was a vestige of colonialism and an impediment to the creation of a socialist state. The FSLN leaders developed a program that called for the emancipation of peasants, workers, women, blacks, and the repressed peoples of Asia, Africa, and Latin America, but not of the Mesoamerican Indians. They made reference to the non-Mesoamerican indigenous groups of the Caribbean coast in their policy statements, but only in the context of the need to incorporate them into the nation's life.

Nevertheless, in the 1970s thousands of people who still thought of themselves as Mesoamericans resided in communities in and around the cities of Managua, Masaya, Granada, and León. These people could no longer speak the native languages once spoken in the area (Pipil, Chorotega, Subtiaba), but they had retained traditional cultural practices in craftsmanship, political organization, and ritual. More important, they inserted themselves into the ongoing revolutionary struggle in dramatic fashion by spearheading a series of insurrections against the Somoza regime. The most dramatic case was in 1978, when the National Guard interrupted a funeral sponsored by the Indian community of Monimbó (Masaya) in honor of the slain newspaper editor, Pedro Joaquín Chamorro. Over 2,000 Monimbó residents attacked the Guard with stones and fireworks, and during the following two weeks barricaded the streets and fended off the assaults by the Guard. The National Guard finally attacked in mass, accompanied by heavy weapons and aerial bombing. Monimbó was taken only after intense house-to-house fighting, and at the cost of hundreds of lives on both sides.

Similar insurrections led by Indians in Diriamba and the Subtiaba community in León were also crushed after heavy fighting and the loss of many civilian lives. Students of the Nicaraguan Revolution agree that these insurrections, especially the one in Monimbó, were symbolically important for the eventual success of the revolution. What is remarkable is that they were spearheaded by Indians who supposedly did not exist as an identifiable people.

The Sandinistas, whose participation in the events of Monimbó and Subtiaba was extremely limited, have praised the role of the Indians in the revolutionary struggle. As a result, nativistic elements began to be incorporated into Sandinista ideology for the first time. The Ministry of Culture sought to rediscover the country's indigenous roots through preservation of archaeological remains and promotion of native foods and crafts. Native dishes made out of corn, such as tortillas and tamales, were touted as substitutes for wheat products, and the production of prehispanic pottery forms and filigree gourdwork was encouraged by the government. Nevertheless, attempts to recognize the contributions by Mesoamericans to Nicaraguan culture have been modest, and pale in comparison with the rich symbolism and lore built up around Sandino and the heroes and events of the revolution itself. Under the Sandinistas, Nicaragua has remained a profoundly mestizo society, its roots in the ancient Mesoamerican tra-

Box 7.3 *Indians in the Revolution of El Salvador*

The Pipil-speaking Indians of El Salvador neither participated actively in that country's long and vicious revolutionary war nor were they the object of much concern to either insurgent or government forces. In fact, by the 1970s the Indians were virtually invisible within Salvadoran society. The national censuses of the period indicate that about 1 percent of the population were classified as Indians, and of these only a few older persons still spoke the Pipil language or used native dress. Scholars viewed the Indians as largely marginal rural peasants, without land, power, or community organization. Any identity they might have had as a group was thought to be reduced to a lower-class condition of common exploitation. For Salvadorans, Indian identity was ascribed to rural peoples who had dark skin, were poor, spoke bad Spanish, and tended to be self-deprecating. The expression "to behave like an Indian" meant to be stupid, irrational, and surreptitious.

Recent research has revealed, however, that in the 1970s, when the revolution in El Salvador was beginning to take off, over 300,000 persons still identified themselves as Indians—about 10 percent of the total population. Most of them, however, were hiding their native identity from the wider society. The majority of them resided in rural communities in the western states of Ahuachapán, Sonsonate, La Libertad, and San Salvador, where one household in ten still had at least one speaker of the Pipil language. These native peoples exhibited few signs of Indianness to the outside, but they identified themselves and were identified by others as Indians. Anthropologists who visited the communities in recent years found that the Salvadoran Indians were still producing native crafts and carrying out traditional religious practices.

The revolution in El Salvador scarcely took the hidden Indian population into account. Their existence was largely denied by the ruling class, who considered the few who remained a counterproductive sector that had been all but eliminated after the 1931 uprisings. For their part, the revolutionary leaders traced the movement's historical roots back to Farabundo Martí and the rebellion of 1931, but ignored the historical role the Indians had played in those events. FMLN ideology placed great emphasis on the liberation of the peasants and workers of El Salvador, but did not identify these sectors with the Indian heritage. The peasants recruited to the revolution in states like Chalatenango and Usulután had been organized as "theology of liberation" religious associations rather than Indian communities. The Indians tended to stay in the background, shunning both the radical left and the reactionary right. It is surely no coincidence that the western states in El Salvador, where most of the Indians resided, were the very areas that remained largely outside the control of the guerrilla forces.

During the 1980s the government of El Salvador tried to win the "hearts and souls" of its people by introducing mild land and other social reforms. Through the auspices of the National Association of Indigenous Salvadorans (ANIS), the Indians made a modest attempt to resurface as an identifiable group so as to regain some of their lost land holdings. When conflicts broke out over lands involving the Indians, conservative mestizo forces once again raised the 1931 specter of "communist" Indians causing trouble. In 1983 the army seized seventy-four Indian men in the Sonsonate area, executed them, and cast their bodies into a nearby river. In view of all this, ANIS has tried to keep a low profile as it walks a narrow line between the polarized right and left. The fact that this Indian organization survived the civil war at all is a remarkable achievement, given the virulent anti-Indian attitude prevalent in Salvadoran society.

dition still largely unappreciated. The participation of Mesoamerican Indians in the Salvadoran revolution parallels in some ways that of Nicaragua, as shown in Box 7.3.

CONSEQUENCES FOR THE MESOAMERICAN INDIANS OF DEVELOPMENT PROGRAMS IN MEXICO AND CENTRAL AMERICA

Social reality in twentieth-century Mexico and Central America has largely taken the form of a sustained drive to modernize, the concrete manifestations of which have alternated between violent revolution and more peaceful development programs. We have already described the involvement of Mesoamerican Indians in the revolutions of the region, and we now turn to their participation in economic and social development. Let us begin with a look at "indigenismo," the program created specifically to promote development among the Indian peoples of the region.

Indigenismo in Mexico

The Mexican Revolution was ostensibly fought on behalf of the Indians, and its agrarian reforms, though not specifically formulated with the Indians in mind, were thought to have finally restored the lands that the liberals had taken from the Indian communities in times past. After the 1940s, as Mexico began to turn from radical change to economic development and the creation of a modern nation, it became clear that the Indian populations were lagging behind. In many of the more isolated areas of Mexico, pre-revolutionary conditions continued to prevail: The Indians were still enclosed in communities where they retained the ancient Mesoamerican languages and cultures; they were exploited by surrounding mestizo landowners and merchants; and the Indians and mestizos were socially segregated by means of local caste-like stratification systems. Mexican anthropologists termed such Indian areas "refuge regions," and argued that they negated the advances of the revolution by perpetuating colonial structures. The refuge regions could not be allowed to persist if Mexico was to fulfill its goal of creating a modern nation-state.

Development of modern Mexico was to be accomplished through industrialization, political reform, and nationalization. Mexican anthropologists such as Manuel Gamio and Alfonso Caso argued that the creation of a modern nation required common culture, which in turn depended upon a common language, ethnic identity, and set of customs. Nationalism was to be achieved through a process of "acculturation," the blending (*mestizaje*) of the different races, ethnic groups, languages, and customs into a unified "Mexican" culture. During the revolution, Mexico had flirted with the idea of a multinational state similar to the Soviet system, but a unified national culture was the only model seriously contemplated after 1940. This meant that the refuge regions would have to be broken down and the Indians integrated into national life.

The policy that emerged in Mexico became known as "indigenismo" ("Indianism"), and was officially enunciated by President Lázaro Cárdenas at the First Inter-American Indigenist Congress in Pátzcuaro, Mexico, in 1940. The program was later institutionalized in Mexico with the formation of the National Indigenist Institute (INI) under the direction of anthropologist Alfonso Caso.

"Mexico," Caso said, "could opt for no other way than to incorporate the indigenous cultures into the great Mexican community" (Medina and García Mora 1983). Indigenist leaders like Gamio and Caso were both students and advocates of the Indian cultures, and labored diligently to enhance their appreciation in Mexico. They believed that integration of the Indians could be achieved through managed acculturation—a selective blending of elements from both the Indian and Mexican cultures, mediated by indigenist agents. Nevertheless, the overriding indigenist goal was for the Indians to accept the fundamental ideas and institutions of modern Mexican culture.

The indigenists set up coordinating centers in the main refuge regions of Mexico, beginning in 1951 with the Tzeltal-Tzotzil Maya center in highland Chiapas. Gonzalo Aguirre, the foremost intellectual spokesman for indigenismo at the time, was installed as the first director of the center in Chiapas. Aguirre used his position to investigate the structure of refuge regions like highland Chiapas, particularly the highly unequal relationships that existed between the local Maya Indians and the mestizos. The indigenists also tailored programs in education, health, agriculture, and community development to suit the needs of the Indians. The precedent was established that integration of the Indians into the nation would be carried out with due regard for the special social and cultural conditions of the Indians and in a fair and comprehensive fashion. In the following years coordinating centers were set up among other native groups such as the Mixtecs, Zapotecs, and Mixe of Oaxaca; Maya of Yucatán; Mazatecs and Tlapanecs of central and western Mexico; Otomí of Hidalgo; and Tarahumara of northern Mexico.

The Indians of Mexico were subject to acculturation forces even stronger than those emanating from the INI centers. Agrarian industries, for example, were established in most of the refuge regions, in the process expropriating lands and resources from the Indian communities. At the same time, the Mexican government vigorously sought to modernize politics throughout the country, establishing branches of the PRI party in the native communities and reforming traditional political structures such as the civil-religious hierarchies. The Catholic and Protestant churches were also active modernizing agents among the Indians, as they proselytized to replace traditional native beliefs and practices with doctrinal systems more in line with Mexico's increasingly secular society.

By the 1970s, Aguirre, now director of INI, could assert that the main goals of the indigenist program were being achieved. The Indians had been largely "mexicanized," the census of 1970 revealing that only about 10 percent of the population could be classified as Indians. Furthermore, the Indians had been largely "christianized," the culmination of a process begun with the first Spanish missionaries. Most important of all, the Indians were being integrated into national life with little prejudice. Because of acculturation, the Indians had avoided becoming ethnic "minorities" in Mexico; that is to say, cultural groups seeking separate national status. Under President Luís Echevarría (1970–1976), the indigenist program was expanded even further, as thousands of additional bilingual teachers and development agents were assigned to the refuge regions.

Despite Aguirre's optimism about the successes of Mexico's indigenist program, it came under severe attack from two fronts: the Indians themselves, and scholarly critics of its underlying "acculturation" theory. For their part, the Indians have shown a far greater interest in retaining their native identities than expected, as well as resisting many features of the programs designed to integrate them into the national culture. In 1970 at least 3 million people in Mexico still claimed to be Indians, and about one-third of them identified far more with their traditional communities and customs than with the national culture. Much of the resistance to the indigenist programs by Indians has taken the form of either indifference or careful monitoring of proposed changes from the outside. Resistance also took a more violent form during the 1970s and 1980s, as hundreds of thousands of rural Indians joined radical peasant movements to recoup lands lost to agrarian capitalists. Guerrilla warfare broke out in states like Hidalgo, Guerrero, Oaxaca, and Chiapas, and hundreds, perhaps thousands, of Otomí, Huastec, Tarascan, Zapotec, and Maya Indians were tortured and killed by government and private security forces. In some cases, such as the Yaqui and Mayo seizure of lands in Sonora, the government supported aspects of the Indian demands, but overall the response to Indian militancy was extremely harsh.

The scholarly critique of indigenismo came largely after 1968, and has been acrimonious far beyond what might be expected of an academic debate. It split anthropologists and other Mexican social scientists into two hostile and opposed camps: the defenders of the indigenist and other programs for national integration, versus those who favor radical change through renewed revolutionary actions. The opponents of indigenismo in Mexico included illustrious students of Indian history and culture, such as Guillermo Bonfil, Arturo Warman, and Angel Palerm. They argued that the indigenists define the Indian exclusively in cultural terms and that this is misleading: first, because it falsely assumes that Mexican national culture represents a more progressive evolutionary stage than the Indian cultures; and, second, because the focus on Indian culture diverts attention from the Indians' exploited class condition as rural proletariats. These critics claim that the indigenist program is actually destructive to the Indians because it "modernizes their exploitation"; that is, makes the Indians more accessible to the capitalist exploiters.

The critics emphasize that the indigenists overvalue the importance of culture, which in their view is merely "superstructural" to the Indians' underlying class condition. That is why, the critics point out, the indigenists find it so difficult to define what the Indians are. In fact, they argue, the Indians cannot be culturally distinguished from the mestizo peasants and rural proletariats of Mexico. Both are said to be fundamentally Western in culture, and increasingly subject to U.S. influences. It is the Indians' profound dependence on the Mexican nation-state—which in turn is dependent on outside capitalist countries such as the United States—that makes discussion of the "Indian problem" so volatile among Mexican scholars. The fundamental issue at stake is the same issue that led to the original revolutionary struggle in Mexico: liberation from dependency on foreign powers;

that is to say, national sovereignty. Unfortunately, as Aguirre has pointed out, even should the problem of Mexico's dependency on outside powers be resolved this would not eliminate the problem created by Indians who demand to be recognized as culturally distinct ethnic groups with rights of self-determination.

Indigenismo in Central America

Most of the Central American countries ratified the agreements reached in the First Inter-American Indigenist Congress held in Mexico in 1940, and subsequently established National Indigenist Institutes of their own. Only in Guatemala, however, has this institute played a developmental role, and even there its role has been extremely weak compared to Mexico. In El Salvador, Honduras, and Nicaragua the respective institutes have done very little either to aid the Indians in the development process or to incorporate nativistic symbols into national culture. In Nicaragua, the National Indigenist Institute may even have facilitated the loss of communal Indian lands and cultures. Costa Rica's first serious efforts to establish an indigenist organization did not occur until the 1970s, when the government set up the National Commission for Indigenous Affairs (CONAI) and decreed laws to protect Indian lands and provide for self-rule in the Indian territories. Unfortunately, CONAI proved to be ineffective, and the Indian laws were repeatedly violated by thousands of "whites" who invaded the Indian reserves.

Indigenist elements, then, have been virtually nonexistent in the developmental programs of El Salvador, Honduras, Nicaragua, and Costa Rica, and have played only a minor role in Guatemala's developmental reforms. Nevertheless, since Indians make up over half of Guatemala's population, any reform or development plan must necessarily take some account of them. The important reforms of 1944 to 1954 in Guatemala were not strongly indigenist, because, as in Mexico, the Indian communities were seen as impediments to progress and therefore in need of acculturation. Indirectly, however, the Indians benefitted from the reforms. For example, one of the reforms' main goals was to improve the conditions of the poor and working classes by providing them with land, fair labor laws, and agricultural financing. The Indians, along with mestizo peasants and workers, benefitted from these reforms. Furthermore, the holding of fair elections in the rural areas allowed Indians to replace mestizos in the highest political offices of many of the communities, thus seriously weakening the political domination by local mestizos. The redistribution of lands also allowed the Indians to become less dependent on the coffee and sugar plantations, opening the way for more Indians to remain in the communities as peasant farmers. Thus, contrary to much that has been written about the reforms of 1944 to 1954 in Guatemala, they did not weaken the Indian communities.

The military regimes that succeeded the reform government in Guatemala after 1954 were essentially anti-Indian. Unlike the Mexican indigenists, who wanted to integrate the Indians into national life by means of culturally sensitive community development programs, the military governments of Guatemala favored the total eradication of the native cultures as quickly as possible and their replacement with national mestizo culture (the process is known as "ladinoization"). Guatemala's approach to the Indian problem was acculturation with a vengeance. The government's actions toward the Indians were driven not so much by ideas of nationalism as by the need to provide the country's export industries with cheap, easily available labor while at the same time maintaining strict control over the potentially rebellious working classes.

The Indians of Guatemala were subjected to extremely powerful modernization forces in the form of highly exploitative capitalist plantations and aggressive religious leaders—especially reform-minded priests imbued with the social gospel of the "Catholic Action" program. These two forces complemented one another, the plantations proletarianizing the Indians and the Church providing them with a collectivist rationale for their new social condition. By the 1970s more than 20 percent of the Indians had joined peasant cooperative and labor organizations, many of them Church-sponsored. Other Indians residing close to large towns and cities found alternatives to work on the plantations in artisanry, especially weaving, and trade.

Despite these changes, the Indians of Guatemala—like those of Mexico—fiercely resisted the breakdown of their communities and the loss of their cultural identity as Mesoamericans. The same debate taking place in Mexico over whether the Indians should be defined in cultural or class terms was engaged by Guatemalan scholars and political leaders. But the stakes were much higher in Guatemala, for among those who claimed the Indians to be culturally distinct and therefore in need of "special" treatment were members of right-wing death squads; and among those who saw the Indians as socially equivalent to mestizo proletariats were members of left-wing guerrilla organizations. The Indians, of course, were both culturally distinct *and* proletarianized, and they demonstrated this during the bloody revolutionary war of the 1970s and 1980s by joining the insurgent side without abandoning nativistic cultural agendas. Whether a Mexican-type indigenist program could have prevented the civil war in Guatemala is an open question, but its absence certainly hardened the positions of both the insurgent Indians and their military adversaries and helped make it a vicious life-and-death struggle.

MESOAMERICAN CONTRIBUTIONS TO NATIONAL ETHOS

Students of Mexico and Central America have increasingly become aware of the important role played by the Mesoamerican Indians in the emergence of national cultures. The indigenists always accepted this thesis, although they generally conceded that the mestizos rather than the Indians would be the primary carriers of national culture. The critics of indigenismo tended to see the basis of nationalism in class rather than culture, carried forward specifically by the ruling capitalist and middle classes. Nevertheless, the revolutionary experiences of Mexico and Guatemala convinced some critics that the native cultures must be taken into account in the formation of the region's modern nation-states.

This convergence of thinking on the part of the indigenists and some of their critics has been extended to include the possibility of creating "pluralist" nation-states in which the Indian groups are recognized as culturally distinct, self-governing units. Speaking from the side of the critics, Guillermo Bonfil (1981:52) has argued in favor of native groups whose "political struggle necessarily includes recapturing a national identity because it becomes the only way to assure their survival as ethnically differentiated groups." And from the indigenist side, Gonzalo Aguirre speaks in favor of Indian groups who "possess a double identity; their own parochial one and the national one. . . . This would constitute a homogeneous nation-state for practical purposes, but conserve in its bosom a multi-corporate population . . . of ethnic groups who desire to conserve their language, culture and parochial social organizations" (Medina and García Mora 1983:209).

We shall have more to say below on the Indians' own view of national pluralism, but first we must address the question of the extent to which the national cultures of the region show signs of having been influenced by the Mesoamericans. In addressing this question we will not be primarily concerned with surface features of native origin that historically diffused into the national cultures in large numbers—for example, foods; idiomatic expressions; names of geographic locations; arts and crafts; and iconographic themes incorporated into modern architecture, painting, and advertisement. Rather, we are concerned with Mesoamerican elements that have become deeply embedded in the very psyche or "ethos" of national thinking.

Within the region, only in Mexico has this question been seriously addressed, and even in Mexico the proposed answers to it are highly controversial and loudly disputed. Nevertheless, Gonzalo Aguirre's claim that "the cultural symbols that today serve to identify the Mexicans are in part Indian" would seem to be indisputable. Aguirre elaborates as follows:

> The absorption of the Indian personality and values by the national culture is an inexorable process that enriches that culture. . . . Unlike the U.S. and Argentina . . . Mexico elected the personality and values of the Indians to be symbols of national identity. . . . This election was transcendental because the Indian is integrated into a national world that does not discriminate against or deny him, because that would be like denying and discriminating against one's self. (Medina and García Mora 1983:207–208)

Octavio Paz has provided the most influential (and probably the most controversial) analysis of the Indian roots of Mexican national culture in his widely acclaimed book, *The Labyrinth of Solitude* (1961), and other writings (1985). Paz claims that following the revolution the Mexicans created a new national culture, or, as he refers to it, a "hidden collective conscience." The revolution finally gave the mestizo a central place in society and a set of ideas that represented a synthesis of the traditional Indian and creole cultures. To a large extent this synthesis was based on a dialectical process, the negation of both things creole and things Indian. Thus, the emerging culture could be traced to the mestizo's lack of a defined national identity, whether creole or Indian, and therefore to a feeling of orphanhood or bastardness. Mestizo culture seemed to be a residue of inferiority complexes, a certain "servant mentality" carried over by a mestizo group that had to claw its way to power without the benefit of a proud historical tradition or systematically worked-out culture.

Paz particularly calls attention to the collective shout made by the Mexicans each September 15: "Viva México, hijos de la chingada" ("long live Mexico, you sons of the violated mother"). This preoccupation with the violated mother, and hence bastardhood, is part of the burden carried by the mestizos, a burden not born by the Mesoamerican Indians or the Spanish creoles. But the deeply felt symbols that express the Mexicans' hidden conscience have roots in the Spanish and Mesoamerican cultures. Chief among the emerging national symbols was Cuauhtemoc, the Aztec emperor who succeeded Motecuhzoma and led the resistance against the Spanish conquistadors. In the Mexican secular pantheon, Cuauhtemoc became the long-suffering son, bloody but not bowed; the stout warrior. The dialectically opposed symbol to Cuauhtemoc was Cortés, the prototype of the Spanish conquistador. Cortés was the "macho," symbol of power and violation of women, whose name was banned from public discussion but ever present. The hidden message in this symbolism was that the typical Mexican man had lineage from both Cuauhtemoc and Cortés, and thus the power of both the Indian and Spanish heritages.

The Mexican pantheon had female equivalents to Cuauhtemoc and Cortés. First was the Virgin of Guadalupe, the saint adopted by the Indians to represent Tonantzín, the ancient mother goddess of the Aztecs. The Guadalupe symbol in Mexican national culture came to stand for the mother of the poor and weak, the orphans. She was the female counterpart of Cuauhtemoc. The dialectically opposed symbol to Guadalupe was Malinche, the Maya princess who served as translator and mistress to Cortés and his men. Malinche was the "chingada," the violated woman, as were all those traitors who preferred foreign to Mexican ways. The hidden message behind the Guadalupe and Malinche symbols suggested that Mexican mothers, and hence their mestizo offspring, were neither Indian nor Spanish, for they could not have sprung from either a patroness of orphans or a violated woman.

It is noteworthy that the Mexicans granted hero status only to Cuauhtemoc and Guadalupe, both of whom have roots in the Mesoamerican cultures. Since one of them (Cuauhtemoc) was incorruptible, and the other (Guadalupe) virginous, it follows, says Paz, that "The Mexican does not want to be either an Indian or a Spaniard. Nor does he want to be descended from them. He denies them."

Paz's critics point out that Mexico's national culture has been undergoing rapid change as the country increasingly industrializes, and in the process its underlying ethos becomes more oriented to consumerism and middle-class Western values. Even before these changes, it is argued, Paz's "hidden" culture was too simplistic to fit all the regional, ethnic, class, and institutional cultural variations of a large nation like Mexico. Many Mexicans, in fact, not only disagree with Paz's characterization of their culture, but also deeply resent it. While these criticisms have some validity, it would be surprising if the Mexican ethos did not contain Mesoamerican elements, even if in dialectical forms. After all, Mexico has a history that began with an aboriginal civilization of great complexity, witnessed the survival of native peoples as a significant percentage of the population for almost 500 years, and more recently experienced the active participation by millions of Indians in the great modernizing events of the twentieth century. Given this historical background, the Indians and their culture necessarily had to be factored into the equation of modernizing Mexico. Paz's account of Mexico's hidden culture suggests some of the ways that Mesoamerican culture found its way into the emerging national ethos.

Studies of national ethos in the Central American countries are conspicuously lacking, in part because nationalism there remains so incomplete. Only in Costa Rica does a strong national culture exist, and it manifests virtually no indigenous influence. As noted in our discussion above on development in Central America, the Nicaraguans, Salvadorans, and Hondurans also claim to espouse national cultures almost totally devoid of Indian influence. Nevertheless, since they are largely mestizo nations that at one time included large Mesoamerican populations, it is likely that the Indians influenced the emerging national ethos to a greater extent than has been recognized to date. Only future research will reveal the extent to which they might have "hidden" national cultures resembling the one proposed for Mexico.

Guatemala is the one Central American country where we might expect to find a strong Mesoamerican component within its national ethos because of its historically large Indian population. Nevertheless, compared to Mexico, Guatemalan national culture remains weakly developed and poorly studied. We have already seen, for example, that the 1944–1954 reforms in Guatemala did not strongly promote nativistic symbols, certainly less so than in Mexico for the equivalent period of time. Furthermore, Guatemala's post-1954 indigenist programs to promote respect for the Indians and integrate them into national life were extremely weak. And, of course, they were totally scrapped with the onset of the civil war in the 1970s and the government's wholesale attack on the Indians and their cultures.

Despite these developments, Mesoamerican influence on Guatemalan national culture has been substantial. It could not be otherwise, given the fact that a far larger proportion of Guatemala's population is made up of Mesoamerican Indians than in Mexico and the rest of Central America. Robert Carmack (1981) has called attention to some of the Mesoamerican elements in Guatemala's budding national culture. For example, the country's name, like Mexico's, appears to have been taken directly from one of the powerful prehispanic kingdoms of the area. Another of the country's most powerful national symbols is the Popol Vuh, read by all the schoolchildren of Guatemala and endlessly studied and interpreted by Guatemalan scholars and writers.

Perhaps Guatemala's deepest and most complex national symbol of Mesoamerican origin is Tecum, the military leader who led the Quiché Maya forces against the Spanish conquistadors in 1524. According to legend, Tecum was killed by Pedro de Alvarado, the Spanish captain, and today Tecum's burial place is claimed by numerous Indian communities of the western highlands. In many ways, Guatemala's Tecum is the equivalent of Cuauhtemoc in Mexico, the unbowed, valiant Indian warrior; and Alvarado is the equivalent of Cortés, the Spanish conquistador and violator of Indian women and political sovereignty. This Guatemalan secular pantheon is less developed and probably more narrowly shared than Mexico's, but it does exist and seems to express profound but "hidden" native elements.

The parallels between Guatemalan and Mexican national ethos include similar ideas about the mestizos and their origins. The anthropologist Richard Adams points to a hidden "collective conscience" in Guatemala concerning the mestizos ("ladinos"), which is so sensitive and deeply entrenched that almost never is it openly discussed. Even more so than in Mexico the Guatemalan mestizos are defined in racial and ethnic terms, as if to symbolically bridge the historically created chasm of inequality, insecurity, and hatred between the Spaniards and Indians. Luís Cardoza y Aragón, one of Guatemala's most enlightened critics of indigenismo, described this aspect of the national ethos as follows:

> The nation is Indian. This is the truth which first manifests itself with its enormous, subjugating, presence. And yet we know that in Guatemala, as in the rest of America, it is the mestizo who has the leadership throughout the society. The mestizo: the middle class. The revolution of Guatemala [reference to the 1944–1954 reforms] is a revolution of the middle class. . . . And what an inferiority complex the Guatemalan suffers for his Indian blood, for the indigenous character of his nation! . . . The Guatemalan does not want to be Indian, and wishes his nation were not. (Adams 1990:147)

THE SOCIAL DIFFERENTIATION OF CONTEMPORARY MESOAMERICAN INDIANS

We close with an examination of what has remained of Mesoamerican civilization and the place of its native peoples in the modern world of Mexico and Central America. Not surprisingly, the Mesoamerican Indians of today are far less socially homogeneous than they were, for example, around the time of independence from Spain. Most of the Indians at that time were peasants living within the protected confines of corporate rural communities. Today, however, the modernization forces of the twentieth century described above have opened up the communities and stratified the Indians into different classes, segregated them into distinct refuge regions, and forced them to migrate in large numbers to the towns and cities. Nevertheless, perhaps 60 to 70 percent of the people identified today as Indians in Mexico and Central America can still be classified as peasants. Most of these peasant Indians live in rural communities in such Mexican states as Michoacán, Guerrero, Morelos, Puebla, Mexico, Oaxaca, Yucatán, and Chiapas; and in Guatemala.

Approximately 20 percent of the remaining Indians reside in diverse rural settings not closely associated with the traditional native communities. Large numbers of them work in plantations, mines, cattle ranches, and other kinds of rural enterprises. Many of them migrate considerable distances to find work, even to foreign countries; for example, Mexican "braceros" in the United States, Salvadoran cotton pickers in Guatemala, and Nicaraguan coffee harvesters in Costa Rica. These Indians are required to speak Spanish and conform to mestizo ways, and in only a generation or two begin to lose the native languages, dress, and customs. Still, in considerable numbers they continue to identify themselves—and be identified by their mestizo neighbors—as "Indians."

The remaining approximately 10 percent of the region's Indians have left the communities, and in many cases the plantations and mines as well, to find work, education, and political refuge in the towns and cities. They can be found in quite large numbers in Mexican urban centers like Mexico City, Uruapan, Oaxaca, San Cristóbal de Las Casas, and Cancún; and in Central American cities such as Quezaltenango (Guatemala), Guatemala City, Sonsonate (El Salvador), Tegucigalpa (Honduras), and Masaya (Nicaragua). Most of the Indians living in urban contexts are poor and concentrated in marginal zones on the outskirts of the above-mentioned cities. They make a living through artisanry, petty commerce, and manual labor, and are under strong pressures to abandon their native languages and customs. Also residing in the cities, however, are smaller but ever-increasing numbers of educated Indians, largely middle-class merchants, teachers, and public officials. Earlier, during the climax of the developmental phase in the region (1950 to 1970), it seemed as though these educated urban Indians might totally lose their native identity and assimilate into the mestizo population. More recently, however, the trend has been for them to identify with their Indian heritage and, beyond that, to promote its preservation in the context of the wider national culture.

The simple typology of peasant, proletariat, and urban Indians does not cover the full range of social differentiation experienced by the Mesoamerican Indians of contemporary Mexico and Central America. For example, important distinctions exist between peasant Indians who subsist largely through farming and cling to traditional native values and those peasant Indians who are commercialized as artisans and merchants and thus are more receptive to secular ideas. In addition, most native communities have resident "rich" or "bourgeois" Indians, local owners of businesses who tend to be profoundly ambivalent about the traditional native cultures.

It should be noted further that a "frontier" type of Indian is found in the region, made up almost exclusively of native peoples whose ancestors were not part of the Mesoamerican world. They are located mainly in northern Mexico (for example, the Tarahumara, Pima, Seri) and the Caribbean coast of Central America (for example, the Jicaque, Miskito, Talamanca). These frontier Indians live in small, scattered groups, in some cases separated off as "reserve" territories, and retain much of the aboriginal languages and cultures. They generally do not identify with the nations of which they are a part, but instead harbor ideas of political and cultural separatism.

Some scholars and many Indians reject the claim that the Indians have become differentiated into contrasting social types. One prevalent view is that a "pan-Indian" ethnic identity overrides the social differences between the Indians and unites them all, regardless of class, region, language, or nationality. What they share as native peoples is a rejection of Western civilization; an ethic that stresses community solidarity, respect for things Indian, and honesty; and an ethno-ecology that seeks accommodation rather than domination of the earth and its resources.

The views expressed by the pan-Indianists make the important point that cultural or ethnic identity must be taken into account along with economic class in trying to understand the contemporary Mesoamerican Indians. It is also the case, however, that the social divisions between the Indians described above are a necessary consideration if we are to understand the actions of the contemporary Mesoamerican Indians. Their differentiation into peasants, proletariats, or urbanites faithfully reflects, in general terms, the fundamental political-economic forces impinging on them. Clarification of these social differences helps bring into focus the diverse ways that the Mesoamerican Indians have responded to modernization processes, and directs our attention to the dynamic permutations of the Mesoamerican cultural tradition by which they have adapted to the changing world around them.

We conclude, then, by illustrating what life is like for the Mesoamerican Indians living today under these diverse social conditions. As examples of the three social types, we will briefly consider the following specific cases: (1) the Chamula (peasant type); (2) the Otomí (proletarian type); and (3) the Mexico City Indians (urban type).

Chamula and the Mesoamerican Peasants

One of the best-known peasant Indian communities of the Mesoamerican region is Chamula, located in the highlands of Chiapas, Mexico. The Chamula Indians speak the Tzotzil Maya language, and have long had fame as Mexico's prototypically closed and traditional peasant Indian community (Figure 7.10).

Chiapas took a conservative stance toward the military phase of the Mexican Revolution, very similar to the one taken in Oaxaca as described in Box 7.2. The Chamula Indians fought under the leadership of a cacique named Jacinto Pérez "Pajarito" on the side of the landlords who opposed the radical changes proposed by the Zapatista revolutionaries to the north. The Chamula rebels paid dearly for this support when later the Carranza forces came to power, drove them into exile, and captured and executed Cacique Pajarito. Subsequently, during the Cárdenas period, the government replaced Chamula's old civil-religious hierarchy with new municipal authorities more in tune with the revolutionary program. Chamula's communal (ejido) lands were officially recognized, and a Department of Indian Affairs and an indigenous labor union were organized to protect the Indians against debt-peonage.

During the following years the Chamula experienced the powerful pressures of developmental programs in Chiapas. The INI coordinating center established in nearby San Cristóbal de Las Casas initiated a flurry of health, education, and welfare projects designed to improve the economic and social conditions of communities like Chamula. The government also built up the infrastructure of the state, with the construction of new highways, ports, and hydro-electric dams. Industry was encouraged to move into Chiapas, and rich petroleum deposits were discovered in the northern zone of the state.

By the 1980s Chamula had a population of over 50,000 people, all of

Figure 7.10 Chamula Indians carrying goods to the markets and shrines in the town of San Cristóbal de Las Casas. From Ricardo Pozas, *Juan the Chamula: An Ethnological Recreation of the Life of a Mexican Indian,* translated and edited by Lysander Kemp, with the permission of the publishers, University of California Press. Copyright © 1962 by The Regents of the University of California.

whom spoke the Tzotzil language (74 percent of them still could not speak Spanish). The Chamula were scattered across the municipal territory in hamlets, and 92 percent of the economically active population engaged in agricultural pursuits. They cultivated milpas of maize and beans, and husbanded a few animals, such as pigs, cows, and chickens, all on tiny land holdings. Almost none of the Chamula could produce enough food to feed their families, however, and some 77 percent of them were forced to supplement subsistence production with work for wages, either in construction or on the coastal plantations. Two other means of economic survival were the growing of commercial crops, such as vegetables and flowers, and the renting of lands in the lowlands to produce both subsistence and commercial crops. A few families living mainly in the tiny Chamula center became full-time merchants, in some cases purchasing trucks to facilitate transportation of goods. One of their most lucrative commodities was locally produced "moonshine" (*pox*).

The Chamula peasant community became socially stratified as a result of economic developments following the revolution. A fundamental division was created between those Indians involved in commercial activities (merchants of *pox*, producers of commercial crops) and those in wage labor (construction, plantations). The majority of the Chamula were caught in a transitional position between being peasants and being proletariats, although perhaps 30 percent of the Chamula eventually became full-time wage earners. These class divisions in turn led to serious conflicts, one of the most important of which centered on the large numbers of Chamula who converted to evangelical religions. The evangelicals were largely disaffected proletarianized peasants who resented the economic and cultural limitations of the community. They were persecuted, and those who would not renounce the new religions were either killed or driven out of the community. Some of them formed independent agricultural communities in adjacent areas, and thousands of them settled in the marginal zones of San Cristóbal and the state capital of Tuxtla Gutiérrez.

The incipient "bourgeois" class of merchants and commercial farmers in Chamula was made up of the Indians who had been able to take advantage of the developmental programs in Chiapas. The commercial farmers obtained credits, fertilizers, seeds, and irrigation technology from INI and other development agencies. The merchants were early collaborators with the revolutionary government and used political position to get the credits needed to purchase trucks and obtain licenses to establish retail businesses in the community. Some of the commercialized Indians in Chamula, especially the merchants, soon formed an elite group of "progressive" caciques. They gained control over key political and religious institutions, and were able to manipulate community life in such a way that it favored their own interests. Not surprisingly, relations between the members of this elite group of Chamula have been highly competitive, and this has lead to fierce factional struggles within the community.

The highly traditional cultural and language expressions of Chamula would appear to be the result of a synthesis worked out between the ruling Indian caciques and the more peasantized sector of the community. Studies by Gary

Gossen (1974) and others present indisputable evidence that traditional Chamula culture has remained profoundly Mesoamerican and Maya, even though, of course, many cultural elements from Spanish and Mexican sources were incorporated into that culture. Chamula cosmology, for example, retains the mythic idea of cyclic creations, in which each period is a contest between good and bad forces. The world, which centers on Chamula itself, extends upward in the form of celestial layers, each the habitat of sacred powers (for example, "Our Father" the Sun is in the third "sky," "Our Mother" the moon in the second). It extends downward into the underworld, also layered and the habitat of the dead (such as Saint Michael, the earthbearer). The four cardinal directions provide an even more fundamental spatial division of the world, whereby territorial sections, calendrical periods, day and night, seasons, rituals, and practically everything else that takes place in the community are situated according to the particular cardinal direction with which they are associated.

From one perspective, Chamula's social divisions may be seen as a faithful reflection of the more global stratification of the entire Mexican countryside. The Chamula caciques, as with local elites in communities throughout Mexico, either directly exploit the peasant masses or serve as intermediaries for outside mestizos who indirectly exploit them. This is undoubtedly an accurate assessment as far as it goes, but as the rich Chamulan traditional culture demonstrates, class stratification is not the whole story of the peasant Indians of the region. From a more culturalist perspective, native peoples like the Chamula are seen as communities as well as classes, defined primarily by local cultures that in many cases represent highly creative variants of the ancient Mesoamerican tradition. This dual nature of native communities as cultural entities *and* class-stratified divisions generally characterizes the peasant social type throughout the Mesoamerican region.

The Otomí of Mezquital and the Mesoamerican Proletariats

The prototypical Mesoamerican proletariats of Mexico are the Otomí of the Mezquital Valley in the state of Hidalgo. Mezquital is located close to Mexico City, and from the 1930s on became a testing ground for the theories and developmental programs of the post-revolutionary government. As a result, its inhabitants, including the resident Otomí Indians, have been the objects of thorough investigation by Mexican and foreign social scientists.

The large Mezquital Valley occupies over 3,000 square miles of territory, and is located at an altitude that varies between 5,000 and 10,000 feet. Most of the valley is arid and relatively unproductive, except for a small zone along the Tula River where irrigation is possible. The Otomí Indians are scattered across the valley floor, as well as in small villages in the upland zones. Even though estimates place the Otomí valley population today at around 150,000, as many as half that number may now be residing in Mexico City. About 40 percent of the Otomí women are monolingual in the Otomí language, while the men are bilingual in Spanish and Otomí, and in increasing numbers the children monolingual in

Spanish. Many of the Otomí engage in subsistence farming, a hazardous occupation in the harsh environment of the valley. They rely heavily on the maguey plant, which supplies *pulque*, the daily beverage, as well as fibers for weaving coarse cloths (*ayates*) and leaves for roof thatching (Figure 7.11). The Otomí peasants are extremely poor, and the majority of them now depend either part- or full-time on wage labor.

The Otomí Indians along with other peasants from the Mezquital Valley joined with the Zapatista and Villa forces during the revolutionary wars. Their struggle was directed against the landlords of large irrigated estates in the valley who had taken over Otomí lands and converted them into productive farms (in 1900 the Díaz regime diverted Mexico City's sewage waters to the Mezquital Valley to be used for irrigation purposes). The Mezquital revolutionaries succeeded in driving out the landowners, and with the help of Zapata and Villa recovered some of their lands in the form of ejido grants (despite the efforts by Carranza to return the lands to the same wealthy landlords). The struggle for land continued, however, as mestizo caciques and their gunmen fought it out for control over the ejidos. As elsewhere in Mexico, the strongest caciques assumed the office of ejido "commissaries," and usurped many of the best lands for themselves and their clients. The Otomí Indians once again were the big losers.

The notorious poverty and exploitation of the Otomí Indians of the Mezquital Valley led President Cárdenas in the 1930s to form a special commit-

Figure 7.11 A maguey plant of the type found in the Mezquital area.

tee to study the situation and alleviate their poverty. The resulting indigenist program in 1952 was given the title of Indigenous Patrimony of the Mezquital Valley (PIVM) and underwent reorganization along the lines of the INI coordinating centers located in other Indian areas of Mexico. Elaborate PIVM headquarters were built in the town of Ixmiquilpán in the Mezquital Valley. Around this time the Summer Institute of Linguistics (SIL) from the United States also began to operate among the Otomí of Mezquital, and in 1960 established its headquarters in Ixmiquilpán. The SIL missionaries translated the Bible into the Otomí language, and introduced the Protestant religion to the Otomí for the first time.

In recent years dramatic social changes have taken place in the Mezquital Valley, but PIVM and SIL played only limited roles in bringing about these changes. PIVM brought schools, clinics, and new roads to the Otomí of Mezquital, and SIL transcribed the Otomí language to writing and made converts to Protestantism. Nevertheless, their overall impact was marginal. Most PIVM agents were mestizos, whose disdain for the Indians diminished their effectiveness. For their part, the SIL missionaries failed to spread literacy in the Otomí language and the religious conversions caused considerable divisiveness among the Indians. Most social change among the Otomí resulted from developments in transportation and commercial agriculture. An elaborate highway system eventually eliminated the Otomí's geographic isolation, making it possible for them to find work in the mines of Potosí, the streets of Mexico City, or the fields of Texas and California. Equally important, the development of large, irrigated vegetable farms in the valley provided convenient work opportunities for the Indians as farm laborers. The effect of these changes was to transform the Otomí from peasants to wage laborers.

Mexican sociologists such as Roger Bartra have documented the increasing capitalization of the Mezquital Valley, and its impact on the Otomí and lower-class mestizos. They found the Otomí to be profoundly proletarianized, and thus completely integrated into the economic structure of Mexican society. In the process, it is claimed, the Indians lost the last vestiges of native culture, and could no longer be distinguished from the exploited mestizo lower classes. The cacique intermediaries, some of them Otomí, began to disappear too, as rural capitalists and government agents more and more dealt directly with the Indian workers. This represented a shift in native culture as well, since even though the caciques exploited the Indians they did so as "populists" whose authority derived from the promotion of authentic native traditions. Paradoxically, the Indian culture is said to live on only in the minds of the capitalist exploiters who, as indigenists, glorify the Indians and advocate the survival of their cultures at the very time that they bring about the destruction of those same cultures. As Bartra puts it:

> . . . (the capitalist) after contributing to the social disappearance of the Indian, resurrects him to a level of cultural reality; the demagoguery consists in proclaiming that the cultural Indian enters society through the main door—as the guest of honor—while the real Indian has to go through the servants' door, to be integrated—after being robbed of his culture—as a proletariat. (Bartra 1982:93)

Bartra has accurately described some of the social conditions facing proletarian Indians like the Otomí of Mezquital, but two cautionary observations need to be made. First, Bartra and his followers seem to argue that all the Indians of Mexico are in a similar proletarian condition as the Otomí of Mezquital. As we have seen, this is not the case; in Chiapas and other parts of Mexico, peasant communities, local caciques, and Mesoamerican cultural traditions persist as viable social patterns. Second, the loss of native culture is seen by Bartra too categorically, without adequate attention given to the efforts by the Otomí and other proletarian Indians to retain their traditional native cultures and identity. Anthropological studies of the Otomí document the loss of community solidarity and cultural patterns, but also the persistence of important elements of the native cultures at the level of the family and social networks.

The Otomí are painfully aware of their proletarian condition, and in increasing numbers have adopted Protestantism and other forms of modern culture. Nevertheless, they have not forgotten the rich and magical Mesoamerican heritage. This is well illustrated by the following narrative written in the Otomí language by a Mezquital Indian to his fellow Otomí:

> My brother! You are not alone in the world. You have had people who are your true friends for hundreds of years. Surely, you will ask, "Who are they." Brother, I must tell you, then. They are the earth that you walk on; the air that you breathe; the sun that gives you light so that you may see and walk and work, and so that you might live happily in the world. . . . The birds who sing to you out in the countryside are your friends, as are the animals that go about the surface of the earth and beneath the ground, as well. The stars are also your friends, and so is the moon, and the darkness. . . .
>
> Then who are your enemies? . . . Those who tell you that they respect you but who only exploit you daily for your work are your enemies. When you are young they respect you but when you grow old and can't work for them any more, they say that they don't know you. They pay you whatever they want to pay and not what your efforts demand of them. Whenever you sell them anything, they do the same thing to you. Be careful not to make them angry when you ask them for something because they are violent when someone says anything to them that they don't like. What they pay you is not enough for you to feed your family. A salary of hunger is what they give you, and they are always poor-mouthing, saying that they have nothing to give. (Bernard and Salinas Pedraza 1989:602–604)

As noted above, large numbers of proletarianized Indians can also be found in Nicaragua, El Salvador, and Guatemala. Like the Otomí of the Mezquital Valley, these Central American native proletariats have lost much of their Mesoamerican heritage, and in El Salvador and Nicaragua usually are not even identified as Indians. In Guatemala, where they do retain an Indian identity, they became deeply involved in the revolutionary conflict and, as a result, strongly politicized (see the soliloquy above by a proletarianized Guatemalan Indian revolutionary leader). Rigoberta Menchú, winner of the 1992 Nobel Peace Prize, stands as a striking example of the proletarianized Indians of Central America, as suggested in Box 7.4.

Box 7.4 *Rigoberta Menchú and the Proletarian Indians*

Rigoberta was born into a Quiché Maya Indian family in the highlands of Guatemala. As a youth she worked alongside her family on the coastal plantations picking coffee, and later joined a labor organization seeking to improve the working conditions of Indian and mestizo rural workers. Her family eventually espoused the guerrilla cause, for which her father, mother, and brother paid with their lives. Rigoberta herself barely escaped the same fate by fleeing Guatemala for exile in Mexico. During a visit to France she dictated her life story (*I . . . Rigoberta Menchú*), recounting the atrocities committed against the Indian peoples of Guatemala and their struggle to retain the Maya heritage. Rigoberta soon became the chief spokesperson for the exploited Indians of Guatemala, testifying before the United Nations and other international fora. She attempted to return to Guatemala in 1988, but was seized by security officials and forced to go back to Mexico. In 1992 Rigoberta entered Guatemala triumphantly as the Nobel Peace Prize winner, finally protected against assassination by the international acclaim given to her as one of the world's foremost peacemakers.

Rigoberta's proletarian background helps explain her union organizing and sympathy for the revolutionary movement in Guatemala. As with the Otomí, however, she remains firmly Indian in ethnic identity and in her desire to preserve the richness of the Mesoamerican cultural tradition.

The Mexico City Indians and the Mesoamerican Urbanites

One of the largest concentrations of urban Indians today is found in Mexico City, estimated by one anthropologist to number around 250,000 indigenous persons (but surely the true number is much higher). Most of the studies of Indians living in cities within the Mesoamerican region have been carried out in the Mexican capital, beginning with Oscar Lewis's pioneering research on natives from Tepoztlán who migrated to Mexico City. Urban anthropologists subsequently investigated the migration to the city of Mixtecs, Zapotecs, Tarascans, and other Mesoamerican Indians. It should be noted, however, that the impact of urban life on the ethnic identity and cultural ideas of these Indians remains poorly understood.

One of the most striking conclusions from the various studies of Indians in Mexico City is that they have fared quite well. Most of the Indians found stable employment, largely within the labor sector, but in some cases even in the professional sector. Almost universally they claimed to be economically and socially better off than they were in the Indian communities. This claim is supported by statistics that show their incomes and material possessions (houses, consumer goods, utilities) easily surpassing those of the Indians who remained in the original home communities. They also became better educated, more literate in Spanish, and healthier. Somewhat surprisingly, the city Indians also seemed to have more stable family relations than their counterparts in the rural communities. In particular, urban Indian fathers are said to be less "macho," more affectionate toward their children, and less prone to excessive drinking.

The degree to which the Mesoamerican heritage has been a factor in the relatively successful adaptation of Indians to urban life in Mexico City is less clear.

One important trait that the Mesoamericans may bring with them to the city is the ability to organize both formal and informal support groups. The migrants from Tepoztlán early on formed an association known as the Colonia Tepozteca, which not only facilitated adaptation to city life but also helped the migrants retain vital relationships with the home community. Even more striking is a Mixtec association known as the Unión Vecinal (UV), with ties to one of Mexico's most important labor unions (the Confederation of Mexican Workers). The UV helps Mixtec migrants find good jobs in Mexico City's factories, as well as housing in the same neighborhoods. The organizational structure of the UV is similar in important ways to that of the migrants' home communities in Oaxaca, with a hierarchy of officials recruited on the basis of obligatory but unpaid service (*tequío*). The UV members also have become active political players in the original Mixtec communities, where they are able to elect allies to the municipal council.

Many of the Indian migrants to Mexico City do not establish formal organizations, but all of them at least maintain strong informal networks of friendship, mutual aid, and kinship with Indians from the same community or region. These networks function to provide a place to stay for new arrivals from the communities; help in finding employment (one Mixtec Indian was able to find jobs for twenty-one other Mixtec migrants in the same business establishment where he worked); and create a social context for such activities as conversing in one's native tongue, playing sports, finding a spouse, selecting godparents, etc.

The Mesoamerican Indians of Mexico City appear to be particularly well prepared in cultural terms to develop elaborate networks and formal associations. According to one sociologist who studied their activities in Mexico City, they bring with them to the city a "traditional precolonial morality," which among other things imbues them with community spirit, strong family ties, unflinching honesty, and a deeply felt work ethic. The Mesoamerican Indians may also be aided by their long historical acquaintance with urban migration and its associated requirement of flexibility in learning new skills and values. The fact that almost all the urban Indians continue to maintain contact with their native communities is a source of strength too. They identify the communities as a home base, and return often to participate in public celebrations, to conduct family and business matters (many of them retain houses and lands in the communities), and to use special services available there (such as from "curers").

But do the migrants in Mexico City continue to identify themselves as Indians? And, do they retain important elements of the Mesoamerican cultures? No simple answer can be given to these questions, in part because they have not been the subject of close study. Nevertheless, we do know that one's ethnic identification varies according to social class and situational context. Thus, lower-class Indians, who make up the vast majority of Indians in Mexico City, tend to disguise their Indian status in the presence of the mestizos around them. They generally adopt mestizo dress, customs, and language (Spanish), and remain silent about their communities of origin. Some go so far as to denigrate Indian beliefs and practices, although this may be somewhat unusual given the widespread Mexican tolerance for things Indian within the lower classes. At any rate, in dealing with other Indians from their own communities or regions, these lower-class natives fully acknowledge Indian status and share important traditional cultural patterns. The more personal context of the various Indian networks and associations makes it acceptable for them to identify children born in the community of origin as "indios," even though those born in the city may become known as "mexicanos."

The Gómez family, described by Oscar Lewis in his book, *Five Families* (1959), illustrates the situation of lower-class Indians in Mexico City. This family of six inhabited one room of an apartment complex in a poor district of Mexico City. The father, Agustín, mother, Rosa, and two older sons were all born in Tepoztlán, the younger daughter and son in Mexico City. Both Agustín and the oldest son (the second-born son had moved out of the apartment) were city bus drivers, and worked long hours for very low wages. Nevertheless, the family had an inside bathroom, electricity, radio, gas stove, and refrigerator. They considered themselves to be far better off than they were in Tepoztlán. Despite serious strains in the relationship between Agustín and Rosa (Agustín had a common-law wife on the side) and between Agustín and his older sons (the sons were rebelling against his rigid authority), Lewis notes that the family had at least gained some stability and was optimistic about the future.

The Gómez family visited Tepoztlán often, where they made purchases of tortillas and special herbs, and renewed kinship ties. They also occasionally employed the services of curers from the village, and at the time of Lewis's study Rosa was trying to get Agustín to seek help from the community curers in order to break a magical spell that she was certain another woman had cast over him. The family had contacts with other Tepoztecans living in the city, including a family residing in the same apartment complex, but these ties were apparently weak. It is evident from Lewis's account that many Mesoamerican beliefs and practices still held force within the family. For example, food staples were the traditional ones of tortillas and beans, along with the pulque beverage, and other native dishes were consumed as well. The family members were not particularly active Catholics, but in times of crisis they would turn to powerful saints whose roots went back to aboriginal deities (for example, Our Lord of Chalma). The family members believed firmly in visitations by ghosts and in the efficacy of sorcery. Once when Agustín's nephew from Tepoztlán stayed with the family while searching for a job, they heard strange noises at night and became convinced that their guest had the powers of a sorcerer.

Unfortunately, Lewis does not tell us about the Gómez family's perception of their own Indian identity. In at least some contexts, however, they were not above denigrating their Indianness, especially the older sons. Lewis says Agustín considered Rosa to be backward because she accepted so many of the "Indian" beliefs. Hector, the second son, had apparently lost all respect for the family's Indian heritage, which was no doubt one of the reasons why he was forced to lived apart. On one occasion when Rosa tried to give Hector a traditional plate of Tepoztlán food, he exclaimed: "Ay, no! How horrible. Don't give me that! Give it to some Indian, not to me." Hector was clearly ashamed of the family's ethnic background, and told his brother that he would never bring his friends to this home because they lived "like pigs."

In contrast with lower-class Indians, most middle-class people of Indian background in Mexico City no longer identify with the Indians, and have wholeheartedly adopted the mestizo version of Mexican national culture. Nevertheless, a few of them continue to identify themselves as Indians, and have a deep appreciation of the Mesoamerican cultural tradition. Their mode of ethnic identification, however, is the reverse of that of the lower-class Indians: They identify with the Indian heritage publicly, but not privately. That is to say, most of them—teachers, architects, engineers, and businessmen of Indian background—are married to mestizo women, raise their children as mestizos, and in the home live according to the dominant mestizo values. In contrast, publicly they emphasize their Indian identity, and participate in highly visible Indian organizations designed to promote Mexico's Mesoamerican heritage. The attitudes of middle-class Indians in Mexico City are described in Box 7.5.

Box 7.5 *Middle-Class Indians in Mexico City*

In *The Truths of Others* (1977), Alicja Iwanska points out that the middle-class Indians of Mexico City vary in the ways by which they promote the Indian cause. One group, the "realists," adopts an indigenist position: They advocate the incorporation of the peasant Indians into Mexican society but on equitable terms and to the extent possible with preservation of the native cultures. Their theme is, "Let's Mexicanize Indians, not Indianize Mexico." They differ from the INI indigenists only in claiming that educated Indians like themselves rather than governmental agents should mediate between the rural Indians and Mexican society. They claim to understand the problems created by caciques and other "parasites" in the Indian communities, and in the past have organized teams of Indian professionals to visit the communities and provide needed services.

The other group, the "utopians," adopts a nativistic position: They advocate restoring the Mesoamerican cultural traditions of the past as the basis for Mexico's identity as a progressive nation-state. The utopians tend to glorify the Mesoamerican tradition, and engage in revising native histories to conform more closely to their ideas about Mesoamerica's glorious past. One group of utopian "Aztecs," for example, argues that the Spaniards gave their forefathers a bad name by ascribing to them excessive human sacrifices. According to the leaders of this utopian group, references to the Aztecs' practice of human sacrifice should be taken as "poetic metaphors" rather than actual literal facts. Furthermore, they claim that the Aztecs were not organized as an empire, but as a genuine democratic confederacy, founded on the communalistic calpulli. The Aztec calpulli, it is argued, were the model not only for the Mexican ejido but also for the communes of China and kibbutzim of Israel. This group's goals include such ideas as replacing Spanish as the official national language with Nahuatl; gaining control of the national government through the Mexicanidad party; and creating a new national ceremonial calendar based on historical events involving the Aztecs, from aboriginal times to the present day.

Despite the differences between the realist and utopian Indians of Mexico City, they have much in common. Both come from the middle class, although the utopians tend to be wealthier, higher in social status, and probably farther removed from their roots in the rural communities. They are both cultural pluralists in the sense of wanting to preserve the native cultures within the context of Mexico's national culture (the utopians go further in advocating restoration of cultural elements already lost). Both have considerable knowledge about the Mesoamerican cultural tradition, although to a large extent their knowledge is more intellectual understanding than cultural belief. The realists insist on being called "Indians," while the utopians want to be known by their ancient Mesoamerican designations; for example, as "Aztecs," "Maya," or "Purépecha" (Tarascans). Nevertheless, both groups denounce the conquest process by which the term "Indian" was created, and, understandably, both strongly opposed the Quincentenary celebration of Columbus's "discovery," in 1992 arguing that it should have been time for mourning rather than for celebrating.

Reference to the Quincentenary in Box 7.5 is a reminder that in the past few years the center of gravity for urban Indian activity in the Mesoamerican region has shifted from Mexico to Guatemala. Indians from all over the continent gathered in the city of Quezaltenango, Guatemala, in 1992 to denounce the conquest and celebrate 500 years of "indigenous resistance." Guatemala City probably now has more resident Indians than Mexico City, although many of them migrated there seeking political refuge rather than economic opportunity. It is dangerous to be identified as an Indian in Guatemala City, and so the pressures for adopting mestizo ways and disguising native cultural patterns are very strong. It is also dangerous to be seen studying Indians in Guatemala City, and as a result our knowledge of how they feel about their Indian identity and reconstituted Mesoamerican cultural patterns is severely limited.

One thing we do know is that the urban middle-class Indians of Guatemala manifest many of the same characteristics as their counterparts in Mexico City. Because of Guatemala's revolutionary situation and virulent racism, the nativism of the educated Indians there is far more radical and unified than in Mexico. Realist and utopian Maya Indians exist in Guatemala City too, but virtually none of them find assimilation into ladino (mestizo) national culture a viable alternative, and the utopian idea of taking over the state is far too dangerous to advocate in public. Nevertheless, the Indians constitute a majority of Guatemala's national population, and because all Indians recently suffered from a ferocious genocidal attack by the army, the urban and rural Indians have been driven closer together. The idea of a national pluralism that would include a separate Indian nation—an idea that would be patently utopian in Mexico—is taken seriously in the case of Guatemala.

Scarcely had the civil war begun to wind down in Guatemala and a civilian elected president (1985) than middle-class urban Maya began to form nationwide Indian organizations and link them together into an umbrella front known as the Council of Maya Organizations (COMG). One of the leaders of COMG is Demetrio Cojtí Cuxil, a Cakchiquel Maya Indian and professor at the University of San Carlos in Guatemala City. Cojtí has proposed an ambitious program to create an autonomous Maya nation within the Guatemala state, not through violence and force but by means of constitutional change and political dialogue with both the guerrillas and the government. Cojtí's plan would not eliminate the mestizo nation of Guatemala *per se*, but end its dominance over the Indians by giving the Maya an allied but autonomous nation of their own. Both nations would be free to promote their own languages, cultural traditions, and values, and to negotiate the kinds of political relationships that would bind them together in a new, restructured state. In negotiating the constitution of the state, however, the Maya would insist on equal representation in the parliament and governmental agencies, as well as guarantees of the human rights granted to independent "peoples" by the UN and other charters.

Cojtí argues that his plan is for all the Maya Indians of Guatemala, including those in the peasant communities whose particular languages and customs would be respected within the Maya nation. Nevertheless, he admits that the plan derives largely from urban middle-class Indians, and will appear to be overly global (national) to the peasant Indians out in the communities, and too cultural (rather than class-based) to the proletarian Indians of the plantations. The middle-class Indians, therefore, will have to take the lead "in giving priority to the ethnic struggle over the social struggle and to find the way to develop a Maya conscience of our own" (Cojtí 1992).

The implementation of Cojtí's plan will not be an easy task, for as one student of Guatemala has pointed out, its stress on cultural rather than economic issues could easily lead to the co-optation of the Indian leadership by the mestizo state; or if the Indians move too quickly in the political field, they could once again bring down the powerful, repressive apparatus of the state on the Indians. The plan should not be dismissed out of hand, however, as it might possibly succeed, at least in the long run. Should that happen, it would guarantee for many years to come the survival of new and lively variants of at least one strand of the great Mesoamerican cultural tradition.

SUGGESTED READINGS

CARMACK, ROBERT M. 1995 *Quiche-Mayan Rebels of Highland Guatemala: A Political Ethnohistory of Momostenango.* Norman: University of Oklahoma Press.

CHAPIN, MAC (ed.) 1989 Central America and the Caribbean. *Cultural Survival Quarterly,* 13 (3).

COCKCROFT, JAMES D. 1983 *Mexico: Class Formation, Capital Accumulation, and the State.* New York: Monthly Review Press.

CUMBERLAND, CHARLES, C. 1972 *The Mexican Revolution: The Constitutionalist Years.* Austin: University of Texas Press.

DUNKERLEY, JAMES 1988 *Power in the Isthmus: A Political History of Modern Central America.* London: Verso.

GOSSEN, GARY H. (ed.) 1986 *Symbol and Meaning Beyond the Closed Community: Essays in Mesoamerican Ideas.* Studies on Culture and Society, vol. 1, Institute for Mesoamerican Studies. Albany: State University of New York.

KENDALL, CARL, JOHN HAWKINS, and LAUREL BOSSEN 1983 *Heritage of Conquest Thirty Years Later.* Albuquerque: University of New Mexico Press.

NASH, MANNING (ed.) 1967 *Social Anthropology.* Handbook of Middle American Indians, vol. 6, Robert Wauchope, general editor. Austin: University of Texas Press. (Especially chapters 23 and 24.)

SMITH, CAROL A. 1991 Maya Nationalism. *Report on the Americas: The First Nations, 1492–1992,* vol. 25:29–33.

WARMAN, ARTURO 1980 *"We Come to Object": The Peasants of Morelos and the National State.* Baltimore: Johns Hopkins University Press.

Unit II
Selected Topics in Mesoamerican Studies

The six chapters in this unit are not designed to achieve comprehensive or even representative coverage of all relevant aspects of Mesoamerican life. The six topics chosen for inclusion here do reflect one or more of the following: (1) areas in which recent discoveries and new interpretations of the Mesoamerican past have been particularly salient in the past few decades; (2) areas in which social and cultural change has been noteworthy in the recent past; and (3) themes that have increasing relevance to the social and intellectual climate of our time.

As is the case throughout this text, we focus in this unit primarily on native Mesoamericans themselves. However, both the colonial and modern periods have involved Western state policies, national customs, and ideologies that have influenced local practices, both Indian and mestizo. Both spheres, therefore, enter in varying degrees into the discussions presented in this unit.

Chapter 8 The Religious Traditions of Mesoamerica

THE ANCIENT WORLD

From at least 2000 B.C., Mesoamerican religious traditions, like the region itself, began to evolve a distinctive identity. In fact, one of the strongest early expressions on the archaeological record that suggests incipient political and social integration above the level of village cultures occurs in the form of supernatural motifs in what is known as the Olmec Style. This is most clearly expressed in hundreds of objects—rendered in such diverse media as monumental sculpture, carved jade figurines, ceramics, and mosaic pavements—that depict a "baby-faced" human-jaguar motif (Figure 8.1).

Originating around 1150 B.C. in the Central Gulf Coast of Mexico, this distinctive iconography appears to be associated with the ascendancy and expansion of a major cult that came to wield considerable political and ideological influence over large parts of Central and Eastern Mexico by the time of Christ. This iconography appears to link political authority with divine ancestors via the half human–half animal deity. So sudden was the rise of this great style and so notable were the large ceremonial sites, from which it emanated, such as San Lorenzo and La Venta, that the Mexican scholar Miguel Covarrubias (see Chapter 1) advanced in the 1950s the hypothesis that the Olmec civilization and its associated theocratic state apparatus constituted the major formative culture from which multiple subsequent expressions of Mesoamerican civilization evolved (see Chapter 2). There is now increasing evidence that leads us to believe that it was

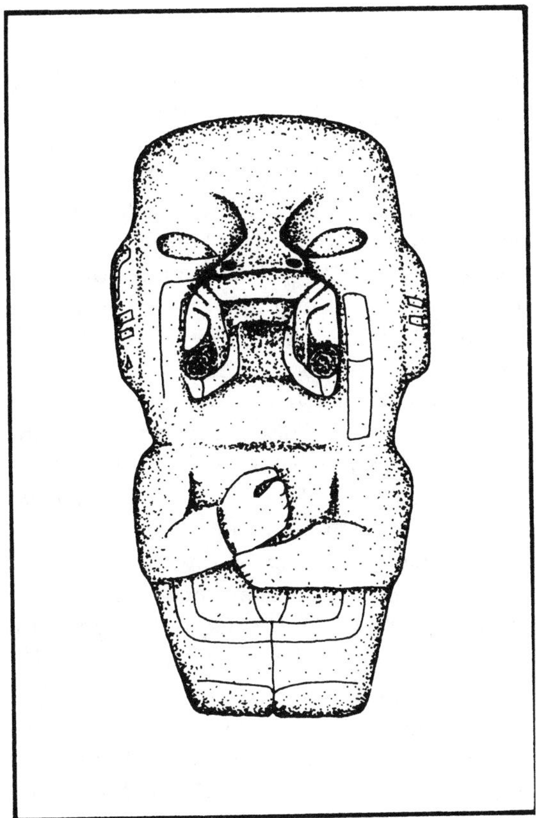

Figure 8.1 A Jade effigy axe (the "Kunz Axe") in the Olmec style. Provenance and date unknown, though central Tabasco, Mexico, circa fifth century B. C. is plausible. Drawing by Ellen Cesarski from a photograph of the original piece in the American Museum of Natural History, New York.

not just the Olmec culture, but rather several such influential Formative period polities, that provided the foundation of Mesoamerican civilization. We can assert with a high degree of certainty that Mesoamerica as we know it, from its inception in the Formative period as a great regional configuration of common ideas and adaptations, did not acquire its singular character through surplus-producing agriculture and village life alone. Mesoamerican civilization evolved, perhaps like all civilizations, as the complex product of *both* the political and economic means to form larger, integrated polities *and* the symbolic forms that rationalized and legitimated the existence of these greater units of integration. To borrow Clifford Geertz's well-known paraphrase of Max Weber, Mesoamericans, past and present, have lived in webs of significance they themselves have spun. Religion clearly ranked as a major political and ideological force in this "created" universe of meaning in ancient Mesoamerica. Here, then, we will synthesize some of the templates by whose agency life and death, well-being and suffering, plenty and poverty, continuity and destruction of life, moral authority and corruption, were understood. We begin with informed speculation about the spiritual traditions of the earliest period of human occupation of the region and then trace patterns in Mesoamerican religious traditions that continue into the present.

Shamanic Roots

The earliest Americans arrived on the continent as fishers, hunters, and gatherers. They lived in small nomadic bands and it is assumed that they had spiritual beliefs and practices that were possibly similar to the shamanic traditions that survive today among the Eskimos of Arctic North America and among the nomadic hunters and gatherers of Amazonia. Such communities as these were scattered throughout Mexico and Central America in what is known as the Paleoindian period (40,000 to 10,000 B.C.) (see Chapter 2). Although any effort to reconstruct their spiritual life must be speculative, modern ethnographies of domestic curing and divination practices in Mesoamerica and elsewhere in the Americas suggest that shamanic belief and supernatural mediation formed a substratum of spirituality in which all Amerindian cultures participated to some degree. We therefore infer that shamanism is a very old, elementary practice that was probably present in ancient Mesoamerica. Consider, for example, the title of a major recent book on the Maya: *Maya Cosmos: Three Thousand Years on the Shaman's Path* (Freidel, Schele, and Parker 1993). Shamanism is thought, in its ancient form, to have been a highly individualistic and pragmatic form of spirituality, the goal of the religious quest being essentially to underwrite human well-being, food supply, and health through interacting with the spirits of animals, plants, geographical features, and deities that were believed to be responsible for hunting, gathering, and fishing resources, and for human destiny. Practitioners were probably not full-time specialists, nor members of organized cults, but individuals who, for their own ends and on behalf of family members, sought to communicate by trance, vision quest, and dream interpretation with the spirits of the natural world.

The Rise of Agriculture and Its Supernatural Charters

The slow process of domestication of food and fiber cultigens during the Archaic period (8000–2000 B.C.) (see Chapter 2) brought with it a vastly increased food-production capacity, a dramatic population increase, and a concomitant evolution of sedentary village life. As new technologies evolved in relation to food production, more complex social forms developed to regulate, defend, and renew the vulnerable infrastructure of settled life: homes, equipment, storage facilities, fields, and water supplies. Among these new social forms, a new configuration of agricultural and ancestral cults appeared. Agricultural practice demanded propitiation of earth, water, solar and lunar deities, along with cults devoted to achieving supernatural protection of domestic plants and to ensuring their continuing fertility. In support of this inference, scholars have noted the extraordinary prominence, in the symbolic representation of this period, of ceramic figurines that portrayed females, sometimes with exaggerated genitalia and breasts (Figure 8.2). This theme has been interpreted to signify a cultural concern with both human and agrarian fertility.

Agriculture and sedentary life also required social control related to

Figure 8.2 A Tlatilco ceramic figurine in what is known as the "Pretty Lady" style. Provenance: Central Mexico, circa 1200 B. C. Courtesy of Gillett G. Griffin.

property rights. The most typical expression of these new forms of social control was the expanded importance of kin groups as the basis of permanent residential patterns and of genealogical reckoning as the basis of ancestral rights to property and access to water for irrigation. These "goals" appear to find expression in the rise of totemic ancestor cult affiliation, the ritual maintenance of the "founder's memory" being closely linked to the identity, property rights, and social status of the corresponding social group.

These patterns probably came to form the ideological foundation of the city-states, kingdoms, and empires that followed in subsequent periods.

The Rise of the Mesoamerican Theocratic States

Upon the base of thousands of village cultures there evolved in what is known as the Preclassic or Formative period (2000 B.C.–A.D. 200) composite and large units of social integration. Characterized by expanding ideological, economic, and political influence, these larger polities built impressive administrative and ritual centers that expressed their growing dominance in regional affairs. Whether or not these urban centers can be called true "cities," it is clear that they evolved as the "greater among equals" in their respective regions with regard to elaborate architectural features such as large pyramids, temples, fortifications, and monumental sculpture. These early centers served not only as administrative and trade foci, but also as seats for the ruling families' ancestor cults and for increasingly centralized celestial, earth, and rain deity cults.

It was during this period that the important early centers, such as La Venta and San Lorenzo, began to exercise religious and political influence over areas far greater than their immediate environs. In such ceremonial centers we see the expression of the trend, as noted above, toward increasing complexity and integration of regional traditions. This was reflected in the emergence and wide diffusion of cults dedicated to major deities. One such case of this pattern can be observed in the ubiquitous distribution of the famous Olmec "were-jaguar" images in the central Gulf Coast and in adjacent regions. It is inferred that these strange beings may have represented divine ancestors by whose moral and political authority the Olmec elite exported their tradition via trade and other, possibly more aggressive, forms of contact. Furthermore, evidence from the Gulf Coast site of Tres Zapotes and other sites farther south and west suggests that the unique Mesoamerican calendrical system, whose sacred astronomical and solar cycles underwrote the political authority of later (Maya) theocratic states, originated with the Olmec and other Formative peoples.

Classic Period Mesoamerican Religion

The Classic period (A.D. 200–900) is considered elsewhere in this text (Chapter 2). Here it is reiterated that we attribute to this period the consolidation of theocratic statecraft throughout Mesoamerica, in hundreds of variants, stretching from Central Mexico to Honduras. All of the city-states of this period were administratively focused on carefully planned ceremonial centers that were characterized by monumental religious architecture and elaborate subsidiary structures. All of the polities appear to have been ruled by hereditary divine kings who lived surrounded by architectural and artistic expressions of their grandeur. The arts, sciences, and writing flourished, all in the service of centralized, divine kingship. It can be said without exaggeration that Mesoamerica's remarkable cultural achievements of this period—running the gamut from astronomy, mathematics, architecture, and urban design to calendrics, writing, sculpture, mural painting, and sophisticated polychrome ceramic art—were all focused on the symbolic representation and legitimation of centralized and unified religious and political authority systems.

Indeed, as far as we have been able to interpret the meaning of the great urban centers of this period, it seems clear that their overall spatial design and major structures expressed nothing less than divine cosmograms. For example, Teotihuacán—which at its peak (circa A.D. 500) had a population of 150,000 and thus ranked as one of the handful of the world's great cities at that time —commemorated the very birthplace of the gods. The Aztecs, who rose to power almost 1,000 years later, remembered Teotihuacán with the greatest of awe. Davíd Carrasco notes that the Aztecs attributed the creation of the fifth age of the cosmos, their own era, to mythical events that took place at Teotihuacán:

> It is told that when yet [all] was in darkness, when no sun had shown and no dawn had broken—it is said—the gods gathered themselves there at Teotihuacán. They spoke . . . "Who will take it upon himself to be the sun, to bring the dawn?" (Sahagún 1952–1982, Book VII:4)

It is not surprising, therefore, to find many of the urban centers of the Classic period dedicated to divine ancestors and their spatial layout to be a replication of the cosmos. For example, the important east-west axis of ceremonial centers was often delimited by major architectural features, just as the central ceremonial plazas were typically laid out in a four-part plan that replicated the four sectors, associated with the cardinal directions, of the divine cosmos. Furthermore, individual structures appear to have been identified with specific deities and parts of the cosmos. For example, in addition to the well-known massive pyramids dedicated to the sun and moon deities, Teotihuacán has an entire temple structure whose iconography is dedicated to a deity whom later cultures identified as Quetzalcoatl (the Feathered Serpent). Murals and other structures at Teotihuacán suggest that supernatural beings associated with rain, water, and vegetation—most prominently a female water deity—were also revered in the great capital.

Sacred ceremonial architecture also dominated the urban centers of the Classic Maya. For example, Palenque, one of the best studied and most thoroughly understood of the ancient Maya cities, contains several elegant temple structures (notably the Temple of the Cross and the Temple of the Foliated Cross, Figures 2.11 and 8.3) that are dedicated to the cosmic tree, from whose trunk and leaves spring maize deities who are in turn linked to sacred ancestors and, ultimately, to the sun deity.

Maya rulers embodied the very life force of the universe and were called Mah K'iná (Great Sun Lord) or Ahau (Lord). Thus, not only the temple centers from which they ruled but also the rulers' bodies themselves constituted living terrestrial cosmograms.

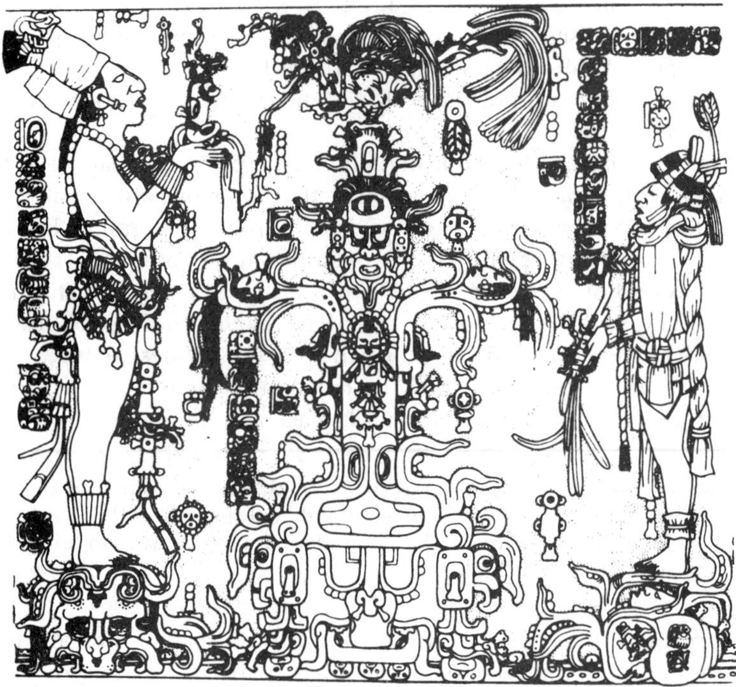

Figure 8.3 The central tablet in the interior of the Temple of the Foliated Cross at the Classic-period Maya city of Palenque, Chiapas, Mexico. Drawing by Linda Schele. Reproduced, with permission, from David Freidel, Linda Schele, and Joy Parker, *Maya Cosmos: Three Thousand Years on the Shaman's Path* New York, NY: William Morrow and Co., 1993, p. 282.

Another prominent feature of Maya urban centers was the ball court, an architectural form whose spatial distribution spans almost all reaches of ancient Mesoamerica (Figure 8.4). In the Maya area, the ball court was, like the cities themselves, a model of the sacred cosmos. This ball court was invariably recessed in the earth, or structurally designed to provide a sunken pavement, often in the shape of a capital "I" (Figure 8.5). The cosmic region represented was the underworld (Xibalbá) from whose precincts primordial life itself sprang via the sun deity's battle with the forces of darkness and death. Hence it was both the Place of Death and the Place of Regenerative Power. The ball game itself appears to have been played as a ritual of cosmic renewal whose purpose was to drive the sun, represented by a heavy natural rubber ball, through a hoop or other structural feature that represented the point of emergence of the sun at dawn. The consequences for the losing team ranged from rituals of humiliation to sacrifice.

It can therefore be said without exaggeration that much of the social, intellectual, and artistic energy of Mesoamerican states of this period focused on highlighting the sacred cosmic authority that ordained and underwrote their existence.

Figure 8.4 A typical Classic period ball court from the Maya site of Copán, Honduras.

The Postclassic Period

The "Postclassic" designation of the period (A.D. 850–1521) is a Eurocentric misnomer, for it attributes to this phase a general "decline" in quality of the arts, engineering, and statecraft. In reality, the beginning of this period in the Maya area is actually an arbitrary date at which the lowland Maya stopped making inscriptions in what is known as their long count calendrical system. This abrupt change in the calendrical recording was also associated with the so-called Maya "collapse"—a time at which many of the major lowland Maya cities were apparently abandoned and in some cases destroyed. Whatever the radical shift of fortune of lowland Maya elite and why it happened (see Chapter 2), life went on, and the subsequent cultural expressions of all parts of Mesoamerica, including the lowland and highland Maya, were substantial to extraordinary. It was, for example, in the Early Postclassic period that the renowned Toltec civilization began its ascendancy as a quasi-mythical "golden age" culture to which many subsequent Mesoamerican cultures, both Maya and Mexican, would look back with reverence and awe.

If the Postclassic was a period of warfare and political expansion on the part of numerous states in their effort to establish larger spheres of interest, it was obviously not a period devoid of political finesse, ideological sophistication, or remarkable achievement in social engineering, trade and marketing, public works, and urban design. To this period of course belong the rise and consolida-

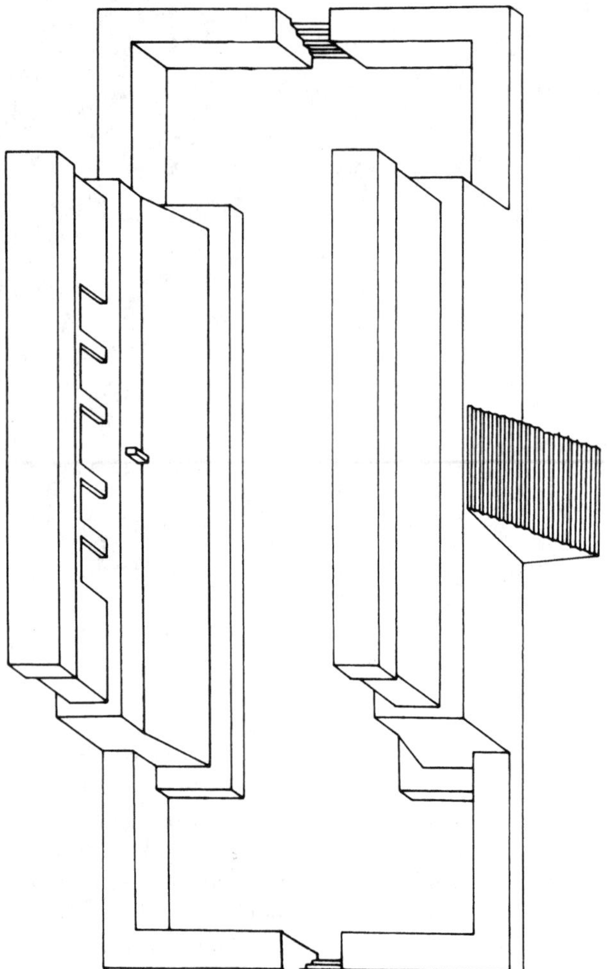

Figure 8.5 A schematic drawing of a Mesoamerican ball court.

tion of the Aztec empire as well as a great number of lesser imperial initiatives in other parts of Mexico and Guatemala.

This period is of particular importance to this text because it is, of course, this phase of ancient Mesoamerican history that is best known to us, for contact period Spanish observers and chroniclers actually witnessed and recorded minute details of this world even as they were destroying it in order to create colonial New Spain. Furthermore, as has been discussed in previous chapters (see chapters 2 and 3), the contact period itself produced massive documentation of ancient Mesoamerican religion, much of it written by Indians themselves in native languages rendered in Latin characters, together with drawings, translation, and commentary in Spanish (see Chapter 12). Thus, although Indian "autoethnography" was undoubtedly biased (in that it was "sponsored" by the Crown and was under the tutelage of priests for reasons having to do with facilitating the missionary enterprise), we can with certainty claim to know a great deal more of sixteenth-century Indian religious thought and practice than we can pretend to know of earlier periods.

For this reason, we are able to offer brief sketches of the main precepts in two contact period religions, those of the Mexica (Aztecs) and, in Box 8.1, of the Maya of Yucatán, based in large part on native testimonies and written texts.

Of Human Destiny in Ancient Mexico. Bernardino de Sahagún's Nahuatl-speaking assistants recorded their soul beliefs in the middle of the sixteenth century as follows:

> It was said
> that in the thirteenth heaven
> [in the uppermost of the heavens]
> our destinies are determined.
> When the child is conceived,
> when he is placed in the womb,
> his destiny (*tonalli*) comes to him there;
> it is sent by the Lord of Duality.
> (Florentine Codex 1969, Book VI, Chapter XXII)

In a recent commentary on this text, the historian Miguel León-Portilla writes:

> In several of the books where divine presences are depicted one finds also the hieroglyphs which denote the *tonalli*, the individual human destinies which, at given moments and places, are brought by the gods. These *tonalli*, destinies, will determine everything in each human life, from birth to death. The tonalli is essentially an individual's *i-macehual*, "that which is granted to one, that which one deserves." Thus, the *tonalli* bears, for all people on earth, the consubstantial origin and imprint of the divine source of life; it is this essence that determines what is going to happen in accordance with prearranged schemes. The unveiling of this predestined plan and propitiation of its divine source are vital to the human condition. (León-Portilla 1993: 46)

When this belief system came into contact with Christianity, its fundamental "otherness" became apparent to the missionaries and other Spanish observers. Jorge Klor de Alva has recently summarized these differences:

> . . . there was no autonomous will at the core of the self since every human being was a microcosm reflecting the forces that made up the cosmos at large. Furthermore, there was no clear boundary between personal will and the supernatural and natural forces that governed the universe. Consequently, acts that were believed truly to harmonize the contrary influences of the gods (saints, spirits, "devils"), rather than right intentions per se, mapped out the terrain of the ethical individual. Therefore, behavior, performance and punctiliousness, rather than will, contemplation or motivation were the key concerns of the Nahua who strove to be moral. (Klor de Alva 1993: 183–184)

Although Aztec state religion was of course enormously more complex than this native theory of self alone reveals, it has been argued that Aztec spirituality as a whole was fundamentally preoccupied with the problem of ascertaining and fulfilling the destiny that humans were given, individually and collectively, by the Lord of Duality. From this logically follows the need for humanity to propitiate and reciprocate for the gift of life. This requirement underlies the theme of human sacrifice, for which the Aztecs were noted but little understood (see Box 8.1).

Box 8.1 *Precepts of Maya Religion*

If Aztec spirituality was preoccupied primarily with the problem of fulfilling and paying for cosmically ordained destiny, the dominant motif of Maya religion was the preoccupation with cosmic time and the organization of human affairs in accordance with the sacred dictates of the many cycles, natural and arbitrary, that comprised it. Ultimately, divine rulership and, hence, the political order, were linked to the creator Sun God and his cosmic pantheon. It is thus to the issue of divinized time that much of the energy of Maya spirituality was directed. The concept of the Maya "chronovision" is here summarized by León-Portilla:

> From at least the time of the first inscriptions of Maya Classic (A.D. 300), the concept of time as an abstraction, derived from the cyclical nature of the sun and the related "day" unit, had primacy in the sphere of Maya culture. Proof of this comes from the ancient word *kinh*, whose meaning is identical in different groups. . . . *Kinh* is primordial reality, divine and without limit. *Kinh* includes, conceptually, all of the cycles and all of the cosmic ages that have existed. . . . The universe of time in which the Maya lived was an ever-changing stage in which one was able to feel the sum of influence and actions of the various divine forces which coincided in a particular period. . . . Since the essence of the nature of *kinh* was cyclical, it was important above all to understand the past in order to understand the present and predict the future. . . . The faces of time, that primordial reality which obsessed the Maya, were objects of veneration. . . . The Maya sages invented a cosmovision. Since it was history, measure of, and prediction about the total reality whose essence was time, it would be more appropriate to call the Maya world view a chronovision. . . . To ignore the primordial importance of time would be to ignore the soul of this culture. (León-Portilla 1968: 62–63, 109–110; translated by G. Gossen)

To this discussion must be added the caveat that time itself was not a deity for the Maya. Time did, however, form the very complex cyclical matrix in which deities acted and therefore, in logical sequence, time also dictated the schedule of human propitiation to them. Finally, it should be noted that Maya chronovision was *both* cyclical and linear; cyclical, in that what was will be again *in pattern*, but will also move forward, as a weaver moves back and forth along the warp, repeating a pattern, but also moving forward, producing variation on the pattern.

It is further worth noting that these fundamental Maya precepts, as with those of the Aztecs, functioned as powerful underlying forces that entered actively into the process of subsequent Christian missionization. Furthermore, there is abundant evidence from the modern era that demonstrates that centuries of contact with Christianity have not eliminated these ancient Mesoamerican ideas: restructured them, yes; transformed them, perhaps; supplanted them, not at all.

THE MESOAMERICAN SPIRITUAL WORLD MEETS THE WEST

By the end of the sixteenth century, well before the Puritans arrived on the rocky shore of what is now Massachusetts, Mesoamerica had been profoundly transformed. New Spain—as Mexico and Central America were called by the Spaniards—was fully established as one of the two linchpins (with Peru) of Spain's New World empire. Hundreds of churches sat on or near the ruins of pyramid mounds that had been the foundations of ancient Mexican and Maya temple shrines. Often, in fact, these ruins provided the building materials for the new colonial structures. Mexico's National Cathedral was built close to the very foundation of the central temple of what had been Tenochtitlán, the Aztec capital. Mexico City, the economic hub of Spain's massive New World operation, had a major university, numerous seminaries, convents, hospitals, plazas, and palaces—all situated in a neatly conceived grid plan. Antigua, Guatemala, also resembled a Renaissance template of ordered colonial life, housing the convent headquarters of a number of religious orders that had the mission of evangelizing America for the Crown. Vast tracts of Mexico and Guatemala had been granted as *encomiendas*, along with their surviving Indian communities, to soldiers and servants of the conquest. Silver mines, cattle ranches, and great estates had emerged in the countryside, all staffed by forced Indian labor (see chapters 4 and 5).

Implementing the Missionary State

The cost of all of this to the Indians of Mesoamerica had been exceedingly high. The physical structures of their temple centers, their books and art forms, lay in ashes and ruins, and their population had been reduced by more than 90 percent, from an estimated 27,000,000 in 1521 (a figure disputed by some scholars) to around 1,200,000 by 1600. European-introduced diseases, to which Mesoamericans were not resistant, along with the abuses of forced labor and forced relocation, were factors in this demographic cataclysm that far outweighed outright slaughter (see the Preface and Chapter 4). The demographic decline was a matter of practical concern to the Spaniards, for they, unlike the Puritans in North America, needed both bodies and souls of Indians to fulfill the ambitious goals that the Crown had set for itself in America. The Laws of the Indies, promulgated in 1542, specifically stipulated that all representatives of the Crown in America were de facto bearers of responsibility for the missionary enterprise; this could not be separated from the more pragmatic goals of the political and economic agenda. This meant that all Crown officials were formally obliged to encourage and support the spiritual conquest of America by persuasion and nurture, for the pope had declared in a bull entitled *Sublimus Deus* that Amerindians were humans with souls worthy of cultivation and redemption who could not be legally or justly enslaved. While the discrepancies between this ideal on the one hand and local practice on the other were surely great, it was nevertheless the case that the Crown was deeply concerned with carrying out the duties of Spain as a "missionary state." This was perhaps nowhere in Spanish colonial history better symbolized than in the triumphal arrival in Mexico of twelve Franciscan priests (popularly known as "apostles") in 1524. In a great state ceremony, they were received by their compatriots as the very architects of a millennial kingdom, the New Jerusalem, on earth. This earthly Christian community, heralding the return of Christ on earth, would be achieved by the conversion of the masses of natives into Christians.

Religious Syncretism and Local Realities

In 1531 (according to a legend that became "canonized" in subsequent centuries; see Chapter 5), just ten years after the Spaniards destroyed the Aztec capital of Tenochtitlán, an Indian named Juan Diego declared that the Mother of Jesus had revealed herself to him. At first, Church authorities were incredulous, and scoffed at the very idea that the Virgin might appear to an Indian. Juan Diego returned to the site of the initial apparition of the Virgin to ask her assistance. She told him (in Nahuatl) to take roses from a nearby bush that was in bloom out of season and roll them up in his cloak. Davíd Carrasco narrates this miracle and its consequences in the following passage:

> He did as he was told, and when he unrolled the cloak a magnificent color image of the Virgin was imprinted upon it. When Juan Diego took the cloak to the Archbishop of Mexico, according to popular legend, the astonishing miracle was accepted and the site of the revelation was chosen for the future cathedral. Today, Mexico's greatest basilica stands at the bottom of the hill [Tepeyac] and is visited every day by thousands of the faithful, who gaze upward at the glass-encased cloak with its miraculously painted image. (Carrasco 1990: 136)

That the site of the apparition of the Virgin was a sacred site that was of significance to the Aztecs and that she chose to reveal herself to an Indian are parts of the story that deserve further discussion, for they have to do with the pragmatics of Spain's colonial agenda. Whether or not the miraculous apparition occurred as legend and Church doctrine narrate the event, it nevertheless illustrates a typical phenomenon of situations of cultural encounter. Both the dominant culture and the vanquished seek—no doubt for different reasons—the means, often articulated through religion, to make sense of the inevitable present by mingling parts of prior cultural forms with new forms, thus creating new syntheses that address new political realities (see Chapter 5). Christianity itself was born this way out of the turmoil of the encounter of Judaism with the expanding Roman Empire, and "Mesoamerican Christianity," in its myriad variants, was born this way.

The original founding of a different cult of the Virgin of Guadalupe, a small dark-skinned image of a Madonna and Child, long antedated the events at Tepeyac Hill, having miraculously appeared, according to legend, to the Spanish faithful several centuries before. Her image is today enshrined in western Spain (in the town of Guadalupe) and was deeply revered long before the conquest. However, her manifestation as a Nahuatl-speaking Mother of Jesus, with Indian features, was something new. Indeed, some scholars note that there is no historical link whatsoever between the two images. Whatever the ironies and accidental convergences in the history of this image, Mexico's Virgin of Guadalupe became nothing less than the patron of Mexico and "Queen of America," and she is revered by tens of millions today. Her story bears significant elements of both the conqueror and the vanquished. In some ways, she can be said to integrate the tensions of Indian and Spaniard, mestizo and Indian, Spaniard and mestizo, into one community of faith and devotion.

The cult of the Virgin of Guadalupe is but one of the thousands of "encounter themes" in post-contact Mesoamerican religion that bear elements that are syncretic. By *syncretic*, we refer to the nature of ideas, deities, and practices that derive from historically distinct traditions that become reinterpreted and transformed in situations of cultural encounter. It is extremely difficult to learn with any certainty just how these myriad syncretic forms took shape in Mesoamerica. The reasons for caution are several.

The process of encounter between Christianity and Mesoamerican spirituality involved hundreds of variants of religious belief and practice, and this pluralism no doubt characterized all types of actors in the American crucible. These variants derived not only from different religious orders and different statuses of individuals in the socioeconomic hierarchy of Spain, but also from different personal biographies. The same muddiness and subjectivity undoubtedly characterized the religious views of Indians who encountered the Europeans. These subjects of Christian evangelism were, in origin, highly diverse: aristocrats and slaves, peasant farmers and traders, artisans and priests, all with different attitudes and loyalties toward former state religions, if any, in their respective roots. Indeed, they often carried no loyalty whatsoever to a former great tradition. To expect, therefore, an easily isolable new phenomenon (that is, the "new Mesoamerican Christianity") is wishful thinking. At best, we can hope for an enlightened dialogue about the subjective expectations and responses of the different types of actors in the encounter in relation to those of the others.

Where have these concerns about the concept of religious syncretism taken us? It is to the recognition that an understanding of the transformed religious order of Mesoamerica in the wake of the conquest is exceedingly complex. The region was, in the first place, a sophisticated and cosmopolitan scene. Mesoamerica, at the time of contact, was the seat of dozens of state theocracies, the Aztec empire being only one of these. All of these ideological power centers constituted "great traditions," in Robert Redfield's sense of the term, signifying that they represented the official ideological canon of the ruling elite and the associated priesthood that controlled the destinies of millions of people of diverse ethnic and linguistic backgrounds who were forced to live as economic tributaries and dependencies of the urban administrative centers. However, the local village cultures that constituted the peasant peripheries of the theocratic states were themselves bearers of religious customs and beliefs that reflected their own local experiences of memory and practice. These local religions expressed what Redfield has called "little traditions" in the sense that they continued to practice highly local spiritual activities even as they had to adapt to larger state demands in terms of their public ceremonial life. Thus, in addition to maintaining obligatory cult affiliations that emanated from the urban centers, precontact Mesoamericans also engaged in local shamanic, ancestral, and agricultural cult practices.

It is therefore reasonable to expect that when the Spanish missionary state decapitated and destroyed the major public foci of precolumbian religious practice, and obliged local elites to become lay catechists—or, at the least, local sponsors—of the new Christian doctrine, they did so in highly diverse ways that were subject to local practice (see Chapter 5). In effect, Christianity became the new great tradition to which all were obliged to pay lip service. Little traditions, whose religious practices had been for millennia focused on rituals of home, lineage, field, and waterhole, did not lose their vitality, though these local foci of religious practice received a new overlay of Christian ideas.

Even God and associated central doctrines of Christianity did not reach the newly converted in ways that the missionaries expected, for they (the Christian concepts) often merged as new semantic overlays with what were already, prior to the conquest, complex, polyvalent ideas. Thus, for example, throughout Mesoamerica in the Colonial period and even today in thousands of Indian communities, Jesus Christ has become one of several manifestations of the ancient sun god. Similarly, the Virgin Mary has become merged with multiple expressions of the ancient moon goddess and other female deities. The Christian saints also became associated with various pre-Christian concepts and deities (as they had in Spain when Christianity encountered native Iberian belief systems).

A good example of this syncretic phenomenon comes to us from Chiapas, where the contemporary Tzotzil Maya have assigned to Saint Jerome the care of people's animal soul companions in the mountains and in the sky. This association appears to be related to the popular Spanish iconographic portrayal of Saint Jerome in the company of a docile lion, an image that is linked to the medieval legend of the saint's life. However, the "success" of this Spanish saint among the Tzotzil Maya appears to be tied less to his virtues as a Christian martyr than to his affinity with the lion. The belief in supernatural co-essences (among them, animals) that share with individuals a kind of predestination was, even in the sixteenth century, a very ancient Mesoamerican concept, being manifest in written hieroglyphic texts dating from around A.D. 150. Saint Jerome's association with this belief system is thus a relatively recent facet of an old and complex Native American spiritual idea. Similar local transformations occurred as the Christian concepts of Satan and the angels were assimilated into local belief and practice. Satan has merged with countless precolumbian forces and beings that were hostile to the order-giving power of the sun god. Christian angels have been assimilated in diverse regions of modern Mesoamerica into various Precolumbian cults to the earth and rain. Thunder and lightning, for example, are known in many contemporary Indian communities of Mesoamerica by some form of the Spanish word for angel ("*ángel*").

When one multiplies all of the above by a factor of many thousands of villages that were subject to Christianization, it becomes clear that the new great tradition, Christianity, was just that and only that. Local practices—little traditions—assimilated Christianity in countless different ways, often with minimal doctrinal maintenance and daily offices left in the hands of Indian sacristans of the village churches. Thus, although some church authorities spoke publicly of the success of the "spiritual conquest," many local priests themselves realized that they were dealing with unfavorable odds (as seen in Box 8.2).

Box 8.2 *Gage's Account of a Little Tradition*

The following account is from a famous seventeenth-century English traveller and Catholic missionary, Thomas Gage, who lived and ministered as a parish priest in highland Guatemala around 1640. The extract given here (originally published in 1648) records a bizarre set of events that surrounded his pious ministry to a dying Maya Indian named Juan Gómez:

> They told me that the report went that Juan Gómez was the chief wizard of all the wizards and witches in the town, and that commonly he was wont to be changed into the shape of a lion, and so to walk about the mountains. That he was ever a deadly enemy to one Sebastián López, an ancient Indian and head of another tribe, and that two days before they had met in the mountain, Gómez in the shape of a lion and López in the shape of a tiger, and that they had fought must cruelly till Gómez, who was the older and weaker, was tired, much bit and bruised, and died of it. And further, that I might be assured of this truth, they told me that López was in prison for it, and that two tribes were striving about it, and that the tribe and kindred of Gómez demanded from López and his tribe and kindred satisfaction, and a great sum of money, or else threatened to make the case known unto the Spanish power and authority. . . .
>
> This struck me to the very heart, to think that I should live among such people, who were spending all they could get by their work and labor upon the church, saints, and in offerings, and yet were so privy to the counsels of Satan. It grieved me that the world I preached unto them did no more good, and I resolved from that time forward to spend most of my endeavors against Satan's subtlety, and to shew them more than I had done the great danger to the souls of these who had made any compact with the Devil. I hoped that I might make them abandon and abjure his works, and close with Christ by faith . . . .
>
> Whilst I was thus musing, there came unto me at least twenty of the chiefest of the town with the two majors, jurats and all the officers of justice, who desired me to forbear that day the burying of Juan Gómez, for that they had resolved to call a crown officer to view his corpse and examine his death, lest they all should be troubled for him, and he be exhumed. I made as if I knew nothing, but enquired of them the reason. Then they related to me how there were witnesses in the town who saw a lion and a tiger fighting, and presently lost the sight of the beasts, and saw Juan Gómez and Sebastián López much about the same time parting one from another, and that immediately Juan Gómez came home bruised to his bed, whence he never rose again, and that he declared upon his deathbed unto some of his friends that Sebastián López had killed him. For this reason they had López in safe custody . . . .

> The crown officer was sent for and came that night and searched Gómez' body. I was present with him, and found it all bruised, scratched, and in many places bitten and sore wounded. Many evidences and suspicions were brought in against López by the Indians of the town, especially by Gómez' friends, whereupon he was carried away to Guatemala [City], and there again was tried by the same witnesses, and not much denying the fact himself, was there hanged. And though Gómez' grave was opened in the church, he was not buried in it, but in another made ready for him in a ditch . . . .(Gage 1958: 275–277)

From an examination of this text, it is evident that Thomas Gage witnessed the tragic aftermath of what, in the view of the Indian community, had been a supernatural battle between the animal soul companions of two powerful shamans. The "lion" and the "tiger" (perhaps a careless English reference to the puma and the jaguar, which are native to Guatemala) were the co-essences of Gómez and López, and hence, their battle in the woods involved both their bodies and the bodies of their human counterparts. Gage's narrative leads us to believe that neither he nor the crown officials fully understood what was going on, though all parties, in the end, ironically concurred in believing that López was guilty as accused.

The Social Organization of the Colonial Church

In a profound sense, Spain stacked its cards against achieving a massive, unified Kingdom of God in New Spain. In the first place, the Crown implemented in Mexico and Central America the policy that it practiced elsewhere in America. Two "states," based on caste and color, were established in the New World: a creole state for Spaniards and their mixed offspring, and an Indian state for Indians. Thus, from local organization to representation before Crown institutions, there were two juridically, spiritually, and demographically separate entities within Spain's New World empire. Separate and unequal Crown laws, civil and ecclesiastical codes, and tax schedules applied to Spanish and Indian communities. Indians were encouraged, even obliged by these laws of caste, to live in, pay tribute from, and attend mass in their own communities through their own Indian puppet authorities. In a system not unlike the system of home rule practiced by the British in India, the local elites were encouraged by the Crown to remain in power as long as they facilitated legal and tributary obligations of Indian subjects to Crown authorities. In exchange for their services in keeping local villages docile and compliant with Crown demands, local caciques (chiefs or bosses) received substantial privileges and tax benefits, often even access to higher education (see Chapter 5).

In terms of Christian religious organization, belief, and practice, this separate and unequal arrangement also prevailed. With the paucity of clergy necessary to service thousands of Indian parishes, Indian lay catechists, often drawn from the old elite classes, were trained in doctrine by the missionaries. They typically received instruction in Spanish and were taught the basic elements of the catechism, with the expectation that they would carry on day-to-day maintenance of the faith in the Indian communities when the Spanish clergy were not present. Known in Mesoamerica as *sacristanes* (sacristans) and *maestros de capilla* (chapel choir masters), these Indian representatives of the Church were often responsible for assisting with the daily office, for translating prayers and canticles into Indian languages, and for serving as the link of the local communities with regional representatives of the Church and with the Crown representatives of the Inquisition who were responsible for overseeing the purity of the faith. The sacristans and choir masters thus became, with the local Indian political elite, individuals who had something to gain in terms of privileges and exemptions from serving as proxy representatives of the Crown. They also had a great deal to do with molding church doctrine and practices to the dictates of local custom.

In another ironic twist of colonial history—ironic in that it contributed to the maintenance of limited Indian authority even under Crown dictates—Spain insisted that local Indian communities organize themselves according to highly prescribed formulas of civil administration and religious cult sponsorship (see Chapter 5). Expressing a certain Renaissance compulsion for bureaucratic symmetry, this was the colonial prototype (later reinterpreted and reinstituted for similar reasons under secular governments in the nineteenth century) for the well-known civil-religious hierarchies (also known as cargo systems) that survive today in hundreds of Indian communities throughout Mexico and Central America.

Religious organization below the occasionally present parish priest (usually a Spaniard or mestizo) and the trusted continuing lay assistants (sacristans and choir masters) consisted of sodalities of local people who were designated—sometimes on a continuing and sometimes on a rotating basis—to sponsor and maintain images of saints, to care for their accoutrements and clothing, and to be responsible for paying for annual festivals in their honor. These cult-maintenance groups were encouraged by the Church in medieval Spain and became even more popular with the Church authorities during the Counterreformation as a means of maintaining approved forms of local community devotion. The system was vigorously encouraged in Mesoamerica as well. Typically, the leaders would bear titles such as *mayordomo* ("steward") and *alférez* ("standard bearer"). They received honor and prestige for their contributions to community life and for their sponsorship of particular saints who were identified as being special patrons and protectors of local health, prosperity, and well-being. These cults also contributed significantly to the maintenance of highly local identities and loyalties, a situation that the Crown favored because it kept Indians separate from creole and mestizo populations and also discouraged the formation of pan-Indian political solidarity against colonial authorities.

Thus, the civil-religious hierarchies gave the appearance of relative homogeneity throughout colonial Mesoamerica, which was, of course, in part their administrative rationale. Indians could be taxed, baptized, indoctrinated, and conscripted for forced labor and other services through an efficient and uniform local authority system—efficient precisely because it was in the hands of Indian petty officials who had something to gain from compliance. The other side of the coin, of course, was that religious events and festivals could be conceived and staged, mingling themes from precontact beliefs and practices, with relative autonomy from Crown and Church authorities. If the cults to the saints—as ubiquitous in the Colonial period as they are today—served the purpose of mobilizing individual communities in corporate celebration of approved icons, they also functioned to maintain the new forms of Indian Christianity as highly distinct from one another and from creole and mestizo beliefs and practices. Even today in many Mesoamerican villages that have mixed ladino (mestizo) and Indian populations, the annual liturgical cycle is staged and understood by both parties to be a parallel and separate, not unified, event.

These organizational factors help to account for the amazing mosaic of local expressions of Indian Christianity that evolved in the colonial era and continue into our time. The emphasis on public celebration also allows us to understand how easily nonpublic beliefs and practices might continue to express significant Precolumbian content and ideas, for the fields, homes, gardens, and pastures were not the preferred foci for staging the Christian liturgical cycles. It is thus the case that highly localized precontact rituals and practices associated with the individual life cycle, family, and domestic life could, with relative ease and impunity, persist and successfully coexist with the more prescribed content of public devotion. This helps to account for the persistence of hundreds of forms of shamanic curing and divination practices in the modern era. Agricultural and fertility rituals, along with related beliefs and practices associated with ancestors and rain, wind, and earth deities, constituted an area in which precontact customs could continue in relative isolation from the vigilance of Crown authorities.

It is helpful, therefore, to consider the myriad syncretic forms that evolved in the colonial era as expressing both prescribed uniformity in the structure (if not content and practice) of public devotion and relatively unmonitored particularity of domestic and individual religious practice, much of which was veiled discreetly from church vigilance. The many expressions of this public-domestic mix of spiritual beliefs and practices are further multiplied by the fact that the linguistic and cultural mosaic of colonial Mesoamerica was, as it is today, enormously diverse.

INTO THE MODERN ERA

If the diverse cultural geography of Mesoamerica—mestizo, Amerindian, European, and Afro-American—was already forged at the time of the independence movements of the early nineteenth century, this pattern of cultural and religious diversity has become more rather than less complex in the nineteenth and twentieth centuries. The reasons for this involved both internal and external forces.

Local Communities under Secular States

Much of the impetus leading to Mesoamerica's increasing religious pluralism came from the detachment of the new nations of the region from the centralized political and religious institutions of Europe. These new nations were avowedly secular and "progressive" in their self-definition. In most of the national constitutions—based, as they were, on French and U.S. models—the Church was disestablished juridically (if not always in practice). This meant that political authority (once one-and-the-same with the Church) no longer had responsibility for the spiritual nurture and protection of Indian communities. This fundamental change, combined with "liberal" land reform legislation that encouraged private as opposed to communal ownership of land, led to massive encroachment of mestizos and creoles on traditional communal landholdings. Whether by legal or illegal means, this erosion of the land and economic base of Indian communities forced large-scale displacement of Indian populations. Many Indian communities were forced into the paradoxical situation of becoming more demographically and socially isolated—their truncated landholdings being in marginal areas deemed undesirable for cattle ranching, commercial agriculture, and mining—just as they were increasingly forced to become migrant laborers in mestizo- and creole-owned ranching and farming operations. Often, economic circumstances forced whole families to abandon their home communities altogether to become debt-slaves on cattle ranches and plantations (see Chapter 6).

One route of escape from this situation—one that continues unabated in certain parts of Mexico and Guatemala even today—was massive migration to urban areas, where better economic opportunities were thought to exist. Urban migration has typically led to assimilation of Indians into the national culture, usually at the lower end of the socioeconomic spectrum (see Chapter 7). As members of the town and city underclasses, newly acculturated Indians have proven to be particularly attractive and willing subjects for Protestant evangelical and Roman Catholic lay missionary activity in our time. These recent urban immigrant populations, together with the rural proletariat, have also emerged as an important constituency of the reform-oriented Theology of Liberation, a radical Roman Catholic movement that developed in Latin America in the wake of the Vatican II reforms of the 1960s.

Nativism, Revitalization, and Separatism

Another internal force that has led to an increasingly complex mosaic of religious belief and practice in the nineteenth and twentieth centuries has been local Indian nativistic or revitalization activity. As liberal, secular governments came to power and (sometimes inadvertently) forced acute economic hardship upon Indian communities, there were several types of local response. One, already noted, was massive migration to ranches, plantations, and cities to find employment in the wake of the alienation of their communal and private landholdings that had been their subsistence base. This typically led to assimilation and "modernization." The counterface, one that occurred with some frequency, was a reactionary force in the remaining, increasingly marginalized Indian communities. It will be recalled from previous discussions in this and other chapters that Crown authority and also the post-independence secular governments had deliberately created and encouraged socially and ethnically separate Indian townships with strong local religious and civil hierarchies (the so-called "closed corporate communities"). The social infrastructure and demographic mass of people who shared an Indian identity were therefore present in such force as to allow Indian towns to seal themselves off socially and spiritually from those whom they regarded as their oppressors. For these reasons, among others, the nineteenth and twentieth centuries saw hundreds of articulate and violent religious movements that focused on Indian nativism and autonomy.

Perhaps the best known of these movements was the "Caste War" of 1848 in Yucatán, Mexico (see Box 6.3, Chapter 6). This uprising created national panic as Maya Indian communities—which clearly comprised the majority population of Yucatán—mobilized syncretized Maya Christian and precolumbian religious symbols and underground books of prophecy, together with an impressive military force, to assert their identity as sovereign people in the region. This movement is widely recognized as the most successful native-controlled, quasi-Christian, separatist alternative religion ever invented by Mesoamericans. Indeed, they came remarkably close to driving the mestizos out of the region altogether.

Another such movement, loosely related to the Caste War, was the so-called War of Saint Rose (1867–1870) of highland Chiapas, Mexico. Tzotzil Maya Indians of the area laid siege to San Cristóbal (the mestizo trade and administrative center of the region) in the name of a cult dedicated to Indian religious separatism. In addition to worshipping a set of sacred images that had been acquired by a woman who declared herself to be the "Mother of God," the cult focused symbolically on the coming of a new Indian Christ. Both Mexican and Indian accounts of the movement affirm that the Chamula Tzotzil people crucified a young man on Good Friday, 1869, claiming that only a newly martyred Indian Sun-Christ was worthy of their homage and respect. The national Catholic establishment was irrelevant to them, as was the political authority of Mexico.

Although this movement, like many others in Mexico and Guatemala, was effectively suppressed by state military intervention, it expressed in powerful terms that Mesoamerica had a hidden minority—the Indian community—that was excluded from economic opportunity, political expression, and religious freedom. Far from being passive and unconscious of their oppressed situation, they recognized their circumstances and, in seeking autonomy, created an Indian political consciousness that was bound inextricably with local religious symbols. This is a pattern that remains clearly visible in our time.

New Tutelage: Indigenismo and Foreign Missionization

Still another internal phenomenon that has contributed, albeit indirectly, to increasing religious diversity has been *indigenismo* (see Chapter 7). Typically associated with periods of secular political reform at the national level (particularly Mexico since the 1930s and Guatemala between 1944 and 1954), indigenismo is a body of public policy aimed at addressing the educational, economic, health, and social needs of long-ignored Indian communities. Although the agenda is ostensibly one of providing social and economic opportunities for Indians, the "subtext" is aimed at accelerated assimilation of Indian communities into the mainstream of national culture. Indigenismo has produced mixed results, the most important of them being the following: (1) the expected tendency of acculturation of Indians into the rural and mestizo mainstream of the respective nations; (2) the resistance to acculturation, as expressed in ideological and religious separatism as discussed above; and (3) the open door policy extended to the activities of European and U.S. missionaries.

Missionary activity, it is argued, must necessarily be tolerated under the premise of freedom of religious affiliation that is guaranteed by most Latin American constitutions, including those of the modern nations of Mesoamerica. Thus, as early as the mid-nineteenth century, U.S. Protestant missionaries began their labors in the area, particularly in Guatemala. In an ironic twist that brings the policy template of indigenismo in the twentieth century together with accelerated missionary activity in our time, governments have perceived that foreign missionary work typically shares the goals of indigenismo: teaching of literacy in Spanish, providing better health care, advocacy of modernization and "progress," and integration of isolated communities into national cultures and economies. In this manner, national "goals" are achieved at little or no cost to the governments themselves. Thus, beginning in the mid-nineteenth century, foreign missionaries have been tolerated, even encouraged by cash-strapped national governments, in that they are thought to bring foreign-financed "community development," the goals of which mesh with those of the nation.

The policy link between various government policies aimed at rural and urban development, on the one hand, and the tolerance and encouragement of missionary activity, on the other, has had an enormous impact on the religious configuration of the modern nations that constitute the formal Mesoamerican world. Dozens of U. S. and European Protestant denominations, Mormons, post–Vatican II reform Catholics, and militant "people's church" advocates within the Theology of Liberation—all can claim extraordinary success in the late twentieth century. Their faithful number in the many millions, almost none of whom can be claimed as loyal to the old order state Catholicism. Already extraordinarily diverse at the time of independence from Europe, Mesoamerican religious belief and practice in the modern period have splintered even further with the successes of the new evangelism. The much sought-after "national integration," in whose name missionary activity has sometimes been encouraged, has not always been achieved; indeed, the converts sometimes achieve the power and influence to change the quality of the national culture itself.

New Immigration

Another force that has contributed to the increasing religious pluralism of Mesoamerican is the substantial non-Iberian immigration into the region, beginning in the early nineteenth century and continuing, though at a diminished rate, in our time. This new immigration of the post-independence era has brought many new strains of religious belief and practice: West Indian Afro-Caribbean cult practitioners; English Protestants; Irish Catholics; Italian Catholics; German Protestants, Jews, and Catholics; Eastern European Roman Catholics, Jews, and Orthodox Christians; Middle Eastern Jews, Moslems, and Christians; Chinese Buddhists; Vietnamese Catholics; even North American Kickapoo Indian traditionalists; and U. S. and Canadian Mennonites. All came in quest of economic opportunity and, in some cases, religious and political asylum. Several of the region's major cities, such as Mexico City, Monterrey, Guadalajara, Guatemala City, and San José (Costa Rica), have hundreds of non–Roman Catholic practicing religious groups. Thus, from city to remote Indian hamlet, modern Mesoamerica does not permit easy generalizations about traits that characterize the whole.

If one adds to all of the above the especially important role of nations like Mexico and Costa Rica in granting political asylum to refugees from other parts of the Hispanic world in the twentieth century, the region begins to look increasingly international in terms of the national and religious traditions represented. Hundreds of thousands of Spanish Republicans, Cubans, Chileans, Salvadorans, Nicaraguans, Argentines, and, most recently, Guatemalan Indians, have found refuge in Mexico, almost all of them for reasons related to political upheavals in their own countries. Costa Rica has also, in proportion to its small size, received enormous numbers (in the hundreds of thousands) of political refugees in the late twentieth century, most recently from Nicaragua and El Salvador.

Thus, the crucible of life and belief has become, in our time, enormously complex in terms of who's who. Like much of the world, Mesoamerica—for millennia a region mingling many variants of great and little traditions—continues in the twentieth century to be a borderland of spiritualities, now involving much of the hemisphere and the globe rather than merely the extent of prehispanic trade networks.

IS THERE A COMMON CORE OF MESOAMERICAN SPIRITUALITY?

While it is relatively easy to speak of certain themes that unify Mesoamerican spirituality, one is confounded at every turn by millions of people for whom the generalization does not hold true. If the Virgin of Guadalupe is called the Patron of Mexico, and indeed the Queen of America, about whom is one speaking in terms of believers? Mexico's approximately 10 million Indians and several million Protestants cannot be said to "revere" the Virgin of Guadalupe as the soul of their belief. She is often relegated to the status of a minor, though duly recognized and respected, deity in Mesoamerican Indian communities that practice variants of Indian Christianity. She is a neutral, secular symbol, sometimes even a threatening pagan icon, to millions of Protestants, Indian and mestizo. Guatemalan and Salvadoran Catholics may or may not take her seriously as a powerful intermediary with God. Many Afro-Caribbean religious practitioners on the Gulf Coast rimland have never heard of her. Where does one turn for generalization?

All of this said, we feel that generalization is possible about a relatively circumscribed segment of Indian Mesoamerica that has been the primary focus of this text. If the limitations are clearly stated, we think that the following sketch of core features of Mesoamerican Indian religions, past and present, will be useful. What we assert here is that these spiritual concerns have dramatic temporal and spatial persistence in Mesoamerican thought—so much, perhaps, that some of these ideas may be found to color the tone of other traditions found in the area.

The Concept of Individual Co-essences

Perhaps linked to a deep shamanic past, Mesoamerican spiritual traditions throughout the region carry a fundamental commitment to the idea that each individual carries a predestined fate that is expressed by a co-essence that is given at the time of conception. Sometimes merely an abstract "destiny," but more often embodied in the person of a deity or an animal or a spirit companion, this co-essence experiences the life journey of the human counterpart through good and ill, often determining, in the supernatural world, what will befall the individual—power or wealth, sickness or health, early death or a fulfilled life, humility or power. The documentation of this spiritual idea dates now (on the basis of hieroglyphic texts) from at least A.D. 150 (Figure 8.6), and has been recently asserted to be the fundamental principle underlying Mesoamerican Classic period rulers' claim to power (see Chapter 11).

Known as the *tonalli* in the Mexican Central Valley (see the discussion earlier in this chapter), past and present, and as the *nagual, chanul,* or *wayel* in the Maya area, this co-essence of the individual plays a powerful role in both affirmative and therapeutic rituals—as in curing—and in negative and aggressive transactions—as in witchcraft (see Box 8.2 on Thomas Gage's seventeenth-century report from Guatemala). The co-essence and its role in individual destiny were once, apparently, determined by calendrical reckoning (birthdate and associated deities). Today, this belief system is made to "speak" via dream interpretation, pulsing of the wrist (allowing the blood to speak), and divination. In both the ancient and modern eras, the co-essence embodies, exalts, and constrains individual power and destiny, for these forces are in essence "from elsewhere." Since this idea constitutes a conceptual foundation for a kind of predestination, it is not unreasonable to link it with a certain skepticism about the capacity of individuals to "make their own way in the world" through their own volition. We know that this belief is strong in Indian communities of the region today. It may also be found to characterize certain aspects of the world view of non-Indians, particularly in Mexico and Guatemala.

Cyclical Time as a Sacred Entity

Whether in its macro-form as a four- or five-part grand creation and restoration cycle that constitutes all of history, or in its micro-form as the metaphor of the day as a minimal cycle of heat, in its calendrical mode, in its astronomical mode,

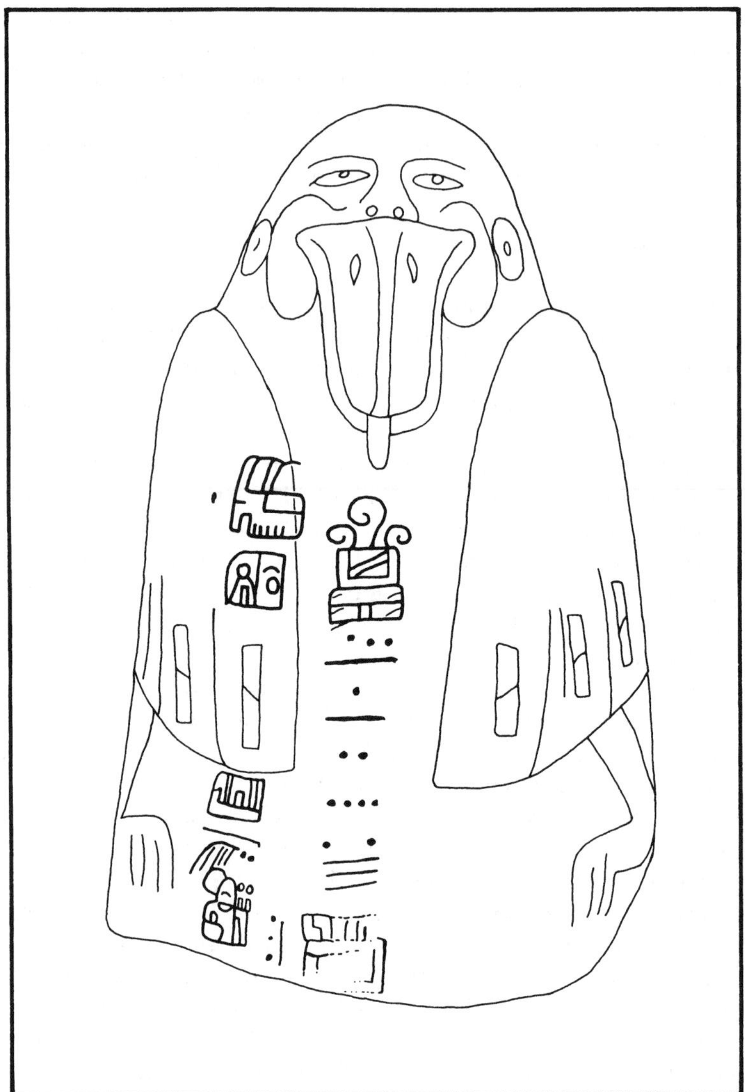

Figure 8.6 The Tuxtla Statuette. Iconography, writing, and long count date are in the Epi-Olmec style. Provenance: San Andrés Tuxtla, Veracruz, Mexico. The date in the inscription corresponds to A. D. 162. The lower four glyphs in the column on the left side of the figure say "The animal soul companion is powerful" (Justeson and Kaufman 1993: 1703). Redrawn after W. H. Holmes, "On a Nephrite Statuette from San Andrés Tuxtla, Mexico," *American Anthropologist* 9 (1907), 691–701.

in its ritual mode, or in the smallest nuances of verbal metaphor and poetics, it is clear that sacred, cyclical solar time has held powerful sway in both the ancient and contemporary Mesoamerican universe. (See the extract from Miguel León-Portilla, above.) Other natural and cultural cycles—such as the human life cycle, the human gestation cycle, the agricultural cycle, and the festival cycle—are all laced into the daily and annual solar cycles to create a cosmos that places humankind in an inherited, sacred, temporal order that demands human maintenance. This is not a system in which the human will is free to indulge its whims or to innovate in the hope of achieving personal or collective gain. It is obvious that this ideological premise occupies a key position in questions of continuity and change in the Mesoamerican present and future, for it possesses, in addition to its cyclical principles, a cumulative, progressive component. But this progressive, linear component is not selfishly pragmatic and not necessarily subject to the human will. It is a spiral that cannot move forward without contemplating and retracing its past positions and prior forms. Competing ideologies, such as Protestantism, Marxism, Reform Catholicism, and development programs, must either acknowledge and accommodate this ancient ideology or demand its eradication. Comfortable coexistence is unlikely, for many of the new ideologies are linear, progressive, secular, and pragmatic. The old Mesoamerican temporal order, in both its cyclical and linear modes, is sacred and highly patterned.

The Structure of the Vertical and Horizontal Cosmos

Both ancient and modern Mesoamerican communities recognize a consistent delimitation of sky, earth, and underworld in the spatial layout of the cosmos, with mediation among these realms as a key intellectual, political, and religious activity. With successful mediation come power, wisdom, even personal health and community survival. Some variant of this spatial structure, with subunit segmentation and corresponding cardinal directional symbolism, occurs throughout Precolumbian Mesoamerica and in hundreds of contemporary communities. Shamanism, heroic narratives, key integrating symbols, and deities themselves (particularly Sun, Moon, Jaguar, Wind, Lightning, Earth Lords, Serpents, Jesus Christ, the Virgin Mary and the saints, even the individual co-essences)—all depend for their power and efficacy upon spatial mobility within all or parts of the tripartite vertical cosmos (sky, earth, and underworld) and the related quadripartite (four-part) horizontal cosmos. Through the mediation of supernatural forces that traverse this spatio-temporal whole, the individual gains access to, and is also constrained by, the whole.

Supernatural Combat and Secular Conflict as Creative and Life-Sustaining Forces

From grand mythical commentaries on the creation and early phases of the universe, to the structure and content of sacred narrative, to the ordering of everyday life—conflict is the genesis and precondition for order. This theme has countless permutations, from the battles of the underworld in the *Popol Vuh* (the sixteenth-century Quiché Maya epic), to the dialectic of the male and female principle in everyday life, to the problem of Indian ethnicity in the complex modern societies of the region today. The theme of conflict as part of creation and life-maintenance does not impress one at first as distinctive. Is it not part of the human condition?

What makes the conflict motif peculiarly Mesoamerican is twofold. First, conflict is divinely ordained. Thus, it is primordial, ubiquitous and easy to rationalize. Second, the parties in the conflicts are often dual aspects of the same supernatural being, social unit, or person. For example, the Passions, who are ritual personages who sponsor the cult to the Sun-Christ deity in the Chamula Tzotzil (Maya) ritual of annual renewal, simultaneously sponsor the ritual warfare that is intended to kill the Sun-Christ deity. The Passions' ritual accomplices, the Monkeys, in the same festival simultaneously represent the pre-cultural forces that helped to kill the Sun-Christ before the First Creation of the mythic era, and function as the policemen who keep order at the festival and defend the sacred symbols of the Sun-Christ's cult. This of course echoes the dual nature of countless deities of the Precolumbian Mesoamerican pantheon (for example, the founding deity of the Aztec cosmos: the Lord of Duality). The issue of duality and subsequent dialogue and conflict between these dual principles is indeed the dynamic force that creates the cosmos in the Maya world, ancient and modern. Dennis Tedlock has noted that the peculiar Mesoamerican twist to this idea is not only that this dynamic tension is sacred, but also that it is complementary rather than oppositional, contemporaneous rather than sequential. This reading of Mesoamerican dualism meshes intelligibly with the principles of cyclical time (noted above) in that the elements in temporal cycles that are not currently active always remain latent, ready to express themselves again in the same formal manner, though perhaps in a different code. Latent elements do not disappear, nor do they get permanently transcended or defeated.

The pattern of complementary dualism also recalls and illuminates the ubiquitous Mesoamerican custom of addressing ancestors, deities, and ritual personages with a bisexual honorific title—for example, "Fathers-Mothers" or "Grandmothers-Grandfathers." Power, divinity, age, and honor seem to evoke the complementary whole (male and female), rather than the everyday mode in which the male has primacy over female in the public arena of community life and female dominates male in many spheres of domestic life. Obviously, public and domestic life coexist now, as they always have, in the Mesoamerican world (see Chapter 9).

Complementary Dualism as a Key to Understanding Religious Process and Social Change in Mesoamerica

Is it not plausible that the male-dominated public arena has been the active assimilator of new codes (new languages, economic systems, political authority systems, state religions) and, thus, seemingly able to respond quickly, even apparently capitulating to the winds of change; while the female-dominated domestic sector simultaneously guards the older order (native languages, agricultural ritual, curing and divinatory knowledge, ancestor cults, shamanistic knowledge) for present and future reference and security? This renders intelligible the enigma that has impressed many scholars and casual observers of Indian communities in Mesoamerica: People seem at once to be modern Mexican or Guatemalan peasants and living shadows of a vanished Precolumbian world. Which is the "true" identity? This may well be a moot question; surely it does not concern the average Mesoamerican rural family. Yet we are, as students and scholars, interested in making sense of what we observe. It seems clear that both identities—Mexican and Indian, Guatemalan and Indian—are, simultaneously, true identities, for Mesoamerican ideology accommodates such complementary duality easily. Perhaps it has also always been so in the ebb and flow of Mesoamerican history, as the little communities of the hinterland absorbed wave after wave of new state ideas and religions that emanated from the urban centers. The public sector voluntarily adapted or involuntarily capitulated to the ideological demands of the more inclusive system, while the domestic sector held fast. This is not unrelated to the fact that female deities have played a singularly important role in the initial moments of Mesoamerican nativistic movements and major syncretic adjustments; the Virgin of Guadalupe herself may be usefully interpreted in this light, for she chose to make her appearance on Tepeyac, a hill that, according to legend, housed a shrine dedicated to the Aztec moon goddess Tonantzín. New political authority and new religions were pragmatically accommodated, yet the integrity of local identity and local knowledge was not annihilated; rather, it was, somewhat conservatively, transformed.

The Extraordinary Power of Spoken and Written Language as a Symbolic Entity in Itself, Beyond Its Neutral Role as Medium for Routine Communication

The great American linguist Edward Sapir wrote long ago of language as "those invisible garments that drape themselves about our spirit." He, of course, was writing about language in general. Mesoamericans, reflecting on their own languages, would agree with Sapir, but would be likely to force the issue to greater hyperbole. Throughout the region, Mesoamericans linked language and dialogue to the dawn of consciousness in the creation of the human condition. In time present as in time past, language, with its wide range of rhetorical, poetic, and musical embellishments, has behaved as a sacred symbol that allows humans to share qualities with, and to communicate with, gods. In effect, beautifully executed speech and song are the only substances, with the possible exception of blood, that the human body can produce that are accessible to, and worthy before, divine beings. The Aztec theory of language, song, and poetics was expressed in the metaphor of plants and flowers. Flowers are the most beautiful, perfect achievement of plants, and also their medium for continuity through seed production. Flowers are also symbols of the transforming sacred power of the sun. So also, song and poetry are the most beautiful realization of the human spirit, making this essence worthy before the deities. If divine beings are pleased, human life is allowed to continue. A variant of these ideas occurs among the Chamula Tzotzil, in which the metatheory of language links high poetic and musical forms of the language to the qualities of divine heat, which are required for communication to and about the Sun-Christ.

It is well known that ancient Mesoamerican writing and mnemonic systems were used to record calendrical, dynastic, and astronomical information of the highest order of political and religious importance. Books were in fact produced, kept, and used by a priestly class. The spiritual and political power that the native Mesoamericans attached to pictographic and hieroglyphic books was such that the conquering Spaniards destroyed them as a first order of business, and did so with particular zeal.

The native languages of Mesoamerica retain today not only their remarkable vitality (as of 1990, over 15 million contemporary Mesoamericans continue to speak over eighty native languages as their first or only language) but also their importance as an art form and as a passive and active political force (see Chapter 13). The late anthropologist Eva Hunt observed, with understatement, that the conservative character of Mesoamerica's native languages may be the single best way to account for the continuity in the region's distinctive symbolic order in our time. It is also worth noting that the written form of language continues to be important in Mesoamerican Indian communities, even in those that are largely nonliterate either in their own languages or in Spanish. For example, the charter proclamation of the Festival of Games in San Juan Chamula, a community that is largely monolingual in Tzotzil and over 90 percent nonliterate, exists only in written form. This document, called the "Spanish letter," is "read" (actually recited from memory) at key moments in the ritual sequence. It is worth noting that the Spanish letter itself is a regional historical synthesis of the conquest, incorporating references to Spanish soldiers who come from Guatemala and Mexico City. The paper on which it is written is a potent ritual symbol and mnemonic device. This function is not unlike the role of the written word in ancient Mesoamerica (see Chapter 11). This also recalls the sacred "Books of Chilam Balam," written in Maya utilizing the Latin alphabet, which persisted throughout the colonial and early modern periods (perhaps even today) as underground books of prophecy.

All of this could be dismissed as a mere curiosity were it not for the fact that literacy and the written word, as symbols of political and religious power and ethnic consciousness, matter a great deal in the ideological warfare that pervades Mesoamerica in our time. All of the major purveyors of new ideology—Protestants, Marxist revolutionaries, Roman Catholic reform-oriented missionaries affiliated with the Theology of Liberation, and advocates of national integration and development—promise some form of political entitlement through literacy. This is old soil, well trodden for 2,000 years. However, two new issues are apparent. First, in all cases, the focus is upon shared entitlement; literacy is not destined to empower only the elite. The second question is, of course, whether the written word will empower in Spanish or in native languages. Interested parties disagree here. However, there is at least good reason to speculate that victory in the new spiritual warfare of Mesoamerica will go to those who offer literacy (and something to read) in native languages. This may partly account for the extraordinary recent success of Protestantism in many of the predominantly Indian areas of Guatemala and Mexico.

We have concluded this chapter by sketching six core features of spirituality that span the linguistic diversity and the ethnic, political, and ecological boundaries of Mesoamerica across several millennia. Because these traits are so widespread and apparently so durable, it is not unreasonable to assert that religion, cosmology, and related symbolic constructions may be among the more important features that unify the native peoples of the region as a distinctive cultural space in both past and present. Although this may be true, we have noted above that there are now tens of millions of Mexicans and Central Americans for whom the core features we have described as characterizing Indian-derived spiritual components of the region certainly do not apply, at least insofar as people would consciously identify themselves. However, although cultural space and individual identity are not necessarily related, it is nevertheless the case that the Indian past and present color the quality of life throughout the region. From mini-shrines that adorn the front of buses and taxis, to the coins in their pockets, to the murals painted on public buildings, Mexicans daily encounter sacred symbols from their Indian past. Guatemala's greatest literary classics—the sixteenth-century Quiché Maya *Popol Vuh* and Miguel Angel Asturias's twentieth-century epic novel *Men of Maize*, for which he received the Nobel Prize in literature—are nothing more and nothing less than root and branch of Maya spiritual ideas. Thus, the realm of spiritual and religious traditions does not lie far removed from the lives of all contemporary peoples residing in the bounds of the ancient Mesoamerican lands.

SUGGESTED READINGS

ANNIS, SHELDON 1987 *God and Production in a Guatemalan Town.* Austin: University of Texas Press.

BROWN, LYLE C., and WILLIAM F. COOPER 1980 *Religion in Latin American Life and Literature.* Waco, Texas: Markham Press Fund of Baylor University Press.

CARRASCO, DAVÍD 1990 *The Religions of Mesoamerica: Cosmovision and Ceremonial Centers.* San Francisco: Harper & Row.

FARRISS, NANCY M. 1987 Remembering the Future, Anticipating the Past: History, Time and Cosmology among the Maya of Yucatán. *Comparative Studies in Society and History* 29:566-593.

GOSSEN, GARY H. (ed.) 1986 *Symbol and Meaning Beyond the Closed Community: Essays in Mesoamerican Ideas.* Studies on Culture and Society, vol. 1, Institute for Mesoamerican Studies. Albany: State University of New York.

GOSSEN, GARY H., and MIGUEL LEÓN-PORTILLA (eds.) 1993 *South and Mesoamerican Native Spirituality: From the Cult of the Feathered Serpent to the Theology of Liberation.* Vol. 4. *World Spirituality: An Encyclopedic History of the Religious Quest.* New York: Crossroad.

INGHAM, JOHN M. 1986 *Mary, Michael and Lucifer: Folk Catholicism in Central Mexico.* Austin: University of Texas Press.

LEÓN-PORTILLA, MIGUEL 1980 *Native Mesoamerican Spirituality.* New York: Paulist Press.

MENDELSON, E. MICHAEL 1967 Ritual and Mythology. In *Social Anthropology*, edited by Manning Nash, pp. 392–415. Handbook of Middle American Indians, vol. 6, Robert Wauchope, general editor. Austin: University of Texas Press.

MYERHOFF, BARBARA G. 1974 *Peyote Hunt: The Sacred Journey of the Huichol Indians.* Ithaca: Cornell University Press.

SANDSTROM, ALAN R. 1991 *Corn Is Our Blood: Culture and Ethnic Identity in a Contemporary Aztec Indian Village.* Norman: University of Oklahoma Press.

STOLL, DAVID 1990 *Is Latin America Turning Protestant? The Politics of Evangelical Growth.* Berkeley: University of California Press.

TEDLOCK, BARBARA 1992 *Time and the Highland Maya*, rev. ed. Albuquerque: University of New Mexico Press.

VOGT, EVON Z. 1993 *Tortillas for the Gods: A Symbolic Analysis of Zinacanteco Rituals.* new ed. Norman: University of Oklahoma Press.

WATANABE, JOHN 1992 *Maya Saints and Souls in a Changing World.* Austin: University of Texas Press.

Chapter 9 Women and Gender in Mesoamerica

The selection of Rigoberta Menchú, a Maya woman from Guatemala, as the Nobel Peace Prize winner in 1992 calls attention to and celebrates women's important contributions to cultural, social, and political processes in the region. In the face of 500 years of continued oppression, exploitation, and forced evangelization, the native population of Mesoamerica struggled to salvage bits and pieces of the revered culture their ancestors bestowed upon them. Women bore major responsibility in this struggle. Men were compelled, through the centuries, to act as intermediaries for Spanish priests and administrators (and, after independence, for ladinos or mestizos), to learn Spanish, and to become increasingly involved in the nonindigenous world. In the privacy of their homes, women continued transmitting the native language, domestic rituals, cooking techniques and traditional foods, and the ancestral arts of weaving, embroidery, and pottery from generation to generation. Kneeling and bound within the ancient backstrap loom, women patiently wove esoteric symbols that encapsulated the indigenous cosmos (Figure 9.1). Thus, grandmothers, mothers, and daughters ensured some continuity of their sacred universe, concealing the meanings of this symbolic language from the ever-suspicious gaze of priests.

Rigoberta's selection also pays tribute to the new woman—indigenous as well as nonindigenous—emerging in the region. Patriarchal national societies in the region traditionally endeavored to confine women's activities and lives to the domestic sphere. Though women, especially those at the lower socioeconomic levels, have always worked hard to support their families, the economic crisis of the

Figure 9.1 Woman weaving on a backstrap loom, a technique dating back more than two thousand years. JEFFREY JAY FOXX/NYC

past decade drove them into the labor force in unprecedented numbers. On the other hand, thousands of women were drawn into their countries' armed struggles. Women's involvement in the economy and in the war has helped them realize that their input is essential to transforming society. It has also encouraged them to overcome their feelings of inadequacy, to speak up, to organize, to become leaders, and to defend their rights. Women have been amazed at their own strength, courage, and effectiveness, since society had been telling them that their abilities were limited to domestic work.

Moreover, as they joined the armed struggle in various ways, women became thoroughly aware of the limitations that the patriarchal order imposed on them. Women found themselves relegated to jobs of secondary importance both on the battlefield and in supportive activities. However, they asserted their rights to equal participation and proved capable of taking on the positions of highest responsibility. Even though most activist women claim that feminism weakens the primary struggle to transform society, they have gained a deeper awareness of the specific problems that *machismo* and patriarchal control create for women. The new Mesoamerican woman, epitomized by Rigoberta Menchú, has become thoroughly politicized, gaining a sense of her own worth and an understanding of society and patriarchy.

This chapter consists of two main sections. The first considers women's roles in Mesoamerican societies from prehispanic to contemporary times. We will describe women's active economic and political participation through the centuries as well as the central part women have played in ensuring the survival of the native cultures that give this region its distinctive shape. Such information has been consistently missing from the record of the human experience in the region; researchers and readers have assumed that women's lives unfolded exclusively within the domestic sphere and that their roles have been of secondary social importance. Feminist research, however, has altered this partial, inaccurate picture generated solely on the basis of the male perspective.

The second section explores important contemporary issues, such as the effect of the economic situation and of the politico-military crisis upon women and gender, and the development of feminist movements in the various countries. Just like ethnicity and class, gender configures the nature of modern Mesoamerican societies, allocating resources, rights, and privileges unequally between men and women, and creating specific controls to guarantee the reproduction of this system. Although there are differences between indigenous and nonindigenous systems, the ideology and practice of male privilege are strongly rooted in the region, determining women's lack of access to educational, economic, and social opportunities. Furthermore, recent economic trends—industrialization in rural areas and the emergence of *maquila* (see Chapter 10)—have introduced gender bias into more egalitarian systems such as those of indigenous groups at a subsistence level.

HISTORICAL DEVELOPMENT OF THE GENDER SYSTEM

The Prehispanic System

What kind of gender system prevailed in Mesoamerica before the arrival of the Spaniards? In the past decade, archaeologists and ethnohistorians working in the region have begun to investigate this topic and apply a feminist perspective to their analysis. For example, recent strides in decoding Maya hieroglyphs and the study of the depictions of men and women in Maya monuments have led to the formulation of initial hypotheses about the gender system of the Classic Maya elite. Drawing from detailed accounts about the social structure and cultural categories of the contemporary Maya, certain researchers define the elite gender system as one of complementary dualism; that is, the male-female pair constitute a dynamic totality in which each plays a different and equally important role and neither is considered whole without the other. The Maya represented power as such a totality, with the female side symbolizing the notion of origins and the male side symbolizing that of authority. Other researchers point out that the Classic Maya characterized women as both conservative and dynamic. For example, in some monuments, women appear to legitimize the ruling lineage and to cement alliances of centers through marriage, whereas in other monuments they appear as central figures in transitional times (Figure 9.2). The information on gender in Classic Maya times, however, is of a preliminary nature; we need considerably more data to piece together a picture.

Many ethnohistorians focus on the Aztecs of Central Mexico in their studies of the prehispanic gender system because of the abundance of written sources available. These sources, however, were mostly written by Spanish men—most of them priests—who projected their own preconceptions on the unfamiliar systems they encountered. Scrutinizing their biases and problems, researchers have been able to sift through these documents and shed light on the lives of Postclassic and Colonial Aztec men and women.

The prehispanic Aztec gender system appears to have combined gender parallelism (where men and women played different but parallel and equivalent roles) with gender hierarchy. Gender parallelism was rooted in the kinship structures and in religious and secular ideology. Men and women were genealogically and structurally equivalent. They inherited property from both their fathers and their mothers, although the older son acted as guardian of the property for his siblings. In the Aztec pantheon, male and female deities were equally important, and deities often exhibited androgynous characteristics. Both men and women

Figure 9.2 Lady Xoc of Yaxchilán, an elite Maya woman who lived in the Classic period, performs a bloodletting ritual. Her tunic displays the diamond-shaped design of the universe that contemporary Maya women still weave into their blouses. Courtesy of Ian Graham, Peabody Museum, Harvard University.

had access to priestly roles, but women did not retain this position for life as men did. Furthermore, men held the highest positions in the religious hierarchy.

Since women owned property and derived an income from their productive activities outside the household (through spinning, weaving, healing, embroidering, etc.), they maintained a measure of independence from their husbands (Figure 9.3). In general, Aztec culture did not consider women as weak, dependent, or helpless. When war came to dominate their way of life, however, bravery and skill became new standards of behavior; men who were defeated or who showed cowardly behavior on the battlefield were said to act like women.

Not only did women peddle their goods in the marketplace, but they shared the positions of market administrators with men; as such, they supervised the prices of products, assigned tributes, and prepared war provisions. Women and men acted as leaders and administrators of their *barrios* and the song houses attached to temples or palaces. Aztec women executed important authority functions, although the highest political and religious offices were restricted to men.

Some authors argue that as Aztec society became increasingly militarized and imperialistic, women lost status. Noble women saw their economic and ritual activities increasingly circumscribed when social stratification increased and royal lineages emerged. On the other hand, the productive roles of common women remained important. The dominance of Huitzilopochtli, the Sun War deity—which displaced the previous pantheon of androgynous and male-female progenitor deities—provides an important clue to changes in the gender system. People

Figure 9.3 In addition to domestic responsibilities such as weaving (left), Mexica women held a variety of roles in their society, from trading in the markets (right) to performing agricultural and priestly duties, and prophesying the future. After Bernardino Sahagún, *Historia General de las Cosas de Nueva España, Códice florentino.* Facsimile of the *Codex Florentinus* of the Biblioteca Medicea Laurenciana, supervised by the Archivo General de la Nación (AGN) de México, Florence, Italy, Book 10. Left figure is from ". . . de otros oficiales como los sastres y texedores" Chapter 10, fs. 22v and 24r; right figure is from ". . .de los que venden mantas" Chapter 17, fs. 44v and 45 r.

usually project their ideal views of society into the supernatural realm, sacralizing and rationalizing a given state of affairs.

Some authors maintain that because Aztec men began to control the new sources of wealth (tribute) and the spoils of conquest, war automatically marginalized women, the household, and domestic production. Others argue, however, that although women did not fight on the battlefield and were thereby excluded from essential sources of status and wealth, their rituals and activities at home had a definite bearing upon the fate of men on the front. Furthermore, the war did not devalue domestic production or activities. Rather, the home and women's activities were invested with military symbolism. For example, labor was equivalent to fighting, and the successful delivery of an infant equivalent to a warrior taking a prisoner. A mother's death in labor was equivalent to getting captured or killed. Box 9.1 provides another example of military symbolism associated with women in Aztec society.

Box 9.1 *Aztec Women and Ritual Sweeping*

Sweeping, cooking, and weaving had important economic, symbolic, and religious connotations. Priests swept the temple and housewives swept their homes. In both cases they defended their dwellings against chaos and dirt. The wife of a warrior had to sweep not only at dawn but also at noon, sunset, and midnight, purifying her home and marking the sun's path. The sun deity would be expected to reciprocate by protecting the woman's husband in the battlefield. Warriors' wives had to prepare special foods, grind toasted maize, and place it in gourds as offerings to the deities. Women carried their weaving shuttles to the temples at night to offer food on behalf of their husbands, sons, or fathers who were fighting. Weaving shuttles symbolized the warriors' weapons and the hope that they would conquer their enemies in battle. Thus, through domestic production, women ensured the survival of their families while the men were away. Furthermore, these activities carried important consequences on the battlefield. The Maya myth text to follow is on ritual sweeping.

> Once the great star appeared, as we say. The sky grew bri—ght [— indicates vowel elongation in original narrative performance] from end to end. "I am the sweeper of the path. I sweep his path. I sweep Our Lord's path for him, so that when Our Lord passes by he finds [the path] already swept." [The star] travels. Then the sun appears. The sun sweeps forth as we say.
>
> But you know, first it's the morning star. Venus is a Chamulan girl. She is from Chamula.
>
> They didn't believe the Chamulan girl when she talked about it.
>
> "We'll see what the ugly Chamulan girl is like! She says she is a star! Could she be a star? She's an awful, ugly, black Chamulan. Isn't the star beautiful? It has rays of light. The star is a beautiful bright r—ed," said the women. They ridiculed that girl for saying she was a star.
>
> They didn't think she was. "Do you think I don't know what you're saying? You are ridiculing me. It's me. I am the one who fixes the path. I sweep off the path. When Our Lord disappears, the ocean dries up. The fish come out when Our Lord passes by there. That's when Our Lord disappears. That's why there is the monkey's sun as we call it [a red sunset]. That's when Our Lord passes over the ocean. That's when night falls. That's when the rays of light can be seen in the distance. I am the sweeper

of the house. I swee—p off the path. I walk just when it grows light, at dawn again. I sweep here beneath the world. The next day when dawn comes, I appear and sweep again, because that is my work. That's what I do. I haven't any other work. That is what my work is. That's why I am a star. *Ve—nus appears early in the dawn*, say the people, but it's me. I sweep the house. [I sweep] his path, Our Lord's path. It isn't just anyone's path," she said.

She sweeps. She sweeps it off constantly. When she disappears then she is travelling inside the earth again. So the star reappears the next day again. She sweeps it off again. She passes under us, beneath the world it seems. She goes and comes out the next day again. Just the same way she appears. That's why the star appears first, it seems. "It's me, I sweep Our Lord's path," she said. The path of the holy sun.

We didn't believe it ourselves, that it was a Chamulan girl, it seems. "If I ever see what it is that sweeps, it seems to be a star, but a Chamulan, I don't believe it!" we said to ourselves.

But she heard it when we were ridiculing her, when the poor girl was mocked. If it weren't so—she wouldn't have heard. But she did hear, so it's true. (Laughlin 1977:253–254)

Essential differences distinguished the status and leverage within the family of noble and common women, not only among the Aztecs but in other areas of Mesoamerica. The productive and reproductive activities of common women were highly valued within a subsistence economy, where husband and wife provided goods and services for each other that could not be obtained otherwise. Marriage was valued by both men and women as the first step to adulthood. For the man, it often implied the beginning of his own patrilineage. In the case of nobility, however, servants and slaves performed many of the household tasks, and polygyny was common. Thus, women were less important except as bearers of legitimate offspring for rulership and as a means—through marriage—of forging political alliances.

Transformations in the Aztec Gender System

By the seventeenth century, new cultural definitions and gender practices introduced by the Spaniards had provoked drastic transformations in the status of women in Central Mexico. Aztec women lost power in the religious and political realms because many of the native institutions in which women had held posts of authority were destroyed. Besides, the imposition of Spanish ideals of women's purity and honor restricted their freedom. Although women retained the rights to own and administer property, and to litigate in the courts, the Spanish patriarchal system encroached on every aspect of their lives, increasingly limiting their autonomy.

Native women had a strong presence in the courts, defending native property during the first fifty years after the conquest (see Box 12.1, Chapter 12). By the seventeenth century, however, they were much less likely to initiate property litigation, and wills made by women were no longer as frequently employed to bolster ownership claims as they had been in the sixteenth century. Likewise, the rates at which women bought, sold, or inherited property decreased dramatically. This indicates a deterioration in women's status. How did this deterioration come about? The patriarchal society instituted by the Spaniards gave fathers and husbands unlimited authority over their wives and children. Two centuries after the arrival of the Spaniards, Aztec women's identity had merged with that of their husbands, and women needed the support of husbands or fathers to present a claim in court. Men became the representatives of women in legal and political matters.

Although Aztec women continued to engage in productive activities crucial to their families' survival, the ideology of female purity and enclosure preached by the Catholic Church further undermined their opportunity to hold formal positions of authority. This ideology created a sharp division between a male social and political domain, and a female domestic domain. In two centuries, patriarchal ideology and its impact on the religious, social, and legal system had transformed precolonial gender parallelism into a system of hierarchical relations between men and women.

Nevertheless, the voices of women did not completely fade away. During the Colonial period, Aztec women led indigenous rebellions against colonial rule, perhaps because the men were working far away from their communities. Women often insulted and vilified outside authorities.

The Gender System Imposed by the Spaniards

There are few colonial sources written by or specifically about women (whether indigenous or Spanish). However, researchers are now probing the abundant colonial documents (such as confessional manuals, censuses, cases brought to ecclesiastical or civil authorities, Inquisition records, and so forth) for information about gender interaction in colonial society.

What were the main characteristics of the new gender system? Priests and Spanish officials alike extolled the patriarchal system as the divine design for humanity. The family epitomized this ideal and served as a model for all social relationships. A husband had control over his wife, his children, and any others in the household. Women and children were always minors under the tutelage of the father. They owed him nearly total obedience. Patriarchal ideology defined the father as the source of authority. His legitimacy rested upon his responsibility to support and look after the well-being of his family. He had the latitude to punish and even strike his wife to correct her behavior. He determined how much discipline his wife and children needed. However, when the husband exercised excessive authority, or when he did not support his family as he was expected to, his wife could appeal to religious or secular authorities. Sometimes women opted to run away, returning to their parents' homes or seeking refuge in convents where they felt safe and were able to find work. There are a few court cases that describe women who fought back—probably in self-defense. However, according to their husbands, these women were resisting rightful authority.

The Spaniards regarded virginity as an essential quality of women before marriage and when they remained single. The honor of the family was inextricably linked with female sexuality and the birth of legitimate children. A woman who engaged in premarital or extramarital affairs tarnished her personal reputation and brought dishonor to the family by begetting illegitimate offspring. The double standard of morality pervaded colonial society; whereas a woman's reputation suffered greatly from liaisons, neither her lover's reputation nor his family's honor suffered any ill consequences. During the first two centuries of colonial rule, emphasis on family honor and concepts of women's virtue and vulnerability led to women's seclusion at home. Convents and retirement houses provided protection for older unmarried women, widows, and abandoned wives. The Church glorified celibacy as one path to perfection; women who followed the Virgin's model were closer to God.

On the other hand, patriarchal ideology maintained that women's will and honor were fragile; that is, that a man could easily convince or force a woman to engage in illicit relationships. In this way society rationalized women's need for "protection" by fathers and other male relatives, as well as by the authorities. When a woman's father would seek redress in court for a man's failure to make good on his marriage promise to her, for elopement, and so forth, vulnerability was used to justify the woman's behavior. Such a strategy promoted the family's aim to force the man to marry her or to pay a dowry for having dishonored her. If the accused man rebutted by bringing up this woman's previous illicit affairs or dubious reputation, the woman had no recourse; the court would only protect a woman who submitted to patriarchal behavioral codes.

Adulterous women were deemed to have committed a serious social offense. On the other hand, adultery by a man was not considered critical, especially if he was discreet and the affair did not lead to the humiliation of his wife and family. Women usually were resigned to their husbands' affairs and were unlikely to sue for divorce or separation on those grounds. Because they depended economically and legally on their husbands, most women attempted to bring the errant spouse back to the family.

Women's Work in Colonial Mexico City

At the end of the eighteenth century and the beginning of the nineteenth, women accounted for one-third of the labor force in Mexico City. While 46 percent of Indian women and 36 percent of "caste" women (those of mixed blood) were engaged in productive activities, only 13 percent of Spanish or creole women worked. These figures illustrate the contrasting situation of women in the different social classes. Poor women (largely Indian and caste) could not comply with the ideal of women's enclosure. Living in conditions of extreme poverty and high mortality rates, lower-class families needed the economic cooperation of husband and wife to survive, albeit in a precarious way. The majority of women found work as domestic servants (a job considered utterly denigrating at the time); others sold fresh produce or cooked foods in corner stands and in the market, worked as waitresses in public eating houses, took in laundry, sewed, sold thread or wove for other people, etc.

In the early Colonial period, many middle-class women were shopkeepers. This was a more prestigious occupation than manual labor, and it enabled women to follow the rule of seclusion since these shops were usually attached to their homes. New possibilities opened for women of this class at the end of the eighteenth and beginning of the nineteenth centuries, when reforms introducing women's education began to take effect. Middle-class women pursued education, and were taught to care for sick or abandoned women in welfare institutions. This type of work was considered reputable. As for elite women, those who wanted a career rather than marriage took religious vows. Other women from this class were involved in the management of properties they had inherited.

Feminists today applaud women's historical efforts to remain productive and socially involved in the face of patriarchal control. Colonial society, however, accorded high status to women who did not work, and stigmatized those who did. Out of pure necessity, lower-class women engaged in labor considered degrading and transgressed the social precept of women's enclosure; thus, their purity and morality were called into question. Given the choice, they might have elected the path of domesticity and patriarchal protection.

Women's Responses to Patriarchal Domination

Since the Church and state colluded to keep women submissive, how were women able to maneuver within this limited space to overcome their powerlessness? Women sought to gain a measure of control over their own lives by practicing witchcraft; seeking direct communication with supernatural beings through trance; and, occasionally, entering a convent. These activities provided a respite from the constrictions imposed on them by colonial society. Any manifestation of power, however, was deemed disruptive and negative. Therefore, women suffered the consequences of attempting to subvert the natural and divine order that required them to be submissive.

Women practiced witchcraft in the hope of gaining some influence over husbands or lovers. Abandoned wives, women whose husbands engaged in extramarital affairs, and those who wanted to retaliate against abusive husbands performed love magic themselves or requested the services of women with esoteric wisdom. In this way, they would entice their husbands back, "stupefy" them, or force the breakup of a relationship with another woman. Interestingly, because of their marginality, Indian and caste women were reputed to have extraordinary magical powers. Engaged in manipulating secret powers, women established interethnic and interclass networks; they communicated secret concoctions, formulas, and prayers, and assisted each other in finding ways to deal with their oppressive situation.

Because the Spanish Inquisition regarded love magic as mere superstition, as delusion grounded in ignorance, it was treated leniently. Spanish officials devalued and trivialized witchcraft, thus dismissing an important source of women's power. On the one hand, this permissive response from the Church allowed love magic to continue. On the other hand, the effectiveness of the Church's preachings on this matter led women to internalize the notion of the evil nature of women's magical faculties and to reject their empowering effects. In documents of the time, women declared explicitly that they would rather put up with abusive or unfaithful husbands than commit the sin of entering into compacts with evil supernaturals and thus challenge the divine order.

During the Colonial period, many nuns or common women attempted to engage in direct communication with the Virgin, Jesus, the saints, or demons. These women usually fell into raptures or trance-like states in which they heard voices or had visions of heaven, hell, or purgatory. Where these women lived in a controlled environment, such as a convent, they were viewed as "mystics." Their confessors enjoined them to go about their lives quietly, since women were thought to be best suited to passive contemplation rather than to intellectual analysis; the formulation of thoughts into arguments or prayers was a prerogative of men. Besides, raptures always bordered on dangerous terrain. Colonial ideology contended that women were easily overcome by passions like hatred and love, and prone to lunatic episodes because of their inherent weakness. The direct communication of women with the supernatural challenged male authority because priests were the only designated intercessors between God and people and because the mystics' experiences gave these women irrefutable authority.

The clergy was hard pressed to find a way to assert its control: Confessors both required the mystics to write down details of their supernatural experience and served as the ultimate judges who decided whether these experiences were legitimate or the product of a deranged mind. On many occasions, the confessors plagiarized the writings of these women to author books and biographies without fully acknowledging the source. Denied access to the public arena and to learning, theology, and disputation, and restricted to a typically female discourse—the language of feeling—women still asserted their voices strongly, bypassing male intermediaries.

Women who did not live in convents but claimed to have mystical experiences had a much harder time legitimizing their claims. The Church dismissed such discourse as deceptions of the Devil, arguing that these women claimed to experience raptures and visions to make money or for all kinds of perverse reasons. Many of them ended up in special asylums. Ana de Aramburu, for example, was judged by the Inquisition and condemned to imprisonment in its secret prisons for having claimed to have been singled out by God. Her attempts to challenge the established order, by finding a legitimate language and a space to speak, proved unsuccessful. An even more important example of a female mystic is Sor Juana, discussed in Box 9.2.

Box 9.2 *Sor Juana, A Colonial Mystic*

Sor Juana Inés de la Cruz, nun and talented poet and writer, lived in Mexico in the seventeenth century. She has been widely acclaimed as a precursor in defending women's rights in the region. Sor Juana took on religious vows as a young woman to avoid marriage, the only alternative open to creole women. In many of her writings, Sor Juana employed language shrouded in humility and self-deprecation to criticize clergy members, including her own confessor, for censuring her work and wanting to silence her. In a critique of a sermon by Father Vieria, a Jesuit, Sor Juana asserts that "it is no light punishment for one (Father Vieria) who thought that no man would dare to answer him to see that an ignorant woman for whom this kind of attack (so alien and so remote for one of her sex) dares to do so; yet the use of arms was alien to Judith and the exercise of justice to Deborah." (From a letter to the Bishop of Puebla, cited in Franco [1989:41].) Here, Sor Juana joins forces with venerable women who, when necessary, acted like men of the times. The most crucial document written by Sor Juana, however, was the *Respuesta a Sor Filotea,* in which she discloses the criticisms and humiliations to which she has been subjected for writing and studying. Working from within the Catholic Church, bulwark of patriarchal ideology, Sor Juana refused to acquiesce to the limitations it imposed on women, and successfully challenged the male authority structure.

Native Women's Roles in Colonial Rebellions in Rural Mesoamerica: The Case of Highland Chiapas

As a result of the lack of specific information and research, the situation of indigenous women living in rural areas, far from the centers of colonial domination, remains largely unknown at this point. Documentation of women's participation in rebellions, therefore, provides valuable insights on the roles and status of women within native communities.

The decimation of the population during the first century of Spanish occupation meant that surviving native men and women had to fulfill the onerous tribute and work obligations imposed by the Spaniards. Spanish priests, colonial administrators, and entrepreneurs competed among themselves to exploit Indian labor. Native women worked extremely hard to produce the yarn and woven goods demanded in the *repartimiento* system. Men had to transport the requisite goods long distances on their own beasts. Exhausted and constantly on the move, men were easy prey to sickness and died young; often, their wives survived them. Households headed by women became a common feature of indigenous life (see Chapter 5).

The central participation in nativistic or revitalization movements epitomizes the important roles women played in the colonial communities. Indigenous peoples sought, through these movements, to bring hope and redemption to the ravaged communities. They attempted to forge alliances with supernatural beings that, on the one hand, would help them carry on, and, on the other, would serve as rallying points to consolidate the native struggle against invasive forces. In highland Chiapas, a young Tzotzil Maya woman named Dominica López had a vision in a cornfield: The Virgin spoke to the woman, requesting that her image be brought into town and a chapel be built for her. The townspeople did as she wished, and Dominica and her husband were named *mayordomos* (stewards) for the Virgin. The Virgin communicated only through Dominica, and she offered to reward the people with an abundant harvest of corn and beans and many children. When the Spaniards realized what a stir this image was creating in surrounding native communities and its quickly expanding number of followers, they took decisive action. The image was carried off to San Cristóbal, where the Spaniards banished it and brought Dominica López and her husband to trial.

At the time of the trial in June 1712, the Virgin appeared again, in the nearby Tzeltal Maya town of Cancuc. María López, another young woman, saw the Virgin and conveyed to her townspeople the Virgin's desire that a chapel be built in her honor on the spot where she appeared. Sebastián Gómez, an indigenous man from nearby San Pedro Chenalhó, claimed to have spoken with the Virgin. He said the Virgin had demanded that a native priesthood replace the Spanish one. Following her orders, Sebastián Gómez ordained a group of Maya men as priests, who took over the functions of the ousted Spanish priesthood. Although these priests were all men, María López became the *mayordoma mayor*; that is, the main steward. María López held the place of honor, standing closest to the image of the Virgin. She was flanked by two native priests who served as her scribes and she conveyed the Virgin's messages to the people (for more on the 1712 rebellion, see Box 5.1).

The Spanish felt threatened by this movement, especially in August 1712, when the rebellious Indians massacred the Spanish population of several highland towns. The Spaniards counterattacked, and finally, after fierce fighting, routed the native rebels. Foreseeing a total military defeat, the Indians appealed to supernatural forces as a last resort to stop the colonial forces. They carried four women, reputedly witches, to the river, invoking female supernatural powers to destroy the enemy. Each woman represented a natural force: earthquake, lightning, flood, and wind.

What do these native uprisings reveal about gender and women in native communities during colonial times? In a general way, they allow us to assess the importance of women in these communities, at a time when severe population decline threatened the survival of the group. The deities that appeared to the young Indian women were female, and probably correspond to *jme'tik*, Our Mother, who in modern Tzotzil Maya cosmology represents both the Moon and Mother Earth and is identified with the Virgin. As the Earth, Our Mother symbolizes fertility—that is, life and renewal of population and crops. She appeared at a time of hunger and hopelessness, offering to bless the Indians with abundant food and children. Dominica López, and later María de la Candelaria, (the name that María López assumed when she became a spokesperson for the Virgin), could be interpreted as symbols of fertility and hope. Furthermore, the association of this cult with the female Earth is confirmed by the recruitment of women witches, representing the forces of nature, to destroy the Spaniards. To this day, the Tzotzil Maya believe that these forces reside in the Earth.

The fact that women assumed the role of stewards in the movement suggests that they were active in the religious organizations of their communities in colonial times. The appointment of women to religious positions was probably an accepted practice.

Women in the Mexican Republic, 1821 to the 1940s

Individual women appear as central figures in the struggles for independence in Mexico and Central America. Up to now, women's participation in these movements has been regarded as restricted to a few exceptional figures. Initial studies of the broader participation of women, however, indicate that they played an active role in the independence movement in Mexico, for example, although it is difficult to assess their numbers or percentage (see Chapter 6). In Mexico City and in Mexican provinces, women hauled messages, arms, and instructions in their baskets from one place to the other. Wealthy women contributed funds to the insurgent cause. One of the most important tasks carried out by women in the independence movement was to attempt to convince soldiers to desert the Royal Army and join the insurgency. In a propaganda document dated 1812, Mexican women were enjoined to enlist in the armed struggle to avenge the deaths of their male relatives by the Spanish army. This document displayed a picture of two women wearing military hats and holding raised swords (Figure 9.4). Although the insurgents praised women's participation as central to the success of the movement, after independence the new republic did not allow women a greater role in political life. Women were not granted the right to vote or hold office. In fact, the opposite happened: Books and newspapers of the period urged women to mind the home and children.

By the end of the nineteenth century, a greater number of women entered into the labor force. At the tobacco and textile factories women had an important presence in the unions. Many unionized women later joined with the opposition to Porfirio Díaz and sought membership in the various political parties and groups that opposed him. Women's participation in the Mexican Revolution was extensive (Figure 9.5). They were incorporated into both the popular and the constitutionalist armies. Because of the promise of lands, peasant women overwhelmingly supported the revolution. They streamed onto the battlefield in large numbers, not only following their husbands to care for their needs, but also acting as nurses, spies, arms providers, and even as combatants on the front. Some women dressed like men in order to get to the front. A battalion exclusively composed of sisters, daughters, and widows of dead soldiers was commanded by a woman. In a few cases, women led male soldiers in combat on specific missions.

Women were startled, however, to learn that the Mexican Constitution of 1917 again denied them the right to vote. Congressmen argued that, although there were a few exceptions, most women had been traditionally restricted to family and home, and, as a consequence, had not yet developed a political awareness. There was no point, therefore, for women to participate in public life.

Figure 9.4 Mexican women heeded the call of this 1812 propaganda document enjoining them to participate in the struggle for their country's independence. "Personajes de un corrido." Archivo General de la Nación (AGN) de Mexico. Peraciones de Guerra: Vol. 406, f. 195 (Catalogue no. 2648).

Women's groups began to emerge in the 1920s. One was the *Consejo Feminista Mexicano* (Mexican Feminist Council), affiliated with the Mexican Communist Party, which tried to engage women, especially those working in factories, in the fight to radically transform the country's socioeconomic structures. The major aim of this group was not the liberation of women but the ultimate conquest of power by proletariats. The Council explicitly dismissed the feminist quest to improve the situation of women, claiming that this played into the hands of the conservative powers and only weakened the revolutionary movement. Another women's group was attached to the ruling revolutionary party. This group's platform pursued the vindication of women's rights, promising to fight against the exploitation of Mexican women; to improve their working conditions; and, more concretely, to organize day care centers, health centers, communal houses, and legal advice centers for women. The two groups clashed with each other as they endeavored to win the hearts and minds of Mexican women.

The ascent of Lázaro Cárdenas to power in 1934 brought the promise of new possibilities for women in the political arena. In 1935 women organized the

Figure 9.5 Mexican women carried out a variety of tasks during the Mexican Revolution, including fighting, nursing the wounded, spying, and providing food and arms to the combatants. Reprinted with permission from Esperanza Tuñón Pablos, *Tambien Somos Protagonistas de la Historia de México, Parte Primera* Mexico City, Mexico: Equipo de Mujeres en Acción Solidaria (EMAS), 1987, p 8.

National Conference of Women, and thus the United Front Pro-Women's Rights (FUPDM) was born. As described in Box 9.3, the Front was an organization that united Mexican women from every ideological, religious, and social persuasion.

Box 9.3 *A Women's Rights Organization in Mexico*

The charter of the United Front Pro-Women's Rights declared its support for basic women's demands, such as equal pay for equal work, the right of women to vote and hold office, and improvement in the working conditions of women. However, the Front presented itself as seeking to improve the general welfare of the population. For example, the Front attempted to influence the government to control the cost of food, rent, and electricity; to improve the salaries of both men and women; to implement an eight-hour working day; and to fight against foreign intervention in Mexican affairs. The Front rejected a purely feminist struggle, claiming that only the joint efforts of men and women would bring about the transformation of society and that a feminist movement would be inevitably divisive.

From 1937 on, the members of the United Front began to focus their activities on the demands for women's vote. In 1937 the Senate once again denied women this right. The Front organized massive protests, inundated the city with posters and fliers, and urged President Cárdenas to remain true to his promise to further the political participation of Mexican women. Responding to this plea, Cárdenas announced that he would initiate reforms leading to the incorporation of women into political life. It was unfair, he argued, that women continue as second-class citizens when they had abundantly proven their commitment to society. Days and months passed, but Cárdenas feared that the women's vote would favor the rightist Catholic opposition party, and thus he did not fulfill his promise.

After Cárdenas, in the confluence of international forces of the early 1940s and the dramatic expansion of industrialization and its concomitant social changes, women had a difficult time regrouping an effective social movement. Politically active women's groups redirected their efforts to charitable organizations, working to improve the situation of the most needy segments of the population. It was not until 1947 that the opportunity was given to women to participate in municipal elections both as voters and as holders of office. Finally, in 1953, President Ruiz Cortínes modified the constitution to grant women full citizen's rights on a par with men.

Rural Native Women in the Mexican Republic, 1821–1940: The Case of Highland Chiapas

Not much changed in the lives of indigenous peoples after independence. In fact, in both Mexico and Central America, their economic situation worsened as the infusion of foreign investment in export products in the second half of the nineteenth century intensified the exploitation of indigenous labor. Furthermore, Catholic priests continued to press the Indians to give up their native beliefs and practices.

In highland Chiapas, a nativistic movement developed as a result of the despair and confusion that prevailed. It began in 1867 when Agustina Gómez Checheb, a young Chamula girl, claimed to have seen three stones falling from the sky while she pastured sheep in the fields. Pedro Díaz Cuscat, an assistant to the priest in Chamula, took over the organization of the cult. He declared that Gómez Checheb had given birth to the stones, and that she was, therefore, "the Mother of God." Through Gómez Checheb the stones talked to the people who came to worship them. She was identified with Saint Rose, an important deity in the Chamula pantheon.

Díaz Cuscat incorporated the cult into the traditional festival cycle and *cofradía* organization. He established a market that attracted a large number of people, who were then recruited into the cult. The movement ended in open confrontation with mestizo authorities, as nine Tzotzil Maya towns participated in the revolt. The confrontation between the Indian and mestizo armies left many people dead on both sides. Like the Virgin cults of 1712, the War of Saint Rose expressed the aspiration of native peoples to establish a cult that would unite them in the worship of a distinct, native deity. The stones that ignited the spark for the rebellion may be interpreted as another expression of the female Earth and its wealth, defined in terms of crops, animals, or money. The participation of women went beyond igniting the spark for the rebellion. They fought alongside their husbands in the battles against mestizo soldiers. According to highland Chiapas folklore, women decided to join in the struggle with the hope that their "cold" female genitals would "cool" the guns (considered a "hot," male item) of the mestizos. This account substantiates the contemporary view held in many highland Chiapas indigenous communities that female genitals are cold in nature—a direct association to the coldness of the Earth's womb. The account also reveals the solidarity of husbands and wives and the decision of men and women to fight their oppressors jointly in a final attempt to rescue their society from seemingly inevitable destruction.

During the Mexican Revolution, indigenous peoples of highland Chiapas were recruited, manipulated, and mistreated by the contending sides. Many native lives were lost. The revolution's promise of land to peasants only began to bear fruit in the region after 1936, when the Cárdenas government embarked on large-scale land reform (see Chapter 7).

From Cárdenas's time to the present, the Mexican government has sought to control and mobilize the indigenous population by effecting changes in the native communities' structure of government. By law each community was required to establish a Constitutional Council that would represent it before state and national authorities. While previously these communities had been governed by civil and religious "cargo" systems headed by respected monolingual elders, since Cárdenas the Mexican government required that Constitutional Councils be constituted by bilingual, experienced men. These conditions led to a drastic transformation of the traditional structure of government in indigenous communities, and to the entrenchment of mestizo power within the communities.

The political changes described above inflicted a severe blow on women. In fact, women had been actively engaged in religious cargos (services) for centuries and had important religious obligations complementary to their husbands' civil positions. In the newly created offices there was no space left for women: first, because Mexican officials, since early colonial times, were accustomed to dealing exclusively with male leaders in indigenous communities; and second, because most indigenous women in highland Chiapas were, and continue to be, monolingual. Their knowledge of and contact with mestizo society and government were, at best, minimal. Even women actively involved in politics in the urban areas had no prospect of gaining public office or suffrage. Therefore, what opportunity did indigenous women have to establish a presence in the newly created councils? Since the 1940s, Constitutional Councils came to stand for a new kind of power in indigenous communities—an elite that is totally male, is strongly secularized, and displays vast economic superiority to the majority of the population. The complementary presence of women, customary in native cargo systems, was lost within the Constitutional Councils.

CURRENT ISSUES IN THE STUDY OF WOMEN AND GENDER

The increase of poverty in the Mesoamerican region and the violent armed confrontations (in Guatemala, El Salvador, and Nicaragua) during the 1980s brought tremendous hardship to the population of the region. But even before these crises, survival had been difficult for the majority of the region's peoples, and large numbers of women were driven out of the domestic sphere and into the informal labor force and armed struggle. As a result of the transformations in their lives, a new awareness of society and self developed. In the 1970s, women's organizations began to develop in earnest, and twenty years later, some of these organizations are advancing feminist causes.

Machismo—the ideology (and corresponding practices) that places a high value on virility as a result of "conquering" a large number of women—is widespread in the region. Machismo shapes the region's patriarchal system in specific ways, placing women under the control of men who may eventually abandon them. Within a system that defines men as the main breadwinners and gives priority to the training and education of men, women frequently must find the means to support their families on their own.

Students of Mexican and Central American society argue that machismo and paternal irresponsibility are less of a problem among indigenous people (especially those living in traditional contexts) than among mestizos or ladinos. Although Indian males engage in extramarital affairs, their culture stresses responsible behavior toward the family. It is more unusual for an indigenous man (as compared to a mestizo) to leave his wife and children to fend for themselves.

The Economic Situation

Responses to the Economic Crisis of the 1980s. The region experienced a drastic economic recession during the 1980s (see Chapter 10). Decreasing standards of living hit the lower classes in a disproportionate way, and among them, women suffered more than men. Several factors contributed to women's vulnerability, their lack of schooling being perhaps one of the most significant. A large proportion of poor women never attend school, or they do so for only one or two years. Additionally, large families prevent these women from seeking formal employment for many years, and lack of access to property and credit minimizes their entrepreneurial possibilities. Malnourishment tends to be twice as high among women as men, making their overall health more precarious. These factors push women into the "informal" sector, which is characterized by low returns, lack of insurance benefits, and little or no job security. Unfortunately, this state of affairs perpetuates women's dependence on their husbands, forcing them to put up with sometimes abusive spouses.

How have women responded to the increasing impoverishment? Mestizo women in the lower strata, in both urban and rural areas, developed a series of strategies to reduce costs and increase income in order to counter the decline in standards of living.

The arrangements devised by Marta Sandoval, a single mestizo mother who lives with her three young children in one of the squatter settlements on the outskirts of San Salvador, illustrate these strategies. To reduce costs, her sister Manuela, with her two children, moved in with Marta. The women hoped to pool their meager resources by sharing rent for the shack where they live, by cooking and eating together, and by helping each other with child care. Marta had lost her janitorial job at a nearby plant several months before, and was leaving at dawn with her six-year-old son to sell newspapers on a busy street corner. Previously, she had paid a neighbor to keep an eye on her children, but now Manuela cares for them. When Marta returns home at noon, Manuela leaves for her job. She washes clothes for a middle-class family three times a week. Though they barely have enough money for their own needs, Manuela and Marta send some money to their parents, who live in a village two hours from the city. The two sisters are happy that they have not had to reduce their food intake as some of their neighbors have. In their settlement, some of the poorest families have begun to search for food in garbage dumps. Under these circumstances, one of the most difficult aspects of life for women such as Marta and Manuela is that, within the prevailing ideology, mothers bear primary responsibility for their children. They often must make critical decisions alone concerning such issues as birth control, abortion, or the abandonment of young babies when conditions are desperate.

Figure 9.6 Deepening poverty in Mesoamerica during the 1980s forced thousands of poor, unskilled women into the labor force, usually in the informal economy.

Before she found work selling newspapers, Marta had tried her hand unsuccessfully at many different jobs in the informal sector. When poverty deepens, people seek any type of work available (Figure 9.6). Among the poorest women, 40 percent are heads of households and the main breadwinners. In such cases, their children and other relatives who may live with them seek additional sources of income to enhance the family's resources. In the 60 percent of households headed by men, wives increase their participation in the informal market, and sometimes children and elderly parents search for an income as well. Poor women increasingly dedicate their energies to working without pay in a family cottage industry, usually under the husband's control. This exacerbates the woman's dependency on her husband. Women rely on older children and relatives to take care of domestic chores and child care in order to free them to work outside the home. Migration to the United States has become an important coping strategy to alleviate poverty; monthly contributions of migrant family members constitute the primary income of many families. In short, among the poorest people in Mexico and Central America, women often have the responsibility for family survival. Their working hours increase enormously as they balance child care, household chores, and urgently needed income-generating activities under extremely precarious conditions (Figure 9.7).

Figure 9.7 In the various economic crises that have gripped the region, women's ingenuity has proved fundamental to survival.

Box 9.4 *Maya Women Ease the Economic Crisis through Domestic Production*

Dominga Quej, an Achí Maya woman from Guatemala, and her family were deeply affected by the economic crisis. Seasonal work in Guatemala's coffee plantations, her family's main source of cash, dwindled considerably. Indigenous women, however, have an advantage over their mestizo counterparts. Their skills in traditional arts are a protection in difficult economic times. Dominga and thousands, perhaps millions, of indigenous women responded to the economic crisis by intensifying domestic production of textiles, pottery, wooden objects, and other craft goods (Figure 9.8). Indeed, although in the past Dominga had always woven some items for sale in addition to weaving her family's clothes, she began to spend many hours weaving for the tourist market in order to compensate for her family's lost income from seasonal plantation work. This strategy, according to researchers, not only enables women like Dominga to improve their economic situation somewhat when recession strikes, but also lets them do so without giving up control over tools, techniques, and work schedules. By working at home or close by, women are able to structure their domestic chores and child care around productive activities. By intensifying artisan production, women resist total incorporation into the capitalist sector, where they would be easy prey for direct exploitation.

Dominga employs techniques handed down from her ancestors, and this enables her and most indigenous women in the area to successfully preserve their own cultural identity and reinforce the values and beliefs they hold dear. Most indigenous men, in contrast, increasingly opt for wage labor—usually away from the community—and expose themselves to strong acculturative forces that threaten their identity and the preservation of their culture. Consequently, women gain leverage over their husbands by being economically active and by becoming symbols of ethnic identity and culture. For the most part, ethnic distinctiveness is still highly regarded by both men and women in traditional society.

As Box 9.4 reveals, in contrast to poor mestizo women, indigenous women in the region—although equally poor and not formally educated—are trained at a young age in the community's traditional arts and thus can cope better.

Gender and Modernization of Indigenous Societies. Gender studies conducted among the Zapotec in Oaxaca, Mexico, and the Maya in Chiapas and Guatemala indicate that the indigenous population living in traditional communities appears to have a more egalitarian gender system than their corresponding socioeconomic class within the mestizo population.

Among the Tzotzil Chamula of highland Chiapas, for example, women and men contribute equally to the family economy. While men tend the milpas and engage in wage labor in distant places, women take care of the children and domestic animals and devote many hours to the production of textiles for sale. In addition, they take over the milpa while their husbands work away from home. The cash contribution of women (as well as the other services they provide) is indispensable to the survival of the family. This interdependence between husband and wife strengthens their relationship.

In Chamula and many other traditional societies, men and women are not considered adults until they marry. A man cannot opt for political or religious office unless he has a wife to fulfill the required complementary duties of his posi-

Figure 9.8 Practicing the ancient arts of spinning and weaving, indigenous women contribute to the survival of their family while preserving their ancestors' culture.

tion. Although women are barred from civil office, the joint participation of husband and wife in the religious *cargo* system (or *cofradía*) enhances communication and cooperation between them, and strengthens the marital bond. Chamulans say that the deities served by husband and wife grant blessings unto the couple, bringing material well-being and improving the spousal relationship. In this way, Chamula culture encourages the interdependence of husband and wife.

This holds true especially in the lower socioeconomic sectors. Among higher-income indigenous people, the interdependence between spouses diminishes. As mentioned above, the male bias of the larger society determines men's greater access to education, credit, and contacts with the outside world. When a man's income is much higher than his wife's, her contribution to the family economy is slighted. She becomes more dependent on her husband's income, thereby losing leverage.

In the past twenty years, many indigenous communities have experienced an intense penetration of modern capital, which has radically altered the gender system. In the Mam Maya town of San Pedro Sacatepéquez in Guatemala, for example, the introduction of capitalism brought about a remarkable rise in the living standards of its population. Similar processes took place among the Zapotec of Teotitlán del Valle with the entry of artisan production in the international markets, and among the Zapotec of the Sierra de Oaxaca when coffee as a major commercial crop replaced a household-oriented system of production. These three communities suffered a transformation from a situation of relative egalitarianism among the population to the gradual development and crystallization of social classes. Gender stratification also evolved as a clear outcome of the massive penetration of capitalism. The position of women deteriorated in a dramatic way.

How did this happen? Because of their advantages, men were able to secure loans; buy trucks; engage in more modern, industrialized production; or forge links with national and international markets to sell their products. Restricted to traditional, nonefficient productive techniques, women's income remained constant or even diminished as the demand for industrial goods in their townships began to replace that of products of the cottage industries (the latter in the hands of women). Whereas, as noted before, in traditional communities women are highly valued as bulwarks of identity and continuity, in rapidly modernizing societies, women become identified with backwardness. Women, thus, lose power and are less likely to be influential in important family decisions. They tend to become increasingly dependent on their husbands, who have ultimate control of the money. Frequently this dependency implies that women have no alternative but to tolerate their husbands' infidelity or mistreatment.

The Incorporation of the Region into the Global Economy. As part of the drive to capitalize on the abundant and inexpensive labor supplies in Third World countries, many international companies have set up assembly operations (*maquilas*) in the region. While industries owned by nationals of Mexico and Central America traditionally have employed mainly men, most maquilas employ women. The explanation for the different employment strategies is found in the prevailing patriarchal ideology: Considered the chief breadwinners for the family, and offered greater opportunities to receive an education and technical training, men gain access to the best jobs—those with benefits, security, and stability. In contrast, conceptualized primarily as housewives and mothers, whose productivity is inevitably and properly limited by these roles and whose income is only supplementary, women do not "merit" training and formal employment. Many parents argue that education is wasted on their daughters since their future domestic roles make it unnecessary. This ideology and the practices it generates led traditionally to the concentration of the female labor force in the informal, self-employed sector of the economy.

Ironically, the "comparative disadvantages" of women—including their culturally shaped submissiveness and docility, and their willingness to accept a lower wage for lack of alternatives—turns women into the most desirable workers for maquilas. Thus, the Mexican economists Arizpe and Aranda (1962:193) argue that the "comparative disadvantages" of women have been translated into "comparative advantages" for companies, capitals, and governments in the international markets.

Exploiting existing values and practices that maintain the subordination and docility of women, maquilas reinforce the traditional patriarchal system. Although this employment provides women with alternatives to self-employment, domestic service, or wage-labor on the land, it does nothing to improve women's economic situation, general educational level, or technical skills. These jobs represent only a temporary palliative for the young women (ages sixteen to twenty-four) who constitute the maquilas' preferred labor force. And so the involvement of the region in the global economy has not created the conditions for long-term development that would bring about major changes in the lives of women. Moreover, this involvement has posed no challenge to the existing gender structures that privilege men.

Politico-Military Crises in Mesoamerica

Women played a central role in the struggle to effect radical changes in the socioeconomic structures of their countries, a struggle that led to civil wars in Guatemala, El Salvador, and Nicaragua from the late 1970s to the late 1980s (see Chapter 7). Similarly, although it is too soon to expect detailed discussions of the process through which women have joined the Zapatista uprising in Chiapas (1994), women do appear to have a large presence in the movement, both as combatants and as supporters (see the Epilogue).

In the early 1960s, the "popular church"—or "church of the poor," as it is sometimes called (that is, grassroots Catholic organizations such as Catholic Action or catechist programs)—sought to incorporate women into its organizations in Mexico, Guatemala, El Salvador, Honduras, and Nicaragua. The main objective was to raise women's awareness of the need to fight the widespread oppression and inequality in their countries. Women attended courses and began to confront openly the ideology of machismo, dealing with and overcoming feelings of inadequacy and training to assume leadership roles in the communities. These analyses helped women to gain a feminist consciousness (see Box 9.5). Given the tremendous social and economic problems of the region, however, the involvement of women in the "church of the poor" led primarily to their extensive politicization.

When armed struggles erupted in Guatemala, El Salvador, and Nicaragua, many women eagerly joined the rebel forces. Among them were poor peasant women, including indigenous women in Guatemala; urban working-class women; and middle-class, educated mestizo women. Many women joined the insurgency as a result of appalling actions perpetrated against their families and communities by the military. Victims of rape, their villages razed to the ground, their close relatives kidnapped and murdered, women felt compelled to protect themselves from the army and avenge the deaths of their loved ones.

Women joined the struggle in a variety of ways: Some went to the front as combatants; others produced propaganda material, occupied local radio stations to gain support for the insurgency, and wrote communiqués for newspapers. In the mountains and villages, women acted as doctors and nurses, and they fed, clothed, and sheltered combatants. Women also provided infrastructural support, allowing the insurgents to convene in their homes, transporting explosives and guns, and acting as messengers.

Many widows, and women whose husbands, fathers, or children had been

Box 9.5 *Taming Macho Ways*

"When I started working with the mothers' clubs in the Catholic Church, it was the first time I realized that we women work even harder than the men do.

"We get up before they do to grind the corn and make tortillas and coffee for their breakfast. Then we work all day—taking care of the kids, washing the clothes, ironing, mending our husband's old rags, cleaning the house. We hike to the mountains looking for wood to cook with. We walk to the stream or the well to get water. We make lunch and bring it to the men in the field. And we often grab a hoe and help in the fields. We never sit still one minute. . . .

"Men may be out working during the day, but when they come home they usually don't do a thing. They want their meal to be ready, and after they eat they either lie down to rest or go out drinking. But we women keep on working—cooking the corn and beans for the next day's meal, watching the children.

"I don't think it's fair that the women do all the work. Maybe it's because I've been around more and I've seen other relationships. But I think that if two people get together to form a home, it should be because they love and respect each other. And that means that they should share everything."

From Medea Benjamin, trans. and ed., *Don't Be Afraid Gringo: A Honduran Woman Speaks from the Heart. The Story of Elvia Alvarado.* New York: HarperCollins, 1989, pp. 51–52.

kidnapped and disappeared, joined human rights organizations such as GAM and CONAVIGUA in Guatemala (Figure 9.9); Mothers and Relatives of the Disappeared in El Salvador; Relatives of Jailed and Disappeared People in Honduras; and Mothers of Heroes and Martyrs in Nicaragua. Women, who constitute the majority of the membership of these organizations, initially entered seeking economic and emotional support and to gain some leverage by functioning within a group (see Box 9.6). Many of them came from the ranks of indigenous peasant women, illiterate and humble. The traumas they suffered and their work in these organizations brought about the politicization of motherhood. These women now stage public protests, pressuring governments to find the whereabouts of their loved ones and to punish the people responsible for their deaths or disappearances. Through their accusations of human rights violations to the international forum, they have procured effective worldwide support for their cause. As a result of their activism, women have gained a deeper understanding of the roots of poverty and violence in their countries and now seek to transform their societies so that their children may have a better future (see Box 9.7). A similar process of awareness and development of activism has taken place in the refugee camps in Mexico, where thousands of Guatemalan Maya widows fled in terror with their children.

Women had to overcome major obstacles in this quest to become active in the insurgency. They needed first to establish child care arrangements that would enable them to leave the home and join the struggle. It was not easy to prevail over their husbands' resistance to their involvement. Even revolutionary men made it difficult for their wives to join in the fight, claiming that women who did this were disregarding the needs of their children and husbands. On the battlefront, leaders and combatants alike opposed women's participation in actual combat, and instead gave women tasks such as caring for the sick, cooking, cov-

Figure 9.9 Like thousands of women in Guatemala, El Salvador, and Nicaragua, this woman, holding a picture of her missing son, joined the opposition movement in her country as a result of a personal tragedy. Jim Tynan/Impact Visuals.

ering for a male combatant, and preparing a mission. Women, however, did not acquiesce; they demanded equality of participation and jobs of greater responsibility. According to many female insurgents, women had to work twice as hard as men and be twice as courageous to be allowed into important positions. Eventually, as the war intensified and women became indispensable, men realized the need to incorporate women fully into the fight and opened the way for their participation at all levels. In the struggle to overthrow Somoza in Nicaragua, and in some of the areas controlled by the guerrillas in El Salvador, women accounted for about a third of the insurgent forces. Some women were even able to rise to leadership positions.

In contrast to the movements in Guatemala, El Salvador, and Nicaragua, from its inception women found a place in the Zapatista rebellion in Chiapas as combatants and in positions of leadership on a par with men. Maya women constitute about one-third of the combat forces and 55 percent of the popular sup-

Box 9.6 *Testimony of a GAM Woman*

"I joined GAM because my compañero, Gustavo Adolfo Castañón Fuentes, was kidnapped on May 24, 1984. He was a student at the University of San Carlos. My husband wasn't alone—he was kidnapped with two other compañeros. It's not easy to talk about this. You lose someone you loved, someone you've shared with. What I've tried to do is just keep going—to get over it. But I can't completely get over it. . . .

"With some members of my husband's family, I began a personal search. Looking back, joining GAM helped me a lot emotionally and spiritually because I could channel my hope, my faith and my struggle. . . .

"If you go to one of our demonstrations, you'll notice that most of us are women. And we're women who have discovered our capacity for struggle, our capacity for resistance. We've been left alone with four, five, six children, and we have to keep going. It gives me great hope.

"Those theories that women are weak or whatever can be overcome. But it won't be easy. We aren't in favor of a struggle between the sexes. Women and men have to come together to forge a new society, and within this new society, we each have to struggle for our place. Only our concrete efforts will achieve this."

From María Ixabel Choxóm López, , "We Aren't Widows." In Emilie Smith-Ayala, *The Granddaughters of Ixmucané: Guatemalan Women Speak.* Toronto: Women's Press, 1991, pp. 119–124.

Box 9.7 *How CONAVIGUA Came to Life*

"Since I was fourteen I joined groups of young Catholics, cooperative groups and literacy groups. We taught women using their own experiences, employing the milpa, a hoe, a broom, to teach them to read and write in connection with their reality.

"Our lives changed after the earthquake of 1976. We devoted our energies to reconstruct our town and villages. Our communal organization was increasingly stronger because everybody participated in the work of reconstruction.

"Then the violence came, in 1979. We were disbanded. Our work became extremely difficult, many women disappeared, others were murdered. The whole population was terrorized. The groups disintegrated. Everybody felt persecuted. . . .

"In 1984, while I was living in the city with my family, my husband was kidnapped and I was left alone with two children. . . . I had to sell vegetables in the city every day with my children. It is thus that I had the opportunity to meet other sisters that were also widows. We supported each other, we began to weave together and our work grew.

"We were here in Guatemala City, all of us widows, when we learned about similar groups in Chimaltenango. There were groups all over the country and we began to communicate. That is how CONAVIGUA came to life; it was not the work of one or two women, but of many, seeking help, seeking corn. In the first Assembly of Widows there were one hundred representatives of the different groups. I was chosen as a member of the board because I was one of the three women, among those 100, who knew how to read, write and speak Spanish. This Assembly opened the eyes of many women. Sharing our problems strengthened us. . . .

"At this point CONAVIGUA has many projects in the areas of agriculture, crafts, health, education, and literacy. We have small local projects in some villages, such as producing straw hats, raising cows and pigs, and setting up electric mills to grind corn.

"Some members of our organization write poetry. We have dancing and singing groups. You can see how much women have learned by the way they write their documents of protest. Now the women don't hide away from their problems any longer, they confront them."

From "Rosalina Tuyuc: Our Lives Changed Since the Earthquake," interview published in *Siglo Veintiuno,* April 20, 1993. Translated by Brenda Rosenbaum.

port of the Zapatista National Liberation Army. During the peace talks between rebel leaders and representatives of the Mexican government, female commanders Ana María, Ramona, and Maribel shared the negotiating table with Subcomandante Marcos, and journalists witnessed the internationally renowned Marcos taking orders from Ramona, a slight woman wearing a multicolored, handwoven *huipil*. Furthermore, the Zapatista movement has acknowledged explicitly and demanded an end to the specific oppression suffered by women. According to a female combatant, many women fight today hoping to enable their daughters to become doctors or lawyers tomorrow.

It is too early to assess the long-term consequences of these armed struggles for the gender relations in the region. The heights in awareness and self-assurance achieved by women as an aftermath of their participation in their countries' civil wars, as well as the new respect men have gained for women's competence, might have lasting effects on their relations as civilian life reclaims society again. If, however, these countries return to the preconflict status quo, the situation of women may rapidly slide back because of the lack of economic and social opportunities and the backlash of the patriarchal resolve to keep male prerogatives intact.

Gender Awareness and the Women's Movement in Mesoamerica

Facing head-on the limitations imposed by gender discrimination and machismo, and breaking ground to establish their rights, women involved in the insurgency have come to realize their strength, competence, and worth in a variety of contexts, and to acknowledge the male bias of society. Most political activists, however, firmly believe that the revolutionary struggle requires the joint participation of men and women and that the quest to further women's rights would weaken the larger plan to transform society.

The countries of the region did not grant women the right to vote and to be elected to political office until the period between the mid-1940s and the mid-1950s. Moreover, in most countries, these rights were not won as a result of energetic action taken by suffragist groups, as happened in Mexico, but as a consequence of the United Nations' pronouncement, after the war, that such rights be adopted.

Although some charitable and politically active women's groups began to emerge in Central America after the 1950s, it was not until the 1970s that a large number of women's groups began to appear in the area. The impetus to create these groups originated in the international sphere, with the UN's declaration of the Decade of Women. Professional women's organizations proliferated in the region, and several women's groups emerged to support the insurgency movements in the area. These groups are described in Box 9.8.

The Zapatista movement in Chiapas seems to be exceptional in its willingness to identify women's oppression as a central problem of society and, consequently, as one of the main targets of its struggle. At the very beginning of the uprising, the EZLN (Ejército Zapatista de Liberación Nacional) proclaimed

Box 9.8 *Women's Organizations in Contemporary Central America*

Just as occurred in Mexico in the 1920s and 1930s, two main types of women's organizations appeared in Central America in the 1970s: those seeking to mobilize women for political programs and those directly addressing women's rights.

While acknowledging women's specific problems, most organizations in those countries sought to mobilize women for the insurgency cause. In revolutionary circles, the fight to improve women's conditions was deemed a "fabrication" of middle-class women. Most revolutionaries, indeed, contend that women were not oppressed by men but by bourgeois society and that "women's problems" would disappear as soon as the revolution changed the exploitative structures of society. AMNLAE (Association of Nicaraguan Women Luisa Amanda Espinoza), the women's section of the Sandinista party, for example, coordinated the integration of women into general revolutionary tasks. After the Sandinistas came into power, women became active in literacy campaigns, local defense and agrarian committees, and mass organizations of different types. Because of its close ties to the Sandinistas, AMNLAE never developed an analysis of women's oppression or responded to women's requests for assistance with problems such as domestic violence, sexual harassment, paternal irresponsibility, and birth control. After years of arduous work with women, AMNLAE realized that specific conditions in women's lives hindered both their involvement in production and their participation in the political process. Finally, in 1987, the FSLN (the Sandinista party in power) promulgated an official document, the *Proclamation on Women*, a recognition of women's specific problems. It acknowledged that women suffer additional exploitation and that their struggles within the revolutionary process were legitimate; it condemned machismo and argued that women's issues could not be discarded until the Contra war was over. The *Proclamation* meant that women's emancipation was of concern to the country's policymakers. After the Sandinistas left power in 1990, independent feminist organizations began making inroads in the women's movement in Nicaragua, creating a feminist awareness and offering medical and legal advice, sex therapy, and gynecological treatment for women.

In Guatemala and El Salvador, most women's organizations geared their efforts to supporting the political struggle. Although awareness of the situation of women has sprung out of the joint participation of men and women in the different arenas of the struggle, the needs of women have not yet been directly addressed. Among these organizations are AMES (Association of Women of El Salvador) and, in Guatemala, CONAVIGUA, the widows' organization, and GAM. In Honduras, women peasant organizations emerged in different areas of the country, with the specific purpose of demanding access to land and property; protesting human rights violations; and demanding services such as education, income-generating projects, and training from their government.

In Costa Rica, by 1990, about 150 women's organizations had come together in a confederation that seeks to create and encourage programs to study gender, supports organizations fighting against the discrimination of women, and struggles to incorporate women in the political processes of the country.

Feminist organizations in the other Central American countries are just beginning to develop. Through radio programs, magazines, and meetings they discuss machismo, help women achieve self-confidence, and fight to incorporate women into social and political programs. Many of these organizations offer a variety of day care facilities to working women, and legal and medical advice and services.

"Women's Revolutionary Laws." Some of these entail the rights of women within the Zapatista rebellion, and others demand that women receive an equal wage for equal work and access to education, health, and community leadership. The most progressive feminist demands, however, given the conservative nature of the gender system in Chiapas, concern the rights of women to determine the size of their families, to select their own husbands, and to be free not to marry against their will. The laws also call for the implementation of severe punishments for rape and domestic violence. Zapatistas included these laws in the list of requests presented to the Mexican government as a prerequisite to ending the armed struggle. As more information on the movement becomes available, it will be interesting to assess the basis for the dramatic difference in the importance accorded to women by the Zapatistas as opposed to the other insurrections in the region.

Organizations working for feminist causes have not been as strong in Chiapas as they have been elsewhere in Mexico. The Mexican feminist movement has been the most active and successful. From its inception early in this century, it has ebbed and flowed in consonance with national and international political climates. The movement has made great strides in the past twenty-five years. There are hundreds of women's organizations working at both state and national levels. These have promoted in-depth analyses of women's situations, successfully disseminated results through the mass media, and regularly held feminist conventions. Mexican women follow with interest feminist discussions presented in magazines, radio, television, and newspapers. Topics such as voluntary pregnancy, birth control, decriminalization of abortion, sterilization, homosexuality, sexual harassment, rape, and domestic violence—hardly ever discussed in the other countries of the region—have been forcefully brought to the Mexican collective consciousness. Dealing with those issues openly has furthered the awareness of women in all social classes of the need to confront patriarchal domination. Thousands of women—especially middle-class, professional, and unionized women, and to a lesser degree women in rural areas—are demanding the right to control their bodies, equality in the job market, and access to decision making in public life. They are pressuring political parties to deal systematically with women's issues in government programs and to include women as candidates in their slates. Even though women are still grossly underrepresented in the highest and medium-rank political positions, they have begun to make inroads and are now increasing their presence in national and state political bodies.

In general, much needs to be done in Mexico and Central America to make the system more gender-equitable. Because of the military conflicts in Central America and the devastating poverty of the majority of the population in the region, gender awareness has been slow to develop. Neither men nor women view the effort to liberate women from the oppressive conditions imposed by patriarchy as a priority at this stage. Nevertheless, the relative political stability and better economic situation of a wider sector of the population in Mexico and Costa Rica have opened windows for feminist awareness and practices. The example of Rigoberta Menchú, as a humble indigenous woman who dared to challenge the established order and who reached the heights of international recognition, will unquestionably remain an inspiration to Mesoamerican women for years to come.

SUGGESTED READINGS

BEHAR, RUTH 1989 Sexual Witchcraft, Colonialism and Women's Powers: Views from the Mexican Inquisition. In *Sexuality and Marriage in Latin America,* edited by Asunción Lavrin, pp. 178–206. Lincoln: University of Nebraska Press.

BENJAMIN, MEDEA (trans. and ed.) 1989 *Don't Be Afraid Gringo: A Honduran Woman Speaks from the Heart. The Story of Elvia Alvarado.* New York: HarperCollins Publishers.

BURKHART, LOUISE 1995 Mexica Women on the Home Front: Housework and Religion in Aztec Mexico. *In Indian Women in Early Mexico: Identity, Ethnicity and Gender Differentiation,* edited by Susan Schroeder, Stephanie Wood and Robert Haskett. Norman: University of Oklahoma Press. (In press.)

COLLINSON, HELEN (ed.) 1990 *Women and Revolution in Nicaragua.* London and Atlantic Highlands, N.J.: Zed Books Ltd.

EBER, CHRISTINE 1995 *Women and Drinking in a Highland Maya Town: Water of Hope, Water of Sorrow.* Austin: University of Texas Press.

FRANCO, JEAN 1989 *Plotting Women: Gender and Representation in Mexico.* New York: Columbia University Press.

KELLOG, SUSAN 1988 Cognatic Kinship and Religion: Women in Aztec Society. In *Smoke and Mist: Mesoamerican Studies in Memory of Thelma D. Sullivan,* 2 vols., edited by J. Kathryn Josserand and Karen Dakin, pp. 666–681. Oxford: B.A.R.

MENCHÚ, RIGOBERTA 1984 *I, Rigoberta Menchú: An Indian Woman in Guatemala,* edited by Elizabeth Burgos-Debray. London: Verso.

NASH, JUNE 1978 The Aztecs and the Ideology of Male Dominance. *Signs* 4:349–362.

1993 Maya Household Production in the World Market: The Potters of Amatenango del Valle, Chiapas, Mexico. In *Crafts in the World Market: The Impact of Global Exchange on Middle American Artisans,* edited by June Nash. Albany: State University of New York Press.

ROSENBAUM, BRENDA 1993 *With Our Heads Bowed: The Dynamics of Gender in a Maya Community.* Studies on Culture and Society, vol. 5, Institute for Mesoamerican Studies. Albany: State University of New York.

SMITH-AYALA, EMILIE 1991 *The Granddaughters of Ixmucané: Guatemalan Women Speak.* Toronto: Women's Press.

STEPHEN, LYNN 1991 *Zapotec Women.* Austin: University of Texas Press.

Chapter 10
The Political and Cultural Economy of Mesoamerica

A young Maya woman is sitting at a sewing machine by the door of a small adobe room, the only source of light. She is putting together a black sport jacket. It is a shiny polyester and cotton blend with a fashionable style. It was designed by her employer, who likes to copy some styles and innovate others. He purchases the materials in the city, designs and cuts the pieces, and then hires young, single women and men to assemble them. The woman is using his sewing machine while other workers whom he employs work at home using their own equipment. Her brothers are working in the corn fields.

This is an example of the wide and complex range of activities that the present-day peoples of the ancient Mesoamerican region practice in order to make a living. The most industrialized sectors currently produce for international markets, assemble goods for the most developed countries using labor-intensive programs, and produce items that require highly developed technologies. Most industrial centers are located in or around urban centers. Labor, however, is drawn heavily from rural areas. In the rural areas, we find producers of diverse crops; foodstuffs; crafts; and smaller, labor-intensive industries, such as the garment producers of the western highlands of Guatemala, exemplified above. Just like their urban counterparts, they are dependent on the whims and fluctuations of international markets.

In this chapter we will introduce the various ways in which people earn a living, and the ways in which they organize themselves in the process of production. This is an introduction to the economies of Mesoamerica. The *economy* is defined here as all those aspects of society related to the production, distribution, and consumption of goods and services. It is of interest to assess in this context the kinds of relations people establish among themselves as they produce a given item. These relations are an indication of the degree of stratification found in a given society. An analysis of some of the technological, social, and cultural changes that people experience enables us to understand the nature of the changing societies in which they live. Our goal is to show that the different actors, producers, and consumers throughout Mesoamerica are undergoing some common processes of differentiation and change. Our focus will be on the native, indigenous peoples as they participate in the national economy, and the strategies they devise to survive under changing and often strenuous conditions. Indigenous peoples participate in a variety of ways in the economies of the region. In some settings, such as agriculture, cattle ranching, and wage labor, they share markets and opportunities with sectors of the mestizo population. The range of activities of native peoples includes semi-subsistence forms, which always include some form of access to markets; various combinations of agriculture and manufactures; wage labor in small family enterprises; and larger industrial settings.

A BRIEF HISTORICAL REVIEW OF PRODUCTION FORMS AND USE OF LABOR

As pointed out elsewhere in this volume (see Chapter 7), there is large ethnic diversity in the region. Over fifty different languages are spoken throughout Mexico, twenty-two in Guatemala, and others in the rest of the region (see Chapter 11). Ethnic diversity often is related to occupational specialization. In fact, specialization of production by village currently characterizes most of the rural areas of the region, except for the most mestizo areas. Within many areas, it is possible to identify products with a particular village. Since the contact period, Spanish priests encouraged villagers to learn new crafts or skills, or to intensify the production of certain products. Spaniards were interested, in part, in the education of the native peoples. However, they were particularly concerned with the Europeans' own well-being, as they required a steady provision of items that they themselves did not intend to produce in the New World. The Europeans had a direct impact on the type and organization of economic activities conducted by the Mesoamericans. Production activities often changed as new products were incorporated or willfully adopted, following the demand generated by the Spaniards. To the already existing network of open markets, the Europeans requested (or more accurately, ordered) the creation of additional markets. Their goal was to serve their own needs, particularly in the newly created administrative towns. With the introduction of new products, new needs were also generated within the native households. New taxes and tributes were imposed, and with the expectation of payment in cash instead of in kind, Mesoamericans had to resort to new occupations. In Chapter 4, we discussed the impact of Spanish institutions, like the *encomienda* and *repartimiento,* on Indian towns. The requirements of forced labor and payment of tributes produced significant changes in the native production forms. In addition, Indians experienced great losses when their coastal lands were separated from the original townships. The coastal *estancias* (ranches), for example, were lands that originally belonged to highland townships but were arbitrarily expropriated by colonial authorities through the *congregaciones* (reunions and forced resettlement of towns). Indians lost access to lands and therefore to the possibility of growing products that were only available in those ecological contexts. They then had to resort to purchasing goods that they originally produced, reducing their chances for self-sufficiency and generating further dependence on the markets.

Indian slavery was declared illegal by the mid-sixteenth century, but some forms of labor that followed, including temporary forced labor, resembled slavery very closely. The work in haciendas and plantations throughout the colonial and independence years has always been described as slave-like. Workers were forced to purchase food and clothing from the owner's store, often at prices much higher than they could afford. As a result, they would regularly become indebted and then be forced to return to (or remain in) the landlord's field for an undetermined time. Debt servitude coexisted with work in mines and textile factories. Besides contract work in the plantations, the eighteenth century was also characterized by the coexistence of several forms of labor, including sharecropping, subsistence agriculture, and wage labor. The need for cash brought more native peoples to wage labor. The nature of the work changed slightly as the emphasis in commercial agriculture moved from cochineal, sugar, cotton, coffee, and fruits in the nineteenth and twentieth centuries. It was in the nineteenth century that most of the remaining communal lands were taken away from peasant townships throughout Mesoamerica. The justification for this was that the lands were not used and fell into the category of "vacant lands."

The forms of labor just outlined were often pursued in multiple forms by individual peasants. A peasant family could own a piece of land for partial subsistence; work seasonally in the plantations; and engage in other forms of contract, wage labor, or independent artisan production. The diverse forms of labor imply different degrees of control on the part of employers-owners over workers. Contract work in the plantations represented the highest degree of control and subjection of work. Sharecropping (working on the owner's lands in exchange for part of the harvest) and wage labor represented intermediate forms of control, with the workers retaining the relative power of resorting to alternative options. Subsistence agriculture and artisanry were the preferred forms from the worker's perspective.

We will describe the current economic practices of Mesoamerican peoples in five major sections. The first section provides some background and contextual information about economies in Mesoamerica. In section two, we consider such basic production strategies as wage labor, petty commodity production, cottage industries, and *maquiladora* industries. Section three is concerned with distribution, with an emphasis on periodic markets and the culture of marketing. In section four, we consider the interplay between economy and culture. The final section consists of a discussion of Mesoamerican economies in the broader context of the world system.

LAND AND LABOR

Peasants in Mesoamerica

A great portion of the population of the region is made up of the peasant sector. The term *peasant* is used to describe diverse populations. Some scholars would prefer to drop the term altogether, but its use continues to be widespread and seems to serve a function. At its most general (and vague) level, "peasant" refers to societies or sectors of societies that are linked to a larger, dominant society or sector. Most people think of peasants in the context of capitalist systems. They are present, however, in other economic systems as well. For example, as rural inhabitants depending on and providing labor to other sectors, peasants were a key part of feudal society. While often associated with isolated rural settlements, some peasants live in smaller urban centers and retain some linkages to agriculture.

Most peasants own at least a small parcel of land, where they have a house and perhaps a garden. Yet many peasants have no land. They must rent land to cultivate crops, or rent a site for their house and then work for wages for other peasants in the nearest towns and cities. Some peasants work seasonally in haciendas and plantations. These people are also called rural proletariats. Other peasants are engaged in commercial activities. They commercialize their own surpluses or act as intermediaries. Some combine wage labor with subsistence production. Others may fish, hunt, gather wild plants, and grow crops. The stereotypical agricultural inhabitant who owns enough land for self-sufficiency and cooks the food he or she produces is rare in the region today. Rather, peasants represent women and men involved in multiple activities. They may be agriculturalists who are connected to other peoples through the marketing system. They may depend strongly on items produced by others in rural towns and in national and international factories. Some scholars believe that the capitalist system exploits rural producers. They see the system as dependent on family labor, low costs, and low prices of products produced by the peasant sector. When we talk about peasants, we need to qualify the production processes people are involved with, and specify their relation to the larger society of which they are part (Figure 10.1).

Rural-Urban Migration

A recent phenomenon observed in the region, which dates especially to the 1950s and 1960s, is the migration of people from rural areas to the cities. The population of the cities is increasing at rates that far exceed the possibilities of

Figure 10.1 Day laborers in Chiapas, Mexico. JEFFREY JAY FOXX/NYC

absorption. Urban primacy, which refers to the concentration of people, resources, and services in one central city, characterizes most Latin American cities, including those of Mexico and Central America. The concentration of elites, industry, and population in cities creates centers that are spatially split along class lines, with areas of the cities clearly marked with respect to specific socioeconomic sectors.

Owing to general population increase, rural areas are also experiencing population increases, but at lower rates than urban centers. The general migration trends have created a new sector of the economy that has been termed the "informal" economy. This sector is formed by independent vendors of a large variety of products. It includes chain vendors who function as franchises of some established product, shoe shiners, and many other occupations whose economic actors were in the past classified as unemployed. Often underestimated, the informal sector constitutes an important part of the larger economies. Most migrants come to the cities because of the lack of land and sources of employment in their rural settings. As dispossessed peasants, they have no land and can only obtain a few days of work as day laborers in their villages. Their only other options for sustenance are occasional work in haciendas and plantations; migration to the cities; or migration to other countries, particularly the United States. We will come back to this issue in the last section of this chapter.

Land Loss and Land Tenure

As in other parts of Latin America, land distribution patterns in Mesoamerica usually correspond to either the latifundio (large estates) or the minifundio (small farms) type. Most land in the area is owned by a few landowners (latifundio). A small fraction of land is divided into thousands of very small plots, often smaller than five acres (minifundio), which are owned by the vast majority of the rural population. These small subsistence plots, where people usually grow some corn, beans, and squash, are not sufficient to provide a family with all their agricultural needs for a year. Families often must purchase basic products. This situation results from a combination of factors, including land expropriations, population increase, and native inheritance laws.

As stated earlier, land dispossession began at the moment of the European invasion and has continued until the present. Some expropriation was carried out through national legislation, while other expropriations took the form of land purchases from peasants, who needed cash and had no other recourse. In Guatemala, the lands were used for the production of indigo (blue dye), cacao, sugar cane, cochineal (a source of red dye), and coffee in the nineteenth century, followed by cotton, bananas, and other products throughout the twentieth century. Early in the nineteenth century, Guatemalan legislation was passed permitting people to rent communal lands and forcing communities to rent "unused" lands. Even when peasants were offered money for their lands, they resisted what they thought would be a major loss of resources. Expropriations continued, and currently some landless peasants are attempting land takeovers at the risk of their lives. In Mexico, peasants were allowed to keep some land, at least until the beginning of the nineteenth century. However, by 1910, most rural families (96 percent) owned no land, and the haciendas controlled the land of the country. Before the revolution, communal Indian holdings were located primarily in the south of Mexico. These were the model for the contemporary *ejido* program, instituted by the Constitution of 1917, which expropriated land from the haciendas and gave it to agrarian communities. This was accomplished in two formats. The first was an individual form, where a small plot was given to one family to work, to pass on to their children, but not to sell, and where pasture and woodlands were community owned and shared. The second was a collective form, where the community worked the land as a unit. Most ejido lands were given individually.

In 1992 an amendment to the Mexican Constitution was passed that allows for the privatization of community-held ejido land. The amendment permits the rental of ejido land, a practice already in effect, and thus formally terminates land redistribution by the government. The new regulations have many implications. Additional inequalities may result from the changes: Who is going to sell their lands? Where will new investments flow? Will this encourage further migration and land concentration? In spite of the fact that half of the cultivated land is now part of ejidos, there continue to be large landholdings in Mexico and, through leases and rental agreements, land concentration is a problem for rural families.

In both Guatemala and Mexico, the problem still is the existence of minifundios and landless peasants. Combined, they constitute half of the total rural population. Contributing to the minifundio system are the local inheritance rules, which often demand the equal distribution of land and other resources among all children, and the further diminishing access to land for each passing generation. Coupled with population increases, all of this has resulted in the development of a large sector of landless peasants. These peasants find themselves forced to leave their towns as they are unable to save enough money to buy or rent land. In most areas, villagers have followed the sometimes implicit rule of not selling land to outsiders. In recent years, however, entrepreneurial peasants have decided to ignore this traditional rule in order to gain access to land at prices that they can afford. This is the case of some villages in western Guatemala such as San Pedro Almolonga, described in Box 10.1.

Box 10.1 *Agricultural Petty Commodity Production: A Case Study of the Quiché Maya Township of San Pedro Almolonga, "The Central American Garden"*

Almolongueños are seen selling vegetables in most markets of the central area of the marketing system of western Guatemala—in the surroundings of Quetzaltenango and Totonicapán. They are quite noticeable: The women wear very bright clothes and elegant hair pieces. The men are said to dress better than others and drive good trucks and jeeps. Located five kilometers from Quezaltenango, on what in 1983 became a paved road, a sign at the entrance of the town states: "Welcome to Almolonga, The Central American Garden (*La Huerta de Centroamérica*)." At present, Almolongueños are successful traders; they sell their vegetables in Guatemala, Mexico, and throughout Central America. They have diversified markets and products and become more prosperous than many of their neighbors.

These are times when many Guatemalan peasants suffer from poverty and malnutrition. In fact, Almolongueños have little land: 86 percent of the plots are less than one *manzana* (or two acres). Furthermore, as is the case in other villages in Guatemala, inheritance rules stipulate that land be subdivided among a person's children in equal parts, making the few available lots insufficient for subsistence or commercial purposes. The situation in Almolonga is consistent with the situation in the region. According to the Agricultural Census of 1979, the region holds 40 percent of the total amount of plots in the country, which in turn comprise only 19 percent of the total amount of land. In addition, population has increased in the highlands as a whole, and in Almolonga it has quadrupled in the last 100 years.

In other communities, change and capitalization implied, for the most part, proletarianization. Instead, Almolongueños chose to exploit the land by trying nontraditional crops and specializing in trade, taking advantage of their closeness to the market in Quezaltenango. At present, there are no communal lands in Almolonga and, with one exception, there is no memory of their existence in the past. On the contrary, many villagers denied it emphatically; Almolongueños, in their view, had always had private property, and the idea of sharing land seems totally foreign to them. Only one old man mentioned in passing that the largest extension of fertile land in the valley (approximately 9 acres) once might have belonged to the town, only to become the Potrero, or grazing field, owned by a mestizo family. The family was forced to sell the land back to the Indians in very small plots of one or two cuerdas. Even after recovering this land, Almolonga's cultivable flat land is less than two square kilometers. To the scarcity of land, Almolongueños responded by purchasing land in Quezaltenango, Salcajá, San Cristóbal Totonicapán, and San Marcos. Almolongueños can pay prices that locals cannot, and old traditional-conservative community models that prevented selling land to outsiders were overridden by the need for cash.

Older people from Almolonga remember well the construction of the Pan-American road by Ubico in the 1930s; they were forced to work on its construction. Mandatory work in the plantations (abolished in 1934) was replaced by the Vagrancy Law. This dictated that landless peasants had to work 100 days a year in the plantations. By then, Almolonga peasants were once again experimenting with vegetables, probably incorporating many new kinds to those that they might have grown in the past.

The earliest reports available for life in Almolonga proceed from Fuentes y Guzmán (1969), who at the end of the seventeenth century described the people as very laborious and dedicated to the production of grains, domestic fowls, and vegetables. In 1763 Almolongueños were reported to be trading bread, pigs, and cacao in the Pacific Coast region. Around the same time, they were producing corn, wheat, wool, and beans. At the end of the eighteenth century, Almolongueños were trading with pork, wood, and wild herbs, and chronicles stated that they were also growing vegetables. The reports of their growing some vegetables already in the seventeenth century are particularly interesting since people today have no memory of their great-grandparents producing any, and the chronicles do not specify which vegetables they did indeed cultivate. Almolongueños say that the production of vegetables is a new activity that developed within the last fifty years.

At the beginning of this century the main activities in Almolonga were milpa agriculture, growing and selling some flowers, and the sale of medicinal wild plants on the coast. By 1925, people remember that their main activity was growing alfalfa and oats for animals that used to graze in their lands. People from Cobán and Cabricán used to bring their animals on their way to the coast. Almolongueños say that they discovered "by accident" (some had revealing dreams; others learned that onions had spontaneously grown in someone's kitchen) that vegetables grow very well in their land. They brought seeds from Sololá, El Salvador, and Oaxaca. Today, they grow 36 percent of the total production of carrots in the country, 42 percent of the beets, 89 percent of the total production of cabbage, and 29 percent of the onions. They have no permanent crops of significance. They like growing vegetables better than alfalfa, because the "idea of alfalfa was not ours" but the mestizo landowners'.

Almolongueños not only do not go to work for wages in the plantations, but they proudly emphasize that they themselves hire people from other highland towns to work for them, including Nahualá and others in the department of Sololá. They suggest that they pay salaries that are higher than what others pay. Unlike many of their neighbors in the region, Almolongueños changed productive activities and techniques at least twice in less than 100 years, thus taking over an important part of the national and international markets.

The use of chemical fertilizers since the late 1960s, generalized throughout western Guatemala, was readily incorporated by Almolongueños. It increased yields, but to the point of abuse and apparent detriment of their township's environmental health. They developed a new and heavily specialized cash production, new technology, sharing the monopoly over vegetables only with the people of Lake Atitlán. To a limited demand in Guatemala, they responded with the development of new markets, and addressed their production to the more solvent mestizo market, since Indians rarely consume the vegetables they produce.

They explain their success as a result of their own effort. People do work hard, from 4:00 or 5:00 in the morning to 6:00 or 7:00 at night. Many are already irrigating their fields at 5:00 A.M. while in other places, as they say, they do not even water or spray with fertilizers. People from neighboring villages admit that Almolongueños work hard, but many suggested that Almolongueños are rich because they obtain their money from supernatural sources. Almolongueños also give credit for their success to the good weather conditions of the township.

Many Almolongueños attribute their situation to the impact of evangelization, suggesting that it is because of the fact that people today dedicate themselves more to work than to vices, such as drinking and womanizing, that they do better in the present. In the process of exploring new markets and diversifying production, Almolongueños have adopted new perspectives on the world. This ideological change predisposed more people to accept the new religion and simultaneously explore economic alternatives. The production of nontraditional crops has been accompanied by capital accumulation and economic differentiation within the town and in the region, as Almolongueños hire workers in other neighboring towns. People refer to their competitiveness, individualism, and interest in profit and accumulation. Growing economic differences and obvious resentment from their neighbors, combined with problems of environmental degradation, raise questions about the limits of the productive strategy adopted by the people of Almolonga.

In Chiapas, Mexico, lack of land has driven peasants to become tenant farmers through a system of sharecropping. By these means, they rent lands and pay rent with part of the harvest. Landless peasants throughout Mexico and Central America have also opted to migrate to the cities and to the United States.

In sum, a large sector of the population in the region is represented by rural inhabitants. Many of these are peasants who have been subjected to policies that have resulted in land loss. The increasing population, along with cultural traditions, has further contributed to their dwindling land resources. There is also widespread migration from rural to urban areas, as many peasants try to support themselves and their families by establishing work opportunities in major urban areas.

PRODUCTION

There are many forms of production within Mesoamerican economies. In this section, we consider four major ones—wage labor, petty commodity production, cottage industries, and maquiladora industries.

Wage Labor

Wage labor involves the payment to individuals of a wage in exchange for labor, so as to transform or produce one or more goods. A common form of rural wage labor in Mexico and Central America involves working on haciendas and plantations. Life for individuals or families who opt to migrate seasonally to coastal areas such as the Pacific Coast in Guatemala is very difficult (Figure 10.2). Relocating individuals or whole families for a few months in a totally different environment has many negative consequences. For people accustomed to highland climates, the intense heat of the coastal zones often makes them susceptible to diseases they do not encounter in their native lands. Unable to cultivate land of their own, and forced to purchase food and other goods that they need for survival, they frequently suffer from malnutrition. Plantations are often far from main towns and

Figure 10.2 Transporting Mexican workers to the lowlands. In Chiapas, Mexico, and Guatemala, overloaded trucks with temporary workers are often seen on the roads enroute to plantations. JEFFREY JAY FOXX/NYC

sources of goods. It is customary that the plantation itself has its own store to provide migrants with all their needs. Because the migrants are paid low wages and are forced to buy at the company store, they soon find themselves in debt. They then are forced to remain working for the same employer or to return the following season, often without having received any cash payments for their labor. This system of supplying migrant workers is so pervasive in Mexico, Guatemala, El Salvador, and other countries in Central America that it has been termed "debt peonage." Once in debt, the workers lose their freedom to leave, and the longer they remain working, the more they owe the landowner. This situation is combined with work that is extremely arduous, involving long hours, whether harvesting cotton, coffee beans, cacao, or fruit; cutting sugar cane; or processing sugar (see Box 10.2).

It is not surprising that highland peasants often are reluctant to go to work on the plantations. They consider this a last resort. Often, contractors will drive through highland towns, encouraging people to get on the truck that will take them to the coast. They sometimes depict misleading salaries and conditions. Contract labor is also called *enganche* ("hook up"), a term that suggests the lack of incentives people have to engage in this type of work owing to the poor labor conditions.

Box 10.2 *Working and Living Conditions on a Guatemalan Cotton Plantation*

"I remember that from when I was about eight to when I was about ten, we worked in the coffee crop. And after that I worked on the cotton plantations further down the coast where it was very, very hot. After my first day picking cotton, I woke up at midnight and lit a candle. I saw the faces of my brothers and sisters covered with mosquitos. I touched my own face, and I was covered too. They were everywhere; in people's mouths and everywhere. Just looking at these insects and thinking about being bitten set me scratching. That was our world. I felt that it would always be the same, always the same. It hadn't ever changed. . . .

"The contracting agents fetch and carry the people from the *Altiplano.* The overseers stay on the *fincas.* One group of workers arrives, another leaves and the overseer carries on giving orders. They are in charge. When you're working, for example, and you take a little rest, he comes and insults you. 'Keep working, that's what you're paid for,' he says. They also punish the slow workers. Sometimes we're paid by the day, and sometimes for the amount of work done. It's when we work by the day that we get the worst treatment. The *caporal* stands over you every minute to see how hard you're working. At other times, you're paid for what you pick. If you don't manage to finish the amount set in a day, you have to continue the next day, but at least you can rest a bit without the overseer coming down on you. But the work is still hard whether you work by the day or by the amount.

"Before we get into the lorry in our village, the labour contractor tells us to bring with us everything we'll need for the month on the *finca*; that is, plates and cups, for example. Every worker carries his plate, his cup, and his water bottle in a bag on his back so he can go and get his *tortilla* at mealtimes. Children who don't work don't earn, and so are not fed. They don't need plates. They share with their parents. The little ones who *do* earn also have plates for their ration of *tortilla.* When I wasn't earning anything, my mother used to give me half her ration. All the mothers did the same. We get *tortilla* and beans free, but they are often rotten. If the food varies a bit and we get an egg about every two months, then it is deducted from our pay. Any change in the food is deducted."

From Rigoberta Menchú, *I, Rigoberta Menchú: An Indian Woman in Guatemala,* edited by Elizabeth Burgos-Debray, translated by Ann Wright. London: Verso, 1984, pp. 22–23.

Petty Commodity Production

Broadly defined, petty commodity production refers to the small-scale production of agricultural or artisan goods oriented toward sale in the markets for a profit. It suggests a shift from production for sustenance to production for the market, with the corresponding intensification of labor. Petty commodity production uses occasional wage labor, whereas capitalist or petty capitalist production makes use of a permanent wage labor force from which a surplus can be extracted, thereby allowing capitalist accumulation. Examples of petty capitalist production include the treadle loom weaving industries of Teotitlán del Valle in the Oaxaca Valley, Mexico, and the garment production center of San Francisco el Alto, Guatemala.

Petty commodity production often requires the incorporation of technological changes and/or the enlargement of the labor force traditionally employed. For example, the production of textiles (cloth, table cloths, shirts, bags) in Totonicapán, Comalapa, and Chichicastenango in Guatemala (Figure 10.3), or Chamula and San Pedro Chenalhó in Chiapas, Mexico, was originally oriented toward subsistence and sale in regional markets. Recently, however, pro-

Figure 10.3 Market scene in Chichicastenango, Guatemala. Furniture and pots from Totonicapán are exhibited on a side street. JEFFREY JAY FOXX/NYC

duction has been intensified and expanded, and accompanied by the incorporation of occasional wage workers and unpaid apprentices. A decrease in the quality of yarns and time invested in products for sale to tourists in local and national markets also has been observed.

The process of intensification of production fosters stratification within and across villages as well as various cultural changes. In Oaxaca, Mexico, brickmakers (an example of rural petty industrial production studied by Scott Cook and others) have had incredible material success. Practiced since the nineteenth century, brickmaking has undergone several changes. It evolved from a temporary peasant artisan occupation practiced by just a few households to a full-time peasant capitalist industry practiced by people who have differentiated themselves into groups of owners and groups of pieceworkers who do not own their business. In San Miguel Totonicapán, Guatemala, a town studied by Carol Smith, weavers are doing quite well since they have intensified the production of textiles for tourists and export. Totonicapán weavers do not seem to have polarized into two classes (owners and wage workers), in contrast with other petty industries.

San Pedro Almolonga in western Guatemala (see Box 10.1) is a town that specializes in the production of vegetables, and is considered to be doing better, on average, than most other towns in the area. There, we observe widespread economic differentiation. To the lack of land in the township, people responded by

Figure 10.4 San Pedro Almolonga, Guatemala. The women are harvesting vegetables to be sold in the Almolonga market. Individual farmers often sell entire baskets of produce to wholesalers who meet them at the market. JEFFREY JAY FOXX/NYC

renting and then purchasing lands in nearby townships. They diversified production strategies, including the development of new markets, the addition of trade partners, the acquisition of new lands, and the production of new cash crops. On the average, those who have opted for trade and intensification of production of vegetables are doing better than those who remain dedicated to agriculture and milpa production (Figure 10.4). Traders seem to be converting to Protestantism in larger proportions than agriculturalists, thus generating a distinct group within the town experiencing profound cultural changes.

An illustration of the impact of commodity production is given in Box 10.3.

Of great interest to students of peasant societies is the issue of their possibilities for capital accumulation and capitalist development. Social scientists wonder whether peasants are in the process of becoming capitalists and disappearing as a group, or whether peasantry is a lifestyle that allows for some but fairly limited changes, including marginal capital accumulation, which would not lead to capitalist development. Are these petty producers developing larger concentrations of capital and greater intensification of both labor and technology, just as large capitalist enterprises do in the developed world? Or are they follow-

Box 10.3 *Petty Commodity Production in the Tzeltal Maya Township of Amatenango del Valle, Chiapas*

In Amatenango del Valle, Chiapas, the intensification of the production of pottery by women has also generated internal stratification. At the same time, according to June Nash, relations between men and women experienced a conflictive shift brought about by the new trend of independent and self-sufficient women. As part of these economic developments, men and women have redefined their roles in the household. Both groups had always contributed to the subsistence of the household, but with production intensification and some degree of economic differentiation, the nature of the contributions of men and women has changed. For one thing, in most cases the hours spent working on the production of a particular commodity have increased. Cash availability from the work of both women and men has created changes in power relations within the household and between men and women in general. Women now have access to the capital they generate owing to an expanded market for the crafts they produce. This has given them more power than they previously had, as they can make decisions related to production and to the household consumption that they did not make before. Men's activities yield comparable or sometimes lower returns, thus affecting intergender dynamics. The practice of productive diversification is not new to peasant households, as already pointed out. However, with intensification, the incorporation of paid help (temporary wage workers) and a different division of labor, the economic process also has changed in nature. For example, the combination of subsistence agriculture with the practice of one or more artisan activities, along with different levels of commercialization, are now considered standard strategies for capitalization.

ing demographic cycles that allow for periods of greater productivity and profits, to be followed by periods of decline, with no significant accumulation of capital?

The first position roughly describes the claims once made by Vladimir Lenin and came to be known as the Marxist or *de-campesinista* (de-peasantizing) perspective. According to this perspective, peasants would slowly become wage workers for industry and service, and a few would become capitalists themselves. The second position roughly describes the argument of Alexander Chayanov, which is known as the *campesinista* (peasantist) perspective. According to this perspective, peasants are seen as a changing but almost perpetual category, sometimes exploited by the capitalist system as they provide cheap foodstuffs to the cities, and sometimes remaining relatively marginal to the capitalist world. Students of Mesoamerican peasants have found evidence to support both viewpoints. Some social scientists have concluded that petty commodity production as a system is limited. Owing to the low level of investment, it does not allow for significant capital accumulation, nor the segregation of the population into two definite classes: one of owners of the means of production (land, labor, and capital) and the other of dispossessed people who constitute a full-time proletariat (wage workers). Others point to the existence of a combination of full-time and part-time wage workers with access to limited resources (that is, a small plot of land). Finally, the presence of people being capitalized and doing significantly better than the average peasant-artisan or cash-crop agriculturalist leads scholars to believe in the possibility of the generation of capitalist accumulation from the peasant-worker workshop or industry. These positions are not necessarily in contradiction with each other, and much research is ongoing to understand and predict future developments among the peasants of Mexico and Central America.

Cottage Industries

Of the several possible ways of generating an income that are now practiced in the region, home work is a relatively recent one and is becoming quite widespread. Home work, or work done at home (also called the "putting out" system), is quite common in the garment industry, but it is also found in several other industries. It is work that requires simple and available technology (a sewing machine, needle and thread, a loom). In general, the employer puts out the raw materials and specific assembling instructions for each piece. In the case of the embroidery industry of Ocotlán, Mexico, "outworkers" get the pieces of material to be embroidered, and sometimes the yarn, and return the assembled piece to the merchant for a lump sum of money. Sometimes arrangements are made to pay piece-rate, and often cash advances are given to the workers. In some cases, different members of the household will be in charge of different parts of the garment or the performance of different tasks. In Teotitlán de Valle, Mexico, Cook observed workers who are independent and work with their own looms and yarn at home, as well as others who own their looms but receive yarn from the merchants.

This type of work presents many advantages to merchants, many of whom are themselves intermediaries. For one thing, they do not need to supply a space to the worker, nor equipment, saving the expenses of electricity (when available) and upkeep. Most of the home workers are women, and this work style allows them to continue with their daily activities of taking care of young children and various house work. The transition from home work to the workshop at the merchant's house or property often implies more expenses for the proprietor-merchant. It also increases his or her control over the production process. Many workers will eventually become the merchant's competitors, as they begin to buy their own raw materials and engage relatives and others with piece work.

Maquiladora Industries

The combination of lack of land and employment opportunities for peasants and urban inhabitants in the region, and the preference of the United States and other developed countries for obtaining an unlimited supply of cheap unskilled labor, has resulted in the creation of a new type of industry: export manufacturing plants, known as *maquiladoras.* Maquiladoras are spread throughout several regions of the Third World, including Latin America and the Caribbean. For example, they are located in the north of Mexico, particularly near the border with the United States, and they are a relatively new development in Guatemala (since the mid-1980s). These industries rely on migrants, some of whom are trying to immigrate to the United States, and others who are simply moving in search of jobs within their own countries. Most of the workers in these plants are women (over 85 percent). Women are considered by employers to be more docile and less inclined to protest and unionize (see Chapter 9). In fact, the assumption is also that women will accept lower wages and harsher conditions than men, and have fewer options than men. Components of goods are sent from developed countries to these Third World countries, and maquila factories assemble them into finished products to export back to the sending country (for example, the United States or South Korea), where they are finally sold. Countries in the Third World are often eager to attract these foreign investments that bring jobs to their countries. For that purpose they offer potential manufacturers not only an unlimited supply of labor but also different incentives in the form of tax exemptions. Labor comes in part from the rural areas, but mostly from the overpopulated urban centers. The conditions in these plants are often poor, not only by U.S. or other developed countries' standards, but by local standards as well. Women are paid little (as low as one or two dollars a day); are forced to work overtime; and are not allowed sufficient breaks, even when pregnant or breast-feeding. To signs of unionization, companies respond by threatening with closure of the plants. They frequently close and move to new locations. Mesoamerican peoples, native and mestizo alike, have painfully linked themselves directly to the international arena through these export-processing enterprises.

DISTRIBUTION

Trade and Markets

Anyone travelling in Mexico and Central America will retain vivid images of the sale of a large array of colorful goods in the local markets. These open markets are spread throughout the region at distances that grow closer to each other as new markets continue to be created, in part as a response to population increase in the region and to improved transportation means and networks. Rural markets were already held in Precolumbian times, of course, and the frequency and number of them increased as colonial authorities would ask—often demand—Indians to hold *plazas* in places that would serve the Spaniards better. Also as a result of requests and impositions from Spanish authorities, enclosed market buildings began to be built in the nineteenth century. Spaniards considered enclosed markets to be more sanitary and "organized." Indians never agreed with Spaniards on this issue, thinking that their traditional open plazas with an abundance of fresh air and sunlight were not only more pleasant but also cleaner and better organized. Certainly, the preferred organizational patterns varied for both groups, and the debate over the best model for a marketplace continues today. As a result, it is common to find enclosed markets in most large towns of Guatemala, Mexico, El Salvador, and Honduras, in combination with some kind of open market that seems to spill outside of the enclosed buildings. Small villages often organize the market in the main plaza in front of the church, or create a special area (often an area covered with cement and sometimes a roof and no walls) for their market. Here, vendors from the region come to sell their products. Larger markets attract both vendors and buyers from a larger radius, while smaller ones attract local buyers and vendors.

It is interesting to note that while rural markets, unlike urban ones, tend to meet once a week (and historically have done so since Precolumbian times), many markets are expanding to two or three days a week. Some towns already hold daily plazas, and the trend points to many more permanent markets. A good example of this is the market in San Francisco el Alto in western Guatemala, the largest in the region. This market used to be held only on Fridays, when over 10,000 people would crowd the hilly streets of the town early Friday morning. In 1980, vendors would arrive in San Francisco at 9:00 or 10:00 on Thursday night and sleep in the plaza to be guaranteed a space. By 1987, people were arriving early on Thursday, and the plaza would begin its activity then. In 1990, people predicted that soon Wednesdays would become an additional day of plaza. The level of commercialization, particularly in traditional textiles and male garments, is so high that San Francisco may become a permanent market center of the western region.

While many direct producers (called *propios* in Guatemala) bring small amounts of produce on each market day, a large number of intermediaries (called *regatones*) may buy from the local producers at their local market and then take them to other markets at longer distances. There is some gender differentiation in this division of labor. Most direct producers who sell at the markets are women. Women prefer to sell in markets close to home, and thus travel shorter distances. They often travel by bus, although some people in the region still walk several miles between marketplaces. Most intermediaries are men. They are long-distance travelers; many of them own trucks and cross regional and national boundaries. In fact, intermediaries are experimenting with new strategies that represent variations from their traditional practices. For example, many do not remain loyal to the traditional products because diversifying the items traded diminishes the risk of businesses going bad. Vendors may set a goal of reaching a distant market, even crossing national borders. They then purchase goods that will be sold at different stops throughout the trip. In turn, they acquire local specialties at each stop, which will be sold at the final destination. This practice of stepped trading, now conducted with the aid of trucks or buses, was already practiced during the colonial and independent years with the help of mules, and, in Precolumbian times, by foot.

Marketing Culture

The complex network of interdependent markets graphically depicts a network of social and political relations among the populations of the different regions. The closeness and intensity of the trading interactions suggest the degree of the participants' immersion in the capitalist system. As these networks expand, so does the universe of the region's inhabitants. Spanish is spoken as a trading language in most markets of Mesoamerica, even where large sectors speak Spanish only as a second language. This is the case in Chiapas, Oaxaca, and western Guatemala, among other areas. Markets provide the means for acquiring ethnic knowledge, and as such, they have been recognized as sites for peaceful interactions, even in times of violence. The practice of bargaining, widespread in Mesoamerica, goes hand in hand with full acceptance of the market as regulator and determinant of prices. Research has shown that the resulting price of each bargaining interaction usually does not change significantly from one trading partner to another. What does change is the length and style of the bargaining itself. The negotiation is longer and more difficult and it starts at higher prices when partners do not know each other well or at all. It is much shorter, faster, and friendlier when the partners know each other and have an established relationship (the asking price is then much closer to the expected sale price). Bargaining thus becomes a ritual of social identification that leads to more fluid economic relations.

ECONOMY AND CHANGE

In the context of the extensive economic and technological changes that we outlined above, how are people's world views affected, if at all? Do people's private, domestic, social lives change along with the many other changes? Mesoamericans have shared basic cultural assumptions since Precolumbian times (see Chapter 8). One of these traditional Mesoamerican traits includes close ties to the earth, which is perceived as the great provider and with whom people establish deep symbolic and ritual connections. The traditional person is thus identified as someone who depends heavily on the earth for resources and, given the choice, would rather have more land than any other resource. The traditional Indian expects his or her children to remain nearby, inherit the land, and keep working it. This Mesoamerican (idealized here) is one who, when resources are available, prefers to invest them in his or her community, often by means of participation in the communal fiestas and the civic and religious brotherhoods (*cofradías*). These investments in food, liquor, costumes for ceremonial dances, ritual paraphernalia, care of the saints, and others provide a return that translates into higher status. There is thus room for some degree of accumulation, where the culturally appropriate form it takes is prestige. Accumulation of other forms of capital, with a lavish lifestyle and display of wealth, is frowned upon. In this world view, emphasis is placed on community values, solidarity, and generosity. Greed and personal ambition are viewed with disdain. Expressions of these beliefs and attitudes toward life, and in particular toward aspects of life related to the economy, are found in the stories people tell to each other—both in old folk accounts and in other stories considered to be actual events that happen to people who behave in certain ways. The moral of many of these stories often suggests that ambition, greed, and desire to have more material means than others are negative values and should be condemned by all. Such traits are perceived as detrimental to the society because they cause "envy." Envy is a bad feeling, generated in part by conspicuous consumption, which, according to the traditional viewpoint, could lead to disease and even death.

Within this economic ideology, there is room, of course, for notions of change and innovation. Agricultural techniques may change slightly, fertilizers may be a welcome addition to depleted soils, acceptance of rentals or sharecropping may be necessary. The traditional native world view is not by any means static, but it is conservative.

Conversations with people who have experienced drastic changes in their lifestyles and economic practices reveal some interesting changes in the way they think about the issues outlined above. Changes in economic ideology, documented in particular for western Guatemala but with sufficient information available from adjacent areas, reveal an increasing number of people who are defining their positions differently, and a transitional group slowly questioning some of their traditional assumptions.

Petty commodity and petty capitalist producers who have intensified production, diversified productive activities, and expanded their commercial practices come to think about the world in very different terms. Such people may indicate that they would much prefer to obtain more money than more land. They see their children leaving the township upon reaching adulthood in order to find new markets and new horizons. They are willing to try new economic ventures and take risks. Some people also indicate that accumulation is something to strive for as long as there is a degree of redistribution involved. In sum, many Mesoamericans now admit that becoming wealthy is something to aspire to, but that it is also important to be generous and not greedy. In this context, by presenting themselves as protectors of reciprocal community obligations, people facilitate the transition to a new ideological framework while trying to protect themselves from envy.

Studies have shown that those who espouse the new economic ideologies tend to be those whose economic status is relatively high, and many are heavily involved in commercial activities (as in western Guatemala) or in petty industrial production (as in Oaxaca). Such people probably experience changes in their economic practices and in perceptions and evaluation of the world around them. As these changes take place, other related cultural changes take place. The world view of the larger capitalist society not only becomes familiar but is partially adopted. Native peoples transform themselves as they transform the work they do and adjust to the changes going on around them. They are also agents in this process, as they become key links in the larger economic system.

An interesting phenomenon occurring among large sectors of Mesoamerican peoples, as well as nonindigenous people living in the region, is the high rate of conversion from Catholicism to Protestantism. This may be one of the most visible cultural changes people have been undergoing during the twentieth century. The introduction of Protestantism in the region is related to the interests of the governments in Mexico and Central America in generating capitalist development and growth together with their conviction that by encouraging foreign investments and bringing in the ideas and styles of the developed countries, development will follow.

Ever since Max Weber elaborated his theories on the rise of capitalism, scholars have pointed to the possible relationship between Protestantism and economic improvement. There seems to be a relationship between people's exposure to certain activities closely associated with the capitalist market (or technological innovations leading to higher economic status) and people's openness to new ideas, including new religious orientations. The ideas of Protestantism (as espoused in Mesoamerica) appear to correspond well with the new occupations and new economic practices in general, providing an articulate conceptual framework that justifies and also encourages the change. Protestants argue that it is good to work hard, and as a result to have more wealth than others. They stress that competition encourages well-being and growth, both individual and social. Furthermore, they stress the importance of investing time in "worthwhile," constructive activities, such as production or healthy distractions, rather than in long ritual celebrations that include heavy drinking and several days away from production. In this context, Protestantism is not itself generating change, but may be providing people with the necessary explanatory and supportive framework for general economic change.

MESOAMERICA IN THE WORLD SYSTEM

Consumption Patterns

Are all the productive systems described in this chapter remnants of precapitalist social formations, survivals of forms about to disappear, or are they full, integral parts of the world capitalist system? An examination of the distribution and consumption pattern of the commodities produced by peasant artisans, petty agricultural producers, and petty industrial producers suggests that these forms are indeed integral to capitalism. Some would even say that capitalism heavily depends on forms like the ones described here.

Fruit and vegetables intensively produced in different areas of Central America reach the tables of most North American households. In some cases, this is a direct result of the efforts of thousands of migratory seasonal workers who work for large landowners on coastal estates; in others, it is the result of the combined effort of small farmers and intermediaries. Prices for those fruits and vegetables are determined by the combined forces of supply and national and international demand; that is, the world market. Box 10.4 shows just how close the connection between the First and Third Worlds can be.

On occasion, craft production for the world market, and in particular the sale to tourists, has compensated for the significant population losses owing to migration to the United States (which is still large). Craft production often allows

Box 10.4 *The Economic Links Between New York and Atitlán*

When a woman from New York goes to a mall and purchases a pair of pants made in Lake Atitlán, Guatemala, or a blouse made in Chiapas, Mexico, she is closing a circle that began with a particular use and aesthetic context generated within the peasant household. The blouse and the pants, however, have gone through a profound transformation in use, style, intent, and (often) quality. The weaver, embroiderer, or garment maker has adapted the product to suit a foreign taste and a foreign need. The textile, originally meant to be used in the making of a man's shirt, is now used to make pants to be worn by both men and women. The blouse, originally hand-embroidered and worn in special ceremonial occasions, is now often machine-embroidered and worn with a pair of jeans in an informal context. The quality of the pieces often has decreased to fit the demand and the pockets of the buyers. The market for peasant crafts has changed the style, dimension, and nature of their production. Tourists visiting the region graphically reveal its producers' embeddedness in the modern world. In fact, as a vivid example of its immersion in the world economy, tourism has actually stimulated the production of craft commodities. Fewer peasants may wonder, "Why would anyone want to hang a woman's blouse on the wall?" or "Is it appropriate for men to wear women's clothes in your country?" They may instead explore ways of increasing their production, while keeping costs down so that they can still compete in the market of exotic handmade goods. In this sense, native crafts are part of the same international division of labor that includes industrial production, and share many of the biases and drawbacks of the larger industrial production. An example is the gendered division of labor, where women increasingly constitute the majority of the lower-paid and more labor-intensive jobs.

peasants who used to migrate to the coastal plantations to remain in their villages, as is the case of the people in many Maya communities of Guatemala.

Cooperatives have been created in Mexico and Guatemala for the purpose of coordinating and managing the export of crafts (Figure 10.5). The Mexican government has sponsored some cooperatives for the purchase of raw materials and the sale of artisan products. Participation in many of these cooperatives has significantly improved the standard of living of many Mesoamerican natives. Women's cooperatives in Guatemala, for example, provide some women—many widowed by the political violence of recent years—with greater skills to commercialize their products, even though their dependence on foreign markets may at some point prove dangerous. Competition with other Third World countries may put some of these workers out of business, and it is increasingly likely that a factory worker in Asia may be producing industrial versions of handmade native designs. Also, in the context of the tourist business and exports of artisan products, native peoples have become increasingly aware of many unjust situations. In particular, unfair prices paid for goods sold in the cities of the region and in other countries may yield profits for the merchants that grossly exceed the payments to the producers. Artisans often feel exploited by local operators of petty capitalist workshops, or putting out merchants.

The incorporation of Mexico and the countries of Central America as fully participating members of the capitalist world market has had a profound impact on people's cultures. We have mentioned some of these developments ear-

Figure 10.5 Exhibit room of the Cooperative Sna Jolobil (Chiapas, Mexico). Here local crafts are sold to tourists. JEFFREY JAY FOXX/NYC

lier; for example, the influx of Protestantism from the United States and its related consequences on people's world views as they engage in new economic activities. New political affiliations result from the combined influence of religion and production. They shape new coalitions of native and non-native workers, and redefine old sectors in light of new problems and class affiliations. Ethnicities are also reconstructed in these new frameworks. As people engage in different economic activities and relate to other people in different terms, they also redefine themselves. The new autonomy of women, counterbalancing the traditional patriarchal structure, is also related to the possibilities that the new markets have created for them. As new gender relations develop, so do new family dynamics, as men and women become part of the new division of labor. Finally, as the products of native peoples are sold and purchased throughout the world, parts of their cultures are also disseminated, although transformed, throughout the world.

Migration to the United States

Any analysis of the economic conditions of the region that includes Central America and Mexico must examine questions about the ongoing migration wave to the

United States. It is hard to find anyone in the rural or urban settings of Mesoamerica who does not have a relative or friend living temporarily or permanently in the United States. And for many people, especially men, this journey seems to be part of the corpus of goals and dreams to be achieved in their lives. It is difficult to generalize which social type is more prone to migrate (or to attempt migration). Some researchers have noted that while scarce land resources and impoverished conditions at home may motivate people to leave, it is often the middle sectors, rather than the totally landless or resource-deprived people, who migrate. Individual cases may point to all socioeconomic sectors of Mesoamerican societies, including the wealthier and/or best educated. Distribution and quality of agricultural land certainly play a crucial role, but migrants come to the United States not only from areas with poor land but also from areas of high-quality land and intensive agricultural production. When competition increases and farm incomes decline, farms tend to diversify through internal and international migration. There are also migrants who leave from urban areas. The latter tend to settle in U.S. cities and remain on a more permanent basis than rural migrants (who tend to employ temporary migration strategies).

While middle sectors are the first to migrate, the networks extend over time to all socioeconomic sectors. The same happens with gender trends. Men are the first to migrate for practically all groups, but over time women and children follow. This is somewhat different for politically motivated migrations, as with the recent Salvadorans and Guatemalans, who tend to migrate as whole families in order to seek refuge in Mexico and the United States from highly repressive conditions in their own countries. As shown in Box 10.5, migration of Mexicans to the United States has a long history.

Box 10.5 *Mexicans Migrate to the United States*

Much of the movement of Mesoamericans into the United States is clandestine, so it has been difficult for students of this phenomenon to estimate migration rates. Mexico alone is the source of 95 percent of all undocumented migrants in the United States, as reported by Jorge Durand and Douglas Massey (1992). It is important to note, however, that much of the migration was induced early in this century by the United States rather than by the sending countries. Growers in the southwestern United States provided incentives to Mexican agricultural workers throughout the nineteenth and early twentieth centuries in order to obtain cheap, reliable labor. Migration was not initiated by individuals in search of a better life, as often depicted, but by North Americans trying to obtain cheap labor to work under conditions that few North Americans would accept. These flows of labor into the United States were revived in 1942, when the Bracero Program was instituted by the U.S. government. This program for temporary workers provided migrants with temporary documents to cross the border and work during limited periods. The program ended in 1964, but other agreements have been instituted to allow temporary migration since then. The notion that the United States does not want these migrants for whom there is no work is fallacious, since it is U.S. growers, and not just in the south, who lobby for immigration measures that will facilitate the availability of migrants willing to take temporary jobs.

Most migrants from Mexico, El Salvador, and Guatemala have settled in California, but there are smaller numbers in Florida; Texas; Washington, D.C.; and the Midwest (especially from the latter two countries). Unlike migrants who came from the communist world and were welcomed as refugees, many of those from Guatemala and El Salvador, once they were denied political asylum, remained in the country illegally; they never were recognized as refugees by the U.S. government.

Not all migrants lack education. Approximately 25 percent of all migrants are professionals who expect a better life in the United States. Mexico sends a large number of professionals, but less than other nationalities. Most of the migrants from Mexico and Central America are manual laborers. Millions of Central Americans and Mexicans have emigrated to the United States, legally and illegally. They are drawn by the possibilities of work or freedom, pushed in part by uncertain economic conditions and political persecution in their own countries. But most are drawn by the restructuring of the world economy, which is generating sources of labor for international capital through a new international division of labor. This is a process that has created new ethnic minorities throughout the world, as the immigrants struggle today to claim a space of their own in their new homelands.

Development and Underdevelopment

The area that corresponds to ancient Mesoamerica has suffered from the effects of underdevelopment as much as, and often more so than, other countries in Latin America. Comparative statistics show that countries like Guatemala and El Salvador compete for last place when it comes to indices of underdevelopment (Mexico and other countries in Central America follow quite closely). Countries like Mexico and Costa Rica have overall better standards of living in the region. They still experience, however, unequal distributive patterns that hurt the peasant and urban informal sectors alike.

Most attempts to explain the roots of underdevelopment in the region agree that the model of agroexport development has been detrimental to the largest sectors of the population. Commercial agriculture in the Colonial period contributed to the concentration of fertile lands in the hands of a small elite. This was by far the primary cause of the impoverishment of the rural populations, even in Mexico, where land reform and the implementation of the ejido system has not resolved land inequities yet. Lands were (and are) used for export crops instead of food crops for local consumption, and the proportion of lands devoted to the former is still increasing. This forces many of the peoples of Central America and Mexico to import food that they traditionally produced. Furthermore, the internationalization of the market has resulted in an accommodation of prices that has generated uneven terms of trade. While some analysts thought that the concentration on a few exports would generate larger funds for investment and give the area a "comparative advantage," in practice there have been detrimental consequences of this development strategy. While prices for agricultural exports have declined, those for the manufactured goods that the people of the region must import have increased, creating uneven trading stances.

The high price of manufactured goods, combined with the great instability of prices of agricultural products, has generated the need for export diversification. The expansion of nontraditional agricultural exports, like beef, has taken over large extensions of good lands in places like Costa Rica and Honduras. The lack of land has generated a differentiated rural population competing among themselves for scarce resources. A most evident expression of this situation is the high level of malnutrition, especially in El Salvador, Guatemala, and Honduras. Furthermore, export agriculture combined with population growth have significantly contributed to environmental degradation. Soils are being exhausted because of intensification of production and excessive use of fertilizers and pesticides. Deforestation is creating further erosion as forested areas are converted to cotton or other export crops or construction timber. As a consequence of all of these factors, landlessness and unemployment have increased in the rural areas. While some people have migrated to the cities, thus becoming part of the lower sectors of urban society, others have resorted to the economic strategies outlined above. Indeed, most community development alternatives seem to point to the need for some form of land reform. Costa Rica and Honduras have a somewhat more equitable land distribution program than Guatemala and El Salvador. Some steps have been taken in Mexico, but the situation there is far from resolved.

When land reform is not an option, the development programs that have proved most successful are those in which community members are allowed a greater degree of participation in the making of decisions and the setting of priorities. Furthermore, the programs that are sensitive to culturally viable initiatives, which attend not only to local needs but to culturally meaningful means of addressing those needs, have also led to promising results. Such is the case of the relocation of Chamulans from the highlands of Chiapas to the rainforest, documented by Duncan Earle (1983). The immigrants from Chamula kept some of their highland patterns and introduced new ones, more appropriate to the lowlands. The goal was to achieve a form of adaptation that was viable from economic, ecological, and social perspectives, and that would prevent the alienation of the resettled group.

Experiences drawn from the repertoire of local and international development agencies repeatedly point to two major consequences of violating the needs and participation of community members. On the one hand, and as suggested above, projects that are not viewed as meaningful to the people do not represent valid alternatives for rural peoples. On the other hand, when agencies erroneously assume community homogeneity—even when the decision-making stage does reach the community—the benefits often remain in the hands of the local elites. The development initiative is thus truncated by the same uneven mechanisms that on a much larger scale generated underdevelopment in the first place.

SUGGESTED READINGS

ANNIS, SHELDON 1987 *God and Production in a Guatemalan Town.* Austin: University of Texas Press.

BROCKETT, CHARLES D. 1990 *Land, Power and Poverty: Agrarian Transformations and Political Conflict in Central America.* Boulder, Colo.: Westview Press.

CAMBRANES, JULIO C. 1985 *Coffee and Peasants in Guatemala.* South Woodstock, Vermont: CIRMA.

CANCIAN, FRANK 1965 *Economics and Prestige in a Mayan Community: The Religious Cargo System in Zinacantan.* Stanford, Calif.: Stanford University Press.

COLLIER, GEORGE 1989 Changing Inequality in Zinacantán: The Generations of 1918 and 1942. *In Ethnographic Encounters in Southern Mesoamerica: Essays in Honor of Evon Zartman Vogt, Jr.*, edited by V. R. Bricker and G. H. Gossen, pp. 111–123. Studies on Culture and Society vol. 3, Institute for Mesoamerican Studies. Albany: State University of New York.

COOK, SCOTT, and LEIGH BINFORD 1990 *Obliging Need: Rural Petty Industry in Mexican Capitalism.* Austin: University of Texas Press.

EHLERS, TRACY BACHRACH 1990 *Silent Looms: Women and Production in a Guatemalan Town.* Boulder, Colo.: Westview Press.

NASH, JUNE (ed.) 1993 *Crafts in Global Markets: Artisan Production in Middle America.* Albany: State University of New York Press.

SMITH, CAROL (ed.) 1990 *Guatemalan Indians and the State, 1540 to 1988.* Austin: University of Texas Press.

WASSERSTROM, ROBERT 1983 *Class and Society in Central Chiapas.* Berkeley: University of California Press.

Chapter 11
Language and Languages in Mesoamerica

WHAT ARE THE LANGUAGES OF MESOAMERICA?

Modern Mesoamerica is an area of great linguistic diversity. Although Spanish is the dominant language of the region, around eighty Native American languages are still spoken within its borders, and English is the official language of Belize. The study of these languages has provided a great deal of information about the cultures, histories, and relationships among Mesoamerican peoples. The native languages of Mesoamerica also share certain linguistic properties that distinguish them from languages to the north and south, and help define one part of what it is to be Mesoamerican.

The indigenous languages of Mesoamerica are listed in Figure 11.1. Any such list is to some extent subjective. Two different types of speech are considered to be the same language if speakers of one type understand speakers of the other; the two types of speech are *mutually intelligible* dialects of a single language. If speakers of the two types of speech cannot understand one another, the two are considered to be distinct languages. These are the clearcut cases.

The subjective element enters when people understand one another partially. People with different purposes make systematically different judgments. For example, missionaries may want to provide everyone with a Bible that they can read and understand; different languages or dialects can be defined by whether their speakers understand a single translation of the Bible well enough. For anthropologists, it may be more important to know the extent to which people in

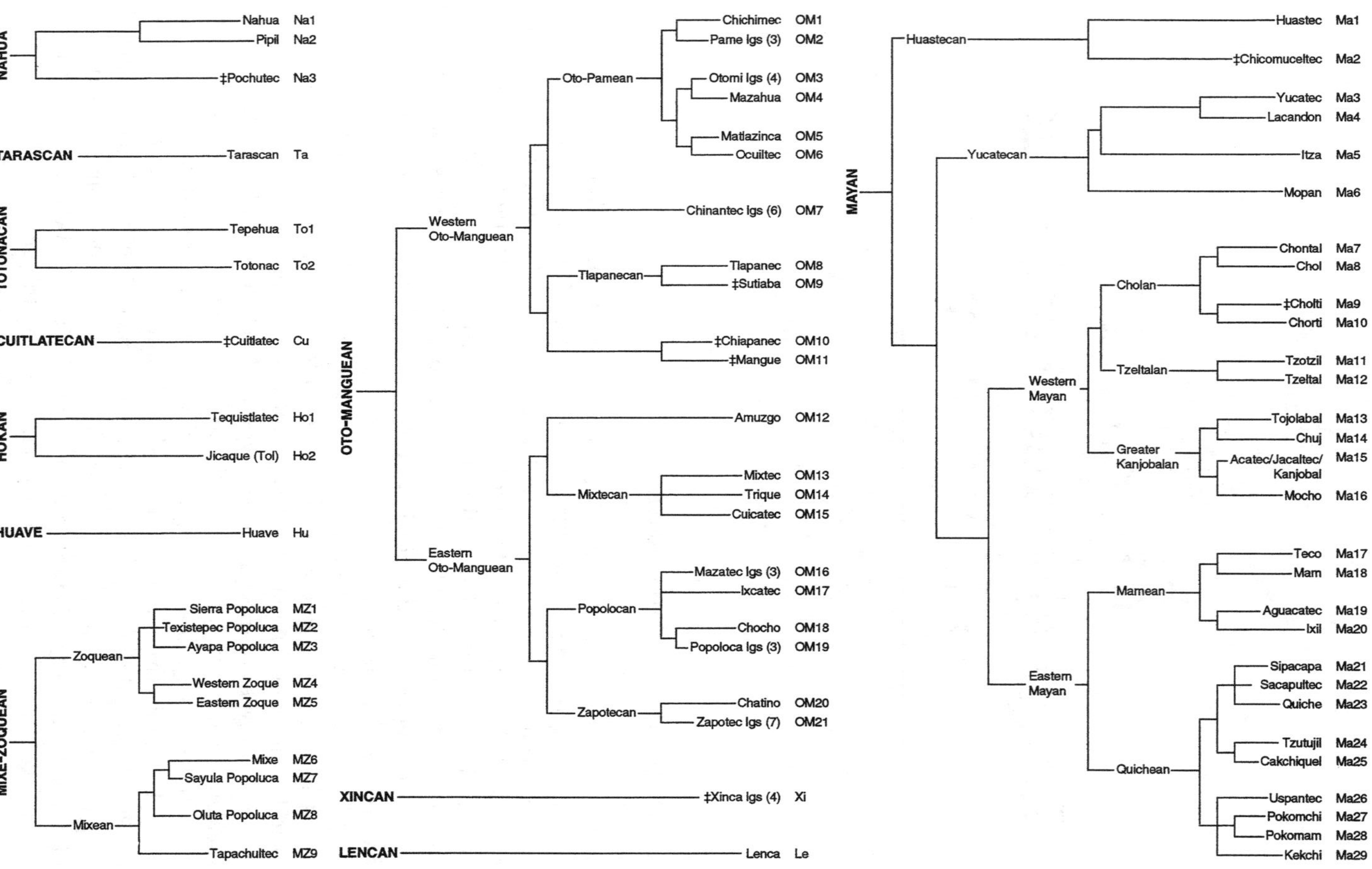

Figure 11.1 "Family Trees" of Mesoamerican Languages. Labels by language names are keys to Figure 11.2. ‡ means "extinct".

contact—for example, in markets—can make themselves understood while using their own language. The list given in Figure 11.1 reflects this general type of perspective. The classification shown is based on the judgments of Terrence Kaufman, a North American linguist who has made a comparative study of most of the languages of Mesoamerica.

The languages given in Figure 11.1 can be *classified,* or grouped into *language families.* A language family is a historically based grouping of languages according to their degree of mutual relationship. The type of relationship involved is historical, and involves the idea of language change.

All languages are constantly changing. In time—certainly after a thousand years or so—a language changes so much that speakers of the different dialects can no longer understand each other. We say that two languages are members of the same language family if they are historically derived from dialects of the same language. The ancestor languages that gave rise to the different languages of Mesoamerica no longer exist, but we can draw conclusions about their properties by comparing the properties of the languages that are descended from them and *reconstructing* a hypothetical ancestral form of the language. Linguists refer to these reconstructed versions of ancestor languages as *protolanguages.* The extinct language that gave rise to the modern Mayan languages, for example, is called *Proto-Mayan*; the ancestor of the Zapotecan languages is *Proto-Zapotecan*; and so on.

Every Mesoamerican language is a member of one of eleven genetic units: Some are families of languages, while others (*isolates*) consist of a single language. The locations of these units and their member languages are indicated on Figure 11.2. Their sizes, in terms of the number of languages composing them, is quite varied. The Oto-Manguean family is the largest, consisting of at least forty distinct languages; the Cuitlatec, Huave, and Tarascan families have a single member each. Box 11.1 describes one language that falls on the margins of the Mesoamerican tradition.

The languages of Mesoamerica have been written in European script since shortly after the Spanish invasion, early in the sixteenth century. The first of these records were made by Franciscan priests as part of their attempt to Christianize the indigenous population of the Americas. Today, missionaries working with the Summer Institute of Linguistics continue to be very important in documenting Mesoamerican languages. An increasing amount of linguistic research, however, is carried out by nonmissionary anthropologists and linguists, who have made important contributions to understanding the structures and histories of these languages.

In addition to the documentation in Spanish-based orthography and in linguists' representations, some of the languages have prehispanic documentation in hieroglyphic records. The greatest number of hieroglyphic texts come from the lowland Mayan area. The texts appear to be in two different Mayan languages—Yucatecan in the north, and Cholan in the south. Hieroglyphic inscriptions thought to be of Zapotec have also been found concentrated in the Valley of Oax-

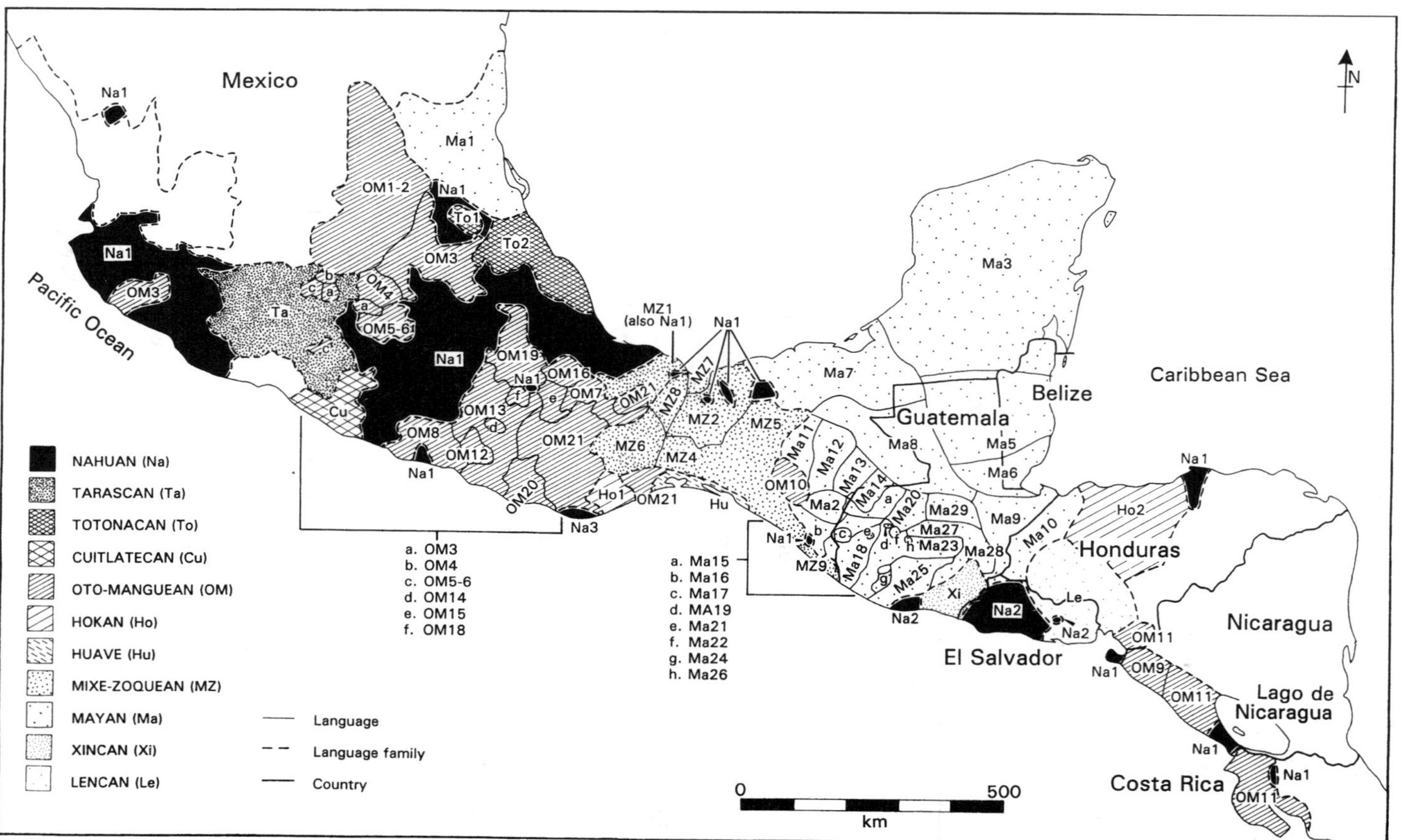

Figure 11.2 Distribution of Mesoamerican Languages.

Box 11.1 *Garífuna—a Language with a Complex History*

One of the most unusual languages spoken in Mesoamerica is the language known as Garífuna, or Black Carib. This language belongs to the Arawakan language family of South America, but it is currently spoken along the Caribbean coast of Belize, Guatemala, and Honduras.

Before the arrival of Europeans in the Caribbean, languages belonging to two different families, Carib and Arawak, were spoken on the Caribbean Islands. The Arawakan people seem to have been residents of these islands for a longer period of time, but many Arawakan populations had been conquered by Carib-speaking people.

This was the case on the island of St. Vincent, in the Lesser Antilles. An older Arawakan population had been largely overrun by Carib-speaking people. As a result of the Carib conquest, many or most Arawakan men were killed, but many Arawakan women survived and married Carib men. Linguists believe that for a period of time there were distinct men's and women's languages on the island. The women's Arawakan language (now called Garífuna) was the one that survived, but the people speaking it continued to be called Caribs.

Also on St. Vincent were a small number of European colonists and a large number of African slaves. Substantial numbers of escaped slaves mixed with the native population of the island, and there was a high rate of intermarriage between the two groups. As a result, most of the speakers of Garífuna have both African and Native American ancestry, and for this reason they are also known as the Black Caribs.

After revolts against the British on St. Vincent, the British government made the decision to deport all the remaining Black Carib people from St. Vincent in 1797. There were 5,080 people shipped from St. Vincent to the island of Roatán, off the coast of Honduras. The modern Garífuna people are the descendants of those who were deported from St. Vincent, and there are now about 30,000 speakers of this language.

As a result of the unusual history of these people, a South American language spoken by people of mixed African and Native American ancestry, Garífuna, has become part of the language diversity that characterizes the Mesoamerican region today.

aca at Monte Albán and other sites associated with the Classic period. Apart from some calendrical portions, these inscriptions are largely undeciphered, but most consist mainly of brief captions containing personal names and dates. A third set of hieroglyphic texts has recently been deciphered. The texts were discovered in the region of the ancient Olmecs, and the language of the inscriptions has been labelled epi-Olmec. The language of these texts is a form of Zoquean that turns out to be older than Proto-Zoquean (the ancestor of the Zoquean languages), but younger than Proto-Mixe-Zoquean.

WHAT ARE MESOAMERICAN LANGUAGES LIKE?

While most people have a fair understanding of what Spanish is like, the structure of the indigenous Mesoamerican languages is substantially different from either English or Spanish. Different native languages of the region also differ substantially from one another. However, the many interactions between speakers of different Mesoamerican languages has had an influence on the structures of the languages involved; to this extent, it makes sense to refer to a "typical Mesoamerican language." In addition, many of the features shared by Mesoamerican languages are not shared with languages just across the northern or southern borders of Mesoamerica. These features are discussed in this section.

Many other features of Mesoamerican languages are specific to individual language families, and did not spread widely. Some of these features occur frequently enough to merit discussion, providing a picture of the individuality of the languages and cultures of the region.

It is in the areas of *syntax*, the rules governing the order and use of words, and *semantics*, the typical relations among meanings of different words or grammatical constructions, that Mesoamerican languages have converged most heavily. The systems of sounds that are used in the languages (*phonology*) and the rules governing the formation of words (*morphology*) are typically rather similar in languages of a single family, but each family is rather different.

Phonology

The languages of Mesoamerica tend to have consonants and vowels that are not radically different from those found in familiar languages like English or Spanish. There are some exceptions, however.

There are cases of vowels unlike those found in most Western European languages. Many languages, for example, have a high central vowel /ɨ/, which is somewhat like the *e* in the English *roses*. Some Chinantecan languages have unusual vowels like /ë/ and /ï/, which are rare in the world's languages. They are made with the tongue in the position for /o/ and /u/, but with the lips spread, rather than rounded. Such vowels are typical of languages like Vietnamese. (Linguists enclose symbols between slashes to represent those sounds that constitute *phonemes* in a given language, i.e., sounds that contrast with one another, in the sense that words in that language may differ only by the substitution of one phoneme for another. For example, /p/ and /b/ are different phonemes in English, because several pairs of words like *pit* and *bit* differ by substituting /p/ and /b/ for each other.)

Distinctions are also made on the basis of the length of a vowel or whether it is followed by a glottal stop (a sound like the one that begins each syllable in the English expression "*uh-oh*"). Length and glottalization may occur on vowels in many families—Oto-Manguean, Totonacan, Mixe-Zoquean, and Mayan. Some Oto-Manguean languages make even more unusual distinctions in vowel type. There are varieties of Zapotec that distinguish vowels according to whether they are pronounced with a creaky voice or not.

Other languages make distinctive use of tone, like that found in Chinese. In these languages, the pitch or tone with which a word is pronounced makes as much of a difference in meaning as do the consonants and vowels in English. The most elaborate tone systems are found in the Oto-Manguean languages, where in some cases it appears that tone has arisen as consonants were lost. Whistled speech (see Box 11.2) exploits tonal clues to word meaning.

Box 11.2 *Whistled Speech in Oaxaca*

Several of the native languages in the highlands of Oaxaca may take on an unusual form—they may be whistled as well as spoken! Cowan (1948) describes the following exchange, which took place in a Mazatec village:

> One day Chumi was standing idly in the doorway of our hut. Irene Flores was working around the hut. No one, it seemed, was paying any attention to the quiet, random whistlings of the boy so nonchalantly leaning against the doorpost. All of a sudden, however, Irene whirled and launched out in a terrific scolding in spoken Mazateco. The whistling had not been as aimless and innocuous as it appeared. The mischievous boy had actually been whistling very meaningful things to the girl, until she could stand the teasing no more.

Whistled speech has been observed in the Zapotec, Chinantec, and Mazatec languages. In all these languages, whistled speech relies on tonal contrasts in the language. In general, the pattern of the whistles follows the pattern of the tones in the spoken language, and is in effect a direct translation of it.

For example, in the following exchange in that language, 1 shows a high tone, 4 shows a low tone, and 2 and 3 show intermediate tones:

A. Hña^{1} khoa^{2} ai^{4}-ni^{3}? "Where are you coming from?"

B. Ni^{3}ʔya^{2} khoa^{2} ai^{4}-nia^{3}. "I'm coming from Huautla."

The whistled version of this exchange is:

A. 1 2 4 3?

B. 3 2 2 4 3.

Notice that the pitch of each whistle is determined by the tone of the corresponding syllable in the spoken version of the exchange. Whistled speech is one of the features that makes Mesoamerica especially interesting as a language area.

The consonants of Mesoamerican languages also sometimes show contrasts that are unfamiliar in European languages. Some Mayan languages include the consonant /q/, which sounds somewhat like /k/, but is articulated further back in the mouth.

Another common consonant in Mesoamerican languages is the *glottal stop*, mentioned above. In Classical Nahuatl texts it is spelled "h," but often it was not spelled at all in the Spanish-based orthographies adopted in the early Colonial period. Today it is usually spelled by an apostrophe or 7, or by the linguistic symbols ʔ.

Other consonants are far more restricted. Nahua and Totonac have a phoneme (sound unit) usually written "tl" by nonlinguists. This sound is made with the tip of the tongue firmly against the base of the upper front teeth, as for a [t]; but when moving to the next sound, air is released at both sides of the tongue while the tip of the tongue remains against the teeth. This sound is distinct from both [t] and [l]. (Linguists enclose symbols between square brackets to give *phonetic* information, the actual pronunciation of sounds in the language, whether those phonetic units constitute separate phonemes or variant pronunciations of a single phoneme. For example [p^h] represents the pronunciation of English /p/ in the word *pit*, with a strong *aspiration* or release of air; you can feel the release if you place your fingers to your lips while pronouncing this word, but not after the *un*aspirated [p] of *spit*.)

It is also common to find that consonants are modified in certain ways when they are *pronounced. Palatalization* involves the addition of a y-like sound to the consonant; for example, t^y and k^y. Palatalized consonants are commonly found in Oto-Manguean, Zoquean, and less commonly in Mayan languages. *Glottalization* involves the addition of a glottal stop to the consonant; for example, t′ and k′. Glottalization is found in Mayan, Tepehua, Xincan, and along the southern border of Mesoamerica in Jicaque. *Aspiration* is characterized by the addition of an h-like sound to the consonant; for example, t^h and k^h. Aspiration is a contrastive feature of Tarascan (and Jicaque). *Prenasalization* involves the addition of nasality to the beginning of the consonant; for example, ^{m}b and ^{n}d. Some Oto-Manguean languages contain prenasalized consonants. Although the descriptions of these processes may make them sound like clusters of sounds, the languages in question treat them as single units for purposes such as grouping sounds into syllables.

All of these features of pronunciation are part of the systematic pattern of the languages in which they occur, in that all or most consonants exhibiting these features have a counterpart not exhibiting it, and vice versa. Thus, every Mayan glottalized consonant corresponds to a plain (unglottalized) consonant; for example, /t′/ vs. /t/, /k′/ vs. /k/, and so on. Palatalization and prenasalization work similarly in languages that have these features. Occasionally, however, the unmodified series of consonants has more members than the modified series; for example, Tarascan has /p/ vs. /p^h/ and /t/ vs. /t^h/, but there is no /k^h/ corresponding to /k/. This is a common pattern not only in Mesoamerica but throughout the world.

One feature that is common in European languages, but rare in the languages of Mesoamerica, is a contrast between consonants based on voicing. *Voicing* refers to the vibration of the vocal cords while producing a consonant, and English has many contrasts based on voicing; for example, /b/ is voiced, while /p/ is voiceless; /d/ is voiced, while /t/ is voiceless; and /g/ is voiced, while /k/ is voiceless. In most Mesoamerican languages, there is no contrast between these pairs of sounds; [p] and [b] are treated as variant pronunciations of the same basic sound.

Morphology

In Mesoamerican languages, the order of elements in a word is strictly defined. Words are made up of a root element plus some number of affixes (that is, prefixes, suffixes, and infixes) that must appear in a definite order. The orders of elements within a word will, of course, vary from language to language, but there are fixed rules of order for any particular language.

Table 11.1 Verbs with Affixes in Three Mesoamerican Languages

Zapotec:	Gu-re-lilaaz-detu-ni? question-habitual-*believe-you(pl)-it* *"Do you believe it?"*
Nahuatl:	Ō-ti-c-āltih-ca-h past-we-him-bathe-had-plural "We had bathed him."
Tzotzil:	Stak′ ch-a-j-kolta. can incompletive-you-I-help "I can help you."

A verb, for example, is usually made up of a verbal root plus affixes that indicate the tense-aspect of the verb, and the person and number of the subject (and object, if there is one). Table 11.1 shows verbs with affixes in three Mesoamerican languages.

Pronominal affixes on nouns and verbs exhibit a number of different patterns. In general, they are based on the category of *person*, defined in terms of the participants in a speech event. A first person affix refers to the speaker *(I)*; second person refers to the addressee *(you)*; and third person refers to a third party who is neither speaker nor addressee *(he, she, it)*.

Some languages have pronouns for combinations of these categories of participant. In several Mesoamerican languages, there are differences between two kinds of first person plural pronoun *(we)*. The inclusive first person plural means "we (including you)," and the exlusive first person plural means "we (not including you)." Sometimes third person pronouns distinguish between humans and nonhumans, as in several Oto-Manguean languages. Differences among pronouns based on respect are also found in Nahuatl and Oto-Manguean. However, third person pronouns are rarely distinguished by gender; that is, "he" and "she" (and often "it") are all indicated by the same pronominal affix or pronoun.

One unusual pattern of pronoun use is widespread enough in Mesoamerica to merit mention. This pattern is one that linguists refer to as *ergative*. In English, the same pronouns are used for both transitive subjects (*He saw him*) and intransitive subjects (*He ran*). An ergative system is one that treats transitive and intransitive subjects differently, grouping the intransitive subject together with the object. If English were an ergative language, we would still have sentences like *He saw him*, but the object pronoun would be used in intransitive sentences like *Him ran*. Mayan and Mixe-Zoquean languages show this sort of ergative pattern in their pronominal affixes.

Syntax

In most Mesoamerican language families, transitive sentences are constructed with their words in a different order than in English or Spanish. Transitive sentences place the verb (V) before the subject (S) and object (O); that is, they exhibit either VOS or VSO order, rather than the SVO order of English and Spanish. Intransitive sentences place the verb before the subject; that is, they exhibit VS order, rather than the SV order of English and Spanish.

In Table 11.2, Zapotec and Nahuatl show VSO orders, and Tzotzil shows VOS. A few languages, such as Huave, Tarascan, and Tequistlatecan, have SVO as the dominant order, but there do not seem to be any languages that have SOV as their primary word order. This is a distinctive feature of the region, since most languages on the northern and southern borders of Mesoamerica do have SOV order.

The universal occurrence of VO order is one of the features pointing to intensive interaction in this region over a long period of time. We can see the influence of other Mesoamerican languages on Nahuatl, which is the southernmost branch of a larger family of languages (Uto-Aztecan). The other members of that larger family outside Mesoamerica generally have SOV as their basic word order, and this probably was the original word order in Nahuatl as well. It appears that Nahuatl word order changed after Nahuatl speakers entered the Mesoamerican world.

Similarly, linguists believe that the Mixe-Zoquean languages once had SOV order, although they are all now verb-initial. This conclusion is now confirmed by hieroglyphic texts in Zoquean, which show this older word order. As of A.D. 162, transitive sentences were all SOV. However, intransitive sentences were either SV or VS, and this may be evidence of an early phase in word order change. The Zoquean languages must have changed to verb-initial order during or after the period of transition between the Formative and Classic periods of the epi-Olmec states (see Chapter 2).

Although verb-initial orders are the most common or basic orders, it is usual for alternative orders to be possible. It is typical in verb-initial languages for the subject to be moved to the front of the sentence when it is being emphasized. In many languages, any ordering of subject, verb, and object is possible, each order emphasizing a different notion. In addition, some Mesoamerican languages do not use the verb at the beginning of the sentence. This is most often a later development within a family that does place the verb first, and is usually found in languages nearest the northern or southern borders of the region. On the

Table 11.2 Word Order in Three Mesoamerican Languages

Zapotec:	Gu-dîxh nigí'u biñiin. completive-pay man boy "The man paid the boy."
Nahuatl:	Qu-itta in cihuā-tl in cal-li. it-see the woman-abs the house-abs "The woman sees the house."
Tzotzil:	7i-s-pet lok´el 7antz ti t´ul-e. cp-it-carry away woman the rabbit-clitic "The rabbit carried away the woman."

southern border, for example, Chortí Mayan is said to prefer SVO order, but the dominant and original pattern in Mayan languages is VOS. Chichimec, on the northern edge, is an SOV language, but the dominant and original pattern in Oto-Manguean languages is VSO (or VOS).

Other features of the grammar of Mesoamerican languages we summarize more briefly (see Table 11.3). When nouns (for example, "arm") are possessed, as in "the man's arm," the typical pattern in Mesoamerican languages is to say "his arm the man" or, less commonly, "the man his arm." The Nahuatl example in Table 11.3 shows this pattern.

Locational notions conveyed by prepositions in English (for example, "on the hill") are conveyed by *relational nouns* in Mesoamerican languages: possessed, (for example, "the hill, its top"), as in Mayan and Nahuatl, or as the head of a compound noun (for example, "the hill top"), as in Mixe-Zoquean and Oto-Manguean. Numerals have a *vigesimal,* or base-20 structure; rather than counting in powers of ten (10s, 100s, 1000s), as we normally do, Mesoamericans count in units that are powers of 20 (20s, 400s, 8000s). Thus a number like fifty-five is expressed as "two twenties plus fifteen."

Other Typical Characteristics

Also widespread are idiomatic expressions that occur throughout the Mesoamerican languages through the process of *loan translation.* This is a process in which an idiomatic expression—for example, the use of "mouth of house" to mean "door"—is translated word for word into other languages and used with the same idiomatic meaning. In addition, some loan translations consist of the use of a word with one meaning for another meaning related to the first metaphorically, if at all. Several such loan translations are found in Mesoamerica, but are rare

Table 11.3 Other Grammatical Features of Zapotec and Nahuatl

Zapotec:	Nuu toy nigí´u leen yuliz-a. there is a man belly house-my "There is a man in my house."
	gal-bi-tsuu twenty-with-ten 'thirty'
Nahuatl:	ī-cihuā-uh Pedro his-wife-poss Peter 'Peter's wife'
	cāl-ihtic cf. ihtitl, 'belly' house-inside 'inside the house'
	ōm-pōhualli on-caxtōlli two-twenty and-fifteen 'fifty-five'

Box 11.3 *Loan Translation*

The influence of Spanish is sometimes disguised by the typical Mesoamerican practice of loan translation, discussed above. Spanish base-10 numeration led to the introduction of words for "thousand" in several native languages that lacked it because they used base-20 systems (naming 20s, 400s, and 8000s). Doris Bartholomew has noted that the Spanish word *mil* ("thousand") was adopted in Nahuatl, but this was also the root of the native Nahua word *milpa*, meaning "cornfield." This Nahua pairing was widely adopted, as a number of indigenous languages came to use their own word for "cornfield" as a numeral for "thousand."

beyond its language borders; for example, "mother of hand" = "thumb", "child of hand" = "finger"; "edge" = "mouth"; "god excrement" or "sun excrement" = "gold" or "silver"; "water mountain" = "town"; "deer snake" = "boa constrictor"; "awake" = "alive" (see Box 11.3).

All of these characteristics typify all Mesoamerican language families, and all are uncharacteristic of the languages at the borders of the prehispanic Mesoamerican region. They are ways of speaking and thinking that are part of what defines Mesoamerica as a cultural unity. Other characteristics that are widespread in Mesoamerica are found also in languages in adjacent areas; they characterize but do not distinguish Mesoamerica as a linguistic region. For example, kinship terms and body parts are normally possessed, and when they are not possessed a special prefix or suffix is added. Words for locations are typically the same as or derived from words for body parts; for example, "head" is used for "top," "foot" for "base," "stomach" for "in." Semantic equivalences typical of the region, but also found outside it, include the use of the same word for "hand" and "arm"; that is, the concepts are not distinct.

Still other characteristics are widely shared among Mesoamerican languages, and rare or absent across its borders, but are missing in only one language family. In such cases, Mayan is most often the family in which the characteristic is missing; this family lies at the southern border of the ancient Mesoamerican world.

LANGUAGE VARIATION AND CHANGE

Dialects of Native Languages

Almost all indigenous languages in Mesoamerica occur in more than one form. In some areas, linguistic diversity is so great that every town has its own dialect or even its own language. This is the case, for example, in much of the Guatemalan highlands. Chicomuceltec was spoken only in and around the town of Chicomucelo; Mochó was spoken in Motozintla and Tuzantán, each having its own dialect; and, in general, each distinct town in the Cakchiquel region has a distinct form of Cakchiquel. The situation is similar for many of the Oto-Manguean languages, especially in Oaxaca. In other areas, linguistic diversity is quite low. The Yucatec language, for example, covers a large part of the Yucatán Peninsula.

Dialect differences are social as well as linguistic facts. When distinct forms of a language are found in different areas, people from one area may have difficulty understanding people from other areas. But this difficulty is not equally great for all participants; more often than not, tests of mutual intelligibility of dialects indicate that speakers of, say, dialect A understand speakers of dialect B more than speakers of dialect B understand speakers of dialect A. Where does this asymmetry come from? It often appears to reflect the density of communication (see Box 11.4).

Communication is pursued most with those one understands the best, all other things being equal. This structuring of communication has two effects. Linguistically, changes in poorly understood dialects are less likely to be noticed and adopted than changes in well-understood dialects, and so the least similar dialects become increasingly dissimilar. Socially, decreasing communication among communities reinforces social distance between them. This is a major trend in dialect evolution; it is the source of the origin of new languages from old, and of the development of language families out of parent languages. When this happens, the effect of the communication bottleneck is that the most closely related languages tend to be located next to one another; the geographic pattern of location is consistent with the degree of relationship among languages unless one or more of the social groups migrates from its ancestral location.

All the changes just discussed have the effect of increasing social and linguistic distance. Some changes, however, have the effect of *integrating* social groups and *decreasing* the distance between dialects. These are changes that take place when speakers of one language or dialect copy the vocabulary or speech patterns of speakers of another. Those doing the copying are speakers of the *borrowing language*; those being copied are speakers of the *source language*. Eventually, some of the copying being done will be internal copying by some speakers of the borrowing language of the patterns acquired by other speakers of that language, which were ultimately acquired by copying the source language.

The differentiation between languages or dialects, and between social groups, occurs probably most often as a result of changes occurring within separate

Box 11.4 *How Languages Diverge and Converge*

It has been found in Cakchiquel Mayan that speakers of dialects in major centers have more difficulty in understanding the Cakchiquel of smaller settlements around them than the latter do in understanding the Cakchiquel spoken in the center. People in the center host the regional market to which people from the surrounding areas come, and they also constitute a larger population than the speakers of dialects from surrounding settlements. As a result, speakers from the settlements interact far more with speakers from the center, relative to their interactions with other Cakchiquel speakers, than do the speakers from the center with any particular group of provincial speakers. Density of interaction, then, accounts for the asymmetry.

speech communities that are not interacting intensively. In some cases, however, continuing interaction helps to drive the differentiation between dialects. Leanne Hinton has shown this for the Mixtec spoken at Chalcatongo and at San Miguel, the next town along the main local highway. There is a social differentiation between the Mixtecs of San Miguel and surrounding hamlets, who are committed to and involved in traditional, local culture, and the Mixtecs of Chalcatongo, who are modernizing and ladinoizing via participation in wider economic networks. The dialects of San Miguel and Chalcatongo turn out to be most similar in the more distant parts of these communities; near the border between the municipios, the differences in the dialects are exaggerated. These Mixtec-speaking communities are using language differences to display social commitments and to call attention to social differences between them. The greater the extent of interaction among members of these groups, the greater the usefulness of devices such as the symbolism of dialect difference for reinforcing group identity and distinctness.

The process of convergence through borrowing can be illustrated by Kekchí, a Mayan language spoken in the highlands of Guatemala. Kekchí has been spreading since the Spanish invasion and probably before. The town of Cobán is the leading economic center, and its dialect is the most highly valued by Kekchí speakers generally; that is, it is the *prestige dialect.* As a result, younger speakers of other Kekchí dialects are copying some of the changes that are taking place or that have already taken place in Cobán. For example, /w/ is pronounced as [kw] in Cobán, ultimately under the influence of Spanish; this change is also being generalized, with /y/ being raised in the same way and pronounced as [ty]. These changes are so recent that younger and older speakers of Cobán Kekchí pronounce /w/ and /y/ differently, even as the change is spreading to other communities. Other, older changes are well entrenched throughout Cobán, and are widespread in Kekchí; for example, speakers of almost all Kekchí dialects have shortened their original long vowels.

These changes in Kekchí are typical of patterns of language change not only in Mesoamerica but throughout the world. One community having a socially favored position is a center of innovations that are adopted by its neighbors. These neighbors typically lag somewhat behind the innovating center. Changed forms at first exist in variation with the original forms, but eventually replace them.

Such changes may be recognized and copied not only by speakers of different dialects but even by speakers of different languages. Relatively casual contact is enough for the borrowing of vocabulary, especially for items or concepts that are newly introduced to the borrowing group. Changes in pronunciation or grammar—that is, in the structure of a language—always involve intensive interaction among speakers of the source and borrowing languages.

In ancient times, the same processes are assumed to have been at work. When linguists detect the effects of these processes, they thereby provide evidence for the existence of interaction among speakers of the languages involved, for the intensity and duration of that interaction, and for the nature of that interaction. Historical reconstruction from the imprint of culture on language is discussed later in this chapter.

Since arrival of the Europeans in Mesoamerica, native languages have suffered greatly in terms of numbers of speakers and social status. Many languages have become extinct, and very few of the millions of speakers of indigenous languages in Mesoamerica have been literate in native languages. This results from several factors. Education and scholarship in the countries of Mexico and Central America have been conducted almost entirely in European languages, preventing speakers of the native languages from achieving literacy in these languages. Further, full access to education has historically been limited to a small percentage of the indigenous people of Mesoamerica.

However, in the last few decades, there has been an upsurge of interest in and attention to the native languages of the area. In Guatemala there are several million speakers of Mayan languages, and owing to the combined efforts of native speakers and linguists, efforts are now under way to provide bilingual education in Spanish and in local Mayan languages (Cakchiquel, Kekchí, Quiché, Mam, and others). Such efforts require the production of textbooks and reading materials in Mayan languages, and the goals of the project are to increase literacy in both Spanish and native languages. Box 11.5 provides an example of how the Zapotec language is being promoted in modern Mexico.

Box 11.5 *Using the Zapotec Language Today*

The Zapotec language has also emerged as an important literary and political force in Oaxaca, Mexico. In Juchitán, Oaxaca, many local political figures make campaign speeches in Zapotec, and the use of the Zapotec language has become a symbol of Juchitán's resistance to Mexico's ruling government. Residents of Juchitán also produce a Zapotec language periodical, *Guchachí Reza* ('Sliced Iguana'), which is a bearer of the growing Zapotec language literacy in Oaxaca. The following poem by Gabriel López Chiñas exemplifies modern pride in the Zapotec language:

They say that Zapotec is going,
no one will speak it now,
it's dead they say, it's dying,
the Zapotec language.

The Zapotec language
the devil take it away,
now the sophisticated Zapotecs
speak Spanish only.

Ah, Zapotec, Zapotec!
those who put you down
forget how much their mothers
loved you with a passion!

Ah, Zapotec, Zapotec!
language that gives me life,
I know you'll die away
on the hour of the death of the sun.

Gabriel López Chiñas

From Gabriel López Chiñas, *El zapoteco* López, Chiñas, Gabriel 1983 El zapoteco. In *La flor de la palabra,* edited by Victor de la Cruz, pp.68–69. Mexico City: Premia Editora. English translation by Nathaniel Tarn, in *Zapotec Struggles: Histories, Politics, and Representations from Juchitán, Oaxaca,* edited by Howard Campbell, Leigh Binford, Miguel Bartolomé, and Alicia Barabas, p. 211. Washington, D. C.: Smithsonian Institution, 1993.

The Impact of Spanish on Native Languages

Most of the language families in Mesoamerica were documented in some form from very early in the sixteenth century. Based on these and later records, we know that some languages once spoken in the region are no longer spoken today. We also know that people rarely give up their own language willingly. What are the languages that have been lost, and why did they die out?

The main direct cause of language loss is a process called *language shift*: The speakers of one language begin using another language in place of it. Typically such speakers are at first bilingual in their native language and a second language whose use is economically or socially advantageous. Over the last few centuries, this second language has usually been Spanish, although sometimes it is an expanding native language such as Kekchí Maya.

The use of native languages is typically associated with traditional practices and institutions, while the use of Spanish is associated with the penetration of mestizo or ladino practices and institutions, including especially regional and national economic systems. Survival or advancement in the local economy via participation in wider economic systems is often facilitated by the use of Spanish. Partly this is because Spanish aids communication among speakers of different indigenous languages, since bilingualism in Spanish is widespread across all languages of Mesoamerica. Partly it is because native languages are usually stigmatized by ladinos, as nonstandard dialects of English are stigmatized among white-collar workers in the United States. In addition, native language use has often been discouraged by national policies. Schools often promote the use of Spanish and avoid the use of indigenous languages. Recently in Guatemala and El Salvador, people have sometimes been regarded as insurgents, and targeted for kidnapping and murder, simply because they spoke Mayan languages.

In such situations, the choice of which language to use often depends upon the nature of the speech situation, and who is involved in it. The native language may be spoken primarily within the family or among close friends, while Spanish is preferred in interactions with more distant acquaintances, or with strangers. But when the native language is seen as a hindrance to social and economic advancement, parents may speak only Spanish to their children.

Once children no longer learn the native language of their people, it is moribund. There are several native languages that few if any children learn. Texistepec Popoluca, for example, is spoken only by people in their fifties or older; there are only two dozen or so fluent speakers of Oluta Popoluca. Other languages are learned by children only after they learn Spanish, as a second language. This is usual in the case of Chontal Mayan.

In some cases, languages die out as the populations that speak them are destroyed. Often, languages are highly localized, spoken in a single village or valley. It might be thought that the speakers of these languages were often killed off in warfare, but this happened rarely if ever in prehispanic Mesoamerica. Rather, the populations usually disappeared as separate entities because they were displaced or dispersed, and came to live among much larger groups that eventually absorbed them.

These language choices influence native people's sense of their own identity. Very frequently in Mesoamerica, a person's ethnic identity and language are identified: To *be* Lacandón is to *speak* Lacandón. The process of language replacement, in this setting, means selecting a different ethnic identity and different social commitments by the very act of language choice. Even the choice of language to use at a particular moment in a particular social setting is complicated by the particular communicative requirements of the situation and the social statement that language choice makes.

Nonetheless, the potential for breakdown of ethnic identity can be overemphasized. The relation between language and ethnicity may have been closer in the past, before Spanish began to replace native languages in large portions of most native groups. Today, however, language, culture, and ethnic identity cannot be equated. With the replacement of native languages by the processes described above, the native language may come to be spoken by a minority of members of the once-associated cultural and ethnic groups, with Spanish now the dominant language. Conversely, members of different ethnic groups may speak the same language.

Although Spanish is far from replacing many of the indigenous languages, all of these languages have been affected by Spanish in their vocabulary and phonology, and probably in their syntax as well. Some have borrowed a great deal of Spanish vocabulary, especially for items and ideas introduced since the conquest. Other languages have resisted the incorporation of Spanish vocabulary, and create new words from native roots and affixes. For example, "horse" was usually designated by a native word for "animal," or for a large animal such as a deer or mountain cow (whereas, in North America, it was typical to adopt the word for "dog," the prime domestic animal). "Chicken" was referred to by the word for "turkey," while "turkey" came to be named with this word plus a modifier or affix. "Rifle" was named with compound nouns such as "shooting stick" or "fire stick" (for additional examples, see Box 11.6). Today, the Mayan Academy is replacing some Spanish loans by such Mayan-based vocabulary.

In the section on the phonology of Mesoamerican languages, we point out that the sound systems of these languages differ from that of Spanish. When Spanish words are adopted, indigenous languages often *nativize* them; that is, they adapt the pronunciation of the Spanish form to the native pattern. Tzotzil *pale* and Oluta Popoluca *pane* are examples, taken over from Spanish *padre*, 'priest'.

Box 11.6 *The Influence of Spanish on Counting*

Numerals are a part of the basic vocabulary of a language, and they are rarely borrowed. This tends to be especially true of the lower numerals, which have more common use in everyday talk than do larger numerals. Some indigenous Mesoamerican languages have replaced their larger numerals by Spanish terms. The point at which native numerals end and Spanish numerals begin varies from language to language.

The Mayan languages illustrate the range of variation. There are five modern Cholan-Tzeltalan languages. The native numerals consisted of basic roots from 1 to 12; for 13 to 19, the numerals are composed of the words for "ten" plus the remaining number. For example, **7ox-lajun* ("thirteen") comes from the roots **7ox* ("three") and **lajun* ("ten"). There were basic words for higher numerals that were powers of 20—at least for 20, 400, and 8000—since, like other Mesoamerican languages, these languages were vigesimal (or base-20). Other numerals were formed, additively or multiplicatively, from smaller numerals.

The Tzeltalan languages, both Tzeltal and Tzotzil, preserve all basic number words. In contrast, all Cholan languages have lost terms for higher numerals. Chol preserves words for 20, 400, and 8000; Chontal only the word for 20; Chortí has lost all of its words for powers of 20. All three have adopted Spanish words for the numerals 13 to 19. In Chol, the unanalyzable numerals for 1 to 12 are all maintained. Chontal adopted Spanish terms for numerals 5 and up; in addition, it has *7un* rather than the expected *jun* for "one," presumably an accommodation to Spanish *uno*, and it has innovated a form *7unk'a7* (from "one hand") for "five." Similarly, some speakers of Chortí adopted Spanish terms for numerals over 5, though others preserve native terms up to 9.

Native vocabulary is often embedded into larger semantic and grammatical structures of a language. Numerals, for example, modify nouns. In addition, special morphemes often attach to numerals. In Cholan-Tzeltalan languages, *numeral classifiers* are attached to numerals in counting. For example, *7ox-tuhl* means "three (animate things)," *7ox-tz'iht* means "three (long thin things)," and *7ox-pis* means "three (measured things)." Classifiers like *-tuhl* and *-tz'iht* were required with all numerals in prehispanic times.

Borrowed vocabulary often does not fit in native structures. In the case of numerals, for example, it is often found that borrowed Spanish nouns are modified by Spanish numerals, even when native numerals exist. A particularly widespread example of this lack of fit is that native affixes may not be attached to borrowed words. In the Cholan-Tzeltalan languages, the native classifiers are never used along with a borrowed numeral.

This happens not only to individual Spanish sounds but also to sequences of them; for example, *cuentas* (= /kwentas/) ("counters, rosary beads") was adopted as *wentax* in several languages.

However, as often happens elsewhere in the world, indigenous languages sometimes adopt Spanish words with their Spanish pronunciation, or a close approximation to it. The result is that some words in the language have *loan phonemes* and phoneme sequences (like consonant clusters) that occur only in Spanish loans into the language. When speakers use words with non-native sounds or sound patterns, this marks the usage as a "hispanism"; this may orient people's attitudes toward the topic addressed through the use of the hispanic rather than a nativized usage. Hispanic pronunciation is normally found only with extensive bilingualism in Spanish and the native language.

WRITING IN ANCIENT MESOAMERICA

Ancient Mesoamerican societies were evidently unique in the New World in that most had some form of writing. Writing existed among speakers of lowland Mayan languages in southeastern Mexico, Guatemala, and Belize; among Zoquean speakers in southern Veracruz and probably in Chiapas; among Zapotec speakers in the Valley of Oaxaca; among Mixtec speakers in Oaxaca; and among Nahuatl speakers in the Valley of Mexico. Texts are also found in other areas of Mesoamerica—at Kaminaljuyú and Izapa in Guatemala, at El Tajín in Veracruz, and at Xochicalco in Morelos, for example—but the languages associated with these scripts have yet to be determined. The content of these hieroglyphic texts is discussed in Chapter 2. In this chapter we sketch some principles of Mesoamerican writing as they relate to language.

How Languages Were Represented

All Mesoamerican scripts made use of *logograms,* signs that represented whole words or roots. This could be through direct depiction (for example, a picture of a knot for the Zapotec day name Knot), depiction of an associated concept (for example, the rain god's face for the Aztec day name Rain), or by abstract signs. This may be the source of all other types of representation found earlier in Mesoamerican iconographic systems.

All well-understood Mesoamerican scripts also used *rebus* representation: Two words pronounced the same, or almost the same, could be spelled by the same sign, though that sign depicted the idea behind only one of the words. In ancient lowland Mayan languages, for example, *tu:n* (earlier *to:n*) meant "year-ending." Another word pronounced *tu:n* referred to long wooden musical instruments, such as trumpets and split log drums. Although the similarity in pronunciation was only coincidental, the first word was sometimes spelled, like the second, using a sign that depicted a split log drum.

These principles may suffice to account for all prehispanic Aztec and Mixtec spellings. These spellings, which served within complex systems of narrative pictographic iconography ("picture writing"), named the gods, people, and places whose depictions they accompanied, as well as the dates in the ritual calendar of the events that were shown. Quite serviceable for conveying such information, rebus and logographic spelling was quite ambiguous from the point of view of linguistic transcription, with many grammatical affixes and words left unrepresented (see Box 11.7).

Fully *textual* systems were more explicit in representing such grammatical elements, typically with *phonetic* signs that represented not words or roots, but simple syllables consisting of a consonant, a vowel, and sometimes another consonant. These signs were heavily used in Mayan and epi-Olmec writing. Whether they were used in the Zapotec writing of Monte Albán is an open question. In any case, for the purpose of decipherment, it is methodologically important to presume at first that basic grammatical morphemes are explicitly represented.

There is an inherent structural mismatch between a spoken language whose syllables can end in consonants and a phonetic spelling using symbols for a consonant followed by a vowel (*CV* signs): Whenever a word contains a consonant that is not followed by a vowel, either a vowel will be spelled that is not actually to be pronounced (like that of the sign ***pi*** in epi-Olmec ***7i-ki-pi-wʉ***, spelling Zoquean ***7i-kip-wʉ***, "they fought them"), or a consonant will not be spelled that *is* to be pronounced (like *j* in *wehj-pa*, "he shouts," spelled ***we-pa***). Weak consonants (*j*, *w*, *y*, and *7*) were especially susceptible to loss: When an extra vowel was inserted, it usually matched the preceding vowel. Rather firm rules or practices characterize the phonetic spellings of epi-Olmec writing; practices in Mayan writing seem to have been more complex and flexible.

One rather common variety of spelling combined both logographic and syllabic principles through the use of a logogram with a *phonetic complement.* In effect, the logogram spelled the word, and the syllabic sign—the phonetic component—indicated part of the pronunciation of that word. For example, the epi-Olmec word for "ten" was *mak*; that for "sky" was *tzap.* In the name of the Venus god Ten Sky, the syllabic sign ***ma*** was placed before the numeral ***10,*** indicating that the word for "ten" begins with the syllable *ma.* Phonetic complements can also spell final consonants, using the same practices as in fully phonetic spellings discussed in the previous paragraph. For example, the sign ***pa*** follows the sign SKY on one occasion, agreeing with the final consonant of *tzap* ("sky"), and with the extra vowel selected to agree with that of *tzap* (see Box 11.8).

Box 11.7 *Ethnocentrism and Writing Systems*

Symbol systems that indicate some words or parts of words but do not indicate other words or grammatical suffixes are sometimes referred to as "mnemonic devices" or jogs to the memory. Others characterize such systems as failed or poor attempts to convey their languages, remarking on how surprising it is that the inadequacies could persist for centuries without being corrected by, for example, making fuller use of phonetic representation. These perspectives mistake the organization and purpose of this kind of symbolic representation, denigrating it as a defective version of our own system or of other systems that are more explicit or complete in what they represent about a language.

It seems unlikely that the Aztec and Mixtec systems were ever meant to represent spoken utterances. What is referred to as "writing" in these representational systems was a means of identifying gods, people, places, and dates. Language was a resource for this task: The roots in place names, for example, were enough to identify a place for someone who knew those names. Ambiguities in these systems do not make them any more defective than does ambiguity in word meaning; in context, we understand which meaning of a word makes the most sense, and the ancient Mixtecs and Aztecs could do the same with their system of representation. In other words, these people made effective *use* of language to help them convey important information; precise replication of the stream of speech was not their goal.

Box 11.8 *Deciphering Epi-Olmec*

Decipherment is a process of accounting for the patterns of sign use in a writing system. In phonetic writing, this usually means accounting for individual signs as corresponding to particular sounds, and for sequences of signs as corresponding to sequences of sounds. If the language is known, the grammatical structure and vocabulary of that language become substantial clues that can be used to decipher the script. These were major clues in the recent decipherment of a hieroglyphic script of ancient southern Veracruz by John Justeson and Terrence Kaufman.

For geographic and historical reasons, most researchers recognized that the script probably represented an ancient Mixe-Zoquean language. Verbs in these languages began with one of a small number of prefixes and suffixes, most of which are syllables. In fact, the most common verb prefix and the most common noun prefix were both pronounced *7i-*; the most common verb suffix was *-wʉ*. This made it easy to recognize the signs that represented these syllables. This, in turn, made it possible to begin an analysis of the text: to identify its nouns and verbs, which led to the identification of additional noun and verb affixes, which led to yet further refinement of the analysis.

Vocabulary could also be identified. Using calendrical statements, it was possible to identify the meanings of several words in the text, including "day," "star," "ten," and "sky." The word for "day," for example, was spelled with two signs. One was postulated as representing the syllable *ja*, the next as *ma*. This *ma* reading is confirmed because the sign that spells *ma* begins the spelling of "star" (*matza7*) and "ten" (*mak*), both of which start with *ma*.

Given a number of these phonetic readings, and a number of grammatical identifications, a rather complete grammatical description of epi-Olmec texts has been worked out. This resulted in the recognition of many features specific to Mixe-Zoquean grammar, which confirmed the Mixe-Zoquean family model. For example, epi-Olmec texts use SOV word order, which can be reconstructed only in Mixe-Zoquean among all the languages of Mesoamerica. These texts also use European-style "nominative-accusative" pronoun patterns in subordinate clauses, but ergative patterns in main clauses. Such independent tests confirm the decipherment and the Zoquean identification of the texts.

How Writing Evolved

The origin of writing was a process that transformed a symbolic system in which language played no crucial role to one in which language was a significant resource for interpreting symbolic statements. The precursor system cannot have used much phonetic representation, since that kind of convention does make crucial use of language. Just what system or systems may have contributed directly to the emergence of writing in Mesoamerica cannot be said with assurance. However, one early symbol system does appear to have been much like writing, using similar nonphonetic representational conventions, but without relating directly to language. This is the Olmec-style iconography on many incised celts, dating to the Early and/or Middle Formative periods.

Most incised celts in the Olmec style depict humans wearing elaborate headgear and gesturing or holding various objects that seem to indicate their social status or such offices as ruler or warrior (Figure 11.3, left). In some cases, however, most of the detail used to represent the figure was eliminated, and only those that convey specific categories of information remain (Figure 11.3, right). For example, instead of depicting a person gesturing, the head is represented (indicating a person) with a headdress (indicating rank or office); the gesture is represented separately, as a disembodied hand or arm in the appropriate posture. Thus, iconic elements were being taken out of the usual figural context of pictorial representation, functioning as symbols for social categories, events, and probably other types of information as well. Some of these symbols seem relatively abstract, as is often true of status symbols, while others seem to be depictions of something directly related to the concept—for example, weapons may indicate warrior status or battles. Thus, a subset of celt iconography uses separate symbols for the kinds of concepts that are represented by the nonphonetic conventions of later Mesoamerican writing, yet their source in standard celt iconography is apparent. The iconography of ceremonial celts is therefore a plausible precursor of writing in Mesoamerica.

Figure 11.3 Arroyo Pesquero Celts. After Peter David Joralemon, "The Olmec Dragon: A Study in Pre-Columbian Iconography," in *Origins of Religious Art and Iconography in Preclassic Mesoamerica,* ed. H. B. Nicholson. Los Angeles, CA: UCLA Latin American Center Publications and Ethnic Arts Council of Los Angeles, 1976, p. 41, fig. 8 e and f.

It might be thought that the earliest writing probably resembled the Mixtec and Aztec systems, which have the most limited forms of representation of language. However, these systems seem to have actually developed ultimately from the Zapotec system, originally a more textual tradition. They contain no traces of syllabic or other phonetic spelling, except for rebus, and it is possible that the scripts from which they emerged also lacked such spelling. As noted above, syllabic spelling has yet to be definitively established in Zapotec texts. It may be that the difficulty in deciphering these early texts lies precisely in a lack of simple phonetic spelling, but the problem is only now being addressed with the necessary linguistic framework for analysis.

As a result of the limited knowledge not only of the Zapotec script, but of all Middle Formative writing, the nature of the earliest Mesoamerican writing systems—those from which the better-known systems emerged—is largely a matter of conjecture. It is generally thought that syllabic spelling emerged out of an earlier system or systems with rebus representation but without a substantial amount of nonrebus syllabic spelling. By the end of the Late Formative period, when readable Mayan and epi-Olmec texts are found, syllabic spelling is firmly a part of both hieroglyphic systems.

We cannot tell whether the epi-Olmec writing system evolved in any significant way; only two texts survive with enough writing to analyze and they are dated within five years of one another. In the case of Mayan writing, some syllabic spelling is found in the earliest datable texts. However, the amount of syllabic spelling gradually increased during the 600 to 700 years in which dated inscriptions are found. So, apparently, did the explicitness with which grammatical affixes were represented. There is a tendency to add phonetic complements first to those logograms that are ambiguous, thereby determining just which word is intended. For example, the sign for the day "Thunder" (in lowland Mayan, *chawuk* or *kawak*) was also used for both *tun* ("year ending") and *ha7b'* ("year"); the word *tun* could be secured as the interpretation by indicating that it ends in *n*, which was done by placing the sign ***ni*** after it. There is also a tendency for fully syllabic spellings of a given word to occur later than logographic spellings with phonetic complements; for example, Mayan *tun* was occasionally spelled ***tu-n(i)*** in the Late Classic period. So, to some extent, fully syllabic spelling seems to be a generalization from the earlier, partially syllabic and partially logographic spellings. In spite of definite trends in this direction, the story of the development of Mayan writing is much more complex than this. Some words have no known logographic spellings, and the earliest instances of such words are spelled syllabically.

LANGUAGE AND HISTORY

Linguists are able to determine a number of facts about the culture and history of Mesoamerica from the imprint that history has left on their languages. When people interact and influence one another's cultures, their languages are among the domains that are affected. When this happens, it is often possible to detect the influence, to determine its linguistic and cultural sources, and to reconstruct the nature of the interaction that brought it about. This is possible because different types of social interaction lead to different types of linguistic change.

Reconstructing Culture from Vocabulary

It is possible for linguists to determine the history of the languages of Mesoamerica by comparing the present state of those languages. There are two basic approaches involved in such comparisons—reconstruction and classification. Linguists can reconstruct ancestral vocabulary and grammatical patterns by comparing the differently changed forms of these ancestral words and patterns as they survive in the modern, descendant languages. These reconstructions constitute a hypothetical description of the ancestral language. As mentioned above, such ancestral languages are known as proto-languages. The forms that are reconstructed for proto-languages are preceded by the asterisk symbol (*) to make explicit the fact that the forms are reconstructed rather than being attested in written records. Today, a large number of proto-Cholan and proto-Yucatecan (Mayan) reconstructions have been verified in Mayan hieroglyphic texts, and Zoquean and Mixe-Zoquean reconstructions in epi-Olmec texts.

Cultural inferences can be drawn from reconstructed vocabularies. For example, if it is possible to reconstruct a large set of terms related to maize cultivation—corncob, cornfield, cornhusk, to double over corn, sweet corn, tortilla, etc.—then we can be quite sure that speakers of the ancestral language were maize agriculturalists. On the other hand, if the descendant languages use forms for such items that do not descend from the same words, then it is less likely that they practiced maize cultivation. As it happens, such vocabulary has been reconstructed for all Mesoamerican language families, so we suppose that ancestral Mayans Mixe-Zoqueans, and Oto-Mangueans all practiced maize cultivation. In contrast, words for a variety of pottery vessels, for cooking and storage, are reconstructible for proto-Mayan and proto-Mixe-Zoquean, but not for proto-Oto-Manguean, and the same is true of words for the hearthstones that support cooking vessels over a fire. We infer from this that ancestral Oto-Mangueans probably did not have pottery vessels and did not boil their food. This makes sense archaeologically: pottery, including boiling pots, is only found thousands of years *after* maize agriculture began in the Oto-Manguean area, the earliest locus of maize cultivation in Mesoamerica.

Language Classification and Migration

Language classification is also a crucial key to culture history. As discussed in the section on dialects, language differences that develop among dialects result in a geographic distribution of languages that places the most closely related languages adjacent to one another—geography recapitulates phylogeny. Exceptions to this pattern result from the movement of groups from their ancestral location. Thus, classification helps us to recognize which groups have moved, and where they came from. In fact, the geographic distribution of Mesoamerican languages generally agrees quite closely with the genetic relations among these languages, so such migration has evidently been relatively rare in this part of the world.

Nonetheless, many obvious cases of the movement of peoples are known. Some linguists believe that Tequistlatecan is a member of the Hokan family, which is widespread in northern North America but rare elsewhere. The Tequistlatecan family includes Tequistlatec in Oaxaca and Jicaque in Honduras. Speakers of these languages must have migrated into Mesoamerica from the north.

Similarly, three Oto-Manguean languages—Sutiaba, Chiapanec, and Mangue—are outside the area in which the other thirty or so Oto-Manguean languages are compactly located. Chiapanec and Mangue form a genetic grouping within Oto-Manguean. Presumably, they moved as a group, stopping first in Chiapas; those who remained became the Chiapanecs, while those who continued on to Nicaragua became the Mangues (see Chapter 3). They must have left from the vicinity of the Tlapanecs, linguistically their closest relatives. In fact, the Mangues were called "Chorotega" (= /chololteka/), and Terrence Kaufman proposes that they were the Early Classic inhabitants of Cholula. The closest linguistic relative of Sutiaba is the Tlapanec language.

Nahuatl is a branch of the Uto-Aztecan family, the only one to enter the region of the Mesoamerican world. Its presence is the result of intrusion into the region, and it has been noted above that several characteristics of Nahuatl have been acquired through contact with other Mesoamerican languages. In fact, Nahuatl has spread into pockets throughout Mesoamerica, interrupted by ancient language groupings of long standing; this pattern also reflects a recent radiation of Nahuatl people.

For Mixe-Zoquean, the situation is complicated. The Mixean languages are split into two areas by Zoquean, and the Zoquean languages are split into two areas by Mixean. The simplest geographic account that is consistent with the identification of the epi-Olmec sites in southern Veracruz with Zoquean is to suppose that Mixean was originally south of Zoquean; most of Mixean moved westward and northward as Chiapanec-Mangue moved into Chiapas and Zoquean expanded southward into Chiapas and Oaxaca. It is possible, then, that the northernmost Olmec settlements were Zoquean and that the southernmost were Mixean; alternatively, Mixean may have been south of the Olmec heartland (see Chapter 2).

Language Contact

It was noted in earlier sections that language contact provides evidence for social interaction. One of the most obvious ways is through the diffusion of vocabulary.

Names of animals and plants have often been borrowed by people entering an ecological zone from people already living there. For example, the Totonac language includes many loan words from Huastec for plants and animals native to the area in which the Totonacs now live. This suggests that the Totonacs entered the region in which they now live at a time when it was occupied by Huastecs, who were displaced by Totonacs. Archaeologically, evidence for the intrusion of new people into the area is found around A.D. 1100. Accordingly, Kaufman proposes that the people of Tajín were Huastecs—that is, people who spoke the Huastec language.

Culturally important contacts are indicated by the borrowing of vocabulary for cultural complexes. For example, several of the names and numerals used in naming days in the ritual calendar of the Oaxaca Mixe are Zoquean words, although the Mixe language has the corresponding names and numerals for use in general, noncalendrical vocabulary. This indicates that the Oaxaca Mixe calendar was strongly influenced by Zoquean speakers, which further indicates a leading role for Zoqueans in some aspects of the ritual life of the Mixe. Mixe-Zoquean names for several important cultigens are found throughout a large number of Mesoamerican languages; these and other important loans have been taken as evidence that the Olmecs spoke Mixe-Zoquean.

As noted above in the discussion of language change (see Box 11.4), one language sometimes changes grammatically by copying the grammatical structures of another. Quite intense levels of interaction must be inferred when this happens. These changes may occur when the source group switches rapidly to the language of a small target group—normally when the small group was a militarily successful elite. The source group uses its own grammatical patterns while acquiring imperfect control of the target language. Alternatively, grammatical copying occurs when two groups are in long-term, intense contact, probably the more common situation in Mesoamerica.

Such grammatical borrowing happened many times and in many places in Mesoamerica. In the discussion of syntax, we mentioned the change of Mixe-Zoquean languages from SOV to verb-initial. It seems likely that this change resulted from the word order of other Mesoamerican languages. The word order change could have happened in one of two ways: (1) Zoquean-speaking epi-Olmec people could have been bilingual with their neighbors speaking other languages, with the epi-Olmecs in a subordinate role relative to these neighbors; or (2) a substantial portion of the epi-Olmec population could have consisted of people who had employed another language as their native tongue, but shifted to Zoquean speech because of cultural domination by Zoqueans. Zapotecs in Oaxaca, Mixes in the Guatemalan highlands, and Mayans were probably in a position to provide such influence.

Similar cases exist for other language groups. Within Mayan, Cholan appears to have had a heavy influence on the vocabulary of Yucatecan, while Yucatecan has influenced the grammar and phonology of Cholan. In Oto-Manguean, the spread of sound changes among different Mixtec languages indicates that the Mixtecs of Tilantongo exerted substantial influence on neighboring kingdoms.

Glottochronology

Another tool often used in linguistic studies is glottochronology. By assuming that basic vocabulary is lost at a relatively constant rate, the time elapsed since two languages had a common ancestor can be determined, provided that it is known that they are in fact related and provided that the basic vocabulary list has been reconstructed. The assumption that vocabulary is lost at a constant rate appears to be at best an approximation, but glottochronology can provide at least a rough estimate for when two or more languages were one. In the cases of migration just discussed, this gives an estimate for when the people speaking these languages migrated.

Glottochronology has been tested against hieroglyphic data in the case of Mayan and Mixe-Zoquean; given that the underlying assumptions of the method are not universally accepted, it is remarkable how exactly the glottochronological dates fit the hieroglyphic evidence. In Mesoamerica, it appears that glottochronology provides a rather reliable guide for cultural chronologies.

CONCLUSION

The languages we have described above are crucially tied to our understanding of the Mesoamerican cultural tradition.

When we attempt to understand the history of this region, the common properties of Mesoamerican languages attest to the long periods of interactions among different Mesoamerican peoples, and the hieroglyphic texts provide us with irreplaceable insights into ancient political systems. Glottochronology and reconstruction allow us to form hypotheses about the cultures and movements of the ancient peoples of Mexico and Central America.

The indigenous languages are also central to understanding preconquest, colonial, and contemporary Mesoamerican views of the world. The voices of native peoples in Mesoamerica have been expressed in both native and colonial languages, but the choice of languages has rarely been neutral. Choosing one or another language or dialect conveys complex messages about colonialism, community, and ethnic identity.

Finally, not only has language served as a medium for the expression of the histories, religions, and dreams of Mesoamerican people, but it has also acted as a conservative force in shaping the content of these expressions as well. Language is one of the strongest links between the achievements of ancient Mesoamerica and the struggles and accomplishments of the peoples in this part of the modern world.

SUGGESTED READINGS

BRICKER, VICTORIA R. (ed.) 1992 *Epigraphy*. Handbook of Middle American Indians, Supplement 5. Austin: University of Texas Press.

CAMPBELL, HOWARD, LEIGH BINFORD, MIGUEL BARTOLOMÉ, and ALICIA BARABAS, (eds.) 1993 *Zapotec Struggles: Histories, Politics, and Representations from Juchitán, Oaxaca*. Washington, D.C.: Smithsonian Institution.

CAMPBELL, LYLE 1979 Middle American Languages. In *The Languages of Native America: Historical and Comparative Assessment*, edited by Lyle Campbell and Marianne Mithun. Austin: University of Texas Press.

COWAN, GEORGE M. 1948 Mazateco whistle speech. *Language* 24:280–286. Reprinted in Dell Hymes, ed., *Language in Culture and Society*, pp. 305–311. New York: Harper & Row, Publishers.

JUSTESON, JOHN S., and TERRENCE KAUFMAN 1993 A Decipherment of epi-Olmec Hieroglyphic Writing. *Science* 271:1703–1711.

HILL, JANE H., and KENNETH C. HILL 1986 *Speaking Mexicano*. Tucson: University of Arizona Press.

KAUFMAN, TERRENCE 1991 "Mesoamerican Languages." In *Encyclopaedia Britannica*, vol. 22, pp. 785–792.

LÓPEZ, CHIÑAS, GABRIEL 1983 El zapoteco. In *La flor de la palabria*, edited by Victor de la Cruz, pp. 68–69. Mexico city: Premia Editora. English translation by Nathaniel Tarn, in *Zapotec Struggles: Histories, Politics, and Representations from Juchitán, Oaxaca*, edited by Howard Campbell, Leigh Binford, Miguel Bartolomé, and Alicia Barabas, p. 211. Washington, D. C.: Smithsonian Institution, 1993.

SUÁREZ, JAIME 1983 *The Mesoamerican Indian Languages*. New York: Cambridge University Press.

Chapter 12
Indigenous Literature in Preconquest and Colonial Mesoamerica

PRECOLUMBIAN LITERATURE

Characteristics of Native Literature

Verbal art in preconquest Mesoamerica was predominantly an art of the spoken word, an art of oratory and of song. When systems of writing were invented, they were rarely if ever used to produce word-for-word transcriptions of speech, such that the reader would repeat the exact words of the writer. Rather, the written text provided a kind of model or key—widely varying in its degree of detail and specificity—that the speaker interpreted orally. The precise words chosen to express the text's meaning could vary among different readers or from one reading to the next. However, particularly in the case of very sacred texts, a particular wording that was considered the true or original one could be memorized and passed along word for word. But always the written form was intended to be the basis for an oral performance: There were no texts whose principal function was to be contemplated in silence and solitude.

When we look at literature from other civilizations, it is wise to keep in mind that what we think of as "reading" is a relatively recent phenomenon—given that writing was first invented around 7,000 years ago. It was not until the time of the Renaissance in Europe, when the invention of movable type made books much easier to produce, that the act of reading came to be separated from that of speaking aloud. Until then, books were normally read out loud. This explains why the English word "lecture," which we now associate with an oral presentation, derives from the Latin word meaning "to read." To give a lecture originally meant to read aloud from a written text. You may know of some college professors who still follow this ancient custom.

To sit alone and read a text solely for the sake of one's personal entertainment or enlightenment is a very different act from the oral delivery of a text. The oral performer is directly engaged in a social transaction with at least one listener, and listeners may participate in various ways in the reading. As we examine native Mesoamerican literary forms, it is important to remember that these texts were (and are) always embedded in face-to-face social exchanges. There are no monologues or soliloquys, only dialogues.

This social dimension applies both to interpersonal communication and to communication with the gods. According to the *Popol Vuh,* a Maya creation myth, the gods created humanity in order to have beings who could speak to them articulately, name their names, and pray to them in lines of poetry. To be able to speak in a formal, polite, and aesthetically appealing manner was a social and ritual obligation. The sacred powers had to be addressed with beautiful prayers and invocations every time one interacted with them, even if one were just lighting the household fire in the morning or picking a few ears of corn from the garden. And social interactions were characterized by formalized dialogue. Even simple, everyday activities like greeting a neighbor involved the ritualized exchange of courteous pleasantries. Conversation was elevated to an art form.

Writing, too, was an art form, not just in respect to the spoken words being represented but also to the *way* they were represented. Speaking was a form of verbal art, and writing was a form of visual art. Mesoamerican writing systems were glyphic, or pictorial. Even when highly conventionalized, the individual glyphs were based on pictures of objects, plants, animals, people, and deities. In Mesoamerican languages, the same verbs refer to writing as to drawing, designing, painting, or embroidering. Much effort went into the execution of written texts: The scribe's goal was not speed, legibility, or efficiency, but rather ornateness and beauty.

We can compare Mesoamerican writing with the medieval European art of illuminating manuscripts, with Chinese calligraphy, or with the beautifully rendered texts from the Koran produced by Islamic artists. But the overlap between word and picture was even greater in Mesoamerica (see Chapter 11). Pictures were meant to be read, to be interpreted through an oral performance. Conventionalized symbols combined with more directly pictorial representations not simply on the same page but in the same image. Even in Maya writing, the most sophisticated Mesoamerican writing system, written texts were very often accompanied by pictures that conveyed some of the same information. The pictures could include glyphs, acting like labels, and the glyphic captions could incorporate small versions of parts of the accompanying picture.

The ability to read such texts was a highly specialized form of knowledge. The writing was intentionally cryptic, full of hidden meanings. It was never immediately obvious how the pictures should be interpreted. This left much space for different interpretations to be made, depending on the reader's goals in the immediate context. In Nahuatl, the verb for "read," *pohua*, also refers to divination, or the discovery of hidden knowledge through arts of magic—as in interpreting omens or telling fortunes. To conjure a meaning out of a pictorial text demanded similarly esoteric skills. Learning to read and write—to paint or carve the pictures and signs and to sing and speak the appropriate words—demanded years of formal training in special schools.

The Maya had phonetic symbols so close to true alphabetic writing that they could easily have written clear and unambiguous texts, readable with little training. But they chose instead to complicate matters by having many different glyphs that could represent the same sounds; by having many different versions of the same glyph; by using glyphs that could have multiple readings—phonetic, pictographic (standing for the thing represented), logographic (standing for a word), or ideographic (standing for a concept); and by mixing phonetic and non-phonetic readings in the same text. The scribes who controlled these skills were influential members of elite families.

Another crucial dimension of Mesoamerican literature is its instrumentality. By this we mean the belief that the reciting of a text could have a real effect on the world, like the casting of a spell. Words were instruments of power; to speak or sing of the world in a certain way could actually make it so. And how much more power might those words have if carved into stone! This assumption may seem naive or superstitious, but it may be equally naive to assume the opposite. Our perceptions of reality depend heavily on our customary modes of describing it; the things we are told over and over again as children form attitudes that last our whole lives. Sometimes a single speech can have an effect on history, changing the way significant numbers of people think and act: Abraham Lincoln's Gettysburg Address and Martin Luther King, Jr.'s, "I Have a Dream" speech are two examples from U.S. history.

What we can know about literature in Precolumbian Mesoamerica is limited in several ways. With the performers and audiences long dead, much of what we would like to know about social contexts and performance techniques is impossible to recover. The written texts that we have may not tell us the full story, or may have the potential to tell us several different versions of a story, such that we cannot know which interpretation might have been used and when. And these surviving written texts are only a tiny fraction of those that were produced.

Another limiting factor is our ability to read and interpret the texts that do survive. This is an area in which tremendous advances have been made in recent years, particularly with respect to the decipherment of the Maya writing system, which scholars once believed would never be decoded. Even when we know what words or concepts are represented by all of the signs, even when we know the names of all the deities and historical personages mentioned or depicted, we are still a far cry from the text's full meaning in its original context. Nevertheless, the texts have taught us a great deal about Precolumbian Mesoamerica.

In Mesoamerica's tropical environment, paper decays quickly if discarded or buried. A handful of texts painted on paper survive from the Postclassic period. The only texts that survive from more ancient times are those inscribed on more durable media: stone sculptures; ceramic vessels; bones; shells; and, though rarely, the walls of caves, tombs, and buildings. Our knowledge of these depends on archaeological discovery and restoration. Many text-bearing objects are looted from their sites and end up in private collections completely divorced from their original contexts. Often they are damaged in the process of removal and transport. Some scholars decline to work with looted materials for fear that their studies might add to the market value of the stolen objects and help to grant legitimacy to the business of looting and collecting.

The largest corpus of such inscriptions are those of the Classic Maya. Classic Maya texts deal primarily with historical information, particularly the genealogies and exploits of rulers. This concern with elite personages extended to the inscribing of their personal effects with messages like "this is Ruler So-and-so's chocolate cup." Such a text hardly constitutes a work of literature, but some Maya inscriptions include hundreds of glyphs. The Hieroglyphic Stairway at the ancient city of Copán, Honduras—the longest stone inscription in the Americas—has approximately 1,300 glyphs.

Texts such as this are historical narratives that set their human protagonists into grand cosmological schemes that span millions of years. The actions of actual Maya leaders are related in the texts to those of primordial deities and to the movements of the moon, stars, and planets. The rulers claim to be descended from deities and to share their birthdays. They assert that their deceased parents and other ancestors have themselves been deified. At the same time, actual historical events such as accession to the throne or the designation of an heir are recorded with precise historical dates. Such glorification of human rulers obviously functioned as political propaganda. But the texts also reveal ancient Maya views of the cosmos and the nature of their historical consciousness, which cast human history in mythological terms. One such text is shown in Figure 12.1.

Though texts produced in a variety of media were important throughout Mesoamerican history, in the following discussion we will focus on books and other documents.

The Precolumbian Codices

The civilizations of Mesoamerica differed from the other native peoples of both North and South America in that only they invented writing systems and created books. The keeping of written records allows people to communicate with others across distances of space and time. It allows people to develop a sense of their own past, their position in regard to a chronologically structured history, which is unavailable to those who depend solely on the spoken word. As keepers of books, Mesoamericans had something in common with the Europeans who conquered them, something that both sides recognized.

Figure 12.1 This Classic Maya relief sculpture, carved at the ancient city of Palenque in A.D. 722, shows the apotheosis, or transformation into a deity, of Kan-Xul, a ruler of Palenque. Kan-Xul is depicted dancing his way out of the underworld to join his mother and father in the heavens. Dumbarton Oaks Research Library and Collections, Washington, D. C.

This mutual recognition—and the distinctiveness of the two traditions—is well illustrated by an anecdote included in one of the first European books that told of Spanish experiences in America. Peter Martyr of Anghiera, who interviewed returning Spaniards and published their stories, collected the following account from a Spaniard named Corrales who, in Panama around 1514, had met a man from the Mesoamerican interior:

> Corrales was reading. The native jumped, full of joy, and by means of an interpreter, exclaimed: How is this? You also have books and use painted signs to communicate with the absent? And saying this, he asked to see the book in the belief that he was about to see the writing he was familiar with, but he discovered it was different. (León-Portilla 1992:317)

The native person's utterance—"you also have books"—conveys his sense of his own culture as a literate one and the importance he placed on this fact. Both he and the Spaniard, unlike the native people of Panama among whom they found themselves, understood the nature and value of books.

Only fifteen books, or fragments of books, are known to survive from preconquest Mesoamerica. Most of these were taken to Europe soon after the Spanish invasion of Mesoamerica and preserved as curiosities. Eventually they found their way from private hands into libraries in England, France, Germany, Austria, and Italy.

These manuscripts are usually called codices (singular, codex). The term "codex" originally meant a manuscript with its pages sewn together on one side. But since the late nineteenth century, scholars of Mesoamerica have used this term to designate any pictorial (or combination written and pictorial) manuscript executed in an indigenous artistic style. Early colonial pictorial manuscripts are included in this designation. Each codex has a name derived from its location, discoverer or former owner, place of origin, or some other criterion.

The codices were constructed of paper made from the bark of a type of fig tree, or of deerhide. The paper or leather was coated on both sides with a layer of gesso or plaster of paris. This provided a smooth, white surface on which to paint. Each codex consisted of a single long, rectangular strip, made by attaching together numerous pieces of paper or hide. This strip, called a tira, was painted on both sides and then was either rolled up like a scroll or, more frequently, folded up accordion-style into a type of book known as a screenfold. A cover made of wood or leather protected the book.

In a screenfold book, the text is divided into a series of individual pages, each separated from its adjoining pages at the folds. The book may be unfolded at any point to reveal two adjoining pages. Typically, the text reads horizontally across two pages at once, either in successive rows going from left to right or in a meandering pattern. Other pages, either adjoining these two or lying at other places in the series, can also be unfolded, such that several pages—or even half of the book, one entire side of the *tira*—may be viewed at once. This is an advantage over the type of book you are now holding in your hands, in which only two pages at a time may be viewed. Also, the screenfold lies flat when unfolded and does not have to be held open. Screenfold-style books were once used in Europe and in China. They are still used today in Southeast Asia for Buddhist literature.

The fifteen preconquest codices divide into three groups based on their style and area of origin. Five of them comprise what is known as the Borgia Group, named after the largest and most beautifully executed member of the group, the *Codex Borgia.* These codices come from somewhere in central Mexico, probably to the south and east of the Mexico City area and very likely a Nahuatl-speaking region. They date to shortly before the Spanish invasion. All of them are screenfold books of ritual and divinatory character. Their content focuses on the 260-day ritual calendar, its use in prognostication, and the deities and religious rites associated with the different days (Figure 12.2). Other calendrical cycles are also represented, particularly the cycle of the planet Venus, which was identified with the deity Quetzalcoatl.

These books are guides for priests and diviners, specialists who had the knowledge needed to interpret the pictures, to generate a spoken narrative based upon the painted illustrations. Depending on the occasion, such a narrative might take the form of a myth telling the exploits of gods shown in the book, a

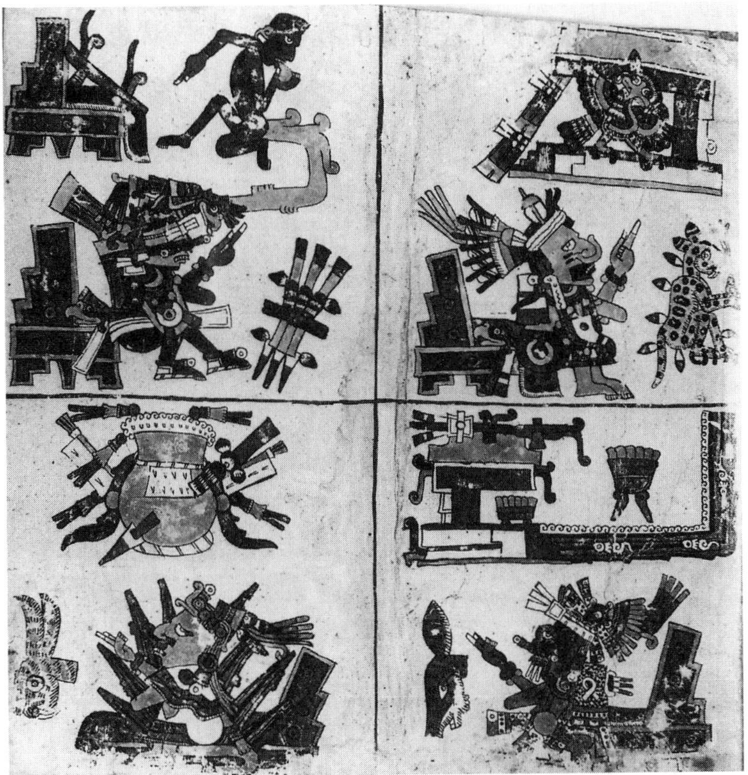

Figure 12.2 *Codex Borgia.* On this page of the screenfold book are depicted the deities associated with four of the twenty day-signs in the 260-day calendar. Reprinted with permission from *Codex Borgia.* Graz, Austria: Akademische Druck- und Verlagsanstalt, 1976, folio 12.

homily advising people on how they ought to behave, a prophecy telling of the future, instructions on how to perform a certain ritual, or some combination of these.

One of the codices in the group, the *Codex Laud,* includes a series of twenty-five pictures to be used for advising couples who planned to marry (Figure 12.3). Each picture shows a man and a woman, depicted with different features, poses, and gestures and accompanied by different objects. The diviner would add together the numerical signs of the prospective bride's and groom's birthdates in the 260-day ritual calendar. This would yield a number from 2 to 26. He or she would then consult the corresponding picture in this section of the codex, and make a pronouncement regarding the couple's future prospects. Given the ambiguous nature of the pictures, the diviner could make a wide variety of predictions combining the interpretation of the signs with knowledge of the two individuals and their families.

Figure 12.3 *Codex Laud.* A page from the marriage prognostication tables. Reprinted with permission from *Codex Laud.* Graz, Austria: Akademische Druck- und Verlagsanstalt, 1966, verso of folio 11.

Another of the codices, the *Fejérváry-Mayer,* shows on its first page a map of the world, as Mesoamericans conceived of it (Figure 12.4). Space is divided among four quadrants representing the four directions. In the space at the middle stands the fire deity, who stands at the *axis mundi* or center of the cosmos—just as the hearth lay at the center of the Mesoamerican home. Each of the four directional quadrants contains a male-female pair of deities, one of the sacred world-trees that held up the sky, and a sacred bird representing the heavens. Additional trees stand at the intercardinal points. The day signs of the 260-day ritual calendar are arranged about the perimeter. Five of the twenty signs are associated with each of the four directions; 260 small circles represent the individual days in the count. In such a manner time and space, history and geography, were united in a single vision of creation.

A colonial Nahuatl text describing the role of the priests in preconquest society eloquently expresses the importance of such ritual and calendrical books:

It is said that they are sages wise in words. . .
and they watch over, they read, they lay out
the books, the black ink, the red ink.
They are in charge of the writings.
It is they who are in charge of us.
They lead us, they tell us the way.
They arrange in order how a year falls,
how the count of the days follows its path,
and they attend to each count of twenty days.
Their charge, their business, their duty
is the sacred words. (Sahagún 1986:140; trans. by L. Burkhart)

The second group of surviving codices comes from the Mixtec civilization in what is now the Mexican state of Oaxaca. There are six of these, and they are known, after one of their number, as the Nuttall Group. Two of these manuscripts, the *Codex Nuttall* and the *Codex Vienna*, are believed to have been sent by

Figure 12.4 The frontispiece of the *Codex Fejérváry-Mayer*, depicting the layout of the earth and the spatial distribution of the ritual calendar's 260 days. Reprinted with permission from *Codex Fejérváry-Mayer*. Graz, Austria: Akademische Druck- und Verlagsanstalt, 1971.

Hernán Cortés to Emperor Charles V. Two others, the *Codex Colombino* and the *Codex Becker I*, remained in Mixtec hands until they were used as evidence in legal suits over land rights, the *Colombino* in 1717 and the *Becker* in 1852.

These Mixtec codices are predominantly genealogical and historical in content. They tell the history of the ruling dynasties of particular towns and cities in the Mixtec region, including the exploits of various individual rulers, both male and female. These histories, however, include many elements of myth and ritual. The historical personages are shown engaging in religious rites and consulting priests and diviners. The mythological origins of the dynasties are also represented, with the lineage founders being, for example, born out of trees or out of the earth. An exception to this pattern is the *Codex Vienna*, which is genealogical on one side but on the other is devoted to mythology—particularly the story of the deity Nine Wind, the Mixtec version of the god that the Nahua called Quetzalcoatl (Figure 12.5).

The third group consists of four manuscripts that come from the Maya region. One of these, the *Codex Madrid*, consists of two parts that were formerly considered to be two separate manuscripts. Another, the *Codex Grolier*, emerged from a private collection in 1971. It had reportedly been discovered by looters in

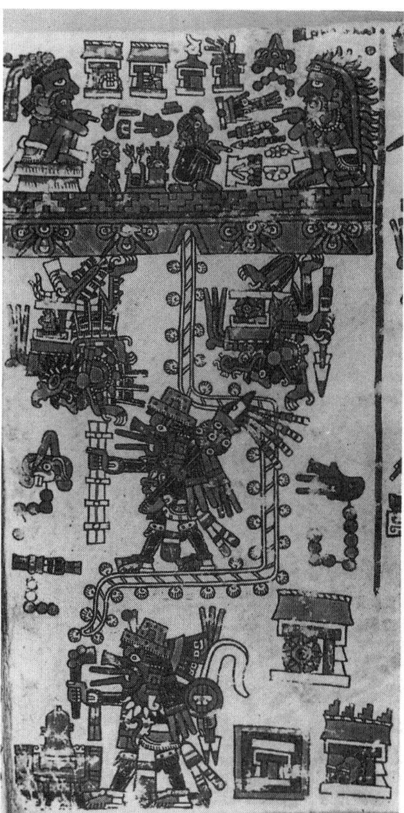

Figure 12.5 This scene from the *Codex Vienna* depicts part of the story of Nine Wind, the Mixtec equivalent of the Aztec deity Quetzalcoatl. Reprinted with permission from *Codex Vindobonensis Mexicanus I*. Graz, Austria: Akademische Druck- und Verlagsanstalt, 1963, folio 48c.

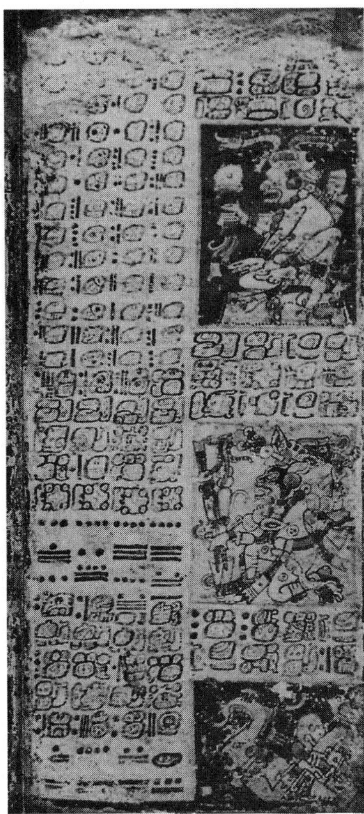

Figure 12.6 *Codex Dresden.* Venus rises in the east as morning star. At bottom is the maize deity, sacrificial victim of the vengeful star: crop failure may be expected at this time. Reprinted with permission from *Codex Dresdensis.* Graz, Austria: Akademische Druck- und Verlagsanstalt, 1975, folio 48.

a dry cave. It is the only Precolumbian codex that was found in an archaeological context. Some scholars believe that it may be a forgery, but the prevailing opinion currently holds it to be authentic.

The Maya codices, like the Borgia Group, are ritual and divinatory in content. The most famous and complete one, the *Codex Dresden,* is thirty-nine leaves in length and is believed to date to the thirteenth century A.D. (Figure 12.6). It is particularly notable for its complex and very accurate astronomical calculations relating to lunar and solar eclipses and the cycles of Venus and Mars. The Maya were Mesoamerica's greatest mathematicians, discoverers of the concept of zero and of positional numeration. The purpose of their astronomical books was not, however, to represent natural phenomena in the manner of what we think of as "science." The astronomical bodies were deities whose actions had effects on human life; knowledge of their movements could help people to pattern their own activities after cosmic models. For example, the rising of the planet Venus as morning star was a time that throughout Mesoamerica was associated with wars and other disasters. Maya rulers would sometimes plan military attacks to coincide with this astronomical event, identifying themselves with the vengeful planet and seeking, at this time so ripe for destruction, to destroy their own enemies.

Thousands more of these Precolumbian books might have come down to us if not for the repressive policies of the Spanish colonial regime. Colonial authorities confiscated and burned many native books, thinking that the Devil's hand lay behind the strange pictures and unfamiliar writing. The religious rituals that went along with some of the texts were also suppressed. With no one performing these rituals, there was no incentive to replace the confiscated texts. Native people who wanted to keep their ancient books had to hide them. In these hiding places the books often rotted away or were eventually forgotten. In some places, though, books of divination survived along with the shamans who consulted them.

Our analysis of Precolumbian literature is greatly assisted by evidence from the Colonial period. Even while nearly all the older manuscripts were destroyed, some new texts were produced that retained preconquest style, at least to some degree. At the same time, European observers wrote about some of the texts and performances that they witnessed themselves or that native people described to them. And native people, once they had mastered the European alphabet, used alphabetic writing to record versions of some of their traditional oral and written texts.

NATIVE LITERATURE OF THE COLONIAL PERIOD

The Colonial Codices

Native people continued to create pictorial manuscripts during the Colonial period, especially through the sixteenth century. Four major changes occur in the tradition. First, ritual and divinatory codices cease to be produced except when commissioned by Europeans seeking ethnographic information on native religion—mainly for the purpose of recognizing and eradicating "idolatry." Such manuscripts resemble their Precolumbian models but functioned in entirely different contexts. Second, alphabetic writing invades the pictorial text, first complementing the pictures and gradually coming to replace them. Third, the native artists adopt some conventions of European art, introducing perspective, landscape, and three-dimensionality into their paintings while still maintaining a representational style easily distinguished from that of European artists. Fourth, entire new genres of pictorial manuscript are created under European sponsorship.

While religious manuscripts were largely suppressed—or at least driven underground—along with the native rituals and priesthood, there continued to be a need for other kinds of manuscripts that had long been in use. The Spanish colonial government tolerated and even encouraged the maintenance of these traditions, for a lot of information useful to Spaniards as well as natives was recorded and preserved in such texts. Spaniards considered native documents to be authentic and accurate representations of dynastic genealogies, imperial organization, and local history. Pictorial manuscripts were accepted as legal evidence by Spanish administrators in cases involving disputes over the inheritance of titles or property, the setting of tribute levels, or rights to land and water.

Probably the largest genre of these nonritual manuscripts that continued to be made by native people for their own use were historical accounts recording the history of a particular community. The account would deal with the origins of the group (often mythological); its migration to its current home; the founding of the community; and notable events in its subsequent history, such as the deaths and successions of rulers, wars, temple dedications, crop failures, comets, and earthquakes. Among the surviving Precolumbian manuscripts, the genealogical records from the Mixtec region fall into this historical category. Indeed, one of them, the *Codex Selden*, is partly preconquest in date but continued to be added to during the Colonial period, up to about 1560. A history of the royal lineage of the town of Añute, it covers a time span from the late eighth century A.D. to the year 1556 (Figure 12.7).

In much of Mesoamerica, these local historical chronicles took the form of a year count. A calendrical symbol representing each year would be painted along the margin. Next to or above this would be painted whatever significant event(s) happened to occur that year. For example, in central Mexican manuscripts, a portrait of a seated ruler accompanied by his name glyph represented the accession of a new king; a depiction of a corpse wrapped in white cloth labelled with the same name glyph was painted for the year that that ruler died. A military victory was shown as a burning temple labelled with the name of the defeated town. A comet was represented as a smoking star, an earthquake as a plot of ground with the calendrical symbol *ollin*, "movement," above it. If nothing noteworthy happened in a particular year, the space would be left blank. Captions in alphabetic writing may explain or elaborate upon the information shown in pictures.

Perhaps what is most striking about these year-count annals, all surviving examples of which are postconquest, is the matter-of-fact way in which they deal with the transition to Spanish colonial rule. The count passes unbroken from pre-

Figure 12.7 One of the last events recorded in the *Codex Selden* is this wedding between a noble Mixtec lord and lady, which occurred in 1546. The groom's calendrical name is 10 Grass; the bride's is 10 Serpent. After *Codex Selden 3135*. Mexico City, Mexico: Sociedad Mexicana de Antropología, 1964, folio 20.

conquest to colonial times. The only difference is that the noteworthy events begin to include the coming of Spanish soldiers, baptism by Catholic friars, deaths and successions of viceroys and bishops as well as local native governors, epidemics, the building of churches, and other previously unimagined occurrences. The scribes simply copied the earlier annals and appended recent events to the traditional account. This shows, perhaps as effectively as any other evidence, that for most native people the Spanish conquest did not represent an end to or even a transformation of their sense of their own identity and history (Figure 12.8).

Other kinds of pictorial manuscripts documented practical aspects of everyday life, such as the boundaries of a community's property, census lists, and records of tribute in goods and labor owed to native rulers or, in colonial times, to Spanish authorities. There is not much of a "literary" aspect to such manuscripts, but we must keep in mind that Mesoamericans could turn the most mundane events into elaborate performances. For instance, a property survey involved a formal tour of all of the boundary markers by the town's dignitaries. At each marker—a pile of stones or, in colonial times, often a cross—musical instruments would be played and speeches would be given, then the group would march in procession to the next. In the course of the tour, the town's history would be

Figure 12.8 A page from the *Codex Aubin*, a year-count chronicling Mexica history from A.D. 1168 to 1608. This page records events of the years 1521 to 1525, including the succession of Cuauhtemoc as Mexica ruler, the occupation of the city by Spaniards, activities of Cortés, a solar eclipse, the coming of the Franciscan friars in 1524, and Cuauhtemoc's death. Reprinted with permission from Charles E. Dibble, ed., *Codex Aubin: Historia de la nación mexicana.* Madrid, Spain: J. Porrúa Turanzas, 1963, p. 87.

recalled and reinterpreted, its relations with neighboring communities reviewed and reestablished. A painted map resulting from such an event is but a dim shadow of the original performance.

The colonial codices that are best preserved and most widely studied are those that were produced for Europeans seeking to know more about native culture and history. These manuscripts tell us not only about Precolumbian traditions but also about the adjustments—in their daily lives and in their interpretations of the past—that native people were making as they learned to cope with their colonial circumstances.

Nearly all of these "ethnographic" codices come from the Nahuatl-speaking region of central Mexico, mainly from Mexico City and its environs. This area was conquered and evangelized earlier and more pervasively than the rest of Mesoamerica. The center of the former Aztec polity as well as the Spanish colony, it was home not only to many artists but also to the Spanish priests and officials who commissioned these works. Close working relationships between friars and native artists and consultants were possible here, especially in the Franciscan schools and college. The result was a florescence of manuscript painting during the mid- to late sixteenth century.

The majority of these codices are organized around the calendar: the 260-day ritual calendar, the 365-day year (broken into eighteen "months" of twenty days each), year counts, or a combination of these. Emphasis is on the deities and ceremonies associated with each calendrical period, sometimes with additional information on noncalendrical rituals or other aspects of native culture. Pictures painted by native artists are accompanied by written glosses, usually in Spanish. A number of these calendrical books are related to one another. These derive from now-lost prototypes ultimately based upon the work of a Franciscan friar, Andrés de Olmos, who began his ethnographic research in 1533. Box 12.1 provides an example of one of these calendrical codices from the Colonial period.

Box 12.1 *Codex Borbonicus*

One of the earliest colonial codices is the *Codex Borbonicus,* once thought by some to be Precolumbian. Most colonial codices are bound along the left-hand margin like European books, but the *Borbonicus* retains the screenfold format. The first part is a 260-day calendar, painted in a style that is purely Precolumbian except for the fact that space has been left next to the painted symbols in order that Spanish glosses may be written in, as they are in some instances (Figure 12.9).

A later section of the *Borbonicus* consists of depictions of the ceremonies performed for the months of the 365-day calendar and the New Fire Ceremony, performed every fifty-two years. This was not something that Precolumbian codices ordinarily included, so there were few conventions regarding how such a document should look. The paintings are spread out across a blank background with much space left empty; this contrasts with the very dense and even distribution of figures across the page in Precolumbian manuscripts. Also, the artist makes some tentative and not altogether successful attempts to show perspective (Figure 12.10). The back of the screenfold is left blank, an unlikely circumstance had the manuscript been made for actual native use.

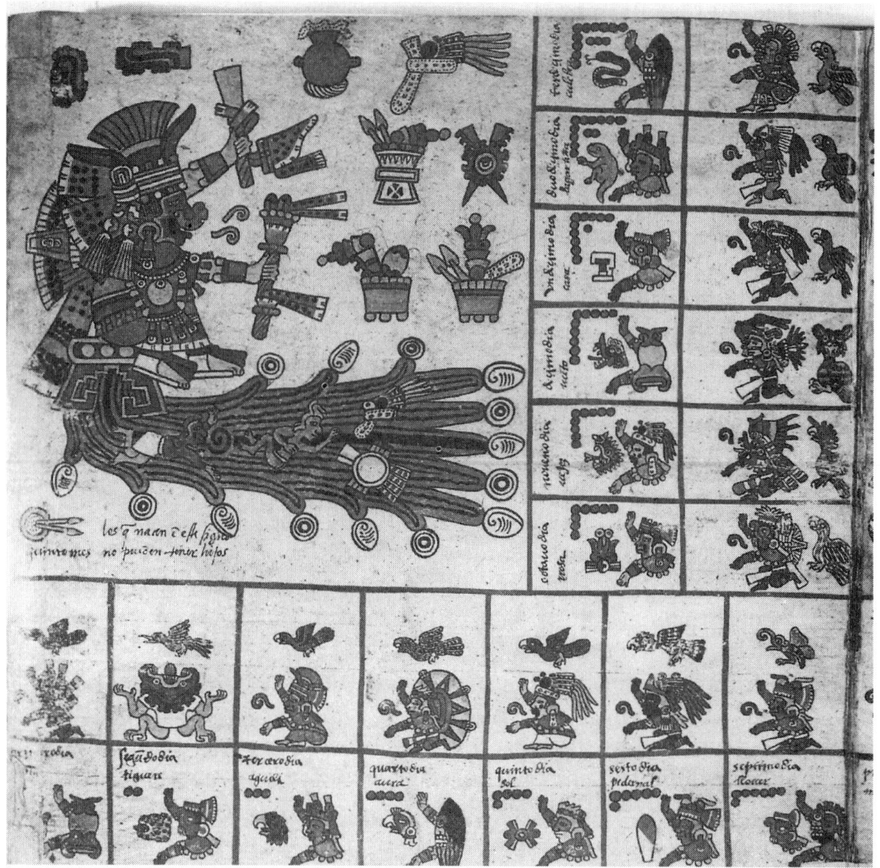

Figure 12.9 *Codex Borbonicus.* A page from the 260-day ritual calendar. The water goddess Chalchiuhtlicue, "She of the Jade Skirt," presides over the thirteen-day period commencing with the day One Reed. Reprinted with permission from *Codex Borbonicus.* Graz, Austria: Akademische Druck- und Verlagsanstalt, 1974, folio 5.

The *Codex Mendoza,* thought to have been commissioned in the early 1540s by the colony's first viceroy, is one of the most beautiful and informative of colonial codices (Figure 12.11). Illustrated by a master artist and glossed in Spanish by a priest, the codex is comprised of three parts. The first two are Precolumbian in style and based on earlier documents: One is a history of the Mexica rulers and their conquests; the second is a catalog of all the tribute those rulers demanded from each of their subject provinces. Such information was of obvious value to Spaniards wanting to know what riches they could wrest from their new territories.

The third section is unique. It deals with the life of the Mexica (Aztec) people: the upbringing of male and female children from birth to marriage (Fig-

Figure 12.10 *Codex Borbonicus.* The New Fire Ceremony: every 52 years all fires were extinguished, and a new fire was kindled in a temple near the Aztec capital. Here four priests bring wood to feed the new fire. The lower two appear to stand on the temple stairs while the upper two float in space: the artist has only partially adopted European conventions of landscape and perspective. Reprinted with permission from *Codex Borbonicus.* Graz, Austria: Akademische Druck- und Verlagsanstalt, 1974, folio 34.

ure 12.12), the different professions for young men, the military and the priesthood with their various ranks, the conducting of warfare, and the operation of the courts of law and the royal palace. To create this pictorial ethnography, the artist had, in a sense, to stand outside of his own culture and look at it analytically, to play the role of interpreter between his own people and the foreigners who now ruled over them. The portrait he drew presents an orderly, disciplined, hierarchical society of a sort that Europeans of the time would be able to respect. The document is both a nostalgic, somewhat idealized recollection of the preconquest social order and an attempt to persuade Spanish viewers of the legitimacy of native society. Sent to Charles V, it was transported to France after French pirates attacked the Spanish fleet; eventually it ended up in the Bodleian Library at Oxford University.

The greatest monument of sixteenth-century ethnography is the work of a Franciscan friar named Bernardino de Sahagún. From the 1540s to the 1580s, Sahagún and a number of indigenous students and collaborators produced a series of ethnographic studies combining pictorial and textual materials, the latter not in Spanish but in Nahuatl. They interviewed experts in different fields,

Figure 12.11 Drawing of the frontispiece of the *Codex Mendoza.* The main scene represents the founding of the Mexica (Aztec) capital, Tenochtitlan, on an island in Lake Texcoco. Below this scene, two of the Mexicas' early military victories are represented. Courtesy of Frances F. Berdan. Reproduced with her permission from Frances F. Berdan and Patricia Anawalt, eds. *The Codex Mendoza, Volume 4: Pictorial Parallel Image Replicas of Codex Mendoza.* Berkeley, CA: University of California Press, 1992, p. 9 (folio 2r).

such as medicine, divination, rhetoric, and the ancient ceremonies. Sahagún's goal was to create an encyclopedia of native culture that not only would assist priests in eliminating "pagan" religion but also would serve as an extended lexicon for the language and a record of native knowledge that was good (in his estimation) and useful.

The culmination of the project is a document known as the *Florentine Codex*, completed in 1577 and now housed in the Laurentian Library in Florence, Italy. Its twelve books are written in Nahuatl, with an accompanying Spanish text summarizing and commenting upon the Nahuatl. Though primarily a written rather than pictorial document, the small paintings by native artists found throughout the text are integral to the work as a whole. The *Florentine Codex* is the longest text in a native language from anywhere in the Americas and the most complete description of a native American culture created before the advent of professional anthropologists (figures 12.13 and 12.14).

We will mention just one more of the great colonial codices, the *Codex Badianus* or *Cruz-Badiano.* This book is an example of how native people combined their own traditions with European genres of writing, even European languages. It is an illustrated herbal, or book of herbal remedies, explaining cures

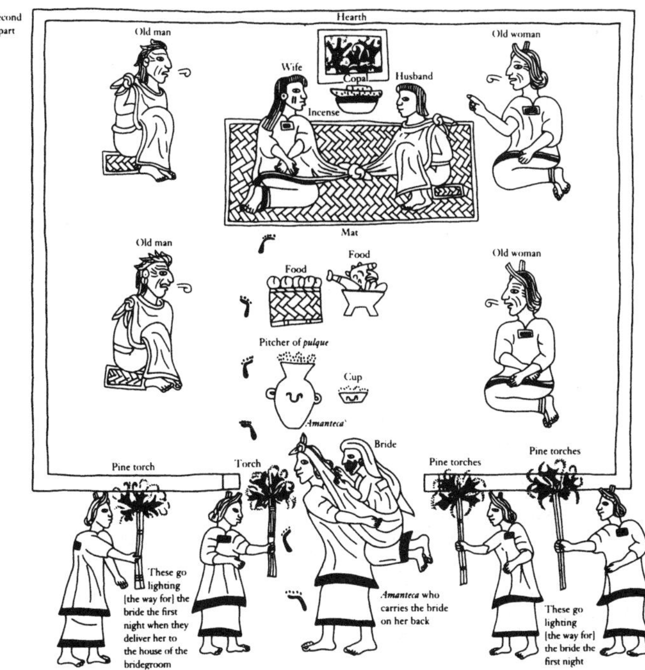

Figure 12.12 *Codex Mendoza.* Drawing of the wedding ceremony: the bride and groom sit on a new mat in the groom's house, their clothing knotted together to symbolize their union, while elderly men and women offer advice. Below, the bride is carried to the groom's house by a woman doctor while other women light the way with torches. Courtesy of Frances F. Berdan. Reproduced with her permission from Frances F. Berdan and Patricia Anawalt, eds. *The Codex Mendoza, Volume 4: Pictorial Parallel Image Replicas of Codex Mendoza.* Berkeley, CA: University of California Press, 1992, p. 127 (folio 61r).

for various ailments and depicting the plants to be used in preparing the medicines. It was produced in 1552 at the Franciscan college in Tlatelolco. A native doctor named Martín de la Cruz wrote the text in Nahuatl based on his own medical knowledge, which already shows some European influence. He left out the incantations and other ritual elements that might have gone along with these remedies. This Nahuatl text was then translated into Latin by a Nahua student at the college, Juan Badiano. Only this Latin version was included in the finished book. An unknown native artist painted the 184 pictures of plants, some of which include glyphic elements. Sent to Spain as a gift for Charles V, the document was discovered in the Vatican Library in 1929 (Figure 12.15).

Alphabetic Writing

We have already mentioned two documents, the *Codex Florentine* and *Codex Badianus,* that include substantial components written by native people using the European alphabet. The combination of pictures and writing in the same document makes it impossible to draw a firm line between pictorial and alphabetic texts. But we will now focus more specifically on the use of the roman alphabet to record native literature.

The existence of a long tradition of books and writing made it easy for Mesoamericans to adopt the alphabet used by their Spanish conquerors. The alphabet was a more efficient—though less aesthetically appealing—method of record-

Figure 12.13 A page from the *Florentine Codex*. A merchant family is hosting a party to celebrate the birth of a child. Women guests receive gifts of flowers and tobacco, enjoy a meal of tamales and turkey, and dance in honor of the new baby. *Florentine Codex*, Book 4, folio 69v. Reprinted with permission from Fray Bernardino de Sahagún, *Historia General de las cosas de Nueva España, Códice florentino.* Facsimile of the *Codex Florentinus* of the Biblioteca Medicea Laurenciana, supervised by the Archivo General de la Nación (AGN) de México, Florence, Italy, 1979.

ing the spoken word than the traditional pictorial systems. Its mastery also granted native people easier access to the bureaucratic apparatus of the colonial administration.

That native people recognized the new kind of writing as consistent with their own literate culture is indicated by its easy assimilation into already existing terminology: The same words were used for books, documents, scribes, paint or ink, and the act of writing, regardless of whether pictorial or alphabetic conventions were employed. As they did with other aspects of European culture introduced by the colonizers, Mesoamericans took alphabetic writing and made it their own, adapting it to their own needs and employing it as a tool for their own survival.

The early friars taught their indigenous students to read and write using the alphabet. They applied the letters of the alphabet to the sounds of the native languages, choosing the letters that, as pronounced in Spanish or Latin, corresponded most closely to native pronunciation. The fit was never perfect: Some linguistic features, such as vowel length and tone, went unrepresented while others enjoyed a surplus of alphabetic characters—the letters *o* and *u* were used interchangeably for a single Nahuatl vowel. But the fit was close enough to make the

Figure 12.14 *Florentine Codex.* Aztec nobles play *patolli,* a game similar to Parcheesi. The playing pieces are black beans; the men gamble on the outcome by betting their ornaments of jade, gold, and feathers. *Florentine Codex,* Book 8, folio 19r. Reprinted with permission from Fray Bernardino de Sahagún, *Historia General de las cosas de Nueva España, Códice florentino.* Facsimile of the *Codex Florentinus* of the Biblioteca Medicea Laurenciana, supervised by the Archivo General de la Nación (AGN) de México, Florence, Italy, 1979.

writing comprehensible. Documents written by and for native people begin to appear perhaps as early as 1528.

Alphabetic writing as used by native people remained closely tied to speech: It was a method of transcribing the way spoken speech actually sounded rather than sequences of individual "words" with standardized spellings. This can be seen in the way that words are often run together if they were spoken without pauses between them; conversely, words are arbitrarily divided at the end of a line, with the flow of sound simply continuing on the next line. Spelling varies considerably, with much of the variation attributable to actual pronunciation differences in local dialects. These points are important because they remind us that we are still dealing with what is primarily an oral literature. Texts could now be transmitted precisely word for word, without the ambiguity inherent in picture

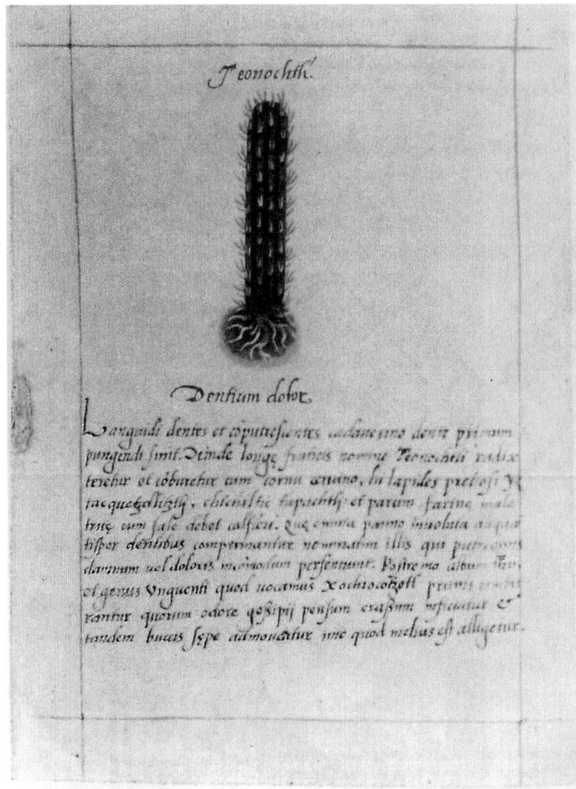

Figure 12.15 A page from the *Codex Badianus.* A species of cactus is employed in a cure for toothache. Reprinted with permission from Emily Walcott Emmart, ed. and trans., *Badianus Manuscript (Codex Berberini, Latin 241), Vatican Library: An Aztec Herbal of 1552.* Baltimore, MD: The Johns Hopkins Press, 1940, folio 17v.

writing, but oral performance remained the mode by which texts were dictated and then read by others.

Even though alphabetic writing was much easier to master than the preconquest writing systems, literacy remained limited to a small minority of the population, principally males of noble rank. Mass literacy was not yet a feature of European societies, and so neither Spaniards nor native nobles felt it necessary to teach the common folk how to read. Literate women appear to have been quite the exception—though not entirely nonexistent—in preconquest society, and this remained the case after the conquest. Control of writing helped the nobles to maintain their positions of authority in the native social structure.

The office of scribe or notary was a standard part of native town government throughout the Colonial period. The records of municipal affairs kept by these scribes and other literate individuals comprise a documentary corpus—some of it in Spanish but most of it in native languages—that has only recently begun to be studied. With the end of the Colonial period, this tradition of local record-keeping vanished along with the administrative structure that had fostered it. Native people literate in their own languages nearly disappear from the Mesoamerican scene until the twentieth century.

Colonial Transcriptions of Oral Literature

Many literary compositions that had formerly been passed along through pictorial writing, oral transmission, or a combination of the two were, during the Colonial period, transcribed using alphabetic writing. As a result, we have access to a great deal of verbal art reflecting native experience before and during Spanish rule. Much of this literature is probably very similar—sometimes virtually identical—to versions used before the Spanish invasion. However, since the texts were transcribed during the Colonial period we can never rule out the possibility that the performers have adapted them in light of their current experiences. Nor should we assume that there was one original or correct Precolumbian version, for all of these texts may have developed and changed over time and existed in multiple versions.

From this rich trove of literary treasures—oratory, poetry, song, myth—we have selected three works representing different regions, different literary genres, and different production contexts. We will describe these texts and give some brief excerpts in English translation.

In some cases, alphabetic transcriptions of traditional literature were executed by native people for their own use and kept within the native community. This is the case with our first example, the *Popol Vuh*, "Book of the Mat" or "Book of Counsel," of the Quiché Maya people of highland Guatemala. The single most important mythological text from Mesoamerica, this sacred book was written down by Quiché noblemen between 1554 and 1558, based on a glyphic text and oral tradition. Statements made within the text imply that these men wished to preserve the story while the glyphic version and the ability to read it still existed, but they also needed to keep the work hidden from Spanish eyes since they lived "in Christendom now" and could no longer perform the text in its traditional ritual contexts. At the beginning of the eighteenth century, a friar working among the Quiché made a copy of the text. This copy, now the only version of the text known to have survived, eventually found its way to the Newberry Library in Chicago.

The *Popol Vuh* tells the history of the world and of the Quiché people from the time of the earth's creation to the early decades of Spanish rule. At the beginning exist only the sky and the primordial sea:

> There is not yet one person, one animal, bird, fish, crab, tree, rock, hollow, canyon, meadow, forest. Only the sky alone is there; the face of the earth is not clear. Only the sea alone is pooled under all the sky; there is nothing whatever gathered together. It is at rest; not a single thing stirs. It is held back, kept at rest under the sky.
>
> Whatever there is that might be is simply not there: only the pooled water, only the calm sea, only it alone is pooled.
>
> Whatever might be is simply not there: only murmurs, ripples, in the dark, in the night. (Tedlock 1985:72)

Then Heart of Sky, Plumed Serpent, and other deities come together and converse in the primordial sea:

> "How should it be sown, how should it dawn? Who is to be the provider, nurturer?"
>
> "Let it be this way, think about it: this water should be removed, emptied out for the formation of the earth's own plate and platform, then comes the sowing, the dawning of the sky-earth. But there will be no high days and no bright praise for our work, our design, until the rise of the human work, the human design," they said.
>
> And then the earth arose because of them, it was simply their word that brought it forth. For the forming of the earth they said "Earth." It arose suddenly, just like a cloud, like a mist, now forming, unfolding. Then the mountains were separated from the water, all at once the great mountains came forth. By their genius alone, by their cutting edge alone they carried out the conception of the mountain-plain, whose face grew instant groves of cypress and pine. (Tedlock 1985:73)

The gods endeavor to create human beings who will appreciate the gods' work, live orderly lives according to the days of the calendar, and pray to them. First they create the animals, but these wander about aimlessly and are incapable of articulate speech. Two more attempts, one using wood and the other mud, also fail to yield the kind of beings the gods have in mind.

The text then digresses into what probably was originally a separate myth. This myth tells how a pair of magically conceived twin brothers defeat the nasty lords of the underworld—gods of death and sickness—and other primordial monsters. These beings had to be destroyed or constrained before the earth could be safe for human society. At the climax of the story, the twins appear in the court of the underworld lords disguised as roving acrobats. They dance and do magic tricks, which include sacrificing first animals and then people and bringing them back to life. Swept away in the excitement, the underworld lords beg that they too may be sacrificed and brought back to life. The boys kill them—but do not bring them back!

The narrative then returns to the gods who are still trying to create human beings. On their fourth try they are successful. They use a dough made from white and yellow corn, ground up by a female deity and mixed with water in which she has rinsed her hands: The oil from her skin turns into the body fat of the four men who are formed from the dough. These four men thank their creators with the following prayer. The text is built with a variety of parallel constructions—the same or similar ideas expressed in two or more ways. For the Quiché and other Mesoamericans, mastery of this poetic strategy signalled good literary style:

> Truly now,
> double thanks, triple thanks
> that we've been formed, we've been given
> our mouths, our faces,
> we speak, we listen,
> we wonder, we move,
> our knowledge is good, we've understood
> what is far and near,
> and we've seen what is great and small

under the sky, on the earth.
Thanks to you we've been formed,
we've come to be made and modeled,
our grandmother, our grandfather. (Tedlock 1975:166)

These very articulate men of corn are actually superior to what the gods intended, for they are able to see and know everything that is in the world. They are too similar to the gods themselves—and a bit too familiar, addressing them as grandparents! The gods therefore dull the men's vision, so that they are able to see only things that are close to them. As compensation, the gods create four women to be the men's wives, and the men are happy once more.

These four couples become the ancestors of the Quiché people. The rest of the *Popol Vuh*, approximately half of the total text, deals with the migrations, wars, settlements, and ruling lineages of the Quiché. Myth passes gradually into history, and we come at the end to the middle of the sixteenth century.

Many other works were written down at the behest of Europeans, with the resulting documents removed from native hands. Some such transactions occurred in an atmosphere of cooperation, as in the case of Sahagún's project: The friar was popular among the native people; teams of native researchers and consultants worked together on the texts. Even in contexts like this, however, the native consultants knew that much of their traditional culture—especially in regard to religious beliefs—was considered by the Spanish priests to be idolatrous or immoral.

Book Six of Sahagún's *Florentine Codex* preserves a collection of Nahuatl orations pertaining to a genre of oral literature the Nahua called *huehuehtlahtolli*, "ancient words" or "speech of the elders." These were formal speeches delivered on special occasions. They are packed with moral philosophy, religious teachings, and poetic devices such as metaphors and parallel constructions. The speeches were first transcribed around 1547, probably in Tlatelolco, the northern part of Mexico City.

Excerpts from one of these orations, a prayer to Tlaloc, the principal rain deity, is presented in Box 12.2.

Sometimes the transcription of oral literature involved coercion. Early in

Box 12.2 *The Prayer to the Rain God Tlaloc*

The following excerpt describes the earth languishing in need of life-giving rain. The "elder sister of the gods" is the corn, sister of the rain gods. "He of the Near, He of the Nigh" is the important deity Tezcatlipoca; by the time the text was transcribed this title was also being applied to the Christian God. Tlaltecuhtli is the earth deity.

And here it is true,
today the crops lie suffering,
the elder sister of the gods lies dragging herself along.

The crops already lie covered with dust,
already they lie wrapped with spider webs,
already they suffer, already they are weary.
And here are the vassals,
the tails, the wings [the common people],
already they are perishing,
for their eyelids are swollen, their lips are parched,
they are bony, they are bent,
they are emaciated.
They are just thin-lipped, pale-throated,
the tails, the wings.
With pallid eyelids go about the little children,
The little babies,
they who toddle, they who crawl,
they who pile up earth and potsherds,
they who sit on the surface of the earth,
and they who lie on the wooden plank,
they who lie on the cradleboard.
And already every person knows torment, exhaustion;
already every person sees anguish.
And there is none whatsoever who is left out,
for already all the little creatures are suffering.
The troupial bird, the roseate spoonbill,
they just drag their wings along,
they tumble over, they fall on their heads,
they open and close their beaks.
And the animals, the four-footed ones
of He of the Near, He of the Nigh,
they just wander about,
they just rise up upon us,
in vain they lick the surface of the earth.
And already they go crazy for water,
already there is dying of thirst,
already there is perishing,
already there is destruction.
Already the vassals, the animals perish.
And here is the one who is our mother, our father,
Tlaltecuhtli.
Already her chest is dry,
no longer can she nourish, no longer can she feed,
no longer is there anything with which she might suckle
that which germinates, that which lies germinating,
that which is the maintenance, the life, of the vassal.
And that which is life,
there is no more,
it has gone away, it has perished. (Sahagún 1969:35–36; trans. by L. Burkhart)

The final appeal to the rain gods at the end of the oration goes as follows:

Oh master, oh precious noble, oh giver of gifts,
may your heart concede it, may it do its job,

may you console the earth,
and all that live upon it,
that travel about on the surface of the earth.
I call to you, I cry out to you,
you who occupy the four quarters,
you the green ones, you the givers of gifts,
you of the mountains, you of the caves!
May you carry yourselves here,
may you come, may you come to console the vassals,
may you come to water things on the earth!
For they lie watching, they lie crying out,
the earth, the animals, the herbs, the stalks.
For they all lie trusting in you.
May you hurry, oh gods, oh our lords! (Sahagún 1969:40; translation revised by L. Burkhart)

The repetition, the elaborate imagery, and the tone of desperation serve not only the aesthetic purpose of creating beautiful and moving poetry. Such a text would have the power also to get the attention of Tlaloc and oblige him to fulfill his function and send the rains.

the seventeenth century a priest named Hernando Ruiz de Alarcón ran an anti-sorcery campaign among Nahuatl-speakers living toward the south and west of Mexico City, in what is now the states of Morelos and Guerrero. This was a relatively rural context compared to the Basin of Mexico, where most of the codices and other ethnographic documents were produced. Ruiz de Alarcón arrested and punished Nahua religious practitioners—men and women whom he believed were in league with the Devil. He understood enough Nahuatl to write down many of the chants these specialists used in their rites of curing and divination. The result is an invaluable collection of Nahuatl ritual poetry, though one gained under unfortunate circumstances.

The chants employ a specialized vocabulary characterized by elaborate metaphors. The practitioners personified the various phenomena involved in the ritual. They granted identities to, for example, the patient's injury or illness, the medicines being used, the fire and the offerings of incense and tobacco that were made to it, and the curer's own hands and fingers. They invoked mythological precedents for the situation at hand, thus casting it in grandiose terms and bringing the sacred power of the myth to bear on the problem.

One of the simplest of the ritual cures is this procedure a woman named María Salome used for curing eye problems. First she addresses the pain, personifying it as a series of serpents and thus giving a concrete form to the patient's sensations. She then threatens the serpent with the water she is about to use to wash the eye. "Jade-Skirted One" is the Nahuatl name for the female water deity: The water here is being treated as a supernatural force.

Well now, please come forth,
1 Serpent,
2 Serpent,

3 Serpent,
4 Serpent:
Why do you harm
The enchanted mirror,
The enchanted eye?
Lie down I know not where,
Remove yourself to I know not where.
But if you do not obey me,
I shall call the Jade-Skirted One,
The Jade-Bloused One:
For she will scatter you,
She will disperse you,
Upon the plain
She will leave you dispersed. (Coe and Whittaker 1982:234)

In a spell for setting broken bones, a curer named Martín de Luna cast himself in the role of the god Quetzalcoatl, or Plumed Serpent. According to a myth recorded in the sixteenth century, this god had stolen one or more bones from the Lord of the Underworld with which to create the human beings of the present age of creation. In one version of the myth, quail startle the fleeing god and he stumbles, breaking the bones. The spell seems to allude to such an episode:

I am the Priest,
I am the Plumed Serpent,
I go to the Land of the Dead,
I go to the Beyond,
I go to the Nine Lands of the Dead;
There I shall snatch up
The bone of the Land of the Dead.
They have sinned—
The priests,
The dust-birds;
They have shattered something,
They have broken something,
But now we shall glue it,
We shall heal it. (Coe and Whittaker 1982:268–269)

The curer identifies the patient's broken bone with this primordial bone over which gods fought and from which humanity was formed. Ruiz de Alarcón dismissed these chants as a combination of superstitious nonsense and diabolical deception. However, it is now recognized that symbolism such as this can work upon the mind and yield healing effects. At the very least, such cures boost the patient's morale, which in turn contributes to recovery.

Native Historians

The tradition of keeping pictorial manuscripts telling of historical events was both reinforced and transformed by the adoption of alphabetic writing. By adding written captions to the records of migrations, genealogies, and year counts, native historians were able to record more detailed information. Previously, the full story that went along with the pictures had had to be passed along by word of mouth. But now, the scribe could record as much as he pleased of these oral interpretations.

Some native historians gave up the pictures altogether and created year-count annals written entirely in alphabetic writing. These still follow the traditional pattern of listing the year and noting one or more important events that occurred therein. But others began to think about their history not as a sequence of separate episodes but in terms of a more continuous narrative, such as European historians—following a pattern established in ancient Greek and Roman times—tended to produce. Instrumental in the development of this new historical consciousness were the native men who were educated according to European models, particularly at Franciscan and Jesuit institutions. Literate in Latin, these men read the same classical sources as learned Europeans.

A few native scholars took the old pictorial chronicles and began to convert them into narrative histories that told the story of a people. Like both the pictorial records and the Old World models, these histories focused on politics and warfare, telling of the glorious deeds of the great men of the past. They also reflect the kinds of issues with which native people were especially concerned: the founding of noble lines and their dynastic history, the granting and inheritance of special titles, the patronage of deities, and the building of temples.

The authors were motivated by a desire not only to preserve information about the past but also to seek legitimacy in the present. The authors play up the roles of their own ancestors and their own communities. They sometimes seek to downplay, or to blame on other groups, practices such as human sacrifice. Some of them wrote in Spanish, clearly intending that their accounts be read by non-native people. They present their history in a style and format that Europeans will understand and respect.

The Texcocan historian Don Fernando de Alva Ixtlilxochitl, author of several Spanish-language chronicles from the early seventeenth century, was the grandson of one of Cortés's principal allies and a direct descendant of Nezahualcoyotl, a long-lived fifteenth-century ruler of Texcoco who was an important ally of the Mexica rulers in Tenochtitlan. Not surprisingly, Alva Ixtlilxochitl emphasizes Texcoco's alliance with the invading Spaniards and also glorifies his ancestor along the lines of the Old Testament's David or Solomon: Nezahualcoyotl becomes an almost super-human patriarch, poet, philosopher, law-giver, judge, and prophet; he is even said to have believed in only one god.

The most prolific historian to write in a native language is a Nahua who gave himself the imposing name Don Domingo de San Antón Muñón Chimalpahin Quauhtlehuanitzin. His writings—eight historical chronicles, a diary, and miscellaneous shorter pieces—comprise the largest body of native-language texts from colonial Mesoamerica that can be attributed to a single author. Most of his work dates to between 1600 and 1620. Chimalpahin was born in 1579 in the town of Chalco Amaquemecan (today's Amecameca de Juárez) in the southeastern corner of the Basin of Mexico. He spent his adult life in Mexico City, employed as a steward or sacristan at a small church. He based his writings on older documents and on interviews with relatives and acquaintances.

Chimalpahin's histories cover a time span from the twelfth century to 1620. Like other native historians, he treats this known period of the past as an unbroken sequence of years, those following the arrival of Cortés not qualitatively different from the preceding span. His accounts focus on his hometown and nearby communities, but also include extensive information regarding the Mexica (who conquered Chalco in the mid-fifteenth century), the Spanish conquest, and events in the colonial capital. Some of his writings take the form of year-count annals.

In some cases men of mixed parentage, products of unions between native noblewomen and Spanish men, wrote histories of the native communities to which they bore maternal ties. Such is the case with Diego Muñoz Camargo's *Historia de Tlaxcala,* written between 1576 and 1595, and Juan Bautista Pomar's *Relación de Texcoco* of 1582. Though these men identify more closely with their Spanish heritage than with their native roots, their familiarity with native culture and their reliance on older documents and oral tradition place their work at some intermediate point between native and Hispanic literature.

A particularly interesting genre of historical document comes into existence later in the Colonial period, becoming especially popular in the eighteenth century. These documents, known as *títulos primordiales,* "primordial titles," give an account of a community's founding, history, and original boundaries. They often include pictures done in a native—though not Precolumbian—style. Some are made out of particularly coarse and ragged native paper. Both the pictures and the rough paper were intended to make the documents look ancient (Figure 12.16).

In essence, these are late-colonial attempts to reclaim a historical tradition that many communities had lost. The ancient-seeming documents are meant to make it look as if the community has preserved these records ever since the early Colonial period. But the information they contain is, in respect to actual historical realities, characterized by inaccurate dates, events placed out of chronological sequence, and events that could not have occurred as described. Mythological elements are included. The original founding of the community may be conflated with its conversion to Christianity. Attempts are made to make the community look good in Spanish terms: The ancestors allied themselves with the Spanish invaders; they welcomed the friars and were baptized immediately. Authorities such as Cortés or early Spanish viceroys are said to have granted the community permanent rights to certain lands.

These documents are an excellent source of insight into how native people viewed their own history during these later colonial times. They also indicate the continued reverence that native people held for ancient documents as a source of community rights and legitimacy, an attitude fostered by the colonial courts, which accepted such ancient documents as evidence in land claims.

The primordial titles proliferated at a time when many native communi-

Figure 12.16 A page from an eighteenth-century "primordial title," from a Nahua village called Santa María Tetelpan, which was used to help defend the village's property in a land dispute. The four men are supposed to be ancestors who founded the community. *Coyoacan Codex, Codex Indianorum 1.* Courtesy of the John Carter Brown Library at Brown University.

ties were experiencing a serious shortage of resources owing to population growth. In the wake of the early colonial demographic collapse, lands that once belonged to these communities were appropriated by Spaniards. When population levels finally rebounded, communities not only recovered a sense of identity and interest in their past, but also found themselves in dire need of more land. Most of these communities had no authentic early documents that could help them reestablish their claims to these lands. Primordial titles were sometimes presented in court to back up such claims. However, Spanish defendants and judges could easily dismiss them as inauthentic by noting their factual inaccuracies.

The Maya of the Yucatán Peninsula continued throughout the Colonial period to keep books of history and prophecy organized around one of the native calendrical systems. Several of these books, known as the *Books of Chilam Balam,* survive in copies written down just after the end of the Colonial period. "Chilam Balam" means priest or spokesperson of the jaguar; this title refers to the official Maya prophet whose words these books purport to represent. These books are written in a highly specialized form of poetic language, full of metaphors and other figures of speech; this makes them quite difficult for scholars to interpret.

The *Books of Chilam Balam* are based on the *katun* calendar. One *katun* corresponded to 20 *tuns,* or "years" of 360 days each; hence, one *katun* was equal to 7,200 days, or 100 days less than 20 of our 365-day years. Thirteen *katuns* comprised a *may,* a unit of 260 *tuns,* or 160 days short of 256 years. The Maya believed that each of the *katuns* within the *may* was characterized by certain kinds of events. To compare this with our calendar, imagine that in every century the decade of the twenties was associated with invasion, the thirties with sickness, the forties with prosperity, the fifties with changes in government, and so forth.

As with the more straightforward chronicles kept by other peoples, these Maya books do not treat the Spanish invasion as a significant discontinuity in history. The coming of the Spaniards is recorded in the same manner as invasions by other native groups and is sometimes confused or conflated with these other conflicts, all of which were remembered as occurring during a certain *katun.*

Indo-Christian Literature

During the Colonial period, a tremendous quantity of textual material was written for use in the context of the Catholic Church. This includes catechistic materials for teaching Catholic doctrine to native people and devotional texts, such as prayers and songs, for native people to use themselves. Some of these works were published. Indeed, the first text ever published in the Americas was a Nahuatl catechism issued in 1539.

Most of this Christian literature was authored by priests. However, even those who were fairly fluent in the native language being used relied extensively on native assistants and interpreters, to the extent that what we really have are collaborative texts in which natives and non-natives participated to varying degrees. In a few cases, the known ones being in the Nahuatl language, native style and imagery are so prevalent that we may consider the texts to be works of native literature. Examples of such Christian literature are given in Box 12.3.

Drama, like song, was a performance genre in which native people participated with enthusiasm. Native-language plays based on Christian subject matter were performed in Mesoamerica beginning in the early 1530s. Unfortunately, scripts from these plays are extremely rare, apart from a few that survive in much

Box 12.3 *Nahua-Christian Songs*

A collection of Nahuatl songs transcribed during the later sixteenth century contains several with predominantly Christian subject matter. These are undoubtedly of native authorship. The following is the opening stanza of a Christmas song composed in 1553 by a Nahua nobleman named Don Francisco Plácido:

> May he be prayed to! Uncover your sacred jewels of turquoise, your compassion, oh you children! May there be jewels of jade, jewels of gold, your rosary beads! With these may we entertain the one who lies now in Bethlehem, the savior of the world! Let us go! Come on! Hurry!
>
> May we depart from the place of waiting, oh our nephews, oh our brothers! Red popcorn flowers are scattering, there where God's compassion has descended to the world!
>
> In a house of quetzal feathers by the side of the road, there you are, you maiden, Saint Mary. Right there you have given birth to the child of God. With various jewels may he be prayed to!
>
> You are simply exalted, as if you surround yourself with jewels. Now he is in your arms, God the child, various jewels! (Bierhorst 1985:254; translation revised by L. Burkhart)

Bernardino de Sahagún and four of his Nahua assistants composed a collection of Nahuatl songs for Christian festivals, published under the friar's name in 1583. In much of the work, the friar seems to take a back seat to the literary skill and creativity of the native authors. A song for Easter morning conjures up a vision of a beautiful garden populated by native species of flower, tree, and bird:

> You green-corn flower, you heart flower, you cacao flower, you red jar flower: put forth a shady ring of fronds, send forth boughs! You have come to arrive in your place of sprouting.
>
> You ceiba tree, you cypress, you fir, you pine: why do you still stand sadly? It is the time, it is the moment for you to renew your flowers, your leaves, for you to send forth boughs, for you to bloom!
>
> You oriole, you blue grosbeak, you mockingbird, you hummingbird: where had you gone? Where had you entered? And all you various spoonbills, you various troupials, come! Let there be flying, let there be unfolding, let there be unfurling of wings! May your speech resound! May there be chattering, may your songs resonate like bells! (Sahagún 1583:59r–59v; trans. by L. Burkhart)

Later in the song this sacred place is identified as the churchyard, the flowers representing the worshipping women, the trees representing the men, and the birds representing visiting angels circling above.

later copies. The earliest known script dates to approximately 1590. It is the oldest manuscript of a drama writtten in any Native American language. A Nahua playwright's adaptation of a Spanish play, it dramatizes a farewell scene between Jesus Christ and the Virgin Mary prior to his going to be crucified. Because of the native playwright's changes and additions—he more than doubled the length of the text—and his skilled use of oral-poetic style, the work, though based on a Spanish source, may be considered a native composition.

This excerpt is one of Christ's speeches, as he strives to persuade his mother that his imminent death is truly necessary. Mary has just suggested that since Christ is all-powerful he could accomplish the redemption of humanity without having to undergo death.

You blessed and perfect maiden,
you noblewoman and sovereign,
you who are my precious mother,
what you have said is very true and correct.
It is true that I have total power.
Everything can be done, whatever I may wish,
since I am divine, I am sovereign.
But first may you know
that in no way will I turn things around.
It is true that I will cause to come true
that which the prophets left foretold.
Regarding me they left it said
that I would rescue people here on earth.
It will certainly come true,
that I will endure everything that they left declared,
which lies written in the sacred book.
Nothing whatsoever will be lost,
even if it is a little spatter of ink.
It will all come true.
And it was he, my precious father, God,
he decreed it,
that is how the words were set down in this way.
And they will not be the least bit broken.
I will cause everything to come true.
Oh my precious mother,
may you not be very sad,
may you not be very distressed on my behalf,
for the rescue of the people has already been left in my hands,
the Sentence has already been set down.
I will endure everything that is hurtful to people.
And this:
already it has come to arrive,
the day of sadness,
the day of sadness and weeping.
For it is necessary that I destroy
the sad fasting-garment of the dead,
the winding-sheet of the dead,
that the people on earth go about wearing.
It is the old error, original sin.
Their souls are dressed in it,
the demon, Lucifer, enslaved them with it.
And this:
oh my precious mother,
if I am not stretched by my arms upon the cross
there on Mount Calvary,
then how will people be rescued?
I speak truthfully to you,

oh my precious mother,
and indeed you know this well.
If I do not cause to come true,
if I do not carry out,
the command of my precious father, God,
then there can be no rescue.
Therefore may you know
that absolutely never will God lie,
he will never break his word,
because he is a truthful divinity.
This:
oh my precious mother,
it is essential that I die,
it is essential for the people of the world. (Burkhart 1996)

The respectful attitude the speaker shows to his mother, the many parallel constructions, and the emphasis on prophecy are all traces of the native author's thinking.

Literature such as this dates mainly to the second half of the sixteenth century and the early seventeenth century. As the native population level reached its lowest point with the epidemics of the 1570s and 1590s, and as the friars who sponsored so much of the work were replaced by parish priests, the production of written literature declined. But the relative scarcity of written records does not mean that native people ceased to sing, pray, and enact dramas as part of their religious life. Rather, the texts employed in such activities became dependent once again on oral tradition.

SUGGESTED READINGS

BIERHORST, JOHN (trans. and ed.) 1992 *History and Mythology of the Aztecs: The Codex Chimalpopoca.* Tucson: University of Arizona Press.

COE, MICHAEL D., and GORDON WHITTAKER (trans. and eds.) 1982 *Aztec Sorcerers in Seventeenth Century Mexico: The Treatise on Superstitions by Hernando Ruiz de Alarcón.* Institute for Mesoamerican Studies Publication 7. Albany: State University of New York.

EDMONSON, MUNRO (trans. and ed.) 1982 *The Ancient Future of the Itza: The Book of Chilam Balam of Tizimin.* Austin: University of Texas Press.

KARTTUNEN, FRANCES, and JAMES LOCKHART (trans. and eds.) 1987 *The Art of Nahuatl Speech: The Bancroft Dialogues.* Nahuatl Studies Series, 2. Los Angeles: UCLA Latin American Center.

LEÓN-PORTILLA, MIGUEL 1969 *Pre-Columbian Literatures of Mexico.* Norman: University of Oklahoma Press.

RECINOS, ADRIÁN, DIONISIO JOSÉ CHONAY, and DELIA GOETZ (trans. and eds.) 1953 *The Annals of the Cakchiquels and Title of the Lords of Totonicapán.* Norman: University of Oklahoma Press.

ROYS, RALPH L. 1967 *The Book of Chilam Balam of Chumayel.* Norman: University of Oklahoma Press.

DE SAHAGÚN, BERNARDINO 1950–1982 *Florentine Codex.* Edited and translated by Arthur J. O. Anderson and Charles E. Dibble. 12 vols. Santa Fe and Salt Lake City: School of American Research and University of Utah.

SMITH, MARY ELIZABETH 1973 *Picture Writing from Ancient Southern Mexico: Mixtec Place Signs and Maps.* Norman: University of Oklahoma Press.

TEDLOCK, DENNIS (trans. and ed.) 1985 *Popol Vuh.* New York: Simon and Schuster.

Chapter 13
The Indian Voice in Twentieth-Century Mesoamerican Literature

THE NINETEENTH-CENTURY HIATUS

With all of the extraordinary legacy of texts and commentary on colonial Mesoamerican verbal arts that we have considered in the previous chapter, it may come as something of a surprise to the reader to find that the nineteenth century appears, by comparison, to be relatively weak with regard to serious scholarly works either by or about Mesoamerican native people. This does not mean that Mesoamerican verbal arts were either moribund or inert in the nineteenth century. Ample testimony to the contrary comes from the powerful role played by oral traditions and underground native books of prophecy in such political movements as the Caste War of Yucatán (1848) (see Chapter 6). One can also infer, from the extraordinary documentation of Indian oral traditions that has been achieved in the twentieth century, that these forms were no doubt thriving in both the formal and informal fabric of life in Indian communities of the nineteenth century. They simply did not get recorded, either by mestizo or creole scholars, for they generally lacked interest in the subject, or by the Indians themselves, for they were for the most part nonliterate in either Spanish or their native languages.

To make sense of this pattern one should recall that the nineteenth century was a period of creole ascendancy in the political, social, and economic arena. The same was true of the arts. The last thing that interested the new creole masters was artistic representation of their region as composed of an ancient or a contemporary Indian substratum; this would merely testify to their "backwardness," both to themselves and to the world community. The name of the artistic game in the period therefore became self-conscious imitation of European and U. S. literary fashions. Such as they were considered, Native Americans in nineteenth-century Mexican and Guatemalan literature, like that of the United States in the same period, came to symbolize the vanquished primitive world, with both its romantically attributed virtues (the "noble savage" theme) and its (then) scientifically and historically assigned vices and afflictions (irrational, prelogical thought; sensuality; cruelty; paganism, etc.). In the end, nineteenth-century representation of Indians, such as it existed, was not about Indians, but about creole views of themselves and of what they were not.

THE REPRESENTATION OF INDIAN VOICES IN TWENTIETH-CENTURY MESOAMERICAN ART AND LITERATURE

Mexico

The beginning of the twentieth century marks both a political and a methodological change in approaches to recording, understanding, and representing the Indian voice in Mesoamerican verbal arts and literature. The political backdrop of this change is manifest in the Mexican Revolution of 1910–1918, which sought nothing less than a redefinition of Mexico, to itself and to the world at large. Along with the radical reforms in land tenure, labor laws, church-state relations, and government stewardship of vital natural resources and industries, the revolution brought massive ideological changes that were reflected in the arts, sciences, and literature. The unifying theme of this intellectual transformation was the celebration of Mexico's Indian past and present as the soul of its national identity. *Indigenista* themes permeated national life, from public policy to creative work in the arts; for example, the symphonic music of Carlos Chávez and the great school of muralist painters, Diego Rivera, José Clemente Orozco, and David Siqueiros. Popular and academic interest in Indian and peasant art forms flourished. Precolumbian architecture and decorative art, as well as contemporary folk art, provided the models and inspiration for expressive forms as diverse as government buildings, schools, clinics, novels, calendar arts, and formal painting. Indeed, the proletarian political focus of the revolution found perhaps its optimal expression in the graphic, plastic, and verbal arts, for these forms were thought to communicate the new revolutionary order more effectively than formal written tracts and abstract public policy statements (Figure 13.1, 13.2, and 13.3).

Not only did Indian and peasant themes enjoy a vogue in popular and academic culture, but there was also abundant public funding to support the scientific collection, study, and publication of native art forms. Nationalism and nation-building justified massive public investment in archaeological and ethnographic research and in restoration of Precolumbian monuments. These same nationalistic causes encouraged scholarship in the area of native languages and oral litera-

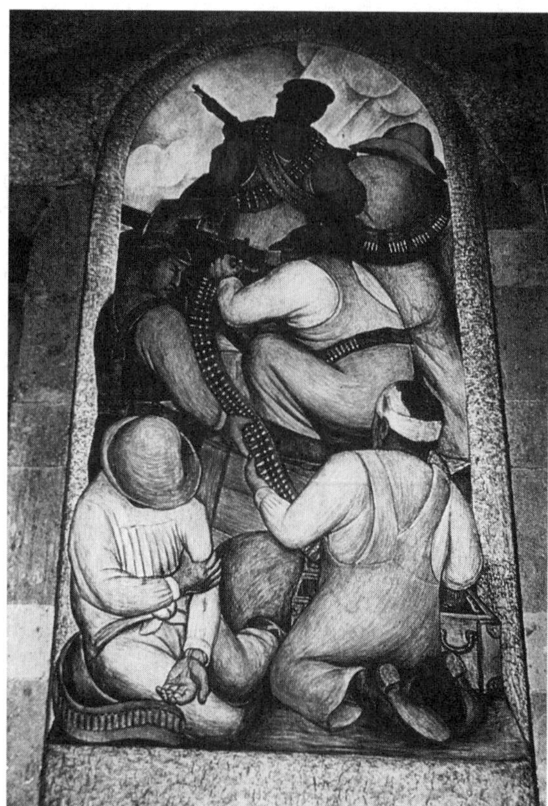

Figure 13.1 "En las trincheras" [In the Trenches], fresco by Diego Rivera in the Ministerio de Educación Pública in Mexico City. Reproduced with permission of the Instituto de Investigaciones Estéticas, Universidad Nacional Autónoma de México.

tures, as well as research on colonial documents written in these languages. Not only Mexicans, but also foreign scholars—including anthropologists, historians, and Protestant missionaries—acquired sophisticated knowledge of Indian languages, thus enabling them to record and document, from live field settings, a substantial archive of modern Indian art and literature. Some of this contemporary material was transcribed and translated from Indian languages that had never before, prior to the twentieth century, had a written literature of any kind.

Another important trend in twentieth-century Mexico has been the revitalization of scholarship on the Indian languages and literatures that have a significant corpus of texts dating from the Colonial period. The most important work in this area has concerned the vast corpus of Nahuatl (Aztec) language texts that were set down in the Colonial period. Beginning in the early twentieth century with Fray Angel Garibay and continuing in the present with the work of his student Miguel León-Portilla and others, there is now a continuing tradition of scholarship in both classic and modern Nahuatl literature at major Mexican universities. Other major linguistic groups whose colonial and modern languages and literatures are regularly taught in Mexican universities are Mixtec and Zapotec (from the Valley of Oaxaca) and Yucatec Maya.

Figure 13.2 "Día de los muertos: la ofrenda," [Day of the Dead: the Offering], fresco by Diego Rivera in the Ministerio de Educación Pública in Mexico City. Reproduced with permission of the Instituto de Investigaciones Estéticas, Universidad Nacional Autónoma de México.

Guatemala

To a certain extent, twentieth-century developments in the study and recording of Guatemalan Indian literatures lag behind those of Mexico, in large part because the popular revolutionary setting that provided the impetus for collection and scholarly creativity on these materials in Mexico developed later in Guatemala and did not become institutionalized as part of the national agenda. The revolutionary parallel in Guatemala occurred in 1944 and lasted only through 1954, at which time the U.S.-backed counterrevolution both directly and indirectly discouraged *indigenista* political and cultural programs. During this brief decade, however, the Guatemalan government sponsored major research projects focusing on the nation's majority Indian population; from that period forward to our time, anthropologists, linguists, and ethnohistorians, many of them foreign, have been relatively free to conduct research there. Although Indian themes in the arts and in popular and institutional culture have never achieved the huge popularity that they have in Mexico, the middle and late twentieth century have produced major discoveries and studies of Guatemalan colonial ethnohistoric documents written in Indian languages. In addition, a signifi-

Figure 13.3 "Orgía: noche de los ricos," [Orgy: Soiree of the Rich], fresco by Diego Rivera in the Ministerio de Educación Pública in Mexico City. Reproduced with permission of the Instituto de Investigaciones Estéticas, Universidad Nacional Autónoma de México (UNAM).

cant corpus of ethnographic literature and important collections of Indian oral traditions have also appeared during this period. In spite of these scholarly advances in the post-1954 era, local and national government interest in the Indian past and present has been, for the most part, focused on the value of Indian "folkloric" themes (for example, Indian festivals and architectural monuments) for promoting tourism.

On the other hand, Indian themes have found their way into Guatemalan literature, as evidenced in Miguel Angel Asturias's *Men of Maize* (1949), which is based on symbolic ideas that come from the *Popol Vuh.* He received the Nobel Prize in Literature for this work, among others, in 1967. More recently, Rigoberta Menchú, herself a Maya, received the 1992 Nobel Peace Prize for her work in promoting social and political justice for the nation's still-oppressed Maya Indian population. Her book *I, Rigoberta Menchú* (1983), an autobiography that documents her life and the dawn of her political consciousness, was a key item of evidence that entered into the decision-making process that led to this great honor. It is symptomatic of the political differences between Mexico and Guatemala that Rigoberta Menchú and her work achieved international fame not for their celebration of traditional Indian themes as a rediscovered part of national identity, but for the author's vivid personal testimonial of the tragic victimization of Indians by the ruling white government in the current climate of civil violence.

Other Central American Nations

It is perhaps a reflection of the mestizo demographic composition of El Salvador, Honduras, Nicaragua, and Costa Rica, together with the still-evolving ethnic composition of Belize, that none of these countries has produced what might be called a distinctively Mesoamerican voice in the arts in the twentieth century (see Chapter 2). Literary creators of such international fame as Rubén Darío and Ernesto Cardenal, both of Nicaragua, have both, for radically different artistic reasons, spoken to issues larger than the nation. Darío self-consciously and very successfully imitated early twentieth-century European literary fashions in his modernist poetry; the Nicaraguan imagery, though often present, was nevertheless not central to his poetic vision or to his international fame. Ernesto Cardenal's great poetic corpus has been tied closely to the theme of Liberation Theology as a cause that pertains to all of Latin America's urban and peasant poor. The Nicaraguan setting in which he lived and worked (eventually as President Daniel Ortega's Minister of Culture) was not really significant as Nicaraguan or Mesoamerican reality per se, but was, rather, emblematic of social and political problems that might be situated anywhere in Latin America. In this sense, both Darío and Cardenal are major literary voices from the region that speak of issues and causes and themes that are beyond, but also pertinent to, Mesoamerica.

THE NATIVE VOICE IN NATIONAL WRITTEN LITERATURES OF MESOAMERICA

In attempting to generalize about the Indian voice in the national literary traditions of Mesoamerica in the twentieth century, it is important to keep in mind that Mexico and Guatemala—fundamentally unlike the United States and also, for reasons just discussed, unlike the rest of Central America—are nations whose cultural, social, and biological identities are profoundly linked to their Indian past and present. It therefore became imperative, as writers sought in the twentieth century to represent national reality and aspirations through literary creations, that the Indian body and soul of these nations be addressed. As noted above, both Mexico and Guatemala have undergone violent civil upheavals in this century—that in Guatemala continues to this day—focusing on the issue of *pan y libertad*, "bread and liberty," which, roughly interpreted, means economic and political justice for all, including marginalized Indians and mestizos. If the nineteenth century was a period of suppression, both political and symbolic, of the Indian cultural component of these nations in the effort to create modern states in the image of France and the United States, the twentieth century has radically reversed this trend, and many of the emblematic literary creations of the modern era clearly reflect this change.

What follows is a small sampler of such works, with brief introductions. It is hoped that the texts will speak clearly for themselves.

Octavio Paz (1914–)

Octavio Paz is among the foremost of many writers and artists in the twentieth century who have sought to define Mexico's singular identity as a modern mestizo nation whose roots are both Indian and Western. In addition to his being an acclaimed national poet, philosopher, and social commentator, he has held major diplomatic posts abroad as well as visiting professorships in Europe and the United States. His book, *The Labyrinth of Solitude* (1950, revised in 1959), from which the excerpt below is taken, was certainly not the first postrevolutionary work to make the point that Mexico's future as a modern nation requires an ongoing dialogue with its Indian past and present. However, it was, without a doubt, one of the most influential statements of this theme, both at home and abroad.

The following excerpt is from the chapter entitled "The Sons of Malinche." In it, Paz deals with two national icons: Mexico's patron saint, the Virgin of Guadalupe, and La Malinche (or Doña Marina, as Spaniards called her), who was Cortés's Indian mistress and interpreter. She is viewed by most Mexicans ambivalently: both as a traitor to the nation's Indian past and as the Mexican Eve (Figure 13.4) (see also Chapter 7):

> In contrast to Guadalupe, who is the Virgin Mother, the Chingada [Malinche] is the violated Mother. Neither in her nor in the Virgin do we find traces of the darker attributes of the great goddesses: the lasciviousness of Amaterasu and Aphrodite, the cruelty of Artemis and Astarte, the sinister magic of Circe or the bloodlust of Kali. Both of them are passive figures. Guadalupe is pure receptivity, and the benefits she bestows are of the same order: she consoles, quiets, dries tears, calms passions. The Chingada is even more passive. Her passivity is abject: she does not resist violence, but is an inert heap of bones, blood and dust. Her taint is constitutional and resides, as we said earlier, in her sex. This passivity, open to the outside world, causes her to lose her identity: she is the Chingada. She loses her name; she is no one; she disappears into nothingness; she is Nothingness. And yet she is the cruel incarnation of the feminine condition.
>
> If the Chingada is a representation of the violated Mother, it is appropriate to associate her with the Conquest, which was also a violation, not only in the historical sense but also in the very flesh of Indian women. The symbol of this violation is doña Malinche, the mistress of Cortés. It is true that she gave herself voluntarily to the conquistador, but he forgot her as soon as her usefulness was over. Doña Marina becomes a figure representing the Indian women who were fascinated, violated or seduced by the Spaniards. And as a small boy will not forgive his mother if she abandons him to search for his father, the Mexican people have not forgiven La Malinche for her betrayal. She embodies the open, the chingado, to our closed, stoic, impassive Indians. Cuauhtémoc and Doña Marina are thus two antagonistic and complementary figures. There is nothing surprising about our cult of the young emperor—"the only hero at the summit of art," an image of the sacrificed son—and there is also nothing surprising about the curse that weighs against La Malinche. This explains the success of the contemptuous adjective *malinchista* recently put into circulation by the newspapers to denounce all

Figure 13.4 "Cortés y la Malinche" [Cortés and Malinche], mural by José Clemente Orozco in the Escuela Nacional Preparatoria, No. 1, Mexico City. Reproduced with permission of the Universisdad Nacional Autónoma de México (UNAM).

> those who have been corrupted by foreign influences. The malinchistas are those who want Mexico to open itself to the outside world: the true sons of La Malinche, who is the Chingada in person. Once again we see the opposition of the closed and the open.
>
> When we shout "¡Viva México, hijos de la chingada!" we express our desire to live closed off from the outside world and, above all, from the past. In this shout we condemn our origins and deny our hybridism. The strange permanence of Cortés and la Malinche in the Mexican's imagination and sensibilities reveals that they are something more than historical figures: they are symbols of a secret conflict we have still not resolved. When he repudiates La Malinche—the Mexican Eve, as she was represented by José Clemente Orozco in his mural in the National Preparatory School—the Mexican breaks his ties with his past, renounces his origins, and lives in isolation and solitude. (Paz 1961:85–87)

Ricardo Pozas Arciniega (1912–)

Ricardo Pozas began in the 1940s, along with many others, to contribute to what would be by the late twentieth century a tidal wave of Mexican scholarly interest in *indigenista* topics in the social sciences. Pozas, a social anthropologist, was among the first Mexican mestizo scholars to conduct extended field research in Indian communities. Pozas's major monograph on the Chamula Tzotzil Maya was published in 1959; unlike most other social scientists, Pozas had a literary bent and contributed, in addition to his ethnographic reports, an extremely popular ethnological reconstruction of the life of a Chamula Tzotzil. The book, entitled *Juan Pérez Jolote* (for the name of the hero), was first published in Spanish in 1952. Pozas used this historical individual (who is, by the way, buried in a marked grave in San Juan Chamula) as a literary and scientific medium to bring to life for a broad sector of the Mexican public the culture of Indian Mexico. The book was even made into a fairly successful motion picture. In the excerpt below (from the 1962 English translation *Juan the Chamula*), Juan Pérez Jolote tells of his homecoming to his Indian village of birth after a ten-year absence during which he fought as a conscripted soldier in the Mexican Revolution.

I went into the house and greeted my father, but he didn't recognize me. I'd almost forgotten how to speak Tzotzil, and he couldn't understand what I was saying. He asked me who I was and where I came from.

"You still don't know me? I'm Juan!"

"What? . . . You're still alive! But if you're Juan, where have you been? . . . I went to the farm twice to look for you."

"I left the farm and went to Mexico City to be a soldier." I was kneeling down as I said this.

"Did you really become a soldier?"

"Yes, papacito."

"Well, I'll be damned! But how come you didn't get killed?"

"Because God took care of me."

Then he called to my mother. "Come here and see your son Juan! The cabrón has come back to life!"

My mother came in and my father asked her, "Do you know who this is?"

I knelt down again. "I'm your Juan, mamacita."

My mother began to cry and said to my father, "Look at him, he's grown up! If you hadn't hit him so much, he wouldn't have run away from us."

My father said, "Well, he's back now, so that's that. Let's go inside."

They gave me a chair and I sat down and looked at them. I couldn't make any conversation because I'd forgotten too much of our language.

They called my brother Mateo and my sister Nicholasa to come see me. "Come here! It's Juan who ran away!"

My brother and sister came in to greet me, but I couldn't talk with them, all I could do was look at them. They didn't remember me, because they'd been so little when I left home.

"He's your older brother," my mother told them. "The one that ran away because his father kept beating him."

Then my sister said, "We thought you must be dead."

"No, thanks to God. He took care of me."

Some of the words I used were Tzotzil, but the rest were Spanish. Everybody laughed at me because I couldn't say things correctly in our language.

And I stayed here, I lived in my own village again. The first night I woke up when my father started blowing on the embers of the cooking fire. I was afraid he'd come over and wake me up by kicking me. But he didn't, because I was a man now! My mother got out of bed and gave him some water so he could wash his hands. She washed hers, too, and began to grind the dough for the tortillas.

We all gathered around the fire to warm ourselves, and I watched the flames, how they surround the comal [tortilla griddle] on which the tortillas were baking. . . . While my mother was making the tortillas I remembered a lot of things I'd forgotten: my mother's dreams, the stories the old people like to tell, their joys and sorrows.

Three hours later the sky grew bright and the sun came up from behind the mountains. My mother put some coals into the clay incense burner and went out to greet the first rays of the sun. She dropped some pieces of copal into the burner, knelt down to kiss the ground, and begged the sun to protect us and give us health. (Pozas Arciniega 1962:44–47)

Ermilo Abreu Gómez (1894–1971)

Ermilo Abreu Gómez was a novelist, poet, journalist, critic, scholar, and educator who taught in Mexico, the United States, and several Latin American universities. His work *Canek: History and Legend of a Maya Hero* (originally published in 1940), which is excerpted in Box 13.1, is a short but complex mosaic of vignettes that take place on a great Yucatec estate in the late nineteenth century. Although it is ostensibly about the peculiar and moving friendship between an invalid creole boy (Guy) of old, aristocratic family background, and a Maya boy (Jacinto Canek) who works as a peon on his aunt's and uncle's henequen plantation, the book is in reality a fictional reconstruction of the living Maya memory of a tragic and terrible moment in white-Indian relations in colonial Yucatán, dating from 1761. This was the date of a rebellion in which the Maya—subscribing to a prophecy (set down in the famous underground book, the *Chilam Balam*) of the imminent return of an Itzá king of the royal lineage of Canek to rescue them from their Spanish oppressors—sought, under just provocation, to make the prophecy come true and to drive the whites into the sea. The leader, for this reason, assumed the name of the prophet, Jacinto Canek. Canek's uprising was squelched and the hero was publicly drawn, quartered, and burned in the plaza of Mérida. From that time forward "Jacinto Canek" became the rallying cry of Yucatec Maya rebellion and separatism, which again flowered in the well-known Caste Wars of

Box 13.1 *Canek: History and Legend of a Maya Hero*

Abreu Gómez's story of Canek actually takes place in multilayered cyclical time: Canek was a Precolumbian royal title; it was the name of a messianic prophet who lived early in the Colonial period; it was the name of the martyred hero of 1761 and thus the rallying cry symbolizing all Maya heroes from 1761 to 1900; and it was the name of Guy's Maya friend who lived at around the time of the historical present that is portrayed in the novel. It is not difficult to read the novel as both an indictment of white Mexico and a bid for Mexican reconciliation with its Indian past.

The following passage, depicting the tenderness of Canek's last days with his frail white friend, evokes several possible interpretations:

When Guy came back from the field he was bent over like a broken cornstalk and was drowsy. Canek laid him down on the grass. He sat beside him and kept watch over his sleep. In the shelter of his care, Canek could feel the boy was resting. Without speaking it, in the peace of his closed eyes, Canek read the message of innocence that lived in Guy's spirit.

Guy can't sleep. The night is sour and the winds from the south beat heavily on the limy earth. A yellow dust clouds the stars. Guy can't stop coughing. Resting his head in Canek's hands he sometimes smiles. Canek tells him ancient tales.

As soon as he woke up, Guy asked for water. He had spent the night sweating and in pain. Canek took the jug with water collected from the morning dew and gave it to him. Guy drank with an almost painful anxiousness. Afterward he asked, "Jacinto, why is dew water so good? "Because it is filled with light from the stars, and starlight is sweet."

"Is it true, Jacinto, that children who die are turned into birds?"

"I don't know, Guy."

"Is it true, Jacinto, that children who die become flowers?"

"I don't know, Guy."

"Is it true, Jacinto, that children who die go to heaven?"

"I don't know, Guy."

"Then Jacinto tell me what does happen to children who die?"

"Children who die, little Guy, awaken."

In the morning Guy was gone. Nobody saw him die. Between the strands of his hammock, he looked asleep. On his pale, delicate lips a light smile also slept. In the corner, not making any noise, Canek cried like a child.

Tía Charo came near, touched his shoulder and said, "Jacinto, you're not family. Why are you crying?" (Abreu Gómez 1979:29–30)

Yucatán, which began in 1848 and lasted in one form or another almost to the end of the nineteenth century.

Gregorio López y Fuentes (1897–1966)

Gregorio López y Fuentes, like Ermilo Abreu Gómez, belongs to the great generation of early twentieth-century Mexican writers who considered Indian themes to be centrally important in the valuation of postrevolutionary national identity. He was both a novelist and a journalist and his novel, *El Indio,* from which the extract below is taken, won for him in 1935 Mexico's first National Prize of Literature. The original edition and current English translations are illustrated by Diego Rivera. This book reveals López y Fuentes to be an artist of both historical and ethnographic sensitivity, yet the book itself is odd in that it is about no particular place or time. The events depicted fictionally suggest that its ethnographic time and place are "somewhere in East Central Mexico sometime before, during and after the Revolution."

The novel is tragic and ironic in that its protagonist is not a person but the collective identity of marginalized Indian Mexico. The village represented here is a Nahuatl-speaking community that could symbolize hundreds of other Indian communities. For centuries the protagonists and their ancestors had fled from the land-grabbing and labor exploitation of white and mestizo Mexicans into the mountain fastnesses. Now, however (at the time of the novel), they are sought out, at the edge of nowhere, by whites and mestizos who demand that the Indians provide knowledge of alleged hidden treasure. Subsequently they also demand from the Indians labor service for public works related to the revolution in progress, which is intended to "liberate" them.

In the passage that follows, Indians have slain one of these abusive Mexicans with a well-engineered rockslide and gird themselves for the consequences:

> All that night the rancheria buzzed with excitement. It was evident that the old men were in council, and the villagers crowded around them, droning like a disturbed beehive.
>
> The men who had just returned from work were told what had happened. Those who had been in their own fields, those who had come up from the valley after their daily labor in the haciendas, and those who had just finished their week as servants in the houses of rich townspeople—all heard and gave their opinions, but they carried no weight. The council of elders would decide.
>
> The most important information was brought by one of the Indians just back from service in the town. He had met two whites on horseback, one of them leading a pack mule, and the other a riderless mount. It was clear from this that the fugitive treasure hunters had abandoned the one who was hit by the rock—maybe buried it—at the bottom of the canyon.
>
> The old men remained sunk in thought for a long time. Beyond question the white man was dead; therefore, they could expect reprisals. The paper the strangers had shown them was proof of their influential connections. And, just as they had been able to obtain credentials, so they would get an order to capture and punish the killers.
>
> The oldest of the huehues [elders] got up from the stone where he had been sitting. The moon rose like a yellow mirror catching the fading light of the sun. The old man's eyes ran over the crowd.
>
> Few, if any, were missing. He beckoned those farthest away to come closer. They all looked alike in the first light of the moon. Their color was the same and their features identical, as if cast by one impulse, the reason for their meeting.
>
> Everybody was silent as the old man spoke. He said the town would take its revenge even if the rancheria was in the right. As had happened before, the death of the white man would be a pretext for annihilation and pillage.
>
> A new cycle of suffering had begun, he explained, and they could survive it only if the whole tribe faced it together, just as they had punished the white man together. He and the other elders, although they were part of the rancheria and had witnessed the act, could not say who pushed the rock that, plunging down the mountainside, had caused the death. Furthermore—and he raised his voice in resentment and anger—to give up the avenger would be an insult to the women of the tribe, for the pursuit of the girl was an outrage to all of them. Likewise, it would be an affront to the men, for the misfortune of the youth who served as guide through the mountains was an injury to them all.
>
> The speaker concluded with an outline of his plan of campaign: abandon the rancheria; take refuge in the mountains as in past epochs of persecution; resist when the situation was favorable; beware of the neighboring tribes whose hatred made them allies of the strangers; and finally, for whoever fell into the hands of the whites, this order—sealed lips. That was their strength!
>
> "No matter," he told them, "if they burn your feet to make you confess our hiding-places. Not a word! If they hang you on a tree to tear from your lips the

names of those who took part in the fight with the whites—not a word! If they twist your arms till they break, to make you tell where we have our provisions—not a word!"

The huehue then turned to the other old men, and they nodded their heads in approval; for in his mouth, the tongue of experience had spoken. The crowd was silent. And silently they scattered. (López y Fuentes 1981:61–64)

Miguel Angel Asturias (1899–1974)

Miguel Angel Asturias, of Guatemala, was awarded the 1967 Nobel Prize for Literature. Widely regarded as one of the great artistic voices of twentieth-century Latin America, he also served in his country's diplomatic corps, including a period as ambassador to France. His literary innovation has been extraordinary. Indeed, he is regarded as the major Mesoamerican voice (along with García Márquez in Colombia and Carpintier in the Caribbean) of the great twentieth-century Latin American literary movement known as magical realism. His novel *Mr. President (Señor Presidente)* has also been credited with the creation of a whole new genre of Latin American fiction, that which deals artistically and politically with the persona of the military dictator.

His many works have focused on two central themes: the literary re-creation of themes in Indian mythology and folklore and the systematic indictment of the economic, social, and political privilege of the creole elite. The work *Men of Maize*, from which the excerpt below is taken, mounts what is essentially an epic framework for addressing both of these themes. The imagery of the book is borrowed from the *Popol Vuh*; yet this contact period Quiché Maya symbolism is cast against a twentieth-century backdrop of social and political conflict over Maya Indian rights to their land, which for them has both sacred and economic value. The overall plot of this quasi-mythical epic story concerns the Indians' heroic quest for repatriation of their lands from their ruthless ladino (mestizo) usurpers.

The following passage evokes the mood of a Maya village religious observance:

Each woman stopped beneath the portico to lift her shawl over hair strummed by the wind from the mountains, each man paused briefly to spit out the butt of a maize-leaf cigarette and take off a hat like a cold tortilla. They were frozen, like hailstones. The church, inside, was a mass of flames. The confraternities, men and women, the oldest of them with bands around their heads, held small bundles of candles between fingers streaming sweat and hot wax. Other candles, a hundred, two hundred, were burning on the floor, fixed directly to the ground, on islands of cypress branches and *choreque* petals. Other candles of various sizes, from highborn ones with silver paper decorations and votive offerings pinned to them, down to the smallest tapers, waxes of less value, in candleholders which looked like tinplate flowerpots. And the candles at the altar adorned with pine branches, *pacaya* leaves. In the center of all this veneration stood a wooden cross painted green and spotted with red to represent the precious blood, and a white altar cloth draped hammock-style over the arms of the cross, also spotted with blood. The people, the color of hog-plum bark, motionless in front of those rigid timbers, seemed to root their supplication in the holy sign of suffering with a whispering of leached ashes. (Asturias 1975:127)

TRADITIONAL INDIAN VERBAL ARTS IN THE TWENTIETH CENTURY

Major works of Mesoamerican Indian literature in a number of genres—narrative, song, poetry, ritual language, and public discourse—have been known and published for centuries (as discussed in Chapter 12). That Mesoamerica has by far the earliest documentation of native verbal expressive culture of any region of the Americas is no doubt related to the fact that the cultures from which most of these texts come (the Nahua, Mixtec, Quiché Maya, Cakchiquel Maya, and Yucatec Maya) had writing systems and the tradition of books and literacy long before contact with the Spanish missionaries under whose aegis their texts were set down in the Latin alphabet in the Colonial period. Although these colonial texts have been rediscovered, studied, and translated in the modern era, the cultural and linguistic traditions from which they come have been limited to those areas that were subject to early and continuing missionary presence, notably—the Mexican Central Valley, the Valley of Oaxaca, highland Guatemala, and Yucatan.

A major addition to this circumscribed pattern of areal coverage of historical texts has emerged only recently with the important breakthroughs in the decipherment of hundreds of Classic lowland Maya hieroglyphic texts. These developments, discussed elsewhere in this text (see Chapter 11), have already revealed a written Maya historical tradition that dates at least to the first century of the Christian era in lowland Chiapas and Guatemala. At least in the Maya area, therefore, the presence of written texts available for study now spans a period of almost 2,000 years.

The twentieth century has provided both the political and the scientific infrastructure to greatly expand our knowledge of Native American art forms to include regions that were hitherto not well known. Indeed, many of the eighty-plus Indian languages still surviving in Mesoamerica (including, as of the 1990s, about 17 million speakers, living primarily in Mexico, Guatemala, and Belize) did not have, even in the mid-twentieth century, any published accounts of their contemporary verbal arts. Now, however, much is known of both the variety and the complexity of this expressive and spiritual world.

It may come as a surprise to the reader to find that oral traditions are not easy to record, transcribe, translate, and interpret in written form. Not only are we dealing with spoken languages that may not even have a standardized written form, but also with a fluid set of art forms that are always changing as they are re-created and used in new contexts. There are no fixed texts, sometimes not even fixed genres, as in, say, the Bible's Genesis 1, verses 1 to 8. What is spoken in what we might classify as verbal art is carried in traditional knowledge that exists only as it is re-created by the pragmatic dictates of myriad social settings that require use of stylized language in an oral culture. These may be everyday events like the following: morning prayers; joke-telling banter among young men as they walk on a mountain path; requests for a loan or a favor from a relative; a toast to ritual kin who offer a friendly drink of rum; a recounting of the day's gossip around the fire at night, with casual reference to similar events in time past; or a warning to children about a spook that will capture them and turn them into tamales if they wander too far from home.

Special forms of language also occur as an accompaniment to ritual events at festivals: for example, long sacred songs, prayers, and ritual language. It is often the case during ritual proceedings that sacred narratives are implicitly present in participants' background knowledge, although they may not be formally recited; they are assumed to be part of everyone's common knowledge. Thus, the task of setting down an oral tradition as a "written literature" and the quest for native theories of language and poetics that characterize these traditions are, necessarily, somewhat artificial undertakings, for, from an oral performer's point of view, that which is useful and beautiful in the spoken word is simply learned and known from cultural experience; it is never a circumscribed, fixed corpus of knowledge.

The quest for adequate descriptions of these fleeting art forms is nevertheless worth the effort, for modern Mexican and Guatemalan Indians, like their Precolumbian forebears, take accomplished and poised use of language extremely seriously. Eloquence in the spoken word, in fact, often ranks as the single most important qualification for leadership and public service in Indian communities. Why and how is this so?

Mesoamerican mythological accounts, past and present, link acquisition of language and dialogue with the dawn of consciousness in the creation of the human condition. In time present as in time past, language, with its wide range of poetic and musical embellishments, has functioned as a sacred symbol that allows humans to share qualities with gods and to communicate with them. In effect, beautifully executed speech and song are the only substances, with the possible exception of blood, the human body can produce that are accessible to and worthy before divine beings. Ancient and modern Nahuatl theory of language, song, and poetics was expressed in the metaphor of plants and flowers. Flowers, according to this theory of "flower and song," are the most beautiful, perfect achievement of plants, and also their medium for continuity through seed production. So also, song and poetry are the most beautiful realization of the human spirit, making these "verbal essences" worthy before the deities. If divine beings are pleased, human life is allowed to continue. A variant of these ideas occurs among the Chamula Tzotzil Maya, whose metatheory of language links high poetic and musical forms of the language to the qualities of divine heat, which are required for communication with, and about, the Sun-Christ deity.

Closely linked to Mesoamerican ideas about the sacred qualities of poetic language are the stylistic conventions through which this elevated quality is achieved. As in many parts of the world, Mesoamerican poetry, ritual speech, and sacred narrative are highly redundant. Moreover, this redundancy is most typically expressed in variants of couplet poetry. Munro S. Edmonson has described this stylistic pattern for Quiché Maya narrative as follows:

> A close rendering of the Quiché will inevitably give rise to semantic couplets, whether they are printed as poetry or prose. In no case, so far as I can determine, does the Quiché text embellish this relatively simple poetic device with rhyme, syllabification or meter, not even when it is quoting songs. The form itself, however, tends to produce a kind of "keying," in which two successive lines may be quite diverse but must share key words which are closely linked in meaning (Edmonson 1971:xii).

The couplet may be merely semantic in structure, as in this example from a Zinacanteco Tzotzil narrative:

> He was very sick now,
> He wasn't at all well now;

or it may follow closely parallel syntax, as in this line from a Zinacanteco court declaration:

> What do they say is my crime, Sir?
> What do they say is my evil, Sir?

or it may be expressed in fixed formulaic couplets, as in this typical introductory invocation that is used in Chamula Tzotzil prayers:

> I have come before your feet,
> I have come before your hands,
> With my spouse,
> With my companion.

It is important to note that the couplet pattern and multiple forms of such redundancy do not by any means characterize all of Mesoamerican verbal art. Readers will see in the examples that follow in this section that different linguistic traditions and different performers within these traditions do not follow couplet structure with any rigidity or absolute consistency. Furthermore, different scholars who have collected and transcribed oral texts from Mesoamerican traditions do not always agree on how best to translate the pattern of native oral style into Western languages. There is, however, a "center of gravity" to Mesoamerican oral literary style that tends, like so many aspects of their expressive and spiritual universe, to complementarity, duality, and opposition.

Three examples of contemporary Mesoamerican verbal art are provided in the pages that follow. The first case study, from the Chamula Tzotzil of Chiapas, Mexico, provides a broad portrait of the content, structure, and poetics of a living oral tradition. The second case study, from the Huichol of Western Mexico, presents a long didactic or instructional text dictated by a shaman. The purpose is to explain the meaning of a native ritual practice, that of the peyote vision quest. In this case study, we will see how different genres of stylized language move freely in and out of the flow of ordinary conversational language. The third example, from the Nahuatl-speaking people of Central Mexico, presents an extract from what is now regarded as one of the first major Nahuatl-language texts to be transcribed in the twentieth century. Transcribed and translated by Fernando Horcasitas from a remarkable narrator, Doña Luz Jiménez, it recounts a Nahua Indian view of the Mexican Revolution.

The Tzotzil Maya of Chiapas, Mexico

This case study comes from the research of Gary H. Gossen. The goal of the description below is to illustrate the importance and the extraordinary diversity and coherence of stylized language use in a Mesoamerican Indian community, San Juan Chamula, the largest (around 100,000 people as of 1990) of twenty Tzotzil Maya–speaking *municipios* found in highland Chiapas today.

What is a literature? The term becomes feeble when one tries to apply it to nonliterate oral traditions. For literate traditions, the term carries some evaluative nuance; literature contains exemplary works of recognized genres: short story, poetry, essay, and so forth. For oral traditions, the task of considering them as literatures becomes enormously more difficult, for while there may be a native view of what counts as a native genre in the tradition, it is ultimately up to those of us who care to take them seriously as literatures to classify culturally significant genres and provide good examples of them. One cannot provide the wood smoke and laughter or adequately transcribe the delight that listeners find in a well-turned sexual pun. Nor can one reproduce the complex cadence of spoken Tzotzil in the silent fog on a muddy mountain path as an old man tells you of his father's encounter with an earth lord. Much, therefore, is lost in sketching and oral tradition whose very life is ephemeral, highly variable, and always linked to a particular performance context that will never again be quite the same.

Whether you look or whether you listen, you cannot spend time even as a casual visitor in a Tzotzil community without coming away impressed by the intensity and vitality of public ritual life. There are no scripts or notes, of course; only knowledge, precedent, and advisers. All that is done—the processions, the songs, the seemingly endless prayers and exchanges of ritual language—is carried in the oral tradition. In similar fashion, the daily round of domestic life in Tzotzil households typically begins with prayers to the Sun-Christ and other deities at the household shrine, and ends with tortillas, beans, gossip, and joking around the fire.

Most narrative accounts of Tzotzil history emphasize the learning of *batz'i k'op* (the "true language," or Tzotzil) and its specialized forms—such as prayer, ritual speech, and song—as the diagnostic moment in human "progress" through the four-period creation cycle. As it was in progress as a species, so it is with

Tzotzils as they move through the life cycle. Infants are classified as monkeys *(mashetik)*—precultural beings without language—until they are named and baptized, usually in the first two years of life. According to Tzotzil theories of self and individual being, a human life is a cycle of heat, beginning as a cold fetus and acquiring ever-increasing measures of spiritual heat as the individual moves through the life cycle. Language-learning and increasing sophistication in language use, particularly in punning and joking behavior, are signs of increasing social maturity. Skillful use of language, like sexual maturity and wealth, is likened to powerful heat, the desired and the desirable. Those men and women who achieve rank and status in shamanistic careers and public ritual life do so in part through their linguistic competence. So complex are the specialized linguistic requirements of civil and religious officeholders and shaman that formal and informal apprenticeship is the norm. Major civil and religious offices carry as a requirement the engagement of ritual advisers *(yahvotik)*, typically past holders of the office, whose task is to accompany the officials and to teach them proper ritual behavior, prayers, songs, and ritual formulas. Aspiring shamans must not only dream to receive their calling, but also find (and sometimes pay) a mentor from whom to learn prayers and other specialized knowledge. Musicians (those of string ensembles—harp and guitar) occupy a culturally important role as ritual accompanists and as informal ritual advisers. A prestigious musician not only knows song sequences involving hundreds of formal couplets but also is able to prompt ritual officials and assistants about matters of etiquette, protocol, and specialized language use.

If specialized language use is crucial to the success of a "public service" career, it is also laced into the fabric of countless everyday social transactions. To borrow money, to ask a favor, to ask for help, to share a drink of rum, to enlist a ritual kinsman *(compadre)* for the baptism of one's child, even to pay a visit to one's neighbor's house—all require the use of formal language, a style of speech that is formulaic and fixed rather than spontaneous and free-form (see Box 13.2).

Box 13.2 is a transcription of a casual visit of two *compadres* (ritual kinsmen), as recorded in Zinacantán by Robert Laughlin. There has apparently been a misunderstanding. The visitor seeks to assuage bad feelings by offering rum, talk, and camaraderie.

A bewildering number of processes, abstractions, and things can be

Box 13.2 *Formal Speech Between Compadres of Zinacantán*

Maryan: (He offers a bottle of rum to Romin.) I am paying you a visit here. Grant a little pardon for our tiny bit of cold water [ritual deprecation of the gift of rum], since you suffered the pain and the hardship. You sustained the lowly soul, the lowly spirit of God's humble angel.

Romin: God, are your lordly heads still anxious, your lordly hearts, My Father, My Lord? That should have been all, I wish nothing. My Father, I wish nothing. My Lord, I wish nothing, my holy companion, my holy compadre. Thank you so much. May God repay you a little. It isn't that I have said a thing, it seems.

Maryan: This way it has always been from the beginning, from the start, grant a very little pardon. God, compadre, grant the holy pardon, a little, a bit. I have come holding in my possession, the sunbeams, the shade of Our Lord [another ritual reference to rum]. Thanks for suffering the lordly pains, enduring the lordly hardship, you sustained the lowly soul, the lowly spirit of God's humble angel [speaker reference to himself in the mode of self-deprecation], the way you, too, are measured as a lordly man, as a lordly person.

Romin: God, thanks, then, thanks. They say there is still a little, a bit. Well, see here, compadre, it seems that now you offered me the little, the bit, it seems. I partook of the lordly liquor at your table. Let's share the little, the bit, it seems of what you offered me, too. It's not as if I am fine, by myself, proper by myself. It won't happen that I will go by myself to drink next to the house, of course [meaning that he does not regard this merely as an opportunity to have a casual drink of rum]. (Laughlin 1975:17)

The reader can easily infer that the formal use of language matters a great deal in Tzotzil everyday life. To gain some understanding of the complexity of this sphere of human affairs is indispensable for an appreciation of the vitality of this community.

glossed as *k'op*, which refers to nearly all forms of verbal behavior, including oral tradition. The term *k'op* can mean word, language, argument, war, subject, topic, problem, dispute, court case, or any number of forms of verbal lore.

Chamula recognize that correct use of language (that is, their own dialect of Tzotzil) distinguishes them not only from nonhumans, but also from their distant ancestors, and from other contemporary Indian- and Spanish-speaking groups. According to Chamula narrative accounts, no one could speak, sing, or dance in the distant past. These were among the reasons why the sun creator destroyed the experimental people of the First and Second creations. The more recent people learned to speak Spanish and then everyone understood one another. Later, the nations and *municipios* were divided because they began quarrelling. The sun deity changed languages so that people would learn to live together peacefully in small groups. Chamula came out well in the long run, for their language, *batz'i k'op* ("the true language"), was the best of them all.

The taxonomy of *k'op*, which appears as Box 13.3 and in Figure 13.5, was

Box 13.3 *A Folk Taxonomy of Chamula Verbal Behavior*

"Ordinary Language" is restricted in use only by the dictates of the social situation and the grammaticality or intelligibility of the utterance. It is believed to be totally idiosyncratic and without noteworthiness in style, form, or content; it is everyday speech. As one moves from left to right in this taxonomy, progressively more constraints of various sorts apply to what one says (content) and how one says it (form) (Figure 13.5).

The intermediate category ("language for people whose hearts are heated") contains kinds of verbal behavior that are neither "ordinary language" nor "pure words." They are restricted with regard to form (that is, how people will speak), but are unpredictable as far as content is concerned. A common Chamula explanation for this kind of emotional speech emphasizes the individual idiosyncratic qualities of the performance: "It comes from the heart of each person." The term referring to all of these intermediate forms ("language for people whose hearts are heated") implies an elevated, excited, but not necessarily religious attitude on the part of the speaker.

Within "pure words," the criterion of time association is the most important one in distinguishing the secular forms ("recent words," associated with the Fourth Creation) from those having greater ritual and etiological significance ("ancient words," associated with the First, Second, and Third creations). "Recent words" are colder, for they do not refer to the full four-cycle period of creations, destructions, and restorations. "Ancient words" are hotter, for they refer to events and supernatural beings that date from the very beginning of time. "Ancient words," therefore, comprise the sacred narratives and forms of language used for religious transactions (see Figure 13.5).

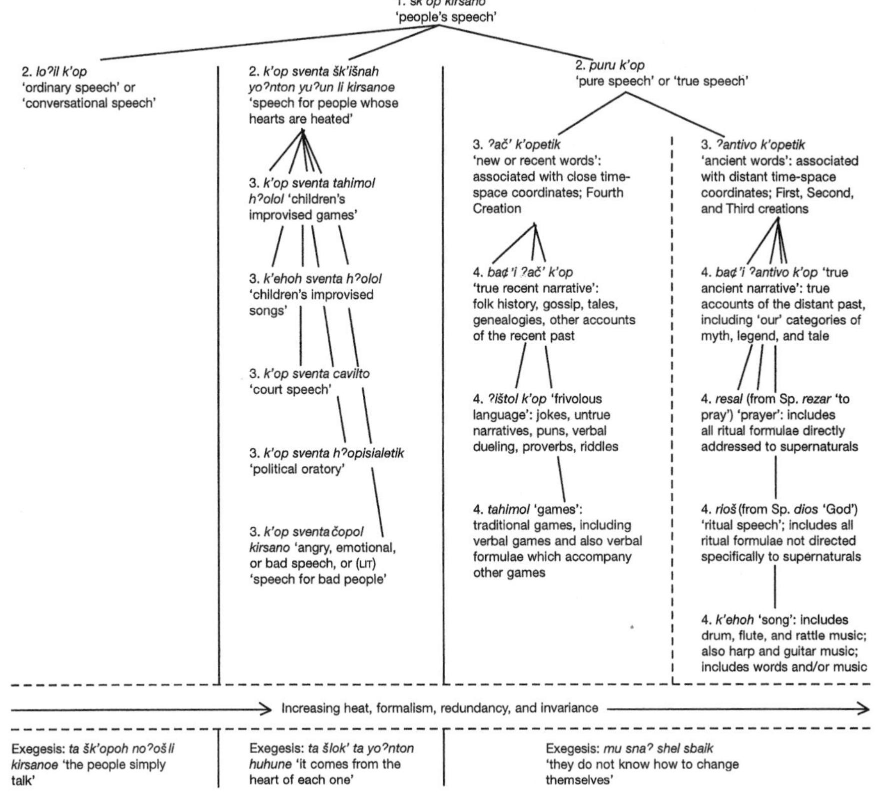

Figure 13.5 A Folk Taxonomy of Chamula Verbal Behavior. After Gary H. Gossen, "Tzotzil Literature," in *The Handbook of Middle American Indians Supplement, Volume 3: Literatures,* volume editor Munro S. Edmonson, general editor Victoria R. Bricker. Austin, TX: University of Texas Press, 1985, p. 81.

elicited several separate times from six male assistants ranging in age from eighteen to sixty-five over the period of one year. The information contained therein should be more or less self-explanatory.

The following prayer text exemplifies the great beauty of Chamula "ancient words." This comes from the induction ceremony of the Steward for San Juan. This is among the most prestigious of many religious offices held by members of the community, for San Juan is the patron saint of the community. The date is December 22, and the new official stands before the home of the outgoing Steward for San Juan. An assistant places a lighted censer before the patio shrine and the whole party together, ritual adviser and incoming steward (*martoma*, from Spanish *Mayordomo*) leading, begins to pray for the success of their coming year of ritual service:

Have mercy, Lord.
    Great Juan,
    Great Patron.
How is it that I come before your feet?
    How is it that I come before your hands?
With my spouse,
    With my companion.
    With your guitar,
    With your gourd rattle,
    With your servant, the musician,
    With your servant, the gruel-maker,
    With your servant, the cook,
    With your fireworks,
    With your hand cannons.
Your children are gathered together,
    Your offspring are gathered together,
For you to see,
    For you to witness.
Great San Juan,
    Great Patron.
Now you are to be delivered at my feet.
    Now you are to be entrusted to my hands.
Now I am your new servant;
    Now I am your new attendant.
I shall be as father to you,
    I shall be as mother to you.
    For one year the same as for one day.
Great San Juan,
    Great Patron,
There is incense for you,
    There is smoke for you.
I shall lift you,
    I shall carry you,
    For one year the same as for each day.
My Lord, Jesus, your children are gathered together,
    For you to see,
    For you to witness.
One alone cannot assume your care;
    A man alone cannot do your will.
What a good thing it is!
    What an undertaking!

That your children are gathered together,
    That your offspring are gathered together,
To stand up for you,
    To stand firmly for you.
May nothing befall us,
    May nothing harm us.
May your flowery countenance shine in white radiance,
    May your flowery face shine in soft brilliance.
That you may watch over us,
    That you may care for us,
    And your musicians
    And your cannoneers
    And your cook.
May nothing befall us,
    May nothing harm us.
Great San Juan,
    Great Patron.
Now you are to be delivered at my feet,
    Now you are to be delivered into my hands,
    And those of my spouse, my companion;
    And those of my father and my mother;
    And those of your children, your offspring,
For you to witness,
    For you to see,
    For one year as for each day.
Great San Juan,
    Great Patron,
I search over the earth,
    I search over the heavens,
Man of the cane of authority,
    Ladino of the staff.
Patron of Heaven,
    Lord of Glory.
Our Father Saint Matthew, Our Lord,
    Our Father Saint Matthew, Jesus.
Mother of Heaven,
    Mother of Glory.
Father of the Cross,
    Father of the Passion.
How is it that you come before my feet?
    How is it that you commend your self to my hands?
Great San Juan,
    Great Patron.
    For one year as for each day.
(Adapted from Gossen 1970:330–334; Gossen 1985:64, 76–82)

The Huichol of Western Mexico

The Huichol, numbering some 40,000 in the late twentieth century, live in the relatively remote mountainous areas of the states of Nayarit, Jalisco, Durango, and Zacatecas. In the Precolumbian era they lived at the northwestern periphery of the Mesoamerican heartland. Being mountain dwellers and seminomads, they did not in the Precolumbian or Colonial periods, nor do they today, participate fully in the centralized political and social arrangements that have long characterized the region. Their social, political, and economic world has always been an order somewhat separate from that of the heartland, sharing certain elements with it but remaining nevertheless at the margins of it.

The text excerpt below in Box 13.4 is about the sacred journey into the Huichol past that they reenact ritually via their ceremonial peyote hunt. This material, recorded by Barbara Myerhoff in the 1970s, constitutes a formal instructional speech that interprets the meaning of this ritual practice to children. Dictated by a shaman named Ramón Medina Silva, this account reveals the central importance of this sacred pilgrimage to the desert, their legendary homeland.

Box 13.4 *Huichol Journey to Find Their Life*

The text to follow, though cast in somewhat complex metaphorical language, nevertheless succeeds in communicating the religious urgency of the sacred journey. The "birds" of the text refer both to the pilgrims who actually participate and to the listeners who, via the narrative, participate vicariously and magically. The text provides a fine example of the manner in which sacred narrative, exegesis of text, and ritual language all occur together in a single discourse.

> "Look," he tells them, "it is this way. We will fly over this little mountain. We will travel to Wirikuta, where the sacred water is, where the peyote is, where Our Father comes up."
>
> And from there they fly, like bees, straight, they go on the wind as one says, this way. As though they were a flock of doves, very beautiful, like the singing turtle doves. They fly evenly. You can see that they become as little tiny bees, very pretty. They continue from hill to hill. They fly from place to place as the mara'akame [shaman] tells them. The mara'akame goes with Kauyumari, Kauyumari who tells him everything. He protects them all. A little girl is missing a wing because the father or the mother have committed many sins. If they are missing a wing, the mara'akame puts it back on. Then she flies with the rest of them.
>
> So they continue to travel. As they come to a place, the mara'akame points it out. So that they will know of it, how it was when Our Grandfather, Our Father, Our Great Grandparent, Our Mothers, when they went to Wirikuta, when Elder Brother Deer Tail, Maxa Kwaxí-Kauyuimari, crossed over there and the children of the first Huichols went there, so that they became cured.
>
> That is what the drum says on our rancho. When it is beaten. There the children fly. The mara'akame leads them on the wind. They land on one of the rocks. It is as though they were clinging to the rock, very dangerous. The mara'akame tells them, "Look, children, you are not familiar with these paths. There are many dangers, there are many animals that eat children, that threaten people. You must not separate, you must stay close together, all of you." And the children are very glad, very happy. . . .
>
> "At last," he prays, "Our Mother, Our Fathers, all you who are in Wirikuta, those who are eaten as peyote, we are on our way to Wirikuta." He says to the children, "Act and feel like eagles, you will go there on your wings." They give instructions to one another, they learn. One tells the other, "Light your candle," and he answers, "Yes, very well." Mara'akame takes tinder, he takes flint, he takes steel for striking fire.

They do this five times and they light the candles and worship there and go on their way. They travel and come to a place they call Las Cruces, where the cross is. They exclaim, "Oh, look, we really have come far, yes we have come far. And how will we be able to go on?" And they say, "Well, it is because we are going to Wirikuta, where the peyote grows, where our ancestors traveled. We have to get rid of our sins, everything. . . ."

Where it is called Wirikuta, where Our Mother Peyote dwells, there they arrive. When he has beaten the drum, when he stands by the sacred pools, when he has spoken to the Mothers and the Fathers, to Our Father, to Our Grandfather, to Our Great Grandparent, when he has laid his offerings down, when their votive bowls are in their place, when their arrows are in their place, when their wristbands are in their place, when their sandals are in their place, then it will be good, then we will have life.

The children are happy, all, they are contented. Because now they are blessed. The offerings are made, the deer tail plumes are in their place, the arrows are to the south, to the north, to the east, up above. He holds them out. The horns of the deer are in their place, no matter what kind. The mara'akame says, "Oh, Our Father, Our Grandfather, Our Mothers, you all who dwell here, we have arrived to visit you, to come and see you here. We have arrived well." And when they arrive, they kneel and Our Father, Our Grandfather, Our Elder Brother, embrace them.

"What did you come for, my children?" they ask. "You have come so far, why did you travel so far?"

They answer, "We came to visit you so that we will know all, so that we will have life."

"All right," they say, "it is well," and they bless them. And there they remain but ten minutes, a very few minutes, to speak with Our Father, Our Grandfather, with all of them there. And then the Mother gives them the blessing and they leave. (Myerhoff 1974:179–184)

Small groups of Huichols undertake this journey at great personal cost, in order to "find their life," past and present, via prayer, song and vision quest as they "hunt" and consume the sacred peyote cactus. Through this sacred hallucinogenic substance, which is closely linked with maize and deer symbolism in their cosmology, Huichols affirm their social bonds with one another and with their ancestors and founding deities.

The Sierra Nahuatl of Central Mexico

The text excerpt that is presented below comes from one the first major Nahuatl language testimonies transcribed in the twentieth century. The source is Fernando Horcasitas's transcription and translation of an oral historical account of the time of the Mexican Revolution. Dictated by a virtuoso narrator, Doña Luz Jiménez, the entire large text from which the extract below is taken (*Life and Death in Milpa Alta: A Nahuatl Chronicle of Díaz and Zapata*, originally published in Nahuatl and Spanish in 1968) illustrates the extraordinary value of listening to historical accounts of key events from diverse points of view.

The eyewitness perspective of the Mexican Revolution from the point of view of a small Nahua village will make any "authentic" version of this event seem just that: official history. In particular, Doña Luz Jiménez's account reveals that President Porfirio Díaz, known to most of the revolutionaries (and to most modern Mexicans) as a ruthless dictator and hated symbol of the old order, was in fact well respected in her village. Furthermore, Emiliano Zapata, the great revolutionary leader of central and southern Mexico (see Chapter 7), emerges from Doña Luz's chronicle with mixed reviews: handsome and well-spoken, but nevertheless responsible for actions and policies that she finds reprehensible.

Here begins her account of how the first events related to the Revolution came to Milpa Alta, located in the mountains just south of Mexico City.

The heavens did not thunder to warn us that the tempest was coming. We knew nothing about the storms nor about the owlish wickedness of men.

One day gunfire was heard between the hills of Teuhtla and Cuauhtzin. We were told that it was the Federals fighting against the men of Morelos. There was a lot of shooting. It was the first time we had heard such a thing, and all of Milpa Alta trembled.

The men of Morelos kept passing through the village and it was said they were on their way to Xochimilco. I do not know why they were against Porfirio Díaz.

These men from Cuernavaca and Tepoztlan spoke our language. They were only peasants, and we did not know why the Federals were afraid of them.

This was the first thing we heard of the Revolution. One day a great man by the name of Zapata arrived from Morelos. He wore good clothes—a fine broad hat and spats. He was the first great man to speak to us in Nahuatl. All his men were dressed in white—white shirts, white pants, and they all wore sandals. All these men spoke Nahuatl more or less as we spoke it. Señor Zapata also spoke Nahuatl. When all these men entered Milpa Alta, we understood what they said. Each of the Zapatistas carried pinned to his hat a picture of his favorite saint, so that the saint would protect him. Each bore a saint in his hat.

Zapata stood at the head of his men and addressed the people of Milpa Alta in the following way: "Come join me! I have risen in arms, and I have brought my countrymen with me. We don't want Our Father Díaz to watch over us any more. We want a better president to care for us. There isn't enough to eat or to buy clothes. I want every man to have his own plot of land. He will sow it and reap corn, beans, and other grains. What do you people say? Will you join us?"

Nobody answered. The days passed. The barracks of Zapata and Everardo González were set up in the village. González was told to stay in Milpa Alta to watch over the village. General Zapata was received in the following way. Everyone in the village went out to receive him. Crowds of men and women came with flowers in their hands. A band played and fireworks burst; and when he had entered, the band played the diana [a Mexican patriotic song].

Several months went by, and Our Father Porfirio Díaz and the Secretary Justo Sierra were not worried about the Revolution. Their great passion was the Mexican people. Wherever there were four children, they were given clothing. Girls were given a blouse and skirt, and boys were given a shirt and trousers.

Perhaps Señores Díaz and Sierra believed this: "Fathers and mothers will thus learn how to give an education to their children. They will send them to school."

The hopes of these great men were fulfilled, and everybody in the village obeyed them. . . .

One day the Zapatistas came down and burned the town hall, the courthouse, and several homes. One of these houses belonged to a rich man by the name of Luis Sevilla.

His house was burned to the ground. It was enough to break your heart to hear the bursting of the grains of corn and the beans. All his domestic animals died in the burning of that house. The next day, the Zapatistas came down again to the village and forced our men to take fodder and water to their horses. All of these things were caused by the Zapatistas.

When the men of Zapata entered the town, they came to kill. They killed the rich because they asked for large amounts of money which the rich were not willing to give up. Then they would take the rich men to the woods and murder them there. They also carried off girls. People said that they took them to the woods and raped them there. These maidens were abandoned forever in the woods, never to return to their homes. No one knew whether they were devoured by wild animals or whether the Zapatistas murdered and buried them there. (Doña Luz Jiménez, from the transcription and translation of Fernando Horcasitas 1972:125–135)

NEW INDIAN WRITING IN MESOAMERICA

In addition to the incorporation of Native Mesoamerican voices into the national literatures, ethnohistories, and anthropological studies in the late twentieth century, it must also be noted that Indian scholars and artists are now increasingly active in producing their own historical and literary texts. In both Guatemala and Mexico, this new generation of Indian writers became visible in the 1980s with the founding of such organizations as the *Academia de Cultura Maya* and the *Instituto Lingüístico Francisco Marroquín* in Guatemala, and the Tzotzil Writers' Cooperative *(Sna Jtz'ibahom)*, located in San Cristóbal de las Casas, Chiapas, Mexico. These organizations and others like them have encouraged not only the creation of literature in native languages—including readings and performances of their work at home and abroad—but also the teaching of literacy in these languages.

It should be noted that local and national governments of both Mexico and Guatemala have recognized these organizations, but that funding has been hard to obtain, for their goals are in some respects at odds with other government policies that encourage acculturation and literacy in Spanish. Still other opposition has come from Protestant missionary organizations that, prior to the rise of these native cultural movements, held a virtual monopoly (largely in the form of Biblical and other religious texts) on the production of written materials in native languages. For these reasons, the new Indian cultural organizations have been for the most part self-supporting, depending on funds generated by the sale of their publications and by private donations. The published works of these organizations are available in low-cost editions and usually carry a dual language text in the Indian language and Spanish. The subject matter varies from the re-telling of traditional folktales, to the interpretation of recent historical events, to extensive biographical and autobiographical texts. In some cases, ancient Maya and Spanish colonial texts are being translated and interpreted in modern Indian languages. The following brief excerpts will provide a sampling of this "new" Indian literary creation.

"About Pajarito and Chamula in 1911"

This work, dated 1991, is Publication 8 of the Writers' Cooperative (*Sna Jtz'ibahom*, or *Cultura de los Indios Mayas, A. C.*). of San Cristóbal de las Casas. This organization was founded in the late 1970s by a group of Tzotzil, Tzeltal, and Tojolabal Indian writers, with the assistance of Robert Laughlin of the Smithsonian Institution of Washington, D.C. Although initially supported by private donors (notably Cultural Survival, Inc., and the *Fundación Interamericana*), the organization has become to a certain extent self-supporting. The publication series is supported by the Mexican government's *Consejo Nacional para la Cultura y las Artes.*

The book whose preface is reproduced below derives from oral sources about a famous Chamula Tzotzil historical figure, Jacinto Pérez Chishtot, who was the leader of a violent political and religious movement of 1910 and 1911. He and his followers sought, under the tutelage of the conservative Bishop Francisco Orozco y Jiménez, to place the town of San Juan Chamula in the political camp of the counterrevolutionary forces of the Chiapas theater of the early years of the Mexican Revolution. "Pajarito," as the leader was known in Spanish (meaning "Little Bird," from his Tzotzil surname Chishtot), has not fared well in Mexican official history, for he was eventually executed as a counterrevolutionary by the Mexican army. However, the following introduction to the Tzotzil re-telling of these violent events of 1911 leads us to entertain a more complex reading of his life and political career than that given in official histories, where he is simply written off as a counterrevolutionary "crazy." As in the case of Doña Luz Jiménez's Nahuatl chronicle, the rendering of historical events depends a great deal on where one stands in the flow of these events, and, above all, who one is in terms of local identities and affiliations.

As we shall now see, one person's counterrevolutionary is another's ethnic hero. Pajarito emerges from this account as an Indian ethnic martyr who tragically died at the hands of self-interested and deceitful ladinos, both revolutionaries and counterrevolutionaries.

> This account of the life and work of the famous "Pajarito" presents another facet of this well-known historical figure. We see here both an ironic and ambiguous side to his character that differs somewhat from the official accounts of him that appear in history books. This point of view is possible because the account recorded here was narrated by the son of one of Pajarito's closest political allies and co-religionists who fought side by side with him in his ill-fated uprising against the Mexican authorities.
>
> Because of the personal anecdotal origin of what is told here, we are able to understand that Pajarito's violent military activities were in fact being manipulated by other non-Indian political interests. In fact, goals quite opposite those that Pajarito believed he was fighting for, were in fact pushing him onto the field of battle.

Now, as we stand some 75 years removed from these events, we must be aware that the circumstances have become clouded with false framing and contextualization. We are now in a position to free ourselves from these assertions about our past, for we begin to sense a feeling of liberation from the long tradition of racism that Ladinos have imposed on us and our own past.

Although it can hardly be argued that Pajarito's people were justified in perpetrating all of their bloody activities, it is nevertheless the case that they were in fact being manipulated, however briefly, by Ladino power plays. (Sna Jtz'ibahom 1991:5; translation by Gary H. Gossen)

Victor Montejo's Testimony: Death of a Guatemalan Village (1987)

Victor Montejo, a Jacaltec Maya from Guatemala, has become one of the more prominent members of a new generation of Mesoamerican Indian writers and artists whose work has appeared in Spanish and English editions. Montejo's work in English has included a poetic rendering of a Jacaltec sacred narrative (*El Kanil, Man of Lightning,* 1982) and a retelling of Jacaltec children's stories (*The Bird Who Cleans the World,* 1991), as well as the hair-raising eyewitness account of the current Guatemalan civil conflict, *Testimony: Death of a Guatemalan Village* (1987). The excerpt from *Testimony* that appears below is chosen not only for its artistic merit but also for its political content. It reflects the plain social and historical truth that Mesoamerican Indians have spent many centuries as the de facto underclass of New Spain and of the modern nations of the region. As is discussed elsewhere in this book (see Chapter 7), Guatemala has not yet emerged from the tyranny of these social and political arrangements.

Testimony records Montejo's eyewitness account of the Guatemalan army's massacre of a Jacaltec Indian village on September 9, 1982, when the civil patrol of Tzalalá, where Montejo was a schoolteacher, mistook an army detachment dressed in olive fatigues for leftist guerrillas and fired on them. This massacre included members of Montejo's own family. These events took place in a period in which many of the departments of northwestern Guatemala (most of them with a majority Maya population) were under military occupation. The justification was that all of the region's inhabitants, being Indians, either were subject to leftist insurgency or were themselves guerrilla sympathizers.

Reproduced here are the final passages of *Testimony*:

I returned innumerable times to report to the base commander, until he was relieved from his post. He was replaced by another lieutenant who had stored up in his being all the deadly poisons. I hesitated to present myself before him but finally had to do it to avoid intrigues and greater dangers.

"I know nothing of you," he said to me the first time, which was fine with me.

But some days later I learned he was carrying out a probe about me and my associations in town and in the village.

When I next reported to the commander, he said to me:

"You will have to report here without fail. And don't duck out on me because I'm not one to be fooled with, as you did with my predecessor. I just came from el Quiché and I know how to clean up towns infested by guerrillas."

"Be assured, I will comply with the order."

Around this time the school semester was coming to a close. I had written final evaluations for my pupils and prepared to fill out the end of term reports and lead the closing ceremonies. The last days of October resembled a sick burro reluctant to move a step. More corpses kept appearing in the outskirts of town, and machine gun volleys shattered the silence every night. The army infested the town with secret agents who sowed distrust and fear among the neighbors. Once more I began to fear the prospect of a late-night kidnapping; my sleep grew fitful and my dreams were stalked by nightly terrors.

With the rise to power of Efraín Ríos Montt, all remaining human rights were abolished, and the army became the sole arbiter of the lives of Guatemalans.

As the situation deteriorated day by day, I became convinced that I had to protect my life somewhere else, and so one dark night I fled with my wife and children in the firm expectation of returning when peace and tranquility will have returned to the beloved land of the quetzal. (Montejo 1987:112)

Rigoberta Menchú's *I, Rigoberta Menchú* (1983)

It is fitting to conclude this chapter with the voice of Rigoberta Menchú, the Quiché Maya woman of Guatemala who won the 1992 Nobel Peace Prize. Chief among the credentials that won for her this well-deserved honor was her autobiographical account *I, Rigoberta Menchú.* In this work she recorded, via oral testimony in Spanish (her second language), her extraordinary life as an Indian peasant woman who saw her own family (mother, father, and brother) cruelly murdered by the Guatemalan army for their alleged involvement in anti-government activities under the military regime of President Romeo Lucas García, who came to power in 1978. (The reader will note that Menchú is responding to the same period and the same national tragedy as Montejo, whose work is discussed and excerpted immediately above.) The social context of Rigoberta Menchú's testimony is considered elsewhere in this volume (see Chapters 7 and 9). However, for the present context, it is useful to recall that Guatemala in the late twentieth century remains, not unlike the former Apartheid system of South Africa, a caste society. A minority population of Hispanic identity controls most of Guatemala's land and means of production and also suppresses political expression and ethnic affirmation of the majority population of Maya Indian identity. While she addresses her Guatemalan experience in particular, she regards her testimony as a manifesto on behalf of all of Latin America's marginalized indigenous peoples.

In the following extract from *I, Rigoberta Menchú*, the author considers the political and ethnic power of Maya views of the human soul. This discussion is directly related to the concept of individual co-essences (discussed in Chapter 8) as a key trait of Native Mesoamerican religious belief and practice. The author concurs with our assertion that co-essences are important, but she takes it a step further, suggesting that Indian "souls" provide an esoteric language of self-definition that helps Indian communities to affirm their identity, even in circumstances of oppression and discrimination:

> Every child is born with a *nahual.* The *nahual* is like a shadow, his protective spirit who will go through life with him. The *nahual* is the representative of the earth, the animal world, the sun and water, and in this way the child communicates with nature. The *nahual* is our double, something very important to us. We conjure up an image of what our *nahual* is like. It is usually an animal. The child is taught that if he kills an animal, that animal's human double will be very angry with him because he is killing his *nahual.* Every animal has its human counterpart and if you hurt him, you hurt the animal too. . . .
>
> We Indians have always hidden our identity and kept our secrets to ourselves. This is why we are discriminated against. We often find it hard to talk about ourselves because we know we must hide so much in order to preserve our Indian culture and prevent it being taken away from us. So I can only tell you very general things about the *nahual.* I can't tell you what my *nahual* is because that is one of our secrets. (Menchú 1984:18–20)

With Rigoberta Menchú's commentary we come, in a sense, full circle. Native Mesoamericans, once a literate people before contact with Europe, are regaining this form of independent empowerment through literacy and through artistic and scholarly activity in both Native American and Western languages.

SUGGESTED READINGS

BIERHORST, JOHN 1990 *The Mythology of Mexico and Central America.* New York: William Morrow.

BURNS, ALLAN F. 1983 *An Epoch of Miracles: Oral Literature of the Yucatec Maya.* Austin: University of Texas Press.

EDMONSON, MUNRO S. (ed.) 1985 *Literatures.* Supplement to the Handbook of Middle American Indians, vol. 5, Victoria R. Bricker, general editor. Austin: University of Texas Press.

GOSSEN, GARY H. 1974 *Chamulas in the World of the Sun: Time and Space in a Maya Oral Tradition.* Cambridge: Harvard University Press.

1993 On the Human Condition and the Moral Order: A Testimony from the Chamula Tzotzil of Chiapas, Mexico. In *South and Meso-American Native Spirituality: From the Cult of the Feathered Serpent to the Theology of Liberation,* edited by Gary H. Gossen and Miguel León-Portilla, pp. 414–435. New York: Crossroad.

KARASIK, CAROl (ed.), and ROBERT M. LAUGHLIN (trans.) 1988 *The People of the Bat: Mayan Tales and Dreams from Zinacantán.* Washington, D.C.: Smithsonian Institution Press.

LAUGHLIN, ROBERT M. 1977 *Of Cabbages and Kings: Tales from Zinacantán.* Smithsonian Contributions to Anthropology, no. 23. Washington, D.C.: Smithsonian Institution Press.

PAZ, OCTAVIO 1961 *The Labyrinth of Solitude: Life and Thought in Mexico.* New York: Grove Press. (English translation of the revised Spanish edition, 1959) *El laberinto de la soledad.* Mexico City: Fondo de Cultura Económica.

TAGGART, JAMES M. 1983 *Nahuat Myth and Social Structure.* Austin: University of Texas Press.

TEDLOCK, DENNIS 1993 *Breath on the Mirror: Mythic Voices and Visions of the Living Maya.* San Francisco: Harper.

Epilogue: Mexican Spring, 1994

Mesoamericans themselves have recently acted and spoken in dramatic ways that provide a fitting conclusion to this text. As this is written, in the spring of 1994, two closely related current events that link the destiny of Mesoamerica to our own lives as U.S. citizens saturate the media. We refer to the North American Free Trade Agreement (NAFTA) and the Zapatista Insurgency Movement that began in Chiapas, Mexico, on January 1, 1994, the very day that NAFTA went into effect. The coincidence of these two events was no accidental convergence. The rebels, members of the Ejército Zapatista de Liberación Nacional (EZLN), launched the insurgency movement on this day in order to make a political statement.

While we do not fully understand as of this writing the entire political agenda that Zapatista rebels have in mind, several things are clear. The initial composition and constituency of the movement consisted of poor, marginalized Indians, most of whom claim Maya identity—Tzeltals, Tzotzils, Tojolabals, and Zoque. They belong to a greater Indian community that constitutes almost half of the population of the state of Chiapas. The drama of the initial phase of the movement (January 1994) involved the temporary capture and occupation of four major towns and cities. One of these was San Cristóbal de las Casas, the historical administrative center of the region under Spanish colonial rule. It remains to this day the major Mexican mestizo political, cultural, and economic center of highland Chiapas. Thus, its capture, however brief, impressed millions of Mexicans, including Indian communities all over the nation, as a major symbolic statement. The grievances of the insurgents, claimed during the first days of the rebellion and reiterated in February at the first round of peace negotiations, focused on the Mexican government's purported lack of interest in the welfare of the Indian peasants in the areas of land reform, health care, education, cultural acknowledgment, political representation, and electoral enfranchisement. Mexico's ruling political apparatus—embodied in the PRI (Partido Revolucionario Institucional, or Institutional Party of the Revolution)—was targeted as the key focus of the rebels' wrath. They asserted that the PRI had forsaken its revolutionary commitment to Mexico's poor and oppressed in its zeal to cooperate with Canada and the United States as a trading partner. This agenda, the rebels stated, has already channelled Mexico's political energy and financial resources out of agrarian reform and into corporate interests linked to NAFTA. This accusation is not without foundation, for in 1992 the PRI-controlled legislature reformulated Article 27 (the centerpiece pertaining to agrarian reform) of the 1917 Constitution in such a way that all existing federally sponsored land grants *(ejidos)* could be treated as private property, thus opening up the possibility of their alienation. Furthermore, the prospects for future outright land grants to landless petitioners—a policy that had been consecrated as a central goal of revolutionary agrarian reform—now seem greatly diminished if not gone altogether.

Thousands of Maya Indian peasants have focused world attention on these issues through the medium of the Zapatista insurrection. The ripple effect of this movement is already apparent all over Mexico and will surely bring in its wake a revision or reappraisal of Mexico's current political and economic system. The climate is becoming ominous. On March 23, 1994, the PRI candidate for the Mexican presidency—in effect, Mexico's president-elect—Luis Donaldo Colosio, was assassinated, plunging Mexico into one of its worst political crises since the chaotic period of post-revolutionary reconstruction in the 1920s.

It is not our place to judge or second-guess the affairs of our neighbors. Nevertheless, the events in Chiapas will have an impact on us in the future, and our national interests have already contributed to the form that they have taken. Furthermore, it is clear that the Mesoamerican Indians have been principal players in the unfolding drama in Mexico, and therefore, the contents of this text are profoundly relevant to an understanding of its characters and plot. Let us illustrate this last point with a few examples from the preceding chapters that shed light on the momentous events taking place in Chiapas.

Our geographic summary of the Mesoamerican region (Chapter 1) allows us to place the Chiapas rebels in space as inhabitants of the lowlands; specifically, a corner of the Gulf Coast lowland natural area. As indicated in the text, lowland native populations have tended to practice extensive agriculture and therefore to live in rather dispersed settlements. Thus, the rebels' home base is a somewhat isolated and marginal area compared with much of the region, an ideal setting for incubating revolutionary activities.

Our account of the Mesoamerican languages (Chapter 11) specifies the linguistic identity of the rebels as being of the Maya family, with Tzeltal Maya serving as their lingua franca. Some of the special features of that language family are worth considering in any attempt to understand the basis of communication among the diverse rebel groups. Our discussion of the influence of Spanish on the native languages of Mesoamerica also helps to clarify why Spanish serves as another lingua franca for the rebels, as well as being the mother tongue of the rebel leader, "Sub-Commandante Marcos."

Each historical period for Mesoamerica described in the text provides useful background information for an understanding of the ongoing rebellion in Chiapas. The summary of Mesoamerican prehistory (Chapter 2) indicates that the area of the rebels' home base was the site of important Classic Maya city-states, such as Toniná and Yaxchilán. Following the dramatic Maya collapse, the area became sparsely populated, most of the major sites being located to the east in the area of Lake Petén. Our account of the Spanish contact period (Chapter 3) indicates that at this time the area was inhabited by small Lacandón- and Chol-speaking societies, which were probably in peripheral relationship with the Itzá Maya kingdom centered on Lake Petén. This peripheral position would explain why the peoples residing in the area under discussion were not brought under Spanish rule until the eighteenth century.

From our account of the Colonial period (Chapter 5), we learn that Bartolomé de Las Casas once served as bishop in the capital of the Chiapas province and that the Maya Indians of Chiapas were organized into corporate communities and exploited for their labor and goods. Exploitation was particularly egregious in the Tzeltal area. As a result, in 1712 the Indians of Cancuc rebelled against the colonial overlords, declared the death of the Spanish god and king, and tried to set up their own religious kingdom on earth. Some 150 years later, the Indians of Chiapas once again rebelled against exploiting overlords, this time creole rulers of the Mexican republic (Chapters 6 and 9). Although the uprising was short lived, the rebels did manage to lay siege to the regional capital of San Cristóbal in 1869 and strike fear into the hearts of the ruling class. There was precedence, then, for the Chiapas rebellion of January 1994, and the takeover of San Cristóbal. There can be no doubt that the modern-day rebels were inspired by the example of their rebellious ancestors.

Our discussion of modern historical developments in the Mesoamerican region (Chapter 7) deals with many issues related to the ongoing rebellion in Chiapas. This chapter helps explain, for example, why Emiliano Zapata, the only leader of the Mexican Revolution to earnestly seek a return of lands to the Indians, was chosen as the defining symbol of the rebel movement (Zapatista Liberation Army). Paradoxically, Zapata's original movement was largely rejected by the Indians of Chiapas. The chapter also clarifies why the present-day Chiapas rebels complain about the ineffectiveness of Mexico's National Indigenist Institute (INI), for as we learned, the INI program was designed more to *assimilate* the Indians into Mexican culture than to provide them with the means for true economic development. In addition, the distinction made in the chapter between the more conservative peasant Indians in places like Chamula and the more radical, proletarianized Indians in places like the rebels' lowland home base helps explain the revolutionary propensities of these latter-day Zapatistas. It is also worth noting that the middle-class origin of the rebel leader, Sub-Commandante Marcos, supports the argument made in the chapter that leadership for twentieth-century revolutions usually is provided by "ambitious middle-class radicals" meeting up with rebellious peasants in the countryside.

The topical chapters of the book provide many insights into the events of the Chiapas rebellion. Thus, for example, our account of Mesoamerican religion (Chapter 8) describes the complex splintering of Mesoamerican beliefs and practices in the encounter with modern variants of Christianity. It is pointed out that Catholic Liberation Theology has been especially influential with proletarianized Mesoamerican Indians, and this appears to be true for the Chiapas rebels as well. In our description of the role of women in Mesoamerican society (Chapter 9), the prominent place of women in the Chiapas rebellions of the past and present is noted, as is the relatively strong position of women even in peasant Indian communities such as Chamula. This helps to explain the presence of women in leadership positions within the Zapatista rebel organization, including the female "captain" who was killed while leading the charge in the attempted takeover of Las Margaritas.

The most basic economic demands being made by the Chiapas rebels receive clarification in our account of economic conditions among the Indians of Mesoamerica (Chapter 10). This chapter describes the landless condition of most Indians, in part the result of the breakup of the ejido system in the case of Mexico, and their desperate attempts to survive through sharecropping, land takeovers, indebted wage labor, and production of commodities to sell in the market. These are exactly the economic problems that characterize the communities from which the rebels come in the eastern corner of Chiapas. The Zapatistas' claim that NAFTA will only exacerbate their problems finds confirmation in our discussion in this chapter of "underdevelopment" in the region.

As the Chiapas rebellion moves from a military to a more pragmatic phase, it will become increasingly important to listen to and understand the voices of the Mesoamerican rebels themselves. Our summary of native literature, both past (Chapter 12) and present (Chapter 13), will be useful for interpreting their messages. For a penetrating look into the thinking of rebellious Mesoamerican Indians, we can turn to such written accounts as Gregorio López y Fuentes's *El Indio*; or for the specific case of Chiapas, to Ricardo Pozas's *Juan Pérez Jolote*. We must also pay particular attention to Mesoamerican Indians' own art forms, both oral and written. The rebels are demanding that the Mesoamerican legacy be taught in all of Mexico's schools. Based on our experience in preparing this text, we suggest that the incorporation of literature about Indians and by Indians would be one effective way to meet this rebel demand.

Glossary

acculturation: the process by which a subordinate culture changes to become more like the dominant culture during culture contact situations.

Alcalde mayor: Spanish royal official charged with the administration of a district known as an Alcaldía Mayor. Other district officials were known as corregidores.

altepetl: Nahuatl term for a town or city (city-state) that had its own deities, religious and civil administrative structures, markets, and land base.

amaranth: a short, bushy plant with small black seeds that were an important source of food in Precolumbian Mesoamerica.

Archaic period: the period from around 8000 B.C. to 2000 B.C. when many plants were domesticated and people became more sedentary.

Aztec: a general term used for Nahuatl-speaking peoples of Late Postclassic Central Mexico; people from Aztlán.

Bajío: a highland basin located along the drainage of the Lerma River around Guanajuato, historically important for agricultural production and mining.

ball game: a game played with a rubber ball on a formal court throughout ancient Mesoamerica. The game was played primarily for ritual purposes.

barrio: territorial division of a town or city.

cabildo: town council and municipal office building.

cacao: the beans from the cacao tree from which chocolate is made.

cacique: in the Colonial period, a native ruler or chief (from the Arawak language); in modern times, a small-town political boss.

calmecac: the schools for the children of the Aztec nobility.

calpulli: Aztec territorial unit corresponding to a village, a town, or a neighborhood (barrio) within a city.

castas: in the Colonial period, categories in a social hierarchy based on biological heritage with respect to European, African, and Native American ancestry and combinations thereof.

caudillo: a military or political leader or dictator.

centralist: in ninteenth-century Mesoamerica, those who supported the traditional power of large landholders, the army, and the Catholic Church, and favored centralized political and economic power.

chia: a sage plant whose seeds were used in ancient Mesoamerica for oil and in a drink.

Chichimec: a general term applied to the nomadic peoples originally from, in some cases, the northern desert area of Mexico. The term was used to denote ethnic groups in ancient Mesoamerica.

chiefdom: a complex society characterized by social inequality, limited full-time occupational specialization, and economic and political institutions headed by hereditary authority (a chief).

chinampa: Nahuatl term for raised field, a highly productive farming method in which artificial plots are created in swamps or shallow lake-beds from layers of mud and vegetation.

chronicle: a historical record; annals.

científicos: generally, the elite scientists and technicians who created the economic infrastructure in nineteenth-century Mesoamerica; in nineteenth-century Mexico, the group of intellectuals, landowners, and bankers who served as advisers under the Porfirio Díaz regime in Mexico.

Classic period: the period from approximately A.D. 200 to A.D. 900, marked in many areas by the development of large-scale political states and a florescence in the arts.

codex (plural, codices): generally, any preconquest or colonial manuscript with pictorial content produced by native artists. Codices are frequently named for their location, discoverer or former owner, or place of origin. Preconquest codices were constructed of fig tree bark paper (amate) or deerhide, coated with a layer of plaster, and then painted and rolled up like a scroll or folded up accordion-style into a screenfold. Codices dating to the Colonial period may be painted on European paper and bound like a book. Known codices record historical, religious, astronomical, or economic information.

cofradía: religious confraternity dedicated to the cult of a particular saint or aspect of the Christian deity.

compadrazgo: ritual kin ties between godparents and biological parents.

CONAVIGUA: National Coordinator of Guatemalan Widows. Human rights group formed by widows from Chimaltenango, Guatemala. The group was founded in 1988 in order to counter the "abuse, rape, and exploitation" by the Guatemalan right wing military forces.

congregación: Spanish colonial policy of concentrating Indian populations of different and dispersed communities into a single new community.

conversos: Jewish converts to Christianity.

core: in world-system theory, the dominant region or regions that are the recipients of resources (luxury goods and labor) from the peripheral regions.

corregidor: Spanish royal official charged with the administration of a district known as a Corregimiento; corregidor de indios was in charge of an Indian district; similar in functions to the acalde mayor.

creoles: Spaniards born in the New World.

dialect: variation within one language.

doctrina: a parochial or parish district made up of Indian communities.

domestication: the process by which humans select for specific traits thereby causing the evolution of wild plants or animals into forms advantageous to human use.

ejido: community lands; in twentieth-century Mexico, the program that expropriated land from large landholders and redistributed the land to agrarian communities.

encomienda: system that rewarded certain individuals (encomenderos) with the rights to goods and labor of a specific group of native people; the encomendero was responsible for Christianizing the natives.

epistemology: the study of theories or the theory of knowledge.

estancia: farm or ranch, usually for livestock.

ethos: the characteristic spirit and cultural patterns of a people.

expropriate: taking control of productive goods, as when a government takes control of what was once private property.

extensive agriculture: agricultural practices that utilize relatively simple technology; requires large areas for cultivation. An example is swidden or slash-and-burn agriculture; contrasts with intensive agriculture.

federalist: in nineteenth-century Mexico and Central America, those who supported liberal ideals of social progress, a secular state, and regional political and economic power.

feminism: a movement that promotes equal

rights and opportunities for women; an approach that analyzes the concept of gender and the meaning of sexual differences.

fiscal: in indigenous communities, a religious official who acts as the priest's assistant and oversees the affairs of the local church.

Formative period: the period from around 2000 B.C. to A.D. 200, during which many societies in the Mesoamerican region became more complex; Preclassic period.

friar: a member of a Catholic religious order such as the Franciscans or Dominicans; may be an ordained priest or a lay brother.

GAM: Mutual Support Group. Human rights group originally formed by Indian widows of men who were killed or "disappeared" as part of the violence (1970s and 1980s) in Guatemala.

gender: culturally prescribed behaviors, roles, and relationships between the sexes.

genre: class or category, such as speech genres.

halach uinic: prehispanic Mayan term for the ruler of a town or region; governor.

henequen: a plant that produces fiber used for cordage.

indigenismo: public policy and institutions that address the educational, economic, health, and social needs of the Indian population, with the underlying goal of assimilating Indians into the national culture.

indigo: a plant from which blue dye is produced.

intensive agriculture: agricultural practices that use labor-intensive techniques to produce high yields. Examples include terracing, irrigation, and raised fields; contrasts with extensive agriculture.

ladino: in the Colonial period, an acculturated or Spanish-speaking Indian; in the modern period, a non-Indian, a mestizo, or a person of European or mixed descent.

latifundio: a large rural estate; plantation.

Liberation Theology: movement within the Catholic Church in which criticism of oppression and exploitation is central to the practice of theology.

long count: a dating system used primarily by the lowland Classic Maya in which a particular day was defined as occurring in a specific baktun (cycle of about 400 years), katun (cycle of about twenty years), tun (cycle of 360 days), uinal (cycle of twenty days), and kin (day), also including the appropriate date in the 260-day secular calendar.

macehual (plural, macehualtin): Nahuatl term for commoner or vassal.

machismo: an ideology and its practices that place a high value on male dominance and virility.

maestro de cantor: Indian official in charge of liturgy and catechism; choirmaster.

maize: corn *(Zea mays)*; the staple food of Mesoamerica.

maquiladora: export manufacturing factories.

mayordomo: caretaker or custodian (steward).

mendicants: members of Catholic religious orders who live by a vow of poverty and are dependent on donations, such as the Franciscans, Augustinians, and Dominicans.

mestizaje: the process by which a mestizo population is created through biological and cultural mixing.

mestizo: a person of mixed white, Indian, and in many cases African descent; as used in colonial *casta* system, a mestizo would *not* have African ancestry.

Mexica: the Nahuatl-speaking group that founded Tenochtitlan and came to dominate Central Mexico; the Aztecs of Tehochtitlán.

milpa: a plot of land planted with maize and beans and often chile as well.

minifundio: a small rural estate or farm plot.

modernization: the practice of emulating European models for progress based on the assumption that Latin American countries could catch up with Europe and the United States through capitalist economic development.

moriscos: Moorish converts to Christianity.

morphology: in linguistics, the system for the formation of words in a language.

mulatto: person of mixed white and African/African-American ancestry.

myth: a narrative, usually involving supernatural forces, that accounts for historical and natural phenomena and expresses deeply held cultural values.

nagual (nahual): the magical companion animal or force of humans, and the individual who is believed to have the power to transform him/herself into that magical entity.

nativistic movement: an attempt by native groups and their charismatic prophet leaders to achieve religious and/or political autonomy and recognition of ethnic identity. These movements often turn violent when efforts are made to suppress them by force.

obraje: textile workshop or factory, primarily for woolens, in which forced labor is typical.

obsidian: a volcanic glass-like rock used to make sharp tools like arrow points and knives.

orthography: in linguistics, the use of phonetic symbols to express sounds and words.

Paleoindian period: the period that began with the earliest arrival of humans (40,000 to 20,000 years ago) in the Americas and ended around 8000 B.C. This period was characterized by populations with a nomadic lifestyle.

patriarchy: a social system in which fathers are dominant in the family relations.

peasant: a person belonging to a society or sectors of society subject to providing surpluses to a larger, dominant society; they support themselves to some extent through agricultural labor.

peninsulares: Spaniards born in Spain and living in the New World.

periphery: in world-system theory, the subordinate regions that supply the core with resources.

petty commodity production: small-scale production of agricultural or artisan goods for sale in markets for profit.

phonology: the sound systems of a language.

pilli (plural, pipiltin): Nahuatl term for a noble.

Pleistocene: the geological period of colder climate that began about 100,000 years ago and ended about 10,000 years ago.

polygyny: marriage pattern in which one man has two or more wives simultaneously.

positivism: the ninteenth-century philosophy that maintains that no knowledge is possible beyond that which can be discovered through empirical facts and hypothesis testing.

Postclassic period: the period from approximately A.D. 900 to the time of Spanish contact (ca. 1520).

Preclassic period: same as the Formative period.

proletariat: wage laborers.

pulque: a native Mesoamerican alcoholic beverage made from the fermented juice of the maguey plant (also called agave or century plant).

reconquista: the process by which Christian Spaniards reconquered the Iberian Peninsula from the Muslim Moors of North Africa (who had conquered the peninsula in the early eighth century).

reducción: same as congregación.

repartimiento: in the Colonial period, various institutions for exploiting Indian goods, labor, and wealth; a labor draft, forced distribution of goods, or forced production of goods.

rural proletariat: individuals from traditional agricultural rural areas who rely on wage labor.

secular clergy: Catholic priests who do not belong to a religious order.

sedentism: a way of life characterized by permanent or semi-permanent settlements.

semantics: in linguistics, relations among meanings of different words or grammatical constructions.

semi-periphery: in world-system theory, the regions that mediate between core and periphery, often through trade.

shaman: part-time religious specialist who possesses magical powers through links with a supernatural source.

sharecropping: the system by which farmers rent land and pay owners with part of their harvest.

state: a large, complex society characterized by social stratification, full-time occupational specialists, and political and economic institutions that allow the central authorities to monopolize the use of force.

stela (plural, stelae): stone slab erected as a monument, often sculpted with hieroglyphic texts and scenes depicting ceremonies or mythical events.

subaltern: generally, someone of inferior status, especially relative to the ruling class.

swidden: slash-and-burn agriculture, an extensive agricultural method in which the vegetation of a plot is cut and burned, cultivated until the soil is depleted, and left fallow to recover before the cycle begins again.

syncretism: ideas and practices derived from distinct traditions that are reinterpreted and transformed during the process of cultural contact.

syntax: in linguistics, rules governing the order and use of words.

Tlaloc: Aztec rain god, same as the rain deity

in other regions of Mesoamerica; Chac (Maya), Cocijo (Zapotec).

tlamene: Nahuatl-derived term for Indian carriers; they usually employed the tiempline.

tlatoani (plural, tlatoque): Nahuatl term for the ruler of a town or region (literally, "speaker").

tonalli: an individual's destiny or co-essence as indicated by the calendar; also a day-sign in the Aztec 260-day calendar.

Treaty of Tordesillas: 1493 treaty between Spain and Portugal that gave Spain the rights to all lands to the west of a certain line and Portugal the rights to all lands to the east of the line; in the Americas only Brazil lies to the east of this line.

vigesimal: base-20 numerical system; the typical system in ancient Mesoamerica.

world-system: a model articulated by Immanuel Wallerstein and others of a social system that supersedes political boundaries and is characterized by unequal exchange between core, semi-peripheral, and peripheral regions, and an international division of labor.

Bibliography

Abreu Gómez, Ermilo 1979 *Canek: History and Legend of a Maya Hero.* Translated with an introduction by Mario L. Dávila and Carter Wilson. Berkeley: University of California Press. (English translation of the original, 1940, *Canek.* Mexico City: Ediciones Canek.)

Aguirre Beltrán, Gonzalo 1983 Indigenismo en México: Confrontación de problemas. In *La Quiebra Política de la Antropología Social en México,* edited by A. Medina and Carlos Garcia Mora, pp. 195–212. Mexico City: Universidad Nacional Autónoma de México.

Arizpe, Lourdes, and Josefina Aranda 1986 Women Workers in the Strawberry Agribusiness in Mexico. In *Women's Work: Development and the Division of Labor by Gender,* edited by Eleanor Leacock and Helen I. Safa, pp. 174–193. Greenwood, Massachusetts: Bergin and Garvey Publisher.

Arrom, Silvia Marina 1985 *The Women of Mexico City.* Stanford, Calif.: Stanford University Press.

Asturias, Miguel Angel 1949 *Men of Maize.* Translated by Gerald Martin. New York: Delacorte Press/St. Lawrence. (English translation of the original Spanish edition, 1949, *Hombres de Maíz.* Buenos Aires: Editorial Losada, S. A.)

Benjamin, Medea (trans. and ed.) 1989 *Don't Be Afraid Gringo: A Honduran Woman Speaks from the Heart. The Story of Elvia Alvarado.* New York: HarperCollins.

Behar, Ruth 1989 Sexual Witchcraft, Colonialism and Women's Powers: Views from the Mexican Inquisition. In *Sexuality and Marriage in Latin America,* edited by Asunción Lavrin, pp. 178–206. Lincoln: University of Nebraska Press.

Berdan, Frances F. 1982 *The Aztecs of Central Mexico: An Imperial Society.* New York: Holt, Rinehart and Winston.

Bierhorst, John (trans. and ed.) 1985 *Cantares Mexicanos: Songs of the Aztecs.* Stanford, Calif.: Stanford University Press.

Blanton, Richard, and Gary Feinman 1984 The Mesoamerican World System. *American Anthropologist* 86:673–682.

Boyer, Richard 1989 Women, *la Mala Vida,* and the Politics of Marriage. In *Sexuality and Marriage in Latin America,* edited by Asunción Lavrin, pp. 252–286. Lincoln: University of Nebraska Press.

Bricker, Victoria Reifler 1981 *The Indian Christ, The Indian King: The Historical Substrate of Maya Myth and Ritual.* Austin: University of Texas Press.

Burkhart, Louise M. 1992 Mujeres Mexicas en "el frente" del hogar: trabajo doméstico y religión en el México Azteca. *Mesoamerica* 23: 23–54.

___. 1996 *Holy Wednesday: Drama and Redemption in Early Colonial Nahua Mexico.* Philadelphia: University of Pennsylvania Press.

Carmack, Robert M. 1973 *Quichean Civilization: The Ethnohistoric, Ethnographic, and Archaeological Sources.* Berkeley: University of California Press.

Carrasco, David 1990 *Religions of Mesoamerica: Cos-*

movision and Ceremonial Centers. New York: Harper & Row.

COE, MICHAEL D., and GORDON WHITTAKER (trans. and eds.) 1982 *Aztec Sorcerers in Seventeenth Century Mexico: The Treatise on Superstitions by Hernando Ruiz de Alarcón.* Institute for Mesoamerican Studies Publication no. 7. Albany: State University of New York.

COLLINSON, HELEN (ed.) 1990 *Women and Revolution in Nicaragua.* London, Atlantic Highlands, N.J.: Zed Books Ltd.

CONTRERAS, J. DANIEL 1951 *Una Rebelión Indígena en el Partido de Totonicapán en 1820: El Indio y la Independencia.* Guatemala City: Imprenta Universitaria.

COOK, SCOTT, and LEIGH BINFORD 1990 *Obliging Need: Rural Petty Industry in Mexican Capitalism.* Austin: University of Texas Press.

CORTÉS, HERNANDO 1962 *Five Letters of Cortés to the Emperor.* Translated by J. Bayard Morris. New York: W. W. Norton.

CUMBERLAND, CHARLES C. 1968 *Mexico: The Struggle for Modernity.* London: Oxford University Press.

DAVIES, NIGEL 1973 *The Aztecs: A History.* Norman: University of Oklahoma Press.

___. 1977 *The Toltecs Until the Fall of Tula.* Norman: University of Oklahoma Press.

DÍAZ DEL CASTILLO, BERNAL 1956 *The Discovery and Conquest of Mexico.* Translated and edited by A. P. Maudslay. New York: Farrar, Straus and Giroux.

DIEHL, RICHARD A. 1983 *Tula: The Toltec Capital of Ancient Mexico.* New York: Thames and Hudson.

DURAND, JORGE, and DOUGLAS MASSEY 1992 Mexican Migration to the United States: A Critical Review. *Latin American Research Review* 27:3–42.

EARLE, DUNCAN 1983 Los Mayas del Altiplano en las Tierras Bajas: Un caso de Autodesarrollo. *Mesoamérica* 5:186–194.

EBER, CHRISTINE 1991 *Before God's Flowering Face: Women and Drinking in a Tzotzil Maya Community.* Ph.D. dissertation. State University of New York at Buffalo. Ann Arbor: University Microfilms.

EDMONSON, MUNRO S. 1971 *The Book of Counsel: the Popol Vuh of the Quiché Maya of Guatemala.* Middle American Research Institute Publication 35. New Orleans: Tulane University.

EHLERS, TRACY BACHRACH 1990 *Silent Looms. Women and Production in a Guatemalan Town.* Boulder: Westview Press.

FARRISS, NANCY 1984 *Maya Society under Colonial Rule: The Collective Enterprise of Survival.* Princeton, N.J.: Princeton University Press.

FLANNERY, KENT V., editor 1985 *Guila Naquitz: Archaic Foraging and Early Agriculture in Oaxaca, Mexico.* New York: Academic Press.

FRANCO, JEAN 1989 *Plotting Women. Gender and Representation in Mexico.* New York: Columbia University Press.

FREIDEL, DAVID, LINDA SCHELE, and JOY PARKER 1993 *Maya Cosmos: Three Thousand Years on the Shaman's Path.* New York: William Morrow and Co.

FUENTES Y GUZMÁN, FRANCISCO 1969 [1690] *Recordación Florida.* Biblioteca de Autores Españoles, No. 230, 259. Madrid.

GAGE, THOMAS 1958 [1648] *Thomas Gage's Travels in the New World.* Edited with an Introduction by J. Eric S. Thompson. Norman: University of Oklahoma Press.

GARCÍA, ANA ISABEL and ENRIQUE GOMÁRIZ 1989 *Mujeres Centroamericanas.* 2 vols. San José, Costa Rica: FLACSO.

GOSNER, KEVIN 1992 *Soldiers of the Virgin: The Moral Economy of a Colonial Maya Rebellion.* Tucson: University of Arizona Press.

GOSSEN, GARY H. 1970 *Time and Space in Chamula Oral Tradition.* Unpublished Ph.D. Dissertation, Department of Anthropology, Harvard University.

___. 1985 Tzotzil Literature. In *Literatures,* edited by Munro S. Edmonson, pp. 64–106. Supplement to the Handbook of Middle American Indians, vol. 3. Austin: University of Texas Press.

GOSSEN, GARY H., and RICHARD LEVENTHAL 1993 The Topography of Ancient Maya Religious Pluralism: A Dialogue with the Present. In *Lowland Maya Civilization in the Eighth Century A.D.,* edited by J.A. Sabloff and J.S. Henderson, pp. 185–218. Washington, D.C.: Dumbarton Oaks.

GROVE, DAVID C., (ed.) 1987 *Ancient Chalcatzingo.* Austin: University of Texas Press.

Haugaard, Lisa 1992 Interesting Times: Nicaragua in Revolution. *NACLA Report on the Americas* XXXVI (3):18–24.

HORCASITAS, FERNANDO (translator and editor) 1972 *Life and Death in Milpa Alta: a Nahuatl Chronicle of Díaz and Zapata,* Norman: University of Oklahoma Press. (Translation of the original Spanish edition, 1968, *De Porfirio Díaz a Zapata.* Universidad Nacional Autónoma de México, Instituto de Investigaciones Históricas, Mexico City.)

JONAS, SUSANNE 1974 Guatemala: Land of Eternal Struggle. In *Latin America: The Struggle with Dependency and Beyond,* edited by R. H. Chilcote and J. C. Edelstein, pp. 93–219. New York: John Wiley & Sons.

KELLOG, SUSAN 1988 Cognatic Kinship and Religion: Women in Aztec Society. In *Smoke and Mist: Mesoamerican Studies in Memory of Thelma D. Sullivan,* 2 vols., edited by J. Kathryn Josserand and Karen Dakin, pp. 666–681. Oxford: B.A.R.

___. 1995 *From Parallel and Equivalent to Separate but Unequal: Tenochc Women, 1500–1700.* In *Indian Women in Early Mexico: Identity and Gender Differentiation,* edited by Susan Schroeder, Stephanie Wood, and Robert Haskett. Norman: University of Oklahoma Press. (In Press).

KLOR DE ALVA, J. JORGE 1988 Sahagún and the Birth of Modern Ethnography: Representing, Confessing and Inscribing the Native Other. In *The Work of Bernardino de Sahagún: Pioneer Ethnographer of Sixteenth-Century Aztec Mexico,* edited by J. Jorge Klor de Alva, H. B. Nicholson, and Eloise Quiñones Keber, pp. 31–52. Institute for Mesoamerican Studies. Albany: State University of New York.

KRAMER, WENDY, W. GEORGE LOVELL, and CHRISTOPHER H. LUTZ 1991 Fire in the Mountains: Juan de Espinar and the Indians of Huehuetenango 1525-1560. In *Columbian Sequences,* vol. 3, edited by David Hurst Thomas, pp. 263–282. Washington, D.C.: Smithsonian Institution Press.

LAUGHLIN, ROBERT M. 1975 *The Great Tzotzil Dictionary of San Lorenzo Zinacantán.* Smithsonian Contributions to Anthropology No. 19. Washington, D.C.: Smithsonian Institution Press.

___. 1977 *Of Cabbages and Kings: Tales from Zinacantán.* Smithsonian Contributions to Anthropology No. 23. Washington, D.C: Smithsonian Institution Press.

LAVRIN, ASUNCIÓN 1981 Women and Religion in Spanish America. In *Women and Religion in America,* vol. 2, edited by Rosemary Radford Ruether and Rosemary Skinner Keller, pp. 42–78. San Francisco: Harper and Row.

___. 1989 Sexuality in Colonial Mexico: A Church Dilemma. In *Sexuality and Marriage in Colonial Latin America,* edited by Asunción Lavrin, pp. 47–95. Lincoln: University of Nebraska Press.

LEÓN-PORTILLA, MIGUEL 1962 *The Broken Spears: The Aztec Account of the Conquest of Mexico.* Boston: Beacon Press.

___. 1968 *Tiempo y realidad en el pensamiento maya.* Instituto de Investigaciones Históricas, Universidad Nacional Autónoma de México, México City. (English translation, 1973. *Time and Reality in the Thought of the Maya.* Boston: Beacon Press.)

___. 1992 Have We Really Translated the Mesoamerican 'Ancient Word'? In *On the Translation of Native American Literatures,* edited by Brian Swann, pp. 313–338. Washington, D.C.: Smithsonian Institution Press.

___. 1993 Those Made Worthy by Divine Sacrifice: The Faith of Ancient Mexico. In *South and Meso-American Native Spirituality: From the Cult of the Feathered Serpent to the Theology of Liberation,* edited by Gary H. Gossen and Miguel León-Portilla, pp. 41–64. New York: Crossroad.

LEWIS, OSCAR 1963 *Life in a Mexican Village: Tepoztlán Restudied.* Urbana: University of Illinois Press.

LOCKHART, JAMES 1991 *Nahuas and Spaniards: Postconquest Central Mexican History and Philology.* Stanford, Calif.: Stanford University Press.

LÓPEZ Y FUENTES, GREGORIO 1981 *El Indio.* New York: Frederick Ungar. (English translation of the original Spanish edition, 1935, *El Indio.*)

MENCHÚ, RIGOBERTA 1984 *I, Rigoberta Menchú: An Indian Woman in Guatemala.* London: Verso. (English translation of the original Spanish edition, 1983, *Me llamo Rigoberta Menchú y así me nació la conciencia.* Barcelona: Editorial Argos Vergara.)

MONTEJO, VICTOR 1987 *Testimony: Death of a Guatemalan Village,* translated by Victor Perera. Willimantic, Conn.: Curbstone Press.

MYERHOFF, BARBARA G. 1974 *Peyote Hunt: The Sacred Journey of the Huichol Indians.* Ithaca: Cornell University Press.

NASH, JUNE 1978 The Aztecs and the Ideology of Male Dominance. *Signs* 4:2:349–362.

___. in press Household Production and the World Crisis. In *Crafts in Global Markets: Changes in Artisan Production in Middle America,* edited by June Nash. Albany: State University of New York Press.

NICHOLSON, H. B. 1971 Religion in Pre-Hispanic Central Mexico. In *Archaeology of Northern Mesoamerica,* Pt. 1., edited by Gordon F. Ekholm and Ignacio Bernal, pp. 395–446. Handbook of Middle American Indians, vol. 10, Robert Wauchope, general editor. Austin: University of Texas Press.

PAZ, OCTAVIO 1961 *The Labyrinth of Solitude: Life and Thought in Mexico.* New York: Grove Press. (English translation of the revised Spanish edition, 1959, *El laberinto de la soledad.* Mexico City: Fondo de Cultura Económica.)

POZAS ARCINIEGA, RICARDO 1962 *Juan the Chamula: An Ethnological Re-creation of the Life of a Mexican Indian.* Berkeley: University of California Press. (English translation of the original Spanish edition, 1952, Juan Pérez Jolote: Biografía de un tzotzil. Mexico City: Fondo de Cultura Económica).

Recinos, Adrian 1980 *Memorial de Solola, Anales de los Cakchiqueles.* Mexico City: Fondo de Cultura Económica.

RECINOS, ADRIAN (ed.) 1984 Título de la Casa Ixcuin-Nehaib, Señora del Territorio de Otzoya. In *Crónicas Indígenas de Guatemala,* edited by Adrian Recinos, pp. 69–94. 2nd Ed., 1984, Academia de Geografía e Historia de Guatemala.

REED, NELSON 1964 *The Caste War of Yucatan.* Stanford, Calif.: Stanford University Press.

ROSENBAUM, BRENDA 1992 Mujer Maya, Tejido e Identidad Etnica. Un Ensayo Histórico. In *La Indumentaria y el Tejido Mayas a través del Tiempo,* edited by Linda Asturias de Barrios and Dina Fernández García, pp. 157–169. Guatemala: Museo Ixchel.

___. 1993 *With Our Heads Bowed: The Dynamics of Gender in a Maya Community.* Studies on Culture and Society, vol. 5, Institute for Mesoamerican Studies. Albany: State University of New York.

ROYS, RALPH L. 1933 *The Book of Chilam Balam of Chumayel.* Washington, D.C.: Carnegie Institution of Washington, Publication 438.

SABLOFF, J.A., and E.W. ANDREWS V. (eds.) 1985 *Late Lowland Maya Civilization.* Albuquerque: University of New Mexico Press.

SAHAGÚN, BERNARDINO 1583 *Psalmodia christiana.* Mexico City: Pedro Ocharte.

___. 1950–1982 *Florentine Codex: General History of the Things of New Spain.* Translated and edited by Arthur J. O. Anderson and Charles E. Dibble. 12 books. Santa Fe and Salt Lake City: School of American Research and the University of Utah Press.

___. 1986 *Coloquios y Doctrina Cristiana.* Edited and translated by Miguel León-Portilla. Mexico City: Universidad Nacional Autónoma de México.

SCHELE, LINDA, and DAVID FREIDEL 1990 *A Forest of Kings.* New York: Quill William Morrow.

SMITH-AYALA, EMILIE 1991 *The Granddaughters of Ixmucané: Guatemalan Women Speak.* Toronto: Women's Press.

SNA JTZ'IBAHAM (Cultura de los Indios Mayas) 1991 *Sventa Pajaro ta Chamula ta l9ll* [Spanish translation: *Los pajaritos de Chamula*]. Sna Jtzi'bahob [Cultura de los Indios Mayas, A. C.] Publication 8, San Cristóbal de las Casas, Mexico.

STEINSLEGER, JOSÉ 1994 *The Zapatista Women's Revolution.* Mexico Newspak, vol. 3, no. 3, issue 29. February 28–March 13, 1994, pp. 11–12.

STEPHEN, LYNN 1991 *Zapotec Women.* Austin: University of Texas Press.

STEPHENS, JOHN L. 1841 *Incidents of Travel in Central America, Chiapas and Yucatan.* 2 vols. New York: Dover Publications.

___. 1843 *Incidents of Travel in Yucatan.* 2 vols. New York: Dover Publications.

TEDLOCK, DENNIS (trans. and ed.) 1985 *Popol Vuh.* New York: Simon and Schuster.

THOMSON, MARILYN 1986 *Women of El Salvador: The Price of Freedom.* London and Atlantic Highlands, N.J.: Zed Books Ltd.

TUÑÓN PABLOS, ESPERANZA 1987 *También Somos Protagonistas de la Historia de México.* 2 vols. Mexico: EMAS.

TURNER, VICTOR 1974 Hidalgo: History as Social Drama. In *Dramas, Fields, and Metaphors: Symbolic Action in Human Society,* pp. 98–155. Ithaca, N.Y.: Cornell University Press.

TUTINO, JOHN 1986 *From Insurrection to Revolution in Mexico: Social Bases of Agrarian Violence, 1750–1940.* Princeton, N.J.: Princeton University Press.

TWINAM, ANN 1989 Honor, Sexuality and Illegitimacy in Colonial Spanish America. In *Sexuality and Marriage in Colonial Latin America,* edited by Asunción Lavrin, pp. 118–149. Lincoln: University of Nebraska Press.

WEST, ROBERT C. 1964 The Natural Regions of Middle America. In *Natural Environment and Early Cultures,* edited by Robert C. West, pp. 363–383. Handbook of Middle American Indians, vol. 1. Austin: University of Texas Press.

WEST, ROBERT C., and JOHN P. AUGELLI 1989 *Middle America: Its Land and Peoples,* 3rd ed. Englewood Cliffs, N.J.: Prentice Hall.

WOLF, ERIC R. 1959 *Sons of the Shaking Earth.* Chicago: University of Chicago Press.

___. 1969 *Peasant Wars of the Twentieth Century.* New York: Harper & Row.

WOODWARD, RALPH LEE JR. 1976 *Central America: A Nation Divided.* New York: Oxford University Press.

Index